THE POEMS OF EDWARD TAYLOR

29:6:m
1708 83. Meditation. Can. 5.1. ƒ am come into my
             my Garden &c

A Garden, &c. a Paradise indeed,
    Of all Delightfull Beauteous flowers & Sweet
A Cloud of rich perfume these did proceed
    From Sweet & beautif plants) first Adam was to keep
      But Sinning had from this Garden wilde.
    And his Garden, Lord, thou camst too, 's a Garden Style.

A Garden=Church, Set with Choice Herbs & flowers.
    Here Lign=Aloes. & the Tree of Life.
Here trees of Frankincense & Myrrh up towers;
    Here's Sharons Rose & Lillie: Beauties Strife.
    Here's Cassia, Cinnamon, Spices, Nut Megs, Made
    Sweet Calamus: & all Heavens herbs of Grace.

Here's Order Choice, Beds, Allees, all in print.
    Here each Sweet blushing blossom, Sparkling brave
And Beautifull rich Spangled flowers beginne
    with White, Red, Blushe Glory Checke'd Smiles have
    Waving Celestiall aire: their Spirit box
    Of Aromatick Vapors: Spirituall Drops.

This Garden, Lord, thy Church, this Paradise
    Thou turnst into, with thy Choice Spirits Gales
Waving all Plants of Grace gust out like Spice
    Their Sweet perfumed breath that Garden scales.
    And Sacrifice their Spirits Sweet upon
    Their Beauties Altar to thee, Holy One.

This Garden too's yᵉ Soule of thy Redeem'd.
    When thou thy Spirit=plants therein hast Set
In their Compression, nor'd & Choisely Steem'd
    Unbeautifyd with Graces Sugarsett
    O that my Soule thy Paradise once bee.
    That with my Paradise it ee, with thee.

Wralt make thy Garden, Lord, thy Grace my plant:
    Wralt make thy Vineyard, & my plants thy Vine:
Then come into thy Garden: & each rank
    And make my Grape bleed in thy Grapes fine wine
    When thou comst in. My Garden flowers with Spice
    And Blossom Aromatick Praise thee will.

THE POEMS OF

Edward Taylor

EDITED BY

Donald E. Stanford

WITH A FOREWORD BY

Louis L. Martz

NEW HAVEN

Yale University Press

© 1960 by Yale University Press, Inc.
Fourth printing, 1977.
Set in Baskerville type and
printed in the United States of America by
The Murray Printing Company,
Westford, Massachusetts.
All rights reserved. This book may not be
reproduced, in whole or in part, in any form
(except by reviewers for the public press),
without written permission from the publishers.
Library of Congress catalog card number: 60-6432
International standard book number:
0–300–00972–1 (cloth)
0–300–02134–8 (paper)

Published in Great Britain, Europe, Africa, and Asia
(except Japan) by Yale University Press, Ltd.,
London. Distributed in Latin America by Kaiman &
Polon, Inc., New York City; in Australia and New
Zealand by Book & Film Services, Artarmon,
N.S.W., Australia; and in Japan by Harper & Row,
Publishers, Tokyo Office.

FOR YVOR WINTERS

Among the first and farthest

Preface

The dedication acknowledges a long-standing obligation to Yvor Winters, whose lectures on American poetry at Stanford University first brought to my attention the need for a new edition of Edward Taylor and whose poems and critical essays I have studied with increasing admiration for many years.

For his wise guidance and friendly assistance I also owe a special debt to Norman Holmes Pearson, one of the earliest admirers of Taylor and the first editor to put his poems between hard covers.

Louis L. Martz has been of great assistance in interpreting difficult passages in Taylor's manuscript. Of particular interest was his discovery that Taylor entitled his major poems *Preparatory Meditations* and not *Sacramental Meditations,* as has heretofore been supposed. I wish also to thank him for his Foreword. Helge Kökeritz has aided in compiling the Glossary and Notes and in establishing the meanings of a number of difficult words which long eluded my search.

Leon Nemoy has been most helpful in establishing the Hebrew texts.

I acknowledge the courtesy of the late Stanley T. Williams of Yale University. Professor Williams and Barbara Simison of Yale's Sterling Library began an edition of Taylor's poetry when my own edition was nearing completion. I was not aware of their work, nor they of mine. When Professor Williams learned of my edition, he graciously relinquished his lien on the Taylor manuscript. Miss Simison subsequently published a number of the Meditations in the *Yale University Library Gazette,* and I have benefited in several instances from her deciphering of difficult passages.

To the Sterling Library I owe thanks for permission to publish those poems in the Taylor manuscripts which they own, and especially to Marjorie Wynne, librarian of the Rare Book Room of the Yale Library, and her staff, for their courteous assistance.

I am indebted to Donald T. Gibbs, librarian of the Redwood Athenaeum and Library, for his assistance in microfilming and examining the recently discovered Taylor manuscripts in the possession of the Athenaeum, and to his staff for their constant and courteous help; also to Wilmarth Lewis, the late Mrs. William Greenough, and the directors and president of the Redwood Athenaeum for permission to publish excerpts from their manuscripts. Thanks are due Miss Miriam C. Wolcott for permission to examine and publish excerpts from the Taylor manuscripts in the possession of the Westfield Athenaeum, Stephen T. Riley for permission to examine and publish excerpts from the Taylor manuscript owned by the Massachusetts Historical Society, and Mrs. Kathleen T. Doland for permission to examine the Judd manuscripts owned by the Forbes Library.

Dean R. J. Russell and the Research Council of Louisiana State University have been most generous in awarding research grants that have enabled me to complete this edition. The courtesy of the librarians and staffs of the Emmanuel College library, the library of the University of Cambridge, the Folger Library, the Huntington Library, the British Museum, the Library of Congress, the library of Stanford University, and the library of Louisiana State University is gratefully acknowledged.

The editors of *American Literature,* the *New England Quarterly,* the *Transactions of the Colonial Society of Massachusetts,* and the *Yale University Library Gazette* have given their permission for inclusion of poems by Taylor that appeared first in their pages. The Princeton University Press has permitted inclusion of the poems that appeared in Thomas H. Johnson's *The Poetical Works of Edward Taylor.*

Finally, and most important, I am indebted to my wife for her constant assistance and encouragement.

D. E. S.

Baton Rouge

January 1959

Contents

Abbreviations

C   "Christographia." A manuscript by Edward Taylor in the Yale University Library.

CD   "China's Description and Commonplace Book." A manuscript by Edward Taylor in the Yale University Library.

Cent. Dict.   *The Century Dictionary and Cyclopedia*, 12 vols. New York, Century, 1889–1911.

Conj.   Conjectural reading.

CP   "Commonplace Book." A manuscript by Edward Taylor in the Massachusetts Historical Society Collection of manuscripts.

CR   Westfield "Church Record." A manuscript by Edward Taylor in the Westfield Athenaeum.

D   "Dispensatory." A manuscript by Edward Taylor in the Yale University Library.

DAE   *A Dictionary of American English*, ed. Sir William A. Craigie and James R. Hulbert, Chicago, University of Chicago Press, 1938–44.

DB   Sir William Smith, *Dr. William Smith's Dictionary of the Bible*, rev. and ed. by H. B. Hackett, New York, Hurd and Houghton, 1868–70.

DTP   "Diary, Theological Notes, and Poems." A manuscript by Edward Taylor in the Redwood Athenaeum.

EDD   *The English Dialect Dictionary*, 6 vols. London, Henry Frowde, 1898–1905.

ETG   Thomas H. Johnson, "Some Edward Taylor Gleanings," *New England Quarterly, 16* (1943), 280–96.

ETP   Thomas H. Johnson, "Edward Taylor: A Puritan 'Sacred Poet,'" *New England Quarterly, 10* (1937), 290–322.

H   F. E. Hutchinson, ed., *The Works of George Herbert*, Oxford University Press, 1941.

HDB   Madeline S. Miller and J. Lane Miller, *Harper's Bible Dictionary*, New York, Harper's, 1952.

HG   "Harmony of the Gospels." A manuscript by Edward Taylor in the Redwood Athenaeum.

J   Thomas H. Johnson.

M   "Metallographia." A manuscript by Edward Taylor in the Yale University Library.

MGG   Morris A. Neufeld, "A Meditation upon the Glory of God," *Yale University Library Gazette, 25* (1951), 110–11.

MH   "Metrical History of Christianity." A manuscript by Edward Taylor in the Redwood Athenaeum.

OED   *The Oxford English Dictionary*, 12 vols. Oxford, Clarendon Press, 1933.

orig: Originally (used in textual notes to indicate words canceled by Taylor).

PET   Barbara Damon Simison, "Poems by Edward Taylor," *Yale University Library Gazette, 28* (1954), 93–102, 161–70; *29* (1954), 25–34, 71–80.

PW   The "Poetical Works" of Edward Taylor. Manuscript in the Yale University Library.

Reg   *The New England Historical and Genealogical Register.*

RTS   Cotton Mather, *Right Thoughts in Sad Hours*, London, 1689.

SCP   Thomas H. Johnson, "A Seventeenth Century Printing of Some Verses of Edward Taylor," *New England Quarterly, 14* (1941), 139–41.

SMT   Donald E. Stanford, "Sacramental Meditations by Edward Taylor," *Yale University Library Gazette, 31* (1956), 61–75.

TVT   Thomas H. Johnson, "The Topical Verses of Edward Taylor," *Transactions of the Colonial Society of Massachusetts, 34* (1942), 513–54.

UPT   Donald E. Stanford, "Nineteen Unpublished Poems by Edward Taylor," *American Literature, 29* (1957), 18–46.

W   Thomas H. Johnson, *The Poetical Works of Edward Taylor*, Rockland Editions, 1939; Princeton University Press, 1943.

WDB   *The Westminster Dictionary of the Bible*, Philadelphia, Westminster Press, 1944.

WNI   *Webster's New International Dictionary*, Springfield, Mass., Merriam, 1956.

Z   Copies of poems by Edward Taylor found in the binding of the "Poetical Works."

Foreword BY LOUIS L. MARTZ

Bad Poetry in Meditation [handwritten note]

The importance of the present volume lies primarily in the fact that it offers for the first time the complete text of Edward Taylor's major work, the *Preparatory Meditations,* consisting of 217 poems, written from 1682 to 1725, while Taylor was serving as minister to the frontier settlement of Westfield, Massachusetts. Since 128 of these *Meditations* have never before been published, the full range and power of the work have not been manifested; and, as a result, students of Taylor have tended to give at least equal attention to his long doctrinal allegory, *Gods Determinations,* which has been completely available in Thomas Johnson's valuable selection from Taylor's poetry. *Gods Determinations* is a significant work, unique in English poetry; it reveals the workings of the Puritan doctrine of Grace through a framework derived from the old devices of medieval allegory; and it develops, by the blunt insistence of its verse, a certain crude and battering strength. Yet when all is said, *Gods Determinations* remains, I think, a labor of versified doctrine; only a few of its lyrics can approach the best of the *Meditations* in poetical quality. In the end, Taylor's standing as a poet must be measured by a full and careful reading of the *Meditations.*

Such a reading leaves no doubt that Taylor is a true poet, and yet it is a strange experience, hard to evaluate and explain. For Taylor leads us, inevitably, to compare his achievement with the consummate artistry of George Herbert, whose poetry Taylor echoes throughout the *Meditations,* as well as in his other poems. The example of Herbert appears with special force at the beginning of the present volume; in the "Prologue" Taylor five times repeats Herbert's phrase "crumb of dust":

> Lord, Can a Crumb of Dust the Earth outweigh,
> Outmatch all mountains, nay the Chrystall Sky?

It seems a clear echo of Herbert's "The Temper" (I), which also deals with the speaker's sense of inadequacy in attempting the praise of his Lord:

> Wilt thou meet arms with man, that thou dost stretch
> A crumme of dust from heav'n to hell?

And the whole conception of Taylor's poem is perhaps influenced also by a stanza from Herbert's "Longing":

> Behold, thy dust doth stirre,
> It moves, it creeps, it aims at thee:
> Wilt thou deferre
> To succour me,
> Thy pile of dust, wherein each crumme
> Sayes, Come?

The "Prologue" thus prepares us for the strongly Herbertian mode of the first Meditation, with its theme of Love and its familiar exclamations in the presence of the Lord: "Oh! that thy Love might overflow my Heart!" Then, shortly after, we have the three poems that Taylor entitled "The Experience," "The Return," and "The Reflexion"—the only poems in the sequence thus entitled—with their clear reminiscence of the many titles of this kind among Herbert's poetry: "The Answer," "The Reprisall," "The Glance." But these and the other particular echoes of Herbert pointed out in Mr. Stanford's annotations are only the most evident aspects of a pervasive influence. Like Henry Vaughan, Edward Taylor appears to have had a mind saturated with Herbert's poetry, and the result is that a thousand tantalizing echoes of Herbert remain for the most part untraceable because the meditative voice of Herbert has been merged with Taylor's own peculiar voice.

"How sweet a Lord is mine?" "I'le be thy Love, thou my sweet Lord shalt bee." "Then let thy Spirit keepe my Strings in tune." "Blushes of Beauty bright, Pure White, and Red." "My Dear, Deare, Lord I do thee Saviour Call." "What Glory's this, my Lord?" "Oh! Bright! Bright thing! I fain would something say." "Lord speake it home to me, say these are mine." "Oh! that I ever felt what I profess." "What rocky heart is mine?" "Was ever Heart like mine?" "Fain I would sing thy Praise, but feare I feign." "Strang, strang indeed." "I fain would prize and praise thee." "What love, my Lord, dost thou lay out on thine."

> Dull, Dull indeed! What shall it e're be thus?
> And why? Are not thy Promises, my Lord,

> Rich, Quick'ning things? How should my full Cheeks blush
> To finde mee thus? And those a lifeless Word?
> My Heart is heedless: unconcernd hereat:
> I finde my Spirits Spiritless, and flat.   [2.12]

All the above quotations are by Taylor; they would not disrupt the harmony of Herbert's *Temple,* and they could be multiplied a hundred times. Yet the full effect of any single poem by Taylor is never quite Herbertian.

Taylor has, first of all, very little of Herbert's metrical skill. In *Gods Determinations* and in the series of short poems on various "occurrants" Taylor attempts to deal with a great variety of stanza forms, in Herbert's way, but with only moderate success. In his *Meditations* no such variety is tried: every poem is written in the popular six-line stanza used in Herbert's "Church-porch." Taylor's handling of this stanza seldom rises above competence, and all too often he gives a lame effect of counting syllables and forcing rimes:

> I needed have this hand, that broke off hath
> This Bud of Civill, and of Sacred Faith.

> untill my Virginall
> Chime out in Changes sweet thy Praises shall.

> To view those glories in thy Crown that vapor,
> Would make bright Angells eyes to run a-water.

This sort of clumsiness, in some degree, is found in most of the poems.

Another problem arises when we compare the language of Herbert and Taylor, especially their use of terms from daily speech. As the above examples indicate, Taylor frequently attains the neat and flexible delicacy of Herbert's conversations with God, where the poet speaks in the presence of a familiar friend, as in Herbert's "Easter":

> I got me flowers to straw thy way;
> I got me boughs off many a tree:
> But thou wast up by break of day,
> And brought'st thy sweets along with thee.

This is colloquial, but chastened and restrained: Herbert's language never strays far from the middle way of educated conversation. Herbert was bred in courtly circles, and though he knows that "Kneeling ne'er spoil'd silk stocking," he does not allow slang, dialect, or "low" terms to spoil his neatness. If he allows a line like "The worky-daies are the back-part," this is exceptional: it is at once absorbed into a more discreet context. But consider these lines by Taylor:

> Thus my leane Muses garden thwarts the spring
>> Instead of Anthems, breatheth her ahone.
> But duty raps upon her doore for Verse.
> That makes her bleed a poem through her searce. [2.30]

Terms like "ahone" and "searce" bring us up abruptly; they lie outside the mainstream of the language, along with dozens of other terms scattered profusely throughout the poetry: *I'st, bedotcht, brudled, crickling, flur, frim, gastard, glout, keck, paintice, riggalld, skeg, slatch, snick-snarls, tantarrow'd, weddenwise, an hurden haump.* Words like these, whether coinages, phonetic spellings, or Leicestershire dialect, require a sizable glossary, such as that provided at the end of the present volume. And the problem is compounded by the fact that Taylor's range runs at the same time to the far end of the learned spectrum: *epinicioum, dulcifi'de, enkentrism, enucleate, officine, fistulate, obsignation, aromatize, theanthropie, bituminated.* Even John Donne, who likes to mingle learned and colloquial terms, does not display in his poetry so wide a range as this; and for Herbert, of course, extremes in either direction are to be avoided: he follows Ben Jonson's dictum: "Pure and neat language I love, yet plain and customary."

The problems presented by Taylor's strangely assorted diction are inseparable from a third difficulty: his use of the homeliest images to convey the most sacred and reverend themes. Here again Herbert leads the way, with his "Elixir":

> All may of thee partake:
> Nothing can be so mean,
>> Which with his tincture (for thy sake)
> Will not grow bright and clean.

> A servant with this clause
> Makes drudgerie divine:
> Who sweeps a room, as for thy laws,
> Makes that and th' action fine.

But with Herbert these homely images are handled with a bland understatement, a deft restraint:

> You must sit down, sayes Love, and taste my meat:
> So I did sit and eat.

And in this love, more then in bed, I rest.

> This day my Saviour rose,
> And did inclose this light for his:
> That, as each beast his manger knows,
> Man might not of his fodder misse.
> Christ hath took in this piece of ground,
> And made a garden there for those
> Who want herbs for their wound. ["Sunday"]

Herbert thus succeeds by the total poise of his poem: where every syllable is taut, we cannot doubt the speaker's word. But what shall we say of Taylor's treatment of Jonah as the "type" of Christ?

> The Grave him swallow'd down as a rich Pill
> Of Working Physick full of Virtue which
> Doth purge Death's Constitution of its ill.
> And womble-Crops her stomach where it sticks.
> It heaves her stomach till her hasps off fly.
> And out hee comes Cast up, rais'd up thereby. [2.30]

Or this treatment of the sinner's state?

> Mine Heart's a Park or Chase of sins: Mine Head
> 'S a Bowling Alley. Sins play Ninehole here.
> Phansy's a Green: sin Barly breaks in't led.
> Judgment's a pingle. Blindeman's Buff's plaid there.
> Sin playes at Coursey Parke within my Minde.
> My Wills a Walke in which it aires what's blinde. [2.18]

Or this account of the operations of Grace?

> Shall things run thus? Then Lord, my tumberill
>   Unload of all its Dung, and make it cleane.
> And load it with thy wealthi'st Grace untill
>   Its Wheeles do crack, or Axletree complain.
>   I fain would have it cart thy harvest in,
>   Before its loosed from its Axlepin. [1.46]

A brief acquaintance with Taylor's poetry might easily lead us to dismiss him as a burlap version of Herbert, a quaint primitive who somehow, despite the Indians, managed to stammer out his rude verses well enough to win the title of "our best Colonial poet." Such a judgment would be utterly wrong. Taylor is not a primitive: he is a subtle, learned man who kept his Theocritus and Origen, his Augustine and Horace, with him in the wilderness. We have the inventory of his library: it would have done credit to a London clergyman, and for one on the Westfield frontier it is all but incredible—until we realize that the Puritan minister of New England did not come to make terms with the wilderness: he came to preserve the Truth in all its purity and wonder. Taylor's *Meditations* represent a lifelong effort of the inner man to apprehend that Truth.

2

As we read more deeply and more widely in his poetry, we gradually become aware of the tenacious intelligence that underlies these surface crudities: a bold, probing, adventurous intellect that deliberately tries to bend the toughest matter toward his quest for truth. Consider closely, as a representative example, Meditation 32 of the first series, on the text: "1 Cor. 3.22. Whether Paul or Apollos, or Cephas." We need the whole context of those names: *For all things are yours; whether Paul, or Apollos, or Cephas, or the world, or life, or death, or things present, or things to come; all are yours; and ye are Christ's; and Christ is God's.*

> Thy Grace, Deare Lord's my golden Wrack, I finde
>   Screwing my Phancy into ragged Rhimes,

Tuning thy Praises in my feeble minde
    Untill I come to strike them on my Chimes.
    Were I an Angell bright, and borrow could
King Davids Harp, I would them play on gold.

But plung'd I am, my minde is puzzled,
    When I would spin my Phancy thus unspun,
In finest Twine of Praise I'm muzzled.
    My tazzled Thoughts twirld into Snick-Snarls run.
    Thy Grace, my Lord, is such a glorious thing,
    It doth Confound me when I would it sing.

There is an effect of deliberate roughness here, of struggling for
adequate expression, climaxed in the vigorous line: "My tazzled
Thoughts twirld into Snick-Snarls run." And now, to work his
way out of this ragged state, the speaker in the next two stanzas
turns to analyse the meaning of God's Love and Grace in lines
that gradually become clear, more harmonious, more fluent:

Eternall Love an Object mean did smite
    Which by the Prince of Darkness was beguilde,
That from this Love it ran and sweld with spite
    And in the way with filth was all defilde
    Yet must be reconcild, cleansd, and begrac'te
    Or from the fruits of Gods first Love displac'te.

Then Grace, my Lord, wrought in thy Heart a vent,
    Thy Soft Soft hand to this hard worke did goe,
And to the Milke White Throne of Justice went
    And entred bond that Grace might overflow.
    Hence did thy Person to my Nature ty
    And bleed through humane Veans to satisfy.

There, in the middle stanza of the poem, the central act of Grace
is brought home, with perfect clarity and cadence, to the speaker's
mind. As a result, his "Snick-Snarls" disappear, and he bursts
forth into spontaneous praise:

Oh! Grace, Grace, Grace! this Wealthy Grace doth lay
    Her Golden Channells from thy Fathers throne,

Into our Earthen Pitchers to Convay
   Heavens Aqua Vitae to us for our own.
   O! let thy Golden Gutters run into
   My Cup this Liquour till it overflow.

He pauses, then, to analyse the meaning of these images which
have burst out so unexpectedly:

Thine Ordinances, Graces Wine-fats where
   Thy Spirits Walkes, and Graces runs doe ly
And Angells waiting stand with holy Cheere
   From Graces Conduite Head, with all Supply.
   These Vessells full of Grace are, and the Bowls
   In which their Taps do run, are pretious Souls.

The term "Ordinances" refers specifically to the sacraments of
Communion and Baptism, held by Taylor to be the "Seales of
the Covenant of Grace" (see Glossary: "Sacraments"); but more
generally, the term includes the Decrees and Determinations sig-
nified by those sacraments. These are the vats of wine from which
Grace runs to save the human soul. Realizing now the immensity
and the richness of the gift, the speaker has achieved his wish to
"play on gold": Grace conveyed through those "Golden Chan-
nells" and "Golden Gutters" has brought to the speaker's soul a
"Golden Word":

Thou to the Cups dost say (that Catch this Wine,)
   This Liquour, Golden Pipes, and Wine-fats plain,
Whether Paul, Apollos, Cephas, all are thine.
   Oh Golden Word! Lord speake it ore again.
   Lord speake it home to me, say these are mine.
   My Bells shall then thy Praises bravely chime.

The poem, I believe, creates a total effect of rough integrity,
moving from a ragged opening to the smooth Herbertian phras-
ing of the close. The rough phrasing, the colloquialism, the
vividly concrete imagery, the Herbertian echoes all play their part
in a total pattern. I will not argue that such a control is always
present in Taylor's *Meditations*: there is, as I have implied, a fre-
quent clumsiness that has no function; and one cannot defend

his excesses in developed imagery, as when he shows the prisoners
of sin thus released by "the Blood of thy Covenant":

> And now the Prisoners sent out, do come
>   Padling in their Canooes apace with joyes
> Along this blood red Sea, Where joyes do throng . . . [2.78]

But frequently, even in poems with grave flaws, the underlying
control is greater than we might at first think, and sometimes the
flaws recede into insignificance as the whole poem comes into
focus.

At the same time, we must reckon with the fact that the *Medi-
tations* are written in sequences, sometimes with tight links be-
tween the poems. The poem we have just considered, for example,
is part of a sequence of seven Meditations (1.31–37) written on
consecutive aspects of the above-quoted passage from I Corin-
thians 3:21–23. What I have called the tenacity of Taylor's in-
telligence is enforced when we realize that these seven Medita-
tions, like the others, were composed at intervals of about two
months, and sometimes longer, for Communion Sundays; in this
case the poems are dated as follows: 17 February 1688/9; 28 April
1689; 7 July 1689; 25 November 1689; 19 January 1689/90; 16
March 1689/90; and 4 May 1690. These Meditations, then, are
the outgrowth of a planned series on sequential texts, running
over a period of fifteen months. Longer and more striking se-
quences appear: the thirty meditations on "Types" that begin
Taylor's second series; the subsequent series on the nature, love,
and power of Christ (2.31–56), which includes the sequence
(2.42–56) associated with a group of fourteen sermons preserved
by Taylor under the title *Christographia;* the series (2.102–11)
in which Taylor deals with the doctrine of the Lord's Supper;
and lastly, the long series on sequential texts from Canticles
(2.115–53), running from September 1713 to February 1719.

It is worth noting, too, that Taylor started renumbering his
Meditations when he began the series of poems on typology—
that is to say, on events and personages of the Old Testament
that were interpreted as prefigurations of the New Testament.
This would seem to be a clear indication that the 49 opening
meditations constitute a unit of some kind. The number 49 is

probably significant after the manner of the times; it is the perfect multiple of seven, a number whose significance Taylor celebrates in Meditation 21 of the second series:

> What Secret Sweet Mysterie under the Wing
> Of this so much Elected number lies?

In seventeenth-century thought the number 7 and its multiples signified perfection, and it may be that a meditative quest toward the perfect apprehension of God's Love is the key to this opening series. Certainly Love is its theme, as the opening Meditation declares, foreshadowing the struggle of the whole series toward a joyous realization of this Love:

> Oh! that thy Love might overflow my Heart!
> To fire the same with Love: for Love I would.
> But oh! my streight'ned Breast! my Lifeless Sparke!
> My Fireless Flame! What Chilly Love, and Cold?
> In measure small! In Manner Chilly! See.
> Lord blow the Coal: Thy Love Enflame in mee.

Toward the close of the series, after many expressions of desire and longing, the efforts of the lover come to focus more and more upon the promised glories in Heaven, beginning with Meditation 41, on the text "I go to prepare a Place for you":

> Reason, lie prison'd in this golden Chain,
> Chain up thy tongue, and silent stand a while.
> Let this rich Love thy Love and heart obtain
> To tend thy Lord in all admiring Style.

Then the sequence moves through meditations on the "Throne," the "Crown of Life," the "Crown of Righteousness," the "Crown of Glory," and the "White Raiment," to conclude with a sequence of three poems on the text "Enter thou into the joy of thy Lord." Meditation 48 achieves the assurance of an affectionate realization:

> When I, Lord, eye thy Joy, and my Love, small,
> My heart gives in: what now? Strange! Sure I love thee!
> And finding brambles 'bout my heart to crawl
> My heart misgives mee. Prize I ought above thee?

Such great Love hugging them, such small Love, thee!
Whether thou hast my Love, I scarce can see.

·   ·   ·

Yet when the beamings, Lord, of thy rich Joys,
    Do guild my Soule, meethinks I'm sure I Love thee.
They Calcine all these brambly trumperys
    And now I'm sure that I prize naught above thee.

And Meditation 49 gives the effect of a formal conclusion, since
it offers a sustained prayer for the continued operations of Grace
upon his sinful soul:

A Lock of Steel upon my Soule, whose key
    The serpent keeps, I fear, doth lock my doore.
O pick't: and through the key-hole make thy way
    And enter in: and let thy joyes run o're.

Thus, as the full effect of an individual Meditation often en-
folds and sustains a number of flaws in detail, so a weak poem may
be enfolded and sustained by the part it plays in a developing
sequence. The flaws are there, and we do not overlook them; yet
the poems, in the large, succeed in creating a highly original
world, designed upon a special plan. It is a world where the Puri-
tan doctrine of Grace operates to consecrate, within the soul of
one of the Elect, every object, every word, every thought that
passes through his anguished, grateful, loving mind. To under-
stand the workings of that world, we need to explore the meaning
of that key word which Taylor repeated in his titles, more than
two hundred times: "meditation."

3

For a Puritan minister of New England in the year 1682, the
word "meditation" would have retained, certainly, some of the
grimmer implications that it held among the older generation of
Puritan ministers, for whom the word signified, primarily, a rig-
orous self-examination designed to uncover the sins of fallen man.
The eminent Connecticut divine Thomas Hooker, for example,
devotes seventy-five pages of his treatise *The Application of Re-
demption* (London, 1657) to a vigorous exhortation toward the

"Meditation of sins" as "a special means to break the heart of a sinner" (pp. 208–83). Meditation, he declares, "is as it were the register and remembrancer, that looks over the records of our daily corruptions, and keeps them upon file." Moreover, "Meditation is that which encreaseth the weight of the evil of sin, presseth it down upon the Conscience, and burdens the heart with it until it break under it. It gleans up, and rakes together al the particulars, adds dayly to the load, and laies on until the Axletree split asunder, and the heart fails and dies away under the apprehension of the dreadfulness of the evil." Thus "daily meditation flings in one terror after another," "holds the heart upon the rack under restless and unsupportable pressures," with the result that "the sinner is forced to walk and talk with [sin], to wake and sleep with it, to eat and drink his sins." In this way, "by serious meditation we sew them all up together, we look back to the linage and pedegree of our lusts, and track the abominations of our lives, step by step, until we come to the very nest where they are hatched and bred, even of our original corruption" (pp. 208, 212–13, 219, 221, 271).

But in Edward Taylor's day other aspects of the word "meditation" were operating in Puritan circles, aspects that served to modify and ameliorate the fearsome rigor of the older generation. The clearest indication of these newer tendencies, I think, may be found by turning to the most important Puritan treatise on meditation written during the seventeenth century, the fourth part of Richard Baxter's famous work *The Saints Everlasting Rest* (London, 1650). Baxter's works were well known in New England; Taylor's own library contained two of Baxter's treatises, although the *Everlasting Rest* is not one of them. We should recall, too, that Taylor did not leave England until 1668, when he was about the age of 25; he was already highly educated and apparently designed for the ministry; he is said to have attended Cambridge University, and, as Mr. Stanford points out, he was at once admitted to Harvard with advanced standing. Taylor, then, came to maturity in England at just the time when the temporary victory of the Puritan Commonwealth had released into new areas the powerful energies of English Puritanism, long constricted by the fierce struggle for survival.

Baxter's treatise on meditation is one of many signs that English Puritanism, in its mid-century moment of dominance, was reaching out into areas hitherto neglected: the place of the mystical Platonist Peter Sterry as Cromwell's chaplain and the presence of John Milton and Andrew Marvell in the inner circles of Cromwell's government will testify to the rich expansion of outlook that occurred in this brief interval. Richard Baxter's treatise, with ten editions appearing in the years 1650–70, played its part in this development by urging Puritans to undertake what his title page calls "the Diligent Practice of that Excellent unknown Duty of *Heavenly Meditation*"—formal meditation on the joys of Heaven. A brief account of Baxter's mode of meditation will help to show how closely Taylor's poetry accords with the expanding outlook of contemporary Puritanism.

Meditation in his sense of the term, Baxter declares, is "unknown" among his people, largely because they have spent so much time in running "from Sermon to Sermon," or in examining their souls for "signs of their sincerity," or in passively awaiting the gift of "Enthusiastick Consolations" (Pt. IV, pp. 5, 147; I quote from the London edition of 1653). Baxter is clearly attempting to add another dimension to the state of mind that Perry Miller has acutely described in the second chapter of *The New England Mind: The Seventeenth Century,* where he deals with that "unceasing self-examination" by which the Puritan attempted to assure himself that he was indeed regenerated, sanctified, elected. To be sure, the word "meditation" is well known and often used among these people, but, Baxter says, they do not understand its true meaning: "They have thought that Meditation is nothing but the bare thinking on Truths, and the rolling of them in the understanding and memory" (IV, 151). And no one, he notes, in a passage that may bear a special import for the study of Taylor's poetry—no one is more prone to this error than "those that are much in publick duty, especially Preachers of the Gospel."

> O how easily may they be deceived here, while they do nothing more then read of Heaven, and study of Heaven, and preach of Heaven, and pray, and talk of Heaven? what, is not this the Heavenly Life? O that God would reveal to our

hearts the danger of this snare! Alas, all this is but meer prep-
aration: This is not the life we speak of, but it's indeed a
necessary help thereto. I entreat every one of my Brethren in
the Ministry, that they search, and watch against this Temp-
tation: Alas, this is but gathering the materials, and not the
erecting of the building it self; this is but gathering our
Manna for others, and not eating and digesting our
selves . . . [IV, 122]

And therefore Baxter says to all his people: "this is the great task
in hand, and this is the work that I would set thee on; to get these
truths from thy head to thy heart, and that all the Sermons which
thou hast heard of Heaven, and all the notions that thou hast
conceived of this Rest, may be turned into the bloud and spirits of
Affection, and thou maist feel them revive thee, and warm thee at
the heart" (IV, 151).

Taylor's *Meditations* seem to bear exactly this relation to his
sermons, as his full title makes clear: "Preparatory Meditations
before my Approach to the Lords Supper. Chiefly upon the Doc-
trin preached upon the Day of administration." Norman Grabo,
in his forthcoming edition of Taylor's *Christographia,* will show
how sermon and Meditation correspond, bearing the same dates
and, with one exception, the same biblical text. The sermon pre-
pares the ground, the doctrine, for the Meditation; while the
act of meditation in turn prepares the preacher to receive and
administer the sacrament, and to deliver his sermon on that day
with "the bloud and spirits of Affection." These poems, then, are
properly called *Preparatory Meditations* (not *Sacramental Medi-
tations,* as they have hitherto been called, after a title added by
another hand, above Taylor's own title): they preserve, in the
finest verbal form that Taylor could give, his efforts "to get these
truths" from his head to his heart.

Baxter, in a long exposition, makes clear every aspect of the art
of meditation as he wished his people to practice it. The method,
as I have tried to show in *The Poetry of Meditation,* is essentially
the same as that which had been advocated, over the preceding
century, by Catholic handbooks of devotion. It consists of three
essential acts, corresponding to the old division of the faculties

— Meditation is an art or a method —

or "powers" of the soul into Memory, Understanding, and Will.
Thus the work of meditation, for Baxter, proceeds by "the set
and solemn acting of all the powers of the soul" (IV, 146). This
meditation, he explains, is "set and solemn" because it is per-
formed "when a Christian observing it as a standing duty, doth
resolvedly practise it in a constant course" (IV, 153). First, he
directs, "you must by *cogitation* go to the Memory (which is the
Magazine or Treasury of the Understanding); thence you must
take forth those *heavenly doctrines,* which you intend to make
the subject of your *Meditation.*" Then, after "you have fetcht
from your memory the *matter* of your *Meditation,* your next
work is to present it to your *Judgment:* open there the case as
fully as thou canst" (IV, 186–7). He has explained earlier that the
"great Instrument that this Work is done by, is Ratiocination,
Reasoning the case with your selves, Discourse of mind, Cogita-
tion, or Thinking; or, if you will, call it Consideration." This
Consideration, he declares, "doth, as it were, open the door, be-
tween the Head and the Heart" (IV, 178–9).

He particularly urges that the work of Consideration be carried
on by means of *Soliloquy,* "which is nothing but a pleading the
case with our own Souls," or, he adds, "a Preaching to ones self."
"Why thus must thou do in thy *Meditation* to quicken thy own
heart: Enter into a serious debate with it: Plead with it in the
most moving and affecting language: Urge it with the most
weighty and powerful *Arguments*" (IV, 209–10). And so, through
the vigorous use of the understanding, the soul is aroused to feel
the Affections (emotions or feelings) of the Will, which, according
to Baxter, should be developed in a certain order: Love, Desire,
Hope, Courage (Resolution), and, lastly, Joy.

I believe that anyone who reads carefully through the first 49
Meditations of Edward Taylor will quickly sense how closely
the poetry accords with such advice by Baxter. It is not essential,
of course, to believe that Taylor learned this mode of meditation
from Baxter's treatise. By 1682 Baxter's influence had been widely
disseminated throughout English Puritanism; and during Tay-
lor's youth in England exhortations to this kind of meditation
were available in Catholic or Anglo-Catholic treatises. The chief
point is that both Baxter and Taylor, while maintaining all the

central Puritan tenets, were participating in one of the central movements of religious devotion in the seventeenth century.

The entire process is accompanied by two other elements which are, in Baxter's view, essential to success in meditation, and are of the utmost importance for Taylor's poetry. The first of these is Prayer: requests to God "may be intermixed or added, and that as a very part of the duty it self." Such constant prayer, Baxter says, "keeps the Soul in mind of the *Divine Presence;* it tends also exceedingly to quicken and raise it; so that as God is the highest Object of our *Thoughts,* so our viewing of him, and our speaking to him, and pleading with him, doth more elevate the soul, and actuate the affections, then any other part of *Meditation* can do" (IV, 214).

And secondly, we have the advice stressed by Kenneth Murdock in the second chapter of his study *Literature and Theology in Colonial New England.* As one is aided by the upward looks of Prayer, so the meditative man may be constantly aided by downward looks: the senses themselves should be used "to make your *thoughts* of *Heaven* to be piercing, affecting, raising *thoughts.*" The time has come, Baxter believes, for Puritanism to moderate its mistrust of sensory aids in the service of religion. "Why sure it will be a point of our Spiritual prudence, and a singular help to the furthering of the work of Faith, to call in our Sense to its assistance . . . Sure it is both possible and lawful, yea, and necessary too, to do something in this kind; for God would not have given us either our senses themselves, or their usual objects, if they might not have been serviceable to his own Praise, and helps to raise us up to the apprehension of higher things" (IV, 216–17). Following the lead of Scriptural imagery, we must make every effort to apprehend the joys of heaven with our senses: "get the liveliest Picture of them in thy minde that possibly thou canst; meditate of them, as if thou were all the while beholding them, and as if thou were even hearing the *Hallelujahs,* while thou art thinking of them; till thou canst say, Methinks I see a glimpse of the Glory! Methinks I hear the shouts of Joy and Praise!" (IV, 220–21). And he continues for twenty more pages to suggest various ways in which sensory objects and personal experiences may be used constantly "to quicken your

was designed to prepare the minister for Divine Communion — the Lord's Supper

affections, by comparing the unseen delights of Heaven, with those smaller which you have seen, and felt in the flesh" (IV, 242).

4

Taylor's imagery

In Baxter's arguments for the use of sensory images in meditation we have, I believe, the grounds of justification for Taylor's bold and often unseemly use of common imagery. For Baxter's support of this way of meditation is thoroughly and vehemently argued: "He that will speak to mans understanding must speak in mans language, and speak that which he is capable to conceive." "Go to then," he exclaims, "When thou settest thy self to meditate on the joyes above, think on them boldly as Scripture hath expressed them. Bring down thy conceivings to the reach of sense, Excellency without familiarity, doth more amaze then delight us: Both Love and Joy are promoted by familiar acquaintance" (IV, 218–19). Baxter is speaking at this point particularly of meditation upon the Everlasting Rest in Heaven; but he points out elsewhere (IV, 208) that the same methods may be used "for the acting of the contrary and more mixed passions"—such as "hatred and detestation of sin," grief, shame, repentance, and so on.

The whole of the spiritual life, then, is to be apprehended in sensory and colloquial terms. Everything that exists may be used to promote this "familiar acquaintance": thus Taylor uses a rolling pin, roast mutton, a bowling alley, a "Bucking tub," a "Titimouses Quill," milk pails, a "Drippen pan," a "Dish clout," a "Trough of Washing-Swill." "Nothing that is available in human experience is to be legislated out of poetry," says R. P. Warren in a classic essay of modern criticism; Edward Taylor clearly agrees. Are we searching for the nature of Love? Here is the way to bring it home to the heart:

> O! what a thing is Love? who can define
>   Or liniament it out? Its strange to tell.
> A Sparke of Spirit empearld pill like and fine
>   In't shugard pargings, crusted, and doth dwell
>   Within the heart, where thron'd, without Controle
>   It ruleth all the Inmates of the Soule.

It makes a poother in its Secret Sell
  Mongst the affections: oh! it swells, its paind,
Like kirnells soked untill it breaks its Shell
  Unless its object be obtained and gain'd.
  Like Caskd wines jumbled breake the Caske, this Sparke
  Oft swells when crusht: untill it breakes the Heart. [2.66]

Or perhaps we are searching for a way to drive home the horrors
of sin:

My Sin! my Sin, My God, these Cursed Dregs,
  Green, Yellow, Blew streakt Poyson hellish, ranck,
Bubs hatcht in natures nest on Serpents Eggs,
  Yelp, Cherp and Cry; they set my Soule a Cramp.
  I frown, Chide, strik and fight them, mourn and Cry
  To Conquour them, but cannot them destroy.

I cannot kill nor Coop them up: my Curb
  'S less than a Snaffle in their mouth: my Rains
They as a twine thrid, snap: by hell they're spurd:
  And load my Soule with swagging loads of pains.
  Black Imps, young Divells, snap, bite, drag to bring
  And pick mee headlong hells dread Whirle Poole in.

                                              [1.39]

As these examples indicate, Taylor has a way of shifting im-
petuously from image to image in his effort to define and bring
home the spiritual import; in the above four stanzas the images
work without confusion, but elsewhere, as earlier critics of Taylor
have noted, he jumps from image to image in a way that tends
to shake the poem apart: Meditation 37 in the first series will
provide examples of this weakness. But a more serious flaw in
Taylor's handling of imagery seems to arise from the opposite
tendency: he frequently hangs on to an image until he has
strained it by excessive ingenuity: Meditation 38 in the first
series seems to me an example of this sort of excess.

  Yet when all his flaws in dealing with imagery have been ac-
knowledged, even at his worst he retains an attractive vigor; and
at his best he can produce an analysed image of a subtlety that
equals Herbert:

> I have no plea mine Advocate to give:
>   What now? He'l anvill Arguments greate Store
> Out of his Flesh and Blood to make thee live.
>   O Deare bought Arguments: Good pleas therefore.
>   Nails made of heavenly Steel, more Choice than gold
>   Drove home, Well Clencht, eternally will hold. [1.39]

Thus the nails driven through the flesh of Christ on the Cross are made to symbolize the certainty, as well as the means, of Christ's effective advocacy.

At other times the casual introduction of a homely image or expression is enough to give life to a passage that seems doomed to dryness; thus Taylor deals with Joseph as a Type of Christ:

> Is Josephs glorious shine a Type of thee?
>   How bright art thou? He Envi'de was as well.
> And so was thou. He's stript, and pick't, poore hee,
>   Into the pit. And so was thou. They shell
>   Thee of thy Kirnell. He by Judah's sold
>   For twenty Bits, thirty for thee he'd told.
>
> Joseph was tempted by his Mistress vile.
>   Thou by the Divell, but both shame the foe.
> Joseph was cast into the jayle awhile.
>   And so was thou. Sweet apples mellow so. [2.7]

Sweet apples mellow so. One can endure a good deal of Taylor's clumsiness for one such effect of "familiar acquaintance."

But in the final analysis the success of Taylor's homely images and earthy language must depend on how they function in the whole poem. Here again, I believe, the meditative discipline that lies behind and within the poetry has enabled Taylor to give many of his poetical meditations a firm and operative structure. For the most part, his Meditations are working at the achieved level of the Affections. Like the "Divine Meditations" (Holy Sonnets) of John Donne, the sonnets of Gerard Manley Hopkins, or the poems of George Herbert, Taylor's Meditations represent the peaks and pinnacles of the meditative process on which the poet's spiritual life is based:

And now his shining Love beams out its rayes
    My Soul, upon thy Heart to thaw the same:
To animate th'Affections till they blaze;
    To free from Guilt, and from Sins Slough, and Shame.
    Open thy Casement wide, let Glory in,
    To Guild thy Heart to be an Hall for him.

My Breast, be thou the ringing Virginalls:
    Ye mine Affections, their sweet Golden Strings,
My Panting Heart, be thou for Stops, and Falls:
    Lord, let thy quick'ning Beams dance o're the Pins. [1.18]

But at the same time this music of the Affections will frequently, and indeed usually, reflect in some measure the stages by which the soul has reached such a level of religious experience. Consequently, in Taylor's meditative poems, as in Donne's or Herbert's or Hopkins', we can often trace clearly, preserved in miniature, the whole process of a meditation, in Baxter's meaning of the term. One example must serve: Meditation 29 of the first series, on the text: "Joh. 20.17. My Father, and your Father, to my God, and your God." The context is important, for the words are spoken by the risen Jesus in the garden of the sepulcher, after Mary Magdalene has mistaken him for the gardener; the garden of the Gospel has provided Taylor with a setting from which the hand of Meditation can draw forth from the Memory the following vivid picture:

My shattred Phancy stole away from mee,
    (Wits run a Wooling over Edens Parke)
And in Gods Garden saw a golden Tree,
    Whose Heart was All Divine, and gold its barke.
    Whose glorious limbs and fruitfull branches strong
    With Saints, and Angells bright are richly hung.

With the situation thus firmly established, Consideration then projects the speaker's own plight upon the scene, and explains, with careful analysis, the exact relation of Man to God by developing the central image of a "Grafft" upon that Tree.

Thou! thou! my Deare-Deare Lord, art this rich Tree
    The Tree of Life Within Gods Paradise.

I am a Withred Twig, dri'de fit to bee
    A Chat Cast in thy fire, Writh off by Vice.
    Yet if thy Milke white-Gracious Hand will take mee
    And grafft mee in this golden stock, thou'lt make mee.

Thou'lt make me then its Fruite, and Branch to spring.
    And though a nipping Eastwinde blow, and all
Hells Nymps with spite their Dog's sticks thereat ding
    To Dash the Grafft off, and it's fruits to fall,
    Yet I shall stand thy Grafft, and Fruits that are
    Fruits of the Tree of Life thy Grafft shall beare.

I being grafft in thee there up to stand
    In us Relations all that mutuall are.
I am thy Patient, Pupill, Servant, and
    Thy Sister, Mother, Doove, Spouse, Son, and Heire.
    Thou art my Priest, Physician, Prophet, King,
    Lord, Brother, Bridegroom, Father, Ev'ry thing.

I being grafft in thee am graffted here
    Into thy Family, and kindred Claim
To all in Heaven, God, Saints, and Angells there.
    I thy Relations my Relations name.
    Thy Father's mine, thy God my God, and I
    With Saints, and Angells draw Affinity.

Reason has opened the case as fully as it can, and the door be-
tween the head and the heart now stands ajar: the poem concludes
with a surge of the Affections toward gratitude and praise:

My Lord, what is it that thou dost bestow?
    The Praise on this account fills up, and throngs
Eternity brimfull, doth overflow
    The Heavens vast with rich Angelick Songs.
    How should I blush? how Tremble at this thing,
    Not having yet my Gam-Ut, learnd to sing.

But, Lord, as burnish't Sun Beams forth out fly
    Let Angell-Shine forth in my Life out flame,
That I may grace thy gracefull Family
    And not to thy Relations be a Shame.

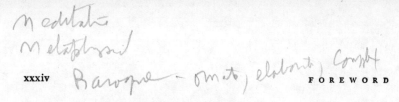

Make mee thy Grafft, be thou my Golden Stock.
Thy Glory then I'le make my fruits and Crop.

5

Some readers will no doubt prefer to describe the action of this analysed conceit as "metaphysical" or, perhaps, "baroque." I do not mean to quarrel with these terms, both well established in critical discussion, and each with its own particular use. I must confess, however, that both seem less accurate than the term "meditative," when applied to Taylor's *Preparatory Meditations*. For Baxter's kind of meditation is, like poetry, a verbal action developed through every resource that language can offer.

Near the close of his treatise Baxter sets forth an elementary "Example" of a full meditation "for the help of the unskilful." This is written in concrete, colloquial, highly charged language which in places sounds like Taylor's poetry—or even like Herbert's poetry—turned into prose:

> What thinkest thou, O my Soul, of this most blessed state? What! Dost thou stagger at the *Promise of God* through unbelief? . . . Can *God* lie? or he that is the *Truth* it self, be false? Foolish wretch! What need hath God to flatter thee, or deceive thee? why should he promise thee more then he will perform? Art thou not his *Creature?* a little crumb of dust? [IV, 259]

One might hesitate to attribute that phrase "crumb of dust" to a memory of Herbert, were it not for the fact that later in the meditation (IV, 278) we find Baxter quoting a whole stanza from "*Herberts Poems,* The Glance," and three pages after this, Herbert's entire poem "Dotage," and ten pages after this, a stanza (considerably altered) from Herbert's "Mans medley." Then, after a few pages of concluding advice, Baxter places at the very end of his volume "A Poem of Master G. Herbert; In His Temple": one of Herbert's longest poems, covering three pages here—the poem "Home":

> Come dearest Lord; pass not this holy season;
>   My flesh and bones and joynts do pray;

And even my verse, when by the rhyme and reason
The word is, Stay, say's ever, Come.
O shew thy self to me,
Or take me up to thee.

Thus Baxter himself indicates how meditation and poetry converge. Baxter, Herbert, The Psalms, the Canticles—these are enough to suggest the literary traditions which made it possible for Edward Taylor to compose his poetical meditations in the wilderness. They will suggest, too, Taylor's place in literary history as the last heir of the great tradition of English meditative poetry that arose in the latter part of the sixteenth century, with Robert Southwell as its first notable example, continued on through the religious poetry of John Donne (and also in those of his secular poems that have powerful religious elements), reached a fulfillment in the *Temple* of George Herbert, went abroad to include the baroque motifs of Richard Crashaw, found another home in Henry Vaughan's uneven but inspired meditations on the "creatures," strengthened the fiber of Andrew Marvell's slender muse, and, so far as England was concerned, died at the death of Thomas Traherne in 1674, with both his prose meditations and their companionate poems unpublished. But as Crashaw had gone abroad to preserve and extend his Catholic allegiance, so, at the end of the line, in 1668, Edward Taylor sailed for New England, and there, surrounded by the rude and dangerous life of the frontier, composed his Puritan and meditative poems.

What I have said thus far has been concerned with enforcing Taylor's relation to the traditions of English culture. Is there anything in Taylor's poetry that could be called distinctively American? In the whole large range of his *Preparatory Meditations* and *Gods Determinations,* there is almost nothing (except for an occasional canoe or rattlesnake) that one could single out to suggest a specifically American allusion. In some ways Edward Taylor may seem to bear out the charge brought against New England Puritanism by William Carlos Williams in his *In the American Grain* (pp. 110 f.): that the Puritans refused to *touch* —that they set up a "resistance to the wilderness"—"with a ground all blossoming about them." Williams speaks of the "rigid clarity" of their religion, "its *inhuman* clarity, its steel-like thrust from the heart of each isolate man straight into the tabernacle of Jehovah without embellishment or softening." "Its firmness is its beauty . . . Its virtue is to make each man stand alone, surrounded by a density as of the Lord: a seed in its shell." It is true that, so far as local allusion is concerned, Taylor's *Meditations*, one might think, could as well have been written in England—or in India, or in Egypt.

Yet the fact remains that no such poetry was being written in the England of Taylor's day; and indeed, poetry with Taylor's peculiar quality could not, I think, have been written at all in England, even by Taylor himself. For the writer in England, wherever he may be living, works within a certain conditioning imposed by the context of that intimate island's culture: he knows the ways of other learned, literary men; he senses the current modes of writing; and even though he believes in freedom of language, as Baxter does, the writer is nevertheless tacitly and unconsciously influenced by the accepted conventions of public speech and writing in that culture. George Herbert lived in Bemerton, a country parson, and yet he could walk from there to the high and ancient culture of Salisbury. But in Taylor's frontier settlement these guide-lines fall away; cultivated conversation becomes rare; the minister's work is solely occupied with humble folk; his daily life is rude, simple, concerned with the bare, stark facts of survival in a village that is at times little more than a stockade. Even the intellectual life must be limited to the essentials: Taylor's library at his death contained only one work of English poetry: the poems of Anne Bradstreet.

Thus the poet's conversations with God are spoken in a language that the meditative poet, living in England, would never use. For the soul, in meditation, is to speak as the man himself has come to speak; any other language would be dishonest and pretentious. So Taylor speaks in this peculiar mixture of the learned and the rude, the abstract and the earthy, the polite and the vulgar; for such distinctions do not exist in the wilderness.

The result is often lame and crude; in some respects the writer needs the support and guidance of an established culture; but

since he in himself is almost the sole bearer and creator of what-
ever culture his village will possess, he must do what he can
with whatever materials lie at hand. Out of his very deficiencies
he creates a work of rugged and original integrity. The result
helps to mark the beginning of an American language, an Ameri-
can literature.

Introduction BY DONALD E. STANFORD

Edward Taylor was born about 1642 [1] in or near the town of Sketchley, Leicestershire, England. The exact place [2] and year of his birth have not been established. Of his family and his early life in England we know little. The poet mentions two brothers, Joseph and Richard, in his Diary,[3] and the names of these two brothers and a sister-in-law, Alice, appear on an acrostic letter [4] which Taylor wrote before coming to this country. In his "Relation" upon the founding of the Westfield Church [5] he spoke of a strict Christian mother who maintained religious discipline in her home.

Taylor was educated for the ministry. He may have spent several years at the University of Cambridge, but the information concerning his student days is uncertain. However, it should be noted that when he entered Harvard in 1668 he was given advanced standing and his name was put at the foot of his class list, a custom which, according to F. B. Dexter,[6] indicated that a student had had previous college or university training. In his Diary Taylor states that on his voyage to America he read the New Testament in Greek. He probably taught school for a short time at Bagworth, Leicestershire, but was dismissed upon refusal to take the oath required by the Act of Uniformity of 1662: "the ejection of 2,000 dissenting clergymen in 1662," says Sibley, "and the per-

---

1. There is much conflicting evidence concerning the date of Taylor's birth, estimates ranging from 1642 to 1646. According to his obituary in the Boston News Letter (Aug. 7–14, 1729) he was eighty-five at the time of his death in 1729. His tombstone states that he died at the age of eighty-seven.

2. According to a note by John Sibley in his Biographical Sketches of Graduates of Harvard University (3 vols. Cambridge, 1881), 2, 534, Ezra Stiles thought that it was Coventry; Sibley himself gives Sketchley; Stiles' uncle, in the Literary Diary of Ezra Stiles, ed. Franklin B. Dexter (New York, 1901), states that it was Hinckley.

3. The manuscript of the Diary is in the Redwood Athenaeum, Newport, R.I. See Appendix 2, below. It has been published in Proceedings of the Massachusetts Historical Society, 18 (1880), 5–18.

4. In DTP.

5. CR, pp. 81–83. See Appendix 2.

6. "On Some Social Distinctions at Harvard and Yale," Proceedings of the American Antiquarian Society, new ser. 9 (1893–94), 46–47.

secutions which that class of Christians suffered, induced him to a voluntary exile." [7]

On April 26, 1668, Taylor embarked for New England. The Diary of his voyage indicates that, as one would expect of a Puritan landsman, he spent a good deal of time reading the Bible and being seasick. The Diary is of particular interest in that it reveals the author's concern with curious facts of natural history, a characteristic which his grandson, Ezra Stiles, also notes in a sketch of his grandfather.[8] The description (p. 12) of a fish is typical: "We saw a great fish, called a Dubartas, with a head like a notted boar, his back like a great scalded Hogs, his colour like a pilled [peeled] oake; his length (I suppose) was four yards; when we saw him first we took it to have been a piece of a tree, and made to him to get it for firewood."

Taylor landed in Boston on July 5, 1668. He carried letters addressed to Increase Mather, with whom he spent two nights, and to John Hull, the mintmaster, with whom he stayed until he was ready to enter Harvard. On July 14 he had an interview at Harvard with the president, Charles Chauncy. He returned to Cambridge on July 22, staying the night with President Chauncy. He was admitted to Harvard on July 23 and became a pupil of Thomas Graves, senior fellow, the same who was nailed into his own classroom by some of his pupils who disliked his austerity. Our poet was a witness of the prank but not a participant. During his three years at Harvard, Taylor was the college butler, a position usually given to a mature and responsible upper classman.[9]

There is no curriculum extant for the years 1668–71, when Taylor was at Harvard. However, an examination of the Chaunceian Code of 1655 (which is incomplete) and of the program of studies drawn up by Tutor Henry Flynt in 1723 indicates the probable schedule of Taylor's studies.[10] In his sophomore year he reviewed Hebrew, Greek, logic, and rhetoric; continued divinity;

7. Sibley, *2*, 397.
8. In M.
9. The duties of the college butler are described in the "College Book": see *Publications of the Colonial Society of Massachusetts*, *15* (1925), 46–48.
10. Samuel Eliot Morison, *Harvard College in the Seventeenth Century* (2 vols. Cambridge, Harvard University Press, 1936), *1*, 144–47.

and began physics. In his junior year he continued physics and
started ethics, metaphysics, and geography. In his senior year he
reviewed languages, logic, and physics and took up mathematics
(geometry and arithmetic) and astronomy. The study of divinity
was probably continued through all three years. Of the cur-
riculum offered to Taylor and his contemporaries, Samuel Eliot
Morison says: "Harvard was attempting to reproduce the whole
Arts curriculum of Cambridge, and a little more: the medieval
Trivium and Quadrivium (without Music); the Three Philoso-
phies; the Learned Tongues; and a smattering of classical belles-
lettres. It is not a specialized course for Protestant pastors, but a
Christian gentleman's education that is offered to the youth of
New England." [11]

In his second year at Harvard, Taylor became acquainted with
John Steadman and his wife Elizabeth, who was "lying . . . un-
der trouble of Spirit," and evidently in his attempt to heal Mrs.
Steadman of her spiritual afflictions he provoked a certain
amount of neighborhood gossip, for he says in his diary that he
considered giving up his place at commencement. He was gradu-
ated with his class, however, in 1671. Among his classmates was
Samuel Sewall, the famous diarist and witchcraft judge, Taylor's
roommate at Harvard, and his lifelong friend.

At the time of Taylor's graduation, the new frontier town of
Westfield, Massachusetts, which had been incorporated in 1669,
was in need of a minister. On November 17, 1671, Thomas
Dewey, sent as messenger from Westfield, came to Taylor with
a letter from Increase Mather, pastor of the second church at
Boston, and invited Taylor to go with him to Westfield. Taylor
consulted with several friends, including President Chauncy
and Increase Mather, and after considerable indecision agreed
to accompany Dewey. They set out November 27 just after a
heavy snowfall. Taylor described the journey graphically in his
diary (p. 20): "the snow being above Mid-Leg deep, the way
unbeaten, or the track filled up again, and over rocks and moun-
tains, and the journey being about an 100 miles, and Mr. Cooke
of Cambridge told us it was the desperatest journey that ever
Connecticut men undertooke." On December 3 the new minister

11. Ibid., p. 150.

preached his first sermon at Westfield, from Matthew 3:2. And one year later the townspeople voted their "earnest desire" that Taylor remain as their minister; fifteen acres of land were given to him, and a new meetinghouse was built at the confluence of Great River and Little River to which, for many years, the worshipers were called to meeting by the roll of a drum.[12]

On November 5, 1674, Taylor married Elizabeth Fitch, the third child of the distinguished Reverend James Fitch of Norwich, Connecticut. A love letter, a curious mixture of Christian piety and the tender passion expressed in elaborate artificial rhetoric, from the poet to his intended bride begins as follows:

> My Dove: — I send you not my Heart, For that I hope is sent to Heaven long since, and unless it hath utterly deceived me it hath not taken up its Lodgen in any one's bosom on this side the Royal City of the Greate King. But yet the Most of it that is allowed to be layed out upon any Creature doth solely and singly fall to your share.[13]

The first Mrs. Taylor lived for approximately fifteen years after her marriage and bore eight children.[14] Of these, five died as infants, a tragedy which Taylor mentions in the elegy on his wife, "Five Babes thou tookst from me before this Stroke . . ." [15] The first-born, Samuel, married Margaret Moseley on January 5, 1704/5; the third child, James, died in 1701 at Barbados, where he had gone on a commercial venture. Meditation 40 (second series) contains a touching reference to his death. Bathshuah married Colonel John Pynchon in 1702. By this marriage and

12. John H. Lockwood, *Westfield and Its Historic Influences* (2 vols. Springfield, Mass., 1922), *1*, 139; B. B. Edwards, "Complete List of the Congregational Ministers in the Old County of Hampshire, MS.," *American Quarterly Register, 10* (1838), 401.

13. PW. For publications of this letter see Appendix 1.

14. Samuel, Aug. 27, 1675; Elizabeth, Dec. 27, 1676, *d.* Dec. 25, 1677; James, Oct. 12, 1678; Abigail, Aug. 6, 1681, *d.* Aug. 22, 1682; Bathshuah, Jan. 17, 1683/4; Elizabeth, Feb. 5, 1684/5, *d.* July 26, 1685; Mary, July 3, 1686, *d.* May 15, 1687; Hezekiah, Feb. 18, 1687/8, *d.* Mar. 3, 1688. Information from George Sheldon, *A History of Deerfield Massachusetts* (Deerfield, Mass., 1895), *2*, Pt. II, 334. The names of Taylor's children are spelled according to the baptismal record kept by Taylor in CR.

15. PW.

that of Samuel the Taylor family became allied with the most prominent family of the upper Connecticut Valley and the most prominent family of Westfield.[16]

Mrs. Taylor died on July 7, 1689. The elegy composed by her husband is, in spite of the frequently stereotyped language, one of the more moving of Taylor's topical poems.

In 1692 Taylor married again, a Ruth Wyllys of Hartford who came from a distinguished family; her grandfathers, John Haynes and George Wyllys, were governors of Connecticut. There were six children [17] by this marriage. The five daughters all married clergymen. Kezia, the fifth daughter, who married the Reverend Isaac Stiles of New Haven, became the mother of Ezra Stiles, the president of Yale College. The sixth child, Eldad, became the father of John Taylor, a well-known minister of Deerfield and one of the incorporators of Deerfield Academy.

In the year 1674, the date of Taylor's first marriage, Philip, son of Massasoit, was laying his grandiose plans for driving the English out of the colonies; and the next year, in June, King Philip's War began with the sacking of the town of Swanzey. During this catastrophe, in which one of every ten men of military age in the Bay Colony was lost and two-thirds of the villages were destroyed or damaged,[18] the townspeople of Westfield were kept in a constant state of alarm, although by good fortune they never suffered a serious attack. In the spring of 1676 the Council of the Bay Colony proposed that the citizens of Westfield move to Springfield for their better protection against the Indians. A letter [19] written by Taylor for a committee of the citizens of Westfield to the Council explains their decision to remain firm in the protection of their homes in Westfield. Of this decision

16. Lockwood, p. 160.

17. Ruth, April 16, 1693, m. Dec. 1717, Rev. Benj. Colton of West Hartford; Naomi, Mar. 30, 1695, m. June 1720, Rev. Ebenezer Devotion of Suffolk; Ann, July 7, 1696, m. June 1720, Rev. Benj. Lord of Norwich; Mehetable, Aug. 14, 1699, m. Rev. William Gager of Lebanon; Kezia, April 4, 1702, m. June 1, 1725, Rev. Isaac Stiles of New Haven; Eldad, April 10, 1708, m. 1732, Rhoda Dewey. Sheldon, p. 334; CR.

18. John Gorham Palfrey, *History of New England* (5 vols. Boston, 1882), *3*, 214–15.

19. Published in Lockwood, pp. 234–36.

J. C. Greenough writes: "Had the settlers of Westfield and Northampton retreated from their outposts, other settlements in the Connecticut Valley would have lost heart, and this valley might have been deserted of English settlers . . . There are other Thermopylaes and other Marathons than those that have honored the soil of Greece." [20]

With the end of Philip's War, Taylor and his congregation could turn their attention to the organizing of their church. In the spring of 1679 Taylor wrote in his Church "Records" (p. 2):

> But God, whose designs shall never fall to the ground, hath not only shew'd himself gratious in the one respect, but also in the other and therefore after he had stilled the noise of war, hath in some measure restrain'd the Adversary of the Gospel and hath recollected that little strength that he hath preserved, so far as that this spring 1679 we came to determine an entrance into a church state the latter end of the sixt month.

Invitations were sent to the Reverend James Fitch of Norwich (who could not attend) and to the ministers and congregations of other neighboring towns. After a week of fasting and prayer, the organization of the church took place on August 27, 1679. Elders and messengers from Windsor, Springfield, Northampton, and Hadley were present, the most famous of these being the Reverend Solomon Stoddard, the grandfather of Jonathan Edwards.

The Church "Records" note (p. 3) that there was considerable discussion as to the confession of faith. Taylor wished to profess "the doctrine laid out in the catechism of the Assembly of Divines at Westminster," but the elders and messengers of the neighboring churches insisted that he draw up his own personal profession of faith, which he did in seventy pages, folio.[21]

In addition to the profession of faith, each of the six founda-

20. "Historical Relation of Springfield and Westfield," *Papers and Proceedings of the Connecticut Valley Historical Society*, 2 (1904), 259.

21. The headings of the profession of faith run from pp. 5 to 75 in CR. Some headings are fully and minutely explicated, others are briefly defined or merely named. Sections on the Sacraments (Baptism and the Lord's Supper) are fully explicated, as are the sections on Heaven and Hell.

tion men of the new church was called upon to give an account of his own personal spiritual experience which entitled him to be a member of the church. Of particular interest is Taylor's spiritual "Relation." He states that a person is brought to Christ by a conviction of his sin and misery through the fall, and by repentance and the belief that there is remedy through grace. He tells his congregation that he was first convinced of his own sinful nature by listening to an account of the fall of Adam and Eve given to him by his sister. "But oh! this account came in upon me in such a strong way that I am not able to express it, but ever since I have had the notion of sin and its naughtiness remain and the wrath of God on the account of the same." [22] He also pays tribute to his mother, who taught him to hate disobedience and lying and warned him of the punishment of fire and brimstone which awaits unrepentant sinners. It should be noted that with respect to belief in original sin and fear of damnation Taylor appears in this spiritual "Relation" to be completely in accord with the orthodox Calvinism of the seventeenth-century New England Congregational Church. Likewise, the relations of the six lay brethren of Taylor's church contain somewhat abnormal and extravagant accounts of mystical experiences and an awareness of the enormity of personal sin and fear of eternal damnation.

When the relations were concluded, Taylor preached a sermon from Ephesians 2:22. The Reverend Mr. Lockwood, who read this sermon in the twentieth century, writes, "It is not a rash statement to make, that there is not now a man living who could write such a sermon." [23] Lockwood was impressed by the sermon's complicated structure, its evidence of learning, and its length.

After the sermon the brethren entered into church covenant by solemnly obligating themselves to walk in the way of Christ, and Solomon Stoddard then gave in the name of the churches the right hand of fellowship. Thus was organized the church to which Edward Taylor was to devote almost fifty more years of his life. The responsibility of the church rested, for a long time,

22. CR, p. 81.
23. Lockwood, *1*, 116.

on Taylor alone, for no other officers were elected until 1692.[24]

From 1679 on, information concerning Taylor's life is meager. That he was an effective preacher we know from a remark in his friend Samuel Sewall's "letter book": "I have heard him preach a Sermon at the Old South upon short warning which as the phrase in England is, might have been preached at Paul's Cross." [25] And that he ministered to his congregation's physical as well as their spiritual needs we learn from a statement by his grandson, Ezra Stiles, "He was physician for the town all his life." [26] That the town took good care to protect him during the Indian troubles of King William's, Queen Anne's, and Father Rale's Wars we can surmise from the following entry in the town record:

> March 21, 1700
> The inhabitants especially those that live on the Town plot had a meeting to consider about fortifying for thar security, did agree and vote that four houses should be securely fortified and Mr Taylors Fort repaired if needed.[27]

It is worth noting that Taylor, although a relatively obscure parson of a small frontier town, was held in affection and esteem throughout his life by the distinguished judge Samuel Sewall. There are many references to him in Sewall's diary and letter book. From these we learn that Taylor kept in touch with the affairs of Boston and the outside world, and that on at least one occasion he was invited to preach in the Old South Church.[28]

Although there is no extant contemporary description of Taylor, we can infer something of his personality and character from Ezra Stiles' account of him:

> He was an excellent classic[al] scholar, being Master of the three learned Languages, a great Historian and every way a very Learned Man. . . . He was a vigorous Advocate for

24. CR, p. 123.
25. "The Letter Book of Samuel Sewall," *Collections of the Massachusetts Historical Society*, 6th ser. 2 (1886–88), 274.
26. In M. See Appendix 2.
27. Lockwood, *1*, 295.
28. Sewall, *2*, 274.

Oliver Cromwell, civil and religious Liberty. A Congrega-
tionalist in opposition to Presbyterian Church Discipline.
. . . [He] greatly detested King James, Sir Edmond Andross
and Randolph: gloried in King William and the Revolution
of 1688: felt for the dissenters in all their apprehension in
Queen Anne's reign . . . A man of small stature, but firm;
of quick Passions, yet serious and grave. Exemplary in Piety,
and for a very sacred Observance of the Lord's Day.[29]

In 1716 the citizens of Westfield began to consider the need
for a new meetinghouse for their growing congregation and
their aged pastor. A committee was appointed to look into the
matter, but the business soon became bogged down in one of
those petty feuds so dear to the hearts of New England farmers.
It was a question of the exact location of the new building. The
matter took four years to decide. But finally, on May 20, 1720,
the town voted to begin building. The same meeting also voted
that

all men belonging to the Town shall asist in the work of
raising the meeting house from 17 years of age and upwards
on pain and penalty of 3 shillings per day for every days
neglect dureing the time of Raising, except all such as shall
make a satisfactory excuse unto the Comitey that have the
charge of the mater.

It was voated that the Comitey shall have liberty to pre-
pare 4 or 5 barels of beer at the Town charge for the Con-
sern above mentioned.[30]

On June 22, 1721, efforts were made to get Taylor to go to the
new church:

At the same meeting it was voated that if Mr. Taylor will
go to the new meeting house to carry on the public worship,
that the Comitey have liberty to remove some of the timber
and Carey from the old meeting house and use it toward
finishing the new meeting house.[31]

29. See M.
30. Lockwood, *1*, 313.
31. Ibid., p. 314.

Evidently the aged minister, now close to eighty, was less than enthusiastic about the efforts of his townsmen, and evidently he had expressed his sentiments to his old friend Samuel Sewall, for we find in Sewall's letter book, interspersed with comments on old age and other matters, this statement: "He had an aversion to it, because it was not built just in the same spot the former sorry house was. The new one is built upon a little knowl, that it might be out of the way of the Overflowing of the River. I writ to Mr. Taylor to incline him to remove to his New House . . ."[32] The new meetinghouse was occupied by Taylor and his congregation toward the end of 1721, but the building was not completed until after 1725.

In 1721 Taylor was ill, and he was helped by his son-in-law the Reverend Benjamin Lord of Norwich, Connecticut. Deacon Noble and Captain Ashley were sent to Taylor the next year to talk with him about the selection of a colleague. In 1723 Isaac Stiles was requested to help Taylor in his ministerial duties. Nemiah Bull was called from Long Island in 1725 to fill the place left vacant by Stiles; he preached his first sermon on January 13, 1725, and was ordained October 26, 1726. Taylor was present at the ordination.[33]

In his final years Taylor was an invalid. On December 27, 1728, this vote appeared in the town records: "to rais 10£ for Ms Hitable Taylor to inable her to provide help to tend Mr. Taylor."[34] He died June 24, 1729. His tombstone, which still stands in the old burying ground at Westfield, bears the following inscription, now partially obliterated:

Here rests ye Body of ye Revᵈ Mr Edward Taylor ye Aged, Venerable, Learned & Pious Pastor of ye Church of Christ in this Town, who after He had served God & his Generation Faithfully for Many Years fell asleep June 24, 1729 in ye 87ᵗʰ Year of his Age.[35]

32. Sewall, 2, 145–46.
33. Lockwood, 1, 320–21.
34. Ibid., p. 148.
35. "A List of Gravestones in the Mechanic Street Cemetery, Westfield Massachusetts, 1939," Westfield Athenaeum, Westfield, Mass., 1939 (typewritten bound MS), p. 184. Mrs. Ruth Taylor, according to her tombstone, died Jan. 27, 1730.

THEOLOGY [36]

An understanding of Taylor's theological position is necessary for an appreciation of his poetry, since the themes of almost all of his poems are his theological ideas. At the time of his ordination Taylor indicated that he believed in the doctrines set forth by the Westminster Confession, which defined the official doctrine of the New England Congregational Church during the seventeenth century. The Westminster Confession is thoroughly Calvinistic and it is, in all essential matters, in agreement with the theology of Calvin's *Institutes*. The evidence of Taylor's poetry, sermons, notes on divinity, and profession of faith in the Church "Records," as well as of his lifelong pastorship of the Westfield Church unmarked, as far as we know, by any deviations on his part from orthodox theology or church polity, indicates that he was completely in accord with the Calvinistic beliefs of his time. On the subjects of predestination, God's decrees, the salvation of the elect and the punishment of the reprobate, Taylor's beliefs appear to be identical with those of Samuel Sewall, the Mathers, and Michael Wigglesworth—beliefs popularized in Wigglesworth's "The Day of Doom," a poem with which Taylor informs us his first wife was very familiar: "The Doomsday Verses much perfum'de her Breath." [37]

The fundamental ideas of Taylor's theology may be briefly summarized as follows: All men, as a result of the fall of Adam and Eve, are justly condemned by the wrath of God to everlasting punishment in hell. God, however, is merciful as well as just, and out of his infinite mercy he foreordained, before the foundations of the world were laid, that a few men, the elect, should be saved and exalted in heaven above the angels through the intercession of His only begotten Son, Jesus Christ. Christ, by his active and passive obedience, purchased salvation for the elect and, although the incarnation took place at a specific time, the benefits of redemption were extended to the elect through all the ages. Taylor believed that men were first under an injunction to obey God through the exercise of good works—the Covenant

---

36. For individual terms, see also below, Glossary.
37. From the elegy on his wife, in PW.

of Works—but that, after the fall, men had forfeited the benefits of this covenant and the Covenant of Grace became operative. God, by his promise that the seed of Eve would bruise the
serpent's head, gave a covenant to the elect [38] that they through
faith in Christ would be saved. Under the Covenant of Grace
men were saved through faith only and not through works;
however, a decision to lead a Christian life and become a member of the Congregational Church was considered evidence that
a man was probably of the elect.

Theoretically the individual could be assured by the working
of God on his spirit that he was destined to be saved, but in fact
every Puritan, including Taylor, had his moments of fear and
doubt which gave his religious life a dramatic intensity—"All,
Lord, or None at all! This makes me dread" defines the alternatives of his faith. He was destined for heaven or hell; there was
no purgatory.

Taylor's religion was completely deterministic as evidenced
by his long poem *Gods Determinations* and by passages in his
sermons. Every event, to the fall of the last leaf, has been foreordained by God. Man is nothing: God is everything. Man is
completely incapable of achieving his salvation without sanctifying Grace which comes from God alone. To modern eyes, Calvinism is a grim theology, and partly because of its grimness,
partly because of its internal inconsistencies (man cannot save
himself yet should exert every effort to lead a good life and
achieve saving faith), the kind of Calvinism in which Taylor believed gradually broke down. With its emphasis on original sin,
the theology encouraged morbid tendencies which Taylor himself did not entirely escape; there are passages in the *Meditations* where the poet describes his personal sinfulness, which
make unpleasant reading today; and in the *Metrical History of
Christianity* attributed to Taylor there are a number of passages
in which the physical tortures of the martyrs are described in unnecessary detail. Also, the God of Taylor is somewhat tyrannical
for modern tastes:

38. According to Taylor's notes in his Diary, the Covenant of Grace in New
Testament times was not confined to the elect. Some who were under the
Covenant of Grace might eventually be rejected by God.

Thou Law deliverest: Thine Authority
      Cannot be idle; nor exceed the right.
Hence such as will not with thy rule Comply,
      Thou with thy iron Scepter down wilt smite.
This Power will raise the dead, and judge all too.
His own will Crown with Life. To hell foes throw.[39]

But of course there is another side to Taylor's theology. The
God of wrath was also a God of mercy. Although the greater
part of mankind was doomed to eternal flames, a few (the saints)
would be exalted above the angels; and Taylor, by temperament
less morbid than Wigglesworth, often chose to emphasize this
aspect of his beliefs; indeed, his most moving Meditations deal
with the sweetness of God's grace and the glorification of the
Puritan saints.

During the years 1701–03 Taylor wrote a series of sermons en-
titled "Christographia," in which he explicated one of his favor-
ite themes—the mystery of the union of the divine and human
natures in Christ, the mystical union between the members of
the Church and Christ, and the glorification of these members
as a result of this union. Meditations 42, 43, 44, 45, 48, 49, 52,
53, 54, and 56 (all of the second series) bear the same date and
text as the sermon for that day.[40] For example the third sermon
of "Christographia," preached on December 28, 1701, and Medi-
tation 44 of the same date both have as their text John 1:14, the
word was made Flesh. This passage from the sermon describes
the mystical union:

> The Person of Christ is most Glorious. He is the King of
> Glory. Now all the glory of his Person is derived to his Man-
> hood by the way of this personall Union. And by the
> Mysticall Union to every Child of God. . . . Oh! then men-
> tain the Glory of Christ by a Christ like life. It is your high-
> est Honour, and it is your giving the Highest honour to

39. Meditation 53 (second series), below, p. 176.
40. The title page of the sermons states that there are fifteen sermons;
however No. 14 is missing. Meditation 47 has the same date as the corre-
sponding sermon but a different text. Meditation 55, corresponding with the
missing Sermon 14, is not in PW.

Christ. It will be your greatest Comfort: and the most com-
fortable Communion with Christ will be the best improve-
ment of your Union to Christ: And of Christ's Union to
God. For the Personall Union is to Communicate the God-
head Excellency unto the Manhood to accomplish it to act
gloriously. The Mysticall Union is to Communicate the
Personall Excellency into the heart and Life of every
Member that the functions thereof may be mannaged with
a Godlike glory upon them and so then to act thus will be
to the Glory of God, the Glory of the Personall Union, the
Glory of Christ's Person, the Glory of the Mysticall Union,
to the Glory of Grace, to the glory of Profession, to the
Glory of each Member of the Body and to the glorious Con-
solation of the soul and its eternall salvation.

The glorification of human nature as a result of the mystical
union with Christ is thus described in Meditation 44 (second
series), p. 162:

> You Holy Angells, Morning-Stars, bright Sparks,
> Give place: and lower your top gallants. Shew
> Your top-saile Conjues to our slender barkes:
> The highest honour to our nature's due.
> Its neerer Godhead by the Godhead made
> Than yours in you that never from God stray'd.

In the series of Meditations numbering 102 through 111, writ-
ten from June 10, 1711, to December 1712, Taylor carefully
explicated his interpretation of the sacrament of the Lord's
Supper. He attacked the Catholic theory of transubstantiation
and the Lutheran doctrine of consubstantiation, and defined his
own notion that the sacrament is a spiritual banquet in which
Christ is present in a real spiritual sense and in which the par-
ticipant enjoys a real spiritual and mystical union with the
Lord.[41] This was the series of Meditations in which Taylor was
particularly concerned with the innovations of the Reverend
Solomon Stoddard of Northampton, who was advocating that
men in an unregenerate condition should be allowed to partake
of the sacrament that they might find therein a means of regen-

41. See Donald E. Stanford, "Edward Taylor and the Lord's Supper,"
American Literature, 27 (1955), 172–78.

eration.[42] Taylor rejected Stoddard's innovations with vehemence, asserting that the Lord's Supper was for the regenerate only.

A number of Taylor's poems cannot be understood without an awareness of the typology behind them. Taylor's typology was the result of reading the entire Bible as a continuous history of God's chosen people; it had its origins in the Middle Ages, but it was emphasized and elaborated by the Puritans, who based their whole theology on the Bible and constantly sought in it answers to their spiritual and material problems; it was the result, in part, of constantly reading the Old Testament in terms of the New Testament, of looking for events in the Old Testament which foreshadowed events in the New Testament. Thus the ram which was sacrificed in place of Isaac foreshadowed Jesus who was sacrificed for man. The ram was the type; Jesus was the antitype. Similarly, Jonah's experience with the whale was a type of Jesus' burial and resurrection. Other types of Christ were Moses, Noah, and Joseph. The type of Christian baptism was Circumcision. The Jewish Passover was a type of the Lord's Supper.

Many of the Meditations were inspired by the Song of Solomon, always referred to by Taylor as Canticles and always understood according to the allegorical interpretation of the period. The two chief personages in Canticles are the bride and the bridegroom. Christ is the bridegroom and the Church (in Puritan terms, the Saints) is the bride.

In the *Preparatory Meditations* there are certain recurrent themes: the sinfulness and insignificance of natural man and conversely the glorification of the elect; the Atonement; the sweetness of God's grace; the power, the glory, and the absolute sovereignty of God; and the ecstatic experience of the mystical union between the believer and Christ celebrated by the sacrament of the Lord's Supper. With respect to this last theme, it has often been said that the Puritans were plain, blunt men with little talent for mysticism; the fact is, however, some of the

---

42. *The Doctrine of Instituted Churches Explained and Proved from the Word of God*, London, 1700; also see his sermon, *The Inexcusableness of Neglecting the Worship of God under a Pretence of Being in an Unconverted Condition*, Boston, 1708. See also below, p. lvii.

Puritans, at least, in contemplating the sacrament and the spiritual union between themselves and Christ were often moved to ecstasies which might be called mystical. There are examples, for instance, in Cotton Mather's Diary as well as in Taylor's poetry; and this mystical experience had solid doctrine behind it, for Calvin had written: "If it be true that the visible sign is given to us to seal the donation of the invisible substance, we ought to entertain a confident assurance, that in receiving the symbol of his body, we at the same time truly receive the body itself." [43]

Taylor, like most New England Puritans, was particularly moved by the doctrine of the Atonement and Redemption:

> Infinities fierce firy arrow red
> >Shot from the splendid Bow of Justice bright
> Did smite thee down, for thine. Thou art their head.
> >They di'de in thee. Their death did on thee light.[44]

and by the power and the glory of an absolute sovereign God:

> God is Gone up with a triumphant Shout
> >The Lord with sounding Trumpets melodies.
> Sing Praise, sing Praise, sing Praise, sing Praises out,
> >Unto our King sing praise seraphickwise.
> >Lift up your Heads ye lasting Doore they sing
> >And let the King of Glory Enter in.[45]

In passages such as these the poet, although expressing theological conceptions which were consistent with the somewhat narrow and outmoded dogma of his time and place, struck a universal note which can still move the modern reader.

TAYLOR'S MANUSCRIPTS

According to tradition, Taylor at the beginning of his career was too poor to buy books; he therefore borrowed books and made copies of them for his own use. Sprague writes:

> Unable through the poverty alike of himself and his parishioners, to purchase his necessary professional books, all or

43. John Allen, trans., *Institutes of the Christian Religion by John Calvin* (2 vols. Philadelphia, The Westminster Press, 1936), 2, 651.

44. Meditation 112 (second series), below, p. 287.

45. Meditation 20 (first series), below, pp. 34–35.

nearly all those used by him were in manuscript, which he had transcribed as he had found opportunity. . . . His manuscripts were all handsomely bound in parchment by himself, of which tradition says he left, at his death, more than a hundred volumes. Fourteen of these were in quarto. Many of the smaller ones were of his own composition.[46]

Of these hundred or so manuscripts, only thirteen are extant,[47] six in the Yale Library, three in the Westfield Athenaeum, three in the Redwood Library and Athenaeum, and one in the manuscript collection of the Massachusetts Historical Society. The most important of these, as far as Taylor's poetic reputation is concerned, is the manuscript (untitled by Taylor) usually referred to as "Poetical Works" (PW), in the Yale Library. It contains all the *Preparatory Meditations,* which have been referred to by previous writers on Taylor as the *Sacramental Meditations.* This latter title, however, written across the top of the page bearing Meditation 1, was added in later years by Ezra Stiles. Taylor called his major work *Preparatory Meditations.* Also in PW are the long and important poem *Gods Determinations,* a few interesting minor lyrics, a number of conventional elegies, a curious poem on the bones of a "giant" dug up at Claverack, New York, and Taylor's love letter to Elizabeth Fitch. In the binding of this manuscript were discovered copies of several *Preparatory Meditations* and metrical paraphrases of scripture. The paraphrases may have been composed by Taylor, or they may have been copied from the work of other poets. Also at Yale are Taylor's "Manuscript Book" with rough drafts of several poems, showing that Taylor carefully reworked his poetry; "China's Description and Commonplace Book" (CD), the first part of which contains extracts from a book on China by the Jesuit priest Louis LeComte, while the second part records divine providences, monstrosities, and other unusual phenomena, revealing Taylor's constant interest in these subjects; "Metallographia" (M), mainly a copy of extracts from John Webster's book on chemistry and alchemy; a "Dispensatory" (D), which

46. William B. Sprague, *Annals of the American Pulpit* (9 vols. New York, 1866), *1,* 179.

47. A detailed description of the Taylor manuscripts is in Appendix 2.

is a curious collection of lore on the "medicinable" properties of gems, herbs, drugs, etc., used by Taylor in his capacity as town physician; and "Christographia" (C), a collection of sermons dealing chiefly with the mystery of the union of the divine and human natures in Christ.

At the Westfield Athenaeum is Taylor's public record of his church, with information on the gathering of the church, a baptismal record, and a long profession of faith. Also at Westfield is an extract of a translation of a book on the Council of Trent by Pietro Polano [Paolo Sarpi], published in 1629. Recently Mr. Francis E. X. Murphy discovered at the Westfield Athenaeum Taylor's copy of Origen's *Contra Celsus* and *De principiis* in English.

In 1951 the Redwood Library and Athenaeum, at Newport, Rhode Island, received from the library of Taylor's great-great-great-grandson, the Reverend Roderick Terry, three interesting and important Taylor manuscripts. The first of these, the Diary, contains, besides Taylor's colorful diary, several pages of theological notes he probably wrote before coming to New England, and about fifty pages of poetry by Robert Wild, Ralph Wallis, George Wither, some unidentified poets, and Taylor himself. The poems by Taylor are his earliest known verse. The second manuscript, of over 400 pages, is a metrical history of Christianity from the beginning until 1100, and from the beginning of Queen Mary's reign to 1558. The sufferings of the Christian martyrs are emphasized and their tortures are described in detail. Interspersed with the narrative portions are a number of moving poems in praise of God's mercy and justice. The third manuscript, a large folio volume, is a commentary and harmony of the gospels, composed by Taylor, according to Ezra Stiles, between 1690 and 1710.

Finally, in the collection of manuscripts of the Massachusetts Historical Society is Edward Taylor's "Commonplace Book" (CP),[48] consisting of copies of letters by Taylor and by his con-

---

48. Described by William P. Upham in *Proceedings of the Massachusetts Historical Socety*, 2d ser. *13* (1899), 124–29, and presented to the society's collection in 1900. It has not been referred to by any writers on Taylor since that date.

temporaries, treatises against kneeling at the Lord's Supper, "wonderful" narratives, etc. Of greatest interest is a bitter letter dated February 13, 1688, to Solomon Stoddard assailing him for his plan to liberalize the requirements for admission to the Lord's Supper. "It seems to carry the Intrest of Christ from him and to do as the Philistins, to make a Cow to carry the Arke . . . bold sinners will be flesht to finde such an Advocate for their Cause as Mr. Stoddard . . . the Glory of your Ministry is Gone if your Church tare to pieces . . . Nay, in a Word, Gods faithfull Ones in following Ages will be ready to date the beginning of New England's Apostasy in Mr. Stoddards Notions . . ." Stoddard delayed his answer to this attack until June. He then wrote Taylor a brief note stating that he was moved to his decision by the will of God and the spreading corruption of religion. That Taylor found this answer unsatisfactory is evident in the next few pages of the Commonplace Book, for he writes a brief account of how Stoddard in 1690, after "many if not almost all the Ancient members of the Church were dead" and the ruling Elders were absent because of sickness, persuaded a majority of his congregation to favor his liberalization of the Lord's Supper. This account is followed by six arguments in the form of syllogisms proving that the Lord's Supper is not, as Stoddard proposed, a converting ordinance. Taylor was obviously disturbed for many years by Stoddard's practice, for in 1711 and 1712 he wrote a series of Meditations on the subject.[49]

EDITIONS OF THE POETRY [50]

Taylor did not publish his poems and he forbade his heirs to publish them.[51] Consequently the poems remained almost unknown and unread until Thomas H. Johnson, noting a reference to the poetry in Sibley's biographical sketch of Taylor, examined the manuscript of the "Poetical Works," [52] which had lain in

49. See below, pp. 265–84.
50. See also below, Appendix 1.
51. Two stanzas of "Upon Wedlock and Death of Children" were published in Cotton Mather's *Right Thoughts in Sad Hours,* London, 1689.
52. See "The Crow's Nest," *Colophon* (June 1939), pp. 101–4.

the Yale University Library since 1883. He published a selection of the poems in the *New England Quarterly* in 1937,[53] and the next year Norman Holmes Pearson anthologized several of Johnson's selections in *The Oxford Anthology of American Literature*.[54] Critical interest in Taylor was aroused by these publications, and after Johnson published an enlarged selection of the poems in 1939[55] Taylor became widely accepted as America's foremost Colonial poet. Much of Taylor's poetry, however, has not appeared in print until this edition, which presents all the extant Meditations.

Gods Determinations appeared in part in Johnson's selection in the *New England Quarterly*, 1937 (ETP), as follows: "Christs Reply," "The Soul admiring the Grace of the Church Enters into Church Fellowship," "The Glory of and Grace in the Church set out," "The Souls Admiration hereupon," "The Joy of Church Fellowship rightly attended," "Prologue," and excerpts of thirty-four other lines. The entire poem was published in *W*.

In this text 128 Meditations are published for the first time. They are: (first series) "The Return," 4, 5, 9, 11, 14–15, 17, 27, 44; (second series) 1, 2, 5, 6, 9, 10, 12, 13, 15, 20, 21, 22, 23, 24, 31, 32, 34, 35, 36, 38, 39, 44, 45, 47, 48, 50, 51, 52, 53, 54, 58, 59, 60A, 61, 63, 66, 67A, 68A, 67B, 68B, 70, 71, 72, 73, 74, 81, 83, 85, 86, 87, 89, 90, 91, 92, 93, 94, 96, 97, 98, 99, 100, 101, 102, 103, 113, 115, 116, 117, 118, 119, 120, 121, 122, 123A, 123B, 125, 126, 127, 128, 129, 130, 131, 132, 133, 134, 135, 136, 137, 138, 139, 140, 141, 142, 143, 144, 145, 146, 147, 148, 149, 150, 151, 152, 153, 154, 155, 156, 157A, 157B, 158, 159, 160, 161A, 161B, 162, 163, 164, 165.

Of the *Miscellaneous Poems* five are here published for the first time: "A Fig for thee, Oh! Death!" "Graces Bright Shine," "The Sparkling Shine of Gods Justice," "The Martyrdom of Deacon Laurence," and "The Persian Persecution." The elegies on Taylor's wife and on Samuel Hooker were first published in TVT.

Information concerning first publication of Taylor's poetry

53. See ETP.
54. Ed. William Rose Benét and Norman Holmes Pearson, pp. 60–63.
55. See *W*.

and publication in Johnson's *Poetical Works of Edward Taylor* has been entered after the date of each poem. Complete information about all first publications of Taylor's poems will be found in Appendix 1.

THE TEXT

The text of the poems has been established from two manuscripts—the "Poetical Works" (PW) in the Yale Library and the "Metrical History of Christianity" (MH) in the Redwood Library and Athenaeum. Capitalization and spelling of these manuscripts have been followed exactly, except that capitalization of the letter *S* is arbitrary (Taylor made little or no distinction between a capital *S* and a lower case *s*), and the names of various speakers in the dialogues of *Gods Determinations* have been capitalized, although usually they appear in lower case in PW. Abbreviations have been written out. Taylor's punctuation has been retained, except that periods, which Taylor frequently omitted at the ends of sentences, have been silently added. The poet sometimes used periods where the modern writer would use commas to set off subordinate elements of a sentence; the resulting fragmentary sentences have been allowed to stand as they appear in the manuscript. The few deviations in punctuation from the manuscript to correct obvious errors, avoid extreme awkwardness, or clarify difficult syntax have all been noted. Biblical quotations in the epigraphs appear exactly as they are in PW, except that periods have occasionally been added at the end of quotations for the sake of uniformity; similarly, the use of the period after meditation numbers has been regularized, as has the terminal punctuation of the titles in *Gods Determinations*.

Variant readings in copies of the Meditations found in the binding of PW (see below, p. 506) have been collated after the symbol Z. The abbreviation "orig:" indicates canceled words and passages in PW. Occasional illegible words, or torn-away passages, have been indicated by asterisks (see, e.g., Meditation 32, p. 140).

In PW almost every Meditation bears the date in the upper left hand corner of the page. This date has been placed between the title and the text of each Meditation, but in the same form

Taylor used. In dating his poems, Taylor counted March as the
first month of the year. The editor has inserted the abbreviation
for each month in brackets.

PW has been followed in the numbering of the Meditations
through 139, except that the letters *A* and *B* have been used to
distinguish two poems bearing the same number. The Medita-
tions were numbered by Taylor from 1 to 49 and from 1 to 156.
In this text the first group is designated "first series" and the
second group "second series," although they were not so distin-
guished by Taylor. As indicated below, PW repeats some num-
bers and omits others. Beginning with number 140 of this edition,
I have renumbered, but the original chronological sequence has
been followed, and the number in PW has been entered in the
textual notes.

In PW the page containing Meditation 1 (second series) and
the first six stanzas of Meditation 2 is between Meditation 3 (first
series) and "The Experience." There are no Meditations num-
bered 55, 57, and 88. Two are numbered 60, 67, and 68. Begin-
ning with 123, the Meditations in PW are numbered as follows:
123, 123, 125, 126, 127, 128, 129, 130, 131, 132, 133, 134, 135, 136,
137, 138 [number originally 128], 139 [number originally 129],
129, 130, 131, 134, 135, 136, 137, 138, 139, 140, 141, 142, 143, 144,
[145], 146, 147, 148, 148 [another version of the preceding], 149,
150, 151, 152, 153 [rough draft], 152, 153, 154, 155, 156. The last
twenty-eight Meditations are out of place, situated between the
"Prologue" and Meditation 1 of the first series. Meditation 148
has two versions, as does Meditation 152. The first of 152, dated
"12m 3 day 1722," comes after 151. The second, dated "22 3m
1723," is after the rough draft of 153. A rough draft of the first
three stanzas of 153 is between the two versions of 152. This
rough draft differs considerably from the fair copy, particularly
in stanzas two and three. However, the rough draft is so confused
that collation with the fair copy is impossible, and the draft has
been omitted from this text, except that conjectural readings for
lines 1 and 3 of the fair copy of 153 have been taken from it. The
date of the two drafts is the same.

For the sake of uniformity, stanza indention has been regu-
larized, even though in PW some stanzas have irregular indention.

Gods Determinations is printed in full just as it appears in PW.

Of the Miscellaneous Poems, the series numbered 1 to 8 was chosen because of its literary value; the elegy on Taylor's wife and "A Fig for Thee, Oh! Death!" are of biographical interest. The elegy on Hooker is perhaps the best of Taylor's exercises in this genre.

METRICAL HISTORY

The excerpts from the *Metrical History* illustrate a recently discovered, unpublished work which, in spite of its uneven literary quality, is of considerable historical interest. This long poem of over 430 pages has as its chief source the *Ecclesiastica Historia Integram Ecclesiae* by Matthias Flacius and others, commonly known as *The Magdeburg Centuries*. Taylor owned a six-volume folio edition of this work, similar to the 1562 edition published in Basel, a copy of which is in the Yale Library. This was the first history of the Church told from the Protestant point of view. The sixth volume ends with the twelfth century. Taylor's poem relates the history of Christianity from the beginning until the twelfth century, resumes the narrative with the beginning of Queen Mary's reign, and ends in the year 1558. The poem describes in considerable detail the martyrdoms and persecutions suffered by the Christians through the centuries. At the end of each century there are usually one or more poems on God's grace, patience, justice, etc. which serve as a general commentary on the preceding narrative. Several sections are devoted to miracles, remarkable providences and heresies.

In *The Magdeburg Centuries* each century is described under certain chapter headings, and these chapter headings and numbers are repeated for each century. Taylor followed a similar plan in his poem, drawing his material from the following chapters and headings: "Caput III De persecuutione et tranquillitate Ecclesiae," used for his martyrdoms; "Caput V De haeresibus et erroribus manifestis," used for his account of heresies; "Caput X De Vitis Episcoporum," used for his surveys of a century—its preachers, saints, etc.; "Caput XIII De Miraculis et Prodiguis," used for his miracles. A three-volume folio edition of John Foxe, *Actes and Monuments,* was owned by Taylor, who drew heavily from it

lxii

for his description of the first ten persecutions of the Christian
Church (there are many verbal parallels between Foxe's text and
the poem), and he probably used the same book for his informa-
tion concerning the martyrdoms under Queen Mary.

The subject of "Graces Bright Shine" comes from the last book
of the New Testament, the Revelation of St. John the Divine, a
long explication of which Taylor wrote to Samuel Sewall (in CP).
See below, Appendix 2.

Taylor's source for the "Martyrdom of Deacon Laurence" is
Foxe's *Actes and Monuments* (1610), *1*, 64–65; and for the "Per-
sian Persecution," *The Magdeburg Centuries, 2*, 150–151.

Prologue

Lord, Can a Crumb of Dust the Earth outweigh,
    Outmatch all mountains, nay the Chrystall Sky?
Imbosom in't designs that shall Display
    And trace into the Boundless Deity?
        Yea hand a Pen whose moysture doth guild ore   5
        Eternall Glory with a glorious glore.

If it its Pen had of an Angels Quill,
    And Sharpend on a Pretious Stone ground tite,
And dipt in Liquid Gold, and mov'de by Skill
    In Christall leaves should golden Letters write   10
        It would but blot and blur yea jag, and jar
        Unless thou mak'st the Pen, and Scribener.

I am this Crumb of Dust which is design'd
    To make my Pen unto thy Praise alone,
And my dull Phancy I would gladly grinde   15
    Unto an Edge on Zions Pretious Stone.
        And Write in Liquid Gold upon thy Name
        My Letters till thy glory forth doth flame.

Let not th'attempts breake down my Dust I pray
    Nor laugh thou them to scorn but pardon give.   20
Inspire this Crumb of Dust till it display
    Thy Glory through't: and then thy dust shall live.
        Its failings then thou'lt overlook I trust,
        They being Slips slipt from thy Crumb of Dust.

Thy Crumb of Dust breaths two words from its breast,   25
    That thou wilt guide its pen to write aright
To Prove thou art, and that thou art the best
    And shew thy Properties to shine most bright.
        And then thy Works will shine as flowers on Stems
        Or as in Jewellary Shops, do jems.   30

See below, Appendix 2, item 33, for the position of this poem in PW.
1 outweigh,] PW outweigh   10 In Christall leaves] orig: And golden letters
in   13 which] orig: and   29 Works will shine as flowers on Stems] orig:
Glorious Works as flowers on Stems

Preparatory Meditations before my
Approach to the Lords Supper. Chiefly
upon the Doctrin preached upon
the Day of administration

1. Meditation

Love

Mysticism?

Theantropy?

Westfield 23. 5m [July] *1682.* Pub. ETP, W.

What Love is this of thine, that Cannot bee
    In thine Infinity, O Lord, Confinde,
Unless it in thy very Person see,
    Infinity, and Finity Conjoyn'd?
    What hath thy Godhead, as not satisfide   5
    Marri'de our Manhood, making it its Bride?

Oh, Matchless Love! filling Heaven to the brim!
    O're running it: all running o're beside
This World! Nay Overflowing Hell; wherein
    For thine Elect, there rose a mighty Tide!   10
    That there our Veans might through thy Person bleed,
    To quench those flames, that else would on us feed.

Oh! that thy Love might overflow my Heart!
    To fire the same with Love: for Love I would.
But oh! my streight'ned Breast! my Lifeless Sparke!   15
    My Fireless Flame! What Chilly Love, and Cold?
    In measure small! In Manner Chilly! See.
    Lord blow the Coal: Thy Love Enflame in mee.

2. Meditation on Can. 1.3. Thy Name is an Ointment poured out.

12. 9m [Nov.] *1682.* Pub. PET.

My Dear, Deare, Lord I do thee Saviour Call:
    Thou in my very Soul art, as I Deem,

At the top of the page in PW: "Sacramental Meditations for 35 y. from 1682 to 1725. Preparatory Meditations before my Approach to the Lords Supper. Chiefly upon the Doctrin preached upon the Day of administration." The original date *1717* has been crossed out and changed to "1725." The figure *35* has not been corrected. On the same page: "By Rev. Edward Taylor A.M. Attest Ezra Stiles his Grandson 1786." The words "Sacramental Meditations for 35 y. from 1682 to 1717" are in the hand of Ezra Stiles. The correction "1725" is in another hand.   Med. *2, 2 Soul art, as I Deem,*] orig: Soul indeed art I Deem,

Soe High, not High enough, Soe Great; too small:
   Soe Deare, not Dear enough in my esteem.
Soe Noble, yet So Base: too Low; too Tall: 5
   Thou Full, and Empty art: Nothing, yet ALL.

A Precious Pearle, above all price dost 'bide.
   Rubies no Rubies are at all to thee.
Blushes of burnisht Glory Sparkling Slide
   From every Square in various Colour'd glee   10
   Nay Life itselfe in Sparkling Spangles Choice.
   A Precious Pearle thou art above all price.

Oh! that my Soul, Heavens Workmanship (within
   My Wicker'd Cage,) that Bird of Paradise
Inlin'de with Glorious Grace up to the brim   15
   Might be thy Cabbinet, oh Pearle of Price.
   Oh! let thy Pearle, Lord, Cabbinet in mee.
   I'st then be rich! nay rich enough for thee.

My Heart, oh Lord, for thy Pomander gain.
   Be thou thyselfe my sweet Perfume therein.   20
Make it thy Box, and let thy Pretious Name
   My Pretious Ointment be emboxt therein.
   If I thy box and thou my Ointment bee
   I shall be sweet, nay, sweet enough for thee.

Enough! Enough! oh! let me eat my Word.   25
   For if Accounts be ballanc'd any way,
Can my poore Eggeshell ever be an Hoard,
   Of Excellence enough for thee? Nay: nay.
   Yet may I Purse, and thou my Mony bee.
   I have enough. Enough in having thee.   30

3 *Soe High*] orig: Too high   *Soe Great*] orig: too Great   4 *Soe*] orig: Too
in] orig: to   23 *thy box*] Z the box   PW orig: the box   *my Ointment*] Z the
Ointment   27 *an Hoard*] Z a Hord   29 *my Mony*] Z the Money

17–18: Cf. Herbert's "To All Angels and Saints," line 14: "Thou art the
cabinet where the jewell lay." Cf. also Herbert's "Ungratefulness," lines 7–12.
19–20: Herbert's "Odour" describes the sweetness of Christ's name "My
Master" in terms of perfumes. This poem may be the origin of Taylor's many
figures involving perfumes.

3. Meditation. Can. 1.3. Thy Good Ointment

11. 12m [Feb.] *1682.* Pub. ETG.

How sweet a Lord is mine? If any should
    Guarded, Engarden'd, nay, Imbosomd bee·
In reechs of Odours, Gales of Spices, Folds
    Of Aromaticks, Oh! how sweet was hee?
    He would be sweet, and yet his sweetest Wave   5
    Compar'de to thee my Lord, no Sweet would have.

A Box of Ointments, broke; sweetness most sweet.
    A surge of spices: Odours Common Wealth,
A Pillar of Perfume: a steaming Reech
    Of Aromatick Clouds: All Saving Health.   10
    Sweetness itselfe thou art: And I presume
    In Calling of thee Sweet, who art Perfume.

But Woe is mee! who have so quick a Sent
    To Catch perfumes pufft out from Pincks, and Roses
And other Muscadalls, as they get Vent,   15
    Out of their Mothers Wombs to bob our noses.
    And yet thy sweet perfume doth seldom latch
    My Lord, within my Mammulary Catch.

Am I denos'de? or doth the Worlds ill sents
    Engarison my nosthrills narrow bore?   20
Or is my smell lost in these Damps it Vents?
    And shall I never finde it any more?
    Or is it like the Hawks, or Hownds whose breed
    Take stincking Carrion for Perfume indeed?

4 *was hee*] Z were hee   7 *Ointments*] Z Ointment   19 *denos'de*] Z benosde
Worlds ill sents] Z world with sents   20 *Engarison*] Z Ingarrison'd
narrow bore] Z or bore   21 *it Vents*] Z the vents   24 *Take*] Z Count

  18 ff.: Johnson suggests (ETG, p. 285) that Taylor uses *mammulary*
throughout the poem to refer to the olfactory system, but there is no evi-
dence for a meaning other than the normal 'nipples' or 'breasts.'

This is my Case. All things smell sweet to mee: 25
     Except thy sweetness, Lord. Expell these damps.
Breake up this Garison: and let me see
       Thy Aromaticks pitching in these Camps.
       Oh! let the Clouds of thy sweet Vapours rise,
       And both my Mammularies Circumcise.   30

Shall Spirits thus my Mammularies suck?
       (As Witches Elves their teats,) and draw from thee
My Dear, Dear Spirit after fumes of muck?
       Be Dunghill Damps more sweet than Graces bee?
       Lord, clear these Caves. These Passes take, and keep.   35
       And in these Quarters lodge thy Odours sweet.

Lord, breake thy Box of Ointment on my Head;
       Let thy sweet Powder powder all my hair:
My Spirits let with thy perfumes be fed
       And make thy Odours, Lord, my nosthrills fare.   40
       My Soule shall in thy sweets then soar to thee:
       I'le be thy Love, thou my sweet Lord shalt bee.

The Experience.

Undated. Pub. ETP, *W*.

Oh! that I always breath'd in such an aire,
       As I suckt in, feeding on sweet Content!
Disht up unto my Soul ev'n in that pray're
       Pour'de out to God over last Sacrament.
       What Beam of Light wrapt up my sight to finde   5
       Me neerer God than ere Came in my minde?

Most strange it was! But yet more strange that shine
       Which filld my Soul then to the brim to spy
My Nature with thy Nature all Divine
       Together joyn'd in Him thats Thou, and I.   10

30 *Mammularies*] Z Mammilaries   31 *Mammularies*] Z Mammilaries
35 *These*] PW these   38 *all*] Z well   40 *And make thy Odours, Lord,*] Z Thine
Odors set to be   42 *I'le*] Z I'st   8 *spy*] Z see   10 *I*] Z me

Flesh of my Flesh, Bone of my Bone. There's run
Thy Godhead, and my Manhood in thy Son.

Oh! that that Flame which thou didst on me Cast
Might me enflame, and Lighten ery where.
Then Heaven to me would be less at last 15
So much of heaven I should have while here.
Oh! Sweet though Short! Ile not forget the same.
My neerness, Lord, to thee did me Enflame.

I'le Claim my Right: Give place, ye Angells Bright.
Ye further from the Godhead stande than I. 20
My Nature is your Lord; and doth Unite
Better than Yours unto the Deity.
Gods Throne is first and mine is next: to you
Onely the place of Waiting-men is due.

Oh! that my Heart, thy Golden Harp might bee 25
Well tun'd by Glorious Grace, that e'ry string
Screw'd to the highest pitch, might unto thee
All Praises wrapt in sweetest Musick bring.
I praise thee, Lord, and better praise thee would
If what I had, my heart might ever hold. 30

The Return.

Undated. Unpublished.

Inamoring Rayes, thy Sparkles, Pearle of Price
Impearld with Choisest Gems, their beams Display
Impoysoning Sin, Guilding my Soule with Choice
Rich Grace, thy Image bright, making me pray,
Oh! that thou Wast on Earth below with mee 5
Or that I was in Heaven above with thee.

11 *There's*] PW there's   15 *Heaven to me would be*] Z heaven would be heaven
less   *less at last*] Z to me at last   26 *tun'd*] Z tuned   *Glorious*] Z thy
27 *to the highest*] Z up to th'highest   28 *Praises wrapt in*] Z praise rapt up in
PW orig: Praises wrapt up in   30 *might*] Z did   4 *thy*] Z thine

Thy Humane Frame, with Beauty Dapled, and
  In Beds of Graces pald with golden layes,
Lockt to thy Holy Essence by thy hand,
  Yields Glances that enflame my Soul, that sayes   10
  Oh! that thou wast on Earth below with mee!
  Or that I was in Heaven above with thee.

All Love in God, and's Properties Divine
  Enam'led are in thee: thy Beauties Blaze
Attracts my Souls Choice golden Wyer to twine   15
  About thy Rose-sweet selfe. And therefore prayes
  Oh! that thou wast on Earth below with mee!
  Or, that I was in Heaven above with thee.

A Magazeen of Love: Bright Glories blaze:
  Thy Shine fills Heaven with Glory; Smile Convayes 20
Heavens Glory in my Soule, which it doth glaze
  All ore with amoring Glory; that she sayes,
  Oh! that thou wast on Earth below with mee!
  Or, that I was in Heaven above with thee!

Heavens Golden Spout thou art where Grace most Choice 25
  Comes Spouting down from God to man of Clay.
A Golden Stepping Stone to Paradise
  A Golden Ladder into Heaven! I'l pray
  Oh! that thou wast on Earth below with mee
  Or that I was in Heaven above with thee.   30

Thy Service is my Freedom Pleasure, Joy,
  Delight, Bliss, Glory, Heaven on Earth, my Stay,
In Gleams of Glory thee to glorify.
  But oh! my Dross and Lets. Wherefore I say
  Oh! that thou wast on Earth below with mee: 35
  Or that I was in Heaven above with thee.

If off as Offall I be put, if I
  Out of thy Vineyard Work be put away:
Life would be Death: my Soule would Coffin'd ly,
  Within my Body; and no longer pray   40

7 *with*] PW whith 16 *And*] PW and 38 *Out of*] PW Outed

Oh! that thou wast on Earth below with mee:
But that I was in Heaven above with thee.

But I've thy Pleasant Pleasant Presence had
    In Word, Pray're, Ordinances, Duties; nay,
And in thy Graces, making me full Glad,   45
    In Faith, Hope, Charity, that I do say,
    That thou hast been on Earth below with mee.
    And I shall be in Heaven above with thee.

Be thou Musician, Lord, Let me be made
    The well tun'de Instrument thou dost assume.   50
And let thy Glory be my Musick plaide.
    Then let thy Spirit keepe my Strings in tune,
    Whilst thou art here on Earth below with mee
    Till I sing Praise in Heaven above with thee.

4. Meditation. Cant. 2.1. I am the Rose of Sharon.

*Note here
Christ is
feminine*

180

22. 2m [April] 1683. Unpublished.

My Silver Chest a Sparke of Love up locks:
    And out will let it when I can't well Use.
The gawdy World me Courts t'unlock the Box,
    A motion makes, where Love may pick and choose.
    Her Downy Bosom opes, that pedlars Stall,   5
    Of Wealth, Sports, Honours, Beauty, slickt up all.

Love pausing on't, these Clayey Faces she
    Disdains to Court; but Pilgrims life designs,
And Walkes in Gilliads Land, and there doth see
    The Rose of Sharon which with Beauty shines.   10
    Her Chest Unlocks; the Sparke of Love out breaths
    To Court this Rose: and lodgeth in its leaves.

53 *Whilst*] Z While   PW orig: While   54 *with*] Z to   2 *out will let it when I
can't well Use*] Z will bring't out when I it well can use   3 *gawdy*] Z gilded
t'unlock] Z t'unscrew   4 *A*] Z And   7 *on't*] Z here   11 *Her Chest*] Z The
Chest 12 *lodgeth*] Z lodges

No flower in Garzia Horti shines like this:
   No Beauty sweet in all the World so Choice:
It is the Rose of Sharon sweet, that is   15
   The Fairest Rose that Grows in Paradise.
   Blushes of Beauty bright, Pure White, and Red
   In Sweats of Glory on Each Leafe doth bed.

Lord lead me into this sweet Rosy Bower:
   Oh! Lodge my Soul in this Sweet Rosy bed: 20
Array my Soul with this sweet Sharon flower:
   Perfume me with the Odours it doth shed.
   Wealth, Pleasure, Beauty Spirituall will line
   My pretious Soul, if Sharons Rose be mine.

The Blood Red Pretious Syrup of this Rose   25
   Doth all Catholicons excell what ere.
Ill Humours all that do the Soule inclose
   When rightly usd, it purgeth out most clear.
   Lord purge my Soul with this Choice Syrup, and
   Chase all thine Enemies out of my land.   30

The Rosy Oyle, from Sharons Rose extract
   Better than Palma Christi far is found.
Its Gilliads Balm for Conscience when she's wrackt
   Unguent Apostolorum for each Wound.
   Let me thy Patient, thou my Surgeon bee.   35
   Lord, with thy Oyle of Roses Supple mee.

18 *on*] orig: of   23 *line*] orig: live
24 *pretious*] Z Deare deare   27 *Soule inclose*] Z Soul up grace [?] inclose
28 *usd*] Z tooke   *most*] Z full   30 *my land*] Z that Land
land] orig: hand   33 *when she's wrackt*] Z Pains, exact
34 *each*] Z its   PW orig: all   36 *thy*] Z this

   25 ff.: The rose as a symbol of Christ, of Christ's blood, and of Christ's
grace is common in Christian typology. The notion of Christ's blood as a
medicine or cordial is also common. The rose and other flowers were used as
purges and medicines in the seventeenth century. For the church considered
as a rose see Herbert's "Church-rents and schismes." For the rose and other
flowers as purges see Herbert's "The Rose," line 18; "Providence," line 78;
"Life," line 15. For Christ's blood or Christ's grace considered as a cordial
see Herbert's "The Sacrifice," line 159; "The Glance," line 6; "Whitsunday,"
line 18; "The Odour," line 9; "Sighs and Groans," line 28.

No Flower there is in Paradise that grows
    Whose Virtues Can Consumptive Souls restore
But Shugar of Roses made of Sharons Rose
    When Dayly usd, doth never fail to Cure.   40
    Lord let my Dwindling Soul be dayly fed
    With Sugar of Sharons Rose, its dayly Bread.

God Chymist is, doth Sharons Rose distill.
    Oh! Choice Rose Water! Swim my Soul herein.
Let Conscience bibble in it with her Bill.   45
    Its Cordiall, ease doth Heart burns Causd by Sin.
    Oyle, Syrup, Sugar, and Rose Water such.
    Lord, give, give, give; I cannot have too much.

But, oh! alas! that such should be my need
    That this Brave Flower must Pluckt, stampt, squeezed bee,
And boyld up in its Blood, its Spirits sheed,   51
    To make a Physick sweet, sure, safe for mee.
    But yet this mangled Rose rose up again
    And in its pristine glory, doth remain.

All Sweets, and Beauties of all Flowers appeare   55
    In Sharons Rose, whose Glorious Leaves out vie
In Vertue, Beauty, Sweetness, Glory Cleare,
    The Spangled Leaves of Heavens cleare Chrystall Sky.
    Thou Rose of Heaven, Glory's Blossom Cleare
    Open thy Rosie Leaves, and lodge mee there.   60

My Dear-Sweet Lord, shall I thy Glory meet
    Lodg'd in a Rose, that out a sweet Breath breaths.
What is my way to Glory made thus sweet,
    Strewd all along with Sharons Rosy Leaves.
    I'le walk this Rosy Path: World fawn, or frown   65
    And Sharons Rose shall be my Rose, and Crown.

37 *there is in Paradise*] Z in Paradise there is
40 *usd, doth never fail*] Z usen never fails
42 *its*] Z as   46 *ease doth*] Z eases   50 *must*] Z should   53 *Rose*] orig: flower
rose up again] Z rose after this   54 *And in its pristine*] Z In'ts Pristine
doth remain] Z beautifull it is   56 *Glorious*] Z beautious
57 *Beauty, Sweetness, Glory*] Z glory, Sweetness, breadth, and Beauty
Cleare,] PW Cleare.   58 *cleare*] Z broad   59 *Blossom Cleare*] Z blossom so
cleare   61 *Glory*] Z beauty   63 *Glory*] Z heaven

The Reflexion.

8⁰

Undated. Pub. ETP, *W*.

Lord, art thou at the Table Head above
    Meat, Med'cine, sweetness, sparkling Beautys to
Enamour Souls with Flaming Flakes of Love,
    And not my Trencher, nor my Cup o'reflow?
    Be n't I a bidden Guest? Oh! sweat mine Eye.   5
    Oreflow with Teares: Oh! draw thy fountains dry.

Shall I not smell thy sweet, oh! Sharons Rose?
    Shall not mine Eye salute thy Beauty? Why?
Shall thy sweet leaves their Beautious sweets upclose?
    As halfe ashamde my sight should on them ly?   10
    Woe's me! for this my sighs shall be in grain
    Offer'd on Sorrows Altar for the same.

Had not my Soule's thy Conduit, Pipes stopt bin
    With mud, what Ravishment would'st thou Convay?
Let Graces Golden Spade dig till the Spring   15
    Of tears arise, and cleare this filth away.
    Lord, let thy spirit raise my sighings till
    These Pipes my soule do with thy sweetness fill.

Earth once was Paradise of Heaven below
    Till inkefac'd sin had it with poyson stockt   20
And Chast this Paradise away into
    Heav'ns upmost Loft, and it in Glory Lockt.
    But thou, sweet Lord, hast with thy golden Key
    Unlockt the Doore, and made, a golden day.

Once at thy Feast, I saw thee Pearle-like stand   25
    'Tween Heaven, and Earth where Heavens Bright glory all

2 *Beautys*] Z beauty
to] orig: show   5 *Guest*] PW Guess   6 *with Teares: Oh! draw thy fountains
dry.*] Z my Cup with tears *** pass by?   7 *smell thy sweet, oh!*] Z catch the
sweet of   8 *not mine Eye salute thy Beauty? Why?*] Z I not greet thy Beauty
with mine eye   9 *Beautious sweets*] Z Beauty bright   23 *hast*] Z do
24 *Unlockt*] PW Unlock   *made*] Z make   25 *Pearle-like*] PW Pearle like

In streams fell on thee, as a floodgate and,
    Like Sun Beams through thee on the World to Fall.
    Oh! sugar sweet then! my Deare sweet Lord, I see
    Saints Heavens-lost Happiness restor'd by thee.   30

Shall Heaven, and Earth's bright Glory all up lie
    Like Sun Beams bundled in the sun, in thee?
Dost thou sit Rose at Table Head, where I
    Do sit, and Carv'st no morsell sweet for mee?
    So much before, so little now! Sprindge, Lord,   35
    Thy Rosie Leaves, and me their Glee afford.

Shall not thy Rose my Garden fresh perfume?
    Shall not thy Beauty my dull Heart assaile?
Shall not thy golden gleams run through this gloom?
    Shall my black Velvet Mask thy fair Face Vaile?   40
    Pass o're my Faults: shine forth, bright sun: arise
    Enthrone thy Rosy-selfe within mine Eyes.

5. Meditation. Cant. 2.1. The Lilly of the Vallies.

2. 7m [Sept.] *1683*. Unpublished.

My Blessed Lord, art thou a Lilly Flower?
    Oh! that my Soul thy Garden were, that so
Thy bowing Head root in my Heart, and poure
    Might of its Seeds, that they therein might grow.
    Be thou my Lilly, make thou me thy knot: 5
    Be thou my Flowers, I'le be thy Flower Pot.

My barren heart thy Fruitfull Vally make:
    Be thou my Lilly flouerishing in mee:

37 *my*] orig: thy   40 *fair Face Vaile*] Z face up vale   4 *Seeds, that they therein might*] Z Lillie *** therein to

Oh Lilly of the Vallies. For thy sake,
    Let me thy Vally, thou my Lilly bee.   10
    Then nothing shall me of thyselfe bereave.
    Thou must not me, or must thy Vally leave.

How shall my Vallie's Spangling Glory spred,
    Thou Lilly of the Vallies Spangling
There springing up? Upon thy bowing Head   15
    All Heavens bright Glory hangeth dangling.
    My Vally then with Blissfull Beams shall shine,
    Thou Lilly of the Vallys, being mine.

[6.] Another Meditation at the same time.

Undated. Pub. *W.*

Am I thy Gold? Or Purse, Lord, for thy Wealth;
    Whether in mine, or mint refinde for thee?
Ime counted so, but count me o're thyselfe,
    Lest gold washt face, and brass in Heart I bee.
    I Feare my Touchstone touches when I try   5
    Mee, and my Counted Gold too overly.

Am I new minted by thy Stamp indeed?
    Mine Eyes are dim; I cannot clearly see.
Be thou my Spectacles that I may read
    Thine Image, and Inscription stampt on mee.   10
    If thy bright Image do upon me stand
    I am a Golden Angell in thy hand.

Lord, make my Soule thy Plate: thine Image bright
    Within the Circle of the same enfoile.
And on its brims in golden Letters write   15
    Thy Superscription in an Holy style.
    Then I shall be thy Money, thou my Hord:
    Let me thy Angell bee, bee thou my Lord.

Another Meditation] PW Another Mediation
4 *and*] Z but   15 *brims*] Z brim

*Polyptotonic play on Still,
Grace, Tincture*

Christ is divine distiller

7. Meditation. Ps. 45.2. Grace in thy
      lips is poured out.

10.12m [Feb.] *1683.* Pub. ETP, *W.*

Thy Humane Frame, my Glorious Lord, I spy,
    A Golden Still with Heavenly Choice drugs filld;
Thy Holy Love, the Glowing heate whereby,
    The Spirit of Grace is graciously distilld.
    Thy Mouth the Neck through which these spirits still.   5
    My Soul thy Violl make, and therewith fill.

Thy Speech the Liquour in thy Vessell stands,
    Well ting'd with Grace a blessed Tincture, Loe,
Thy Words distilld, Grace in thy Lips pourd, and,
    Give Graces Tinctur in them where they go.   10
    Thy words in graces tincture stilld, Lord, may
    The Tincture of thy Grace in me Convay.

That Golden Mint of Words, thy Mouth Divine,
    Doth tip these Words, which by my Fall were spoild;
And Dub with Gold dug out of Graces mine   15
    That they thine Image might have in them foild.
    Grace in thy Lips pourd out's as Liquid Gold.
    Thy Bottle make my Soule, Lord, it to hold.

2 *Heavenly Choice drugs filld*] Z Heavens sweet drugs is filld   *filld;*] PW filld
10 *Give*] Z Carry
13 *Words,*] PW Words   *Divine,*] PW Divine   16 *thine*] Z thy
18 *Thy Bottle make my Soule, Lord, it to hold*] Z Lord, make my heart thy
Bottle this *** to hold

    16. *foild* (see also Glossary). Taylor hopes his words will be adorned with
the golden image of Christ.

8. Meditation. Joh. 6.51. I am the Living Bread.

Emblem 1982

8. 4m [June] *1684*. Pub. ETP, *W*.

I kening through Astronomy Divine
    The Worlds bright Battlement, wherein I spy
A Golden Path my Pensill cannot line,
    From that bright Throne unto my Threshold ly.
    And while my puzzled thoughts about it pore   5
    I finde the Bread of Life in't at my doore.

When that this Bird of Paradise put in
    This Wicker Cage (my Corps) to tweedle praise
Had peckt the Fruite forbad: and so did fling
    Away its Food; and lost its golden dayes;   10
    It fell into Celestiall Famine sore:
    And never could attain a morsell more.

Alas! alas! Poore Bird, what wilt thou doe?
    The Creatures field no food for Souls e're gave.
And if thou knock at Angells dores they show   15
    An Empty Barrell: they no soul bread have.
    Alas! Poore Bird, the Worlds White Loafe is done.
    And cannot yield thee here the smallest Crumb.

In this sad state, Gods Tender Bowells run
    Out streams of Grace: And he to end all strife   20
The Purest Wheate in Heaven, his deare-dear Son
    Grinds, and kneads up into this Bread of Life.
    Which Bread of Life from Heaven down came and stands
    Disht on thy Table up by Angells Hands.

Did God mould up this Bread in Heaven, and bake,   25
    Which from his Table came, and to thine goeth?
Doth he bespeake thee thus, This Soule Bread take.

2 *Battlement*] Z Battlements   8 *Wicker*] Z vitall
22 *Grinds, and kneads up*] Z Doth knead up there
this] Z the   23 *came*] Z comes   27 *Doth he bespeake*] Z And there bespeakes

Come Eate thy fill of this thy Gods White Loafe?
Its Food too fine for Angells, yet come, take
And Eate thy fill. Its Heavens Sugar Cake.   30

What Grace is this knead in this Loafe? This thing
    Souls are but petty things it to admire.
Yee Angells, help: This fill would to the brim
    Heav'ns whelm'd-down Chrystall meele Bowle, yea and
      higher.
    This Bread of Life dropt in thy mouth, doth Cry.   35
    Eate, Eate me, Soul, and thou shalt never dy.

9. Meditation. Joh. 6.51. I am the
        Living Bread.

7.7m [Sept.] *1684.* Unpublished.

Did Ever Lord such noble house mentain,
    As my Lord doth? Or such a noble Table?
'T would breake the back of kings, nay, Monarchs brain
    To do it. Pish, the Worlds Estate's not able.
    I'le bet a boast with any that this Bread   5
    I eate excells what ever Caesar had.

Take earth's Brightst Darlings, in whose mouths all flakes
    Of Lushous Sweets she hath do croude their Head,
Their Spiced Cups, sweet Meats, and Sugar Cakes
    Are but dry Sawdust to this Living Bread.   10
    I'le pawn my part in Christ, this Dainti'st Meate,
    Is Gall, and Wormwood unto what I eate.

The Boasting Spagyrist (Insipid Phlegm,
    Whose Words out strut the Sky) vaunts he hath rife
'The Water, Tincture, Lozenge, Gold, and Gem,   15

28 *Come Eate*] Z Eate, Soule   4 *Pish,*] PW Pish. Z nay
9 *Cups, sweet*] Z Cups and sweet   *Meats, and Sugar*] Z Meats, Sugar
11 *this*] Z his

Of Life itselfe. But here's the Bread of Life.
I'le lay my Life, his Aurum Vitae Red
Is to my Bread of Life, worse than DEAD HEAD.

The Dainti'st Dish of Earthly Cookery
    Is but to fat the body up in print.   20
This Bread of Life doth feed the Soule, whereby
    Its made the Temple of Jehovah in't.
      I'le Venture Heav'n upon't that Low or High
      That eate this Living Bread shall never dy.

This Bread of Life, so excellent, I see   25
    The Holy Angells doubtless would, if they
Were prone unto base Envie, Envie't mee.
    But oh! come, tast how sweet it is. I say,
      I'le Wage my Soule and all therein uplaid,
      This is the sweetest Bread that e're God made.   30

What wonder's here, that Bread of Life should come
    To feed Dead Dust? Dry Dust eate Living Bread?
Yet Wonder more by far may all, and some
    That my Dull Heart's so dumpish when thus fed.
      Lord Pardon this, and feed mee all my dayes,   35
      With Living Bread to thy Eternall Prayse.

10. Meditation. Joh. 6.55. My Blood is Drinke indeed.

26. 8m [Oct.] 1684. Pub. ETG.

Stupendious Love! All Saints Astonishment!
    Bright Angells are black Motes in this Suns Light.
Heav'ns Canopy the Paintice to Gods tent
    Can't Cover't neither with its breadth, nor height.
      Its Glory doth all Glory else out run,
      Beams of bright Glory to't are motes i'th'sun.   5

My Soule had Caught an Ague, and like Hell
    Her thirst did burn: she to each spring did fly,
But this bright blazing Love did spring a Well
    Of Aqua-Vitae in the Deity,   10
    Which on the top of Heav'ns high Hill out burst
    And down came running thence t'allay my thirst.

But how it came, amazeth all Communion.
    Gods onely Son doth hug Humanity,
Into his very person. By which Union   15
    His Humane Veans its golden gutters ly.
    And rather than my Soule should dy by thirst,
    These Golden Pipes, to give me drink, did burst.

This Liquour brew'd, thy sparkling Art Divine
    Lord, in thy Chrystall Vessells did up tun,   20
(Thine Ordinances,) which all Earth o're shine
    Set in thy rich Wine Cellars out to run.
    Lord, make thy Butlar draw, and fill with speed
    My Beaker full: for this is drink indeed.

Whole Buts of this blesst Nectar shining stand   25
    Lockt up with Saph'rine Taps, whose splendid Flame
Too bright do shine for brightest Angells hands
    To touch, my Lord. Do thou untap the same.
    Oh! make thy Chrystall Buts of Red Wine bleed
    Into my Chrystall Glass this Drink-Indeed.   30

How shall I praise thee then? My blottings Jar
    And wrack my Rhymes to pieces in thy praise.
Thou breath'st thy Vean still in my Pottinger
    To lay my thirst, and fainting spirits raise.
    Thou makest Glory's Chiefest Grape to bleed   35
    Into my cup: And this is Drink-Indeed.

Nay, though I make no pay for this Red Wine,
    And scarce do say I thank-ye-for't; strange thing!
Yet were thy silver skies my Beer bowle fine

19 *brew'd*,] PW brew'd.   29 *Oh!*] orig: And

I finde my Lord, would fill it to the brim.   40
Then make my life, Lord, to thy praise proceed
For thy rich blood, which is my Drink-Indeed.

11. Meditation. Isai. 25.6. A Feast
       of Fat things.

31. 3m [Mar.] *1685*. Unpublished.

A Deity of Love Incorporate
    My Lord, lies in thy Flesh, in Dishes stable
Ten thousand times more rich than golden Plate
    In golden Services upon thy Table,
        To feast thy People with. What Feast is this!   5
        Where richest Love lies Cookt in e'ry Dish?

A Feast, a Feast, a Feast of Spiced Wine
    Of Wines upon the Lees, refined well
Of Fat things full of Marrow, things Divine
    Of Heavens blest Cookery which doth excell.   10
        The Smell of Lebanon, and Carmell sweet
        Are Earthly damps unto this Heavenly reech.

This Shew-Bread Table all of Gold with white
    Fine Table Linen of Pure Love, 's ore spred
And Courses in Smaragdine Chargers bright   15
    Of Choicest Dainties Paradise e're bred.
        Where in each Grace like Dainty Sippits lie
        Oh! brave Embroderies of sweetest joy!

Oh! what a Feast is here? This Table might
    Make brightest Angells blush to sit before.   20
Then pain my Soule! Why wantst thou appitite?
    Oh! blush to thinke thou hunger dost no more.
        There never was a feast more rich than this:
        The Guests that Come hereto shall swim in bliss.

21 *Why*] PW why   24 *Guests*] PW Guess

Hunger, and Thirst my Soule, goe Fasting Pray,
    Untill thou hast an Appitite afresh:
And then come here; here is a feast will pay
    Thee for the same with all Deliciousness.
    Untap Loves Golden Cask, Love run apace:
    And o're this Feast Continually say Grace.   30

12. Meditation. Isai. 63.1. Glorious in his Apparell.

19. 5m [July] *1685.* Pub. *W.*

This Quest rapt at my Eares broad golden Doores
    Who's this that comes from Edom in this shine
In Died Robes from Bozrah? this more ore
    All Glorious in's Apparrell; all Divine?
    Then through that Wicket rusht this buss there gave,   5
    Its I that right do speake mighty to save.

27 *here;*] PW here.

3: *Died Robes from Bozrah?* Probably, robes of wool from Bozrah sheep, dyed red. The red robe representing Christ's blood at the Passion was a common symbol in Christian typology; it derives from Isa. 63:1 ff.: "Who is this that cometh from Edom, with dyed garments from Bozrah? . . . I have trodden the winepress alone; and of the people there was none with me: for I will tread them in mine anger, and trample them in my fury; and their blood shall be sprinkled upon my garments, and I will stain all my raiment." Cf. Herbert's "The Sacrifice," lines 157–60: "Then with a scarlet robe they me array; / Which shews my bloud to be the onely way / And cordiall left to repair mans decay; / Was ever grief like mine?" Cf. also Herbert's "The Agonie," line 10, and Crashaw's "On our crucified Lord Naked, and bloody" (L. C. Martin, ed., *Crashaw's Poetical Works,* Oxford, 1927), p. 100:

> Th'have left thee naked Lord, O that they had;
>   This Garment too I would they had deny'd,
> Thee with thy selfe they have too richly clad,
>
> Opening the purple wardrobe of thy side.
>   O never could bee found Garments too good
> For thee to weare, but these, of thine owne blood.

I threw through Zions Lattice then an Eye
    Which spide one like a lump of Glory pure
Nay, Cloaths of gold button'd with pearls do ly
    Like Rags, or shooclouts unto his he wore.   10
    Heavens Curtains blancht with Sun, and Starrs of Light
    Are black as sackcloath to his Garments bright.

One shining sun guilding the skies with Light
    Benights all Candles with their flaming Blaze
So doth the Glory of this Robe benight   15
    Ten thousand suns at once ten thousand wayes.
    For e'ry thrid therein's dy'de with the shine
    Of All, and Each the Attributes Divine.

The sweetest breath, the sweetest Violet
    Rose, or Carnation ever did gust out   20
Is but a Foist to that Perfume beset
    In thy Apparell steaming round about:
    But is this so? My Peuling soul then pine
    In Love untill this Lovely one be thine.

Pluck back the Curtains, back the Window Shutts: 25
    Through Zions Agate Window take a view;
How Christ in Pinckted Robes from Bozrah puts
    Comes Glorious in's Apparell forth to Wooe.
    Oh! if his Glory ever kiss thine Eye,
    Thy Love will soon Enchanted bee thereby.   30

Then Grieve, my Soul, thy vessell is so small
    And holds no more for such a Lovely Hee.
That strength's so little, Love scarce acts at all.
    That sight's so dim, doth scarce him lovely see.
    Grieve, grieve, my Soul, thou shouldst so pimping bee,   35
    Now such a Price is here presented thee.

All sight's too little sight enough to make
    All strength's too little Love enough to reare
All Vessells are too small to hold or take
    Enough Love up for such a Lovely Deare.   40

16 *ten thousand wayes*] PW ten thosand wayes

How little to this Little's then thy ALL.
For Him whose Beauty saith all Love's too small?

My Lovely One, I fain would love thee much
    But all my Love is none at all I see,
Oh! let thy Beauty give a glorious tuch   45
    Upon my Heart, and melt to Love all mee.
    Lord melt me all up into Love for thee
    Whose Loveliness excells what love can bee.

13. Meditation. Col. 2.3. All the
        Treasures of Wisdom.

27.7m [Sept.] *1685.* Pub. PET.

Thou Glory Darkning Glory, with thy Flame
    Should all Quaint Metaphors teem ev'ry Bud
Of Sparkling Eloquence upon the same
    It would appeare as dawbing pearls with mud.
    Nay Angells Wits are Childish tricks, and like   5
    The Darksom night unto thy Lightsom Light.

Oh! Choicest Cabbinet, more Choice than gold
    Or Wealthist Pearles Wherein all Pearls of Price
All Treasures of Choice Wisdom manifold
    Inthroned reign. Thou Cabinet most Choice   10
    Not scant to hold, not staind with cloudy geere
    The Shining Sun of Wisdom bowling there.

Thou Shining Golden Lanthorn with pain'd Lights
    Of Chrystall cleare, thy golden Candles flame,
Makes such a Shine, as doth the Sun benights.   15
    Its but a Smoaky vapor to the Same.
    All Wisdom knead into a Chrystall Ball,
    Shines like the Sun in thee, its azure Hall.

Thou rowling Eye of Light, to thee are sent
    All Dazzling Beams of Shine the Heavens distill.   20
All Wisdoms Troops do quarter in thy Tents
    And all her Treasures Cabin in thy tills.
      Be thou, Lord, mine: then I shall Wealthy bee,
      Enricht with Wisdoms Treasures, Stoughd in thee.

That little Grain within my golden Bowle,   25
    Should it attempt to poise thy Talent cleare,
It would inoculate into my Soule,
    As illookt Impudence as ever were.
      But, loe, it stands amaizd, and doth adore,
      Thy Magazeen of Wisdom, and thy Store.   30

14. Meditations. Heb. 4.14. A Great
15.   High Priest.

14. 9m [Nov.] *1685. 10. 11m* [Jan.] *1685.* Unpublished.

Raptures of Love, surprizing Loveliness,
    That burst through Heavens all, in Rapid Flashes,
Glances guilt o're with smiling Comliness!
    (Wonders do palefac'd stand smit by such dashes).
      Glory itselfe Heartsick of Love doth ly   5
      Bleeding out Love o're Loveless mee, and dy.

Might I a glance of this bright brightness shew;
    Se it in him who gloriously is dresst:
A Gold Silk Stomacher of Purple, blew
    Blancht o're with Orient Pearles being on his Breast: 10
      And all his Robes being answerable, but
      This glory seen, to that unseen's a Smut.

Yea, Beauteous Hee, in all his Glory stands,
    Tendring himselfe to God, and Man where hee
Doth Justice thus bespeake, Hold out thy hands: 15
    Come, take thy Penworths now for mine of mee.

I'le pay the fine that thou seest meet to set
    Upon their Heads: I'le dy to cleare their debts.

Out Rampant Justice steps in Sparkling White,
    Him rends in twain, who on her Altar lies   20
A Lump of Glory flaming in her bright
    Devouring Flames, to be my Sacrifice
    Untill her Fire goes out well Satisfide:
    And then he rose in Glory to abide.

To Heav'n went he, and in his bright Throne sits   25
    At Gods right hand pleading poor Sinners Cases.
With Golden Wedges he of Promise, splits
    The Heav'ns ope, to shew what Glory 'braces.
    And in its thickness thus with Arms extended,
    Calls, come, come here, and ever be befriended.   30

Frost bitten Love, Frozen Affections! Blush;
    What icy Chrystall mountain lodge you in?
What Wingless Wishes, Hopes pinfeatherd tush!
    Sore Hooft Desires hereof do in you spring?
    Oh hard black Kirnell at the Coare! not pant?   35
    Encastled in an heart of Adamant!

What strange Congealed Heart have I when I
    Under such Beauty shining like the Sun
Able to make Frozen Affection fly,
    And Icikles of Frostbitt Love to run.   40
    Yea, and Desires lockt in an heart of Steel
    Or Adamant, breake prison, nothing feel.

Lord may thy Priestly Golden Oares but make
    A rowing in my Lumpish Heart, thou'lt see
My Chilly Numbd Affections Charm, and break   45
    Out in a rapid Flame of Love to thee.
    Yea, they unto thyselfe will fly in flocks
    When thy Warm Sun my frozen Lake unlocks.

Be thou my High Priest, Lord; and let my name
    Ly in some Grave dug in these Pearly rocks   50

40 *Frostbitt*] orig: Frostbitten

Upon thy Ephods Shoulder piece, like flame
    Or graved in thy Breast Plate-Gem: brave Knops.
    Thou'lt then me beare before thy Fathers Throne
    Rowld up in Folds of Glory of thine own.

One of these Gems I beg, Lord, that so well   55
    Begrace thy Breast Plate, and thy Ephod cleaver
To stud my Crown therewith: or let me dwell
    Among their sparkling, glancing Shades for ever.
    I'st then be deckt in glory bright to sing
    With Angells, Hallelujahs to my King.   60

16. Meditation. Lu. 7.16. A Greate
        Prophet is risen up.

6. 1m [Mar.] *1685/6.* Pub. UPT.

Leafe Gold, Lord of thy Golden Wedge o'relaid
    My Soul at first, thy Grace in e'ry part
Whose peart, fierce Eye thou such a Sight hadst made
    Whose brightsom beams could break into thy heart
    Till thy Curst Foe had with my Fist mine Eye   5
    Dasht out, and did my Soule Unglorify.

I cannot see, nor Will thy Will aright.
    Nor see to waile my Woe, my loss and hew
Nor all the Shine in all the Sun can light
    My Candle, nor its Heate my Heart renew.   10
    See, waile, and Will thy Will, I must, or must
    From Heavens sweet Shine to Hells hot flame be thrust.

Grace then Conceald in God himselfe, did rowle
    Even Snow Ball like into a Sunball Shine
And nestles all its beams buncht in thy Soule   15
    My Lord, that sparkle in Prophetick Lines.
    Oh! Wonder more than Wonderfull! this Will
    Lighten the Eye which Sight Divine did spill.

What art thou, Lord, this Ball of Glory bright?
    A Bundle of Celestiall Beams up bound   20
In Graces band fixt in Heavens topmost height
    Pouring thy golden Beams thence, Circling round
    Which shew thy Glory, and thy glories Way
    And ery Where will make Celestiall Day.

Lord let thy Golden Beams pierce through mine Eye   25
    And leave therein an Heavenly Light to glaze
My Soule with glorious Grace all o're, whereby
    I may have Sight, and Grace in mee may blaze.
    Lord ting my Candle at thy Burning Rayes,
    To give a gracious Glory to thy Prayse.   30

Thou Lightning Eye, let some bright Beames of thine
    Stick in my Soul, to light and liven it:
Light, Life, and Glory, things that are Divine;
    I shall be grac'd withall for glory fit.
    My Heart then stufft with Grace, Light, Life, and Glee
    I'le sacrifice in Flames of Love to thee.

17. Meditation. Rev. 19.16. King of Kings.

13. 4m [June] *1686*. Unpublished.

A King, a King, a King indeed, a King
    Writh up in Glory! Glorie's glorious Throne
Is glorifide by him, presented him.
    And all the Crowns of Glory are his own.
    A King, Wise, Just, Gracious, Magnificent.   5
    Kings unto him are Whiffles, Indigent.

What is his Throne all Glory? Crown all Gay?
    Crown all of Brightest Shine of Glory's Wealth?
This is a Lisp of Non-sense. I should say,
    He is the Throne, and Crown of Glory 'tselfe.   10

21 *fixt in*] orig: fixt up in

Should Sun beams come to gilde his glory they
Would be as 'twere to gild the Sun with Clay.

My Phancys in a Maze, my thoughts agast,
   Words in an Extasy; my Telltale Tongue
Is tonguetide, and my Lips are padlockt fast   15
   To see thy Kingly Glory in to throng.
   I can, yet cannot tell this Glory just,
   In Silence bury't, must not, yet I must.

This King of King's Brave Kingdom doth Consist
   Of Glorious Angells, and Blesst Saints alone   20
Or Chiefly. Where all Beams of Glory twist,
   Together, beaming from, lead to his throne
   Which Beams his Grace Coiles in a Wreath to Crown
   His, in the End in Endless Bright Renown.

His Two-Edg'd Sword, not murdering Steel so base,   25
   Is made of Righteousness, unspotted, bright
Imbellisht o're with overflowing Grace
   Doth killing, Cure the Sinner, kills Sin right.
   Makes milkwhite Righteousness, and Grace to reign,
   And Satan and his Cubs with Sin ly slain.   30

Were all Kings deckt with Sparkling Crowns, and arm'd
   With flaming Swords, and firy Courage traind
And led under their King Abaddon, Charmd
   In battell out against their foes disdaind
   One smiling look of this bright Shine would fell   35
   Them and their Crowns of Glory all to Hell.

Thou art my king: let me not be thy Shame.
   Thy Law my Rule: my Life thy Life in Mee.
Thy Grace my Badge: my Glory bright thy Name.
   I am resolv'd to live and dy with thee.
   Keep mee, thou King of Glory on Record.   40
   Thou art my King of Kings, and Lord of Lords.

11 *gilde*] orig: guilde   12 *gild*] orig: guild   20 *Saints*] PW Saint
35 *smiling*] PW smiting[?]

18. Meditation. Isai. 52.14. His Vissage
was marr'd more than any man.

29. 6m [Aug.] *1686.* Pub. UPT.

Astonisht stand, my Soule; why dost not start
    At this surprizing Sight shewn here below?
Oh! let the twitch made by my bouncing Heart
    Gust from my breast this Enterjection, Oh!
    A Sight so Horrid, sure its Mercies Wonder   5
    Rocks rend not at't, nor Heavens split asunder.

Souls Charg'd with Sin, Discharge at God, beside
    Firld up in Guilt, Wrapt in Sins Slough, and Slime.
Wills wed to Wickedness, Hearts Stonifide
    Flinty Affections, Conscience Chalybdine   10
    Flooding the World with Horrid Crimes, arise
    Daring Almighty God Contemptuouswise.

Hence Vengeance rose with her fierce Troops in Buff,
    Soul-piercing Plagues, Heart-Aching Griefs, and Groans,
Woes Pickled in Revenges Powdering Trough: 15
    Pain fetching forth their Proofs out of the boanes.
    Doth all in Flames of Fire surround them so
    Which they can ne're o'recome, nor undergo.

In this sad Plight the richest Beauty Cleare
    That th'bravest Flower, that bud was big with, wore,   20
Did glorify those Cheeks, whose Vissage were
    Marr'd more than any mans, and Form spoild more.
    Oh! Beauty beautifull, not toucht with vice!
    The fairest Flower in all Gods Paradise!

Stept in, and in its Glory 'Counters all.   25
    And in the Belly of this Dismall Cloud,
Of Woes in Pickle is gulpht up, whose Gall
    He dranke up quite. Whose Claws his Face up plow'd.

Yet in these Furrows sprang the brightest Shine
That Glory's Sun could make, or Love Enshrine.   30

Then Vengeance's Troops are routed, Pickled Woe
Heart-aching Griefes, Pains plowing to the boanes,
Soul piercing Plagues, all Venom do foregoe.
The Curse now Cures, though th'Griefe procureth groans.
As th'Angry Bee doth often lose her Sting,   35
The Law was Cursless made in Cursing him.

And now his shining Love beams out its rayes
My Soul, upon thy Heart to thaw the same:
To animate th'Affections till they blaze;
To free from Guilt, and from Sins Slough, and Shame.   40
Open thy Casement wide, let Glory in,
To Guild thy Heart to be an Hall for him.

My Breast, be thou the ringing Virginalls:
Ye mine Affections, their sweet Golden Strings,
My Panting Heart, be thou for Stops, and Falls: 45
Lord, let thy quick'ning Beams dance o're the Pins.
Then let thy Spirit this sweet note resume,
ALTASCHATH MICHTAM, in Seraphick Tune.

19. Meditation. Phil. 2.9. God hath
        highly exalted him.

14.9m [Nov.] *1686.* Pub. *W.*

Looke till thy Looks look Wan, my Soule; here's ground.
The Worlds bright Eye's dash't out: Day-Light so brave
Bemidnighted; the sparkling sun, palde round
With flouring Rayes lies buri'de in its grave
The Candle of the World blown out, down fell.   5
Life knockt a head by Death: Heaven by Hell.

Alas! this World all filld up to the brim
With Sins, Deaths, Divills, Crowding men to Hell.

For whose reliefe Gods milkwhite Lamb stept in
    Whom those Curst Imps did worry, flesh, and fell.   10
    Tread under foot, did Clap their Wings and so
    Like Dunghill Cocks over their Conquourd, Crow.

Brave Pious Fraud; as if the Setting Sun:
    Dropt like a Ball of Fire into the Seas,
And so went out. But to the East come, run: 15
    You'l meet the morn Shrinde with its flouring Rayes.
    This Lamb in laying of these Lyons dead;
    Drank of the brooke: and so lift up his Head.

Oh! sweet, sweet joy! These Rampant Fiends befoold:
    They made their Gall his Winding sheete; although   20
They of the Heart-ach dy must, or be Coold
    With Inflamation of the Lungs, they know.
    He's Cancelling the Bond, and making Pay:
    And Ballancing Accounts: its Reckoning day.

See, how he from the Counthouse shining went,   25
    In Flashing Folds of Burnisht Glory, and
Dasht out all Curses from the Covenant
    Hath Justices Acquittance in his hand
    Pluckt out Deaths Sting, the Serpents Head did mall
    The Bars and Gates of Hell he brake down all.   30

The Curse thus Lodgd within his Flesh, and Cloyde,
    Can't run from him to his, so much he gave.
And like a Gyant he awoke, beside,
    The Sun of Righteousness rose out of's Grave.
    And setting Foot upon its neck I sing   35
    Grave, where's thy Victory? Death, Where's thy Sting?

9 *milkwhite*] PW mikewhite

1978

20. Meditation. Phil. 2.9. God hath
highly Exalted him.

9.11m [Jan.] *1686*. Pub. *W*.

View all ye eyes above, this sight which flings
    Seraphick Phancies in Chill Raptures high,
A Turffe of Clay, and yet bright Glories King
    From dust to Glory Angell-like to fly.
    A Mortall Clod immortalizde, behold,   5
    Flyes through the Skies swifter than Angells could.

Upon the Wings he of the Winde rode in
    His Bright Sedan, through all the Silver Skies
And made the Azure Cloud his Charriot bring
    Him to the Mountain of Celestiall joyes.   10
    The Prince o'th'Aire durst not an Arrow spend
    While through his Realm his Charriot did ascend.

He did not in a Fiery Charriot's Shine,
    And Whirlewinde, like Elias upward goe.
But th'golden Ladders Jasper rounds did climbe   15
    Unto the Heavens high from Earth below.
    Each step trod on a Golden Stepping Stone
    Of Deity unto his very Throne.

Methinks I see Heavens sparkling Courtiers fly,
    In flakes of Glory down him to attend: 20
And heare Heart Cramping notes of Melody,
    Surround his Charriot as it did ascend
    Mixing their Musick making e'ry string
    More to inravish as they this tune sing.

God is Gone up with a triumphant Shout   25
    The Lord with sounding Trumpets melodies.

Pa 47

   13–18: The figure of God ascending to heaven on a ladder is inconsistent
with the figure of God ascending in a chariot in the preceding and following
stanzas.

Sing Praise, sing Praise, sing Praise, sing Praises out,
    Unto our King sing praise seraphickwise.
    Lift up your Heads ye lasting Doore they sing
    And let the King of Glory Enter in.   30

Art thou ascended up on high, my Lord,
    And must I be without thee here below?
Art thou the sweetest Joy the Heavens afford?
    Oh! that I with thee was! what shall I do?
    Should I pluck Feathers from an Angells Wing,   35
    They could not waft me up to thee my King.

Lend mee thy Wings, my Lord, I'st fly apace.
    My Soules Arms stud with thy strong Quills, true Faith,
My Quills then Feather with thy Saving Grace,
    My Wings will take the Winde thy Word displai'th.   40
    Then I shall fly up to thy glorious Throne
    With my strong Wings whose Feathers are thine own.

21. Meditation. Phil. 2.9. God hath
Highly Exalted Him.

13. 1m [Mar.] *1686/7.* Pub. MGG.

What Glory's this, my Lord? Should one small Point
    Of one small Ray of't touch my Heart 'twould spring
Such joy as would an Adamant unjoynt
    If in't, and tare it, to get out and sing.
    T'run on Heroick golden Feet, and raise   5
    Heart Ravishing Tunes, Curld with Celestiall praise.

Oh! Bright! Bright thing! I fain would something say:
    Lest Silence should indict me. Yet I feare
To say a Syllable lest at thy day
    I be presented for my Tattling here.   10

32 *below?*] PW below   41 *up to*] orig: unto

Course Phancy, Ragged Faculties, alas!
　　And Blunted Tongue don't Suit: Sighs Soile the Glass.

Yet shall my mouth stand ope, and Lips let run
　　Out gliding Eloquence on each light thing?
And shall I gag my mouth, and ty my Tongue,   15
　　When such bright Glory glorifies within?
　　That makes my Heart leape, dancing to thy Lute?
　　And shall my tell tale tongue become a Mute?

Lord spare I pray, though my attempts let fall
　　A slippery Verse upon thy Royall Glory.
I'le bring unto thine Altar th'best of all   20
　　My Flock affords. I have no better Story.
　　I'le at thy Glory my dark Candle light:
　　Not to descry the Sun, but use by night.

A Golden Throne whose Banisters are Pearles,   25
　　And Pomills Choicest Gems: Carbuncle-Stayes
Studded with Pretious Stones, Carv'd with rich Curles
　　Of Polisht Art, sending out flashing Rayes,
　　Would him surround with Glory, thron'de therein.
　　Yet this is to thy Throne a dirty thing.   30

Oh! Glorious Sight! Loe, How Bright Angells stand
　　Waiting with Hat in hand on Him alone
That is Enthron'de, indeed at Gods right hand:
　　Gods Heart itselfe being his Happy Throne.
　　The Glory that doth from this Person fall,   35
　　Fills Heaven with Glory, else there's none at all.

22. Meditation. Phil. 2.9. God hath Highly Exalted him.

12.4m [June] 1687. Pub. PET.

When thy Bright Beams, my Lord, do strike mine Eye,
　　Methinkes I then could truely Chide out right

My Hide bound Soule that stands so niggardly
    That scarce a thought gets glorified by't.
    My Quaintest Metaphors are ragged Stuff,   5
    Making the Sun seem like a Mullipuff.

Its my desire, thou shouldst be glorifi'de:
    But when thy Glory shines before mine eye,
I pardon Crave, lest my desire be Pride.
    Or bed thy Glory in a Cloudy Sky.   10
    The Sun grows wan; and Angells palefac'd shrinke,
    Before thy Shine, which I besmeere with Inke.

But shall the Bird sing forth thy Praise, and shall
    The little Bee present her thankfull Hum?
But I who see thy shining Glory fall   15
    Before mine Eyes, stand Blockish, Dull, and Dumb?
    Whether I speake, or speechless stand, I spy,
    I faile thy Glory: therefore pardon Cry.

But this I finde; My Rhymes do better suite
    Mine own Dispraise than tune forth praise to thee.   20
Yet being Chid, whether Consonant, or Mute,
    I force my Tongue to tattle, as you see.
    That I thy glorious Praise may Trumpet right,
    Be thou my Song, and make Lord, mee thy Pipe.

This shining Sky will fly away apace,   25
    When thy bright Glory splits the same to make
Thy Majesty a Pass, whose Fairest Face
    Too foule a Path is for thy Feet to take.
    What Glory then, shall tend thee through the Sky
    Draining the Heaven much of Angells dry?   30

What Light then flame will in thy Judgment Seate,
    'Fore which all men, and angells shall appeare?
How shall thy Glorious Righteousness them treate,

13–14: Cf. Herbert's "Employment (1)," lines 17–20: "All things are busie;
onely I / Neither bring hony with the bees, / Nor flowers to make that, nor
the husbandrie / To water these." Cf. also Herbert's "Praise (1)," lines 17–20:
"O raise me then! Poore bees, that work all day, / Sting my delay, / Who
have a work, as well as they, / And much, much more."

Rend'ring to each after his Works done here?
Then Saints With Angells thou wilt glorify: 35
And burn Lewd Men, and Divells Gloriously.

One glimps, my Lord, of thy bright Judgment day,
And Glory piercing through, like fiery Darts,
All Divells, doth me make for Grace to pray,
For filling Grace had I ten thousand Hearts.
I'de through ten Hells to see thy Judgment Day   40
Wouldst thou but guild my Soule with thy bright Ray.

23. Meditation. Cant. 4.8. My Spouse.

21. 6m [Aug.] 1687. Pub. UPT.

Would God I in that Golden City were,
With Jaspers Walld, all garnisht, and made swash,
With Pretious Stones, whose Gates are Pearles most cleare
And Street Pure Gold, like to transparent Glass.
That my dull Soule, might be inflamde to see   5
How Saints and Angells ravisht are in Glee.

Were I but there, and could but tell my Story,
'Twould rub those Walls of Pretious Stones more bright:
And glaze those Gates of Pearle, with brighter Glory;
And pave the golden Street with greater light.   10
'Twould in fresh Raptures Saints, and Angells fling.
But I poore Snake Crawl here, scarce mudwalld in.

May my Rough Voice, and my blunt Tongue but spell
My Tale (for tune they can't) perhaps there may
Some Angell catch an end of't up, and tell   15
In Heaven, when he doth return that way,
He'l make thy Palace, Lord, all over ring,
With it in Songs, thy Saint, and Angells sing.

8 'Twould] PW T'would   11 'Twould] PW T'would

I know not how to speak't, it is so good:
  Shall Mortall, and Immortall marry? nay,   20
Man marry God? God be a Match for Mud?
   The King of Glory Wed a Worm? mere Clay?
   This is the Case. The Wonder too in Bliss.
   Thy Maker is thy Husband. Hearst thou this?

My Maker, he my Husband? Oh! strange joy!   25
  If Kings wed Worms, and Monarchs Mites wed should,
Glory spouse Shame, a Prince a Snake or Fly
   An Angell Court an Ant, all Wonder would.
   Let such wed Worms, Snakes, Serpents, Divells, Flyes.
   Less Wonder than the Wedden in our Eyes.   30

I am to Christ more base, than to a King
  A Mite, Fly, Worm, Ant, Serpent, Divell is,
Or Can be, being tumbled all in Sin,
   And shall I be his Spouse? How good is this?
   It is too good to be declar'de to thee.   35
   But not too good to be believ'de by mee.

Yet to this Wonder, this is found in mee,
  I am not onely base but backward Clay,
When Christ doth Wooe: and till his Spirit bee
   His Spokes man to Compell me I deny.   40
   I am so base and Froward to him, Hee
   Appears as Wonders Wonder, wedding mee.

Seing, Dear Lord, its thus, thy Spirit take
  And send thy Spokes man, to my Soul, I pray.
Thy Saving Grace my Wedden Garment make: 45
   Thy Spouses Frame into my Soul Convay.
   I then shall be thy Bride Espousd by thee
   And thou my Bridesgroom Deare Espousde shalt bee.

26 *Worms*] PW Worm 27 *Shame,*] PW Shame 48 *shalt bee*] orig: by mee

24. Meditation. Eph. 2.18. Through him we
    have—an Access—unto the Father.

6. 9m [Nov.] 1687. Pub. PET.

Was there a Palace of Pure Gold, all Ston'de
    And pav'de with Pearles, whose Gates Rich Jaspers were,
And Throne a Carbuncle, whose King Enthronde
    Sat on a Cushion all of Sunshine Cleare;
    Whose Crown a Bunch of Sun Beams was: I should   5
    Prize such as in his favour shrine me Would.

Thy Milke white Hand, my Glorious Lord, doth this:
    It opes this Gate, and me Conducts into
This Golden Palace whose rich Pavement is
    Of Pretious Pearles: and to this King also.   10
    Thus Thron'de, and Crown'd: whose Words are 'bellisht all
    With brighter Beams, than e're the Sun let fall.

But oh! Poore mee, thy sluggish Servant, I
    More blockish than a block, as blockhead, stand.
Though mine Affections Quick as Lightning fly
    On toys, they Snaile like move to kiss thy hand.   15
    My Coal-black doth thy Milke white hand avoide,
    That would above the Milky Way me guide.

What aim'st at, Lord? that I should be so Cross.
    My minde is Leaden in thy Golden Shine.
Though all o're Spirit, when this dirty Dross   20
    Doth touch it with its smutting leaden lines.
    What shall an Eagle t'catch a Fly thus run?
    Or Angell Dive after a Mote ith'Sun?

What Folly's this? I fain would take, I thinke,   25
    Vengeance upon myselfe: But I Confess,
I can't. Mine Eyes, Lord, shed no Tears but inke.
    My handy Works, are Words, and Wordiness.

Earth's Toyes ware Knots of my Affections, nay,
Though from thy Glorious Selfe they're Stoole away.   30

Oh! that my heart was made thy Golden Box
Full of Affections, and of Love Divine
Knit all in Tassles, and in True-Love Knots,
To garnish o're this Worthy Worke of thine.
This Box and all therein more rich than Gold,   35
In sacred Flames, I to thee offer would.

With thy rich Tissue my poore Soule array:
And lead me to thy Fathers House above.
Thy Graces Storehouse make my Soule I pray.
Thy Praise shall then ware Tassles of my Love.   40
If thou Conduct mee in thy Fathers Wayes,
I'le be the Golden Trumpet of thy Praise.

25. Meditation. Eph. 5.27. A Glorious
          Church.

22. 11m [Jan.] *1687*. Pub. ETP, *W*.

Why should my Bells, which Chime thy Praise, when thou
My Shew-Bread, on thy Table wast, my King,
Their Clappers, or their Bell-ropes want even now?
Or those that can thy Changes sweetly ring?
What is a Scar-Fire broken out? No, no.   5
The Bells would backward ring if it was so.

Its true: and I do all things backward run,
Poor Pillard I have a sad tale to tell:
My soule starke nakt, rowld all in mire, undone.
Thy Bell may tole my passing Peale to Hell.   10
None in their Winding sheet more naked stay
Nor Dead than I. Hence oh! the Judgment Day.

When I behold some Curious Piece of Art,
Or Pritty Bird, Flower, Star, or Shining Sun,

Poure out o'reflowing Glory: oh! my Heart   15
    Achs seing how my thoughts in Snick-Snarls run.
    But all this Glory to my Lord's a spot
    While I instead of any, am all blot.

But, my sweet Lord, what glorious robes are those
    That thou hast brought out of thy Grave for thine?   20
They do outshine the Sun-Shine, Grace the Rose.
    I leape for joy to thinke, shall these be mine?
    Such are, as waite upon thee in thy Wars,
    Cloathd with the Sun, and Crowned with twelve Stars.

Dost thou adorn some thus, and why not mee?   25
    Ile not believe it. Lord, thou art my Chiefe.
Thou me Commandest to believe in thee.
    I'l not affront thee thus with Unbeliefe.
    Lord, make my Soule Obedient: and when so,
    Thou saist Believe, make it reply, I do.   30

I fain the Choicest Love my soule Can get,
    Would to thy Gracious selfe a Gift present
But cannot now unscrew Loves Cabbinet.
    Say not this is a Niggards Complement.
    For seing it is thus I choose now rather
    To send thee th'Cabbinet, and Pearle together.   35

26. Meditation. Act. 5.31. To Give—
Forgiveness of Sins.

15.1m [Mar.] 1688. Pub. PET.

My Noble Lord, thy Nothing Servant I
    Am for thy sake out with my heart, that holds,
So little Love for such a Lord: I Cry

       ·   ·   ·   ·   ·

31 *Choicest*] PW Coicest   4 This line is missing in PW

How should I be but angry thus to see   5
My Heart so hidebound in her Acts to thee?

Thou art a Golden Theame: but I am lean,
A Leaden Oritor upon the same.
Thy Golden Web excells my Dozie Beam:
Whose Linsy-Wolsy Loom deserves thy blame.   10
Its all defild, unbiasst too by Sin:
An hearty Wish for thee's scarce shot therein.

It pitties mee who pitty Cannot show,
That such a Worthy Theame abusd should bee.
I am undone, unless thy Pardons doe   15
Undoe my Sin I did, undoing mee.
My Sins are greate, and grievous ones, therefore
Carbuncle Mountains can't wipe out their Score.

But thou, my Lord, dost a Free Pardon bring.
Thou giv'st Forgiveness: yet my heart through Sin,   20
Hath naught but naught to file thy Gift up in.
An hurden Haump doth Chafe a Silken Skin.
Although I pardons beg, I scarce can see,
When thou giv'st pardons, I give praise to thee.

O bad at best! what am I then at worst?   25
I want a Pardon: and when pardon'd, want
A Thankfull Heart: Both which thou dost disburst.
Giv'st both, or neither: for which Lord I pant.
Two such good things at once! methinks I could
Avenge my heart, lest it should neither hold.   30

Lord tap mine Eyes, seing such Grace in thee,
So little doth affect my Graceless Soule.
And take my teares in lue of thanks of mee,
New make my heart: then take it for thy tole.
Thy Pardons then will make my heart to sing   35
Its Michtam-David: With sweet joy Within.

11 *Its all defild*] orig: That all defild

27. Meditation. Col. 1.19. In Him
should all Fulness Dwell.

1. *5m* [July] *1688*. Unpublished.

Oh! Wealthy Theam! Oh! Feeble Phancy: I
    Must needs admire, when I recall to minde,
That's Fulness, This it's Emptiness, though spy
    I have no Flowring Brain thereto inclinde.
    My Damps do out my fire. I cannot, though   5
    I would Admire, finde heate enough thereto.

What shall I say? Such rich rich Fullness would
    Make stammering Tongues speake smoothly, and Enshrine
The Dumb mans mouth with Silver Streams like gold
    Of Eloquence making the Aire to Chime.   10
    Yet I am Tonguetide stupid, sensless stand,
    And Drier drain'd than is my pen I hand.

Oh! Wealthy Box: more Golden far than Gold
    A Case more Worth than Wealth: a richer Delph,
Than Rubies; Cabbinet, than Pearles here told   15
    A Purse more glittering than Glory 'tselfe
    A Golden Store House of all Fulness: Shelfe,
    Of Heavenly Plate. All Fulness in thyselfe.

Oh! Godhead Fulness! There doth in thee flow
    All Wisdoms Fulness; Fulness of all Strength: 20
Of Justice, Truth, Love, Holiness also
    And Graces Fulness to its upmost length
    Do dwell in thee. Yea and thy Fathers Pleasure.
    Thou art their Cabbinet, and they thy Treasure.

All Office Fulness with all Office Gifts
    Imbossed are in thee, Whereby thy Grace,   25
Doth treat both God, and Man, bringst up by hifts
    Black Sinner and White Justice to imbrace.

3 *That's*] PW Thats   22 *to*] orig: unto

Making the Glory of Gods Justice shine:
And making Sinners to Gods glory Climbe.   30

All Graces Fulness dwells in thee, from Whom
    The Golden Pipes of all Convayance ly,
Through which Grace to our Clayie Panchins Come.
    Fullness of Beauty, and Humanity.
        Oh! Glorious Flow're, Glory, and Sweetness splice,   35
        In thee to Grace, and sweeten Paradise!

But, oh! the Fathers Love! herein most vast!
    Angells engrave't in brightest Marble, t'see
This Flower that in his Bosom sticks so fast,
    Stuck in the Bosom of such stuffe as wee   40
        That both his Purse, and all his Treasure thus,
        Should be so full, and freely sent to us.

Were't not more than my heart can hold, or hord,
    Or than my Tongue can tell; I thus would pray,
Let him in Whom all Fulness Dwells, dwell, Lord   45
        Within my Heart: this Treasure therein lay.
        I then shall sweetly tune thy Praise, When hee
        In Whom all Fulness dwells, doth dwell in mee.

28. Meditation. Joh. 1.16. Of His Fulness
        wee all receive: and Grace—

2.7m [Sept.] 1688. Pub. W.

When I Lord, send some Bits of Glory home,
    (For Lumps I lack) my Messenger, I finde,
Bewildred, lose his Way being alone
        In my befogg'd Dark Phancy, Clouded minde.
        Thy Bits of Glory packt in Shreds of Praise   5
        My Messenger doth lose, losing his Wayes.

3 lose] orig: and lose

Lord Cleare the Coast: and let thy sweet sun shine.
  That I may better speed a second time:
Oh! fill my Pipkin with thy Blood red Wine:
  I'l drinke thy Health: To pledge thee is no Crime.   10
  Although I but an Earthen Vessell bee
  Convay some of thy Fulness into mee.

Thou, thou my Lord, art full, top full of Grace,
  The Golden Sea of Grace: Whose springs thence come,
And Pretious Drills, boiling in ery place.   15
  Untap thy Cask, and let my Cup Catch some.
  Although its in an Earthen Vessells Case,
  Let it no Empty Vessell be of Grace.

Let thy Choice Caske, shed, Lord, into my Cue
  A Drop of Juyce presst from thy Noble Vine.   20
My Bowl is but an Acorn Cup, I sue
  But for a Drop: this will not empty thine.
  Although I'me in an Earthen Vessells place,
  My Vessell make a Vessell, Lord, of Grace.

My Earthen Vessell make thy Font also: 25
  And let thy Sea my Spring of Grace in't raise.
Spring up oh Well. My Cup with Grace make flow.
  Thy Drops will on my Vessell ting thy Praise.
  I'l sing this Song, when I these Drops Embrace.
  My Vessell now's a Vessell of thy Grace.   30

29. Meditation. Joh. 20.17. My Father,
            and your Father, to my God,
            and your God.

11.9m [Nov.] *1688*. Pub. *W*.

My shattred Phancy stole away from mee,
  (Wits run a Wooling over Edens Parke)

21 *My*] PW By   27 *My*] PW my

And in Gods Garden saw a golden Tree,
    Whose Heart was All Divine, and gold its barke.
    Whose glorious limbs and fruitfull branches strong   5
    With Saints, and Angells bright are richly hung.

Thou! thou! my Deare Deare Lord, art this rich Tree
    The Tree of Life Within Gods Paradise.
I am a Withred Twig, dri'de fit to bee
    A Chat Cast in thy fire, Writh off by Vice.   10
    Yet if thy Milke white-Gracious Hand will take mee
    And grafft mee in this golden stock, thou'lt make mee.

Thou'lt make me then its Fruite, and Branch to spring.
    And though a nipping Eastwinde blow, and all
Hells Nymps with spite their Dog's sticks thereat ding   15
    To Dash the Grafft off, and it's fruits to fall,
    Yet I shall stand thy Grafft, and Fruits that are
    Fruits of the Tree of Life thy Grafft shall beare.

I being grafft in thee there up do stand
    In us Relations all that mutuall are.   20
I am thy Patient, Pupill, Servant, and
    Thy Sister, Mother, Doove, Spouse, Son, and Heire.
    Thou art my Priest, Physician, Prophet, King,
    Lord, Brother, Bridegroom, Father, Ev'ry thing.

I being grafft in thee am graffted here   25
    Into thy Family, and kindred Claim
To all in Heaven, God, Saints, and Angells there.
    I thy Relations my Relations name.
    Thy Father's mine, thy God my God, and I
    With Saints, and Angells draw Affinity.   30

My Lord, what is it that thou dost bestow?
    The Praise on this account fills up, and throngs
Eternity brimfull, doth overflow
    The Heavens vast with rich Angelick Songs.
    How should I blush? how Tremble at this thing,   35
    Not having yet my Gam-Ut, learnd to sing.

4 *Divine,*] PW Divine.   12 *make mee*] mee Conj.   29 *Father's*] PW Fathers

But, Lord, as burnish't Sun Beams forth out fly
     Let Angell-Shine forth in my Life out flame,
That I may grace thy gracefull Family
     And not to thy Relations be a Shame.   40
     Make mee thy Grafft, be thou my Golden Stock.
     Thy Glory then I'le make my fruits and Crop.

30. Meditation. 2 Cor. 5.17.—He is
          a New Creature.

6. 11m [Jan.] 1688. Pub. W.

The Daintiest Draught thy Pensill ever Drew:
     The finest vessell, Lord, thy fingers fram'de:
The statelist Palace Angells e're did view,
     Under thy Hatch betwixt Decks here Contain'd
     Broke, marred, spoild, undone, Defild doth ly   5
     In Rubbish ruinde by thine Enemy.

What Pittie's this? Oh Sunshine Art! What Fall?
     Thou that more Glorious wast than glories Wealth!
More Golden far than Gold! Lord, on whose Wall
     Thy scutchons hung, the Image of thyselfe!   10
     Its ruinde, and must rue, though Angells should
     To hold it up heave while their Heart Strings hold.

But yet thou stem of Davids stock when dry
     And shrivled held, although most green was lopt
Whose sap a sovereign Sodder is, whereby   15
     The breach repared is in which its dropt.
     Oh Gracious Twig! thou Cut off? bleed rich juyce
     T'Cement the Breach, and Glories shine reduce?

Oh Lovely One! how doth thy Loveliness
     Beam through the Chrystall Casements of the Eyes   20
Of Saints, and Angells sparkling Flakes of Fresh

1 ever] PW every

Heart Ravishing Beauty, filling up their joyes?
And th'Divells too; if Envies Pupills stood
Not peeping there these sparkling Rayes t'exclude?

Thou Rod of Davids Root, Branch of his Bough   25
    My Lord, repare thy Palace, Deck thy Place.
I'm but a Flesh and Blood bag: Oh! do thou
    Sill, Plate, Ridge, Rib, and Rafter me with Grace.
    Renew my Soule, and guild it all within:
    And hang thy saving Grace on ery Pin.   30

My Soule, Lord, make thy Shining Temple, pave
    Its Floore all o're with Orient Grace: thus guild
It o're with Heavens gold: Its Cabbins have
    Thy Treasuries with Choicest thoughts up filld.
    Pourtray thy Glorious Image round about   35
    Upon thy Temple Walls within, and Out.

Garnish thy Hall with Gifts, Lord, from above
    With that Rich Coate of Male thy Righteousness,
Truths Belt, the Spirits Sword, the Buckler Love
    Hopes Helmet, and the Shield of Faith kept fresh.   40
    The Scutchons of thy Honour make my Sign
    As Garland Tuns are badges made of Wine.

New mould, new make me thus, me new Create
    Renew in me a spirit right, pure, true.
Lord make me thy New Creature, then new make   45
    All things to thy New Creature here anew,
    New Heart, New thoughts, New Words, New wayes likewise.
    New Glory then shall to thyselfe arise.

39 *Spirits*] orig: Plate

31. Meditation. 1 Cor. 3.21.22. All
                things are yours.

17. *12m* [Feb.] *1688.* Pub. UPT.

Begracde with Glory, gloried with Grace,
    In Paradise I was, when all Sweet Shines
Hung dangling on this Rosy World to face
    Mine Eyes, and Nose, and Charm mine Eares with Chimes.
    All these were golden Tills the which did hold   5
    My evidences wrapt in glorious folds.

But as a Chrystall Glass, I broke, and lost
    That Grace, and Glory I was fashion'd in
And cast this Rosy World with all its Cost
    Into the Dunghill Pit, and Puddle Sin.   10
    All right I lost in all Good things, each thing
    I had did hand a Vean of Venom in.

Oh! Sad-Sad thing! Satan is now turnd Cook:
    Sin is the Sauce he gets for ev'ry Dish.
I cannot bite a bit of Bread or Roote
    But what is sopt therein, and Venomish.   15
    Right's lost in what's my Right. Hence I do take
    Onely what's poison'd by th'infernall Snake.

But this is not the Worst: there's worse than this.
    My Tast is lost; no bit tasts sweet to mee,   20
But what is Dipt all over in this Dish
    Of Ranck ranck Poyson: this my Sauce must bee.
    Hell Heaven is, Heaven hell, yea Bitter Sweet:
    Poison's my Food: Food poison in't doth keep.

What e're we want, we cannot Cry for, nay,   25
    If that we could, we could not have it thus.
The Angell's can't devise, nor yet Convay

4 *Nose,*] PW Nose.   21 *Dish*] PW Dish.

Help in their Golden Pipes from God to us.
But thou my Lord, (Heart leape for joy and sing)
Hast done the Deed: and't makes the Heavens ring.   30

By mee all lost, by thee all are regain'd.
    All things are thus fall'n now into thy hande.
And thou steep'st in thy Blood what Sin had stain'd
    That th'Stains, and Poisons may not therein stand.
      And having stuck thy Grace all o're the same   35
      Thou giv'st it as a Glorious Gift again.

Cleare up my Right, my Lord, in thee, and make
    Thy Name stand Dorst upon my Soule in print,
In grace I mean, that so I may partake
    Of what I lost, in thee, and of thee in't.   40
      I'l take it then, Lord, at thy hand, and sing
      Out Hallelujah for thy Grace therein.

32. Meditation. 1 Cor. 3.22. Whether
Paul or Apollos, or Cephas.

28. 2m [Apr.] *1689.* Pub. PET.

Thy Grace, Dear Lord's my golden Wrack, I finde
    Screwing my Phancy into ragged Rhimes,
Tuning thy Praises in my feeble minde
    Untill I come to strike them on my Chimes.
      Were I an Angell bright, and borrow could   5
      King Davids Harp, I would them play on gold.

But plung'd I am, my minde is puzzled,
    When I would spin my Phancy thus unspun,
In finest Twine of Praise I'm muzzled.
    My tazzled Thoughts twirld into Snick-Snarls run.   10
      Thy Grace, my Lord, is such a glorious thing,
      It doth Confound me when I would it sing.

Eternall Love an Object mean did smite
   Which by the Prince of Darkness was beguilde,
That from this Love it ran and sweld with spite   15
   And in the way with filth was all defilde
   Yet must be reconcild, cleansd, and begrac'te
   Or from the fruits of Gods first Love displac'te.

Then Grace, my Lord, wrought in thy Heart a vent,
   Thy Soft Soft hand to this hard worke did goe,   20
And to the Milke White Throne of Justice went
   And entred bond that Grace might overflow.
   Hence did thy Person to my Nature ty
   And bleed through humane Veans to satisfy.

Oh! Grace, Grace, Grace! this Wealthy Grace doth lay   25
   Her Golden Channells from thy Fathers throne,
Into our Earthen Pitchers to Convay
   Heavens Aqua Vitae to us for our own.
   O! let thy Golden Gutters run into
   My Cup this Liquour till it overflow.   30

Thine Ordinances, Graces Wine-fats where
   Thy Spirits Walkes, and Graces runs doe ly
And Angells waiting stand with holy Cheere
   From Graces Conduite Head, with all Supply.
   These Vessells full of Grace are, and the Bowls   35
   In which their Taps do run, are pretious Souls.

Thou to the Cups dost say (that Catch this Wine,)
   This Liquour, Golden Pipes, and Wine-fats plain,
Whether Paul, Apollos, Cephas, all are thine.
   Oh Golden Word! Lord speake it ore again.
   Lord speake it home to me, say these are mine.   40
   My Bells shall then thy Praises bravely chime.

13 *an*] orig: did an
24 *bleed*] orig: bled   26 *Golden*] PW Goldens   27 *Pitchers*] PW Pilchers
37 *that Catch*] orig: Catching

   38: Golden Pipes. The figure probably comes from Zech. 4:12. Cf. Herbert's
"The Pearl," lines 1–2, and "Whitsunday," lines 17–18.

33. Meditation. 1 Cor. 3.22. Life is
          youres.

7. 5m [July] 1689. Pub. W.

My Lord my Life, can Envy ever bee
          A Golden Vertue? Then would God I were
Top full thereof untill it colours mee
          With yellow streaks for thy Deare sake most Deare,
          Till I be Envious made by't at myselfe,   5
          As scarcely loving thee my Life, my Health.

Oh! what strange Charm encrampt my Heart with spite
          Making my Love gleame out upon a Toy?
Lay out Cart-Loads of Love upon a mite?
          Scarce lay a mite of Love on thee, my Joy?   10
          Oh, Lovely thou! Shalt not thou loved bee?
          Shall I ashame thee thus? Oh! shame for mee!

Nature's amaz'de, Oh monstrous thing Quoth shee,
          Not Love my life? What Violence doth split
True Love, and Life, that they should sunder'd bee?   15
          She doth not lay such Eggs, nor on them sit.
          How do I sever then my Heart with all
          Its Powers whose Love scarce to my Life doth crawle.

Glory lin'de out a Paradise in Power
          Where e'ry seed a Royall Coach became   20
For Life to ride in, to each shining Flower.
          And made mans Flower with glory all ore flame.
          Hells Inkfac'de Elfe black Venom spat upon
          The same, and kill'd it. So that Life is gone.

Life thus abusde fled to the golden Arke,   25
          Lay lockt up there in Mercie's seate inclosde:
Which did incorporate it whence its Sparke
          Enlivens all things in this Arke inclosde.

Oh, glorious Arke! Life's Store-House full of Glee!
  Shall not my Love safe lockt up ly in thee?   30

Lord arke my Soule safe in thyselfe, whereby
  I and my Life again may joyned bee.
That I may finde what once I did destroy
  Again Conferde upon my soul in thee.
    Thou art this Golden Ark; this Living Tree   35
    Where life lies treasurde up for all in thee.

Oh! Graft me in this Tree of Life within
  The Paradise of God, that I may live.
Thy Life make live in mee; I'le then begin
  To bear thy Living Fruits, and them forth give.   40
  Give mee my Life this way; and I'le bestow
  My Love on thee my Life, and it shall grow.

34. Meditation. 1 Cor. 3.22. Death is
Yours.

25. 9m [Nov.] 1689. Pub. PET.

My Lord I fain would Praise thee Well but finde
  Impossibilities blocke up my pass.
My tongue Wants Words to tell my thoughts, my Minde
  Wants thoughts to Comprehend thy Worth, alas!
    Thy Glory far Surmounts my thoughts, my thoughts   5
    Surmount my Words: Hence little Praise is brought.

But seing Non-Sense very Pleasant is
  To Parents, flowing from the Lisping Child,
I Conjue to thee, hoping thou in this
  Will finde some hearty Praise of mine Enfoild,
  But though my pen drop'd golden Words, yet would   10
  Thy Glory far out shine my Praise in Gold.

Poor wretched man Deaths Captive stood full Chuffe
  But thou my Gracious Lord didst finde reliefe,

14 *reliefe*,] PW reliefe

Thou King of Glory didst, to handy cuff   15
    With King of Terrours, and dasht out his Teeth,
    Plucktst out his sting, his Poyson quelst, his head
    To pieces brakest. Hence Cruell Death lies Dead.

And still thou by thy gracious Chymistry
    Dost of his Carkass Cordialls make rich, High,   20
To free from Death makst Death a remedy:
    A Curb to Sin, a Spur to Piety.
    Heavens brightsom Light shines out in Death's Dark Cave.
    The Golden Dore of Glory is the Grave.

The Painter lies who pensills death's Face grim   25
    With White bare butter Teeth, bare staring bones,
With Empty Eyeholes, Ghostly Lookes which fling
    Such Dread to see as raiseth Deadly groans,
    For thou hast farely Washt Deaths grim grim face
    And made his Chilly finger-Ends drop grace.   30

Death Tamde, Subdude, Washt fair by thee! Oh Grace!
    Made Usefull thus! thou unto thine dost say
Now Death is yours, and all it doth in't brace.
    The Grave's a Down bed now made for your clay.
    Oh! Happiness! How should our Bells hereby   35
    Ring Changes, Lord, and praises trust with joy.

Say I am thine, My Lord: Make me thy bell
    To ring thy Praise. Then Death is mine indeed
A Hift to Grace, a Spur to Duty; Spell
    To Fear; a Frost to nip each naughty Weede.   40
    A Golden doore to Glory. Oh I'le sing
    This Triumph o're the Grave! Death where's thy Sting?

15 *didst,*] PW didst   18 *Hence*] PW hence   23 *Death's*] PW Death
26 *Teeth,*] PW Teeth   31 *Washt*] PW Whasht   40 *naughty*] Conj.

34: The Grave's a Down bed . . . Cf. Herbert's "Death," lines 21–24:

    Therefore we can go die as sleep, and trust
        Half that we have
    Unto an honest faithfull grave;
    Making our pillows either down, or dust.

35. Meditation. 1 Cor. 3.22. Things Present.

19. 11m [Jan.] *1689*. Pub. PET.

Oh! that I ever felt what I profess.
 'Twould make me then the happi'st man alive.
Ten thousand Worlds of Saints can't make this less
 By living on't, but it would make them thrive.
 These Loaves and Fishes are not lessened   5
 Nor Pasture over stock, by being fed.

Lord am I thine? art thou, Lord, mine? So rich!
 How doth thy Wealthy bliss branch out thy sweets
Through all things Present? These the Vent-holes which
 Let out those Ravishing Joys our Souls to greet? 10
 Impower my Powers sweet Lord till up they raise
 My 'Fections that thy glory on them blaze.

How many things are there now, who display'th?
 How many Acts each thing doth here dispense?
How many Influences each thing hath?   15
 How many Contraries each Influence?
 How many Contraries from Things do flow?
 From Acts? from Influences? Who can show?

How Glorious then is he that doth all raise
 Rule and Dispose and make them all Conspire 20
In all their Jars, and Junctures, Good-bad wayes
 To meliorate the self same Object higher?
 Earth, Water, Fire, Winds, Herbs, Trees, Beasts and Men,
 Angells, and Divells, Bliss, Blasts, advance one stem?

Hell, Earth, and Heaven with their Whole Troops come 25
 Contrary Windes, Grace, and Disgrace, Soure, Sweet,
Wealth, Want, Health, Sickness, to Conclude in Sum
 All Providences Works in this good meet?

4 *on't*,] PW on't.

Who, who can do't, but thou, my Lord? and thou
Dost do this thing. Yea thou performst it now.   30

Oh, that the Sweets of all these Windings, spoute
    Might, and these Influences streight, and Cross,
Upon my Soule, to make thy Shine breake out
    That Grace might in get and get out my dross!
    My Soule up lockt then in this Clod of Dust   35
    Would lock up in't all Heavenly Joyes most just.

But oh! thy Wisdom, Lord! thy Grace! thy Praise!
    Open mine Eyes to see the same aright.
Take off their film, my Sins, and let the Rayes
    Of thy bright Glory on my peepholes light.   40
    I fain would love and better love thee should,
    If 'fore me thou thy Loveliness unfold.

Lord, Cleare my Sight, thy Glory then out dart.
    And let thy Rayes beame Glory in mine eye
And stick thy Loveliness upon my heart,   45
    Make me the Couch on which thy Love doth ly.
    Lord make my heart thy bed, thy heart make mine.
    Thy Love bed in my heart, bed mine in thine.

36. Meditation. 1 Cor. 3.22. Things
            to come yours.

16. 1m [Mar.] *1689*. Pub. UPT.

What rocky heart is mine? My pincky Eyes
    Thy Grace spy blancht, Lord, in immensitie.
But finde the Sight me not to meliorize,
    O Stupid Heart! What strang-strange thing am I?
    I many months do drown in Sorrows Spring   5
    But hardly raise a Sigh to blow down Sin.

30 *Yea*] PW yea   5 *Spring*] orig: Springs   6 *Sin*] orig: Sins

To find thee Lord, thus overflowing kinde,
　　And t'finde mee thine, thus overflowing vile,
A Riddle seems onrivetted I finde.
　　　　This reason saith is hard to reconcile.　　　　　10
　　　　Dost Vileness choose? Or can't thy kindness shown
　　　　Me meliorate? Or am I not thine own?

The first two run thy glory would to Shame:
　　The last plea doth my Soule to hell Confine.
My Faith therefore doth all these Pleas disdain.　　　　15
　　　　Thou kindness art, it saith, and I am thine.
　　　　Upon this banck it doth on tiptoes stand
　　　　To ken o're Reasons head at Graces hand.

But Did I say, I wonder, Lord, to spie
　　Thy Selfe so kind; and I so vile yet thine?　　　　20
I eate my Word: and wonder more that I　　　　·
　　　　No viler am, though all ore vile do shine.
　　　　As full of Sin I am, as Egge of meate.
　　　　Yet finde thy golden Rod my Sin to treate.

Nay did I say, I wonder t'see thy Store　　　　25
　　Of kindnesses, yet me thus vile with all?
I now Unsay my Say: I wonder more
　　　　Thou dash me not to pieces with thy maule,
　　　　But in the bed, Lord, of thy goodness lies
　　　　The Reason of't, which makes my Wonders rise.　　　　30

For now I wonder t'feele how I thus feele.
　　My Love leapes into Creatures bosoms; and
Cold Sorrows fall into my Soule as Steel,
　　　　When faile they, yet I kiss thy Love's White hand.
　　　　I scarce know what t'make of myselfe. Wherefore　　　　35
　　　　I crave a Pardon, Lord, for thou hast Store.

How wondrous rich art thou? Thy Storehouse vast
　　Holdes more ten thousand fold told ore and ore
Than this Wide World Can hold. The doore unhasp.
　　　　And bring me thence a Pardon out therefore.　　　　40
　　　　Thou Stoughst the World so tite with present things
　　　　That things to Come, though crowd full hard, cant in.

30 of't,] PW of't　　34 *I kiss*] Conj.　　39 *Wide*] Conj.

These things to Come, tread on the heels of those.
    The presents breadth doth with the broad world run.
The Depth and breadth of things to come out goes   45
    Unto Times End which bloweth out the Sun.
    These breadth and length meate out Eternity.
    These are the things that in thy Storehouse ly.

A Cockle Shell contains this World as well
    As can this World thy Liberallness contain.   50
And by thy Will these present things all fell
    Unto thy Children for their present gain;
    And things to Come too, to Eternity.
    Thou Willedst them: they're theirs by Legacy.

But am I thine? Oh! what strange thing's in mee?   55
    Enricht thus by thy Legacy? yet finde
When one small Twig's broke off, the breach should bee
    Such an Enfeebling thing upon my minde.
    Then take a pardon from thy Store, and twist
    It in my Soule for help. 'Twill not be mist.   60

I am asham'd to say I love thee do.
    But dare not for my Life, and Soule deny't.
Yet wonder much Love's Springs should lie so low
    Thy loveliness its Object shines so bright.
    Shall all the Beams of Love upon me shine?   65
    And shall my Love Love's Object still make pine?

I'me surely made a Gazing Stock to all.
    The Holy Angells Wonder: and the Mock
Of Divells (pining that they misse it all)
    To see these beams gild me a Stupid Stock.   70
    Thy Argument is good, Lord point it, come
    Let't lance my heart, till True Loves Veane doth run.

But that there is a Crevice for one hope
    To creep in, and this Message to Convay
That I am thine, makes me refresh. Lord ope   75

46 *Times*] orig: the End of Times   66 *Love Love's*] orig: Love's Object
70 *gild*] orig: guild

The Doore so wide that Love may Scip, and play.
My Spirits then shall dance thy Praise. I'me thine.
And Present things with things to come are mine.

37. Meditation. 1 Cor. 3.23. You are
          Christ's.

4. 3m [May] 1690. Pub. ETG.

My Soule, Lord, quailes to thinke that I should bee
    So high related, have such colours faire
Stick in my Hat, from Heaven: yet should see
    My Soule thus blotcht: Hells Liveries to beare.
    What Thine? New-naturizd? Yet this Relation
    Thus barren, though't 's a Priviledg-Foundation?

Shall I thy Vine branch be, yet grapes none beare?
    Grafft in thy Olive stand: and fatness lack?
A Shackeroon, a Ragnell, yet an Heire?
    Thy spouse, yet, oh! my Wedden Ring thus slack?
    Should Angel-Feathers plume my Cap, I should
    Be swash? but oh! my Heart hereat grows Cold.

What is my Title but an empty Claim?
    Am I a fading Flower within thy Knot?
A Rattle, or a gilded Box, a Flame
    Of Painted Fire, a glorious Weedy Spot?
    The Channell ope of Union, the ground
    Of Wealth, Relation: yet I'me barren found?

What am I thine, and thou not mine? or dost
    Not thou thy Spouse joyn in thy Glory Cleare?
Is my Relation to thee but a boast?
    Or but a blustring say-so, or spruice jeere?
    Should Roses blow more late, sure I might get,
    If thine, some Prim-Rose or sweet Violet?

9 *Ragnell,*] PW Ragnell.   15 *gilded*] orig: guilded

Make me thy Branch to bare thy Grapes, Lord, feed   25
    Mee with thy bunch of Raisins of the Sun.
Mee stay with apples; let me eate indeed
    Fruits of the tree of Life: its richly hung.
      Am I thy Child, Son, Heir, thy Spouse, yet gain
      Not of the Rights that these Relations claim?   30

Am I hop't on thy knees, yet not at ease?
    Sunke in thy bosom, yet thy Heart not meet?
Lodgd in thine Arms? yet all things little please?
    Sung sweetly, yet finde not this singing sweet?
      Set at thy Table, yet scarce tast a Dish   35
      Delicious? Hugd, yet seldom gain a Kiss?

Why? Lord, why thus? Shall I in Question Call
    All my Relation to thyselfe? I know
It is no Gay to please a Child withall
    But is the Ground whence Priviledges flow.   40
      Then ope the sluce: let some thing spoute on me.
      Then I shall in a better temper bee.

38. Meditation. 1 Joh. 2.1. An Advocate
With the Father.

6. 5m [July] 1690. Pub. ETP, W.

Oh! What a thing is Man? Lord, Who am I?
    That thou shouldst give him Law (Oh! golden Line)
To regulate his Thoughts, Words, Life thereby.
    And judge him Wilt thereby too in thy time.
      A Court of Justice thou in heaven holdst   5
      To try his Case while he's here housd on mould.

How do thy Angells lay before thine eye
    My Deeds both White, and Black I dayly doe?

28 *Fruits of the*] PW Fruits the
3 *Words*] orig: his Words   8 *I dayly*] orig: before***

How doth thy Court thou Pannellst there them try?
    But flesh complains. What right for this? let's know.   10
    For right, or wrong I can't appeare unto't.
    And shall a sentence Pass on such a suite?

Soft; blemish not this golden Bench, or place.
    Here is no Bribe, nor Colourings to hide
Nor Pettifogger to befog the Case   15
    But Justice hath her Glory here well tri'de.
    Her spotless Law all spotted Cases tends.
    Without Respect or Disrespect them ends.

God's Judge himselfe: and Christ Atturny is,
    The Holy Ghost Regesterer is founde.   20
Angells the sergeants are, all Creatures kiss
    The booke, and doe as Evidences abounde.
    All Cases pass according to pure Law
    And in the sentence is no Fret, nor flaw.

What saist, my soule? Here all thy Deeds are tri'de.
    Is Christ thy Advocate to pleade thy Cause?   25
Art thou his Client? Such shall never slide.
    He never lost his Case: he pleads such Laws
    As Carry do the same, nor doth refuse
    The Vilest sinners Case that doth him Choose.   30

This is his Honour, not Dishonour: nay
    No Habeas-Corpus gainst his Clients came
For all their Fines his Purse doth make down pay.
    He Non-Suites Satan's Suite or Casts the Same.
    He'l plead thy Case, and not accept a Fee.   35
    He'l plead Sub Forma Pauperis for thee.

My Case is bad. Lord, be my Advocate.
    My sin is red: I'me under Gods Arrest.
Thou hast the Hint of Pleading; plead my State.
    Although it's bad thy Plea will make it best.   40
    If thou wilt plead my Case before the King:
    I'le Waggon Loads of Love, and Glory bring.

39 *Hint*] PW Hit

39. Meditation. from 1 Joh. 2.1. If any
          man sin, we have an Advocate.

9. 9m [Nov.] *1690.* Pub. PET.

My Sin! my Sin, My God, these Cursed Dregs,
    Green, Yellow, Blew streakt Poyson hellish, ranck,
Bubs hatcht in natures nest on Serpents Eggs,
    Yelp, Cherp and Cry; they set my Soule a Cramp.
    I frown, Chide, strik and fight them, mourn and Cry   5
    To Conquour them, but cannot them destroy.

I cannot kill nor Coop them up: my Curb
    'S less than a Snaffle in their mouth: my Rains
They as a twine thrid, snap: by hell they're spurd:
    And load my Soule with swagging loads of pains.   10
    Black Imps, young Divells, snap, bite, drag to bring
    And pick mee headlong hells dread Whirle Poole in.

Lord, hold thy hand: for handle mee thou may'st
    In Wrath: but, oh, a twinckling Ray of hope
Methinks I spie thou graciously display'st.
    There is an Advocate: a doore is ope.   15
    Sin's poyson swell my heart would till it burst,
    Did not a hope hence creep in't thus, and nurse't.

Joy, joy, Gods Son's the Sinners Advocate
    Doth plead the Sinner guiltless, and a Saint.
But yet Atturnies pleas spring from the State
    The Case is in: if bad its bad in plaint.   20
    My Papers do contain no pleas that do
    Secure mee from, but knock me down to, woe.

I have no plea mine Advocate to give: 25
    What now? He'l anvill Arguments greate Store
Out of his Flesh and Blood to make thee live.
    O Deare bought Arguments: Good pleas therefore.

17 *swell*] PW 'swell   22 *plaint*] PW paint

Nails made of heavenly Steel, more Choice than gold
　　Drove home, Well Clencht, eternally will hold.　　30

Oh! Dear bought Plea, Deare Lord, what buy't so deare?
　　What with thy blood purchase thy plea for me?
Take Argument out of thy Grave t'appeare
　　And plead my Case with, me from Guilt to free.
　　These maule both Sins, and Divells, and amaze　　35
　　Both Saints, and Angells; Wreath their mouths with praise.

What shall I doe, my Lord? what do, that I
　　May have thee plead my Case? I fee thee will
With Faith, Repentance, and obediently
　　Thy Service gainst Satanick Sins fulfill.　　40
　　I'l fight thy fields while Live I do, although
　　I should be hackt in pieces by thy foe.

Make me thy Friend, Lord, be my Surety: I
　　Will be thy Client, be my Advocate:
My Sins make thine, thy Pleas make mine hereby.　　45
　　Thou wilt mee save, I will thee Celebrate.
　　Thou'lt kill my Sins that cut my heart within:
　　And my rough Feet shall thy smooth praises sing.

40. Meditation. 1 Joh. 2.2. He is a
Propitiation for our Sin.

12m [Feb.] *1690/1*. Pub. ETG.

Still I complain; I am complaining still.
　　Oh! woe is me! Was ever Heart like mine?
A Sty of Filth, a Trough of Washing-Swill
　　A Dunghill Pit, a Puddle of mere Slime.
　　A Nest of Vipers, Hive of Hornets; Stings.　　5
　　A Bag of Poyson, Civit-Box of Sins.

2: *Was ever Heart like mine?* This question, repeated several times, is prob-
ably an echo of the refrain in Herbert's "The Sacrifice": "Was ever grief like
mine?"

Was ever Heart like mine? So bad? black? Vile?
    Is any Divell blacker? Or can Hell
Produce its match? It is the very Soile
    Where Satan reads his Charms, and sets his Spell.   10
    His Bowling Ally, where he sheeres his fleece
    At Nine Pins, Nine Holes, Morrice, Fox and Geese.

His Palace Garden where his courtiers walke.
    His Jewells Cabbinet. Here his Caball
Do sham it, and truss up their Privie talk   15
    In Fardells of Consults and bundles all.
    His shambles, and his Butchers stale's herein.
    It is the Fuddling Schoole of every sin.

Was ever Heart like mine? Pride, Passion, fell.
    Ath'ism, Blasphemy, pot, pipe it, dance   20
Play Barlybreaks, and at last Couple in Hell.
    At Cudgells, Kit-Cat, Cards and Dice here prance.
    At Noddy, Ruff-and-trumpt, Jing, Post-and-Pare,
    Put, One-and-thirty, and such other ware.

Grace shuffled is away: Patience oft sticks   25
    Too soon, or draws itselfe out, and's out Put.
Faith's over trumpt, and oft doth lose her tricks.
    Repentance's Chalkt up Noddy, and out shut.
    They Post, and Pare off Grace thus, and its shine.
    Alas! alas! was ever Heart like mine?   30

Sometimes methinks the serpents head I mall:
    Now all is still: my spirits do recreute.
But ere my Harpe can tune sweet praise, they fall
    On me afresh, and tare me at my Root.
    They bite like Badgers now nay worse, although   35
    I tooke them toothless sculls, rot long agoe.

My Reason now's more than my sense, I feele
    I have more Sight than Sense. Which seems to bee
A Rod of Sun beams t'whip mee for my steele.
    My Spirits spiritless, and dull in mee   40

17 *stale's*] orig: stall's   26 *Put*] orig: Putsh   40 *and dull*] orig: abide

For my dead prayerless Prayers: the Spirits winde
Scarce blows my mill about. I little grinde.

Was ever Heart like mine? My Lord, declare.
    I know not what to do: What shall I doe?
I wonder, split I don't upon Despare.   45
    Its grace's wonder that I wrack not so.
    I faintly shun't: although I see this Case
    Would say, my sin is greater than thy grace.

Hope's Day-peep dawns hence through this chinck. Christs name
    Propitiation is for sins. Lord, take   50
It so for mine. Thus quench thy burning flame
    In that clear stream that from his side forth brake.
    I can no Comfort take while thus I see
    Hells cursed Imps thus jetting strut in mee.

Lord take thy sword: these Anakims destroy: 55
    Then soake my soule in Zions Bucking tub
With Holy Soap, and Nitre, and rich Lye.
    From all Defilement me cleanse, wash and rub.
    Then wrince, and wring mee out till th'water fall
    As pure as in the Well: not foule at all.   60

And let thy Sun, shine on my Head out cleare.
    And bathe my Heart within its radient beams:
Thy Christ make my Propitiation Deare.
    Thy Praise shall from my Heart breake forth in streams.
    This reeching Vertue of Christs blood will quench   65
    Thy Wrath, slay Sin and in thy Love mee bench.

49 *Hence* canceled at beginning of line   50 *sins*] orig: our sins
take] orig: take it   56–7 Two lines written between 56 and 57 have been
canceled: Oh! wash mee well and all my Sin out rub, / Then rince, and wring
mee cleare out: till th' water f***.   62 *its*] orig: these

41. Meditation. Joh. 14.2. I go to
        prepare a Place for you.

24. 3m [May] *1691*. Pub. UPT.

A Clew of Wonders! Clusterd Miracles!
    Angells, come whet your sight hereon. Here's ground.
Sharpen your Phansies here, ye Saints in Spiricles.
    Here is enough in Wonderment to drownd's.
    Make here the Shining dark or White on which   5
    Let all your Wondring Contemplations pitch.

The Magnet of all Admiration's here.
    Your tumbling thoughts turn here. Here is Gods Son,
Wove in a Web of Flesh, and Bloode rich geere.
    Eternall Wisdoms Huswifry well spun.   10
    Which through the Laws pure Fulling mills did pass.
    And so went home the Wealthy'st Web that was.

And why thus shew? Hark, harke, my Soule. He came
    To pay thy Debt. And being come most Just
The Creditor did sue him for the same,   15
    Did winn the Case, and in the grave him thrust.
    Who having in this Prison paid the Debt.
    And took a Quittance, made Death's Velvet fret.

He broke her Cramping tallons did unlute
    The sealed Grave, and gloriously up rose.   20
Ascendeth up to glory on this Sute,
    Prepares a place for thee where glorie glowes.
    Yea yea for thee, although thy griefe out gush
    At such black Sins at which the Sun may blush.

What Wonder's here? Big belli'd Wonders in't   25
    Remain, though wrought for Saints as white as milk.
But done for me whose blot's as black as inke.
    A Clew of Wonders finer far than Silke.

3 *Saints*] PW Saint   *Spiricles*] PW Spirit'les   25 *in't*] PW in't.

Thy hand alone that wound this Clew I finde
Can to display these Wonders it unwinde.   30

Why didst thou thus? Reason stands gasterd here.
    She's overflown: this Soares above her Sight.
Gods onely Son for Sinners thus appeare,
    Prepare for Durt a throne in glory bright!
    Stand in the Doore of Glory to imbrace   35
    Such dirty bits of Dirt, with such a grace!

Reason, lie prison'd in this golden Chain.
    Chain up thy tongue, and silent stand a while.
Let this rich Love thy Love and heart obtain
    To tend thy Lord in all admiring Style.
    Lord screw my faculties up to the Skill   40
    And height of praise as answers thy good Will.

Then while I eye the Place thou hast prepar'de
    For such as I, I'le sing thy glory out
Untill thou welcome me, as 'tis declar'de
    In this sweet glory runing rounde about.   45
    I would do more but can't, Lord help me so
    That I may pay in glory what I owe.

42. Meditation. Rev. 3.22. I will give
              Him to sit with me in my Throne.

2. 6m [Aug.] *1691.* Pub. *W.*

Apples of gold, in silver pictures shrin'de
    Enchant the appetite, make mouths to water.
And Loveliness in Lumps, tunn'd, and enrin'de
    In Jasper Cask, when tapt, doth briskly vaper:
    Brings forth a birth of Keyes t'unlock Loves Chest,   5
    That Love, like Birds, may fly to't from its nest.

38 *silent*] PW silence   41 *screw*] orig: screw up
42 *thy*] orig: this   45 *me, as*] orig: me there, as   Med. *42, me*] PW we
2 *appetite,*] PW appetite.   6 *Love*] orig: new Love

Such is my Lord, and more. But what strang thing
    Am I become? Sin rusts my Lock all o're.
Though he ten thousand Keyes all on a string
    Takes out, scarce one, is found, unlocks the Doore.   10
      Which ope, my Love crincht in a Corner lies
      Like some shrunck Crickling: and scarce can rise.

Lord ope the Doore: rub off my Rust, Remove
    My sin, And Oyle my Lock. (Dust there doth shelfe).
My Wards will trig before thy Key: my Love   15
    Then, as enliven'd, leape will on thyselve.
      It needs must be, that giving handes receive
      Again Receivers Hearts furld in Love Wreath.

Unkey my Heart; unlock thy Wardrobe: bring
    Out royall Robes: adorne my Soule, Lord: so,   20
My Love in rich attire shall on my King
    Attend, and honour on him well bestow.
      In Glory he prepares for his a place
      Whom he doth all beglory here with grace.

He takes them to the shining threashould cleare   25
    Of his bright Palace, cloath'd in Grace's flame.
Then takes them in thereto, not onely there
    To have a Prospect, but possess the same.
      The Crown of Life, the Throne of Glorys Place,
      The Fathers House blancht o're with orient Grace.   30

Can'an in golden print enwalld with jems:
    A Kingdome rim'd with Glory round: in fine
A glorious Crown pal'de thick with all the stems
    Of Grace, and of all Properties Divine.
      How happy wilt thou make mee when these shall   35
      As a bless't Heritage unto mee fall?

Adorn me, Lord, with Holy Huswifry.
    All blanch my Robes with Clusters of thy Graces:
Thus lead me to thy threshold: give mine Eye
    A Peephole there to see bright glories Chases.   40
      Then take mee in: I'le pay, when I possess,
      Thy Throne, to thee the Rent in Happiness.

43. Meditation. Rev. 2.10. A Crown
of Life.

8.9m [Nov.] *1691*. Pub. PET.

Fain I would sing thy Praise, but feare I feign.
    My Sin doth keepe out of my heart thy Feare,
Damps Love: defiles my Soule. Old Blots new stain.
    Hopes hoppled lie, and rusty Chains worn cleare.
    My Sins that make me stand in need of thee,   5
    Do keep me back to hugge all Sin I see.

Nature's Corrupt, a nest of Passion, Pride,
    Lust, Worldliness, and such like bubs: I pray,
But struggling finde, these bow my Heart aside.
    A Knot of Imps at barly breaks in't play.   10
    They do inchant me from my Lord, I finde,
    The thoughts whereof proove Daggers in my minde.

Pardon, and Poyson them, Lord, with thy Blood.
    Cast their Curst Karkasses out of my Heart.
My Heart fill with thy Love: let Grace it dub.   15
    Make this my Silver Studs by thy rich art.
    My Soule shall then be thy sweet Paradise.
    Thou'st be its Rose, and it thy Bed of Spice.

Why mayn't my Faith now drinke thy Health, Lord, ore,
    The Head of all my Sins? And Cast her Eye,   20
In glorifying glances, on the Doore
    Of thy Free Grace, where Crowns of Life do lie?
    Thou'lt give a Crown of Life to such as bee
    Faithfull to Death. And shall Faith faile in mee?

A Crown of Life, of Glory, Righteousness,   25
    Thou wilt adorn them with, that will not fade.
Shall Faith in mee shrinke up for Feebleness?
    Nor take my Sins by th'Crown, till Crownless made?

2 *Feare,*] PW Feare.

Breath, Lord, thy Spirit on my Faith, that I
    May have thy Crown of Life, and Sin may dy.   30

How Spirituall? Holy shall I shine, when I
    Thy Crown of Righteousness ware on my Head?
How Glorious when thou dost me glorify
    To ware thy Crown of Glory pollished?
    How shall I when thy Crown of Life I ware   35
    In lively Colours flowrish, fresh, and fair? `

When thou shalt Crown me with these Crowns I'l bend
    My Shallow Crown to crown with Songs thy Name.
Angels shall set the tune, I'le it attend:
    Thy Glory'st be the burden of the same.   40
    Till then I cannot sing, my tongue is tide.
    Accept this Lisp till I am glorifide.

44. Meditation. 2 Tim. 4.8. A Crown of Righteousness.

17. _11m_ [Jan.] _1691_. Unpublished.

A Crown, Lord, yea, a Crown of Righteousness.
    Oh! what a Gift is this? Give Lord I pray
An Holy Head, and Heart it to possess
    And I shall give thee glory for the pay.
    A Crown is brave, and Righteousness much more.   5
    The glory of them both will pay the score.

A Crown indeed consisting of fine gold
    Adherent, and Inherent Righteousness,
Stuck with their Ripe Ripe Fruits in every fold
    Like studded Carbuncles they do it dress.   10
    A Righteous Life doth ever ware renown
    And thrusts the Head at last up in this Crown.

41 _then_] PW when

A Milk whit hand sets't on a Righteous Head.
    An hand Unrighteous can't dispose it nay
It's not in such an hande. Such hands would bed   15
    Black Smuts on't should they fingers on it lay.
      Who can the Crown of Righteousness suppose
      In an Unrighteous hand for to dispose.

When once upon the head its ever green
    And altogether Usde in Righteousness,   20
Where blessed bliss, and blissfull Peace is seen,
    And where no jar, nor brawler hath access.
      Oh! blessed Crown what hold the breadth of all
      The State of Happiness in Heavens Hall.

A Crown of Righteousness, a Righteous Head,   25
    Oh naughty man! my brain pan turrit is
Where Swallows build, and hatch: Sins black and red.
    My head and heart do ach, and frob at this.
      Lord were my Turret cleansd, and made by thee
      Thy Graces Dovehouse turret much might bee.   30

Oh! make it so: then Righteousness pure, true
    Shall Roost upon my boughs, and in my heart
And all its fruits that in Obedience grew
    To stud this Crown like jems in every part.
      Ist then be garnisht for this Crown, and thou   35
      Shalt have my Songs to diadem thy brow.

Oh! Happy me, if thou wilt Crown me thus.
    Oh! naughty heart! What swell with Sin? fy, fy.
Oh! Gracious Lord, me pardon: do not Crush
    Me all to mammocks: Crown and not destroy.   40
      Ile tune thy Prayses while this Crown doth come.
      Thy Glory bring I tuckt up in my Songe.

13 *on a*] orig: upon   34 *To stud*] orig: T'bestud   *this*] orig: thy

45. Meditation. 1 Pet. 5.4. Ye shall
receive a Crown of Glory.

24. 2m [Apr.] *1692*. Pub. UPT.

A Crown of Glory! Oh! I'm base, its true.
    My Heart's a Swamp, Brake, Thicket vile of Sin.
My Head's a Bog of Filth; Blood bain'd doth spew
    Its venom streaks of Poyson o're my Skin.
    My Members Dung-Carts that bedung at pleasure,   5
    My Life, the Pasture where Hells Hurdloms leasure.

Becrown'd with Filth! Oh! what vile thing am I?
    What Cost, and Charge to make mee Meddow ground?
To drain my Bogs? to lay my Frog-pits dry?
    To stub up all my brush that doth abound?   10
    That I may be thy Pasture fat and frim,
    Where thy choice Flowers, and Hearbs of Grace shine trim?

Vast charge thus to subdue me: Wonders play
    Hereat like Gamesters; 'bellisht Thoughts dresst fine,
In brave attire, cannot a finger lay   15
    Upon it that doth not besmut the Shine.
    Yet all this cost and more thou'rt at with me.
    And still I'm sad, a Seing Eye may see.

Yet more than this: my Hands that Crown'd thy Head
    With sharpest thorns, thou washest in thy Grace.   20
My Feet that did upon thy Choice Blood tread
    Thou makest beautifull thy Way to trace.
    My Head that knockt against thy head, thou hugg'st
    Within thy bosom: boxest not, nor lugg'st.

Nay more as yet: thou borrow'st of each Grace   25
    That stud the Hearts of Saints, and Angells bright

5 *bedung*] orig: with filth bedung   *pleasure,*] PW pleasure
14 *Gamesters;*] PW Gamesters   23 *hugg'st*] PW hugg' with
end of word worn away

Its brightest beams, the beams too of the place
　　　Where Glory dwells: and all the Beames of Light
　　　Thy, and thy Fathers Glorious Face out spread,
　　　To make this Crown of Glory for my head.　　　　30

If it was possible the thoughts that are
　　　Imbellisht with the riches of this tender
Could torment such as do this bright Crown Ware,
　　　Their Love to thee Lord's lac'de so streight, and slender.
　　　These beams would draw up Griefe to cloude this Glory,　35
　　　But not so then; though now Grace acts this Story.

My Pen enravisht with these Rayes out strains
　　　A sorry Verse: and when my gold dwells in
A Purse guilt with the glory bright that flames
　　　Out from this Crown, I'le tune an higher pin.　　　　40
　　　Then make me Lord heir of this Crown. Ile sing
　　　And make thy Praise on my Heroicks ring.

46.　Meditation. Rev. 3.5. The same shall
　　　　be cloathed in White Raiment.

17. 5m [July] *1692*. Pub. PET.

Nay, may I, Lord, believe it? Shall my Skeg
　　　Be ray'd in thy White Robes? My thatcht old Cribb
(Immortal Purss hung on a mortall Peg,)
　　　Wilt thou with fair'st array in heaven rig?
　　　I'm but a jumble of gross Elements　　　　　　5
　　　A Snaile Horn where an Evill Spirit tents.

A Dirt ball dresst in milk white Lawn, and deckt
　　　In Tissue tagd with gold, or Ermins flush,
That mocks the Starrs, and sets them in a fret
　　　To se themselves out shone thus. Oh they blush.　　10
　　　Wonders stand gastard here. But yet my Lord,
　　　This is but faint to what thou dost afford.

27 *brightest*] PW brighest　　34 *Lord's*] PW Lord,s

I'm but a Ball of dirt. Wilt thou adorn
    Mee with thy Web wove in thy Loom Divine
The Whitest Web in Glory, that the morn   15
    Nay, that all Angell glory, doth ore shine?
    They ware no such. This whitest Lawn most fine
    Is onely worn, my Lord, by thee and thine.

This Saye's no flurr of Wit, nor new Coin'd Shape
    Of frollick Fancie in a Rampant Brain.   20
It's juyce Divine bled from the Choicest Grape
    That ever Zions Vinyarde did mentain.
    Such Mortall bits immortalliz'de shall ware
    More glorious robes, than glorious Angells bare.

Their Web is wealthy, wove of Wealthy Silke   25
    Well wrought indeed, its all brancht Taffity.
But this thy Web more white by far than milke
    Spun on thy Wheele twine of thy Deity
    Wove in thy Web, Fulld in thy mill by hand
    Makes them in all their bravery seem tand.   30

This Web is wrought by best, and noblest Art
    That heaven doth afford of twine most choice
All brancht, and richly flowerd in every part
    With all the sparkling flowers of Paradise
    To be thy Ware alone, who hast no peere   35
    And Robes for glorious Saints to thee most deare.

Wilt thou, my Lord, dress my poore wither'd Stump
    In this rich web whose whiteness doth excell
The Snow, though 'tis most black? And shall my Lump
    Of Clay ware more than e're on Angells fell?   40
    What shall my bit of Dirt be deckt so fine
    That shall Angelick glory all out shine?

Shall things run thus? Then Lord, my tumberill
    Unload of all its Dung, and make it cleane.
And load it with thy wealthi'st Grace untill   45
    Its Wheeles do crack, or Axletree complain.

19 *flurr*] orig: flux[?]

I fain would have it cart thy harvest in,
Before its loosed from its Axlepin.

Then screw my Strings up to thy tune that I
    May load thy Glory with my Songs of praise.   50
Make me thy Shalm, thy praise my Songs, whereby
    My mean Shoshannim may thy Michtams raise.
    And when my Clay ball's in thy White robes dresst
    My tune perfume thy praise shall with the best.

47. Meditation on Matt. 25.21. Enter thou
        into the joy of thy Lord.

9. 8m [Oct.] 1692. Pub. ETG.

Strang, strang indeed. It rowell doth my heart
    With pegs of Greefe, and tents of greatest joy:
When I wore Angells Glory in each part
    And all my skirts wore flashes of rich die
    Of Heavenly Colour, hedg'd in with rosie Reechs,   5
    A spider spit its Vomit on my Cheeks.

This ranckling juyce bindg'd in its cursed stain
    Doth permeat both Soul and Body: soile
And drench each Fibre, and infect each grain.
    Its ugliness swells over all the ile.   10
    Whose stain'd mishapen bulk's too high, and broad
    For th'Entry of the narrow gate to God.

Ready to burst, thus, and to burn in hell:
    Now in my path I finde a Waybred spring
Whose leafe drops balm that doth this venom quell   15
    And juyce's a Bath, that doth all stains out bring
    And sparkling beauty in the room convay.
    Lord feed me with this Waybred Leafe, I pray.

53 dresst] PW dress   54 best] Conj.

7: bindg'd (see also Glossary): The spider vomit enters soul and body,
drenching and swelling each fiber.

My stain will out: and swelling swage apace.
    And holy Lusters on my shape appeare.   20
All Rosie Buds: and Lilly flowers of grace
    Will grace my turfe with sweet sweet glory here.
      Under whose shades Angells will bathing play
      Who'l guard my Pearle to glory, hous'd in clay.

Those Gates of Pearle, porter'd with Seraphims,   25
    On their carbuncle joynts will open wide.
And entrance give me where all glory swims
    In to the Masters Joy, e're to abide.
      O sweet sweet thought. Lord take this praise though thin.
      And when I'm in't Ile tune an higher pin.   30

48. Meditation on Matt. 25.21. Enter
into the Joy of thy Lord.

10m ? [Dec.] *1692*. Pub. UPT.

When I, Lord, eye thy Joy, and my Love, small,
    My heart gives in: what now? Strange! Sure I love thee!
And finding brambles 'bout my heart to crawl
    My heart misgives mee. Prize I ought above thee?
      Such great Love hugging them, such small Love, thee!   5
      Whether thou hast my Love, I scarce can see.

My reason rises up, and chides my Cup
    Bright Loveliness itselfe. What not love thee!
Tumbling thy Joy, Lord, ore, it rounds me up.
    Shall loves nest be a thorn bush: not thee bee?   10
      Set Hovells up of thorn kids in my heart!
      Avant adultrous Love. From me depart.

The Influences my vile heart sucks in
    Of Puddle Water boyld by Sunn beams till

22 *sweet sweet*] orig: sweetest   12 *From*] PW from

Its Spiritless, and dead, nothing more thin   15
    Tasts wealthier than those thou dost distill.
    This seems to numb my heart to think that I
    Should null all good to optimate a toy.

Yet when the beamings, Lord, of thy rich Joys,
    Do guild my Soule, meethinks I'm sure I Love thee.   20
They Calcine all these brambly trumperys
    And now I'm sure that I prize naught above thee.
    Thy beams making a bonefire of my Stack
    Of Faggots, bring my Love to thee in'ts pack.

For when the Objects of thy Joy impress   25
    Their shining influences on my heart
My Soule seems an Alembick doth possess
    Love stilld into rich Spirits by thy Art.
    And all my pipes, were they ten thousand would
    Drop Spirits of Love on thee, more rich than gold.   30

Now when the world with all her dimples in't
    Smiles on me, I do love thee more than all:
And when her glory freshens, all in print,
    I prize thee still above it all. And shall.
    Nay all her best to thee, do what she can,   35
    Drops but like drops dropt in a Closestoole pan.

The Castings of thy Joy, my Lord therefore
    Let in the Cabbin of my Joy rise high,
And let thy Joy enter in mee before
    I enter do into my masters joy.
    Thy joyes in mee will make my Pipes to play   40
    For joy thy Praise while teather'd to my clay.

22 *prize*] orig: love   32 *Smiles*] PW Smile
37 *Castings*] conj.   41 *make*] PW makes

49. Meditation. Matt. 25.21. The joy
        of thy Lord.

26. 12m [Feb.] *1692.* Pub. *W.*

Lord, do away my Motes: and Mountains great.
    My nut is vitiate. Its kirnell rots:
Come, kill the Worm, that doth its kirnell eate
    And strike thy sparkes within my tinderbox.
    Drill through my metall-heart an hole wherein   5
    With graces Cotters to thyselfe it pin.

A Lock of Steel upon my Soule, whose key
    The serpent keeps, I fear, doth lock my doore.
O pick't: and through the key-hole make thy way
    And enter in: and let thy joyes run o're.   10
    My Wards are rusty. Oyle them till they trig
    Before thy golden key: thy Oyle makes glib.

Take out the Splinters of the World that stick
    Do in my heart: Friends, Honours, Riches, and
The Shivers in't of Hell whose venoms quick   15
    And firy make it swoln and ranckling stand.
    These wound and kill: those shackle strongly to
    Poore knobs of Clay, my heart. Hence sorrows grow.

Cleanse, and enlarge my kask: It is too small:
    And tartarizd with worldly dregs dri'de in't.   20
It's bad mouth'd too: and though thy joyes do Call
    That boundless are, it ever doth them stint.
    Make me thy Chrystall Caske: those wines in't tun
    That in the Rivers of thy joyes do run.

Lord make me, though suckt through a straw or Quill,   25
    Tast of the Rivers of thy joyes, some drop.

11 *Wards*] orig: Oyl   18 *Hence*] PW hence   22 *are,*] PW are.

'Twill sweeten me: and all my Love distill
    Into thy glass, and me for joy make hop.
    'Twill turn my water into wine: and fill
    My Harp with Songs my Masters joyes distill.   30

28 *glass,*] PW glass.

Preparatory Meditations

Note how this poem has 3
part Structure I define in my essay

I Meditation on Sin, Confession — (Despair)

II Glory of Christ + on the Elect (Joy)

III Prayer that Christ's glory (Hope)
may exalt him

1. Meditation. Col. 2.17. Which are Shaddows of things to come and the body is Christs.

3 Parts

[16] *93. Unpublished.*

1978

Oh Leaden heeld. Lord, give, forgive I pray.
 Infire my Heart: it bedded is in Snow.
I Chide myselfe seing myselfe decay.
 In heate and Zeale to thee, I frozen grow.
 File my dull Spirits: make them sharp and bright:
 Them firbush for thyselfe, and thy delight.   5

My Stains are such, and sinke so deep, that all
 The Excellency in Created Shells
Too low, and little is to make it fall
 Out of my leather Coate wherein it dwells.   10
 This Excellence is but a Shade to that
 Which is enough to make my Stains go back.

The glory of the world slickt up in types
 In all Choise things chosen to typify,
His glory upon whom the worke doth light,   15
 To thine's a Shaddow, or a butterfly.
 How glorious then, my Lord, art thou to mee
 Seing to cleanse me, 's worke alone for thee.

The glory of all Types doth meet in thee.
 Thy glory doth their glory quite excell: 20
More than the Sun excells in its bright glee
 A nat, an Earewig, Weevill, Snaile, or Shell.
 Wonders in Crowds start up; your eyes may strut
 Viewing his Excellence, and's bleeding cut.

Oh! that I had but halfe an eye to view   25
 This excellence of thine, undazled: so
Therewith to give my heart a touch anew
 Untill I quickned am, and made to glow.
 All is too little for thee: but alass
 Most of my little all hath other pass.   30

1 *I*] orig: my 4 *thee,*] PW thee. 16 *To thine's*] orig: Is but
22 *nat,*] PW nat.

Then Pardon, Lord, my fault: and let thy beams
    Of Holiness pierce through this Heart of mine.
Ope to thy Blood a passage through my veans.
    Let thy pure blood my impure blood refine.
    Then with new blood and spirits I will dub   35
    My tunes upon thy Excellency good.

2. Meditation. Coll. 1.15. The First Born of Every Creature.

Undated. Unpublished.

Oh! Golden Rose! Oh. Glittering Lilly White
    Spic'd o're With heavens File divine, till Rayes
Fly forth whose Shine doth Wrack the strongest Sight
    That Wonders Eye is tent of, while't doth gaze
    On thee. Whose Swaddle Bonde's Eternity.   5
    And Sparkling Cradle is Rich Deity.

First Born of e'ry Being: hence a Son
    Begot o'th'First: Gods onely Son begot.
Hence Deity all ore. Gods nature run
    Into a Filiall Mould: Eternall knot.   10
    A Father then, and Son: persons distinct.
    Though them Sabellians contrar'ly inckt.

This mall of Steell falls hard upon those foes
    Of truth, who make the Holy Trinity
Into One Person: Arrians too and those   15
    Socinians calld, who do Christs Deity
    Bark out against. But Will they, nill they, they
    Shall finde this Mall to split their brains away.

Come shine, Deare Lord, out in my heart indeed
    First Born; in truth before thee there was none   20
First Born, as man, born of a Virgin's seed:
    Before or after thee such up ne'er sprung.

Hence Heir of all things lockt in natures Chest:
And in thy Fathers too: extreamly best.

Thou Object of Gods boundless brightest Love,   25
    Invested with all sparkling rayes of Light
Distill thou down, what hony falls above
    Bedew the Angells Copses, fill our Sight
    And hearts therewith within thy Father's joy.
    These are but Shreads under thy bench that ly.   30

Oh! that my Soul was all enamored
    With this First Born enough: a Lump of Love
Son of Eternall Father, Chambered
    Once in a Virgins Womb, dropt from above.
    All Humane royalty hereby Divin'de.   35
    The First Born's Antitype: in whom they're shrin'de.

Make mee thy Babe, and him my Elder Brother.
    A Right, Lord grant me in his Birth Right high.
His Grace, my Treasure make above all other:
    His Life my Sampler: My Life his joy.   40
    I'le hang my love then on his heart, and sing
    New Psalms on Davids Harpe to thee and him.

3. Meditation. Rom. 5.14. Who is the
      Figure of Him that was to come.

    15. 8m [Oct.] *1693*. Pub. ETP, *W*.

Like to the Marigold, I blushing close
    My golden blossoms when thy sun goes down:
Moist'ning my leaves with Dewy Sighs, half frose
    By the nocturnall Cold, that hoares my Crown.
    Mine Apples ashes are in apple shells
    And dirty too: strange and bewitching spells!   5

28 *Copses*,] PW Copses.   29 *Father's*] PW Father

    5: Apples ashes. The *apples* here are Apples of Sodom (Dead Sea Fruit)—of
fair appearance but turning to smoke and ashes when plucked,

When Lord, mine Eye doth spie thy Grace to beame
　　Thy Mediatoriall glory in the shine
Out Spouted so from Adams typick streame
　　And Emblemiz'd in Noahs pollisht shrine　　　　　　　10
　　Thine theirs outshines so far it makes their glory
　　In brightest Colours, seem a smoaky story.

But when mine Eye full of these beams, doth cast
　　Its rayes upon my dusty essence thin
Impregnate with a Sparke Divine, defacde,　　　　　　　15
　　All Candid o're with Leprosie of Sin,
　　Such Influences on my Spirits light,
　　Which them as bitter gall, or Cold ice smite.

My brissled sins hence do so horrid peare,
　　None but thyselfe, (and thou deckt up must bee　　　20
In thy Transcendent glory sparkling cleare)
　　A Mediator unto God for mee.
　　So high they rise, Faith scarce can toss a Sight
　　Over their head upon thyselfe to light.

Is't possible such glory, Lord, ere should　　　　　　　25
　　Center its Love on me Sins Dunghill else?
My Case up take? make it its own? Who would
　　Wash with his blood my blots out? Crown his shelfe
　　Or Dress his golden Cupboard with such ware?
　　This makes my pale facde Hope almost despare.　　　30

Yet let my Titimouses Quill suck in
　　Thy Graces milk Pails some small drop: or Cart
A Bit, or Splinter of some Ray, the wing
　　Of Grace's sun sprindgd out, into my heart:
　　To build there Wonders Chappell where thy Praise　　35
　　Shall be the Psalms sung forth in gracious layes.

9 *Out Spouted*] orig: Spouted out　　11 *makes*] PW make
23 *high*] PW hugh

abraham

4. Meditation. Gal. 4.24. Which things are an Allegorie.

24. 10m [Dec.] *1693.* Pub. PET.

My Gracious Lord, I would thee glory doe:
    But finde my Garden over grown with weeds:
My Soile is sandy; brambles o're it grow;
    My Stock is stunted; branch no good Fruits breeds.
    My Garden weed: Fatten my Soile, and prune   5
    My Stock, and make it with thy glory bloome.

Sin

O Glorious One, the gloriou'st thought I thincke
    Of thee falls black as Inck upon thy Glory.
The brightest Saints that rose, do Star like, pinck.
    Nay, Abrams Shine to thee's an Allegory,   10
    Or fleeting Sparke in th'Smoke, to typify
    Thee, and thy Glorious Selfe in mystery.

Should all the Sparks in heaven, the Stars there dance
    A Galliard, Round about the Sun, and stay
His Servants (while on Easter morn his prance   15
    Is o're, which old wives prate of) O brave Play.
    Thy glorious Saints thus boss thee round, which stand
    Holding thy glorious Types out in their hand.

But can I thinck this Glory greate, its head
    Thrust in a pitchy cloude, should strangled ly
Or tucking up its beams should go to bed   20
    Within the Grave, darke me to glorify?
    This Mighty thought my hearts too streight for, though
    I hold it by the hand, and let not goe.

Light Dark

Then, my Blesst Lord, let not the Bondmaids type   25
    Take place in mee. But thy blesst Promisd Seed.

25: Bondmaids. Cf. Gal. 4:22–24: "For it is written, that Abraham had two sons, the one by a bondmaid, the other by a freewoman. But he who was of the bondwoman was born after the flesh; but he of the freewoman was by promise. Which things are an allegory."

Distill thy Spirit through thy royall Pipe
    Into my Soule, and so my Spirits feed,
    Then them, and me still into praises right
    Into thy Cup where I to swim delight.   30

Though I desire so much, I can't o're doe.
    All that my Can contains, to nothing comes
When summed up, it onely Cyphers grows
    Unless thou set thy Figures to my Sums.
    Lord set thy Figure 'fore them, greate, or small.   35
    To make them something, and I'l give thee all.

5. Meditation on Gal. 3.16. And to¯thy
      Seed Which is Christ.

4. 1m [Mar.] *1693/4.* Unpublished.

Art thou, Lord, Abraham's Seed, and Isaac too?
    His Promisd Seed? That One and Only Seed?
How can this bee? Paul certainly saith true.
    But one Seed promisd. Sir this Riddle read.
    Christ is the Metall: Isaack is the Oar.   5
    Christ is the Pearle, in Abraham's tread therefore.

Christ's Antitype Isaac his Type up spires
    In many things, but Chiefly this because
This Isaac, and the Ram caught in the briars
    One Sacrifice, fore shew by typick laws   10
    Christs Person, all Divine, joynd whereto's made
    Unperson'd Manhood, on the Altar's laid.

The full grown Ram, provided none knows how,
    Typing Christ's Manhood, made by God alone
Caught in the brambles by the horns, must bow,   15
    Under the Knife: The manhoods Death, and Groan.

6 *tread*] Conj.   11 *joynd whereto's made*] orig: unto it tys
12 *on*] orig: and   *Altar's laid*] orig: Altar lys   14 *Christ's*] PW Christ

Yet Isaac's leaping from the Altar's bed,
Foretold its glorious rising from the Dead.

But why did things run thus? For Sin indeed,
   No lesser price than this could satisfy.   20
Oh costly Sin! this makes mine intraills bleed.
    What fills my Shell, did make my Saviour die.
    What Grace then's this of God, and Christ that stills
    Out of this Offering into our tills?

Lord with thine Altars Fire, mine Inward man   25
   Refine from dross: burn out my sinfull guise
And make my Soul thine Altars Drippen pan
    To Catch the Drippen of thy Sacrifice.
    This is the Unction thine receive; the which
    Doth teach them all things of an happy pitch.   30

Thy Altars Fire burns not to ashes down
   This Offering. But it doth roast it here.
This is thy Roastmeate cooked up sweet, brown,
    Upon thy table set for Souls good cheer.
    The Drippen, and the meate are royall fair   35
    That fatten Souls, that with it welcomd are.

My Trencher, Lord, with thy Roast Mutton dress:
   And my dry Bisket in thy Dripping Sap.
And feed my Soul with thy Choice Angell Mess:
    My heart thy Praise, Will, tweedling Larklike tap.   40
    My florid notes, like Tenderills of Vines
    Twine round thy Praise, plants sprung in true Love's Mines.

6. Meditation on Isai. 49.3. Thou art
        my Servant, Oh, Israel.

27. 3m [May] *1694*. Unpublished.

I fain would praise thee, Lord, but finde black **Sin,**
   To stain my Tunes my Virginalls to spoile.
Fetch out the same with thy red blood and bring
   My Heart in kilter, and my Spirits oyle.
   My Theme is rich: my Skill is poore untill   5
   Thy Spirit makes my hand its holy quill.

I spy thyselfe, as Golden Bosses fixt
   On Bible Covers, shine in Types out bright,
Of Abraham, Isaac, Jacob, where's immixt
   Their streaming Beames of Christ displaying **Light.**   10
   Jacobs now jog my pen, whose golden rayes
   Do of thyselfe advance an holy blaze.

His Name as Jacob, saith there's stow'd in thee
   All Wisdom to mentain all Pious Skill
And that the Divells Heels should tript up bee   15
   By thee alone, thou dost his brains out spill.
   The Name of Israel in Scutcheons shows
   Thou art Gods Prince to batter down his Foes.

His Fathers blessing him, shews thou camest down
   Full of thy Fathers blessing: and his Griefe   20
That thou shouldst be a man of Grief: a Crown
   Of Thorns thou wer'st to purchase us reliefe.
   Isr'el by Joseph's had to Egypt, and
   Joseph thee thither, and from thence did hand.

Jacob doth from his Father go and seek   25
   A Spouse and purchasd by his service two.

21 *Grief:*] PW Grief

Thou from thy Father came'st thy Spouse most meek
    Of Jews, and Gentiles down to purchase, Wooe
    And gain, and as Twelve Stems did from him bud
    Thou twelve Apostles sentst, the Church to stud.   30

In all those Typick Lumps of Glory I
    Spy thee the Gem made up of all their shine
Which from them all in thickest glory fly
    And twist themselves into this Gem of thine.
    And as the Shine thereof doth touch my heart,   35
    Joy sincks my Soule seeing how rich thou art.

How rich art thou? How poore am I of Love
    To thee, when all this Glory at my Doore
Stands knocking for admission: and doth shove
    To ope't, and Cabbinet in't all her Store?   40
    Make Love inflamed rise, and all entwine
    About Thyselfe her Object all in Shine.

Lord pardon mee, my Sin, and all my trash:
    And bring my Soule in Surges of rich flame
Of love to thee. I truely Envie dash   45
    Upon my selfe, my hidebound selfe for shame,
    I fain would prize and praise thee, but do sende
    My Flame up smootherd by a Carnall minde.

Oh! blow my Coale with thy blesst Bellows till
    It Glow, and send Loves hottest Steams on thee.   50
I shall be warm; and thou mine arms shalt fill
    And mine Embraces shall thy Worship bee.
    I'le sacrifice to thee my Heart in praise,
    When thy Rich Grace shall be my hearty Phrase.

28 *down*] orig: camest   47 *thee,*] PW thee.   53 *praise,*] PW praise.

7. Meditation. Ps. 105.17. He sent a man
        before them, even Joseph, who
        was sold etc.

5. 6m [Aug.] *1694.* Pub. *W.*

All Dull, my Lord, my Spirits flat, and dead
    All water sockt and sapless to the skin.
Oh! Screw mee up and make my Spirits bed
    Thy quickening vertue For my inke is dim,
    My pensill blunt. Doth Joseph type out thee?   5
    Haraulds of Angells sing out, Bow the Knee.

Is Josephs glorious shine a Type of thee?
    How bright art thou? He Envi'de was as well.
And so was thou. He's stript, and pick't, poore hee,
    Into the pit. And so was thou. They shell   10
    Thee of thy Kirnell. He by Judah's sold
    For twenty Bits, thirty for thee he'd told.

Joseph was tempted by his Mistress vile.
    Thou by the Divell, but both shame the foe.
Joseph was cast into the jayle awhile.   15
    And so was thou. Sweet apples mellow so.
    Joseph did from his jayle to glory run.
    Thou from Death's pallot rose like morning sun.

Joseph layes in against the Famine, and
    Thou dost prepare the Bread of Life for thine.   20
He bought with Corn for Pharaoh th'men and Land.
    Thou with thy Bread mak'st such themselves Consign
    Over to thee, that eate it. Joseph makes
    His brethren bow before him. Thine too quake.

4 *dim*] orig: thin
10 *They*] PW they   *thee* at end of line canceled   14 *Divell,*] PW Divell.

Joseph constrains his Brethren till their sins   25
    Do gall their Souls. Repentance babbles fresh.
Thou treatest sinners till Repentance springs
    Then with him sendst a Benjamin like messe.
    Joseph doth Cheare his humble brethren. Thou
    Dost stud with Joy the mourning Saints that bow.   30

Josephs bright shine th'Eleven Tribes must preach.
    And thine Apostles now Eleven, thine.
They beare his presents to his Friends: thine reach
    Thine unto thine, thus now behold a shine.
    How hast thou pensild out, my Lord, most bright   35
    Thy glorious Image here, on Josephs Light.

This I bewaile in me under this shine
    To see so dull a Colour in my Skin.
Lord, lay thy brightsome Colours on me thine.
    Scoure thou my pipes then play thy tunes therein.   40
    I will not hang my Harp in Willows by.
    While thy sweet praise, my Tunes doth glorify.

8. Meditation. Rom. 5.8. God commends his Love unto us, in that while we were yet sinners, Christ died for us.

14. 8m [Oct.] *1694*. Pub. UPT.

Thou pry'st thou screw'st my sincking Soul up to,
    Lord th'Highest Vane amazements Summit Wears
Seeing thy Love ten thousand wonders do
    Breaking Sins Back that blockt it up: us snares.

40 *then play thy tunes therein*] orig: thy tunes then blow therein

28: *Benjamin like messe.* The feast Joseph made for his brothers, at which Benjamin's was five times as much as the others' (Gen. 43, esp. verse 34).

The Very Stars, and Sun themselves did scoule,   5
    Yea Angells too, till it shone out, did howle.

Poore sinfull man lay grovling on the ground.
    Thy wrath, and Curse to dust lay grinding him.
And Sin, that banisht Love out of these bounds
    Hath stufft the world with curses to the brim.   10
    Gods Love thus Caskt in Heaven, none can tap
    Or breake its truss hoops, or attain a Scrap.

Like as a flock of Doves with feathers washt,
    All o're with yellow gold, fly all away
At one Gun crack: so Lord thy Love Sin quasht   15
    And Chased hence to heaven (Darksom day).
    It nestles there: and Graces Bird did hatch
    Which in dim types we first Pen feather'd catch.

God takes his Son stows in him all his Love,
    (Oh Lovely One), him Lovely thus down sends   20
His rich Love Letter to us from above
    And chiefly in his Death his Love Commends,
    Writ all in Love from top to toe, and told
    Out Love more rich, and shining far than gold.

For e'ry Grain stands bellisht ore with Love,   25
    Each Letter, Syllable, Word, Action sounde
Gods Commendations to us from above,
    But yet Loves Emphasis most cleare is found
    Engrav'd upon his Grave Stone in his blood
    He shed for Sinners, Lord what Love? How good?   30

It rent the Heavens ope that seald up were
    Against poore Sinners: rend the very Skie
And rout the Curse, Sin, Divell, Hell (Oh Deare,)
    And brake Deaths jaw bones, and its Sting destroy.
    Will search its Coffers: fetch from thence the Dust   35
    Of Saints, and it attend to glory just.

My God! this thy Love Letter to mee send.
    Thy Love to mee spell out therein I will.

13 *with*] orig: whose   32 *Sinners:*] PW Sinners   33 *Deare*] conj.

And What choice Love thou dost mee there commend,
    I'le lay up safely in my Souls best till.   40
    I'le read, and read it; and With Angells soon
    My Mictams shall thy Hallelujahs tune.

9. Meditation. Deut. 18.[15] The Lord thy God
          will raise up unto thee a Prophet—like
          unto mee.

16. 10m [Dec.] *1694*. Unpublished.

Lord, let thy Dazzling Shine refracted fan'de
    In this bright Looking Glass, its favour lay
Upon mine Eyes that oculated stand
    And peep thereat, in button moulds of clay.
    Whose glory otherwise that Courts mine eye   5
    Will all its sparkling family destroy.

Yea let thy Beams, better ten thousand times
    Than brightest Eyebright, cherishing revive
The Houshold that possesseth all the Shrines
    In Visions Palace, that it well may thrive.   10
    Moses is made the Looking glass: in which
    Mine Eyes to spie thee in this Type I pitch.

Poor Parents bring him in, when bondage state
    On Israel lay: and so it was with thee.
He's persecuted. All male babes a late   15
    Are to be slain. Thy case was such we see.
    He's sav'de by miracle: and raisd up by
    A sire reputed. So thy matters ly.

Was he most Meeke, Courageous, Faithfull, Wise?
    These all shine bright in thee, out shine the Sun.   20
Did he his Father then in law suffice

15 *All*] PW all

With faithfull service? So thou well hast done.
Did he a gentile Wed? Thy Spouse so shines.
Was he a Mediator? This thee twines.

Did he Gods Israel from Egypt through   25
    The Red Sea lead, into the Wilderness?
Thou bringst Gods Israel from bondage too
    Of Sin into the World here through no less
    Than thy red blood: and in this Chace t'assoile
    The firy Serpents, whose black venoms boile.   30

He Fasted fourty days, and nights, did give
    Them Gods own Law: Thou didst the very same.
The Morall Law whereto we ought to live.
    The Gospell Law to laver out our Shame.
    Then Israel's Church-hood, Worship, Ministry   35
    He founded: which thou didst too gospelly.

He did confirm his Office Worke with Wonders,
    And to the Covenant annexed Seals.
Thou thine in miracles, and more in numbers.
    And Gospell Seals unto thy Church out dealst.   40
    He intercession made, and pardon gain'd
    Unto his people. Thou didst so, its fam'de.

He led them to the border of God's Land,
    Sang like a Swan his dying Song (Well known)
Laid down his hilts: and so discharg'd his hand.   45
    Dy'de, Buri'de, Rose, and went to glories throne.
    All which shine gloriously in thee that wee
    Do Moses finde a Well drawn Map of thee.

Good God! what grace is this takes place in thee?
    How dost thou make thy Son to shine, and prize   50
His glory thus? Thy Looking-glass give mee.
    And let thy Spirit wipe my Watry eyes.

24 *thee*] orig: 'bout thee   26 *Wilderness?*] PW Wilderness
30 *Serpents,*] PW Serpents.   31 *did give*] orig: then gave   34 *our*] orig: their
42 *so,*] PW so.

That I may see his flashing glory darte
Like Lightening quick till it infire my heart.

I long to see thy Sun upon mee shine,   55
    But feare I'st finde myselfe thereby shown worse.
Yet let his burning beams melt, and refine
    Me from my dross, yet not to singe my purse.
    Then of my metall make thy Warbling harp:
    That shall thy Praise deck't in sweet tunes out warp.   60

10. Meditation. Which our Fathers that Follow'd
        after, brought in with Jesus, into
        the Possession of the Gentiles.
        Acts. 7.45.

10. 12m [Feb.] *1694*. Unpublished.

Moses farewell. I with a mournfull teare
    Will wash thy Marble Vault, and leave thy Shine
To follow Josuah to Jordan where
    He weares a Type, of Jesus Christ, divine.
    Did by the Priests bearing the Arke off Cut   5
    Her Stream, that Isr'el through it drieshod foot.

58 *dross,*] PW dross.

Cf. Josh. 4, describing the journey of the priests bearing the ark of the covenant. They were permitted to pass over Jordan on dry ground; as a memorial of this event, Joshua ordered twelve stones, representing the twelve tribes of Israel, to be placed in the midst of Jordan and twelve more to be placed in Gilgal, site of the first encampment west of the Jordan. The place was named Gilgal, according to Josh. 5:9, because the Israelites who had been born during the march through the wilderness were circumcised there: "This day I have rolled away [*galliothi*] the reproach of Egypt from off you. Wherefore the name of the place is called Gilgal unto this day." Rahab (line 43) was a harlot of Jericho who aided Joshua's spies on behalf of the Israelites (Josh. 2).

Doth twelve men call who in the Channell raise
    Twelve Stones, and also other twelve up take
And Gilgal stud therewith, like pearles that blaze
    In Rings of Gold, this passage to relate.   10
    All speaking Types of Christ whose Ministry
    Doth Jordans Streams cut off, that 'fore them fly.

And brings the Church into the Promisd Coast
    And singles out his twelve Apostles who
Twelve flaming Carbuncles before his host   15
    Out of the Channell take, and them bestow
    As Monuments upon its banck most fair,
    Twelve Articles th'Apostles Creed doth bare.

Now Farewell Wilderness, with all thy Fare.
    The Water of the Rock, and Mannah too.   20
My Old-New Cloaths my Wildernesses Ware,
    The Cloud and Pillar bright, adjue adjue.
    You onely in the Wilderness did flower
    As flowring Types. With Angells now I bower.

Let Gilgal speake for mee, where Egypts Stain   25
    Lapt in my Foreskin up clipt off off took.
I feed on Can'ans Wheat, Mannah's plump grain.
    All Evangelicall our Bakers Cooke.
    I drink the Drink of Life and weare Christs Web
    And by the Sun of Righteousness am led.   30

Our Joshua doth draw his Troops out to
    The Lunar coast, this Jericho the World
And rounds it while the Gospell Levites blow
    Their Gospell Rams Horn Trumpets till down hurld
    Its walls lie flat, and it his sacrifice   35
    Doth burn in Zeale, whose Flame doth sindge the Skies.

As Joshuah doth fight Haile Stones smite down
    The Can'anites: so Christ with Haile Stones shall
Destroy his Enemies, and breake their Crown.
    The Sun and Moon shall stand to see them fall   40

The Heavens Chrystall Candlestick-like stand
Holding for him their Candles in their hand.

Yet such as Rahab like come o're to him
    His Grace implanteth in his Golden Stock.
As Joshuah did each Tribe his lot out fling   45
    So Christ doth his in Glory portions lot.
    As Joshua fixt Gods Worship, and envest
    Them with the Promise. Christ thus his hath blest.

That blazing Star in Joshua's but a Beam
    Of thy bright Sun, my Lord, fix such in mee.   50
My Dish clout Soul Rence Wring, and make it clean.
    Then die it in that blood that fell from thee.
    And make the Waiting men within my heart
    Attend thy sweetest praise, in evry part.

11. Meditation. Jud. 13.3. The Angell of the
            Lord appeared to the Woman, etc.

19. 3m [May] *1695*. Pub. *W.*

Eternall Love burnisht in Glory thick,
    Doth butt, and Center in thee, Lord, my joy.
Thou portrai'd art in Colours bright, that stick
    Their Glory on the Choicest Saints, Whereby
    They are thy Pictures made. Samson Exceld   5
    Herein thy Type, as he thy foes once queld.

An Angell tells his mother of his birth.
    An Angell telleth thine of thine. Ye two
Both Males that ope the Womb in Wedlock Kerfe
    Both Nazarited from the Womb up grew.   10

49 *Beam*] orig: Ray   51 *clean*] Conj.   2 *butt*] PW but

He after pitchy night a Sunshine grows
And thou the Sun of Righteousness up rose.

His Love did Court a Gentile spouse, and thine
Espous'd a Gentile to bebride thyselfe.
His Gentile Bride apostatizd betime.   15
    Apostasy in thine grew full of Wealth.
    He sindgd the Authours of't with Foxes tails.
    And foxy men by thee on thine prevaile.

The Fret now rose. Thousands upon him poure.
    An asses Jaw his javling is, whereby   20
He slew a Thousand, heap by heap that hour.
    Thou by weake means makest many thousands fly.
    Thou ribbon like wast platted in his Locks
    And hence he thus his Enemies did box.

He's by his Friend betray'd, for money sold,   25
    Took, bound, blindfolded, made a May game Flout
Dies freely with great sinners, when they hold
    A Sacred Feast. With arms stretcht greatly out,
    Slew more by death, than in his Life he slew.
    And all such things, my Lord, in thee are true.   30

Samson at Gaza went to bed to sleep.
    The Gazites watch him and the Soldiers thee.
He Champion stout, at midnight rose full deep.
    Took Gaza's Gate on's back away went hee.
    Thou rose didst from thy Grave and also tookst   35
    Deaths Doore away throwing it off o'th'hooks.

Thus all the shine that Samson wore is thine,
    Thine in the Type. Oh. Glorious One, Rich glee.
Gods Love hath made thee thus. Hence thy bright shine
    Commands our Love to bow thereto the Knee.   40
    Thy Glory chargeth us in Sacrifice
    To make our Hearts and Love to thee to rise.

11 *grows*] orig: rose
18 *on*] orig: do   22 *makest*] PW make'st   26 *made a May game Flout*]
orig: and made a may game   *May*] PW may   27 *hold*] orig: did hold
28 *greatly out*] orig: out to***ain   32 *and*] orig: as   36 *o'th'*] PW oth
42 *thee*] orig: life

But woe is me! my heart doth run out to
    Poor bits of Clay: or dirty Gayes embrace.
Doth leave thy Lovely Selfe for loveless show: 45
    For lumps of Lust, nay sorrow and disgrace.
    Alas, poore Soule! a Pardon, Lord, I crave.
    I have dishonourd thee and all I have.

Be thou my Samson, Lord, a Rising Sun,
    Of Righteousness unto my Soule, I pray.   50
Conquour my Foes. Let Graces Spouts all run
    Upon my Soule O're which thy sunshine lay.
    And set me in thy Sunshine, make each flower
    Of Grace in me thy Praise perfum'd out poure.

12. Meditation. Ezek. 37.24. David my
Servant shall be their King.

7. 5m [July] 1695. Unpublished.

Dull, Dull indeed! What shall it e're be thus?
    And why? Are not thy Promises, my Lord,
Rich, Quick'ning things? How should my full Cheeks blush
    To finde mee thus? And those a lifeless Word?
    My Heart is heedless: unconcernd hereat: 5
    I finde my Spirits Spiritless, and flat.

Thou Courtst mine Eyes in Sparkling Colours bright,
    Most bright indeed, and soul enamoring,
With the most Shining Sun, whose beames did smite
    Me with delightfull Smiles to make mee spring.   10
    Embellisht knots of Love assault my minde
    Which still is Dull, as if this Sun ne're shin'de.

David in all his gallantry now comes,
    Bringing to tende thy Shrine, his Royall Glory,

51 *run*] PW run.   4 *And*] PW and   13 *now*] orig: doth

Rich Prowess, Prudence, Victories, Sweet Songs,   15
    And Piety to Pensill out thy Story;
        To draw my Heart to thee in this brave shine
        Of typick Beams, most warm. But still I pine.

Shall not this Lovely Beauty, Lord, set out
    In Dazzling Shining Flashes 'fore mine Eye,   20
Enchant my heart, Love's golden mine, till't spout
    Out Streames of Love refin'd that on thee lie?
        Thy Glory's great: Thou Davids Kingdom shalt
        Enjoy for aye. I want and thats my fault.

Spare me, my Lord, spare me, I greatly pray,   25
    Let me thy Gold pass through thy Fire untill
Thy Fire refine, and take my filth away.
        That I may shine like Gold, and have my fill
        Of Love for thee; untill my Virginall
        Chime out in Changes sweet thy Praises shall.   30

Wipe off my Rust, Lord, with thy wisp me scoure,
    And make thy Beams pearch on my Strings their blaze.
My tunes Cloath with thy Shine, and Quavers poure
    My Cursing Strings on, loaded with thy Praise.
        My Fervent Love with Musick in her hand,   35
        Shall then attend thyselfe, and thy Command.

13. Meditation. Ps. 72. The title. A
        Psalm for Solomon.

1. 7m [Sept.] *1695.* Unpublished.

I fain would praise thee, Lord, but when I would,
    I finde my Sin my Praise dispraises bring.
I fain would lift my hands up as I should,
    But when I do, I finde them fould by Sin.

34 *My*] orig: Upon my

I strive to heave my heart to thee, but finde   5
  When striving, in my heart an heartless minde.

Oh! that my Love, and mine Affections rich
  Did spend themselves on thee and thou hadst them.
I strive to have thy Glory on them pitch
  And fetch thee them. Hence Solomon thy jem,   10
  And glorious Type thy Sparkling Beams out flings
  But in the same my Love but little springs..

Was He a bud of Davids stock? So thou.
  Was he a King? Thou art a King of Kings.
Was He a Make-peace King? Thy royall brow   15
  Doth weare a Crown which peace Eternall brings.
  Did He Excell in Wisdome? Thine doth flame.
  And thou art Wisdom's Storehouse whence his came.

I may aver he's of all fallen men
  The perfect'st piece that Nature ever bred.   20
Thy Human nature is the perfect'st jem
  That Adams offspring ever brudled.
  No spot nor Wrinckle did it ever smite.
  Adams in Paradise was ne're so bright.

Did He Gods Temple Build, in glory shown?   25
  Thou buildst Gods House, more gloriously bright.
Did he sit on a golden ivery Throne
  With Lions fenc'd? Thy Throne is far more White
  And glorious: garded with Angells strong.
  A Streame of fire doth with the Verdict come.   30

Did he his Spouse, a glorious Palace build?
  The Heavens are thy Palace for thy Spouse.
Gods house was by his pray're with Glory filld.
  God will for thine his Church in Glory house.
  Did Sheba's Queen faint viewing of his glory?   35
  Bright Angells stand amazed at thy Story.

13 *stock*] PW stok   20 *ever bred*] orig: bred
24 *ne're*] orig: not   25 *shown*] orig: bright   *shown?*] PW shown.
27 *Throne*] PW Thone   36 *amazed*] PW amaze'd   *at*] orig: stand at
The original version of this line was probably: Bright Angells then amaz'd
stand at thy Story

But hence griefe springs, finding these rayes of Light
   Scarce reach my heart, it is so ditcht with Sin.
I scarce can see I see it, or it smite
     Upon my Love that it doth run to him.
     Why so? my Lord! Why so? Shall Love up shrink?
     Or mine Affection to thee be a Shrimp?   40

Oh! feed me at thy Table, make Grace grow
   Knead in thy Bread, I eate, thy Love to mee,
And spice thy Cup I take, with rich grace so,   45
     That at thy Table I may honour thee.
     And if thy Banquet fill mee with thy Wealth,
     My growing Grace will glorify thyselfe.

14. Meditation. Col. 2.3. In whom are hid all the Treasures of Wisdom, and Knowledge.

3d. 9m [Nov.] *1695.* Pub. PET.

Halfe Dead: and rotten at the Coare: my Lord!
   I am Consumptive: and my Wasted lungs
Scarce draw a Breath of aire: my Silver Coard
     Is loose. My buckles almost have no tongues.
     My Heart is Fistulate: I am a Shell.   5
     In Guilt and Filth I wallow, Sent and Smell.

Shall not that Wisdom horded up in thee
   (One key whereof is Sacerdotall Types)
Provide a Cure for all this griefe in mee
     And in the Court of Justice save from Stripes,   10
     And purge away all Filth and Guilt, and bring
     A Cure to my Consumption as a King?

Shall not that Wisdom horded in thee (which
   Prophetick Types enucleate) forth shine

37 *springs,*] PW springs.   43 *Table,*] PW Table.
47 *Wealth,*] PW Wealth.   6 *wallow,*] PW wallow.   10 *Stripes,*] PW Stripes.

With Light enough a Saving Light to fix   15
    On my Poore Taper? And a Flame Divine?
    Making my Soule thy Candle and its Flame
    Thy Light to guide mee, till I Glory gain?

Shall not that Wisdom horded in thee up
    (Which Kingly Types do shine upon in thee)   20
Mee with its Chrystall Cupping Glasses cup
    And draine ill Humours wholy out of mee?
    Ore come my Sin? And mee adorn with Grace
    And fit me for thy Service, and thy Face?

How do these Pointers type thee out most right   25
    As Graces Officine of Wisdom pure
The fingers Salves and Medicines so right
    That never faile, when usd, to worke a Cure?
    Oh! that it would my Wasted lungs recrute.
    And make my feeble Spirits upward shute.   30

How Glorious art thou, Lord? Cloathd with the Glory
    Of Prophets, Priests, and Kings? Nay all Types come
To lay their Glory on thee. (Brightsome Story).
    Their Rayes attend thee, as Sun Beams the Sun.
    And shall my Ulcer'd Soule have such reliefe?   35
    Such glorious Cure? Lord strengthen my beliefe.

Why dost not love, my Soule? or Love grow strong?
    These glorious Beams of Wisdom on thee shine.
Will not this Sunshine make thy branch green long,
    And flowrish as it doth to heaven climbe?   40
    Oh! chide thyselfe out of thy Lethargie,
    And unto Christ on Angells wings up fly.

Draw out thy Wisdom, Lord, and make mee just.
    Draw out thy Wisdom. Wisdoms Crown give mee.
With shining Holiness Candy my Crust: 45
    And make mee to thy Scepter bow the knee.
    Let thy rich Grace mee save from Sin, and **Death**:
    And I will tune thy Praise with holy Breath.

25 *most*] orig: up   39 *green long*] orig: Green and Long

15. Meditation. Mat. 2.23. He shall bee
      called a Nazarite.

Westfield 12. 10m [Dec.] *1695/6*. Unpublished.

A Nazarite indeed. Not such another.
    More rich than Jasper, finer far than Silke
More cleane than Heavens froth the Skies out pother:
    Purer than snow: and Whiter far than Milke.
    In Bodie ruddier than Rubies, nay   5
    Whose pollishing of Sapphire's brave, and gay.

Devoted by thy Father and thy selfe
    To all Examplary Holy Life.
Grace's Chiefe Flower pot on highest shelfe
    In all God's Hall. Here Holiness is rife.   10
    And higher Herbs of Grace can never grow
    In Bulk, or Brightness, than before us flow.

Thy Typick Holiness, more sweet than Muske,
    Ore tops the paltry Dainties of Strong Drinke:
Or Vines whose Fruite is Casked in an huske,
    And Kirnells with hard Stones: though from their Chink: 15
    Bleeds royall Wine: and grapes Sweet Raisens make
    The Wine will soure. Types may not of it take.

The letter of the Law of Nazarites
    Concerns thee not. The Spirit oft is meet   20
For thee alone. Thou art the Vine t'invite
    The Grape without Husk, Stone, The Raisen Sweet.
    Yea, thou thyselfe, the Wine, and Strong Drink art.
    E're sweet, nere Vinegar, or soureing sharp.

Thy Head that wares a Nazaritick Crown   25
    Of Holiness Deckt with its purple Hair

2 *Jasper*,] PW Jasper.   7 *selfe*] PW selfe.   18 *Types*] PW types
20 *The*] PW the   24 *sweet*,] PW sweet.   25 *that*] orig: doth
26 *Deckt*] orig: set

Dide in the Blood thy Grape shed when presst down
    Derides the Rasor. Saints there nestled are.
    And when thy Vow is o're, under the wing
      Of their Peace offering thy praise they'l sing.   30

Thou never wast defiled by the Dead.
    No Dead thing ever, yet disstained thee.
Life from thy Fingers ends runs, and ore spred
    Itselfe through all thy Works what e're they bee.
    Thy Thoughts, Words, Works are lively, frim, do still   35
    Out Spirituall Life. Thy Spirit doth them fill.

Pare off, my Lord, from mee I pray, my pelfe.
    Make mee thy Nazarite by imitation
Not of the Ceremony, but thy selfe,
    In Holiness of Heart, and Conversation.   40
    Then I shall weare thy Nazarite like Crown
    In Glory bright with Songs of thy Renown.

16. Meditation. Lu. 1.33. He shall reign
over the house of Jacob forever.

Westfield 9. 1m [Mar.] *1695/6.* Pub. UPT.

Thou art, my Lord, the King of Glory bright.
    A glory't is unto the Angells flame
To be thy Harauld publishing thy Light
    Unto the Sons of Men: and thy rich Name.
    They are thy Subjects. Yea thy realm is faire.   5
    Ore Jacobs House thou reignest: they declare.

Their brightest glory lies in thee their king.
    My Glory is that thou my king maist bee.
That I may be thy Subject thee to sing
    And thou may'st have thy kingdoms reign in mee.   10
    But when my Lips I make thy Scepter Kiss
    Unheartiness hatcht in my heart doth hiss.

Rich Reason, and Religion Good thus cry,
    Be Subject, Soule: of Jacobs house be one.
Here is a king for thee, Whom Angells fly
    To greet and honour sitting on his throne.
    Sins mutiny, and marr his intrest brave.
    My Pray'res grow Dead. Dead Corps laid in the grave.

The lowly Vine Grows fruitfull clusters, Rich.
    The Humble Olive fat with oyle abounds.
But I like to the fiery Bramble, Which
    Jumps at a Crown am but an empty Sound.
    A guilded Cask of tawny Pride, and Gall,
    With Veans of Venom o're my Spirits sprawle.

Like to the Daugh all glorious made when dresst
    In feathers borrowed of other birds
Must need be King of birds: but is distresst,
    When ery bird its feather hath, and Curbd
    Doth glout, and slouch her Wings. Pride acts this part.
    And base Hypocrisy. Oh! rotten heart!

Blesst Lord, my King, where is thy golden Sword?
    Oh! Sheath it in the bowells of my Sin.
Slay my Rebellion, make thy Law my Word.
    Against thine Enemies Without within.
    Implant mee as a branch in Gods true vine
    And then my grape will yield thy Cup rich wine.

Shall I now grafted in thy Olive tree
    The house of Jacob, bramble berries beare?
This burdens me to thinke of, much more thee.
    Breake off my black brire Claws: mee scrape, and pare.
    Lord make my Bramble bush thy rosie tree.
    And it will beare sweet Roses then for thee.

Kill my Hypocrisie, Pride Poison, Gall.
    And make my Daugh thy Turtle Dove ore laid
With golden feathers: and my fruites then shall

Flock Dovelike to thy Lockers, oh! Choice trade.
My Cooing then shall be thy Musick in,
The House of Jacob, tun'de to thee, my King.

17. Meditation. Eph. 5.2. And gave himselfe for
us an offering, and a Sacrifice to God.

Westfield 16. 6[m] [Aug.] 1696. Pub. UPT.

Thou Greate Supream, thou Infinite first One:
    Thy Being Being gave to all that be
Yea to the best of Beings thee alone
    To serve with Service best for best of fee.
    But man the best servd thee the Worst of all   5
    And so the Worst of incomes on him falls.

Hence I who'me Capable to serve thee best
    Of all the ranks of Beings here below
And best of Wages win, have been a pest
    And done the Worst, earn'd thus the Worst of Woe.   10
    Sin that imploys mee findes mee worke indeed
    Me qualifies, ill qualities doth breed.

This is an hell indeed thus to be held
    From that which nature holdst her chiefe delights
To that that is her horrour and refelld   15
    Ev'n by the Law God in her Essence writes.
    But for reliefe Grace in her tender would
    Massiah cast all Sacrifices told.

I sin'd. Christ, bailes. Grace takes him Surety,
    Translates my Sin upon his sinless Shine.   20
He's guilty thus, and Justice thus doth eye
    And sues the band, and brings on him the fine.
    All Sacrifices burn but yet their blood
    Can't quench the fire, When laid upon the Wood.

18 *Massiah cast*] orig: Did Cast Massiah

The type thy Veane phlebotomizd must bee   25
    To quench this Fire: no other blood nor thing
Can do't. Hence thou alone art made for mee
    Burnt, Meat, Peace Sin, and Trespass Offering.
    Thy blood must fall: thy life must go or I
    Under the Wrath of God must ever fry.   30

This fire upon thee burnt, and is allay'd
    For all of thine. Oh make mee thine I pray.
So shall this Wrath from mee be retrograde.
    No fire shall sindge my rags nor on them stay.
    New qualify mee. I shall then on go   35
    Anew about thy Service, and it do.

What Grace in God? What Love in Christ thus spring
    Up unto men, and to my poore poore heart?
That so thy burning fire no Sparke can fling
    Or sparkle on such Tinder, This impart   40
    Unto thy Servant. This will be my Health:
    And for a gift to thee I send myselfe.

Oh! that my Love, was rowld all ore and ore
    In thine, and Candi'd in't, and so refin'd
More bright than gold, and grown in bulke, far more   45
    Than tongue can tell of each best sort, and kind.
    All should be thine, and I thine own will be.
    Accept my gift, no better is with mee.

Then own thine own. Be thou my Sacrifice,
    Thy Father too, that he may father mee,   50
And I may be his Child, and thy blood prize,
    That thy attonement may my clearing bee.
    In hope of Which I in thy Service sing
    Unto thy Praise upon my Harp within.

25 *The*] PW **They**   50 *too*] PW **to**

18. Meditation. Heb. 13.10. Wee
        have an Altar.

Westfield 18. 8m [Oct.] *1696*. Pub. *W*.

A Bran, a Chaff, a very Barly yawn,
     An Husk, a Shell, a Nothing, nay yet Worse,
A Thistle, Bryer prickle, pricking Thorn
     A Lump of Lewdeness, Pouch of Sin, a purse
     Of Naughtiness, I am, yea what not Lord?   5
     And wilt thou be mine Altar? and my bord?

Mine Heart's a Park or Chase of sins: Mine Head
     'S a Bowling Alley. Sins play Ninehole here.
Phansy's a Green: sin Barly breaks in't led.
     Judgment's a pingle. Blindeman's Buff's plaid there.   10
     Sin playes at Coursey Parke within my Minde.
     My Wills a Walke in which it aires what's blinde.

Sure then I lack Atonement. Lord me help.
     Thy Shittim Wood ore laid With Wealthy **brass**
Was an Atoning altar, and sweet smelt: 15
     But if ore laid with pure pure gold it was
     It was an Incense Altar, all perfum'd
     With Odours, wherein Lord thou thus was bloom'd.

Did this ere during Wood when thus orespread
     With these erelasting Metalls altarwise   20
Type thy Eternall Plank of Godhead, Wed
     Unto our Mortall Chip, its sacrifice?
     Thy Deity mine Altar. Manhood thine.
     Mine Offring on't for all men's Sins, and **mine?**

This Golden Altar puts such weight into   25
     The sacrifices offer'd on't, that it
Ore weighs the Weight of all the sins that flow

12 *it aires*] orig: they aire   24 *all men's Sins*] orig: Sins of all
26 *on't*] orig: up on't

In thine Elect. This Wedge, and beetle split
The knotty Logs of Vengeance too to shivers:
And from their Guilt and shame them cleare delivers.   30

This Holy Altar by its Heavenly fire
Refines our Offerings: casts out their dross
And sanctifies their Gold by its rich 'tire
And all their steams with Holy Odours boss.
Pillars of Frankincense and rich Perfume   35
They 'tone Gods nosthrills with, off from this Loom.

Good News, Good Sirs, more good than comes within
The Canopy of Angells. Heavens Hall
Allows no better: this atones for sin,
My Glorious God, Whose Grace here thickest falls.   40
May I my Barly yawn, Bran, Bryer Claw,
Lay on't a Sacrifice? or Chaff or Straw?

Shall I my sin Pouch lay, on thy Gold Bench
My Offering, Lord, to thee? I've such alone
But have no better. For my sins do drench   45
My very best unto their very bone.
And shall mine Offering by thine Altars fire
Refin'd, and sanctifi'd to God aspire?

Amen, ev'n so be it. I now will climb
The stares up to thine Altar, and on't lay   50
Myselfe, and services, even for its shrine.
My sacrifice brought thee accept I pray.
My Morn, and Evning Offerings I'le bring
And on this Golden Altar Incense fling.

Lord let thy Deity mine Altar bee   55
And make thy Manhood, on't my sacrifice.
For mine Atonement: make them both for mee
My Altar t'sanctify my gifts likewise

30 *shame*] Conj.   44 *thee?*] PW thee.
46 *bone.*] PW bone?   49 *Amen,*] PW Amen.   52 *brought thee*] orig: brought
to thee

That so myselfe and service on't may bring
    Its worth along with them to thee my king.   60

The thoughts whereof, do make my tunes as fume,
    From off this Altar rise to thee Most High
And all their steams stufft with thy Altars blooms,
    My Sacrifice of Praise in Melody.
      Let thy bright Angells catch my tune, and sing't.   65
      That Equalls Davids Michtam which is in't.

19. Meditation. Can. 1.12. While the King
      sits at his Table, my Spicknard
      sends forth the Smell thereof.

Westfield 7. 10m [Dec.] *1696*. Pub. PET.

Lord dub my tongue with a new tier of Words
    More comprehensive far than my dull Speech
That I may dress thy Excellency Lord
    In Languague welted with Emphatick reech.
      Thou art my King: my Heart thy Table make   5
      And sit thereat untill my Spicknard wake.

My Garden Knot drawn out most curiously
    By thy brave hand set with the bravest Slips
Of Spicknard: Lavender that thence may fly
    Their Wealthy Spirits from their trunks and tips.   10
      That Spicknard Oyle, and Oyle of Spike most sweet
      May muskify thy Palace with their Reeke.

Then sit at thy round Table with delight
    And feast in mee, untill my Spicknard bloome,
And Crown thy head with Odour-Oyle rich bright   15
    And croud thy Chamber with her sweet perfume.

3 *Excellency*] PW Excelleny   4 *welted*] Conj.   *reech*] Conj.

The Spicknard in my knot then flourish will:
And frindge thy Locks with odour it doth still.

And when thou at thy Circuite Table sitst
　　Thine Ordinances, Lord, to greet poor hearts　　　20
Such Influences from thyselfe thou slipst
　　And make their Spicknard its sweet Smell impart.
　　So make my Lavender to spring, and sent.
　　In such attire her Spirits ever tent.

And as thou at thy Table sitst to feast
　　Thy Guests there at, Thy Supper, Lord, well drest,　　25
Let my sweet Spicknard breath most sweet, at least
　　Those Odours that advance thy Glory best.
　　And make my heart thine Alabaster Box
　　Of my Rich Spicknard to perfume thy locks.　　　30

If this thou grant, (and grant thou this I pray)
　　And sit my King at thy rich table thus,
Then my Choice Spicknard shall its Smell display,
　　That sweetens mee and on thee sweet doth rush.
　　My Songs of Praise too sweeten'd with this fume　　35
　　Shall scale thine Eares in Spicknardisick Tune.

20. Meditation. Heb. 9.11. By a Greater, and more Perfect Tabernacle.

7. 12m [Feb.] 1696. Unpublished.

Didst thou, Lord, Cast mee in a Worship-mould
　　That I might Worship thee immediatly?
Hath Sin blurd all thy Print, that so I should
　　Be made in vain unto this End? and Why?
　　Lord print me ore again. Begon, begon,　　　5
　　Yee Fly blows all of hell: I'le harbour none.

20 *Even* at beginning of line canceled　　*Thine*] PW thine
26 *Guests*] PW Guess

That I might not receive this mould in vain
    Thy Son, my Lord, my Tabernacle he
Shall be: me run into thy mould again.
    Then in this Temple I will Worship thee.   10
    If he the Medium of my Worship stand
    Mee, and my Worship he will to thee hand.

I can't thee Worship now without an House.
    An house of Worship here will do no good,
Unless it type my Woe, in which I douse,   15
    And Remedy in deifyed Blood.
    Thy Tabernacle, and thy Temple they
    Such Types arose. Christ is their Sun, and Ray.

Thou wast their Authour: Art Christs too and his.
    They were of Choicest Matters. His's th'best blood.   20
Thy Spirits over shaddowing form'd them, This
    Did overshaddow Mary. Christ did bud.
    The Laver, Altar, Shew Bread, Table Gold
    And Golden Light and Oyle do Christs Shine hold.

The Efficacy that's lodgd in them all   25
    Came from thyselfe in influences, nay
Their Glory's but a painted Sun on th'Wall
    Compar'd to thine and that thou dost display.
    How glorious then art thou, when all their glory
    Is but a Paintery to thy bright Story.   30

Thou art the Laver to wash off my Sin:
    The Altars for atonement out of hand:
The Sweet Sweet Incense cast the fire within
    The Golden Table, where the Shew bread stand.
    The Golden Candlestick with holy Light   35
    Mentain'd by holy Oyle in Graces Pipe.

The flames whereof, enmixt with Grace assaile
    With Grace the heart in th'Light that takes the Eye
To light us in the way within the Vaile
    Unto the Arke in which the Angells prie   40

24 *Oyle*] PW Oyle.   26 *influences,*] PW influences.
37 *assaile*] orig: out throws   38 *With Grace the*] orig: Grace on the

Having the Law stand in't, up Coverd under
    The Mercy Seate, that Throne of Graces Wonder.

Thou art my Tabernacle, Temple right,
    My Cleansing, Holiness, Atonement, Food,
My Righteousness, My Guide of Temple Light   45
    In to the Holy Holies, (as is shewd)
        My Oracle, Arke, Mercy Seat: the place
        Of Cherubims amazde at such rich grace.

Thou art my Medium to God, thou art
    My Medium of Worship done to thee,   50
And of Divine Communion, Sweet heart!
        Oh Heavenly intercourse! Yee Angells see!
        Art thou my Temple, Lord? Then thou Most Choice
        Art Angells Play-House, and Saints Paradise.

Thy Temples Influences stick on mee,   55
    That I in Holy Love may stow my heart
Upon thyselfe, and on my God in thee,
        And with thy Holiness guild Every part
        Of me. And I will as I walke herein
        Thy Glory thee in Temple Musick bring.   60

**21. Meditation. Col. 2.16.17. In respect of
           an Holy Day, of a New Moon, or a
           Sabbath. Which are figures.**

16. 3m [May] 1697. Unpublished.

Rich Temple Fair! Rich Festivalls my Lord,
    Thou makest to entertain thy Guests most dresst
In dishes up by SEVENS which afford
        Rich Mystery under their brims expresst.
        Which to discover clearly, make the brain   5
        Of most men wring, their kirnells to obtain.

44 *Atonement*] orig: my Atonement

Each Seventh Day a Sabbath Gracious Ware.
    A Seventh Week a yearly Festivall.
The Seventh Month a Feast nigh, all, rich fare.
    The Seventh Yeare a Feast Sabbaticall.   10
    And when seven years are seven times turnd about
    A Jubilee. Now turn their inside out.

What Secret Sweet Mysterie under the Wing
    Of this so much Elected number lies?
What Vean can e're Divine? Or Poet sing?   15
    Doubtless most Rich. For such shew God most Wise.
    I will adore the same although my quill
    Can't hit the String that's tun'd by such right Skill.

Sharpen my Sight my Lord that I may spie
    A lively Quickness in it jump for joy   20
And by the breaking of the Shell let fly
    Such pleasant Species as will folly stroy.
    Out of these Feasts, although the Number Seven
    I leave untill my Soul is housd in Heaven.

And here I beg thy aide Mine eyes refine   25
    Untill my Sight is strong enough to spy
Thyselfe my Lord deckt all in Sun Like Shine.
    And see myselfe cloathd in thy Beams that fly.
    My Sight is dim: With Spectacles mee suite
    Made of a pair of Stars it to recrute.   30

Make mee thy Lunar Body to be filld
    In full Conjunction, with thy Shining Selfe
The Sun of Righteousness: whose beams let guild
    My Face turnd up to heaven, on which high Shelfe
    I shall thy Glorys in my face that shine,   35
    Set in Reflected Rayes. Hence thou hast thine.

Moon-like I have no light here of mine own.
    My shining beams are borrowd of this Sun,
With which when 'ray'd its Rayes on mee are shown
    Unto this World as I it over run.   40

12 *Jubilee*] orig: Jubilee Steps in
23 *Out of these*] orig: These Feasts could   38 *Sun,*] PW Sun.

My black Side's Earthward Yet thy beams that flew
    Upon mee from thy face, are in its view.

Hence Angells will in heaven blow up aloud
    For joy thy Trumpet on my new Moon day
And in its Prime, the Golden Rayes that shroud   45
    Within thy Face will guild my Edges gay.
        Oh! Happy Change. The Sun of Righteousness
        With's healing Wings my moon doth richly dress.

And though this world doth eye thy brightness most
    When most in distance from thyselfe I'm backt,   50
Yet then I most am apt even from this Coast
    To be Ecclipsed, or by its fogs be blackt.
        My back at best, and dark side Godward bee,
        And pitchy clouds do hide thy face from mee.

Oh! let not Earth nor its thick fogs I pray   55
    E're slip between me, and thy lightsome Rayes
But let my Cloathing be thy Sunshine Ray.
        My New-Moon Trumpet then shall sound thy praise.
        I then in sweet Conjunction shall with thee
        The Sun of Righteousness abiding bee.   60

[*The following four stanzas appear after the conclusion of this
poem in PW. They have been crossed out and appear, in slightly
altered form, as the conclusion of Meditation 22.*]

But now I from the New Moon Feast do pass
    And pass the Passo're o're unto Gods Seales,
And come to Whitsuntide, and turn its glass
    To search for pearles amongst its sands and meals.
        For Israel had not fifty dayes been out   5
        Of Egypt, ere at Sinai Law did spout.

So Christ our Passover had not passt ore
    Full fifty dayes before in fiery wise
The Law of Spirit and of Life much more
    Went out from Zion. Gospell Law did rise.   10

9 *and*] orig: of

The Harvest of the former yeare is in'd.
    Injoy'd, and Consecrated Thanks for't pay'd.
All holding out the Right in things we sind
    Away restored is, and they all made
    Fit for our use, and that we thankfully   15
    Ourselves unto the using them should ply.

Then make me to this Penticost repare.
    Make mee thy Guest, Lord, at this feast, and live
Up to thy Gospell Law. And let my Fare
    Be of the two Wave Loaves this Feast doth give.   20
    If th'Prophets Seedtime spring my harvest I
    Will, as I reape't, sing thee my harvest joy.

22. Meditation. 1 Cor. 5.7. Christ our
Passover is sacrificed for us.

Undated. Unpublished.

I from the New Moon of the first month high
    Unto its fourteenth day When she is Full
Of Light the Which the Shining Sun let fly
    And when the Sun's all black to see Sins pull
    The Sun of Righteousness from Heaven down   5
    Into the Grave and weare a Pascall Crown.

A Bond Slave in Egyptick Slavery
    This Noble Stem, Angellick Bud, this Seed
Of Heavenly Birth, my Soul, doth groaning ly.
    When shall its Passo're come? When shall't be Freed?   10

13 *the*] orig: hereby the   22 *sing*] orig: make sing
1 *month*] PW mon'th orig: pass   2 *Full*] PW Full,

   10: Passo're, Passover. Three feasts were enjoined by Mosaic law upon the
Hebrews: (1) the Passover, celebrated on the fourteenth day of Nisan, the
first month of the Hebraic year (corresponding to March–April), followed
by the Feast of Unleavened Bread, which began on the fifteenth day and
lasted for seven days; (2) the Feast of Weeks—also called Pentecost, or Harvest

The Lamb is slaine upon the fourteenth day
    Of Month the first, my Doore posts do display.
Send out thy Slaughter Angell, Lord, and slay
    All my Enslaving 'Gypsies Sins, while I
Eate this rost Mutten, Paschall Lamb, Display   15
    Thy Grace herein, while I from Egypt high.
    I'le feed upon thy Roast meat here updresst,
    With Bitter hearbs, unleaven'd bread the best.

I'le banish Leaven from my very Soule
    And from its Leanetoe tent: and search out all   20
With Candles lest a Crum thereof should rowle
    Into its Corners or in mouseholes fall,
    Which when I finde I'le burn up, and will sweep
    From every Corner all, and all cleane keep.

My Bunch of Hyssop, Faith, dipt in thy blood   25
    My Paschall Lamb, held in thy Bason bright
Baptize my Doore Posts shall, make Crimson good.
    Let nothing off this Varnish from them wipe,
    And while they weare thy Crimson painted dy,
    No Slaughter Angell shall mine house annoy.   30

Lord, purge my Leaven out: my Tast make quick:
    My Souls strong Posts baptize with this rich blood

---

of First Fruits—held on the fiftieth day of the Passover season; and (3) the
Feast of Tabernacles—or Feast of Booths, or Feast of the Ingathering (Suk-
koth)—lasting seven days, held during the full moon of Tishri, the seventh
month (September–October).

In this poem Taylor apparently has in mind all three feasts. According
to biblical tradition, the first Passover was celebrated when the Lord com-
manded Moses and Aaron to prepare for departure from Egypt. A lamb in
its first year was killed at sunset on the fourteenth day, and its blood was
sprinkled on the side posts and lintel of the house of the family celebrating
the Passover; the lamb was then roasted whole and eaten with unleavened
bread and bitter herbs (Exod. 12). Killing a lamb in its first year symbolized
God's determination to smite the first-born of the Egyptians; the blood was a
sign to the Destroying Angel to pass over the house so marked.

The Feast of Tabernacles, or Feast of Booths, is referred to in detail in
Meditation 24 (second series), p. 125.

21: lest a Crum thereof should rowle. Ritual cleanliness was essential in
the celebration of the Passover.

By bunch of Hyssop, then I'le also lick
 Thy Dripping Pan: and eat thy Roast Lamb good,
 With Staff in hand, Loins Girt, and Feet well shod 35
 With Gospell ware as walking to my God.

I'le Goshen's Ramesis now leave apace.
 Thy Flag I'le follow to thy Succoth tent.
Thy sprinkled blood being my lintells grace
 Thy Flesh my Food With bitter herbs attent 40
 To minde me of my bitter bondage State
 And my Deliverance from all such fate.

I'le at this Feast my First Sheafe bring, and Wave
 Before thee, Lord, my Crop to sanctify
That in my first Fruits I my harvest have 45
 May blest unto my Cyckle Constantly.
 So at this Feast my harp shall Tunes advance
 Upon thy Lamb, and my Deliverance.

But now I from the Passover do pass.
 Easter farewell, rich jewells thou did shew, 50
And come to Whitsuntide; and turn the Glass
 To search her Sands for pearles therein anew.
 For Isra'l a fift'th day from Egypt broke,
 Gave Sinai's Law, and Crown'd the mount with Smoke.

And Christ oure Passover had not passt o're 55
 Full fifty dayes before in fiery guise
He gave Mount Zions Law from graces store.
 The Gospell Law of Spirit and Life out highs
 In fiery Tongues that did confound all those
 At Pentecost that Zions King oppose. 60

The Harvest of the year through Grace now inn'd,
 Enjoyd and Consecrated with Right praise,
All typefying that the right we sind
 Away's restor'd by Christ: and all things raisd

50 *farewell*,] PW farewell *shew*,] PW shew
64 *raisd*] orig: made

 43: First Sheafe. The Omer, or first sheaf of the harvest, was offered to the
priest (Lev. 23:10–14).
 45–46: have / May blest, i.e. may have blessed.

Fit for our use, and that we thankfully   65
   Unto the use thereof ourselves should ply.

Lord make me to the Pentecost repare,
   Make me thy Guest too at this Feast, and live
Up to thy Gospell Law: and let my fare
   Be of the two white Loaves this feast doth give.   70
   If Prophets Seeding yield me harvest, I
   Will as I reap sing thee my harvest joy.

23. Meditation. 1 Joh. 2.2. He is the
           Propitiation for our Sins.

17. 7m [Sept.] *1697*. Unpublished.

Greate Lord, yea Greatest Lord of Lords thou art,
   And King of Kings, may my poor Creaking Pipe
Salute thine Eare; This thought doth sink my heart
   Ore burdened with over sweet Delight.
     An Ant bears more proportion to the World   5
     Than doth my piping to thine eare thus hurld.

It is a Sight amazing strange to see
   An Emperour picking an Emmets Egge.
More strange it's that Almighty should to mee
   E're lend his Eare. And yet this thing I beg.   10
     I'm small and Naught, thou mayst much less me spare
     Than I the Nit that hangeth on my hair.

But oh thy Grace! What glory on it hings,
   In that thou makest thy Son to bare away
The marrow of the matter choice that Clings   15
   Unto the Service of Atonment's day?
     This was his Type, He is its Treasure rich
     That Reconciles for Sin that doth us ditch.

4 This line is repeated at top of page in PW and canceled.

Sins thick and threefold at my threshold lay
  At Graces threshold I all gore in Sin.   20
Christ backt the Curtain, Grace made bright the day,
  As he did our Atonement full step in.
   So Glorious he. His Type is all unmeet
   To typify him till aton'd and sweet.

A'ron as he atonement made did ware   25
  His milke white linen Robes, to typify
Christ cloath'd in human flesh pure White, all fair,
  And undefild, atoneing God most High.
   Two Goates he took, and lots to know Gods will,
   Which he should send away: and Which, should kill. 30

Dear Christ, thy Natures two are typ't thereby
  Making one Sacrifice, Humane, Divine.
The Manhood is Gods Lot, and this must dy.
  The Godhead as the Scape Goate death declines.
   One Goat atones, one beares all Sin away.   35
   Thy natures do this work, each as they lay.

Aaron the blood must catch in's Vessell to hold.
  Lord let my Soule the Vessell be of thine.
Aaron must in a Censar all of Gold
  Sweet incense burn with Altars fire Divine   40
   To Typify the Incense of thy Prayer
   Perfuming of thy Service thou didst beare.

Aaron goes in unto the Holy place
  With blood of Sprinkling and sprinkles there
Atones the Tabernacle, Altars face   45
  And Congregation, for defild all were.
   Christ with his proper blood did enter in
   The Heavens bright, propitiates for Sin.

Aaron then burns the Goat without the Camp
  And Bullock too whose blood went in the Vaile. 50
Christ sufferd so without the Gate Deaths Cramp,
  And Cramped Hell thereby. The Divells quaile.

21 *day,*] PW day. 47 *proper blood*] PW proper, blood.

Thus done with God Aaron aside did lay
His Linen Robes, and put on's Golden Ray.

And in this Rich attire he doth apply   55
Himselfe before the peoples very eyes,
Unto the other Service, richly high
To typify the gracious properties
Wherewith Christs human nature was bedight
In which he mediates within Gods Sight.   60

What wonder's here? Shall such a sorry thing
As I have such rich Cost laid down for mee
Whose best at best as mine's not worth a Wing
Of one poore Fly, that I should have from thee
Such Influences of thy goodness smite mee   65
And make me mute as by delight envite mee?

Lord let thy Gracious hand me chafe, and rub
Till my numbd joynts be quickn'd and compleat,
With Heate and Spirits all divine, and good,
To make them nimble in thy Service Greate.   70
Oh! take my ALL thyselfe, all though I bee
All bad, I have no better gift for thee.

Although my gift is but a Wooden toole
If thou receive it, thou wilt it enrich
With Grace, thats better than Apollo's Stoole.   75
Thy Oracles 'twill utter out the which
Will make my Spirits thy bright golden Wyers,
ALTASCHAT Michtam tune in Angells Quires.

66 *mee?*] PW mee.   69 *good,*] PW good.

Meditation 24. Joh. 1.14. ἐσκήνωσε[ν]
ἐν ἡμῖν Tabernacled amongst us.

25. 10m [Dec.] 1697. Unpublished.

My Soul would gazing all amazed stand,
    To see the burning Sun, with'ts golden locks
(An hundred sixty six times more than th'land)
    Ly buttond up in a Tobacco box.
    But this bright Wonder, Lord, that fore us playes   5
    May make bright Angells gasterd, at it gaze.

That thou, my Lord, that hast the Heavens bright
    Pav'd with the Sun, and Moon, with Stars o're pinckt,
Thy Tabernacle, yet shouldst take delight
    To make my flesh thy Tent, and tent with in't.   10
    Wonders themselves do seem to faint away
    To finde the Heavens Filler housd in Clay.

Thy Godhead Cabbin'd in a Myrtle bowre,
    A Palm branch tent, an Olive Tabernacle,
A Pine bough Booth, An Osier House or tower   15
    A mortall bitt of Manhood, where the Staple
    Doth fixt, uniting of thy natures, hold,
    And hold out marvels more than can be told.

Thy Tabernacles floore Celestiall
    Doth Canopie the Whole World. Lord; and wilt   20
Thou tabernacle in a tent so small?
    Have Tent, and Tent cloath of a Humane Quilt?
    Thy Person make a bit of flesh of mee
    Thy Tabernacle, and its Canopee?

Wonders! my Lord, Thy Nature all With Mine   25
    Doth by the Feast of Booths Conjoynd appeare

1 would] orig: doth   3 more] orig: bigger

26: Feast of Booths, one of the three Passover feasts: also called Sukkoth, also Feast of Tabernacles (see p. 120, note to line 10). During this festival

Together in thy Person all Divine
    Stand House, and House holder. What Wonder's here?
    Thy Person infinite, without compare
    Cloaths made of a Carnation leafe doth ware.   30

What Glory to my nature doth thy Grace
    Confer, that it is made a Booth for thine
To tabernacle in? Wonders take place.
    Thou low dost step aloft to lift up mine.
    Septembers fifteenth day did type the Birth   35
    Of this thy tabernacle here on earth.

And through this leafy Tent the glory cleare
    Of thy Rich Godhead shineth very much:
The Crowds of Sacrifices which swarm here
    Shew forth thy Efficacy now is such   40
    Flowing in from thy natures thus united
    As Clears off Sin, and Victims all benighted.

But yet the Wonder grows: and groweth much,
    For thou wilt Tabernacles change with mee.
Not onely Nature, but my person tuch.
    Thou wilst mee thy, and thee, my tent to bee.   45
    Thou wilt, if I my heart will to thee rent,
    My Tabernacle make thy Tenement.

Thou'lt tent in mee, I dwell in thee shall here.
    For housing thou wilt pay mee rent in bliss: 50
And I shall pay thee rent of Reverent fear
    For Quarters in thy house. Rent mutuall is.

42 *Sin,*] PW Sin.   46 *my*] PW my,

---

families lived in tents or booths made of boughs, in remembrance of the
forty years' wandering of their nomadic ancestors. This celebration fell into
abeyance among the Hebrews but was revived in the time of Ezra, as re-
counted in Neh. 8:13–18—a passage Taylor had in mind when he wrote the
third stanza of Meditation 24. Taylor considered the Feast of Booths to be a
type of Christ's incarnation: "if it [the Annunciation] be . . . just before the
Conception it will Cast the birth of our Lord Christ into September a sum-
mer Month wherein the Jews kept the Feast of Tabernacles, a type of Christs
Incarnation" (HG, 28).

Thy Tenent and thy Teniment I bee.
Thou Landlord art and Tenent too to mee.

Lord lease thyselfe to mee out: make mee give   55
    A Leafe unto thy Lordship of myselfe.
Thy Tenent, and thy Teniment I'le live.
    And give and take Rent of Celestiall Wealth.
    I'le be thy Tabernacle: thou shalt bee
    My Tabernacle. Lord thus mutuall wee.   60

The Feast of Tabernacles makes me sing
    Out thy Theanthropy, my Lord, I'le spare
No Musick here. Sweet Songs of praises in
    The Tabernacles of the Righteous are.
    My Palmifer'd Hosannah Songs I'le raise   65
    On my Shoshannims blossoming thy praise.

Meditation 25. Numb. 28.4.9. One Lamb shalt thou offer in the Morning, and the other at Even. And on the Sabbath day two Lambs etc.

6. 1m [Mar.] *1698*. Pub. PET.

Guilty, my Lord, What can I more declare?
    Thou knowst the Case, and Cases of my Soule.
A Box of tinder: Sparks that falling o're
    Set all on fire, and worke me all in Shoals.
    A Pouch of Passion is my Pericarde.   5
    Sparks fly when ere my Flint and Steele strike hard.

I am a Dish of Dumps: yea ponderous dross,
    Black blood all clotted, burdening my heart,
That Anger's anvill, and my bark bears moss.

60 *wee*] orig: bee   4 *fire,*] PW fire.

My Spirits soakt are drunke with blackish Art.   10
If any Vertue stir, it is but feeble.
Th'Earth Magnet is, my heart's the trembling needle.

My Mannah breedeth Worms: Thoughts fly blow'd are.
    My heart's the Temple of the God of Flies.
My Tongue's an Altar of forbidden Weare   15
    Fansy a foolish fire enflam'd by toys
    Perfum'de with reeching Offerings of Sins
    Whose steaming reechs delight hobgoblings.

My Lord, is there no help for this with thee?
    Must I abuse, and be abused thus?   20
There Morn, and Even Sacrifices bee:
    To cleans the Sins of Day, and Night from us.
    Christ is the Lamb: my Pray're each morn and night
    As Incense offer I up in thy Sight.

My morn, and evening Sacrifice I bring   25
    With Incense sweet upon mine Altar Christ,
With Oyle and Wine two quarters of an Hin
    With flower for a Meat Offering all well spic'dt,
    On bended knees, with hands that tempt the Skies.
    This is each day's atoning Sacrifice.   30

And thou the Sabbath settledst at the first
    And wilt continue it till last. Wherefore,
Who strike down Gospell Sabbaths are accurst.
    Two Lambs, a Meat, and Drinke offering God more
    Conferd on it than any other Day   35
    As types the Gospell Sabbaths to display.

Here is Atonement made: and Spirituall Wine
    Pourd out to God: and Sanctified Bread
From Heaven's givn us: What! shall we decline
    With God Communion, thus to be fed?   40
    This Heavenly fare will make true Grace to thrive.
    Such as deny this thing are not alive.

32 *till last*] orig: untill the last   36 *As types*] orig: To typify

I'le tend thy Sabbaths: at thine Altar feed.
  And never make thy type a nullitie.
The Ceremonies cease, but yet the Creede   45
  Contained therein, continues gospelly,
    That make my feeble Spirits will grow frim.
    Hence I in Sabbath Service love to swim.

My Vespers, and my Mattins Ile attend:
  My Sabbath Service carry on I will.   50
Atoning Efficacy God doth send
  To Sinners in this path, and grace here stills.
    Still this on me untill I glory Gain.
    And then Ile sing thy praise in better Strain.

Meditation 26. Heb. 9.13.14. How much more shall the blood of Christ, etc.

26. 4m [June] *1698*. Pub. UPT.

Unclean, Unclean: My Lord, Undone, all vile
  Yea all Defild: What shall thy Servant doe?
Unfit for thee: not fit for holy Soile,
  Nor for Communion of Saints below.
    A bag of botches, Lump of Loathsomeness: 5
    Defild by Touch, by Issue: Leproust flesh.

Thou wilt have all that enter do thy fold
  Pure, Cleane, and bright, Whiter than whitest Snow
Better refin'd than most refined Gold:
  I am not so: but fowle: What shall I doe?   10
    Shall thy Church Doors be shut, and shut out mee?
    Shall not Church fellowship my portion bee?

How can it be? Thy Churches do require
  Pure Holiness: I am all filth, alas!
Shall I defile them, tumbled thus in mire?   15

46 *gospelly,*] PW gospelly.
1 *Undone,*] PW Undone.   15 *them, tumbled*] orig: them entering, tumbled

1982

Emblem

    Or they mee cleanse before I current pass?
    If thus they do, Where is the Niter bright
    And Sope they offer mee to wash me White?

The Brisk Red heifer's Ashes, when calcin'd,
    Mixt all in running Water, is too Weake   20
To wash away my Filth: The Dooves assign'd
    Burnt, and Sin Offerings neer do the feate
    But as they Emblemize the Fountain Spring
    Thy Blood, my Lord, set ope to wash off Sin.

Oh! richest Grace! Are thy Rich Veans then tapt   25
    To ope this Holy Fountain (boundless Sea)
For Sinners here to lavor off (all sapt
    With Sin) their Sins and Sinfulness away?
    In this bright Chrystall Crimson Fountain flows
    What washeth whiter, than the Swan or Rose.   30

Oh! wash mee, Lord, in this Choice Fountain, White
    That I may enter, and not sully here
Thy Church, whose floore is pav'de with Graces bright
    And hold Church fellowship with Saints most cleare.
    My Voice all sweet, with their melodious layes   35
    Shall make sweet Musick blossom'd with thy praise.

Meditation 27. Upon Heb. 9.13.14. How much more shall the Blood of Christ etc.

4. 7m [Sept.] *1698.* Pub. UPT.

My mentall Eye, spying thy sparkling Fold
    Bedeckt, my Lord, with Glories shine alone,
That doth out do all Broideries of Gold:
    And Pavements of Rich Pearles, and Precious Stone

24 *off*] orig: away   *Upon Heb.*] PW upon Heb.   2 *shine*] orig: glittering
shine

Did double back its Beams to light my Sphere   5
Making an inward Search, for what springs there.

And in my Search I finde myselfe defild:
Issues and Leprosies all ore mee streame.
Such have not Enterance. I am beguild:
My Seate, Bed, Saddle, Spittle too's uncleane.   10
My Issue Running Leprosy doth spread:
My upper Lip is Covered: not my Head.

Hence all ore ugly, Nature Poysond stands,
Lungs all Corrupted, Skin all botch't and scabd
A Feeble Voice, a Stinking Breath out fand   15
And with a Scurfy Skale I'me all ore clagd.
Robes rent: Head bare, Lips Coverd too, I cry,
Unclean, Unclean, and from thy Camp do fly.

Woe's mee. Undone! Undone! my Leprosy!
Without a Miracle there is no Cure.   20
Worse than the Elephantick Mange I spie
My Sickness is. And must I it endure?
Dy of my Leprosy? Lord, say to't nay,
I'le Cure thee in my wonder working way.

I see thy Gracious hand indeed hath caught   25
Two Curious pritty pure Birds, types most sure
Of thy two Natures, and The one is brought
To shed its blood in running waters pure
Held in an Earthen Panchin which displays
Thy Blood and Water preacht in Gospell dayes.   30

The slain Dove's buri'de: In whose Blood (in water)
The Living Turtle, Ceder, Scarlet twine,
And Hysop dipted are (as an allator)
Sprinkling the Leper with it Seven times
That typify Christs Blood by Grace applide   35
To Sinners vile, and then they're purifide.

Sprindge Lord mee With it. Wash me also in
The Poole of Shiloam, and shave mee bare

34 *Sprinkling*] orig: And Sprinkled   38 *Shiloam,*] PW Shiloam.

With Gospells Razer. Though the Roots of Sin
    Bud up again, again shave off its hair.
    Thy Eighth dayes Bath, and Razer make more gay,   40
    Than th'Virgin Maries Purifying day.

My Tresspass, Sin, and my Burnt Sacrifices
    My Flowre and Oyle, for my meate Offering
My Lord, thou art. Whether Lambs or Doves up rise   45
    And with thy Holy Blood atonement bring,
    And put thy Blood upon my Right Eare fair
    Whose tip shall it, its Onely jewell, Ware.

And put it Gold-Ring-like on my Right Thumbe
    And on my Right Greate toe as a Rich Gem.   50
Thy Blood will not Head, Hand nor Foot benum,
    But satisfy and cleans all fault from them.
    Then put thy Holy Oyle upon the place
    Of th'Blood of my Right Eare, Thumb, Toe. Here's Grace.

Then Holiness shall Consecrate mine Eare.   55
    And sanctify my Fingers Ends, and Toes.
And in my hearing, Working, Walking here
    The Breath of Sanctifying Grace out goes.
    Perfuming all these Actions, and my life.
    Oh! Sweetest Sweet. Hence Holiness is rife.   60

Lord, Cleanse mee thus with thy Rich Bloods Sweet Shower
    My Issue stop: destroy my Leprosy.
Thy Holy Oyle upon my Head out poure
    And cloathe my heart and Life with Sanctity.
    My Head, my Hand and Foot shall strike thy praise,   65
    If thus besprinkled, and Encamp thy Wayes.

45 art. Whether] orig: art alone. Whether   51 Thy] Conj.
66 besprinkled,] PW besprinkled.

    54: th'Blood of my Right Eare. Cf. Exod. 29:20: "Then shalt thou kill the
ram, and take of his blood, and put it upon the tip of the right ear of Aaron,
and upon the tip of the right ear of his sons, and upon the thumb of their
right hand, and upon the great toe of their right foot, and sprinkle the blood
upon the altar round about."

Meditation 28. Isai. 32.2. A man shall be
for a hiding place from the Winde.

11. 10m [Dec.] 1698. Pub. UPT.

That Bowre, my Lord, which thou at first didst build
    Was pollished most gay, and every ranck
Of Creatures in't shone bright, each of them filld
    With dimpling Glory, Cield with golden planck
    Of smiling Beauty. Man then bore the Bell: 5
    Shone like a Carbuncle in Glories Shell!

How brave, and bright was I then, Lord, myselfe?
    But woe is mee! I have transgresst thy Law,
Undone, defild, Disgrac'd, destroy'd my Wealth,
    Persu'de by flaming Vengeance, as fire dry straw.   10
    All Ranks I broake, their Glory I benighted
    Their Beauty blasted, and their Bliss befrighted.

Hence Black-Blew, Purple Spots of Horrid guilt,
    Rise in my Soule. Mee Vengeance hath in Chase
To spill my blood, 'cause I her Glory spilt,   15
    And did the Creatures Glory all disgrace.
    Shall I fall by the Venger's hand, before
    I get within the Refuge Citie's doore?

Oh! give me Angells Wings to fly to thee,
    My Lord, all stumbling stones pick out of th'way.   20
Thou art my Refuge City, and shalt bee.
    Receive me in, let not th'Avenger slay.
    I do attempt to over run my Sin:
    And fly to thee, my Refuge. Let mee in.

Ive by my Sin a man, the Son of man   25
    Slain, and myselfe, Selfe Murderer, I slew.

2 most] orig: with most   14 Chase] PW Chrase

Yet on the Golden Wings of Faith which fan
    The Gospell Aire the Altars Horns I wooe,
    Renouncing all my Sins, and Vanity
    And am resolv'd before the same to dy.   30

Accept me, Lord, and give my Sailes thine Aire,
    That I may swiftly sayle unto thyselfe.
Be thou my Refuge and thy Blood my faire.
    Disgrace my Guilt, and grace me with thy Wealth.
    Be thou my Refuge City, take mee in.   35
    And I thy Praise will on Muth Labben sing.

Meditation 29. 1 Pet. 3.20. While the Ark was Building.

5.12m [Feb.] *1698.* Pub. PET.

What shall I say, my Lord? with what begin?
    Immence Profaneness Wormholes ery part.
The World is saddlebackt with Loads of Sin.
    Sin Craks the Axle tree of this greate Cart.
    Floodgates of Firy Vengeance open fly   5
    And Smoakie Clouds of Wrath darken the Skie.

The Fountains of the Deep up broken are.
    The Cataracts of heaven do boile ore
With Wallowing Seas. Thunder, and Lightenings tare
    Spouts out of Heaven, Floods out from hell do roare.   10
    To overflow, and drownd the World all drownd
    And overflown with Sin, that doth abound.

Oh! for an Ark: an Ark of Gopher Wood.
    This Flood's too stately to be rode upon

36: *Muth Labben.* The phrase occurs in the title to the ninth Psalm: "To
the chief Musician upon Muth-labben"; it may have been the opening words
of a melody to which this Psalm was to be sung (*HBD*). Taylor probably con-
sidered it the name of a musical instrument.

By other boats, which are base swilling tubs.   15
    It gulps them up as gudgeons. And they're gone.
  But thou, my Lord, dost Antitype this Arke,
    And rod'st upon these Waves that toss and barke.

Thy Humane Nature, (oh Choice Timber Rich)
    Bituminated ore within, and out   20
With Dressing of the Holy Spirits pitch
    Propitiatory Grace parg'd round about.
    This Ark will ride upon the Flood, and live
    Nor passage to a drop through Chink holes give.

This Ark will swim upon the fiery flood: 25
    All Showrs of fire the heavens rain on't will
Slide off: though Hells and Heavens Spouts out stood
    And meet upon't to crush't to Shivers, still
    It neither sinks, breaks, Fires, nor Leaky prooves,
    But lives upon them all and upward mooves.   30

All that would not be drownded must be in't
    Be Arkd in Christ, or else the Cursed rout
Of Crimson Sins their Cargoe will them sinke
    And suffocate in Hell, because without.
    Then Ark me, Lord, thus in thyselfe that I   35
    May dance upon these drownding Waves with joye.

Sweet Ark, with Concord sweetend, in thee feed
    The Calfe, and Bare, Lamb, Lion at one Crib.
Here Rattlesnake and Squerrell jar not, breed.
    The Hawk and Dove, the Leopard, and the Kid   40
    Do live in Peace, the Child, and Cockatrice.
    As if Red Sin tantarrow'd in no vice.

Take me, my Lord, into thy golden Ark.
    Then when thy flood of fire shall come, I shall
Though Hell spews streams of Flames, and th'Heavens spark   45
    Out Storms of burning Coals, swim safe ore all.
    I'le make thy Curled flames my Citterns Wire
    To toss my Songs of Praise rung on them, higher.

17 *Arke*,] PW Arke.   21 *Spirits*] orig: Ghost's

Meditation 30. Math. 12.40. As Jonah was
        three Dayes, and three nights in the
        Whales belly. So must etc.

9. 2m [Apr.] *1699*. Pub. *W*.

Prest down with sorrow, Lord, not for my Sin
        But with Saint 'Tony Cross I crossed groane.
Thus my leane Muses garden thwarts the spring
        Instead of Anthems, breatheth her ahone.
        But duty raps upon her doore for Verse.   5
        That makes her bleed a poem through her searce.

When, Lord, man was the miror of thy Works
        In happy state, adorn'd with Glory's Wealth
What heedless thing was hee? The serpent lurks
        Under an apple paring, and by stealth   10
        Destroy'd her Glory. O poor keeper hee
        Was of himselfe: lost God, and lost his Glee.

Christ, as a Turtle Dove, puts out his Wing.
        Lay all on me, I will, saith hee, Convay
Away thy fault, and answer for thy sin.   15
        Thou'st be the Stowhouse of my Grace, and lay
        It and thyselfe out in my service pure
        And I will for thy sake the storm Endure.

Jonas did type this thing, who ran away
        From God and shipt for Tarsus, fell asleep.   20
A storm lies on the Ship. The Seamen they
        Bestir their stumps, and at wits end do weep.
        Wake, Jonas, who saith Heave me over deck.
        The Storm will Cease then, all lies on my neck.

They cast him overboard out of the ship.   25
        The tempest terrible, lies thereby still.

12 *himselfe:*] PW himselfe.   21 *Ship. The*] PW Ship. the

A Mighty Whale nam'd Neptunes Dog doth skip
    At such a Boon, Whose greedy gorge can't kill
    Neither Concoct this gudgeon, but its Chest
    Became the Prophets Coffin for the best.   30

He three dayes here lies trancifi'de and prayes.
    Prooves working Physick in the Fishes Crop.
Maybe in th'Euxine, or the Issick Bay
    She puking falls and he alive out drops.
    She vomits him alive out on the Land   35
    Whence he to Ninive receives command.

A sermon he unto the Gentiles preacht,
    Yet fortie dayes, and Ninus is destroy'd.
Space granted, this Repentance doth them teach
    God pardons them, and thus they ruine 'void.   40
    Oh! Sweet Sweet Providence, rich Grace hath spic'te
    This Overture to be a type of Christ.

Jonas our Turtle Dove, I Christ intend
    Is in the ship for Tarsus under saile.
A fiery storm tempestiously doth spend   45
    The Vessill, and its hands. All Spirits faile.
    The ship will sink or Wrack upon the rocks
    Unless the tempest cease the same to box.

None can it Charm but Jonas. Christ up posts
    Is heaved overboard into the sea.   50
The Dove must die. The storm gives up its Ghost
    And Neptune's Dogg leapes at him as a Prey.
    Whose stomach is his Grave where he doth sleep,
    Three Dayes sepulchred, Jonas in the Deep.

The Grave him swallow'd down as a rich Pill   55
    Of Working Physick full of Virtue which
Doth purge Death's Constitution of its ill.
    And womble-Crops her stomach where it sticks.

---

36 *command*] orig: with command   40 *'void*] PW void   46 *All*] PW all
51 *The storm*] PW the storm

It heaves her stomach till her hasps off fly.
And out hee comes Cast up, rais'd up thereby.   60

In glorious Grace he to the Heathen goes
    Envites them to Repentance, they accept.
Oh! Happy Message squandering Curst foes.
    Grace in her glorious Charriot here rides deckt.
    Wrath's Fire is quencht. And Graces sun out shines.   65
    Death on her deathbed lies, Consumes and pines.

Here is my rich Atonement in thy Death,
    My Lord, nought is so sweet, though sweat it cost.
This turns from me Gods wrath: Thy sweet sweet breath
    Revives my heart: thy Rising up o're bosst   70
    My Soule with Hope seeing acquittance in't.
    That all my sins are kill'd, that did mee sinke.

I thanke thee, Lord. Thy death hath deadned quite
    The Dreadfull Tempest. Let thy Dovy wings
Oreshadow me, and all my Faults benight   75
    And with Celestiall Dews my soule besprindge.
    In Angells Quires I'le then my Michtams sing,
    Upon my Jonath Elem Rechokim.

Meditation 31. Joh. 15.13. Greater Love
    hath no man etc.

4. 4m [June] *1699.* Unpublished.

Its said H * * * * * * * * * * * * * * doth enjoy
    A Tree of Gold whose Root is deemd t'have birth

73 *Thy*] PW thy   74 *Let*] PW let   78 *Jonath*] PW Jonah

    78: *Jonath Elem Rechokim.* The meaning of this phrase is obscure. It is
found only once in the Bible—as heading of the fifty-sixth Psalm, where it
may indicate the modulation of the Psalm. According to the *Biour* to Men-
delssohn's Version of the Psalms, the phrase is the name of a musical instru-
ment, and this seems to be Taylor's meaning.

At Centre of the Earth whose Spirits fly
    Ore all its body blossoming on the earth.
    Leaves dance and Fruits grow on its twigs and limbs.   5
    That make a golden Smile on Spanish Kings.

Yet this rich vegitable tree of Gold
    Is but a Toade Stoole bowre compar'd to thee
My blessed Lord, whose tent of Humane mould
    Shines like Gods Paradise, Where springs the tree   10
    Of Pure, Pure Love that doth thy friends enfold
    In richer Robes than all those Leaves of gold.

Thy Love-Affection, rooted in the Soyle,
    Of Humane Nature, springing up all ore
With Sanctifying Grace, of brightest file   15
    Brings Loads of Love to sinfull man all gore.
    Here is greate Love, greaten'd by influences
    To which thy Godhead to the same dispenses.

No Spirits ever yet were founde within
    The golden Tree of Humane nature, bud,   20
Or blossom such a Love, or Lovely thing
    As this thy nature doth so greate so good.
    The Plant's set in a Soile Pure, faultless, stronge,
    Its fruite sores to the highst pitch, Good, Greate, and Longe.

There is no Sin can touch this Lovely Love.   25
    Its Holy, with a perfect Holiness.
Its grown unto the highst Degree, above
    All Stuntedness, or stately Stintedness.
    The Soile is faultless, and doth give its Strength.
    The Plant doth beare its fruite of largest length.   30

This Love in thee most pure, and perfect stands
    A Relative, and hath its object here
Which it befriends with all good things, and hands
    In holy wayes to heavenly Glory cleare.
    Oh! happy such as with it are befriended: 35
    With perfect Love, to perfect bliss they're tended.

Make me thy Friend: Befriend me with thy Love.
    Here's cloaths more rich than Silk or Cloth of gold.

I'le in the Circuite of thy Friendship moove
    So thy Warm Love enspire mine Organs would.   40
    My Garden will give sweet, and Lovely Flowers
    If thou distill thereon thy Love in Showres.

Lord, let thy Sunshine-Love my Dial grace.
    Then what a Clock it is, it will display.
The glory of the Sunshine on it's Face   45
    Will take the light and tell the time of Day.
    My Hammer then shall greet this Shine as well
    With praise * * * * * * * * * tun'de on my bell.

Meditation 32. Joh. 15.13. Greater Love hath no man than this, that a man lay down his Life for his friends.

30. 5m [July] *1699*. Unpublished.

Oh! that I could, my Lord, but chide away
    That Dulness and the Influences which
Thy All wise Providence doth brieze, display,
    Unedging of my Spirits, them down pitch,
    Although thy quick'ning Love might make them spring   5
    With its Warm Sun Shine till like birds they sing.

That Love of * * * * in thy Person dwells
    All Wonderful in Birth, in Natures shine
In Union too, o're leaping Reason's Shells
    One made of twoness Humane, and Divine   10
    Of Infinite, and Finite, (take my Word)
    Compound, and Uncompound compose a Third.

That Love I see that in thy Person dwells,
    So Great and Good, nothing too good appears

42 *distill*] orig: upon it distill   6 *till*] Conj.   *birds*] PW bird
13 *see that*] Conj.   14 *and*] Conj.

For it to give to such on whom it fell. 15
    Although it shine on mee I hang mine Eares,
    Although it smiles thy * * * doth scowle
    In some Things whence my * * * seems fowle.

* * * Love One Object * * *
    Thy Life (that Wond'rous Life) * * * is One 20
Thy people * * * the other though they snug
    In Satans Arms, in Sin and Wrath ore grown
    This Object then much * * *
    Unless thy Love from * * *

Love borrows Wisdome's Eyes and with them lookes 25
    O're Nature's Cabbinet of Jewells bright
And then attemps th'Accounts down in Gods Books
    If Credit may be made and they made right.
    But here she findes the Sums so greate, the Debt
    Exceed the Worth in Nature's Cabinet. 30

Alass! what now? shall Satans wiles out wit
    Wisdom itselfe and take away Christs eye
His portion from him, and off tare and split
    The Object of his Love and * * *
    Oh! Cursed Elf * * * the fool 35
  * * * dost thy beams of * * * Wisdome's toole.

How doth she now, my Lord, spy out the Way
    Her object and thy merit to set free?
She Comes to thee, and makes thy person pay
    Seing sufficient worth alone in thee. 40
    Hence to the Debtor goes to end the strife
    Ore payes their debts in laying down her Life.

The Better object of thy Love, Christs Love,
    Surrenders up to ruin to redeem
The Other Object of it and remove 45
    That Wrath that else would ever on it been,

16 *mee*] Conj.   25 *borrows*] Conj.
41 *Debtor*] Conj.   *strife*] PW striefe   42 *debts*] Conj.   *down her*] Conj.

Which done it did resume the Life down laid
And both its Objects from the Curse free made.

O let thy lovely streams of Love distill
   Upon myselfe and spoute their spirits pure   50
Into my Viall, and my Vessell fill
     With liveliness, from dulness me secure.
     And I will answer all this Love of thine
     When with it thou hast made me all Divine.

What wilt thou, Lord, deny mee this, that would   55
   Not once deny to lay thy Choice Life downe?
To make a Cabbinet of't more worth than gold,
     To give to thine, and buy them Glories Crowne,
     My Heart shall harbor better than   *   *   *
     If thou my dross dost but refine from mee.   60

Lord! make my Leaden Whistle metall good,
   That in thy Service it may split an haire.
If thou wilt whet it on thy Holy Rub
     Twill trim my Life of sin, and make mee fair.
     And I will sing a song of Love to thee   65
     In a Seraphick tune and full of glee.

Meditation 33. Joh. 15.13. Greater Love hath no man than this, that a man lay down his Life for his Friend.

1. 8m [Oct.] *1699.* Pub. *W.*

Walking, my Lord, within thy Paradise
   I finde a Fruite whose Beauty smites mine Eye
And Taste my Tooth that had no Core nor Vice.
     An Hony Sweet, that's never rotting, ly

55 *that*] Conj.   57 *of't*] Conj.   59 *harbor*] Conj.   61 *Whistle*] Conj.

Theanthropy   *Lobster Claws*

Under a Tree, which view'd, I knew to bee   5
    The Tree of Life whose Bulk's Theanthropie.

And looking up, I saw its boughs all bow
    With Clusters of this Fruit that it doth bring,
Nam'de Greatest LOVE. And well, For bulk, and brow,
    Thereof, of th'sap of Godhood-Manhood spring.   10
    What Love is here for kinde? What sort? How much?
    None ever, but the Tree of Life, bore such,

Who is the Object of this Love? and in
    Whose mouth doth fall the Apple of this tree?
Is't Man? A Sinner? Such a Wormhol'de thing?   15
    Oh! matchless Love, Laid out on such as Hee!
    Should Gold Wed Dung, should Stars Wooe Lobster Claws,
    It would no wonder, like this Wonder, cause.

Is sinfull Man the Object of this Love?
    What then doth it for this its Object doe,   20
That doth require a purging far above
    The whiteness, Sope and Nitre can bestow,
    (Else Justice will its Object take away
    Out of its bosome, and to hell't convay?)

Hence in it steps, to justice saith, I'll make   25
    Thee satisfaction, and my Object shine.
I'l slay my Humane Nature for thy sake
    Fild with the Worthiness of thy Divine
    Make pay therewith. The Fruite doth sacrifice
    The tree that bore't. This for its object dies.   30

An Higher round upon this golden scale
    Love cannot Climbe, than to lay down the Life
Of him that loves, for him belov'd to bale,
    Thereby to satisfy, and end all strife.

15 *Is't*] PW Is   18 *It would*] PW 'Twould[?]   20 *doe,*] orig: doe?
21 *That*] orig: It   22 *bestow,*] orig: bestow?
27 *I'l slay my Humane Nature*] orig: The Humane Nature slayeth
34 *satisfy,*] PW satisfy.

Thou lay'st, my Lord, thy Life down for thy Friend   35
And greater Love than this none can out send.

Then make me, Lord, thy Friend, I humbly pray
    Though I thereby should be deare bought by thee.
Not dearer yet than others, for the pay
    Is but the same for others as for mee.   40
    If I be in thy booke, my Life shall proove
    My Love to thee, an Offering to thy Love.

34. Meditation. Rev. 1.5. Who loved us
        and washed away our Sins in
        his Blood.

26. 9m [Nov.] *1699.* Unpublished.

Suppose this Earthy globe a Cocoe Nut
    Whose Shell most bright, and hard out challenge should
The richest Carbunckle in gold ring put
    How rich would proove the kirnell it should hold?
    But be it so, who then could breake this Shell,   5
    To pick the kirnell, walld within this Cell?

Should I, my Lord, call thee this nut, I should
    Debase thy Worth, and of thee basely stut.
Thou dost its worth as far excell as would
    Make it to thine worse than a worm eat nut.   10
    Were all the World a sparkling pearle, 't would bee
    Worse than a dot of Dung if weighd with thee.

What Elemented bit was that, thine eyes
    Before the Elements were moulded, ey'd?
And it Encabbineting Jewell wise
    Up in thy person, be'st nigh Deified?   15
    It lay as pearle in dust in this wide world,
    But thou it tookst, and in thy person firld.

To finde a Pearle in Oister Shells's not strange:
    For in such rugged bulwarks such abound.   20
But this Rich Gem in Humane Natures grange
    So bright could by none Eye but thine be found.
    Its mankind flowr'd, searst, kneaded up in Love
    To Manna in Gods moulding trough above.

This bit of Humane Flesh Divinizd in   25
    The Person of the Son of God; the Cell ˙
Of Soule, and Blood, where Love Divine doth swim
    Through veans, through Arteries, Heart flesh, and fell,
    Doth with its Circkling Arms about entwinde
    A Portion of its kindred choice, Mankinde.   30

But these defild by Sin, Justice doth stave
    Off from the bliss Love them prepar'de, untill
She's satisfide, and sentence too she gave
    That thou should feel her vengeance and her will.
    Hence Love steps in, turns by the Conduit Cock: 35
    Her Veans full payment on the Counter drop.

Now Justice satisfi'de, Loves Milke white hand
    Them takes and brings unto her Ewer of blood
Doth make Free Grace her golden Wisp, and Sand
    With which she doth therein them Wash scoure, rub   40
    And Wrince them cleane untill their Beauty shows
    More pure, and white, than Lilly, Swan, or Rose.

What love, my Lord, dost thou lay out on thine
    When to the Court of Justice cald they're judg'd.
Thou with thy Blood and Life dost pay their fine   45
    Thy Life, for theirs, thy Blood for theirs must budge.
    Their Sin, Guilt, Curse upon thyselfe dost lay:
    Thy Grace, thy Justice, Life on them Convay.

Make such a Change, my Lord, with mee, I pray.
    I'le give thee then, my Heart, and Life to th'bargen.   50
Thy golden Scepter then my Soule shall sway
    Along my Path unto thy Palace garden.

21 *this*] orig: t' finde this

Wash off my filth, with thy rich blood, and I
Will stud thy praise with thankfull melody.

Meditation 35. Joh. 15.5. Without me yee can do nothing.

3. 1m [Mar.] *1699/1700.* Unpublished.

My Blessed Lord, that Golden Linck that joyns
   My Soule, and thee, out blossoms on't this Spruice
Peart Pronown MY more spiritous than wines,
   Rooted in Rich Relation, Graces Sluce.
   This little Voice feasts mee with fatter Sweets   5
   Than all the Stars that pave the Heavens Streets.

It hands me All, my heart, and hand to thee
   And up doth lodge them in thy persons Lodge
And as a Golden bridg ore it to mee
   Thee, and thine All to me, and never dodge.   10
   In this small Ship a mutuall Intrest sayles
   From Heaven and Earth, by th'holy Spirits gales.

Thy Ware to me's so rich, should my Returns
   Be packt in sparkling Metaphors, out stilld
From Zion's garden flowers, by fire that burns   15
   Aright, of Saphire Battlements up filld
   And sent in Jasper Vialls it would bee
   A pack of guilded Non-Sense unto thee.

Such * * * * Golden Palace Walled round
   With Walls made of transparent Silver bright   20
With Towers of Diamonds and in't is found
   A Throne of Sparkling Carbuncle like light
   Wherein sits Crownd one with the Sunn. The same
   Would be but Smoak compar'd to thy bright flame.

53 *with*] orig: and with   *and I*] orig: I   8 *up*] Conj.   10 *me, and*] orig: me
run, and   16 *Battlements*] Conj.   17 *sent*] Conj.   23 *one*] Conj.

Thy Humane frame's a Curious Palace, raisd   25
   Of th'Creame of Natures top Perfection here
Where Grace sits Sovereign that ere ore blazd
    The splendent beams of precious Stones most clear.
    Whose Mace, and Scepter richer Matter shine,
    Than Berill, Amathyst or Smaregdine.   30

Here is a Living Spring of power which tapt
   All-doing influences hence do flow.
What we have done undone us hath, (sad hapt)
    That we without thee now can nothing do.
    We cannot do what do we should, (in Summ)   35
    Nor undo what undoes us, by us done.

We have our Souls undone, Can't undo this.
    We have Undone the Law, this can't undo:
We have undone the World, when did amiss,
    We can't undoe the Curse that brings in Woe.   40
    Our Undo-Doing can't undo, its true.
    Wee can't our Souls, and things undone, renew.

Without thee wee can nothing do, its sure.
    Thou saidst the same. We finde thy Saying true.
Thou canst do all things: all amiss canst cure,   45
    Undo our Undo-doing, make all new.
    Thou madst this World: dost it thy play-house keep
    Wherein the Stars themselves play Hide-and-Seek.

It is thy Green, where all thy Creatures play
    At Barly-Breake and often lose their fleece.   50
But we poore wee our Soules a wager lay
    At Nine-Mens Morrice, and at Fox and Geese.
    Let me not play myselfe away, nor Grace.
    Nor lose my Soule, My Lord, at prison base.

Reclaim thy Claim: finde me refinde; I'm thine.   55
    Without thee I can nothing do, Dispense,
Thyselfe to me, and all things thine are mine,

33 *sad*] Conj.   41 *undo*,] PW undo.   48 *play*] orig: do play
50 *fleece*] Conj.   51 *wager lay*] Conj.   57 *all*] orig: when all

I'le not account of what thou countst offence.
Give me thy Power to work, and thou shalt finde
Thy Work attended with my hand, and minde.   60

36. [Meditation.] Col. 1.18. He is the Head of the Body.

19. 3m [May] *1700*. Unpublished.

An Head, my Lord, an honourable piece;
    Nature's high tower, and wealthy Jewelry;
A box of Brains, furld up in reasons fleece:
    Casement of Senses: Reason's Chancery:
    Religions Chancell pia-mater'd ore   5
With Damask Roses that Sweet wisdom bore.

This is, my Lord, the rosie Emblem sweet,
    Blazing thyselfe out, on my mudd wall, fair,
And in thy Palace, where the rosy feet
    Of thy Deare Spouse doth thee her head thus ware.   10
    Her Head thou art: Head glory of her Knot.
    Thou art her Flower, and she thy flower pot.

The Metall Kingdoms had a Golden head,
    Yet had't no brains, or had its brains out dasht.
But Zions Kingdome fram'd hath better sped,   15
    Through which the Rayes of thy rich head are lasht.
    She wares thee Head, thou art her strong defence
    Head of Priority, and Excellence.

Hence art an head of Arguments so strong
    To argue all unto thyselfe, when bent   20
And quickly tongue ty, or pluck out the tongue
    Of all Contrary pleas or arguments.
    It makes them weake as water, for the tide
    Of Truth and Excellence rise on this Side.

23 *water,*] PW water.

Lord, let these barbed Arrows from thy bow   25
    Fly through mine Eyes, and Eares to strike my heart.
And force my Will, and Reason to thee so
    And stifle pleas made for the other part
    That so my Soule, rid of their Sophistry
    In rapid flames of Love to thee may fly.   30

My Metaphors are but dull Tacklings tag'd
    With ragged Non-Sense. Can such draw to thee
My stund affections all with Cinders clag'd,
    If thy bright beaming headship touch not mee?
    If that thy headship shines not in mine eyes,   35
    My heart will fuddled ly with wordly toyes.

Lord play thy Excellency on this pin
    To tongue ty other pleas my gadding heart
Is tooke withall. Chime my affections in
    To serve thy Sacred selfe with Sacred art.   40
    Oh! let thy Head stretch ore my heart its wing
    And then my Heart thy Headships praise shall sing.

37. Meditation. Col. 1.18. He is the Head, etc.

14.5m [July] *1700.* Pub. PET.

It grieves mee, Lord, to thinke thy famous Name
    Should not be guilded ore with my bright Love.
Yet griev'd I am to thinke thy splendid fame
    Should be bedotcht by such poore Stuff I moove,
    That thy Bright Pearle, impald in gold, My Theme,   5
    Should by my addle brains, finde a dull veane.

Thou art an Head, the richest, that e're wore
    A Crown of Glory, where the Kirnell lies
Of deepest Wisdom, boxt in Brains, that sore

32 *thee*] PW the   35 *eyes,*] PW eyes.   39 *my*] orig: all my

In highest Notions, of the richest Sise   10
　　Compar'd whereto man's Wisdom up doth rise
　　Like Childrens catching speckled Butterflies.

Thou art the Head of Causes to thy Church:
　　Its Cause of Reconciliation art,
Thou it Redeemdst, and hast gi'n hell the lurch.   15
　　Thou Sanctifiest it in Life, and Heart.
　　Thou dost it Form, Inform, Reform, and Try
　　Conform to thee, marre her Deformity.

A Glorious Heade of Choicest influence
　　More rich than Rubies, golden rivlets lie   20
Convaying Grace along these channells thence
　　To heart, hand, foot, head, tongue, to eare, and eye.
　　That man, as th'golden Tree, golde blossoms shoots.
　　And glorifieth God with golden fruites.

A Royall Head of Majesty to make   25
　　Heade of thy foes thy footstoole Stepping Stone.
Thou giv'st forth Holy Laws, and up dost take
　　The Ruling Scepter over every one.
　　The Golden Rule is ever in thy hand
　　By which thine walk unto the golden Strand.   30

Be thou my Head: and of thy Body make mee
　　Thy Influences in my Cue distill.
Guild thou my Chamber with thy Grace, and take mee
　　Under thy Rule, and rule mee by thy Will.
　　Be thou my head, and act my tongue whereby   35
　　Its tittle-tattle may thee glorify.

32 *Cue*] orig: Cew

38. Meditation. Col. 1.18. He is the Head of
    the Body, the Church, who is the
    Beginning.

22.7m [Sept.] *1700.* Unpublished.

If that my Power was answerable to
    My minde, my Lord, my little mite would rise
With something in its hand of Worth to 'stow
    And send to thee through the bright azure Skies.
      For next unto Infinity, I finde   5
      Its Love unto thyselfe of boundless kinde.

Its Love, Desire, Esteem of thee all scorn
    Confining limits, whose Dimensions stand
Immeasurable, but my Power's down born,
    Its impotency; Cannot heave a Sand   10
      Over a Straw, that all the fruites my Will
      Can e're produce can't   *   *   *   or one Sin kill.

This Wracks my heart, and low my person layes
    And rowles mee in the dust at thoughts hereon.
That thou, who dost deserve all glorious praise   15
    Should with an Empty Will, whose power is none
      Be paid, indeed; But yet, (O pardon mee)
      I want a power, not will to honour thee.

Thou Wisdom art, Wisdom's the heads Chiefe thing,
    Thou the Beginning art of Gods Creation.   20
And therefore art of Excellence the Spring
    And the Beginning of all Holy Station.
      First born from th'Dead: Sun like thy Excellence
      All Good things doth like Sunbeames forth dispense.

All Love, and Praise, all Service, Honour bright   25
    From all the Sons of men is but thy due.

9 *Immeasurable,*] PW Immeasurable.   13 *low*] orig: layes

Thou their beginning art: they and their might
    Should sing thy glory out and it forth show.
    But, oh my Shame, I have no Power nor Skill
    To do the Same, onely an Empty Will.   30

But, O my Lord, thou the Beginning art,
    Begin to draw afresh thine Image out
In Shining Colours, on my Life, and Heart
    Begin anew thy foes in mee to route.
    Begin again to breize upon my Soule   35
    Breize after brieze untill I touch the goale.

Thou the Beginning art of Order, and
    Art Head of Principalities and Power
Archont of Kings, Archangell to the Band
    Of Angells, and Archangells in their flower.
    Thou art, Lord, Principall: whose Beings run   40
    And all best things, like Sun beames from the Sun.

Be ever, Lord beginning till I end,
    At carrying on thine Intrest in my Soule.
For thy beginning will my marrd minde mende
    And make it pray Lord, take mee for thy tole.   45
    If mee as Wheate thy Tole-Dish doth once greet
    My tune's to thee Al-tashcheth Mictam Sweet.

39. Meditation. Col. 1.18. The First Born from the Dead.

10m [Dec.] *1700.* Unpublished.

Poor wither'd Crickling, My lord, am I
    Whose shrunke up Skin hidebounds my kirnell so
That Love its Vitall Sparke's so squeezd thereby
    'T must breake the prisons Walls ere it can go

41 *whose*] Conj.   42 *things, like*] orig: things hence, like

Unto thyselfe. Hence let thy warm beams just   5
Make it to grow that it may breake its husk.

Love like to hunger'll breake through stone strong Walls.
    Nay brazen Walls cannot imprison it
Up from its object, when its object calls
    In Beams attractive falling on it thick.   10
    My Chilly Love sick of the Ague lies.
    Lord touch it with thy Sun shine, make it rise.

Death shall not deaden it, while thy Sun shines.
    The keyes of Hell, and Death are at thy Side.
Thy Conquoring Powre draws ore the grave thy lines,   15
    Whose darksom Dungeon thy dead body tri'de.
    Thou hast Death's Shady Region Conquoured
    Rose, as the Sun, up First born from the Dead.

First Fruits of them that sleep to sanctify
    The Harvest all, thou art. Thou art therefore   20
The First born from the Dead in Dignity
    In kinde, Cause, Order, to dy, and rise no more,
    As those raisd up before must, whose Erection
    Rather Reduction was than Resurrection.

Thy Humane Nature in the Cock-Pit dread,   25
    Like as the morning birds when day peeps, strout
Stands Crowing ore the Grave, laid Death there dead,
    And ore its Carkass neckt, doth Crow about,
    Throws down the Prison doors, comes out, and lay
    Them ope that th'Prisoners may come away.   30

But Lord strike down the iron Gate also
    Of Spirituall Death. Unprison thus my Soule.
Breath in the Realm of Life on it bestow,
    And in thy Heavenly Records me enrowle.
    And then my bird shall Crow thus roosted high   35
    Death, where's thy Sting? Grave, where's thy Victory?

7 *hunger'll*] orig: hunger will   18 *Rose*] orig: And Rose   20 *Thou*] PW thou
therefore] orig: still therefore   26 *Like as the*] orig: And like the
Like] PW like   34 *Heavenly Records*] orig: Records   36 *Victory?*] PW Victory.

The Golden Twist of Unity Divine
    Lord make the Ligaments to ty mee fast
Unto thyselfe, a Member with this twine
    Binde me to thee, For this will ever last.   40
    My Tunes shall rap thy prayses then good Store
    In Death upon the Resurrection Doore.

40. Meditation. Col. 1.18. That in all things
        he might have the Preheminence.

1701. Pub. ETG.

Under thy Rod, my God, thy smarting Rod,
    That hath off broke my James, that Primrose, Why?
Is't for my sin? Or Triall? Dost thou nod
    At me, to teach mee? or mee sanctify?
    I needed have this hand, that broke off hath   5
    This Bud of Civill, and of Sacred Faith.

But doth my sickness want such remedies,
    As Mummy draind out of that Body spun
Out of my bowells first? Must th'Cure arise
    Out of the Coffin of a pious son?   10
    Well: so be it. I'le kiss the Rod, and shun
    To quarrell at the Stroake. Thy Will be done.

Yet let the Rose of Sharon spring up cleare,
    Out of my James his ashes unto mee,
In radient sweet and shining Beames to cheer   15
    My sorrowfull Soule, and light my way to thee.
    Let thy Preheminence which, Lord, indeed
    Ore all things is, me help in time of need.

8 *draind out*] orig: draind of out

    This poem was written upon the death of Taylor's son James, who died in the West Indies on January 30, 1701.

Thy Humane nature so divinely ti'de
    Unto thy Person all Divine's a Spring   20
So high advanc'd, that in it doth reside
    Preheminence large over ev'ry thing.
    Thy Humane flesh with its Perfections shine
    So 'bove all others Beauties in their prime.

The like ne're seen in Heaven, nor Earth so broad.   25
    Adorn'd with Graces all, grown ripe in glory.
Thy Person with all Excellency stowd
    Perfections shine is lodgd in ev'ry story.
    Here all Created, all Creating faire,
    And Increated Eminences are.   30

Here all Preheminence of Offices
    Priest, Prophet-King-Hood too, their glorys rise
Conferrd on thee, my Lord, and all their Keyes
    That open us thy shining Mysteries
    Which do enflame our hearts their heads to run   35
    Under the shining Wings of this bright Sun.

Lord lead my sight to thy Preheminence.
    Raise thou in mee right feare of thee thereby.
My Love to thee advance till it Commence
    In all Degrees of Love, a Graduate high.   40
    When thy Preheminence doth ply this pin,
    My Musick shall thy Praises sweetly bring.

41. Meditation. Heb. 5.8. He learned by the things which he suffered.

6. 5m [July] *1701.* Pub. PET.

That Wisdom bright whose vastness for extent
    Commensurates Dimension infinite
A Palace built with Saphir-Battlement
    Bepinkt with Sun, Moon, Starrs, all gold-fire bright,

Plac'de man his Pupill here, and ev'ry thing,   5
    With loads of Learning, came to tutor him.

But he (alas) did at the threashould trip
    Fell, Crackt the glass through which the Sun should shine
That darkness gross his noble Soule doth tip.
        Each twig is bow'd with loads of follies Rhime.   10
        That ev'ry thing in tutoring, is a toole
        To whip the Scholler that did play the foole.

The Case thus stands: Hence matters up arose
    More sweet than Roses, and out-shine the Sun:
That Living Wisdom put on dying Cloaths: 15
        In mortal roabs to Sorrows Schoole house run.
        The Vessell full can hold no more, doth goe
        To Schoole to learn, whose learning cannot grow.

Christ, where all Wisdom's Treasures hidden are,
    Is Schollar, Suffering's his Tutor-Master: 20
Obedience, is his Lesson, which (as fair
        As Light in th' Sun) flows from him, yea and faster.
        But how should he learn any learning more
        In whom all Learning's ever lodg'd before?

Surely it must be said, the Humane Hall,   25
    Though furnished with all Ripe Grace, yet was
Not all ore Window, that no beame at all
        Of further light could have into it pass.
        He grew in Wisdom, Wisdom grew in him
        As in's, though's Godhead other wayes did't bring.   30

Though Grace in Christ forever perfect was
    And he e're perfectly was free from Sin
His progress yet in Knowledg needs must pass
        The Passes, humane modes, admit the thing.
        Hence learnd Obedience in his Suff'ring-Schoole.   35
        Experience taught him (though a Feeble toole).

O Condescention! Shall the Heavens do
    Low Conjues to the Earth? or Sun array
Itselfe with Clouds, and to a Glow worm go
      For Light to make all o're the World light day?   40
      That thou should learn in Sorrows Schoole, in whom
      All learning is, and whence all learnings come?

Wonder, my Soule, at this great Wonder bright
    And in this frame, Lord, let my heart to thee
On Angells Wings fly, out of Earths Eyesight.   45
      Obedience learn in Sorrows Schoole of thee
      Till right Obedience me hath handed in
      Among thy Palace Songs thy praise to sing.

42. Meditation. Heb. 10.5. A Body hast thou prepared mee. σῶμα δὲ κατηρτίσω μοι

31. 6m [Aug.] *1701*. Pub. PET.

I fain would prize thee, Lord, but finde the price
    Of Earthy things to rise so high in mee
That I no pretious matter in my choice
      Can finde within my heart to offer thee.
      The price of worldly toyes is grown so deare,   5
      They pick my purse. Thy Gaine is little there.

But oh! if thou one Sparke of heavenly fire
    Wilt but drop on my hearth; its holy flame
Will burn my trash up. And refin'de desire
      Will rise to thee in th'Curlings of the same,   10
      As Pillars of Perfumeing incense rise,
      And Surges bright of Glory, 'bove the Skies.

6 *Thy*] PW thy

Oh! that my Soul was Walled round about
    With Orient Pearle fetcht out of holy Mine
And made a Castle, where thy Graces stoute   15
    Keep garison against my foes and thine.
    Then they each peeping thought sent Scout of Sin
    Would quickly take, and gibbit up therein.

But oh! the Swarms of enemies to thee
    (Bold Sawceboxes) make in these quarters spoile,   20
Make insurrection 'gainst the motions free
    Of thy good Spirit: Lord, come, scoure the Ile
    Of these and quarter here each flourishing grace.
    The Whole will then be in a Wealthy Case.

Thou for this end, a Body hadst preparde,   25
    Where Sin ne'er set a foot, nor shewd its head
But ev'ry grace was in it, and Well far'de.
    Whose fruite, Lord, let into my heart be shed.
    Then grace shall grace my Soule, my Soule shall thee
    Begrace, and shall thy gracefull Palace bee.   30

Thy Body is a Building all like mine,
    In Matter, Form, in Essence, Properties.
Yet Sin ne'er toucht it, Grace ne'er ceast in't'shine.
    It, though not Godded, next to th'Godhead lies.
    This honour have I, more than th'Angells bright.   35
    Thy Person, and my Nature do Unite.

Oh! Thanks, my Lord, accept this dusty thing:
    If I had better, thou should better have.
I blush, because I can no better bring:
    The best I do possess, I for thee save.
    Wash in thy blood, my gift till white it bee: 40
    And made acceptable to God by thee.

In humble wise I thee implore to make
    Me, what thou, and thy Father ever love.
Empt me of Sin: Fill mee with Grace: and take   45

20 *make in these quarters spoile*] orig: *these quarters spoile* changed to *these*
quarters all do spoile changed to *do all these quarters spoile*   27 *it,*] PW it.

Up while I'me here, my heart to thee above.
My Soule shall sing Thanksgiving unto thee,
If thou wilt tune it to thy praise in mee.

Meditation 43. Rom. 9.5. God blessed forever.

26. 8m [Oct.] *1701.* Pub. PET.

When, Lord, I seeke to shew thy praises, then
    Thy shining Majesty doth stund my minde,
Encramps my tongue and tongue ties fast my Pen,
    That all my doings, do not what's designd.
      My Speeche's Organs are so trancifide   5
      My words stand startld, can't thy praises stride.

Nay Speeches Bloomery can't from the Ore
    Of Reasons mine, melt words for to define
Thy Deity, nor t'deck the reechs that sore
    From Loves rich Vales, sweeter than hony rhimes.   10
      Words though the finest twine of reason, are
      Too Course a web for Deity to ware.

Words Mentall are syllabicated thoughts:
    Words Orall but thoughts Whiffld in the Winde.
Words Writ, are incky, Goose quill-slabbred draughts,   15
    Although the fairest blossoms of the minde.
      Then can such glasses cleare enough descry
      My Love to thee, or thy rich Deity?

Words are befould, Thoughts filthy fumes that smoake,
    From Smutty Huts, like Will-a-Wisps that rise   20
From Quaugmires, run ore bogs where frogs do Croake,
    Lead all astray led by them by the eyes.
      My muddy Words so dark thy Deity,
      And cloude thy Sun-Shine, and its Shining Sky.

47 *thee,*] PW thee.   8 *melt*] orig: smelt[?]

Yet spare mee, Lord, to use this hurden ware.   25
    I have no finer Stuff to use, and I
Will use it now my Creed but to declare
    And not thy Glorious Selfe to beautify.
      Thou art all-God: all Godhead then is thine
      Although the manhood there unto doth joyne.   30

Thou art all Godhead bright, although there bee
    Something beside the Godhead in thee bright.
Thou art all Infinite although in thee
    There is a nature pure, not infinite.
      Thou art Almighty, though thy Humane tent   35
      Of Humane frailty upon earth did sent.

He needs must be the Deity most High,
    To whom all properties essensiall to
The Godhead do belong Essentially
    And not to others: nor from Godhead go   40
      And thou art thus, my Lord, to Godhead joynd.
      We finde thee thus in Holy Writ definde.

Thou art Eternall; Infinite thou art;
    Omnipotent, Omniscient, Erywhere,
All Holy, Just, Good, Gracious, True, in heart,   45
    Immortal, though with mortall nature here.
      Religious worship hence belongs to thee
      From men and angells: all, of each degree.

Be thou my God, and make mee thine Elect
    To kiss thy feet, and worship give to thee: 50
Accept of mee, and make mee thee accept.
    So I'st be safe, and thou shalt served bee.
      I'le bring thee praise, buskt up in Songs perfum'de,
      When thou with grace my Soule hast sweetly tun'de.

27 *now*] orig: onely now   33 *in*] orig: there b[e] in   41 *thou*] orig: thus thou
44 *Erywhere*] orig: Ubitary   46 *here*] orig: weary[?] wary[?]
48 *all*] orig: from men and all

Meditation 44. Joh. 1.14. The word was made Flesh.

28. 10m [Dec.] *1701.* Unpublished.

The Orator from Rhetorick gardens picks
    His Spangled Flowers of sweet-breathd Eloquence
Wherewith his Oratory brisk he tricks
    Whose Spicy Charms Eare jewells do commence.
    Shall bits of Brains be candid thus for eares?   5
    My Theme claims Sugar Candid far more cleare.

Things styld Transcendent, do transcende the Stile
    Of Reason, reason's stares neere reach so high.
But Jacob's golden Ladder rounds do foile
    All reasons Strides, wrought of THEANTHROPIE.   10
    Two Natures distance-standing, infinite,
    Are Onifide, in person, and Unite.

In Essence two, in Properties each are
    Unlike, as unlike can be. One All-Might
A Mite the other; One Immortall fair.   15
    One mortall, this all Glory, that all night.
    One Infinite, One finite. So for ever:
    Yet ONED are in Person, part'd never.

The Godhead personated in Gods Son
    Assum'd the Manhood to its Person known,   20
When that the Manhoods essence first begun
    That it did never Humane person own.
    Each natures Essence e're abides the same.
    In person joynd, one person each do claim.

Oh! Dignifide Humanity indeed: 25
    Divinely person'd: almost Deifide.
Nameing one Godhead person, in our Creed,

11 *infinite,*] PW infinite.   18 *Person,*] PW Person.   25 *Oh!*] PW Oh.

The Word-made-Flesh. Here's Grace's 'maizing stride.
The vilst design, that villany e're hatcht
Hath tap't such Grace in God, that can't be matcht.　　30

Our Nature spoild: under all Curses groans
　　Is purg'd, tooke, grac'd with grace, united to
A Godhead person, Godhead-person owns
　　Its onely person. Angells, Lord its so.
　　This Union ever lasts, if not relate　　35
　　Which Cov'nant claims Christs Manhood, separate.

You Holy Angells, Morning-Stars, bright Sparks,
　　Give place: and lower your top gallants. Shew
Your top-saile Conjues to our slender barkes:
　　The highest honour to our nature's due.　　40
　　Its neerer Godhead by the Godhead made
　　Than yours in you that never from God stray'd.

Here is good anchor hold: and argument
　　To anchor here, Lord, make my Anchor stronge
And Cable, both of holy geer, out sent　　45
　　And in this anch'ring dropt and let at length.
　　My bark shall safely ride then though there fall
　　On't th'strongest tempests hell can raise of all.

Unite my Soule, Lord, to thyselfe, and stamp
　　Thy holy print on my unholy heart.　　50
I'st nimble be when thou destroyst my cramp
　　And take thy paths when thou dost take my part.
　　If thou wilt blow this Oaten Straw of mine,
　　The sweetest piped praises shall be thine.

32 *purg'd, tooke, grac'd*] orig: tooke, washt, grac'd
34 *Angells*] orig: Lord of Angells　　37 *Angells*] PW Angell
45 *out*] orig: to hold fast and out　　53 *mine,*] PW mine.

45. Meditation. Col. 2.3. In whom are hid
all the Treasures of Wisdom.

15.12m [Feb.] *1701.* Unpublished.

My head, my Lord, that ivory Cabinet
    'S a nest of Brains dust, dry, ne're yet could Ware
The Velvet locks of Vertue for its deck
    Or golden Fleece of Wisdoms virdent hair.
      The Scull without, not fring'd with Wisdom fleece.   5
      The pan within a goose pen full of geese.

There Reason's wick yarn-like ore twisted Snarles
    Chandled with Sensuall tallow out doth blaze
A smoaky flame upon its hurden harles
    That Wil-a-Wisps it into boggy wayes.   10
      Melt off this fat, my Reason make thy Candle
      And light it with thy Wisdom's flames that spangle.

Thy Person's Wisdoms Sparkling Treasury:
    Consisting of two natures: One of which
Runs parallell with blest infinity   15
    All treasures here of Wisdom ever pitch.
      Wise Counsills all, of everlasting date,
      And Wisdom them t'effect, here sits in state.

Th'other's a Locker of a Humane frame
    With richer than Corinthian Amber tills   20
And Shelves of Emralds. Here to deck the same
    All Wisdom that's Created comes, and fills.
      Created Wisdom all and all its Wealths
      Of Grace are treasur'de in these Tills and Shelfes.

Like to a Sparkling Carbuncle up Caskt   25
    Within a Globe of Chrystall glass most cleare
Fills 't all with Shine which through its sides are flasht

Col. 2.3.] PW Col. 23.
2 *dust,*] PW dust.   5 *fring'd*] orig: ruff   18 *t'effect*] orig: to effect

And makes all glorious Shine: so much more here
These treasures of thy Wisdom shine out bright
In thee. My Candle With thy Flame, Lord, Light.   30

Or as the Sun within its Azure bowre
    That guilds its Chrystall Walls with golden rayes
It from its bowl like body, light out poures
    Exiling darkness, making glorious dayes
    All Wisdom so, and Wisdoms Treasures all   35
    Are shining out in thee, their Arcinall.

Unlock thy Locker, make my faith Key here
    To back the Wards. Lord ope the Wicket gate
And from thine Emrald Shelves, and Pinchase there
    A beame of every sort of Wisdom take   40
    And set it in the Socket of my Soule
    To make all day within, and night controle.

And from these tills, and drawers take a grain
    Of evry sort of Sanctifying grace
Wherewith impregnate thou the former beame.   45
    Set in my Soule a lamp to light that place
    That so these beames let in, may generate
    Grace in my Soule, and so an Holy State.

If wisdom in the Socket of my heart
    And Grace within its Cradle rockt do shine   50
My head shall ware a frindg of Wisdoms art.
    Thy grace shall guild this pilgrim life of mine.
    Thy Wisdom's Treasure thus Conferrd on mee
    Will have my glory all Conferrd on thee.

31 *Azure*] orig: Chr[ystall?]   39 *Shelves*] PW Slelves
48 *Soule,*] PW Soule.   50 *Grace within its Cradle rockt do*] orig:
in its Cradle Grace rockt there do

46. Meditation. Col. 2.9. The Fulness of the Godhead dwelleth in him bodily.

10.3m [May] *1702.* Pub. PET.

I drown, my Lord. What though the Streame I'm in
    Rosewater bee, Or Ocean to its brinkes
Of Aqua Vitae where the Ship doth swim?
    The Surges drown the Soul, oreflowd, that sinks.
    A Sea of Liquid gold with rocks of pearle   5
    May drownd as well as Neptune's Fishy Well.

Thy Fulness, Lord, my Filberd cannot hold.
    How should an acorn bowle the Sea lade dry?
A Red rose leafe the Suns bright bulk up fold?
    Or halfe an Ants egge Canopy the Sky?   10
    The world play in a Sneale horn Hide, and Seek
    May, ere my thimble can thy fulness meete.

All fulness is in thee my Lord, and Christ.
    The fulness of all Excellence is thine.
All's palac'de in thy person, and bespic'de.   15
    All Kinds, and Quantities of't in thee shine.
    The Fulness of the Godhead in respect
    Unto the Manhood's in thy person kept.

Hence all the Properties, that Godhead hath,
    And all their Godhead Operations brave,   20
Which are the Fulness Godhead forth display'th,
    Thy person for their Temple ever have.
    All always as transcendent Stones bright, set,
    Encabin'd are in thee their Cabbinet.

Oh! what a Lord and Lordship's here my Lord?   25
    How doth thy Fulness, fill thy Hall with Shine?

Col. 2.9.] PW Col. 3.9   *The Fulness*] PW The the Fulness
5 *A Sea*] orig: Will drown A Sea
6 *Neptune's*] PW Neptune   23 *always*] PW alwaye

Some Rayes thereof my Cottage now afford
    And let these golden rayes its inside line.
    Thy Fulness all, or none at all, Will goe
    Together, and in part will never flow.   30

All, Lord, or None at all! this makes mee dread.
    All is so Good, and None at all so bad.
All puts faith to't: but none at all strikes dead.
    I'le hope for all, lest none at all makes sad.
    Hold up this hope. Lord, then this hope shall sing   35
    Thy praises sweetly, spite of feares Sad Sting.

47. Meditation. Joh. 5.26. The Son hath life in himselfe.

12. 5m [July] *1702.* Unpublished.

Noe mervaile if my mite amaized bee
    Musing upon Almighties Mighty ALL
In all its Fulness socketed in thee
    As furniture, my Lord, to grace thy Hall.
    Thy Work requires that so the Case should goe.   5
    But oh! what Grace doth hence to Sinners flow?

I strike mine oare not in the golden Sea
    Of Godhead Fulness, thine essentially.
But in the Silver Ocean make my way
    Of All Created Fulness, thine Most high.   10
    Thy Humane Glass, God wondrously did build:
    And Grace oreflowing, with All fulness Filld.

Thou dost all Fulness of all Life possess.
    Thy Life all varnisht is with virdent flowers
'Bove Sense and Reason in their brightest dress.
    Lifes best top gallant ever in thee towers.   15
    The Life of Grace that Life of Life within
    Thy knot in heavenly Sparks is flourishing.

Besides thy proper Lifes tall fulness-Wealth,
    There's Life in thee, like golden Spirits, stills,   20
To ery member of thy Mystick Selfe,
    Through secret Chases into th'vitall tills
    Or like the Light embodi'd in the Sun
    That to each living thing with life doth run.

A Well of Living Water: Tree of Life   25
    From whom Life comes to every thing alive:
Some Eate and Drink Eternall Life most rife.
    Some life have for a while by a reprive.
    Who in this well do let their bucket down
    Shall never in the lake of Lethe drown.   30

Lord, bath mee in this Well of Life. This Dew
    Of Vitall Fruite will make mee ever live.
My branch make green: my Rose ware vivid hew
    An Holy and a fragrant sent out give.
    My kirnell ripe shall rattle out thy praise   35
    And Orient blush shall on my actions blaze.

48. Meditation. Rev. 1.8. The Almighty.

13.7m [Sept.] *1702.* Unpublished.

O! What a thing is Might right mannag'd? 'Twill
    That Proverb brain, whose face doth ware this paint.
(Might ore goe's Right) for might doth Right fulfill
    Will Right revive when wrong makes Right to faint.
    Might hatches Right: Right hatches Might, they are   5
    Each Dam, and Chick, to each: a Lovely paire.

Then Might well mannag'd riseth mighty: yet
    Doth never rise up to Almightiness.
Almightiness nere's in a mortall bit.

24 *each living thing*] orig: each thing alive

But, Lord, thou dost Almightiness possess.   10
Might in it's fulness: all mights Fulness bee
Of ery Sort and Sise stow'd up in thee.

But what am I, poor Mite, all mightless thing!
    That cannot rive a rush, that I should e're
Adventure t'dress Almighty up, or bring   15
    Almightiness deckt in its mighty geere?
    Then spare my Stutting Stamring, inky Quill,
    If it its bowells on thy Power distill.

My Mite (if I such Solicisms might
    But use) would spend its mitie Strength for thee   20
Of Mightless might, of feeble stronge delight.
    Its little ALL thy Sacrifice showld bee.
    For thee't would mock at all the Might and Power
    That Earth, and Hell possess: and on thee shower.

A Fig for Foes, for Divells, Hell, and all   25
    The powres of darkness, thou now on my Side
Their Might's a little mite, Powers powerless fall.
    My Mite Almighty will not let down slide.
    I will not trust unto this Might of mine:
    Nor in my Mite distrust, while I am thine.   30

Thy Love Almighty is, to Love mee deare,
    Thy Grace Almighty mee to save: thy Truth
Almighty to depend on. Justice cleare
    Almighty t'justify, and judge. Grace shewth.
    Thy Wisdom too's Almighty all to eye,   35
    And Holiness is such to sanctify.

If thy Almightiness, and all my Mite
    United be in sacred Marriage knot,
My Mite is thine: Mine thine Almighty Might.
    Then thine Almightiness my Mite hath got.   40

12 *stow'd*] orig: stored   15 *up,*] PW up.
24 *shower*] orig: pow[er]   30 *Mite*] orig: Migh[t]   35 *eye,*] PW eye.

My Quill makes thine Almightiness a String
Of Pearls to grace the tune my Mite doth sing.

49. [Meditation.] Joh. 1.14. Full of Grace.

8. 9m [Nov.] *1702.* Pub. PET.

Gold in its Ore, must melted be, to bring
 It midwift from its mother womb: requires
To make it shine and a rich market thing,
 A fining Pot, and Test, and melting fire.
 So do I, Lord, before thy grace do shine   5
 In mee, require, thy fire may mee refine.

My Flame hath left its Coale, my fire's gone t'bed:
 Like Embers in their ashie lodgen gray.
Lord let the Influences of thy head
 Most graciously remoove this rug away.   10
 If with the Bellows of thy grace thou blow
 My ashes off, thy Coale will shine, and glow.

Thy Clay, and Mine, out of one pit are dug:
 Although with Spades of vastest differing kinde.
Thine all bright Godhead; mine of mortall Wood.   15
 Thine shod with Glory; Mine with Sin all rin'de.
 Thy Soule, and Mine made of one minerall
 And each made regent o're their Clayie Hall.

But oh! alas! mine's Wall is worm-hold, and
 My House and Household sogd with noisom Sin   20
And no reliefe can have in Creature's hand
 While thine all Sparkling Shines without, and in,
 Fild with all Grace, and Graces Fullness all
 Adorning of thy Household and thy Hall.

41 *makes thine Almightiness a String*] orig: shall thine Almightiness forth
sing 6 *may mee refine*] orig: mee to refine 9 *of thy*] orig: of kick thy
15 *of*] orig: all

But woe is mee. Unclean I am: my Slips!   25
    Lord, let a Seraphim a live Coale take
Off of thine Altar, with it touch my lips.
    And purge away my Sins for mercys sake.
    I thus do pray finding thy Cask within
    With Grace, and graces fulness fild to th'brim.   30

I empty, thou top full, of Grace! Lord, take
    A Gracious Cluster of thy glorious grace
And busk it in my bosom, Sweet to make
    It, and my life: and gracious, in thy face.
    If thou with gracious Sweetness sweeten mee   35
    My Life with Grace sweetly perfum'de shall bee.

Can I a graceless member be of thee,
    While that thy hand's a Spring of Grace? and Heart
All gracious is to give? Then influence mee
    With thy free Grace. Thou art my lovely marke.   40
    When thy rich Grace doth tune my Song, sung high
    Thy Glory then shall rise its melody.

50. Meditation. Joh. 1.14. Full of Truth.

27. 10m [Dec.] 1702. Unpublished.

The Artists Hand more gloriously bright,
    Than is the Sun itselfe, in'ts shining glory
Wrought with a stone axe made of Pearle, as light
    As light itselfe, out of a Rock all flory
    Of Precious Pearle, a Box most lively made   5
    More rich than gold Brimfull of Truth enlaid.

Which Box should forth a race of boxes send
    Teemd from its Womb such as itselfe, to run
Down from the Worlds beginning to its end.
    But, o! this box of Pearle Fell, Broke, undone.   10
10 *Broke,*] PW Broke.

Truth from it flew: It lost Smaragdine Glory:
Was filld with Falshood: Boxes teemd of Sory.

The Artist puts his glorious hand again
   Out to the Worke: His Skill out flames more **bright**
Now than before. The worke he goes to gain,   15
   He did portray in flaming Rayes of light.
      A Box of Pearle shall from this Sory, pass
      More rich than that Smaragdine Truth-Box was.

Which Box, four thousand yeares, o'r ere 'twas made,
   In golden Scutchons lay'd in inke Divine   20
Of Promises, of a Prophetick Shade,
   And in embellishments of Types that shine.
      Whose Beames in this Choice pearle-made-Box all meet
      And bedded in't their glorious Truth to keep.

But now, my Lord, thy Humane Nature, I   25
   Doe by the Rayes this Scutcheon sends out, finde
Is this Smaragdine Box where Truth doth ly
   Of Types, and Promises, that thee out lin'de.
      Their Truth they finde in thee: this makes them shine.
      Their Shine on thee makes thee appeare Divine.   30

Thou givst thy Truth to them, thus true they bee.
   They bring their Witness out for thee. Hereby
Their Truth appeares emboxt indeed in thee:
   And thou the true Messiah shin'st thereby.
      Hence Thou, and They make One another true   35
      And They, and Thou each others Glory shew.

Hence thou art full of Truth, and full dost stand,
   Of Promises, of Prophesies, and Types.
But that's not all: All truth is in thy hand,
   Thy lips drop onely Truth, give Falshood gripes.   40
      Leade through the World to glory, that ne'er ends
      By Truth's bright Hand all such as Grace befriends.

19 *o'r ere*] PW o'rere
22 *embellishments*] PW embellisments   24 *to*] orig: do
25 *Lord*] orig: Glorious Lord   28 *Promises,*] PW Promises.
31 *thus true they*] orig: this true is   40 *Truth,*] PW Truth.

O! Box of Truth! tenent my Credence in
    The mortase of thy Truth: and Thou in Mee.
These Mortases, and Tenents make so trim,   45
    That They and Thou, and I ne'er severd bee.
    Embox my Faith, Lord, in thy Truth a part
    And I'st by Faith embox thee in my heart.

51. Meditation. Eph. 1.23. Which is his body,
        the fulness of him that filleth
        all in all.

14. 12m [Feb.] *1702.* Unpublished.

My Heart, my Lord, 's a naughty thing all o're:
    Yet if renew'd, the best in mee, 't would fain
Find Words to waft thy praises in, ashore,
    Suited unto the Excellence in thee.
    But easier 't is to hide the Sun up under   5
    Th'black of my naile, than words to weald this Wonder.

Had I Corinthian Brass: nay Amber here
    Nay Ophir Gold transparently refinde.
Nay, th'heavenly Orbs all Quintessenced clear,
    To do the deed, 't would quite deceive my minde: 10
    Words all run wast, so these a nit may Weigh:
    The World in scale, ere I thy wealth display.

Then what doe I, but as the Lady Bee
    Doth tune her Musick in her mudd wall Cell:
My Humming so, no musick makes to thee: 15
    Nor can my bagpipes play thy glory well.

8 *transparently*] PW trasparently   9 *Nay, th'*] PW Nay 'th'
11 *wast,*] PW wast.   *a*] orig: too a

   43 ff.: O! Box of Truth! etc. Taylor, like Herbert, showed an interest in
joinery. Cf. Herbert's "Ungratefulness," lines 28–29, and "Confession," lines
1–6.

  Amaizd I stand to see thee all Compleate:
  Compleated by a body, thou makst neate.

Thy Church, (what though its matter of it here
  Be brightest Saints, and Angells, all Compact   20
With Spirituall Glow, with grace out shining cleare
  And brimfull full of what the World ere lackt)
  Whom thou hast filld with all her fulness, shee
  Thy fulness is, and so she filleth thee.

Oh! wondrous strange. Angells and Men here are   25
  Incorporated in one body tite.
Two kinds are gain'd into one mortase, fair.
  Me tenent in thyselfe my Lord, my Light.
  These are thy body: thou their head, we see
  Thou fillst them first, then they do fill up thee.   30

This gracious fulness thus runs to and fro
  From thee to them: from them to thee again:
Not as the tides that Ebbe, as well as flow.
  The Banks are ever Full, and so remain.
  What mystery's here. Thou canst not wanty bee.   35
  Yet wantest them, as sure as they want thee.

Necessity doth in the middle stand
  Layes hands on both: constrains the body to
The head and head unto the body's band.
  The Head, and Body both together goe.   40
  The Head Compleats the body as its such:
  The Body doth Compleate the Head, as much.

Am I a bit, Lord, of thy Body? Oh!
  Then I do claim thy Head to be mine own.
Thy Heads sweet Influence let to mee flow,   45
  That I may be thy fulness, full up grown.
  Then in thy Churches fullness thou shalt be
  Compleated in a Sense, and sung by mee.

21 *Glow*] PW Glew[?] 34 *Full,*] PW Full. 42 *as*] orig: **and**

52. Meditation. Mat. 28.18. All Power in
         Heaven, and Earth is given mee.

11. 2m [Apr.] *1703*. Unpublished.

What Power is this? What all Authoritie
     In Earth and Heaven too? What Lord is here?
And given All to thee! Here's Majisty.
     All Worldly Power hence slinks away for feare.
     Then blush, my Soule that thou dost frozen ly: 5
     Under the beams of such bright Majesty.

What flying Flakes of Rapid flames of Love
     Scal'de from my heart by those bright beams that bed
Do in thy selfe, up mount to thee above
     Oretoping golden mountains with their head.   10
     But Why, my heart? O! why so drossy now;
     When such Authority doth to thee bow?

One Sprig of this Authority doth beare
     The Tree of Life, that spreads ore heaven quite
And Sinners sprinkles with its Sap t'make faire.   15
     And with its juyce doth quench Gods wrath out right.
     With God it maketh Reconciliation
     By offering, and Holy Intercession.

Within whose Shade my sin scorcht Soule doth bathe
     In Gods bright Sun shine, smiling heart-sweet beams.   20
Whose Rosie sents reviv'de my Spirits have.
     Whose Spirits wash away my guilt and Stains.
     Amongst whose leaves my heart doth shroude its head
     And in whose buds my grounded hopes do bed.

O that I could once frown away my sloath: 25
     And dart my dulness through with glouts that stroy!
That mine Affections, (O! their sluggish growth)

15 *Sap t'make*] orig: juice on

Might with Seraphick Wings, Lord, swiftly fly,
    Unto thine Altar for an Holy Cure
Produced by a Coale thence took most pure.   30

When this is gain'd, a Golden Trumpet I,
    All full of Grace shall be, wherein, in rayse
Of thy bright Priesthoods sweet Authority
    My spirit trumpet shall, tun'd to thy praise
    Till when let this unskilfull ditty still   35
    Tunes in thine Eares, pipd through my sorry quill.

53. Meditation. Mat. 28.18. All Power is
            given me in Heaven, and in earth.

13th. 4m [June] *1703.* Unpublished.

Were not my fancy stagnate, and the Lake
    Of mine affections frozen ore with ice
And Spirits Crampt, or else Catochizate
    The sweet breath'd smells the briezes of the Spice
    My Theme doth vent, would raise such waves upon   5
    The Sea of Eloquence, they'd skip thereon.

Shall I be lumpish when such lightsom showers
    Of livning influences still on mee?
Shall I be lowring, when such lovely flowers
    Spring smiling up, and Court mee too for thee?   10
    When such heart liv'ning glances breake and fly
    Out through the Sides of thy Authority?

Oh! that this, Thine Authority was made
    A Golden Anvill: and my Contemplation
A Smiting Hammer: and my heart was laid   15
    Thereon, and hammerd up for emendation.

34 *My*] orig: The   3-4 *or else Catochizate / The sweet breath'd smells*]
written in margin of PW with sign to insert after *Crampt*
4 *breath'd*] Conj.

And anvilld stoutly to a better frame
To entertain thy rayes that round the same.

Thou hast the golden key, that doth unlock,
    The heart of God: Wisdoms bright Counsills Tower   20
All Power Prophetick This the boundless Stock
    Of Gods Designs displayes in Gospell Shower.
    These gleames may liven our dead Spirits then,
    File bright our rusty brains, and sharpen them.

Thou nothing but the Will of God declarst.   25
    And nothing less: For thine Authority
Should be abusd; if not improov'd, or spar'd.
    If't more or less than Gods good Will descry.
    This cannot be abusd: We therefore must
    The Lesson learn then setst, and therein trust.   30

But here is still another gleame out breakes,
    All Royall Power in heaven, and earth do lodge
In thee, my Lord, this thou wilt not out leake
    Nor smoother up: it will not hast nor dodge.
    A right to mannage all things: therefore thou   35
    Wilt thine secure, and make thy foes down bow.

Thou Law deliverst: Thine Authority
    Cannot be idle; nor exceed the right.
Hence such as will not with thy rule Comply,
    Thou with thy iron Scepter down wilt smite.   40
    This Power will raise the dead, and judge all too.
    His own will Crown with Life. To hell foes throw.

Lord let thy Doctrine melt my Soule anew:
    And let thy Scepter drill my heart in mee:
And let thy Spirits Cotters pierce it through   45
    Like golden rivits, Clencht, mee hold to thee.
    Then thou and I shall ne'er be separate.
    Thy Praise shall be my Glory sung in state.

22 *Designs displayes*] orig: Designs do displayes   *Shower*] PW Showers[?]
36 *secure,*] PW secure.   41 *dead,*] PW dead.

54. Meditation. Matt. 28.18. All Power is given mee In Heaven, and in earth.

22th. 6m [Aug.] *1703*. Unpublished.

Untun'de, my Lord. My Cankard brassy wire
   'S unfit to harp thee Musick. Angells pipes
Are squeaking things: soon out of breath. Desires
   Exceed them; yet screwd highst up are but mites
   To meddle with the Musicking thy glory.   5
   What then's my jews trump meet to tune thy Story?

File off the rust: forgive my Sin, and make
   My Heart thy Harp: and mine Affections brac'de
With gracious Grace thy Golden Strings to shake
   With Quavers of thy glory well begrac'de.   10
   Though small's my mite, its dusty Wings e're will
   Sprindg out thy fame tun'de by thy Spirits Skill.

Three Shining Suns rise in the Chrystall Skies
   Of Mankinde Orbs, and Orbs Angelicall.
Whose Rayes out Shine all pimping Stars that rise   15
   Within these Spheres and Circuite through them all.
   These do evigorate all Action done
   By men and angells right, wherein they run.

The Shine of these three Suns is all the Same,
   Yet sparkling differently according to   20
The Matter form'd therewith, and beares the Name
   Authority, and by the Same doth goe,
   Into a trine of Offices. Hence springs
   Good warrant, for just Prophets, Priests and Kings.

These three are brightest Suns, held in the Skies   25
   Or shining Orb of Man, or Angell kinde.

1 *Cankard*] orig: rusty   7 *off*] PW of   *Sin,*] PW Sin.   11 *mite,*] PW mite.
14 *Orbs,*] PW Orbs.   21 *therewith,*] PW therewith.   22 *Authority,*] PW
Authority.   *goe,*] PW goe.   23 *Offices*] PW Offices

  17: *evigorate*. For envigorate.

And all attain unto a Sovereign Sise
    Of Shine, that hitherto ascend, we finde.
      The brightest brightness, and the mighti'st Might
      Is lodg'd in each one of these Balls of Light.   30

He that hath any one of these, doth weare
    A Supreme Shine. But all these three Suns came
To no man; but alone unto thy Share,
    My Lord, they fall. Thou hast the Sovereign name.
      And all the glorious Sunshine of these three   35
      Bright Suns, shines bright and powerfull out in thee.

Here's three fold glory, Prophet's, Priest's and King's
    Trible Authority bestud thy Crown.
As Mediatour all that Pow're within
    The Heaven, and Earth is thine. O bright Renown.   40
      To view those glories in thy Crown that vapor,
      Would make bright Angells eyes to run a-water.

O! plant mee in thy Priestly Sunshine, I
    Shall then be reconcild to God. In mee
A beame of thy Propheticke Sun imploy.
      'Twill fill my Spirits Eye with light to see.   45
      Make in my heart thy Kingly Sunshine flame.
      'Twill burn my Sin up, sanctify my frame.

My Gracious-Glorious Lord, shall I be thine?
    Wilt thou be mine? Then happy, happy mee!   50
I shall then cloath'd be with the Sun, and shine,
    Crown'd with tweelve Starrs, Moon under foot too see.
      Lord, so be it. My rusty Wires then shall
      Bee fined gold, to tune thee praise with all.

33 *no man*] PW noman   There is no Meditation 55 in PW

37: Prophet's, Priest's and King's. Cf. The Westminster Shorter Catechism: "Christ, as our Redeemer, executeth the offices of a Prophet, of a Priest, and of a King, both in his estate of humiliation and exaltation." As quoted in Philip Schaff, *The Creeds of Christendom* (3 vols. New York, Harper, 1877), 3, 680–81.

56. Meditation. Joh. 15.24. Had I not done amongst
    them the works, that none other man hath
    done, etc.

10. 8m [Oct.] *1703.* Pub. *W.*

Should I with silver tooles delve through the Hill
    Of Cordilera for rich thoughts, that I
My Lord, might weave with an angelick skill
    A Damask Web of Velvet Verse thereby
      To deck thy Works up, all my Web would run   5
      To rags, and jags: so snicksnarld to the thrum.

Thine are so rich: Within, Without. Refin'd.
    No workes like thine. No Fruits so sweete that grow
On th'trees of righteousness, of Angell kinde
    And Saints, whose limbs reev'd with them bow down low.   10
      Should I search ore the Nutmeg Gardens shine
      Its fruits in flourish are but skegs to thine.

The Clove, when in its White-green'd blossoms shoots,
    Some Call the pleasentst sent the World doth show.
None Eye e're saw, nor nose e're smelt such Fruits   15
    My Lord, as thine, Thou Tree of Life in'ts blow.
      Thou Rose of Sharon, Vallies Lilly true
      Thy Fruits most sweet and Glorious ever grew.

Thou art a Tree of Perfect nature trim
    Whose golden lining is of perfect Grace   20
Perfum'de with Deity unto the brim,
    Whose fruits, of the perfection, grow, of Grace.
      Thy Buds, thy Blossoms, and thy fruits adorne
      Thyselfe, and Works, more shining than the morn.

Art, natures Ape, hath many brave things done   25
    As th'Pyramids, the Lake of Meris vast

2 *rich*] orig: Wealthiest   4 *Verse*] PW Velse   14 *show*] orig: know
20 *golden*] orig: glowing

The Pensile Orchards built in Babylon,
  Psammitich's Labyrinth. (arts Cramping task)
  Archimedes his Engins made for war.
  Romes Golden House. Titus his Theater.   30

The Clock at Strasburgh, Dresdens Table-Sight
  Regiamonts Fly of Steele about that flew.
Turrian's Wooden Sparrows in a flight.
  And th'Artificiall man Aquinas slew.
  Mark Scaliota's Lock, and Key and Chain   35
  Drawn by a Flea, in our Queen Betties reign.

Might but my pen in natures Inventory
  Its progress make, 't might make such things to jump

32 *Regiamonts*] orig: Regsamonts

29: Archimedes his Engins. Archimedes, during the siege of Syracuse by
Marcellus, postponed its fall with the military engines he invented (*Cent.
Dict.*).

30: Romes Golden House, palace built by Nero containing porticoes 2800
feet long (*Cent. Dict.*).

30: Titus his Theater, the Colosseum; it was finished by Titus Vespasianus
(40–81 A.D.) (*Cent. Dict.*).

31: Clock at Strasburgh, clock built by mathematician Conrad Dasypodius
in 1574 (*W*).

31: Dresdens Table-Sight. Possibly a reference to a collection of Chinese
porcelains belonging to Augustus II, elector of Saxony (1670–1733) (*W*).

32: Regiamonts Fly of Steele. Taylor has mentioned this fly, as well as other
marvels, elsewhere in his writings: "If Albertus Magnus could make an
Artificiall man that by artificiall Engins did walk and speak; If Regiomon-
tanus made a Wooden Eagle which when the Emperor Maximilian came to
Nuremberg flew a quarter of a mile out of the City to meet him and then
accompanied him to his lodgen and also an Iron fly which at a feast flew
out of his hand and about the room and then returned and lighted on his
hand again, surely the Angels much more can make not by a creating but by
an Artificiall hand Visible Bodies" (HG, 17). Taylor took his information
on Regiomontanus from Peter Heylyn, *Cosmographie* (London, 1657), p. 399;
he copied into CP a number of passages from this work, including a descrip-
tion of Psammitich's Labyrinth (mentioned in line 28).

34: th'Artificiall man Aquinas slew. A talking head or artificial woman
constructed by Albertus Magnus, teacher of Thomas Aquinas. Thomas
destroyed the contrivance because it disturbed him in his studies—or perhaps
because he thought it was a diabolic illusion. See Robert R. Hodges, "Edward
Taylor's 'Artificiall Man,'" *American Literature, 31* (1959), 76–77.

All which are but Inventions Vents or glory
    Wits Wantonings, and Fancies frollicks plump.   40
    Within whose maws lies buried Times, and Treasures
    Embalmed up in thick dawbd sinfull pleasures.

Nature doth better work than Art: yet thine
    Out vie both works of nature and of Art.
Natures Perfection and the perfect shine   45
    Of Grace attend thy deed in ev'ry part.
    A Thought, a Word, and Worke of thine, will kill
    Sin, Satan, and the Curse: and Law fulfill.

Thou art the Tree of Life in Paradise,
    Whose lively branches are with Clusters hung   50
Of Lovely fruits, and Flowers more sweet than spice
    Bende down to us: and doe out shine the sun,
    Delightfull unto God, doe man rejoyce
    The pleasentst fruits in all Gods Paradise.

Lord feed mine eyes then with thy Doings rare,   55
    And fat my heart with these ripe fruites thou bearst.
Adorn my Life well with thy works, make faire
    My Person with apparrell thou prepar'st.
    My Boughs shall loaded bee with fruits that spring
    Up from thy Works, while to thy praise I sing.   60

58. Meditation. Math. 2.15. Out of Egypt have I called my Son.

5. 10m [Dec.] *1703.* Unpublished.

When in Italian flourisht hand I would
    Lord, flourish up thy praise, my Quills too dry,
My Inke too thick and naught (though liquid Gold)
    That will not write, this will not run, nay I

40 *Wantonings,*] PW Wantonings.
There is no Meditation 57 in PW   4 *run,*] PW run.

My Standish finde is empty, Paper loose   5
That drains all blotches from my inkie Sluce.

What shall I then, Lord, doe? Desist thy praise?
    Thou Canst amend it. Steep my Stubborn Quill
In Zions Wine fat, mend my pen, and raise
    Thy right arms Vean, a drop of'ts blood distill   10
    Into mine inkhorn, make my paper tite
    That it mayn't blot. In Sacred Text I write.

Christen mine Eyeballs with thine Eye Salve then,
    Mine Eyes will spy how Isra'ls journying
Into, and out of Egypt's bondage Den   15
    A Glass thy vissage was imbellisht in.
    Hunger Constrains. Jacob to Egypt highs.
    Herod Constrains and Christ to Egypt flies.

God Jacob calls. Jacobs Son Joseph there
    Him brings and nourisht there, and God doth call   20
Jacobs Son Joseph, Jesus brings there, where
    He nourisht him. This spills the Dragons gall
    And broke that aching tooth that at him snapt
    In Herods jaw bone and his Chops it flapt.

God Israel calls from Egypt: up he 'pears.   25
    God calls his Son from Egypt: up he highs.
The Wilderness tries Isr'el 40 years.
    Christ 40 days in Wilderness tride lies.
    The Cockatrice's egg in Jewry hatcht
    He shuns, and Nazareth doth him inlatch.   30

But Isra'ls coming out of Egypt thus,
    Is such a Coppy that doth well Descry
Not onely Christ in person unto us.
    But Spirituall Christ, and Egypt Spiritually.
    Egyptian Bondage whence gates Israel shows   35
    The Spirituall bondage whence Christs children goe.

19 *Joseph*] orig: him   21 *Jacobs*] orig: Jose[ph]   26 *Egypt:*] PW Egypt
28 *Christ*] orig: And Christ   36 *Christs*] orig: from Christs

The Bondage State to Sin and Satan stand,
    In Peckled Black, red hellish Colours laid,
By wicked Pharao and his hellish hand
      On Egypts Bondage in the brickiln trade.   40
      God Israel Calls . . . Pharao and Egypt grin.
      God calls the Soule. Satan now greatens Sin.

God miracles doth work. Wonders out fly,
    Like flocks of birds with golden wings, and Claws.
For Israels Sake, Pharao and Egypt fry   45
      In fiery Wrath. Israel attends Gods Cause.
      So here, when once the Soule doth Gods call heare
      Satan red mad doth rage. Wonders appeare.

Isra'l Complies: runs into fire by this,
    Which Pharao's Wrath, and Egypts rage procure.   50
Now Farewell Goshen; Farewell Rameses.
      Your Pleasures and Commotions we abjure.
      So here the Soule attends Gods Call. Farewell
      Worlds Smiling Sunshine. Tole your passing bell.

Out Israel comes to Succoth, and from thence   55
    To Etham. God his banner ore them bright
Erects His Cloude and firy pillard fence
      A Fence from foes. Lanthorn makes day of night.
      Pharao, and's Peers, horse, hosts and Charet wheels
      Rise and with flaming Swords persue at heels.   60

So here, the Soul Call'd to Effect out goes
    To Succoth, to Gods tabernacles wings,
The firy flag, God, banner ore him throws
      To keep, and Conduct him ins journeyings.
      Though Hell is all in arms, persues him hard,   65
      The Cloud and Fiery Pillar doe him guard.

Isra'l thus bannerd Hiroths mouth attempt
    Whose teeth are Migdol, Baalzephon high.
And throate the red Sea, Pharao's host them pent

43 *work*] orig: hatch[?]   45 *Sake*,] PW Sake.
54 *Tole*] PW tole   65 *arms*,] PW arms.   *hard*,] PW hard.

Behinde up, they then terrifide out Cry.   70
Moses his rod divides the red Sea so
They safely pass't but Pharao't ore doth flow.

So here the Soule on goes into the jaws
    Of Worldly rage with mountains him do round.
Hells armies Chase to tare him with their paws.   75
    The red Sea of Gods wrath seems quite to drownd.
    He Cries, Christs Cross divides the Sea whereby
    He passeth safe, and it his foes doth stroy.

Isra'l sings praise, but yet finds weeping Cheere.
    Wilderness State is his and waters are   80
At Mara bitter. Yet God sheweth here
    A tree whose wood did sweetly them repare.
    So here the Soul sings praise in Christ, yet shall
    The wilderness work griefe, but Christ makes all.

Isra'l to Elim comes. Sweet joyes here findes   85
    Twelve Springs of Water Every tribe a Well,
And Seventy Palm trees fruitfull to their minde
    A type that might things past, and future tell.
    Twelve Patriarchs the wells they sprung from so,
    And Seventy Elders that from them did flow.   90

So here the Soule in Christ at twelve wells, drinks
    Of Living waters, twelve Apostles shewd
Dates bore by seventy Palms set at their brinks
    The Seventy disciples, are this food.
    The Holy Scriptures, and Christs Doctrine are   95
    Waters these Wells, and Dates these Palm trees bare.

Hence Israel goes the red Sea back to see,
    To minde him of the mercy shewn him there,

73 *jaws*] orig: burning jaws   76 *Gods wrath*] orig: Christs blood
79 *praise,*] PW praise.   84 *work*] PW works   *griefe,*] PW griefe.

81–82: *Mara . . . repare.* Marah was a fountain of bitter water in the
wilderness of Shur on the route to Sinai. The Israelites halted there several
days after their passage of the Red Sea. Unable to drink the water, they
complained of their hardships; Moses then cast a certain tree into the waters,
and they were rendered palatable (*WDB;* Exod. 15:23–26).

And thence into the Wilderness goes hee
  Of Sin, where tried, and so to Sinai where   100
  By open Covenant God Israel takes
  His onely Church: and select peoples makes.

Gives him his Laws and ordinances just.
  Erects his Worship, open fellowship
Holds with him in the same wherein he must   105
  In the desert through various Changes trip
  Some very sweet, some of a bitter hande,
  Untill they Come to keep in Canaans land.

So here indeed, the Soul in Christ doth back
  From Elim pass unto the Red Sea deare   110
Of Christ's rich blood the mercy of that track
  To take more in as he about to viere
  Thence through the Wilderness of Sin, to rise
  In Covenant on Zion mount like wise.

And here enricht with Holy Oracles   115
  And fellowship in holy worship so
Through interchanging Course, like miracles,
  The Diaperd Encheckerd works must goe
  Of Providences, Honycombs and Stings
  Till here within Celestiall Canaan sings.   120

What Wisdom's here? My Lord, what Grace? What bright
  Encheckerd Works, more rich than Rubies fair?
Doe thou my Soule with this Rich trade delight
  And bring mee thus into thy promisd aire
  Wherein my Virginalls shall play for joy   125
  Thy Praise with Zions virgins Company.

107 *sweet*,] PW sweet   *hande*,] PW hande   111 *Christ's*] PW Christ
118 *Diaperd*] orig: Diaper of

59. Meditation. 1 Cor. 10.2. Baptized in
        the Cloud.

6. 12m [Feb.] *1703.* Unpublished.

Wilt thou enoculate within mine Eye
    Thy Image bright, My Lord, that bright doth shine
Forth in the Cloudy-Firy Pillar high
    Thy Tabernacles Looking-Glass Divine?
    What glorious Rooms are then mine Eyeholes made.   5
    Thine Image on my windows Glass portrai'd?

Oh! Pillar strange, made of a Cloude, and Fire.
    Whose Stoole is Israels Camp, it sits upon.
Whose Skirts doe Canopy that Camp: Whose Spire
    Doth kiss the Heavens, leading Israel on.   10
    Sure't is Christ's Charret drawn by Angells high.
    The Humane jacket, typ'te, of's Deity.

A Sun by night, to Dayify the dark.
    A Shade by Day, Sunbeames to mollify.
The Churches Pilot out her way to mark: 15
    Her Quarter Master quarters to descry.
    Its Christ's Watch tower over his Churches Host,
    With Angells kept. Tent of the Holy Ghost.

Christs Looking Glass that on his Camp gives Shine.
    Whose backside's pitchy darkness to his foes.   20
A Wall of Fire about his Israel twines
    To burn up all that offer to oppose:
    The Mediatory Province in a Map.
    The Feather in the Tabernacle's Cap.

Christ in this Pillar, Godhead-Man'd doth rise   25
    The Churches King, to guid, support, Defend.
Her Priest to Cleanse her: in the Cloud to baptize.

6 *Image*] PW Images   7 *strange,*] PW strange.   15 *mark*] orig: pry

And Reconcile with Incense that ascends.
Her Prophet too that Lights her in her way
By Night With Lanthorn Fire. With Cloud by day.   30

Then lead me, Lord, through all this Wilderness
    By this Choice shining Pillar Cloud and Fire.
By Day, and Night I shall not then digress.
    If thou wilt lead, I shall not lag nor tire
    But as to Cana'n I am journeying   35
    I shall thy praise under this Shadow sing.

60[A]. Meditation. Joh. 6.51. I am the
                Living Bread, that came down
                from Heaven.

16. 2m [Apr.] 1704. Unpublished.

Count me not liquorish if my Soule do pine
    And long for Angells bread of Heavens wheate
Ground in thy Quorns, Searcde in the Laws Lawn fine
    And bakt in Heavens backhouse for our meate.
    Ist die of Famine, Lord, My Stomach's weak.   5
    And if I live, Manna must be my meate.

I'm sick; my sickness is mortality
    And Sin both Complicate (the worst of all).
No cure is found under the Chrystall Sky
    Save Manna, that from heaven down doth fall.   10
    My Queasy Stomach this alone doth Crave.
    Nought but a bit of manna can mee save.

This Bread came down from heaven in a Dew
    In which it bedded was, untill the Sun
Remoov'd its Cover lid: and did it shew   *Endless*   15
    Disht dayly food, while fourty years do run.

34 *lead,*] PW lead.   7 *sick;*] PW sick.   11 *this*] PW thus[?]

For Isra'ls Camp to feast upon their fill
Thy Emblem, Lord, in print by perfect Skill.

Thou in thy word as in a bed of Dewes
   Like Manna on thy Camp dost fall and light   20
Hid Manna, till the Sun Shine bright remooves
   The Rug, and doth display its beauty bright
   Like pearly Bdellium White and Cleare to set
   The Sight, and Appetite the same to get.

This is a Shining Glass, wherein thy face   25
   My Lord, as Bread of Life, is clearly seen.
The Bread of Life, and Life of lively Grace
   Of such as live upon't do flowrish Green.
   That makes their lives that on it live ascend
   In heav'nly rayes to heaven that have none end.   30

Refresh my Sight, Lord, with thy Manna's eye.
   Delight my tast with this sweet Honied Cake.
Enrich my Stomach with this Cake bread high.
   And with this Angells bread me recreate.
   Lord, make my Soule thy Manna's Golden Pot   35
   Within thine Arke: and never more forgot.

Here's food for ery day, and th'Seventh too:
   (Though't never fell upon the Seventh day
But on the first, and ery week day new)
   And now is on the Camp shour'd ery way.   40
   Yet where it is not rightly usd it turns
   To nauseous sent, and doth occasion worms.

It's first daye's Mess Disht up in Heavenly Dew.
   Lord feede mee all wayes with't: it will enable
Mee much to live up to thy praise anew.   45
   Angells delight, attending on this table.
   If on this Angell fare I'm fed, I shall
   Sing forth thy glory with bright Angells all.

18 *print*] PW prent

60[B]. Meditation. Cor. 10.4. And all drunk
the same spirituall drinke.

30.5m [July] *1704*. Pub. *W.*

Ye Angells bright, pluck from your Wings a Quill.
    Make me a pen thereof that best will write.
Lende me your fancy, and Angellick skill
      To treat this Theme, more rich than Rubies bright.
      My muddy Inke, and Cloudy fancy dark,   5
      Will dull its glory, lacking highest Art.

An Eye at Centre righter may describe
    The Worlds Circumferentiall glory vast
As in its nutshell bed it snugs fast tide,
      Than any angells pen can glory Cast   10
      Upon this Drink Drawn from the Rock, tapt by
      The Rod of God, in Horeb, typickly.

Sea water straind through Mineralls, Rocks, and Sands
    Well Clarifi'de by Sunbeams, Dulcifi'de,
Insipid, Sordid, Swill, Dishwater stands.   15
      But here's a Rock of Aqua-Vitae tride.
      When once God broacht it, out a River came
      To bath and bibble in, for Israels train.

Some Rocks have sweat. Some Pillars bled out tears.
    But here's a River in a Rock up tun'd   20
Not of Sea Water nor of Swill. Its beere.
      No Nectar like it. Yet it once Unbund
      A River down out runs through ages all.
      A Fountain opte, to wash off Sin and Fall.

19 *Pillars*] PW Pillar   22 *it once*] orig: being

   21: Its beere. Taylor's daily familiarity with beer, while he was butler at
Harvard College, did not decrease his respect for this beverage.

Christ is this Horebs Rock, the streames that slide   25
    A River is of Aqua Vitae Deare
Yet costs us nothing, gushing from his side.
    Celestiall Wine our Sinsunk souls to cheare.
    This Rock and Water, Sacramentall Cup
    Are made, Lords Supper Wine for us to sup.   30

This Rock's the Grape that Zions Vineyard bore
    Which Moses Rod did smiting pound, and press
Untill its blood, the brooke of Life, run ore.
    All Glorious Grace, and Gracious Righteousness.
    We in this brook must bath: and with faiths quill   35
    Suck Grace, and Life out of this Rock our fill.

Lord, oynt me with this Petro oyle. I'm sick.
    Make mee drinke Water of the Rock. I'm dry.
Me in this fountain wash. My filth is thick.
    I'm faint, give Aqua Vitae or I dy.   40
    If in this stream thou cleanse and Chearish mee
    My Heart thy Hallelujahs Pipe shall bee.

61. Meditation. Joh. 3.14. As Moses lift up
      the Serpent in the Wilderness
      so must the Son of man be lift up.

17. 7m [Sept.] *1704.* Unpublished.

My Mights too mean, lend your Angelick might
    Ye mighty Angells, brightly to define.
A piece of burnisht brass, formd Serpent like
    To Countermand all poison Serpentine.
    No Remedie could cure the Serpents Bite   5
    But One: to wit, The brazen Serpent's Sight.

2 *brightly*] orig: to brightly   6 *wit*] Conj.

Shall brass the bosoms poison in't Contain
    A Counter poison, better than what beds
In Creatures bosoms? Nay, But its vertue came
    Through that brass Shapt from God that healing sheds.   10
    Its Vertue rode in th'golden Coach of th'eyes
    Into the Soule, and Serpents Sting defies.

So that a Sight of the brazen Serpent hung
    Up in the Banner Standard of the Camp
Was made a Charet wherein rode and run   15
    A Healing vertue to the Serpents Cramp.
    But that's not all. Christ in this Snake shapt brass
    Raist on the Standard, Crucified was.

As in this Serpent lay the onely Cure
    Unto the fiery Serpents burning bite,   20
Not by its Physick Vertue, (that is sure)
    But by a Beam Divine of Grace's might
    Whose Vertue onely is the plaster 'plide
    Unto the Wound, by Faith in Christs blood di'de.

A Sight of th'Artificiall Serpent heales   25
    The venom wound the naturall Serpent made.
A Spirituall Sight of Christ, from Christ down steals.
    A Cure against the Hellish Serpents trade.
    Not that the Springhead of the Cure was found
    In Christs humanity with sharp thorns Crownd.   30

This Brazen Serpent is a Doctors Shop.
    On ev'ry Shelfe's a Sovereign remedy.
The Serpents Flesh the Sovereign Salve is got
    Against the Serpents bite, gaind by the eye.
    The Eyebeames agents are that forth do bring   35
    The Sovereign Counter poison, and let't in.

I by the fiery Serpent bitt be here.
    Be thou my brazen Serpent me to Cure.
My Sight, Lord, make thy golden Charet cleare
    To bring thy remedy unto my Sore.   40

9 *bosoms?*] PW bosoms,

If this thou dost I shall be heald: My wound
Shall sing thy praises: and thy glory sound.

62. Meditation. Can. 1.12. While the King
      sitteth at his table, my Spicknard
      sendeth forth the smell thereof.

18. 9m [Nov.] *1704*. Pub. *W.*

Oh! thou, my Lord, thou king of Saints, here mak'st
    A royal Banquet thine to entertain.
With rich, and royall fare, Celestiall Cates,
    And sittest at the Table rich of fame.
    Am I bid to this Feast? Sure Angells stare,   5
    Such Rugged looks, and Ragged robes I ware.

I'le surely come, Lord fit mee for this feast:
    Purge me with Palma Christi from my Sin.
With Plastrum Gratiae Dei, or at least
    Unguent Apostolorum healing bring.   10
    Give me thy Sage, and Savory: me dub
    With Golden Rod, and with Saints Johns Wort good.

Root up my Henbain, Fawnbain, Divells bit.
    My Dragons, Chokewort, Crosswort, Ragwort, vice,
And set my knot with Honysuckles, stick   15
    Rich Herb-a-Grace, and Grains of Paradise
    Angelica, yea Sharons Rose the best
    And Herba Trinitatis in my breast.

Then let thy Sweetspike sweat its liquid Dew
    Into my Crystall Viall: and there swim.   20
And as thou at thy Table in Rich Shew
    With royal Dainties, sweet discourse as King
    Dost Welcome thine. My Spiknard with its Smell
    Shall vapour out perfumed Spirits Well.

Whether I at thy Table Guest do sit,   25
    And feed my tast: or Wait, and fat mine Eye
And Eare with Sights and Sounds, Heart Raptures fit,
    My Spicknard breaths its sweet perfumes with joy.
    My heart thy Viall with this spicknard fill.
    Perfumed praise to thee then breath it will.   30

63. Meditation. Cant. 6.11. I went down
             into the Garden of Nuts, to see
             the fruits etc.

4. 12m [Feb.] *1704.* Unpublished.

Oh that I was the Bird of Paradise!
    Then in thy Nutmeg Garden, Lord, thy Bower
Celestiall Musick blossom should my voice
    Enchanted with thy gardens aire and flower.
    This Aromatick aire would so enspire   5
    My ravisht Soule to sing with angells Quire.

What is thy Church, my Lord, thy Garden which
    Doth gain the best of Soils? Such Spots indeed
Are Choicest Plots empalde with Palings rich
    And set with slips, herbs best, and best of seed.   10
    As th' Hanging Gardens rare of Babylon
    And Palace Garden of King Solomon.

But that which doth excell all gardens here
    Was Edens Garden: Adams Palace bright.
The Tree of Life, and knowledge too were there   15
    Sweet herbs and sweetest flowers all sweet Delight
    A Paradise indeed of all Perfume
    That to the Nose, the Eyes and Eares doth tune.

But all these Artificiall Gardens bright
    Enameled with bravest knots of Pincks   20

27 *fit,*] PW fit.

And flowers enspangld with black, red and White
    Compar'd with this are truely stincking sincks.
As Dunghills reech with stinking sents that dish
    Us out, so these, when balanced with this.

For Zions Paradise, Christs Garden Deare   25
    His Church, enwalld, with Heavenly Crystall fine
Hath every Bed beset with Pearle all Cleare
    And Allies Opald with Gold, and Silver Shrine.
    The shining Angells are its Centinalls
    With flaming Swords Chaunting out Madrigalls.   30

The Sparkling Plants, Sweet Spices, Herbs and Trees,
    The glorious Shews of aromatick Flowers,
The pleasing beauties soakt in sweet breath lees
    Of Christs rich garden ever upward towers.
    For Christ Sweet Showers of Grace makes on it fall.   35
    It therefore bears the bell away from all.

The Nut of evry kinde is found to grow big,
    With food, and Physick, lodgd within a tower
A Wooden Wall with Husky Coverlid,
    Or Shell flesht ore, or in an Arching bower   40
    Beech, Hazle, Wallnut, Cocho, Almond brave
    Pistick or Chestnut in its prickly Cave.

These all as meate, and med'cine, emblems choice
    Of Spirituall Food, and Physike are which sport
Up in Christs Garden. Yet the Nutmeg's Spice   45
    A leathern Coate wares, and a Macie Shirt,
    Doth far excell them all. Aromatize
    My Soule therewith, my Lord, and spirituall wise.

Oh! Sweet Sweet Paradise, Whose Spiced Spring
    Will make the lips of him asleep to tune   50

30 *Madrigalls*] PW Macridalls
35 *Christ*] PW Christs   41 *Hazle, Wallnut*] PW Hazle Wall, nut
43 *med'cine,*] PW med'cine   44 *are which sport*] orig: which do sport
48 *and*] orig: in

    36: bears the bell (see also Glossary). The phrase also occurs in Herbert's
"The Church-Porch," line 187, and "The Search," line 59.

Heart ravishing tunes, sweet Musick for our king
    In Aromatick aire of blesst perfume
    Open thy garden doore: mee entrance give
    And in thy Nut tree garden make me live.

If, Lord, thou opst, and in thy garden bring   55
    Mee, then thy little Linet sweetly Will
Upon thy Nut tree sit and sweetly sing
    Will Crack a Nut and eat the kirnell still.
    Thou wilt mine Eyes, my Nose, and Palate greet
    With Curious Flowers, Sweet Odors, Viands Sweet.   60

Thy Gardens Odorif'rous aire mee make
    Suck in, and out t'aromatize my lungs.
That I thy garden, and its Spicie State
    May breath upon with such ensweetned Songs.
    My Lungs and Breath ensweetend thus shall raise   65
    The Glory of thy garden in its praise.

64. Meditation. Can. 6.11. To see—if the
Vine Flowrisht, and the Pomegranate bud.

2. 2m [Apr.] *1705.* Pub. PET.

Oh! that my Chilly Fancy, fluttering soe,
    Was Elevated with a dram of Wine
The Grapes and Pomegranates do yield, that grow
    Upon thy Gardens Appletrees and Vines.
    It shouldst have liquour with a flavour fraight   5
    To pensil out thy Vines and Pomgranates.

But I, as dry, as is a Chip, scarce get
    A peep hole through thy garden pales at these,
Thy garden plants. How should I then ere set
    The glory out of its brave Cherry trees?   10

56 *Will*] orig: sing   1 *soe*] orig: low   6 orig: Thy Vine to
paint out and thy Pomgranates

Then make my fancy, Lord, thy pen t'unfold
   Thy Vines and Pomegranates in liquid gold.

Whence come thy garden plants? So brave? So Choice?
   They Almugs be'nt from Ophirs golden land:
But Vines and Pomegranates of Paradise   15
   Spicknard, Sweet Cane, and Cynamon plants here stand.
   What heavenly aire is breezing in this Coast?
   Here blows the Trade winde of the Holy Ghost.

Thy Pomegranates that blushy freckles ware
   Under their pleasant jackets spirituall frize,   20
And Vines, though Feeble, fine, and flowrishing are
   Not Sibmahs, but mount Zions here arise.
   Here best of Vines, and Pomegranates up hight,
   Yea Sharons Rose, and Carmels Lillies White.

These trees are reev'd with Gilliads balm each one   25
   Myrrh trees, and Lign Aloes: Frankincense,
Here planted grow; heres Saffron Cynamon
   Spicknard and Calamus with Spice Ensenc'd.
   Oh fairest garden: evry bed doth beare
   All brave blown flowers whose breath is heavenly aire.   30

Make me thy Vine and Pomegranate to be
   And in thy garden flowrish fruitfully
And in their branches bowre, there then to thee
   In sweetend breath shall come sweet melody.
   My Spirit then engrapd and pomegranat'de   35
   Shall sweetly sing thee o're thy garden gated.

65. Meditation. Can. 6.11. To see the
         Fruits of the Vally.

10.4m [June] *1705.* Pub. PET.

The Vines of Lebanon that briskly grew
   Roses of Sharon in their flowrish fair,

27 *grow;*] PW grow.   2 *Roses*] orig: The Roses

The Lillies of the Vallies Beauteous shew
    And Carmels Glorious Flowery Robes most rare
    In all their lively looks blusht brisk, appeare   5
    Dull Wan lookt things, Lord, to thy Gardens geere.

Engedi's Vineyard, that brave Camphire bower,
    The Cypress Banks and Beds of bravery
And Eshcol's Grapes that royall juyce out shower,
    And Wine of Hesbon in its flavor high   10
    With Elevating Sparks stand shrinking, blush
    To see the flowrish of thy Garden flush.

Mount Olivet with Olive Trees full green,
    The flowrishing Almonds in their smiling ray
And Sibma's vaporing Wines that frolick seem   15
    Are all unmand as tipsy, slink away
    As blushing at their manners to behold
    Thy Nut trees Gardens buds and flowers unfold.

Whose Buds not Gracious but pure Grace do shine.
    Whose blossoms are not sweet but sweetness 'brace   20
Whose Grapes are not Vine berries, but rich Wine:
    Whose Olives Oyle Springs be'n't, but Oyle of Grace.
    When pound and presst, they Cordiall juyce bleed all
    And Spirits Unction. Oh! Sweet Hony fall.

These Buds are better than blown Roses fair: 25
    These Blossoms fairer bee than Carmels hew:
These Vines beare Grapes sweeter than Raisens are.
    These Nuts are better than ere Nutmegs grew.
    Olivets Olive's but a grease pots mate
    To thy Nut Gardens Vine and Pomegranate.   30

In thy Nut Garden make my heart a Bed
    And set therein thy Spicknard, Cypress, Vine
Rose, Olive, Almonds, Pares, Plumbs White, and Red,
    Pomegranats, Spices, Frankincense divine.

---

5 *blusht*] PW blust   15 *that*] orig: and   20 *'brace*] PW brace
22 *Olives Oyle*] orig: Olives are not   24 *Spirits Unction. Oh!*] orig: Unction
of the Spirits   33 *Olive,*] PW Olive   34 *Spices*] orig: Spicknard

If thou dost stud my heart with graces thus   35
My heart shall beare thee fruits perfumed flush.

Make thou my Soule, Lord, thy mount Olivet
   And plant it with thy Olive Trees fair Green,
Adornd with Holy blossoms, thence beset
     With Heavens Olives, Happy to be seen.   40
     Thy Sacred Oyle will then make bright to shine
     My Soul its face, and all the works of mine.

Set thou therein thy Pomegranate of State
   Thy Spice Trees, Cloves and Mace, thy Cynamon.
Thy Lemons, Orenges, Nuts, Almonds, Dates,   45
     Thy Nutmeg trees and Vines of Lebanon
     With Lillies Violets Carnations rare.
     My heart thy Spice box then shall breath sweet aire.

My Vine shall then beare Raisens of the Sun,
   My Grapes will rain May Shower of Sacred Wine.   50
The Smiling Dimples on my Fruits Cheeks hung
     Will as rich jewells adde unto their Shine.
     Then plant my heart with thy rich fruit trees sweet
     And it shall beare thee Fruits stew'd in sweet reech.

66. Meditation. Joh. 15.13. Greater Love
         hath no man than this That a man
         lay down his Life for his Friends.

19. 6m [Aug.] *1705.* Unpublished.

O! what a thing is Love? who can define
   Or liniament it out? Its strange to tell.
A Sparke of Spirit empearld pill like and fine
   In't shugard pargings, crusted, and doth dwell

45 *Almonds,*] PW Almonds   *Life*] PW Live   4 *doth dwell*] orig: filld well

Within the heart, where thron'd, without Controle   5
It ruleth all the Inmates of the Soule.

It makes a poother in its Secret Sell
   Mongst the affections: oh! it swells, its paind,
Like kirnells soked untill it breaks its Shell
   Unless its object be obtained and gain'd.   10
   Like Caskd wines jumbled breake the Caske, this Sparke
   Oft swells when crusht: untill it breakes the Heart.

O! Strange Strange Love! 'Stroy Life and't selfe thereby.
   Hence lose its Object, lay down all't can moove.
For nothing rather choose indeed to dy,   15
   And nothing be, than be without its love.
   Not t'be, than be without its fanci'de bliss!
   Is this Love's nature? What a thing is this?

Love thus ascending to its highest twig,
   May sit and Cherp such ditties. Sing and dy.   20
This highest Note is but a Black-Cap's jig
   Compar'd to thine my Lord, all Heavenly.
   A greater love than such man ne'er mentain'd.
   A greater Love than such thou yet hast gain'd.

Thy Love laid down thy Life hath for thy Sheep: 25
   Thy friends by grace: thy foes by Nature's Crimes.
And yet thy Life more precious is and sweet
   More worth than all the World ten thousand times.
   And yet thy Love did give bright Wisdoms Shine
   In laying down thy precious life for thine.   30

This Love was ne'er adulterate: e're pure.
   Noe Whiffe of Fancy: But rich Wisdomes Beams,
No Huff of Hot affection men endure.
   But sweetend Chimings of Celestiall gleams
   Play'd and Display'd upon the golden Wyer   35
   That doth thy Human Cymball brave, attire.

5 heart,] PW heart.   where] PW whre
8 swells, its] orig: swells also its   11 Caskd wines] PW Caskdwines
13 'Stroy] PW Stroy   Life] PW Live   14 Object,] PW Object.

Thy Love that laid thy life all down for thine
    Did not thereby destroy itselfe at all.
It was preserved in thy Selfe Divine
    When it did make thy Humane Selfe down fall.   40
    And when thy body as the Sun up rose
    It did itselfe like flaming beames disclose.

Lord, let thy Love shine on my Soule! Mee bath
    In this Celestiall Gleame of this pure Love.
O! gain my heart and thou my Love shalt have   45
    Clime up thy golden Stares to thee above.
    And in thy upper Chamber sit and sing
    The glory of thy Love when Entred in.

67[A]. Meditation. Mal. 4.2. But unto you that
             Feare my name, shall the Sun of
             Righteousness arise.

21. 8m [Oct.] *1705.* Unpublished.

My China Ware or Amber Casket bright,
    Filld with Ambrosian Spirits soakt and Bindg'd,
Made all a Mass of Quicken'd metall right,
    Transparent Silver Bowles with flowers Enfringd
    Sent to the Temple by king Ptolemy   5
    Compard thereto are but vile Trumpery.

These Spirits, drawn by heavens Chymistry
    And Casked up, with Cask Conspire into
A Lump of Sacred Fire that actively
    About thy Sacred Selfe entwine and grow   10
    So that this Cask bindgd with these Spirits rise
    A fearer of Jehovah, holy wise.

40 *thy Humane*] orig: thyselfe

In acting of the same with Holy Skill
    And Sanctifying Sight as Shining Eyes
Some soure, and muddy Humors soon do still   15
    When that the Glass is jumbled up arise
    Or in its China ware some spot or Dimple,
    Or Amber Cask unhoopt hath Crack or Wrinkle.

The Spirits and the Vial both are sick.
    The Lump Consisting of them both so trim   20
Is out of trim, sore wounded to the quick
    Distemperd by ill Humors bred therein.
    Some poyson's in the golden Cup of wine,
    That treason works against the king Divine.

I fain would purge the poison out, and Cleare   25
    The liquor from the musty dregs therein.
The Bottle free from Crack, Dint, and bad geer,
    The China Ware from Spot or Wrinkling
    And all the Quickend Lump I fain would Cure
    Of all ill Humors, Sickness, wound, or Sore.   30

But cannot do the same, yet this I finde,
    To them that feare thy Name Lord, there doth rise
The Sun of Righteousness, (this Cheers my minde)
    With healing in his Wings Physicianwise.
    This yields reliefe. Some things in such as do   35
    The Fear is bad: in them diseases grow.

Mine argument let winde into thine heart,
    That hence I do assume seing its sure
None that do feare thee, perfect bee, each part.
    I'm one of them or none of them I'm sure.
    If one of them, my bad Distempers shall   40
    Not it disproove. I don't excell them all.

They want a Cure: and so do I: I'm not
    Pleasd with my mud: Sin doth not tickle mee.
The Wrinkles Crest, or Dints my ware hath got   45

36 *Fear is*] orig: Fear thee are   38 *assume seing*] orig: assume by pious art
39 *perfect*] orig: right perfect   41 *Distempers*] PW Distembers

My Sores and Sicknesses my Sorrows bee.
I'l strive against them till I'st strive no more.
While healing Wings abide, Ile not give o're.

The Objects of the Sun of Righteousness
    Doth with its healing wing rise Cleare upon   50
Have need of healing. I do need no less.
    Our wants for kinde are equall hereupon.
    We both are of our sickness sick. Hence shown
    We both are by the argument proovd one.

Hence this I pray, and pray no less than this.   55
    Grant, Lord, mine Eyes with acute Sight not dim,
Thy Shining Sun of Righteousness may kiss
    And broodled bee under its Healing Wing.
    My Bird like to a Nighting gaile in th'Spring
    With breast on sharpest thorn, thy praise shall sing.   60

68[A].   Meditation. Mal. 4.2. The Sun of
Righteousness, etc.

16. 10m [Dec.] *1705.* Unpublished.

Methinks I spy Almighty holding in
    His hand the Crystall Sky and Sun in't bright:
As Candle and bright Lanthorn lightening,
    The World with this bright lanthorns flaming light
    Endungeoning all Darkness underground,   5
    Making all Sunshine Day Heavenward abound.

The Spirituall World, this world doth, Lord out vie:
    Its Skie this Crystall Lanthorn doth orematch.
Its Sun, thou Art, that in'ts bright Canopy
    Outshines that Candle, Darkness doth dispatch.   10

50 *Cleare*] orig: up Cleare   55 *pray,*] PW pray.   58 *bee*] orig: up bee
59 *gaile*] orig: Gaile

Thy Crystall Globe of Glorious Sunshine furld
Light, Life and heate in't Sundayeth the World.

The World without the Sun,'s as dungeon, darke.
The Sun without its Light would Dungeon spring.
The Moon and Stars are but as Chilly Sparks   15
Of Dying fire. The Sun Cheeres ery thing.
But oh thy Light, Lightsom, delightsom falls
Upon the Soul above all Cordialls.

All Light delights. Yet Dozde wood light is cold.
Some light hath heate yet Darkness doth it **bound**   20
As Lamp and Glowworm light. The Stars do hold
A twinkling lifeless Light. The Sun is found
A Ball of Light, of Life, Warmth to natures race.
But thou'rt that Sun, that shines out Saving Grace.

Doz'de wood-light is but glimmer, with no Smoke.   25
And Candle Light's a smoaky lifeless thing.
The light lodgd in the glowworm's peticoate
Is but a Shew. Star light's nights twinkling.
Moonlight is nightish, Sun makes day: these all
Without our Visive Organs lightless fall.   30

But thou, my Lord no Dozed Wood Shine art.
No Smoky Candle Light rose from thy Wick.
Thy Light ne'er linde the glowworms velvet part.
Thy Shine makes Stars, Moons, Sunlight darkness thick.
Thou art the Sun of Heavens bright light rose in   35
The Heavenly Orbs. And Heavens blesst glories spring.

Were all the trees on earth fir'de Torches made,
And all her Grass Wax Candles set on flame
This Light could not make day, this lightsom trade
Would be a darksom Smoke when Sun shines plaine.   40
But thy Shine, Lord, darkens this Sunshine bright,
And makes the Seing Organ, and its Light.

Within the Horizontall Hemisphere
Of this Blesst Sun, Lord, let mee Mansion have.

22 *Sun is*] orig: Sunlight   34 *Stars*,] PW Stars

Make Day, thou Shining Sun, unto mee cleare   45
    Thy Sorry Servant earnestly doth crave.
    Let not the Moon ere intervene or fix
    Between me and this Sun to make Ecclipse.

O! bright, bright Day. Lord let this Sun Shine flow.
    Drive hence my Sin and Darkness greate profound   50
And up them Coffin in Earths Shade below
    In darkness gross, on th'other side the ground.
    Neer let the Soyle spew fogs to foile the Light
    Of this Sweet Aire pregnant with Sunbeams bright.

How shall my Soule (Such thoughts Enravish mee)   55
    Under the Canopy of this bright Day
Imparadisde, Lightend and Livend bee
    Bathd in this Sun Shine 'mong bright Angells play
    And with them strive in sweetest tunes expresst
    Which can thy glorious praises sing out best.   60

67[B]. Meditation. Mal. 4.2. With Healing in His Wings.

10. 12m [Feb.] *1705.* Unpublished.

Doe Fables say, the Rising Sun doth Dance
    On Easter Day for joy, thou didst ascende.
O Sun of Righteousness; tho't be a glance
    Of Falshoods Spectacles on Rome's nose end?
    And shall not I, furled in thy glorious beams,   5
    Ev'n jump for joy, Enjoying such sweet gleams?

What doth the rising Sun with its Curld Locks
    And golden wings soon make the Chilly world
Shook with an Ague Fit by night shade drops,
    Revive, grow brisk, Suns Eyebright on it hurld?   10

10 *brisk,*] PW brisk.

How should my Soule then sick of th'Scurvy spring
    When thy sweet medicating rayes come in?

Alas! Sweet Sun of Righteousness, Dost shine
    Upon such Dunghills, as I am? Methinks
My Soule sends out such putrid sents, and rhimes   15
    That with thy beams would Choke the aire with Stincks.
    And Nasty vapors ery where, whereby
    Thy rayes should venom'd be that from thee fly.

The Fiery Darts of Satan stob my heart.
    His Punyards Thrusts are deep, and venom'd too.   20
His Arrows wound my thoughts, Words, Works, each part
    They all a bleeding ly by th' Stobs, and rue.
    His Aire I breath in, poison doth my Lungs.
    Hence come Consumptions, Fevers, Head pains: Turns.

Yea, Lythargy, the Apoplectick Stroke: 25
    The Catochee, Soul Blindness, Surdity,
Ill Tongue, Mouth Ulcers, Frog, the Quinsie Throate
    The Palate Fallen, Wheezings, Pleurisy.
    Heart Ach, the Syncopee, bad stomach tricks
    Gaul Tumors, Liver grown; spleen evills Cricks.   30

The Kidny toucht, The Iliak, Colick Griefe
    The Ricats, Dropsy, Gout, the Scurvy, Sore
The Miserere Mei. O Reliefe
    I want and would, and beg it at thy doore.
    O! Sun of Righteousness Thy Beams bright, Hot   35
    Rafter a Doctors, and a Surgeons Shop.

I ope my Case to thee, my Lord: mee in
    Thy glorious Bath, of Sun Shine, Bathe, and Sweate.
So rout Ill Humors: And thy purges bring.
    Administer in Sunbeame Light, and Heate.   40

20 *deep*,] PW deep.   21 *thoughts*] PW thougts
27 orig: Ill Tongue, Mouth ulcers, the Frog, Angina Throate—canceled and
revised as here   29 *Syncopee*,] PW Syncopee.   30 *Cricks*] orig: thick
32 *Scurvy, Sore*] orig: Scurvy e're Sore

Pound some for Cordiall powders very small
    To Cure my Kidnies, Spleen, My Liver, Gaul.

And with the same refresh my Heart, and Lungs
    From Wasts, and Weakness. Free from Pleurisy
Bad Stomach, Iliak, Colick Fever, turns,   45
    From Scurvy, Dropsy, Gout, and Leprosy
    From Itch, Botch Scab. And purify my Blood
    From all Ill Humors: So make all things good.

Weave, Lord, these golden Locks into a web
    Of Spiritual Taffity; make of the same   50
A sweet perfumed Rheum-Cap for my head
    To free from Lythargy, the Turn, and Pain,
    From Waking-Sleep, Sin-Falling Mallady
    From Whimsy, Melancholy Frenzy-dy.

Thy Curled Rayes, Lord, make mine Eare Picker   55
    To Cure my Deafeness: Light, Ophthalmicks pure
To heate my Eyes and make the Sight the Quicker.
    That I may use Sins Spectacles no more.
    O still some Beams. And with the Spirits fresh
    My Palate Ulcerd Mouth, and Ill Tongue dress.   60

And ply my wounds with Pledgets dipt therein.
    And wash therewith my Scabs and Boils so sore,
And all my Stobs, and Arrow wounds come, bring
    And syrrindge with the Same. It will them Cure.
    With tents made of these Beams well tent them all.   65
    They Fistula'es and Gangrenes Conquour shall.

Lord plaster mee herewith to bring soon down
    My Swellings. Stick a Feather of thy Wing
Within my Cap to Cure my Aching Crown.
    And with these beams Heale mee of all my Sin.   70
    When with these Wings thou dost mee medicine
    I'st weare the Cure, thou th'glory of this Shine.

41 orig: Pound for Cordiall powders some rayes very small   67 soon] orig: all
72 thou] orig: then, thou

68[B]. Meditation. Mal. 4.2. Ye shall go forth
and grow as Calves of the Stall.

28. 2m [Apr.] *1706.* Unpublished.

My megre Soule, when wilt thou fleshed bee,
    With Spirituall plumpness? Serpents flesh dost eat
Which maketh leane? Thy bones stick out in thee.
    Art thou Consumptive? And Concoctst not meat?
    Art not a Chick of th'Sun of Righteousness?   5
    Do not its healing Wings thy ailes redress?

Hast not Chang'd place with Mercury? And made
    Thy robes of Broadcloath of the Golden Fleece
Of Wooly Sun beams? (O! Warm Shining trade!)
    Souls freshen sure in Cloaths of such a piece   10
    And gloriously dance on these golden Cords.
    Yet till a Cure is got, Griefe o're them Lords.

And if thou bruddled liest, (though Qualms arise)
    Under the healing wings of this bright Sun
Of Righteousness, as Chicken Chearping wise   15
    Under its Dam, the Cure is surely Done.
    Some healing Beam a Certain med'cine brings
    To all Distemper'd Souls under these wings.

This is the Heavenly Alkahest that brings
    Lean Souls t'ore thrive all Pharao's fattest Ware.   20
Grow like the Stalled Oxe, or Fattlings
    Plump, Fleshy, Fat, Slick, brisk, and rightly fair.
    A spirituall fat of Collops, gracious greate
    Shall Cloath the Whole and make it grace-Compleat.

Though th'Wicker bird Cage is of rusty Wyer: 25
    This Sunshine will imbellish it and bright.
Though th'bird in't of immortall breed, much tire

18 *Distemper'd*] PW Distemer'd

These healing wings will make it fully ripe.
My little Pipkin Soule of heavenly Clay
Shall fatted to the brim with grace grow gay.   30

My Heade, O Sun, hide in thy healing Wing.
    Thy Warmth will to my megre Soule flesh give.
My growth shall Beauty to thine Eyesight bring.
    Thy Sight shall make me plump and pleasant live,
    And all my Growth to thee shall bud with blooms   35
    Of Praises Whistling in Angelick Tunes.

69. Meditation. Cant. 2.2. The Lillie
of the Vallies.

30. 4m [June] *1706.* Pub. PET.

Dull! Dull! my Lord, as if I eaten had
    A Peck of Melancholy: or my Soule
Was lockt up by a Poppy key, black, sad:
    Or had been fuddled with an Hen bane bowle.
    Oh, Leaden temper! my Rich Thesis Would   5
    Try metall to the back, sharp, it t'unfold.

Alas! my Soule, Thy Sunburnt Skin looks dun:
    Thy Elementall jacket's Snake like pi'de.
I am Deform'd, and Uggly all become.
    Soule Sicknesses do nest in mee: and Pride.   10
    I nauseous am: and mine iniquites
    Like Crawling Worms doe worm eat on my joys.

All black though plac'de in a White lilly Grove:
    Not sweet, though in a bed of Lillies rowle,
Though in Physicians shop I dwell, a Drove   15
    Of Hellish Vermin range all ore my Soul.
    All Spirituall Maladies play rex in mee,
    Though Christ should Lilly of my Vally bee.

35 *to thee shall*] orig: shall to thee
Cant. 2.2.] For King James version the text should read Cant. 2.1.

But, Oh! the Wonder! Christ alone the Sun
  Of Righteousness, that he might do the Cure   20
The Lilly of the Vallies is become
  Whose Lillie properties do health restore.
  It's glory shews I'm filthy: yet must spring
  Up innocent, and beautifull by him.

Its Vally State and Bowing Head declare   25
  I'm Haughty but must have a Humble minde.
Its Healing Virtue shew I'm sick: yet rare
  Rich Remedies I'st in this Lilly finde.
  Yea Christ the Lilly of the Vallies shall
  Be to mee Glory, Med'cine, Sweetness, all.   30

The Lillies Beautie, and its Fragrancy
  Shews my ill-favourdness, and Nauseous Stinck:
And that I must be beautifull, fully,
  And breath a Sweetness that the aire must drink.
  This Beauty, Odour, Med'cin, Humble Case   35
  This Vallys Lilly shall my Soul begrace.

Lord, make me th'Vally where this Lilly grows.
  Then I am thine, and thou art mine indeed.
Propriety is mutuall: Glorious shows
  And Oderif'rous breath shall in me breed,   40
  Which twisted in my Tunes, thy praise shall ring
  On my Shoshannim's sweetest Well tun'de string.

33 *beautifull*,] PW beautifull. 36 *begrace*] orig: with grace

70. Meditation. Col. 2.11.12. In whom also ye
     are Circumcised with Circumcision
     made without hands, in putting off
     of the sins of the flesh by the
     Circumcision of Christ, buried with
     him in baptism: etc.

25. 6m [Aug.] *1706*. Unpublished.

I humbly Crave this Riddle to unfold
     Seing, Lord, thou madst man Compleate at first,
How comes't to pass When Natures egge, that holds
     Her Chicken brake, the bird defilde out burst?
     A Callous doth the Heart Disspiritualize   5
     Till Gilgal's Razer doth it Circumcise.

Thy first Free Covenant, Calld not for this:
     Thy Covenant of Graces Quilting kinde,
Shall it require a Seale that Cutting is?
     That fleys the Skin off, that the heart doth rinde?   10
     What is Rebellions Castle made the heart,
     Filld up with filth, to be skin'd off? O sharp.

Hath Sin encrusted thus my heart? Sad! Sad!
     And latcht my Lips? And Eares made deafe, and ditcht?
O! Lord! pare off, I pray, what ere is bad: 15
     And Circumcise my Heart, mine Eares and Lips.
     This in thy Circumcisions heart doth bed.
     The Same in baptism is bosomed.

What must Christs Circumcision pacify
     Gods Wrath? And's Blood of's Circumcision sore,   20
Bring Righteousness, Purge Sin, and Mortify
     Proude Naughtiness? And wash with Grace mee o're?
     And my Uncircumcisedness all slay?
     That I might walke in glorious Graces way?

6 *Till*] orig: Untill   19 *Circumcision*] orig: Blood   22 *mee*] orig: Wash[?]

The Infant male must lose its Foreskin first,   25
 Before Gods Spirit Workes as Pulse, therein
To sanctify it from the Sin in't nurst,
 And make't in Graces Covenant to spring.
 To shew that Christ must be cut off most Pure,
 His Covenantall blood must be mans Cure.   30

And shall this sweet kinde Covenant of Grace
 Ware on't a Seale so keen and Cutting sharp
When it its brightst Edition doth embrace?
 No, no. Baptism is a better marke.
 It's therefore Circumcision's Rightfull Heir   35
 Bearing what Circumcision in't did beare.

Hence me implant in Christ, that I may have
 His Blood to wash away the filth in mee.
And finde his Wounds that are so deep, the grave
 Wherein my Sins ly dead and buri'de bee.   40
 From which let such sweet Exhalations rise
 As shall my Soule deck with an Holy guise.

Lord bed mee in thy Circumcisions Quilt.
 My wounds bathe with New Covenantall blood.
My ears with Grace Lord syringe, scoure off guilt.   45
 My Tongue With holy tasled Languague Dub.
 And then these parts, baptisde thine Organs keep,
 To tune thy Praise, run forth on golden feet.

29 *Pure*,] PW Pure. 36 *what*] orig: in't all

 44: New Covenantall blood. Moses made circumcision the mark of the
new covenant. So Taylor, here, identifies the blood of Christ with the blood
of circumcision; for the blood of Christ was for the Puritans the sign of
what they considered the new covenant—the covenant of Grace.

71. Meditation. 1 Cor. 5.8. Let us keep
the Feast, not with old Leven.

20. 8m [Oct.] *1706.* Unpublished.

Oh! What a Cookroom's here? all Deity
   Thick blancht all ore with Properties Divine
Varnisht with grace that shineth gloriously.
   Pollisht with glorious folds of brightest Shine
   Enricht with Heavens Cookery the best   5
   The Turtle Dove, and Paschall Lamb's here drest.

Oh! Dove most innocent. O Lamb, most White.
   A spotless Male in prime. Whose blood's the Dier
That dies the Doore posts of the Soule most bright.
   Whose body all is rost at justice's fire   10
   And yet no bone is broken, though the Spit
   Whereon its rost runs speare like, thorow it.

This Choicest Cookery is made the Feast
   Where glories king doth entertain his Guests.
Where Pastie past is Godhead, filld at least   15
   With Venison, of Paschall Lamb the best.
   All spic'd and Plumb'd with Grace and disht up right
   Upon Gods Table Plate Divinely bright.

This Spirituall Fare in Ordinances, and
   The Wine bled from the Holy Grape, and Vine,   20
Thats on the Table orderd by God's hand
   The Supper of the Lord, the feast Divine
   God's Gospel Priests this to that Table beare
   Where Saints are Guests and Angells waiters are.

13 *Choicest*] PW Coicest   18 *Plate*] orig: Gods Plate

   7: *Oh! Dove most innocent.* The first-born males of men and beasts be-
longed to God, according to Hebraic law (Exod. 13:2). First-born men were
redeemed with an offering—perhaps a lamb or a pair of turtle doves.

The Wedden garment of Christs Righteousness   25
 And Holy Cloathes of Sanctity most pure,
Are their atire, their Festivall rich dress:
 Faith feeds upon the Paschall Lamb its sure
 That on God's Porslain Dish is disht for them
 And drinks the Cup studded with graces Gem.   30

Let at this Table, Lord, thy Servant sit,
 And load my trencher with thy Paschall Lamb.
My Doore posts dy with the red blood of it.
 The stroying angells weapon therewith sham
 And let my Faith on thy rost mutton feed   35
 And Drinke the Wine thy holy grape doth bleed.

Lord make my Faith feed on it heartily.
 Let holy Charity my heart Cement
Unto thy Saints: and for a Cordiall high
 Make mee partaker of thy Sacrament.   40
 When with this Paschall bread and Wine I'm brisk
 I in sweet Tunes thy sweetest praise will twist.

72. Meditation. Mar. 16.19. Sat down on the right hand of God.

15. 10m [Dec.] *1706. Unpublished.*

Enoculate into my mentall Eye
 The Visive Spirits of the Holy Ghost
My Lord, that I may see the Dignity
 Of thy bright Honour in thy heavenly Coast
 Thou art deckt with as Sunshine bright displaid   5
 That makes bright Angells in it, cast a Shade.

Enrich my Phansy with Seraphick Life,
 Enquicknd nimbly to catch the Beams

26 *pure,*] PW pure. 27 *atire,*] PW atire. 3 *the Dignity*] orig: the ***ght

Thy Honour flurs abroad: in joyous Strife
　　To make sweet Musick on such Happy Themes.   10
　　That in such Raptures, and Transports of joy,
　　To Honour kings I may my Phansy 'ploy.

At God's Right Hand! Doth God mans parts enjoy?
　　This with Infinity can never stande.
Yet so God sayes, His Son to Dignify   15
　　In manhood, said, sit at my right hand.
　　The manhood thus a brighter Honour bears
　　By Deity than Deity ere wares.

The Splendor of the matter of each Story
　　Of th'Heavenly Palace Hall all brightend cleare,   20
The Presence Chamber of the King of Glory
　　Common with thee, to Saints and Angells there.
　　They share with thee in this Celestiall Shine.
　　Although their Share is lesser far than thine.

Yet they in all this glorious Splendor bright,   25
　　So many Suns like, shining on each other,
Encreasing each's glory, fall down right
　　To kiss thy feet, whose Shine this glorie Covers.
　　Their brightest Shine, in Glory's highest Story,
　　Is t'stand before thee in thy bright-bright glory.   30

Thy Honour brightens theirs, as't on theirs falls.
　　Its Royall Honour thou inheritst, Cleare,
A Throne of Glory in bright glories Hall:
　　At Gods right Hand thou sits enthroned there.
　　The Highest Throne in brightest glory thou   35
　　Enjoyest. Saints, and Angels 'fore thee bow.

Come down, bright Angells, Now I claim my place.
　　My nature hath more Honour due, than yours:
Mine is Enthron'de at Gods Right-Hand, through Grace.
　　This Grace for mine and not for yours, endures.   40
　　Yours is not there, unless in part of mine,
　　As Species in their Genus do combine.

22 *Common*] orig: ***s Common　　24 *their*] Conj.　　41 *is*] orig: makes

Hence make my Life, Lord, keep thine Honour bright.
    And let thine Honour brighten mee by grace.
And make thy Grace in mee, thee honour right.   45
    And let not mee thy Honour ere deface.
    Grant me the Honour then to honour thee
    And on my Bells thine Honour chimed shall bee.

73. Meditation. 1 Tim. 3.16. Received into Glory.

9. *12m* [Feb.] *1706*. Unpublished.

Glory! oh Glory! Wonderfull, and more.
    How dost thou Croude with all thy Ranks most bright?
Thou never playdst such Glorious Cast, before
    Nor ever wor'st such flourishing delight.
    Thy heart doth leape for joy, to have the gain   5
    When thou Receivdst my Lord in Glories Flame.

Who can the Ranks of Glory ere relate,
    As they stand up in Honours Palace Hall?
They sparkle Flashing spangles, golden flakes
    Of burnisht shines, with lowly Conjues all   10
    To kisse thy hand, my Lord, and hande thee in
    To tend thee and attend thee, her head spring.

Glory was never glorifide so much,
    She ne're receiv'd such glory heretofore.
As that that doth Embrace her, (it is such,)   15
    As she unto my Lord, doth ope her doore.
    When he receivd was into glory's Sphere
    Glory then found her glory brightest were.

When unto Angell's Glory opens doore,
    Or unto Saints, all to be glorifi'de,   20

47 *honour*] PW hornour

She well bestows herselfe, t'enriche her Store:
    Yet blushes much to eye thy Glories tide.
  When she doth make herselfe thy Cloaths to bee,
    She's cloathd with brighter glory far by thee.

The greatest glory glory doth enjoy,   25
    Lies in her hanging upon thee Wherein
Glory that glorifies thee mightily,
    Is far more glorifide. Hence Glories spring.
    Now Graces Glory, Heavens Glory, and
    Gloryes of Saints, and Angells, guild thy hand.   30

A Glorious Palace, a Bright Crown of Glory
    A glorious train of Saints, and Angells Shine
And glorious exercise as sweetest posy,
    Do sacrifice themselves unto thy Shrine.
    They give their all to thee. And so receive   35
    Therein from thee a much more brighter Wreath.

Let some, my Lord, of thy bright Glories beams,
    Flash quickening Flames of Glory in mine eye
T'enquicken my dull Spirits, drunke with dreams
    Of Melancholy juyce that stupify.
    A Coale from thy bright Altars Glory sure   40
    Kissing my lips, my Lethargy will Cure.

If Envy ere by Sanctifying Skill
    Could gracious be, or be a Grace, I would
I could it on my Spirits Cold and Chill   45
    Well Exercise, that Love thus ever should
    Ly lockt by Melancholy's key up in my Heart.
    And hardly smile when Glories beautyes dart.

Lord make thy beams my frost bit heart to warm.
    Ride on these Rayes into my bosom's chill
And make thy Glory mine affections Charm.   50
    Thy rapid flames my Love enquicken will.
    Then I in Glories Tower thy Praise will sing
    On my Shoshanims tun'd on ev'ry String.

25 *enjoy*,] PW enjoy.   46 *ever*] orig: should ever

74. Meditation. Phi. 3.21. His Glorious
       Body. τῷ σώματι τῆς
       δόξης αυτοῦ

6. 2m [Apr.] *1707.* Unpublished.

I fain would have a rich, fine Phansy ripe
    That Curious pollishings elaborate
Should lay, Lord, on thy glorious Body bright
    The more my lumpish-heart to animate.
        But searching ore the Workhouse of my minde,   5
        I but one there; and dull and meger finde.

Hence, Lord, my Search hand thou from this dark Shop
    (Its foule, and wanteth Sweeping) up unto
Thy Glorious Body whose bright beames let drop
    Upon my heart: and Chant it with the Show.   10
        Because the Shine that from thy body flows,
        More glorious is than is the brightest Rose.

Sun Shine is to this Glory but a Smoke.
    Saints in their brightest Shines are clouds therein.
Bright Angells are like motes i'th'Sun unto't.   15
        Its Beames gild heavens bright Hall, that's sparkling.
        Of all Created Glory, that doth shine
        Thy Bodies Glory is most bright and fine.

The Beauty of Humanity Compleate,
    Where ery organ is adepted right,   20
Wherein such Spirits brisk, do act full neate
        Make Natures operations fully ripe.
        All Harmonizing in their actions done
        That ery twig's with glorious blossoms hung.

And still more sweet: thou'rt with more glory deckt.   25
    The Glory of ripe Grace of brightest kinde

6 *but*] orig: see one but
15 *i'th'*] PW ith'   19 *Compleate,*] PW Compleate.   20 *right,*] PW right.

Like lumps of living Fire, by nothing Checkt
    Thrumping the Stars, as pinking things half blinde.
    This makes thy Bodies glory Choice and fine,
    A spirituall light in Corporall Lanthorn shine.   30

Yea, still more Glory. Oh! thy Humane Frame
    Is th'brightst Temple of the Holy Ghost.
Whose Rayes run through the Whole in brightest flame.
    Hence on thy body campeth Glories Hoast.
    What more can still be said? I add but this.   35
    That Glory bright thy Bodies Tilt-Clothe is.

Oh! Glorious Body! Pull my eye lids ope:
    Make my quick Eye, Lord, thy brisk Glory greet,
Whose rapid flames when they my heart revoke
    From other Beauties, make't for thee more sweet.   40
    If such blest Sight shall twist my heart with thine,
    Thy Glory make the Web, thy Praise the Twine.

75. Meditation. Phil. 3. ult. Our Vile Bodie

τὸ σῶμα τῆς ταπεινώσεως ἡμῶν

1. 4m [June] *1707*. Pub. UPT.

Oh! Strang, my Lord. Here's reason at a set.
    Run out of 'ts Wits, construing Grace's Style.
Nay Shining Angells in an holy fret
    Confounded are, to see our Bodies Vile
    Made Cabinets of Sparkling Gems that far   5
    Out shine the brightest shining heavenly Star.

Mudd made with Muscadine int' mortar Rich,
    Dirt wrought with Aqua-Vitae for a Wall
Built all of Precious Stones laid in it, Which
    Is with leafe gold bespangled, 'maizes all.   10

41 *thine,*] PW thine.   42 *Web,*] PW Web.   2 *Wits,*] PW Wits.

Yet this Amaizment's scarce a minutes Sise
Compar'd unto the matter 'fore our eyes.

Here is a Mudwall tent, whose Matters are
    Dead Elements, which mixt make dirty trade:
Which with Life Animall are wrought up faire   15
      A Living mudwall by Gods holy Spade.
      Yet though a Wall alive all spruice, and crouce
      Its Base, and Vile. And baseness keeps its House.

Nature's Alembick 't is, Its true: that stills
    The Noblest Spirits terrene fruits possess,   20
Yet, oh! the Relicks in the Caldron will
      Proove all things else, Guts, Garbage, Rotteness.
      And all its pipes but Sincks of nasty ware
      That foule Earths face, and do defile the aire.

A varnisht pot of putrid excrements,   25
    And quickly turns to excrements itselfe,
By natures Law: but, oh! there therein tents
      A sparke immortall and no mortall elfe.
      An Angell bright here in a Swine Sty dwell!
      What Lodge of Wonders's this? What tongue can tell?   30

But, oh! how doth this Wonder still encrease?
    The Soule Creeps in't. And by it's too defil'd.
Are both made base, and vile, can have no peace
      Without, nor in: and's of its Shine beguil'd.
      And though this Spirit in it dwells yet here   35
      Its glory will not dwell with such sad geere.

Both grac'd together, and disgrac'd. Sad Case.
    What now becomes of Gods Electing Love?
This now doth raise the Miracle apace,
      Christ doth step in, and Graces Art improove.   40
      He kills the Leprosy that taints the Walls:
      And sanctifies the house before it falls.

And nature here, though mean and base beside,
    With marks and Stains of Sin, and Sin not dead,

14 *dirty*] PW dusty[?]   33 *vile,*] PW vile.

Though mortifi'de and dying, in't reside,   45
    With Graces precious Pearls its flourished.
    And in our bodies very vile and base
    Christ hath enthron'de all sanctifying Grace.

That these dark Cells, and Mudwalld Tents defild,
    With nastiness should Cabinets be made   50
For th'Choicest Pearls in Glories ring enfoild
    Out shining all the shining starry trade.
    Its glorious Wonders, wrought by Graces hand,
    Whereat bright Angells all amaized stand.

Oh! make my Body, Lord, Although its vile,   55
    Thy Warehouse where Grace doth her treasures lay.
And Cleanse the house and ery Room from Soile.
    Deck all my Rooms with thy rich Grace I pray.
    If thy free Grace doth my low tent, perfume,
    I'll sing thy Glorious praise in ery room.   60

76. Meditation. Phi. 3.21. Who shall change
        our vile body, that it may be fashioned
        like his Glorious body.

27. 5m [July] *1707.* Pub. *W.*

Will yee be neighbourly, ye Angells bright?
    Then lend mee your Admiring Facultie:
Wonders presented stand, above my might.
    That call from mee the highest Extasie.
    If you deny mee this: my pimping Soule,   5
    These Wonders pins up in an Auger hole.

If my Rush Candle on its wick ware flame,
    Of Ignis lambens. Oh! bright garb indeed:
What then, when Flakes of flaming Glory train
    From thy bright glorious bulk to 'ray my weed.   10

What my vile Body like thy Glorious, Formd?
What Wonder here? My body thus adornd!

What shall mine hempen harle wove in thy Loome
    Into a web (an hurden web indeed)
Be made its Makers Tent Cloth? I presume.   15
    Within these Curtains Grace keeps Hall, and breeds:
    But shall my hurden-hangings ever ware
    A bright bright Glory like thy body faire?

Meethinks thy smile doth make thy Footstoole so
    Spread its green Carpet 'fore thy feet for joy.   20
And Bryers climb in t'bright Rose that flows
    Out in sweet reechs to meet thee in the sky:
    And makes the sportive Starrs play Hide-and-Seek
    And on thy bodies Glory peeping keep.

And shall not I (whose form transformd shall bee   25
    To be shap'te like thy glorious body, Lord.
That Angells bright, as Gasterd, gaze at mee
    To see such Glory on my dresser board),
    Transported be hereat for very joy,
    Whose intrest lies herein, and gloriously?   30

What shall the frosty Rhime upon my locks,
    Congeale my brains with Chilly dews, whereby
My Phansie is benumbd: and put in Stocks,

21 *And Bryers climb in t'bright Rose that flows*] PW Line heavily corrected.
Last six words of line in text written in margin. An interlinear version of the
marginal words appears to read: *Climb there up in t'bright Rose that Flow.*
Original version of these words illegible. W and Bryers: climb thereup, bright
roses blow

   13: mine hempen harle. The comparison of the body to coarse cloth occurs
in Herbert's "Mans medley," lines 13–18:

      In soul he mounts and flies,
        In flesh he dies.
   He wears a stuffe whose thread is course and round,
      But trimm'd with curious lace,
        And should take place
  After the trimming, not the stuffe and ground.

And thaws not into Steams of reeching joy?
Oh! strange Ingratitude! Let not this Frame   35
Abide, Lord, in mee. Fire mee with thy flame.

Lord, let thy glorious Body send such rayes
        Into my Soule, as ravish shall my heart,
That Thoughts how thy bright Glory out shall blaze
        Upon my body, may such Rayes thee dart.   40
        My Tunes shall dance then on these Rayes and Caper
        Unto thy Praise. When Glory lights my Taper.

77. Meditation. Zech. 9.11. The Pit wherein is no water.

5. 8m [Oct.] 1707. Pub. W.

A State, a State, Oh! Dungeon State indeed.
        In which mee headlong, long agoe Sin pitcht:
As dark as Pitch, where Nastiness doth breed:
        And Filth defiles: and I am with it ditcht.
        A Sinfull State: This Pit no Water's in't.   5
        A Bugbare State: as black as any inke.

I once sat singing on the Summit high
        'Mong the Celestiall Coire in Musick Sweet
On highest bough of Paradisall joy,
        Glory and Innocence did in mee meet.   10
        I, as a Gold-Finch Nighting Gale, tun'd ore
        Melodious Songs 'fore Glorie's Palace Doore.

But on this bough I tuning Pearcht not long:
        Th'Infernall Foe shot out a Shaft from Hell,
A Fiery Dart pilde with Sins poison strong: 15
        That struck my heart, and down I headlong fell.
        And from the Highest Pinicle of Light
        Into this Lowest pit more darke than night.

15 *pilde*] Conj.

A Pit indeed of Sin: No water's here:
    Whose bottom's furthest off from Heaven bright,   20
And is next doore to Hell Gate, to it neer:
    And here I dwell in sad and solemn night,
    My Gold-Fincht Angell Feathers dapled in
    Hells Scarlet Dy fat, blood red grown with Sin.

I in this Pit all Destitute of Light   25
    Cram'd full of Horrid Darkness, here do Crawle
Up over head, and Eares, in Nauseous plight:
    And Swinelike Wallow in this mire, and Gall:
    No Heavenly Dews nor Holy Waters drill:
    Nor Sweet Aire Brieze, nor Comfort here distill.   30

Here for Companions, are Fears, Heart-Achs, Grief
    Frogs, Toads, Newts, Bats, Horrid Hob-Goblins, Ghosts:
Ill Spirits haunt this Pit: and no reliefe:
    Nor Coard can fetch me hence in Creatures Coasts.
    I who once lodgd at Heavens Palace Gate   35
    With full Fledgd Angells, now possess this fate.

But yet, my Lord, thy golden Chain of Grace
    Thou canst let down, and draw mee up into
Thy Holy Aire, and Glory's Happy Place.
    Out from these Hellish damps and pit so low.   40
    And if thy Grace shall do't, My Harp I'le raise,
    Whose Strings toucht by this Grace, Will twang thy praise.

21 *Gate,*] PW Gate.   22 *night*] Conj.   30 *Sweet*] orig: briezes of Sweet
39 *Glory's*] orig: happy

78. Meditation. Zech. 9.11. By the Blood
        of thy Covenant I have sent forth
        thy Prisoners out of the Pit wherein
        is no water.

14. 10m [Dec.] *1707*. Pub. UPT.

Mine Eyes, that at the Beautious Sight of Fruite
    On th'Tree of, Knowledge, drew black venom in
That did bemegerim my brains at root
    That they turnd round, and tippled me int' Sin.
    I thus then in t'Barath'rick pit down fell.   5
    Thats Waterless and next doore is to Hell:

No water's here: It is a Springless Well.
    Like Josephs Pit, all dry of Comforts Spring.
Oh! Hopeless, Helpless Case: In such I fell.
    The Creatures buckets dry, no help can bring: 10
    Oh, here's a Spring: Indeed its Lethe Lake
    Of Aqua-Infernales: don't mistake.

This Pit indeed's Sins Filthy Dungeon State,
    No water's in't, but filth, and mire, Sins juyce.
Wherein I sinke ore Head, and Eares: sad fate,   15
    And ever shall, if Grace hath here no Sluce.
    Its Well Coards whip Coards are: not Coards to draw
    (Like Pully Coards) out of this Dungeons maw.

Yet in the upper room of Paradise
    An Artist anvill'd out Reliefe sure, Good,   20
A Golden Coarde, and bucket of Grace Choice
    Let down top full of Covenantall blood.
    Which when it touches, oh! the happy Cry!
    The doores fly ope. Now's jayle's Deliverie.

2 *Knowledge*] PW Knowled   5 *then in t'Barath'rick*] orig: into th' Barath'rick
14 *in't,*] PW in't.   23 *Cry*] orig: Conj. Life[?] Saile[?]

This is a Spring of Liquour, heavenly, Cleare.
    Its Streams oreflow these banks. Its boundless Grace
Whose Spring head's Godhead, and its Channells where
    It runs, is Manhood veans that Christ keeps Chase
    For it, and when it makes a Springtide Flood
    This Pit is drown'd with Covenantall blood.   30

And now the Prisoners sent out, do come
    Padling in their Canooes apace with joyes
Along this blood red Sea, Where joyes do throng,
    And sayling in the Arke of Grace that flies
    Drove sweetly by Gailes of the Holy Ghost   35
    Who sweetly briezes all along this Coast.

Here's Covenant blood, indeed: and 't down the banks
    Of this dry Pit breakes: Also 'tis a key
T'unlock the Shackles Sin hung on their Shanks
    And wash the durt off: send them cleane away.   40
    The Pris'ners freed, do on this Red Sea swim
    In Zions Barke: and in their Cabbins sing.

Lord let this Covenantall blood send mee
    Poore Prisner, out of Sins dry Dungeon pound.
And on this Red Sea saile mee safe to thee   45
    In which none Israelite was ever drown'd.
    My Sayles shall tune thee praise along this coast
    If waft with Gailes breath'd by the Holy Ghost.

79. Meditation. Can. 2.16. My Beloved is mine and I am his.

8.12m [Feb.] *1707*. Pub. UPT.

Had I Promethius' filching Ferula
    Filld with its sacred theft the stoln Fire:
To animate my Fancy lodg'd in clay,
    Pandora's Box would peps the theft with ire.
    But if thy Love, My Lord, shall animate   5
    My Clay with holy fire, 'twill flame in State.

Fables fain'd Wonders do relate so strange
    That do amuse when heard. But oh! thy Fame
Pend by the Holy Ghost, (and ne'er shall Change
    Nor vary from the truth) is wonders flame   10
    Glazde o're with Heavens Embelishments, and fan'd
    From evry Chaff, Dust, Weedy Seed, or Sand.

What wilt thou change thyselfe for me, and take
    In lew thereof my sorry selfe; whereby,
I am no more mine own, but thine, probate,   15
    Thou not so thine, as not mine too thereby?
    Dost purchase me to be thine own, thyselfe
    And be'st exchange for mee, thyselfe, and wealth?

I'm Thine, Thou Mine! Mutuall propriety:
    Thou giv'st thyselfe. And for this gift takst mee   20
To be thine own. I give myselfe (poore toy)
    And take thee for myne own, and so to bee.
    Thou giv'st thyselfe, yet dost thyselfe possess,
    I give and keep myselfe too neretheless.

1 *Promethius'*] PW Promethiu's   2 With its *** canceled at beginning of
line   *Filld*] PW filld   6 *Clay*] orig: Fan[cy]

    1–2: Promethius' . . . *Fire.* Prometheus stole from the gods enough fire to
make the pitch of a stalk of giant fennel smoulder; from this, men once
again obtained fire (*Oxford Classical Dictionary*).

Both gi'n away and yet retain'd aright.   25
    Oh! Strange! I have thee mine, who hast thyselfe,
Yet in possession Thou hast mee as tite,
    Who still enjoy myselfe, and thee my wealth.
    What strang appropriations hence arise?
    Thy Person mine, Mine thine, even weddenwise?   30

Thine mine, mine Thine, a mutuall claim is made.
    Mine, thine are Predicates unto us both.
But oh! the Odds in th'purchase price down laid:
    Thyselfe's thy Price, myselfe my mony go'th.
    Thy Purchase mony's infinitly high;   35
    Of Value for me: mine for thee, 's a toy.

Thou'rt Heir of Glory, dost Bright image stand
    Ev'n of the God of Glory. Ownest all.
Hast all Wealth Wisdom Glory, Might at hand
    And all what e're can to mans Glory fall.   40
    And yet thou givst thyselfe to purchase mee
    Ev'n of myselfe, to give myselfe to thee.

And what am I? a little bit of Clay.
    Not more, nor better thing at all I give.
(Though give myselfe) to thee as Purchase pay.   45
    For thee, and for thy all, that I may live.
    What hard terms art thou held unto by me.
    Both in thy Sale, and Purchase, laid on thee?

But yet this thing doth not impov'rish thee
    Although thou payest down thy glorious selfe.   50
And my down laying of myselfe I see
    For thee,'s the way for mee to blessed wealth.
    Thou freely givst what I buy Cheape of thee.
    I freely give what thou buyst deare of mee.

The Purchasd Gift, and Given Purchase here   55
    (For they're both Gifts, and Purchases) by each

31 *is made*] orig: runs thus
32 *are*] orig: is   *unto*] orig: to   39 *Might at hand*] orig: Might and Power at
hand   40 *to*] orig: unto   49 *thing*] orig: bargain   56 *Purchases*] *too* has been
inserted after this word and repeated in the margin. The marginal *too* appears
to have been canceled.

For each, make each to one anothers deare,
    And each delight t'heare one anothers Speech.
Oh! Happy Purchase. And oh! Happy Sale:
    Making each others joye in joyous gales.   60

Let this dash out the snarling teeth that grin,
    Of that Damnd Heresy, calld SHERLOSISM,
That mocks, and scoffs the UNION (that blesst thing)
    To Christs Blesst Person, Happy Enkentrism.
    For if thats true, Christs Spouse spake false in this   65
    Saying My Beloved's Mine, and I am his.

Hence, Oh! my Lord, make thou mee thine that so
    I may be bed wherein thy Love shall ly,
And be thou mine that thou mayst ever show
    Thyselfe the Bed my Love its lodge may spy.   70
    Then this shall be the burden of my Song
    My Well belov'de is mine: I'm his become.

57 *one*] PW on   66 *Beloved's*] orig: Beloved is

62: SHERLOSISM, the doctrines of Dr. William Sherlock (1641?–1707), Dean of
St. Paul's—doctrines which Taylor attacked in his sermons as well as in this
Meditation. Sherlock's concept of the Trinity as being composed of three in-
finite distinct minds and substances was condemned at Oxford as heretical.
Sherlock objected to that form of Christianity which made the person of
Christ almost the sole object of Christian religion; he also objected to the
notion of the mystical union between Christ and the members of the
church, and it is this latter objection that Taylor is condemning here.
Taylor's position is the same as that of Edward Polhill, whose *An Answer
to the Discourse of William Sherlock Touching the Knowledge of Christ*
was in Taylor's library. DNB notes that Polhill's writings were strongly
Calvinistic.

80. Meditation. Joh. 6.53. Except you
eate the flesh of the Son of
Man, etc. ye have no Life in you.

6. 1m [Mar.] *1707/8*. Pub. ETG.

This Curious pearle, One Syllable, call'd LIFE,
    That all things struggle t'keep, and we so prize
I'd with the Edge of sharpen'd sight (as knife)
    My understanding sheath'th anatomize
    But finde Life far too fine, I can not know't.   5
    My sight too Dull; my knife's too blunt to do't.

And if you say, What then is Life? I say
    I cannot tell you what it is, yet know
That Various kinds of Life lodg in my clay.
    And ery kinde an Excellence doth show: 10
    And yet the lowest sort so secret lies
    I cannot finde it nor anatomize.

But here I finde, that all these kindes proove Stares
    Whereon I do ascende to heaven to,
My Lord, thyselfe, and so do mock earths Snares   15
    Those snick snarls, and thus my Soul Steps goe
    From Vegetate to Sensitive thence trace
    To Rationall, and thence to th'Life of Grace.

What though I know not what it is? I know,
    It is too good to bee full known by any   20
Poor Perblinde man, that squints on things, although
    It's Life, its quickening Life to very many,
    Yea t'all th'Elect. It is a slip up bred
    Of Godlike life, in graces garden bed.

4 *understanding sheath 'th*] orig: understandings sheath'd
8 *is,*] PW is.   14 *heaven to*] orig: heaven through Grace
17 *trace*] orig: shall trace   21 *things,*] PW things.   22 orig: It is Life,
quickening Life to many   23 *up bred*] orig: likewise

Grace is the Pearle, the Mother Pearle of Pearles   25
   In which this Pearle of Life is kirnell choice.
Christ dropt it in the Soule, which up it ferles
   A Lignum Vitae's chip of Paradise.
   Its Heart and Soule of Saving Grace outspred
   And can't be had till Grace be brought to bed.   30

The Soule's the Womb. Christ is the Spermodote
   And Saving Grace the seed cast thereinto,
This Life's the principall in Graces Coate,
   Making vitality in all things flow,
   In Heavenly verdure brisking holily   35
   With sharp ey'de peartness of Vivacity.

Dead Looks, and Wanness, all things on them weare,
   If this Life Quickens not, Things Spirituall Dead.
The Image too of God is grown thrid bare
   If this Choice Life be n't with Christ's body fed.   40
   All other lives dance on, in hellish wayes
   Eternally, unless this Life out blaze.

Thou art, my Lord, the Well-spring of this life.
   Oh! let this Life send Rivelets in my heart.
That I may by lifes streames in Holy Strife   45
   Conquour that death, at whose dead Looks I start.
   When of this Life my soule with Child doth spring
   The Babe of Life swath'de up in Grace shall sing.

27 *Soule,*] PW Soule.
30 *bed.*] PW bed,   38 *If this Life Quickens not*] orig: Unless this Life them
Quickens   39 *grown*] orig: soil'd   40 *Christ's*] PW Christ

81. Meditation. Joh. 6.53. unless ye eat the
       Flesh of the Son of man, and drink
       his blood, you have no life in you.

2. 3m [May] *1708.* Unpublished.

I fain would praise thee, Lord, but often finde
    Some toy or trinket slipping in between
My heart and thee, that whiffles hence my minde
    From this I know not how, and oft unseen.
      That such should interpose between my Soule   5
      And thee, is matter for mee to Condole.

I finde thou art the Spring of Life, and Life
    Is up Empon'd in thee, that's Life indeed.
Thou art Lifes Fountain and its Food. The Strife
    Of Living things doth for Life Sake proceed.   10
      But he that with the best of Lifes is spic'te
      Doth eate, and drinke the Flesh, and blood of Christ.

What feed on Humane Flesh and Blood? Strang mess!
    Nature exclaims. What Barbarousness is here?
And Lines Divine this sort of Food repress.   15
    Christs Flesh and Blood how can they bee good Cheer?
      If shread to atoms, would too few be known,
      For ev'ry mouth to have a single one?

This Sense of this blesst Phrase is nonsense thus.
    Some other Sense makes this a metaphor.   20
This feeding signifies, that Faith in us
    Feeds on this fare, Disht in this Pottinger.
      Faith feeds upon this Heavenly Manna rare
      And drinkes this Blood. Sweet junkets: Angells Fare.

Christs works, as Divine Cookery, knead in   25
    The Pasty Past, (his Flesh and Blood) most fine

2 *slipping in between*] orig: whiffling off my minde   19 *nonsense*] orig: mere
nonsense

Into Rich Fare, made with the rowling pin
 His Deity did use. (Obedience prime)
Active, and Passive is the Food that all
 That have this Life feed on within thy Hall.   30

Here's Meate, and Drinke for Souls to use: (Good Cheer,)
 Cookt up, and Brewd by Pure Divinity
The juyce tund up in Humane Casks that ne'er
 Were musty made by any Sluttery.
 And tapt by Graces hand whose table hold   35
 This fare in Dishes far more rich than Gold.

Thou, Lord, Envit'st me thus to eat thy Flesh,
 And drinke thy blood more Spiritfull than wine.
And if I feed not here on this rich mess,
 I have no life in mee: no life Divine.   40
 The Spirituall Life, the Life of God, and Grace
 Eternall Life, obtain in me no place.

The Naturall Life the Life of Reason too
 Are but as painten Cloths to that I lack
The Spirituall Life, and Life Eternall View.
 If none of mine, my Glorys face grows black.   45
 And how should I upon this food ere feed,
 If thou give unto me no vitall Seed?

Those Fruits (the Works) that gloriously do shine
 Upon thy Humane Nature Flesh and Blood   50
From thy Divine, are th'Purchase price, and th'Fine
 Set on our heads, and made our Spirituall Food.
 Faith thats the feeding on these pleasant flowers,
 Incorporates thy Flesh and Blood with ours.

Thy Flesh, and Blood and Office Fruites shall bee   55
 My Souls Plumb Cake it eates, as naturally,
In Spirituall wise mixt with my soul, as wee
 Finde food doth with the body properly.
 So that my life shall be mentain'd and thrive
 Eternally when Spiritually alive.   60

32 *Divinity*] PW Divinty 55 *Office Fruites*] orig: its works

Oh! feed mee, Lord, on thy rich Florendine.
　　Made of the Fruites which thy Divinity
As Principall did beare, (more sweet than wine)
　　Upon thy Manhood, meritoriously.
　　If I be fed with this rich fare, I will   65
　　Say Grace to thee with Songs of holy Skill.

82. Meditation. Joh. 6.53. Unless yee eate
　　　　the Flesh of the Son of Man, and
　　　　drinke his blood, ye have no life.

27. 4m [June]. *1708*. Pub. *W.*

My tatter'd Fancy; and my Ragged Rymes
　　Teeme leaden Metaphors: which yet might serve
To hum a little touching terrene Shines.
　　But Spirtuall Life doth better fare deserve.
　　This thought on, sets my heart upon the Rack.   5
　　I fain would have this Life but han't its knack.

Reason stands for it, moving to persue't.
　　But Flesh and Blood, are Elementall things.
That sink me down, dulling my Spirits fruit.
　　Life Animall a Spirituall Sparke ne'er springs.   10
　　But if thy Altars Coale Enfire my heart,
　　With this Blesst Life my Soule will be thy Sparke.

I'm Common matter: Lord thine Altar make mee.
　　Then sanctify thine Altar with thy blood:
I'l offer on't my heart to thee. (Oh! take mee)   15
　　And let thy fire Calcine mine Altars Wood,
　　Then let thy Spirits breath, as Bellows, blow
　　That this new kindled Life may flame and glow.

Some Life with Spoon, or Trencher do mentain
　　Or suck its food through a Small Quill, or Straw: 20

Meditation] PW Medition　　*drinke*] PW drinks　　17 *Bellows,*] PW Bellows)

But make me, Lord, this Life thou givst, sustain
    With thy Sweet Flesh, and Blood, by Gospell Law.
    Feed it on Zions Pasty Plate-Delights:
      I'de suck it from her Candlesticks Sweet Pipes.

Need makes the Old wife trot: Necessity   25
    Saith, I must eate this Flesh, and drinke this blood.
If not, no Life's in mee that's worth a Fly,
    This mortall Life, while here eats mortall Foode.
    That sends out influences to mentaine,
      A little while, and then holds back the same.   30

But Soule Sweet Bread, is in Gods Back house, made
    On Heavens high Dresser Boarde and throughly bakd:
On Zions Gridiron, sapt in'ts dripping trade,
    That all do live that on it do partake,
    Its Flesh, and Blood even of the Deity;   35
      None that do eat, and Drinke, it, ever dy.

Have I a vitall Sparke even of this Fire?
    How Dull am I? Lord let thy Spirit blow
Upon my Coale, untill its heart is higher,
    And I be quickned by the same, and Glow.
    Here's Manna Angells food to fatten them.   40
      That I must eate or be a witherd stem.

Lord, make my Faith thy golden Quill where through
    I vitall Spirits from thy blood may suck.
Make Faith my Grinders, thy Choice Flesh to chew,   45
    My Witherd Stock shall with frim Fruits be stuck.
    My Soule shall then in Lively Notes forth ring
      Upon her Virginalls, praise for this thing.

21 *sustain*] orig: me sustain   29 *That*] orig: This   *to*] orig: that
36 *None that do*] orig: It will the   39 *Coale,*] PW Coale.
40 *same,*] PW same.   43 *where through*] PW where thre'w

83. Meditation. Can. 5.1. I am come into
        my Garden, etc.

29. 6m [Aug.] *1708*. Unpublished.

A Garden, yea a Paradise indeed,
    Of all Delightfull Beauteous flowers and sweet,
(A Cloud of rich perfume hence did proceed
    From sweet breathd plants,) first Adam was to keep.
    But sinning here he's from this Farm exilde,   5
    And th'Farm, Lord, thou camst to, 's a Garden stylde

A Garden-Church, set with Choice Herbs and Flowers.
    Here Lign-Aloes. And th'Tree of Life.
Here trees of Frankincense and Myrrh up towers.
    Here's Sharons Rose and Lillie: Beauties Strife.   10
    Here's Cassia, Cinnamon, Cloves, Nut Megs, Mace.
    Sweet Calamus: and all Heavens herbs of Grace.

Here's Order Choice, Beds, Allies all in print.
    Here bud sweet blushing Blossoms, sparkling brave
And Beautifull rich, spangled Flowers bepinckt   15
    Which White, Red, Blushie, Cherry Cheek't Smiles have,
    Making Celestiall aire their Civit Box
    Of Aromatick Vapors: Spirituall Drops.

This Garden, Lord, thy Church, this Paradise
    Thou comst into, with thy Choice Spirits Gales   20
Making all Plants of Grace gust out like Spice
    Their sweet perfumed breath that us assailes.
    And sacrifice their Spirits sweet upon
    Their Beauties Altar to thee, Holy One.

This Garden too's the Soule, of thy Redeem'd: 25
    When thou thy Spirits plants therein hast set
In their Conversion now most Choicely 'steemd

22 *us*] Conj.

Embeautified with Graces bracelet.
　　If that my Soule thy Paradise once bee:
　　Thou wilt emparadise it e're with thee.　　　　　　30

Make mee thy Garden; Lord, thy Grace my plant:
　　Make mee thy Vineyard, and my plants thy Vine:
Then come into thy Garden: View each ranck:
　　And make my Grape bleed in thy Cup rich wine.
　　When thou comest in, My Garden flowers will smile　　35
　　And blossom Aromatick Praise the while.

84. Meditation. Can. 5.1. I have gatherd
　　　my Myrrh with my Spice.

17. 8m [Oct.] 1708. Pub. UPT.

Hast made mee, Lord, one of thy Garden Beds?
　　And myrrhiz'd mee with bitter Exercise?
Stubd up the Brush, toore up the Turfy head?
　　And Combt it with thy Harrow teeth likewise?
　　Hast set therein thy Myrrhy Trees, that so　　　　5
　　Sweet Spice might in this Garden bed forth flow?

This Bitter myrrh will keep Corruption out
　　Will kill the Worms that Worm hole do my heart:
Will breath sweet breath of rich perfumes about,
　　That sweetest Sents though bitter tast impart.　　10
　　Such med'cine, Lord, I lack my Sin to calm,
　　To kill Corruption and my Soule Embalm.

But doth thy Myrrh tree Flowrish in my Soule?
　　Doth it bleed Myrrh, and Myrrhy blossoms beare?
Do thy Convictions bring mee to Condole　　　　15
　　My Sinfulness with griefe, Hearts bitter fare?
　　And pickle up my Soule in teares whereby
　　My Sins are mortifi'de repentingly?

35 in,] PW in.　　6 forth flow] orig: might glow　　11 my Sin to calm]
orig: to kill my Sin

Is this the State, Lord, of my Garden Bed?
　　And com'st thou in thy Garden, Lord, anew?   20
And gatherst thou thy Myrrh that's therein bred
　　With thy Sweet Spices? Oh! this matter shew.
　　Thy bitter Myrrh that then my Sins doth quell,
　　Will mee revive with its sweet gracious Smell.

How graciously then dost thou deale with mee,   25
　　Wrapping this bitter myrrh in Odours sweet?
Tho'ts bitter rellish yet sweet sented wee
　　Do finde it: when our Senses do it greet.
　　Its bitter kills the Vermin in my Hive:
　　The Sweetness makes my inward man revive.   30

This myrrh in killing putrid vermin Sins,
　　Will keep my Soule from putrifying here,
Will ease the Conscience of its dreadfull Stings:
　　And sweeten all with its perfumed Cheere.
　　Thou art delighted in this Myrrh For Why?   35
　　Thou dost it gather with thy Spice, oh! Joy.

Then spice my Soule, Lord, with sweet myrrh that drops
　　Off of my Myrrh tree in thy garden Bed.
Thou gatherdst with thy Spice, this garden Crops
　　Thy Garden bore thee. Oh! Choice Crop it bred.   40
　　Apply this Myrrh on me, and on mee keep't.
　　My Soules Cure lies indeed in Bitter-Sweet.

If with thy Myrrh, thou curs't my mallody
　　Which hitherto hinders my Songs of Praise
And with its spicy gales that from it fly,   45
　　Thou dost perfume my Spirits, Songs to raise.
　　My Spirits stufft with sweetest joy will bring
　　Thy Glory tun'de on my perfumed String.

31 *vermin*] PW verin   37 *with sweet myrrh that drops*]
orig: with thy sweet myrrh thus got   40 *bore*] PW bores

85. Meditation. Can. 5.1. I have eate my Hony
            Come with my Hony. I have drunk my
            Wine with my Milk.

26. 10m [Dec.] *1708.* Unpublished.

Oh! Angells, stand agastard at my Song;
    The Aire scarce e're sedans such news as this.
The Soule Christs Spouse his garden Bed's become
    Where Christ doth walk in Aromatick bliss.
    Sin slaying Grace he gets as Myrrh and Spice.   5
    Grace Nutritive's his Wine, Milk, Hony Choice.

Repentance, Patience, and Humility
    And Graces such that mortify our Sin
Thou gatherst up as garden fruits with joy,
    Thy bitter Myrrh and Sweet Spice note this thing.   10
    The Exercising of these graces Choice,
    Perfume thy Ambient aire with Holy Spice.

Faith, Hope, and Love with Heavenizing Joy.
    These graces Nutritive to Souls arise
As Honey in its Comb, deliciously   15
    Unto thy Palate in their Exercise
    Thou in the Garden eats as Hony Good,
    And drinkst as wine and milk, sweet Sillibub.

Hast set these Slips, Lord, of the Holy Ghost
    In me thy gardens bed? Do they grow there   20
And bear thee spirituall fruits the which thou dost
    Delight thy Palate with, as Choicest Cheere?
    Oh! Do these graces that thou sets in mee
    Thy Hony, Wine, and Milk Cook up for thee?

Who could believe it, if thou hadst not said
    I'm come into my Garden, in its Shine   25

drunk] PW druk   18 *sweet*] PW sweed   19 *Ghost*] PW Ghost.
21 *the which*] orig: whose

Have got my myrrh with Spice up. (Oh! sweet trade)
    My Hony ate and drunk with milk my Wine?
    Hast Eate and drunk my Holy Fair and Good?
    Hony ints Comb, and Winemilk Sillibub?   30

What thing is this? How sweet? How Good? How brave?
    Oh! Leape my Soule for joy: art thou become
A Spice bed in Christ's Garden where each Wave
    Of spiced aire brieze all his Walks along:
    Oh! dress thy Garden, Lord; it fatten well   35
    That I its bed may with such Fruits excell.

Be thou my Gardener, Lord, make my Soule
    Thy Gardens Knot. Thy Grace my plants set there.
And make my fruits, thy Myrrh and Spice out rowle,
    My Hope, Faith, Charity, thy Chiefe good cheere.   40
    Then Hony, Wine, and Milk Well Spic'de by mee
    Shall disht with Praise, thy entertainment bee.

86. Meditation. Can. 5.1. Eat Oh! Friends. Drink, yea drink abundantly Oh! Beloved.

21.12m [Feb.] *1708.* Unpublished.

Sometimes, my Lord, while that my Soule enwarms
    Heroicks to thy Violl, I did finde
My heart enchanted with thy Ambient Charms,
    That like an Angell, agitate my minde,
    Soaring't as on seraphick wings on high.   5
    But now, like lead, I Cold, and Heavy lie.

Lord, touch it with thine Altars quick, live Coale,
    And then my Spirits, (oh! how brisk? How Quick?)
Will sweetest melody upon thee rowle.

33 *Christ's*] PW Christ   2 *Violl*] PW Viall   9 *sweetest*] orig: sweet

Their Tunes shall with thy praises frisk and skip.   10
When on thy Sillibubb I sup and bib,
Thy wine and milk will make my Notes run glib.

But is it thus? Do graces blossoms grow
    As Myrrh? And Spice? Hony? And Hony Comb?
Yea Wine, and Milk, which as they overflow?   15
    For thee, thou eatst, and drinkst, and sayst come come
    Furnish my Table with the same I'l cry
    Eat here my Friends, drink, drinke abundantly?

Wilt thou me spice with spice that spiceth thee?
    Shall I eat of the Hony Comb thou eatst?   20
Shall I drinke of the Cup thou drinkst of? See!
    Drink of thy Wine and Milk! eat of thy meats?
    What Love? What Honour? Shall I have such share
    And hearty welcome of thy Trencher fare?

Oh that the Quintessence, Lord, of mee here   25
    In the pure Spirits then of Zions Wine
Extracted were all into Praise most cleare
    I'd raise to thee Up Praise. Id all be thine.
    Could I refine myselfe thus melt to praise
    All should be thine on this account, and blaze.   30

Then make mee, Lord, one of thy garden beds
    The Herb of Trinity set in my Heart.
Herb True Love. Herb of Grace with Rosie Sheds,
    Which springing up may beauties sweet impart.
    Then I shall yield thee Hony, Milk and Wine: 35
    And Spice too, sweet to thee, and t'sweeten thine.

Mee gracious make, then Graces fruits I'st beare.
    Which thou, Lord, callst thy Myrrh, thy Spice and Milk
Thy Wine thy Hony too, of which a Share
    To mee to wonderment, impart thou wilt.   40
    Eate at thy Table, and drinke too shall I?
    Then o're this Feast, I will say GRACE for joy.

28 *raise*] PW rise   orig: rise would   29 *refine*] orig: but refine
40 *wonderment*] PW wondement

87. Meditation. Joh. 10.10. I am come
that they might have Life.

17.2m [Apr.] *1709.* Unpublished.

Life! Life! What's That? It is a Taske too hard
    For my Goose Quill with 'Bellisht Definitions
To set it out: It would thereby be marrd:
    My inke would black it, though a gold Edition.
    Its Natures Principall, that makes all brisk,   5
    Peart, Flowerish, Glorious where it consists.

Its such a Thing that makes all things in which
    It doth embower, and while they're with it fraught
To be full Worthy, Beautifull and Rich
    While in them. But when Gone, they're good for naught.   10
    Where ere it is, its th'chiefest excellence:
    And where it is not, is no Worth, nor Sense.

Its such a thing, that all things else attende.
    Earths Golden Fleece, and Flourish, Fruits, and Flower
Of ery sort, their sweet Consent do sende,   15
    To Honour, and mentain it in its Tower.
    Heaven smiles on't and in 'ts Crystall Candle Stick
    Stand Sun, Moon, Stars blazing to Lighten it.

It from the Worlds Birth runs unto its End
    Along Lifes Channells of each sort of things   20
And all their peart Eyde beauty doth them send.
    What of all worldly Glory is the Spring,
    Whose brightest Flower of all this Beauty bright
    Is Humane Life. Oh! a most beautious sight.

This Life adepts mans Person to be made   25
    All Glorious with shining Grace indeed,

2 *'Bellisht*] PW Bellisht   11 orig: Where ere it is, Its such a thing that all
things else attend.   24 *Oh! a most*] orig: Oh it is most[?]   25 *mans*]
orig: his

And in this glory in Gods Holy trade
    Of Grace unto his Glory to proceed.
    But oh! Sin fould this Glory: Man hath lost it:
    Death by a Sinfull Morsell killd and crost it.   30

But oh! what Grace, my Blessed Lord, hast thou?
    What vallue sets't thou on mans life, now vile?
Prize it thou dost 'bove all the world, that Now
    To save't from Death, thou leapest ore the Stile,
    Dy'dst in our Stead, that wee might still have Life   35
    Appeasing Justice, Ending thereby Strife.

But oh! how precious is this Life of Man,
    Seing thou cam'st from heaven for this end
That we might live, Do Satan what he can,
    Myselfe to thee, my Lord, I therefore give.   40
    Give me, Lord, Life and Grace to boot then I
    Will give My Life and Selfe to thee with Joy.

89. Meditation. Joh. 10.10. I am come
       that they might have Life.

12. 4m [June] *1709.* Unpublished.

What Birth of Wonders from thy Fingers ends
    Dropt, when the World, Lord, dropt out of the Womb
Of its Non-Entity for to attende
    Thy Will its Cradle. And its Midwife Strong.
    Non-Entity in Travail full did bare   5
    The World, big belli'd with all Wonders rare.

The Infant born, in'ts Cradle dorment lay,
    As Dead, yet Capable of Ery Form.
A jumbled Lump of all things ery Way
    Not any single birth of its yet born,   10

36 *Ending*] orig: and Ending   There is no Meditation 88 in PW
5 *Travail full*] PW Travell fill

But when this Lump einjoy'd a Vitall Heate
All Kinds of things did from its belly leape.

Life Vegetative now hatcht in the Egge,
    Flourishing some things nobler than the rest.
Life sensitive gives some of these its Head,   15
    Inspiring them with honour next the best.
    And some of which Life Rationall Enfires,
    Cloathd with a Spiritualizing Life, aspires.

This Life thy Fingers freely dropt into
    The Humane shaped Elements and made   20
The same Excell the Rest and nobler goe
    Enspirited with Heavenizing trade.
    But man by Sin hath lost all life, and marr'd
    Himselfe eternally. Death's his reward.

But thou my Lord, before its Execution   25
    Didst Step from heaven down Death to deterr
And that we might have life: making Solution
    Unto the Creditor, dost Grace Conferr,
    Oh! what a thing is life then. Choice? how Good,
    In that thou camst to buy it with thy blood?   30

Life Naturall indeed is in the Bill
    Thou with thy Father drewst up, it to buy.
Life Spirituall much more; which ever Will
    As Heaven doth Earth, all Naturall Life out Vie.
    Life Naturall is Common makes to live   35
    Things Vegetative, and things Sensitive.

The Spirituall Life is never founde but where
    Life Naturall indeed doth make its nest,
Which builds as well in Bruits and Wicked geers
    As in God's Children, and in holy breasts.   40
    But Spirituall Life falls onely to Gods Sons
    And Out in Holy Conversation runs.

13 *hatcht*] PW ha'tcht   22 *Heavenizing*] PW all Heavenizing: *all* canceled?
26 *Didst Step*] orig: Steppest[?] Did Step[?]

It doth Saints Souls and Conversation gild
　　With Godlike Glory of a Gracious Shine
Brightens its Superstructure where it builds 　　　　　　　45
　　A Lofty Tower of Holy Life Divine.
　　The Richest Jewell in the Cabinet
　　Of Nature made, this Spirituall Life is set.

The Spirituall Life is nighst Gods Life in kinde.
　　In Godlike Properties it doth Consist. 　　　　　　　　50
Hence't glorifies the Soule and Life with it lin'de.
　　Lord, in my Soul and Life this life entwist.
　　Thou cam'st that I might live thus. Then grant me
　　This Life. And I shall Glory beare for thee.

90.　Meditation. Joh. 10.28. I give unto
　　　　them Eternal Life.

14. 6m [Aug.] *1709*. Unpublished.

Eternal Life! What Life is this, I pray?
　　Eternity snick snarls my Brains, thought on:
Its the Arithimaticians Wrack each way.
　　It hath begining, yet it end hath none.
　　He that hath been ten thousand years therein, 　　　5
　　'S as far from 'ts end, as when they did begin.

Eternity indeed is Adjunct to
　　The Life of Man. Of all men Good, and Bad.
As to Deaths Darksom Entery they goe
　　They e're shall live and joyous be, or sad. 　　　　　10
　　Eternall life, then is dicotamizd
　　Into a Life of Joy or miseries.

This last is Calld Everlasting Punishment
　　Or Everlasting sad Distruction,

43 *gild*] orig: guild　　48 *made,*] PW made.　　4 *It*] PW If

Or second Death. Not Life. Its Life all shent   15
    Of Good, and filld with Deaths Edition.
    This though the Worms alive, is Living Death,
    A thousand times worse than to have no breath.

Eternall Life then's in a right Sense this.
    That All things blissfull do to it belong   20
Life Naturall, and Spirituall Life's in bliss
    Eternizde in Eternall Joyes that throng.
    Though all by Nature Death indeed doth fine.
    Yet, Lord, thou giv'st Eternall Life to thine.

Oh! what a Lord is mine? How rich? that he   25
    Gives his, Eternall Life: that doth Contain
All Heaven and its Glory, Bliss, and Glee
    Within it, Hee is Rightfull Lord of th'Same.
    For none can give that which he never had:
    Wheather that gift he gives be good, or bad.   30

And though he give this Gift so rich to his
    His Wealth and Glory's not thereby Diminisht.
He hath the Spring of Life, and Life of bliss.
    When they their Pilgrimage have fully finisht,
    Out of His Spring of life and Bliss that flowth,   35
    Confer Eternall Life on them he doth.

Life Naturall (although Essentiall to
    All Living things) and Spirituall Life indeed,
Peculiar to Rationalls also
    Containd are in Christs Gift as in a Seed,   40
    Are both Adjuncted with Eternity
    In that he gives them them Eternally.

Ripe Grace in all its Orient Blossoms bright
    Ripe Glory in its flower of brightest Shine,
Ripe joy upon the highest branch full ripe   45
    Are in this Life Eternall made most fine,
    All blanched o're in orient Glory all
    Do send their Shining Rayes on them to fall.

28 *th'Same*] PW th Same

Oh! Boundless Sea, and Bottomless of Love,
    Confer'd on Saints. Oh! richest gift ere gi'n!   50
Worth more than thousands Worlds: all Heaven above,
    Whole Heavens of Love; and God to boot therein:
      God, Bliss, Joy, Glory, Eternal Life enjoy'de
      Oh! Happiness! Saints Happy shall abide.

Hence, Lord, I kiss thy Feet, and humbly Cry   55
    Give mee this Gift, Eternall Life I pray.
'Twill gild my Harp O're very gloriously,
    And spiritualize my Strings thy tunes to play.
      Life Naturall's the Base: the Spirituall is
      The Meane: the Tenour is Eternall Bliss.   60

Lord, make my Person, subject of thy Gift
    Eternal Life its Adjunct gi'n by thee.
My Person then, thy Well-Tun'de Harp shall lift
    Thy Praises up in Tunes sung forth by mee.
      Then on my Spirituall Wiars harmoniously   65
      Thy Sweetest Tunes shall ring Eternall Joy.

91. Meditation. Matth. 24.27. So also shall
      the coming of the Son of Man be.

2. 8m [Oct.] *1709*. Unpublished.

What once again, My Lord, allowst thou mee,
    Ev'n Mee, poore Dusty thing, thus to enjoy,
With Thee, ev'n thee, 'fore whom, 't's said, Bow the Knee
    Ye Angells bright, Communion Graceously?
      Thou art so glorious, thy Very Feet   5
      Its glory to the Angells bright to greet.

And shall I on thy Table Fare, Lord, feed,
    That is Cookt up by much more Whiter hands
Than ever Angells usd? Thy flesh indeed

65 *Spirituall*] PW Spiritull

Is meate, and Blood is Drink and on it stands.   10
The Waiters are bright Angells all in Shine
Of their White, Holy, Sapphick Robes Divine.

The thoughts hereof entring upon my Heart
Nigh sink, and drown my fainty Soule ev'n in
The Ocean Sea of Flaming Joy best part.   15
As she attempts Magnificat to sing
And plunging down and up herein, oft Cries,
As she pops up her head, *Raptures of Joyes*.

And now, my Lord, me with thy foode sustain:
Mee in good liking make, yea Fat, and fine,   20
To wait on thee when thou hast come again:
For Come thou wilt, and kindely visit thine.
Thou lov'dst our Nature that its blossoms hang
In thy Description. Hence the Son of Man.

Thou art Continually a Comming, its true,   25
In Providences Some, that scowle and lower,
That Thunder sharp and fiery lightening spew.
Yet Roses Some, and Mary golds out shower.
Thou comst in Ordinances too: and dost
The golden gifts give of the Holy Ghost.   30

But still, besides this, there's another which
Our text Embellisheth in glory bright.
Part of thy Exaltations Glory rich
When thou comst with all Angells train of Light.
Then by thy present Comings furnish mee   35
That I when thou shalt come, may wait on thee.

Hence loade my Trencher with thy Flesh Divine:
Its Angells foode. My Soule doth almost sink:
And press thy Grape into my Cup: Rich Wine.
Lord make thy Blood indeed, my dayly drinke.   40
When with thy Fare my Vessels fill to th'brim,
Thy Praise, on my Shoshannims, Lord, shall Ring.

10 *is Drink*] PW as Drink
18 *Raptures of Joyes*] PW Written in large lower case letters
27 *lightening*] PW lighteing

92. Meditation. Math. 24.27. So also shall
        the Coming of the Son of Man be.

27. *9m* [Nov.] *1709*. Unpublished.

It grieves mee, Lord, my Fancy's rusty: rub
    And brighten't on an Angells Rubston sharp.
Furbish it with thy Spirits File: and dub
    It with a live Coale of thine Altars Spark.
    Yea, with thy holly Oyle make thou it slick   5
    Till like a Flash of Lightning, it grow Quick.

My Heart may ake to finde so bright a Theme
    Which brighten might even Angels wits, to bee,
By my thick, Rusty Fancy and dull Veane
    Barbd of its brightsom sparkling Shine by mee.   10
    Quicken my Fancy Lord; and mend my Pen:
    To Flowerish up the same, as brightest Gem.

What is thy Humane Coach thy Soule rides in,
    Bathing in Bright, Heart ravishing glory all
In Gods Celestiall splendent Palace trim,   15
    Full of it's Fulgient Glory of that hall?
    And wilt thou from this glorious Palace come
    Again to us on earth, where Sinners throng?

Methinks I see, when thou appearest thus,
    The Clouds to rend, and Skies their Crystall Doore   20
Open like thunder for thy pass to us
    And thy Bright Body deckt with Shine all Ore
    Flash through the Same like rapid Lightening Waver
    That gilds the Clouds, and makes the Heavens Quaver.

Proud Sinners now that ore Gods Children crow   25
    Would if they could creep into Augur holes,

3 *Furbish*] PW Furbush   9 *and dull Veane*] orig: and Dull Fancy
20 orig: Thy Glorious body Deckt with Shine all o'er:
Canceled and rewritten as 1.22.

Thy Lightening Flashing in their faces so,
    Melts down their Courage, terrifies their Souls.
Thy Rapid Lightning Flashes pierce like darts
    Of Red hot fiery arrows through their hearts.   30

Now Glory to the Righteous is the Song.
    Their dusty Frame drops off its drossiness
Puts on bright robes, doth jump for joy, doth run
    To meet thee in the Clouds in lightning Dress.
    Whose nimble Flashes dancing on each thing   35
    While Angells trumpet-musick makes them sing.

Make Sanctifying Grace, my tapestry,
    My person make thy Lookinglass Lord, clear
And in my Looking Glass cast thou thine Eye.
    Thy Image view that standeth shining there.   40
    Then as thou com'st like Light'ning, I shall rise
    In Glories Dress to meet thee in the Skies.

93. Meditation. Joh. 14.2. In my Fathers
        house are many Mansions.

22. 11m [Jan.] *1709*. Unpublished.

Could but a Glance of that bright City fair,
    Whose walls are sparkling, Pretious Stones, whose Gates
Bright pollisht Splendent Pearls, Whose Porters are
    Swash Flaming Angells, and Whose Streets rich Plates
    Of pure transparent Gold, mine Eyes enjoy,   5
    My Ravisht heart on Raptures Wings would fly.

My Lumpish Soule, enfir'd with such bright flame
    And Quick'ning influences of this Sight
Darting themselves throughout my drossy frame
    Would jump for joy, and sing with greate delight   10

38 *My person make*] orig: And make my person
5 *Gold,*] PW Gold.   8 *Quick'ning influences*] PW Quick'ming infuences

To thee, my Lord, who deckst thy Royall Hall,
With glorious Mansions for thy Saints even all.

Thy Lower House, this World well garnished
    With richest Furniture of Ev'ry kinde
Of Creatures of each Colours varnished   15
    Most glorious, a Silver Box of Winde.
    The Crystall Skies pinkt with Sun, Moon, and Stars
    Are made its Battlements on azure Spars.

But on these Battlements above, thoust placdst
    Thy Upper House, that Royall Palace town,   20
In which these Mansions are, that made thou hast
    For Saints and Angells Dwellings of renown.
    Should we suppose these mansions, Chambers neate
    Like ours, 't would sordid be, not fit this Seate.

But if these Mansions, built so very bright   25
    Beyond the worlds Bright Battlements, yet should
Be of materialls Celestiall right
    Streets of such Houses, of transparent gold
    For Saints and Angells to possess in Glory's
    Would they unfit thy Upper House as Stories.   30

Though we can't ken these Mansions, now, yet this
    Our Faith doth dwell upon while on this Shore
That there are Mansions, in Celestiall Bliss
    For Saints and Angells t'dwell in evermore.
    Then cheer up, Soule, and take the Kings path brave   35
    Unto these Mansions promises do pave.

Bright Jasper Hall Walld with translucid gold,
    Floors pav'd with Pearls, to these are durty Sells.
Then what bright lives ought all men here uphold
    That hope within these mansions ere to dwell?   40
    Adorne my Soule, Lord, with thy Graces here
    Till by their Shine, I'm fitted to dwell there.

24 *'t would sordid be*] orig: 't would be sordid and
28 *transparent*] PW tranparent   31 *now,*] PW now.   40 *mansions*] PW
mansion

Let as I bring thy Glory home, in mee
    Grace shine, and me thy paths tread pav'de with jems,
Unto thy house, wherein these Mansions bee,   45
    And let mee dwell within their Curtain Hems.
    Thy Praise shall then my Virginalls inspire
    To play a Michtam on her golden wyer.

94. Meditation. Joh. 14.2. In my Fathers House are Many Mansions.

19. 1m [Mar.] 1709/10. Unpublished.

Celestiall Mansions! Wonder, oh my Soul!
    Angells Pavillions surely: and no Halls
For Mud walld Matter, wherein Vermins rowle,
    Worm eaten'd ore with Sin, like wormhold Walls.
    Shall Earthen Pitchers set be on the Shelfe   5
    Of such blesst Mansions Heavenly Plate of Wealth?

May I presume to screw a single thought
    Well splic'de with Saving Faith, into my Heart,
That my poore Potshread, all o're good for nought
    May ever in these Lodgens have a part   10
    The influences of the Same would fly
    With rapid flashes through my heart of joy.

Oh! that thy Spirit would my Soule Inlay
    With such rich lining, Graces Web, that would
While in my Loom, me in these Tents convay,   15
    And that thy Sovereign Love might ever hold
    Me in the paths that to these Mansions bring,
    That I might ever dwell with thee therein.

44 Grace] orig: Thy Grace   10 Lodgens have a part] orig: Rest a
part   11 would fly] orig: that fly   15 Tents convay] orig: Lodgens gay

   9: Potshread (i.e. potsherd). Cf. Isa. 45:9.

Oh! that my Meditations all were frindg'd
    With Sanctifying Gifts: and all my wayes   20
Borderd were with Obedience rightly hindg'd
    Lord on thy word thy Honour bright to raise.
    Oh! that my Paths were pavde with Holiness
    And that thy Glory were their shining dress.

Array me, Lord, with such rich robes all ore
    As for their Matter, and their modes usd are   25
Within these Mansions. Dye them all therefore
    Deep in thy blood: to make them gracious Ware.
    If with thy precious robes will't dress me here
    My present tunes shall sing thy praise when there.   30

95. Meditation. Joh. 14.2. I go to prepare a place for you.

14. 3m [May] 1710. Pub. UPT.

What shall a Mote up to a Monarch rise?
    An Emmet match an Emperor in might?
If Princes make their personall Exercise
    Betriming mouse holes, painting with delight!
    Or hanging Hornets nests with rich attire   5
    All that pretende to Wisdome would admire.

The Highest Office and Highst Officer
    Expende on lowest intrest in the world
The greatest Cost and wealthiest treasure far
    Twould shew mans wisdom's up in folly furld.   10
    That Humane Wisdom's hatcht within the nest
    Of addle brains which wisdom ne'er possesst.

But blush, poor Soule, at th'thought of such a thought
    Touching my Lord, the King of Kings most bright
As acting thus, for us all over nought,   15

29 Entire line Conj.   2 might?] PW might   5 nests] PW nest

Worse than poor Ants, or Spider catchers mite
Who goes away t'prepare's a place most cleare
Whose Shine o're shines the shining Sunshine here.

Ye Heavens wonder, shall your maker come
    To Crumbs of Clay, bing'd all and drencht in Sin   20
To stop the gap with Graces boughs, defray
    The Cost the Law transgresst, doth on us bring?
    Thy head layst down under the axe on th'block
    That for our Sins did off the same there lop:

But that's not all. Thou now didst sweep Death's Cave   25
    Clean with thy hand: and leavest not a dust
Of Flesh, or Bone that there th'Elect dropt have,
    But bringst out all, new buildst the Fabrick just,
    (Having the Scrowle of Gods Displeasure clear'd)
    Bringst back the Soule putst in its tent new rear'd.   30

But thats not all: Now from Deaths realm, erect,
    Thou gloriously gost to thy Fathers Hall:
And pleadst their Case preparst them place well dect
    All with thy Merits hung. Blesst Mansions all.
    Dost ope the Doore lockt fast 'gainst Sins that so   35
    These Holy Rooms admit them may thereto.

But thats not all. Leaving these dolefull roomes
    Thou com'st and takst them by the hands, Most High,
Dost them translate out from their Death bed toombs,
    To th'rooms prepar'd filld with Eternall joy.   40
    Them Crownst and thronst there, there their lips be shall
    Pearld with Eternall Praises that's but all.

Lord Let me bee one of these Crumbs of thine.
    And though Im dust adorn me with thy graces
That though all flect with Sin, thy Grace may shine   45
    As thou Conductst me to these furnisht places.
    Make mee, thy Golden trumpet, sounded bee,
    By thy Good Spirits melody to thee.

22 *bring?*] PW bring   27 *that there th'Elect dropt have*] orig: the Elect dropt
there have   40 *th'rooms*] PW th rooms

96. Meditation. Cant. 1.2. Let him kiss
me with the Kisse of his mouth.

9. 5m [July] *1710.* Unpublished.

What placed in the Sun: and yet my ware,
    A Cloud upon my head? an Hoodwinke blinde?
In middst of Love thou layst on mee, despare?
    And not a blinke of Sunshine in my minde?
    Shall Christ bestow his lovely Love on his,   5
    And mask his face? allowing not a kiss?

Shall ardent love to Christ enfire the Heart?
    Shall hearty love in Christ embrace the Soule?
And shall the Spirituall Eye be wholy dark,
    In th'heart of Love, as not belov'd, Condole?   10
    In th'midst of Loves bright Sun, and yet not see
    A Beame of Love allow'd to lighten thee?

Lord! read the Riddle: Shall a gracious heart
    The object of thy love be sick of Love?
And beg a kiss under the piercing Smart,   15
    Of want thereof? Lord pitty from above.
    What wear the Sun, without a ray of light?
    In midst of Sunshine, meet a pitchy night?

Thy foes, whose Souls Sins bowling alley's grown
    With Cankering Envy rusty made, stand out   20
Without all Sense of thy Sweet Love ere shown
    Is no great wonder. Thou lov'st not this rout.
    But wonder't is that such that grudge their hearts
    Hold love too little for thee, should thus smart.

Nay, nay, stand Sir: here's wisdom very cleare.   25
    None sensibly can have thy love decline:
That never had a drop thereof: nor ere

5 *Love*] orig: pure Love   22 *Thou*] PW thou   23 *their*] PW there

Did tast thereof. This is the right of thine.
Such as enjoy thy Love, may lack the Sense
May have thy love and not loves evidence.   30

Maybe thy measures are above thy might.
    Desires Crave more than thou canst hold by far:
If thou shouldst have but what thou would, if right,
    Thy pipkin soon would run ore, breake, or jar.
    Wisdom allows enough: none t'wast is known.   35
    Because thou hast not all, say not, thoust none.

Christ loves to lay thy Love under Constraint.
    He therefore lets not's Love her Candle light,
To see her Lovely arms that never faint
    Circle thyself about, with greate Delight.   40
    The prayers of Love ascend in gracious tune
    To him as Musick, and as heart perfume.

But listen, Soule, here seest thou not a Cheate.
    Earth is not heaven: Faith not Vision. No.
To see the Love of Christ on thee Compleate   45
    Would make heavens Rivers of joy, earth overflow.
    This is the Vale of tears, not mount of joyes.
    Some Crystal drops while here may well suffice.

But, oh my Lord! let mee lodge in thy Love.
    Although thy Love play bow-peep with me here.   50
Though I be dark: want Spectacles to prove
    Thou lovest mee: I shall at last see Clear.
    And though not now, I then shall sing thy praise.
    In that thy love did tende me all my dayes.

28 *This*] PW this

97. Meditation. Can. 1.2. Let him kiss me with the Kisses of his mouth.

3. 7m [Sept.] *1710.* Unpublished.

My onely Lord, when with no muddy Sight,
    Mine Eyes behold that ardent Flame of Love,
Thy Spouse, when that her day Light seemed night
    In passionate affection seemd to move.
        When thou to her didst onely Cease to show   5
        Thy sweet love token: makes me cry out, Oh!

Although in trying, I through grace can finde
    My heart holds such Conclusions in't, that I
Account this World, Silver, and Gold, refinde
    Pearles, Pretious Stones, Riches, and Frïends a toy.   10
        Methinks I could part with them all for thee
        Yet know not what I should if tri'de should bee.

I dare not say, such ardent flames would rise
    Of true Loves passion, in its Blinks or Blisses,
As in thy Holy Spouse's heart that cries   15
    Oh! let him kiss mee with his orall kisses.
        Should he but stop such acts of love and grace
        Making dark Clouds mask up his brightsom face.

If such strong Flame of Love, be made the mark
    And Cata Pantos of true Love, then who   20
Can prove his marriage knot to Christ in's heart

6 *makes me cry out*] orig: she makes me cry   12 *if tri'de should bee*] orig:
should I tride bee

20: *Cata Pantos,* i.e. *kata pantos,* first of the three Aristotelian laws of
method adopted by Peter Ramus: *lex de omni* or *lex kata pantos* 'law of
universal application'; the others were *lex per se* or *lex kath' hauto* 'law of
essential application' and *lex de universali* or *lex kath' holou* 'law of total
application.' Ramist logic was strongly influential in shaping 16th- and 17th-
century New England thought. Walter J. Ong, *Ramus* (Cambridge, Harvard
University Press, 1958), pp. 258–59.

That doth not finde such ardent flames oreflow?
When thy bright Sun-Shine Face doth weare a Cloude
Methinks my Soule in Sorrows thicket shroudes.

Yet pardon, Lord, give me this word again: 25
    I feare to wrong myselfe, or Gracious thee.
This I can say, and can this say mentain,
    If thou withdrawst, my heart soon sinks in mee.
    Though oftentimes my Spirits dulled, grow,
    If so I am, I am not always soe: 30

When thou dost shine, a Sunshine day I have:
    When I am cloudy then I finde not thee:
When thou dost cloud thy face, thy Face I crave.
    The Shining of thy face enlivens mee.
    I live and dy as Smiles and Frowns take place: 35
    The Life, and Death of Joy Lodge in thy face.

But yet methinks my pipkin is too small.
    It holds too little of Loves liquour in't.
All that it holds for thee seems none at all.
    Thou art so dear, it is too cheape a Drink.   40
    If I had more thou shouldst have more of mee
    If Better, better too. I all give thee.

If thou, my Lord, didst not accept a mite
    More than a mountain, if the mite doth hold
More than a mountain of the heart Love right   45
    I should be blankt, my heart would grow so cold.
    A Quarter of a Farthen halfe a mite
    Of Love thou likest well, its heart delight.

Then let thy Loveliness, Lord touch my heart.
    And let my heart imbrace thy loveliness: 50
That my small mite of Love might on thee dart,
    And thy great selfe might my poor love possess.
    My little mite of Love shall musick sweet
    Tune forth on thee, its harp, that heaven shall greet.

44 *mountain,*] PW mountain   48 *well,*] PW well.   53 *mite*] orig: might

98. Meditation. Can. 1.2. Thy Love is
better than Wine.

29. 8m [Oct.] *1710*. Unpublished.

A Vine, my Lord, a noble Vine indeed
    Whose juyce makes brisk my heart to sing thy Wine.
I have read of the Vine of Sibmahs breed,
    And Wine of Hesbon, yea and Sodoms Vine,
    All which raise Clouds up when their Liquour's High   5
    In any one: but thine doth Clarify.

The Choicest Vine, the royallst grape that rose,
    Or ere in Cana'ns Vinyard did take Root,
Did Emblemize thy selfe the True Vine those
    Are not like thee for Nature, nor for fruite.   10
    Thy noble royall nature Ever blesst
    Produceth spiced juyce by far the best.

The Vine deckt in her blosom frindge the Aire
    With sweet perfume. O! Smell of Lebanon!
Her Grapes when pounded and presst hard (hard fare)   15
    Bleed out both blood and Spirits leaving none
    Which too much tooke, the brain doth too much tole,
    Tho't smacks the Palate, merry makes the Soule.

But oh! my Lord, thou Zions Vine most deare,
    Didst send the Wealthi'st juyce and Spirits up to   20
Thy Grape which prest in Zions Wine fat Geere
    Did yield the Welthi'st wine that ere did flow.
    Its Loves Rich liquour spice't with Grace even thine,
    And thus thy love is better far than wine.

This Wine thy Love bleeds from thy grape, how sweet?   25
    To spiritualize the life in every part.
How full of Spirits? And of a spirituall reech,

3 *of Sibmahs*] PW *of* omitted   5 *raise Clouds up*] orig: bring Vapors[?]

To th' blood and Spirits of the gracious heart?
How warming to the Chilly person grown?
And Cordiall to spirituall feeble one?   30

How sweet? how warm? how Cordiall is thy Love
    That bleeds thy grapes sweet Juyce into the Soule?
How brings it Grace, and Heaven from above.
    And drops them in the Heart its Wassell bowle?
    Wine th'Nectar of all juyces with its sapor   35
    Compared to thy love is but a Vaper.

Its not like other wine which took too much,
    Whose Spirits vapor. And do wise men foole.
But this the more is tooke, the Better such
    Servants and Service best, best grace the Schoole.   40
    Lord tun this Wine in me and make my Savour
    Be ever richly filled with its flavour.

Lord make mee Cask, and thy rich Love its Wine.
    Impregnate with its Spirits, Lord, my heart.
And make its heat my heart and blood refine,   45
    And Sweetness sweeten me in ery part.
    Give me to drinke the juyce of this true Vine
    Then I will sing thy Love better than Wine.

99. Meditation. Isa. 24.23. He shall walk
      before his Ancient gloriously.

24.10m [Dec.] *1710*. Unpublished.

Glory! what art? O! Sparkling Spark all bright,
    Thy Shining Robes all gallantry do ware
Dazling the Eye of such as have the Sight
    Of anyone deckt with thy Sparklings rare.

35 *sapor*] orig: Vaper   43 *mee*] orig: my
2 *do*] orig: doth   4 *with*] orig: up with

Guilding the Ambient aire with golden shine   5
    In which its Subjects stande in glory fine.

This pale-fac'de Moon that Silver Snowball like
    That Walkes ints Silver Glory, paints the Skies
The tester of the Bed, where day and night
    Each Creature Coverd ore with glory lies,   10
    She with her Silver Rayes envarnish doth
    In Silver paint, the Skies as out she go'th.

But oh! the Sun, that golden Ball of Glory
    That Walkes in his Celestiall Galleries
In flaming Broad cloth wove, in th'Highest Story,   15
    Of Glories Rayes, and aires fine twine webwise
    Doth make her golden Beams, her tapestry
    Which gilds the heavens ore, hung out on high.

But all this glory pleasent to behold,
    Is but a drop of ink compar'd with thine,   20
My Deare-Dear Lord whose Sparkling glory would
    Enravish all that sees but halfe its Shine.
    The bodies eyes want Strength to beare the Sight
    From sinking when a beam of't on't doth Light.

Thy elementall Frame, that China Dish,   25
    Varnisht with nature's rich perfection o're,
The top of beauty, humane nature's bliss,
    Most naturally deckt with all beauties glore,
    A Crystall Glass, Transparent Silver bowle.
    Or Golden Tabernacle of the Soule.   30

Eyes ne'er beheld Humanity so brave,
    So Beautifull a piece of manhood-frame.
Filld all with graces glory, whose bright Wave
    Is dasht all ore, with orientall flame.
    A Golden Viol full of gracious Grace   35
    Whose flashing Shine out shines the Angells face.

7 that] orig: sparkling
8 That Walkes] orig: Walking   14 That Walkes] orig: Walking
21 Sparkling] PW Sprkling   23 the] PW a   24 on't doth] orig: doth on't

Hence ery thought that in thy heart was hatcht.
    And ery word that from thy lips did fall
And ery act thy person ere dispatcht,
      Came glorifide with graces glory all   40
      That eyes enlighten'd with thy glory, said
      We saw his glory as God's Son's, displaid.

When thou the Curtain backtst a little t'shew
    A little flash of thy greate glory bright
Thy Countenance did shine like lightning: true,   45
      Thy Raiment was as white as Snow, or light.
      Angells adore and Saints admire thy brightness
      And hunger to bee filled with thy likeness.

Lord, make me with thy likeness like to thee.
    Upon my Soule thy Shining Image place.   50
And let thy glorious grace shine bright in mee.
      Enlay my thoughts, my words, and Works with Grace.
      If thou wilt dub mee with bright gracious geere,
      I'le sing thee Songs of Grace in Glories Spheare.

100.   Meditation. Isai. 24.23. The Lord of
       Hosts shall reign in Mount Zion
       and in Jerusalem and before his
       Ancients gloriously.

18. 12m [Feb.] *1710*. Unpublished.

Glory, What art thou? tell us: Dost thou know?
    Its native to our nature to desire
To weare thy Shine. Our Sparkling Eyes bestow
      Their kisses on the Cheeks thou dost attire.
      Our Fancies fed therewith grow lively briske.   5
      Acts always lodged in happy glances frisk.

37 *in*] orig: ere in   4 *the*] orig: thy   5 *Fancies*] PW Fances

Then Glory as a Metaphor, Il 'tende
    And lay it all on thee, my Lord! to bring
My Heart in Flames of love, its rayes out send
    Whose Curled tops shall ever to thee cling.   10
    But all the glory Sunbeams on them beare
    Is but a Smoaky vapour to thy Weare.

To see thee king it in mount Zion bright
    And in Jerusalem, wherein the Shine
Of thy Right Scepter pinkt with Starrs of Light   15
    Thy Gospell Law, and Miracles Divine,
    Enravish may my Soule untill it flies
    To thee upon the Wings of Extasies.

To see thee thron'de in Spirituall Zion Bright,
    Where Sanctifying Grace doth gild the Throne   20
Raisd in the heart In which thou sitst as Light
    And swayst the Realm of thoughts, now gracious grown
    Where Sins arraignd are sentenced and slain
    Will hearts with rapid raptures entertain,

To see thee reign in Heavenly Zion, Oh!   25
    Wherein the Throne of Glory all beset
With Sparkling Angells round about it throw
    Bright flashes of their glory as they step
    Thee to attend, exceeds all Sight each way
    And make might to my Soule, all Heavenly day.   30

The Suns bright Glory's but a smoky thing
    Though it oft 'chants mans fancy with its flashes.
All other glories, that from Creatures spring
    Are less than that: but both are sorry Swashes.
    But thine is purely bright, and spotless cleare   35
    That will inravish in the Heavenly Sphere.

Then set thy Throne, Lord, in my Souls bright Hall:
    And in thy throne let Grace enthroned bee
And let thy Grace gild ore thy Palace Wall

18 *To*] orig: With
32 *'chants*] PW chants   38 *let Grace enthroned bee*] orig: placed in my heart

And let thy Scepter sway and rule in mee.   40
While in my heart thou'rt thron'd my Quill shall greet
Thyselfe with Zions Songs in musick Sweet.

101. Meditation. Isai. 24.23. Then shall the
   Moon be Confounded, and the Sun
   ashamed when the Lord of host shall
   rain in Mount Zion—Gloriously.

15. 2m [Apr.] *1711.* Unpublished.

Glory, thou Shine of Shining things made fine
  To fill the Fancy peeping through the Eyes
At thee that wantons with thy glittering Shine
   That onely dances on the Outside guise
   Yet art the brightest blossom fine things bring   5
   To please our Fancies with and make them sing.

But spare me, Lord, if I while thou dost use
  This Metaphor to make thyselfe appeare
In taking Colours, fancy it to Choose
   To blandish mine affections with and Cheare   10
   Them with thy glory, ever shining best.
   Thus brought to thee so takingly up dresst.

May I but Eye thy Excellency's guise
  From which thy glory flows, all sparkling bright
Th'Property of all thy Properties   15
   Being both inside, and their Outside Light
   The flowing flakes of brightest glories flame
   Would my affections set on fire amain.

Thy Holy Essence, and its Properties
  Divine and Human all this Glory ware.   20

40 *and rule in mee*] orig: in ery part 6 *Fancies*] PW Fances
11 *ever shining*] orig: shining ever 17 *brightest*] PW brighest
18 *set on fire*] orig: all enfire

Thou art Bright Sun Glorie the Beams our Eyes
 Are gilded with which from its body are.
 Magnetick vertue raising Exhalation
 Out of the humble soule unto thy Station.

My blissful Lord, thou and thy properties   25
 And all thy Adjuncts that upon thee throng
Enbedded altogether up arise
 And moulded up into a Splenderous Sun
 And in thy Kingly Glory out do shine
 In Zions mount, outshineing Glories line.   30

Created Glory dangling on all things
 Of brightest sweet breathd flowers and Fields and glaze
The spurred starry Tribes whose sparkling wings
 Flur glory down in Shining Beames and Rayes
 Do blush and are asham'd of all their grace   35
 Beholding that bright Glory of thy Face.

The Silver Candlesticks of th'heaven bright,
 Bearing the Blazing torches round about
The Moon and Sun the Worlds bright Candle's light
 These Candles flames thy Glory blows all out.   40
 These Candle flames lighting the World as tapers,
 Set in thy Sunshine seem like smokie vapors.

The Glory bright of Glorified Saints
 And brightest Glory sparkling out with grace
Comparde with thine my Lord is but as Paint   45
 But glances on them of thy glorious Face.
 Its weak reflection of thy glories Shine,
 Painting their Walls not to compare with thine.

But, Lord, art thou deckt up in glory thus?
 And dost thou in this Glory come and Wooe   50
To bring our hearts to thee compelling us
 With such bright arguments of Glories hew?
 Oh! Adamantine Hearts if we withstand
 Such taking Charming pleas in Glories hand.

22 *are*] orig: run[?] 26 *all*] Conj. 30 *mount*] orig: mont 52 *hew?*] PW hew

Thy splendid glory lapt in Graces mantle   55
    Confer on mee Lord, with thy gracious hand.
Let not my feet upon such glory trample
    But make me for thee and thy Glory stand.
    If that thy Gracious Glory win my Heart
    Thy Glory's Grace I'le on Shoshannims harp.   60

102. Meditation. Mat. 26.26. While they
        were Eating, he took Bread
        and Blessed etc.

10. 4m [June] *1711*. Unpublished.

What Grace is here? Looke ery way and see
    How Grace's Splendor like the bright Sun, shines
Out on my head, and I encentred bee
    Within the Center of its radien lines,
    Thou glories King send out thy Kingly Glory   5
    In shining Institutions laid before mee.

The Basis of thy gracious functions stands
    Ensocketted in thy Essentiall Grace
As its foundation, Rock (not loose loose Sands)
    Bearing the Splendor of this shining face   10
    Th'New Covenant, Whose Articles Divine
    Do far surmount lines wrote in Gold for Shine.

And as the King of Zion thou putst out
    Thy Institutions, Zions Statutes, th'Laws
Of thy New Covenant, which all through out   15
    Thy bright Prophetick trumpet sounds, its Cause.
    To this New Covenant, thou sets thy hand
    And Royall Seale eternally to stand.

59 *Glory win*] orig: Glory doth win   14 *Zions*] orig: these
16 *sounds,*] PW sounds.

A Counterpane indented right with this
    Thou giv'st indeed a Deed of Gift to all   20
That Give to thee their Hearts, a Deed for bliss.
    Which with their hands and Seales they sign too shall.
    One seale they at the Articling embrace:
    The other oft must be renew'd, through grace.

Unto the Articles of this Contract   25
    Our Lord did institute even at the Grave
Of the Last Passover, when off its packt.
    This Seale for our attendance oft to have.
    This Seal made of New Cov'nant wax, red di'de,
    In Cov'nant blood, by faith to be appli'de.   30

Oh! this Broad Seale, of Grace's Covenant
    Bears, Lord, thy Flesh set in its rim aright.
All Crucifide and blood, (Grace hath no want)
    As shed for us, and on us us to White.
    Let's not neglect this gracious law nor breake   35
    But on this Flesh and blood both drinke and Eate.

Seing thou, Lord, thy Cov'nant writst in blood
    My blood red Sins to blot out quite from me
Bathe thou my Soule in this sweet gracious flood,
    Give me thy Grace that I may live to thee.   40
    My heart, thy harp, make, and thy Grace my string.
    Thy Glory then shall be my Song I'l sing.

103. Meditation. Mat. 26.26. As they were
        eating he tooke bread etc.

12. 6m [Aug.] *1711*. Unpublished.

The Deity did call a Parliament
    Of all the Properties Divine to sit

20 *of Gift*] orig: to all   22 *too*] orig: it

About mankinde. Justice her Law out went.
 All Vote man's life to stand or fall by it,
 But Grace gave band securing Gods Elect. 5
 Justice, if Wisdom tended Grace, accepts.

Man out doth come, and soon this Law disgrac't.
 Justice offended, Grace to worke doth Fall
And in the way of Purest wisdom, traced
 New Covenants man and to return him calls. 10
 Erects New Cov'nant worship suited to
 His present State to save him from all Woe.

And in this Course Glory to offer bright
 Through Graces Hand unto Almighty God
Her Credits Good. Justice therein delights. 15
 Rests in her Bill yet Grace prepares a Rod
 That if her subjects her sweet rules neglect,
 She with her golden rod may them Correct.

New Covenant worship Wisdom first proclaims
 Deckt up in Types and Ceremonies gay. 20
Rich Metaphors the first Edition gains.
 A Divine key unlocks these trunks to lay
 All spirituall treasures in them open Cleare.
 The Ark and Mannah, in't, Christ and Good Cheere.

This first Edition did the Cov'nant tend 25
 With Typick Seales and Rites and Ceremonie
That till the Typick Dispensations end
 Should ratify it as Gods Testimony.
 'Mong which the Passover (whose Kirnell's Christ)
 Tooke place with all its Rites, graciously spic't. 30

But when the Pay day came their kirnells Pickt.
 The Shell is cast out hence. Cloudes flew away.
Now Types good night, with Ceremonies strict,
 The Glorious Sun is risen, its broad day.
 Now Passover farewell, and leave thy Place. 35
 Lords Supper seales the Covenant of Grace.

33 *night*,] PW night.

But though the Passover is passt away.
    And Ceremonies that belong'd to it,
Yet doth its kirnell and their Kirnell stay
    Attending on the Seale succeeding it.   40
    The Ceremony parting leaves behinde
    Its Spirit to attend this Seale designd.

As it passt off, it passt its place o're to
    The Supper of the Lord (Choice Feast) to seale
The Covenant of Grace thus, even so   45
    The Ceremoniall Cleaness did reveale
    A Spirituall Cleaness qualifying all
    That have a Right to tend this Festivall.

All must grant Ceremonies must have Sense.
    Or Ceremonies are but senseless things.   50
Had God no reason when, for to dispense
    His Grace, he ope'd all Ceremoniall Springs?
    The reason why God deckt his sacred Shine
    With Senseless Ceremonies, here Divine.

A Typick Ceremony well attends   55
    A Typick Ordinance, these harmonize.
A Spirituall Ordinance the Type suspendes
    And Onely owneth Spirituall Qualities
    To have a right thereto. And this the Will
    The dying Ceremony made, stands still.   60

Morall, and Ceremoniall cleaness, which
    The Pascall Lamb requir'd Foreshow the Guests
Must at the Supper Seale with Spoiles be rich
    Of Sin and be with Saving Grace up dresst.
    God Chose no Ceremonies for their sake   65
    But for Signification did them take.

Give me true Grace that I may grace thy Feast.
    My Gracious Lord, and so sit at thy Table.

51 *Had*] orig: Did
53 *deckt*] PW deck   61 *Ceremoniall*] PW Ceremiall   62 *requir'd*] orig:
requires   67 *Feast*] orig: Table

Thy Spirituall Dainties this Rich Dress at least
   Will have the Guests have. Nothing less is able   70
   To prove their right to't. This therefore bestow.
   Then as I eate, my lips with Grace shall flow.

104. Meditation. Matth. 26.26.27. He tooke
Bread.—And he also tooke the Cup:

30.7m [Sept.] *1711*. Pub. SMT.

What? Bread, and Wine, My Lord! Art thou thus made?
   And made thus unto thine in th'Sacrament?
These are both Cordiall: and both displai'd
   Food for the Living. Spirituall Nourishment.
   Thou hence art food, and Physick rightly 'pli'de   5
   To Living Souls. Such none for dead provide.

Stir up thy Appetite, my Soule, afresh,
   Here's Bread, and Wine as Signs, to signify
The richest Dainties Cookery can Dress
   Thy Table with, filld with felicity.   10
   Purge out and Vomit by Repentance all
   Ill Humours which thy Spirituall Tast forestall.

Bread, Yea substantiall Bread dresst daintily
   Gods White bread made of th'kidnie of Wheate
Ground in his Mill to finest Flowre, we spy,   15
   Searc'de through his strict right Bolter, all compleate
   Moulded up by Gods hand and baked tite
   In Justices hot oven, Gods Cake-bread white.

It is Gods Temple bread; the fine Flower Cake.
   The pure Shew Bread on th'golden Table set,   20
Before the Mercy-Seate in golden Plate,
   Thy Palate for this Zions Simnill whet.

71 *This*] PW this orig: Give this
10 *with*,] PW with.   12 *Spirituall Tast forestall*] orig: Tast do quite

If in this oyled Wafer thou dost eate
   Celestiall Mannah, Oh! the Happy meate.

But that's not all. Here's wine too of brave State.   25
   The Blood, the pure red blood of Zions Grape
Grounde in the Mill of Righteousness to 'bate
   Gods firy wrath and presst into the Shape
   Of Royall Wine in Zion's Sacred bowles
   That Purges Cleanse and Chearish doth poore Soules.   30

This Bread, and Wine hold forth the selfe same thing
   As they from their first Wheat and Vine made flow
Successively into their Beings, bring
   The manner of Christs Manhood and forth show
   It was derived from th'head Humanity   35
   Through Generations all successively.

And as this Bread and Wine receive their forms
   Not fram'd by natures acting, but by Art.
So Christs Humanity was not ere born
   By natures Vertue which she did impart.
   But by Almighty power which acted so   40
   Transendently, did nature overdoe.

These two are of all food most Choice indeed
   Do Emblemise Christ's Elementall frame
Most Excellent and fine, of refinde Seed,
   With Sparkling Grace deckt, and their Works in flame   45
   As grafted in and flowing from his Nature
   And here is food of which his are partaker.

Bread must be broke and Eate Wine pourd out too
   And drunke and so they feed and do delight.   50
Christ broken was upon Gods wheele (its true)
   And so is spirituall bread that feeds aright
   And his Choice blood shead for our Sins is made
   Drinke for our Souls: a Spirituall Drinke displaid.

Food though its ne're so rich, doth not beget   55
   Nor make its Eaters; but their Lives mentain.

44 *Christ's*] PW Christ

This Bread and Wine begets not Souls; but's set
   'Fore spirituall life to feed upon the Same.
   This Feast is no Regenerating fare.
   But food for those Regenerate that are.   60

Spit out thy Fur, my Tongue; renew thy Tast.
   Oh! whet thine Appetite, and cleanly brush
Thy Cloaths and trim thy Soule. Here food thou hast
   Of Royall Dainties, that requires thee thus '
   That thou adorned be in Spirituall State: 65
   This Bread ne're moulds, nor wine entoxicate.

They both are Food, and Physick, purge out Sin
   From right Receivers. Filth, and Faults away:
They both are Cordialls rich, do Comfort bring.
   Make Sanctifying Grace thrive ery day,   70
   Making the spirituall man hate spirituall sloath
   And to abound in things of Holy growth.

Lord, feed me with th'Bread of thy Sacrament:
   And make me drinke thy Sacramentall Wine:
That I may Grow by Graces nourishment   75
   Wash't in thy Vinall liquour till I shine,
   And rai'd in Sparkling Grace unto thy Glory,
   That so my Life may be a gracious story.

105. Meditation. Matt. 26.26. Jesus tooke
       Bread and blessed it, and
       brake it.

23. 10m [Dec.] 1711. Pub. SMT.

If I was all well melted down, refinde
   In graces Furnace and run in the mould

76 *Wash't*] PW wash't orig: And washt
1 *well melted*] orig: melted well   2 *in*] orig: into

Of bright bright Glory, that with Glory shinde
    More bright than glory doth, my Lord I would
    Crown thee therewith thou shouldst have all, except   5
    The dross I in refining did eject.

Hast thou unto thy Godhead nature tooke
    My nature and unto that nature joyn'de
Making a Union thereby, whose root
    Too deep's for reasons delving toole to finde,   10
    Which is held out thus by thy Taking Bread,
    In this sweet Feast in which our Souls are fed?

This Union, that it is, wee clearely see
    But se not How, or What it is; although
We stande and gaze on't, at't amazed bee.   15
    But Why it is Grace graciously doth show.
    These natures thus United have (as't shown)
    Each done by each, what neither could alone.

The Reason of it Grace declares, whose hand
    This Union made; its made (and thinke hereon)   20
That so our Nature Cansell might that Bande.
    She'd forfeited, and Justice sude upon.
    For natures Purse could not the Fine defray.
    Hence she had Gold from Godheads Mint to pay.

This Mystery more rich than massy gold   25
    Our Lord lapt up in a Choice napkin fine
Of Heavenly trade an Ordinance that hold
    The same out doth to us all sweet, Divine,
    That this might live, he in his Dying night
    Portraide it on his Supper last, as light.   30

To shew that he our nature took, he then
    Tooke breade, and wine best Elementall trade,
Designed as the Sign thereof. Which when
    He had his blessing over it display'de
    To shew his Consecration, then it brake,   35
    To signify his Sufferings for our sake.

4 *glory*] PW gl`oly`   12 *Souls*] PW Soals   20 *made;*] PW made.,
35 *brake,*] PW brake.

Hence in this Bread, and Wine thou dost present
    Thyselfe, my Lord, Celestiall Food indeed,
Rich spirituall fare Soul-Food, Faiths nourishment,
    And such as doth all Saving Graces feed.   40
    For which an Heavenfull of thanks, all free,
    Is not too much my Lord to render thee.

Yet my poore Pipe can hardly stut a tune
    Above an hungry thanks unto thy name .
For all this grace, My Lord, My heart perfume   45
    With greater measures, till thy Grace out flame
    And leade mee on in Graces path along
    To Glory, then I'l sing a brighter song.

106. Meditation. Matth. 26.26.27—take
Eate—Drinke yee.

17. 12m [Feb.] *1711*. Pub. SMT.

I fain would Prize, and Praise thee, Lord, but finde
    My Prizing Faculty imprison'd lyes.
That its Appreciation is confinde
    Within its prison walls and small doth rise.
    Its Prizing Act it would mount up so high   5
    That might oremount its possibility.

I fain would praise thee, but want words to do't:
    And searching ore the realm of thoughts finde none
Significant enough and therefore vote
    For a new set of Words and thoughts hereon   10
    And leap beyond the line such words to gain
    In other Realms, to praise thee: but in vain.

Me pitty, parden mee and Lord accept
    My Penny Prize, and penny worth of Praise.
Words and their Sense within thy bounds are kept   15
    And richer Fruits my Vintage cannot raise.

42 *too*] PW to   5 *Act*] Conj.   11 *leap*] orig: leaping

I can no better bring, do what I can:
Accept thereof and make me better man.

With Consecrated Bread and Wine indeed
    Of Zions Floore, and Wine press me sustain.   20
These fruits thy Boddy, and thy blood doth breed
    Thy Pay and Purchase for mee mee to gain.
    Lord make thy Vitall Principall in mee
    In Gospellwise to eate and drink on thee.

These acts of mine that from thy Vitall Spark   25
    In mee being to thyself, my Lord, my Deare,
As formative in touching thee their marke
    Of this thy Sacrament, my Spirituall Cheere.
    Life first doth Act and Faith that's lifes First-born
    Receiving gives the Sacramentall form.   30

Hence its as needfull as the forme unto
    This Choice formation Hypocrites beg on.
Elfes Vizzarded, and Lambskinde Woolves hence goe.
    Your Counterfeted Coine is worse than none.
    Your gilding though it may the Schoole beguile   35
    The Court will Cast and all your gilt off file.

Morality is here no market ware,
    Although it in the Outward Court is free.
A State of Sin this Banquet cannot beare.
    Old and New Cov'nant Guests here don't agree.   40
    The Wedden Robe is Welcome, but the back
    This Supper cloaths not with, that doth it lack.

32 *formation*] PW formatum[?]   38 *is free*] orig: may bee

40: Old and New Cov'nant Guests. Old and new covenant is defined by
Perkins as follows: "The Covenant [of Grace], albeit it be one in substance,
yet is distinguished into the olde and new testament. The old testament or
covenant is that which in types and shadowes prefigured Christ to come,
and to be exhibited. The new testament declareth Christ already come in
the flesh, and is apparently sheewed in the Gospell" (*The Workes of* . . .
William Perkins, 3 vols. London, 1612–13, *1,* 70). See also Glossary, OLD AND
NEW COVENANT

Food is for living Limbs, not Wooden legs:
    Life's necessary, unto nourishment.
Dead limbs must be cut off: the Addle Eggs   45
    Rot by the heat the dam upon them spent.
    A State of Sin that takes this bread and Wine
    From the Signatum tareth off the Signe.

A Principle of life, to eate implies,
    And of such life that sutes the Foods desire.   50
Food naturall doth naturall Life supply.
    And spirituall food doth spirituall life require.
    The Dead don't eate. Though Folly childish dotes
    In th'Child that gives his Hobby horses oates.

To Eat's an Act of life that life out sent   55
    Employing Food. Life's property alive
Yet acts uniting with foods nourishment
    Which spreads o're nature quite to make it thrive.
    Life Naturall and Spirituall Life renewd
    Precedes their Acts, their Acts precede their food.   60

Then form mee Lord, a former here to bee
    Of this thy Sacrament receiving here
And let me in this Bread and Wine take thee:
    And entertain me with thy Spirituall Cheer.
    Which well Concocted will make joy up start,   65
    That makes thy praises leape up from my heart.

107. Meditation. Lu. 22.19. This do in
remembrance of Mee.

13. 2m [Apr.] 1712. Pub. SMT.

Oh! what a Lord is mine? There's none like him.
    Born heir of th'Vastest Realms, and not Confinde,

66 *That*] orig: To   *leape*] orig: to leape

Within, nor o're the Canopy or rim
    Of th'Starry Region, and as vastly kinde.
    But's bright'st Dominion gloriously lies
    In th'Realm of Angells above the Starry Skies.

When man had sin'd he saw that nothing could
    In all's Dominnion Satisfaction make
To milke white Justice, but himselfe, who should
    Then Drinke Deaths health, he did the matter take
    Upon himselfe by Compact, new and good
    On such Conditions that requir'd his blood.

Yet entred he in Cov'nant with God,
    The Father for to do the thing himselfe
Which to perform he took a Humane Clod
    In union to his Godhead, it enwealth,
    That he might in it fully pay the Score
    Of's fallen friends, and them from death restore.

And having in our nature well sufficde
    The hungry law, with active Righteousness
His life did pay our debt. Death him surprizde.
    His blood he made the Law's sufficing mess.
    With Active and with Passive duties hee
    Balanc't th'accounts, and set the Captives free.

But drawing nigh upon Death's Coasts indeed
    He made his Will bequeathing legacies
To all his Children, a Choice Holy seed
    As they did up in Covenant new arise.
    He his last Night them feasts and at that meale
    His Supper institutes his Cov'nant Seale.

Four Causes do each thing produc'd attend:
    The End, Efficient, Matter and the Form.
These last th'Efficient passt through to the End,
    And so obtains the same the babe is born.
    So in this Supper causes foure attend ·
    Th'Efficient, Matter, Form, and now the End.

25 *Coasts*] PW Costs

The Primall End whereof is Obsignation
    Unto the Covenant of Grace most sweet.
Another is a right Commemoration
    Of Christs Rich Death upon our hearts to keep   40
      And to declare his own till he again
      Shall come. This Ordinance doth at these aim.

And Secondary Ends were in Christ's Eye
    In instituting of this Sacrament,
As Union, and Communion Sanctity   45
      Held with himselfe by these usd Elements
      In Union and Comunion which are fit,
      Of Saints Compacted in Church Fellowship.

But lest this Covenant of Grace should ere
    Be held by doubting Saints all Violate   50
By their infirmities as Adams were
      By one transgression and be so vacate
      Its Seale is food and's often to be usd,
      To seale new pardons freshening faith, misusd.

Then make me, Lord, at thy Sweet Supper spy   55
    Thy graces all well flourishing in mee.
And seale me pardon up and ratify
      Thy Covenant with mee, thus gracious bee.
      My Faculties all deckt with grace shall Chime
      Thy praise, with Angells and my grace shall shine.   60

108. Meditation. Matt. 26.26.27. Jesus took
bread—and he took the Cup:

8.4m [June] *1712.* Pub. SMT.

What Royall Feast Magnificent is this,
    I am invited to, where all the fare

41–2 *again / Shall come*] orig: shall come / Again   43 *Christ's*] PW Christ
54 *faith*] orig: the faith   57 *up*] Conj.   58 *mee,*] PW mee.
60 *praise*] PW paise

Is spic'd with Adjuncts, (ornamentall bliss)
 Which are its robes it ever more doth ware?
 These Robes of Adjuncts shining round about   5
 Christs golden Sheers did cut exactly out.

The Bread and Wine true Doctrine teach for faith
 (True Consequence from Truth will never ly)
Their Adjuncts teach Christs humane nature hath
 A Certain place and not Ubiquity.   10
 Hence this Condemns Ubiquitarians
 And whom deny Christs Manhood too it damns.

It Consubstantiation too Confounds.
 Bread still is bread, Wine still is wine its sure.
It Transubstantiation deadly wounds.   15
 Your touch, Tast, Sight say true. The Pope's a whore.
 Can Bread and Wine by words be Carnifide?
 And manifestly bread and Wine abide?

What monsterous thing doth Transubstantiation
 And Consubstantiation also make   20
Christs Body, having a Ubique-Station,
 When thousands Sacraments men Celebrate
 Upon a day, if th'Bread and wine should e're
 Be Con—, or Trans-Substantiated there?

If in Christs Doctrine taught us in this Feast,   25
 There lies No ly. (And Christ can never ly)
The Christian Faith cannot abide at least
 To dash out reasons brains, or blinde its eye.
 Faith never blindeth reasons Eye but cleares
 Its Sight to see things quite above its Sphere.   30

These Adjuncts shew this feast is ray'd in ware
 Of Holiness enlin'de with honours Shine.
Its Sabbath Entertainment, spirituall fare.
 It's Churches banquet, Spirituall Bread and Wine.
 It is the Signet of the Kings right hande,   35
 Seale to the Covenant of Grace Gods bande.

19 *monsterous thing*] orig: monster then
20 *also*] orig: too   31 *in ware*] orig: robes

The Sign, bread, made of th'kidnies of Wheate
    That grew in Zions field: And th'juyce we sup
Presst from the grape of Zions Vine sweet, great
        Doth make the Signall Wine within the Cup.   40
        Those Signals Bread and Wine are food that bear
        Christ in them Crucified, as spirituall fare.

Here is a feast indeed! in ev'ry Dish
    A Whole Redeemer, Cookt up bravely, Good,
Is served up in holy Sauce that is,   45
        A mess of Delicates made of his blood,
        Adornd with graces Sippits: rich Sweet-Meats.
        Comfort and Comforts sweeten whom them eats.

Lord, Make thou me at this rich feast thy Guest
    And let my food a whole redeemer bee.   50
Let Grace Carve him for mee in ev'ry mess:
        And rowle her Cuttings in this Sawce for mee.
        If thou me fatten with this Faire While here.
        Here after shall thy praise be my good Cheere.

109. Meditation. Mat. 26.26.27: And gave
it to his Disciples.

3. 6m [Aug.] 1712. Pub. SMT.

A Feast is said to be for Laughter made.
    Belshazzars Feast was made for Luxury.
Ahashueru's feast for pomp's displayde.
    George Nevill's Feast at Yorks, for gluttony.

    2: *Belshazzars Feast*, the feast climaxed by Daniel's interpretation of the
hand writing on the wall (Dan. 5).
    3: *Ahashueru's feast*, the feast described in Esther 1:1–8. Ahasuerus was a
Persian king—perhaps Xerxes—described as reigning over a hundred and
twenty-seven provinces from India to Ethiopia.
    4: *George Nevill's Feast at Yorks*, the feast celebrating the installment of
George Nevill (ca. 1432–76) as the Archbishop of York in 1470. Taylor's

But thou my Lord a Spirituall Feast hast dresst 5
Whereat the Angells gaze. And Saints are Guests.

Suppose a Feast in such a Room is kept
    Thats deckt in flaming Guildings every where,
And richest Fare in China Chargers deckt
    And set on golden Tables. Waiters there 10
    In flaming robes waite pouring Royall wine
    In Jasper Cups out. Oh! what glories shine?

But all this Glorious Feast seems but a Cloud,
    My Lord, unto the Feast thou makst for thine.
Although the matters thou hast thine allowd,
    Plain as a pike Staffe bee, as Bread and Wine, 15
    This feast doth fall below thine, Lord, as far
    As the bright Sun excells a painted Star.

Thine is a Feast, the Funerall feast to prize
    The Death, Oh! my Redeemer, of the Son 20
Of God Almighty King of Heaven and'ts joys,
    Where spirituall food disht on thy Table comes.
    All Heavenly Bread and Spirituall Wine, rich rare,
    Almighty gives, here's Mannah, Angells Fare.

This Feast indeed yields gracious Laughing ripe 25
    Wherein its Authour laugheth Hell to Scorn:
Lifts up the Soule that drowns in tears, a wipe
    To give th'old Serpent. Now his head piece's torn.
    Thou art, my Lord, the Authour, and beside
    The Good Cheer of this Feast, as Crucifide. 30

The Palace where thou this dost Celebrate
    Is New Jerusalem with Precious Stones
Walld in: all pavde with Gold: and Every Gate,
    A precious pearle: An Angell keeps each one.
    And at the Table head, more rich than gold, 35
    Dost sit thyselfe, and thy rich fare unfold.

9 *Chargers*] PW Charges
16 *bee,*] PW bee.   28 *Now*] PW now   33 *Gate,*] PW Gate.

description of the feast (CP) lists the amounts of food and liquor consumed:
300 tuns of ale, 80 fat oxen, etc.

Thy Table's set with fare that doth Excell
    The richest Bread, and Wine that ever were
Squeezd out of Corn or Vines: and Cookt up well.
      Its Mannah, Angells food. Yea, Heavens Good Cheer.   40
      Thou art the Authour, and the Feast itselfe.
      Thy Table Feast hence doth excell all wealth.

Thou sittest at the table head in Glory,
    With thy brave guests With grace adornd and drest.
No Table e're was set like thine, in Story,   45
      Or with such guests as thine was ever blesst,
      That linings have embroider'd as with gold,
      And upper robes all glorious to behold.

They'r Gods Elect, and thy Selected Ones,
    Whose Inward man doth ware rich robes of Grace,   50
Tongues tipt with Zion Languague, Precious Stones.
      Their Robes are quilted ore with graces lace.
      Their Lives are Checker work of th'Holy Ghost.
      Their 'ffections journy unto Heavens Coast.

The Subjects that at first sat at this feast   55
    With Christ himselfe, faithfull Disciples were
Whose gracious frames 'fore this time so increast
      Into Apostleship that brought them here.
      Who when Christ comes in Glory, saith, they shall
      Sit with him on twelve thrones in's Judgment hall.   60

These sample out the Subjects and the Guests
    That Welcome are unto this Table bright,
As Qualifide Disciples up well drest
      In Spiritual apparell whitend white
      Else Spot there's in this feast. They cannot thrive   65
      For none can eate, or ere he be alive.

Thou satst in flaming Grace at table head.
    Thy flaming Grace falling upon the rest
That with thee sat, did make their graces shed
      Their Odours out most sweet which they possesst.   70

54 *Coast*.] PW Coast,   65 *They*] PW they   67 *in*] orig: at th'Table in

Judas that graceless wretch packt hence before.
That onely gracious ones enjoyd this Store.

Lord Deck my Soule with thy bright Grace I pray:
    That I may at thy Table Welcome bee,
Thy hand Let take my heart its Captive prey   75
    In Chains of Grace that it ne're slip from thee.
    When that thy Grace hath set my heart in trim
    My Heart shall end thy Supper with an Hymn.

110. Meditation. Matt. 26.30. When they
            had sung an Hymn.

5. 8m [Oct.] *1712.* Pub. *W.*

The Angells sung a Carole at thy Birth,
    My Lord, and thou thyselfe didst sweetly sing
An Epinicioum at thy Death, on Earth
    And order'st thine, in memory of this thing
    Thy Holy Supper, closing it at last   5
    Up with an Hymn, and Choakst the foe thou hast.

This Feast thou madst in memory of thy death
    Which is disht up most graciously: and towers
Of reeching vapours from thy Grave (Sweet breath)
    Aromatize the Skies. That sweetest Showers   10
    Richly perfumed by the Holy Ghost,
    Are rained thence upon the Churches Coast.

Thy Grave beares flowers to dress thy Church withall.
    In which thou dost thy Table dress for thine.
With Gospell Carpet, Chargers, Festivall   15
    And Spirituall Venison, White Bread and Wine
    Being the Fruits thy Grave brings forth and hands
    Upon thy Table where thou waiting standst.

75 *Thy hand Let*] orig: Let grace too   3 *at*] orig: ore

Dainties most rich, all spiced o're with Grace,
    That grow out of thy Grave do deck thy Table   20
To entertain thy Guests, thou callst, and place
    Allowst, with welcome, (and this is no Fable)
    And with these Guests I am invited to't
    And this rich banquet makes me thus a Poet.

Thy Cross planted within thy Coffin beares   25
    Sweet Blossoms and rich Fruits, Whose steams do rise
Out of thy Sepulcher and purge the aire
    Of all Sins damps and fogs that Choake the Skies.
    This Fume perfumes Saints hearts as it out peeps
    Ascending up to bury thee in th'reechs.   30

Joy stands on tiptoes all the while thy Guests
    Sit at thy Table, ready forth to sing
Its Hallilujuhs in sweet musicks dress
    Waiting for Organs to imploy herein.
    Here matter is allowd to all, rich, high,   35
    My Lord, to tune thee Hymns melodiously.

Oh! make my heart thy Pipe: the Holy Ghost
    The Breath that fills the same and Spiritually.
Then play on mee thy pipe that is almost
    Worn out with piping tunes of Vanity.   40
    Winde musick is the best if thou delight
    To play the same thyselfe, upon my pipe.

Hence make me, Lord, thy Golden Trumpet Choice
    And trumpet thou thyselfe upon the same
Thy heart enravishing Hymns with Sweetest Voice.   45
    When thou thy Trumpet soundst, thy tunes will flame.
    My heart shall then sing forth thy praises sweet
    When sounded thus with thy Sepulcher reech.

Make too my Soul thy Cittern, and its wyers
    Make my affections: and rub off their rust   50
With thy bright Grace. And screw my Strings up higher

23 *to't*] PW to'te   29 *it out peeps*] orig: they out peepe.   46 *thy*] orig: this

And tune the same to tune thy praise most Just.
Ile close thy Supper then with Hymns, most sweet
Burr'ing thy Grave in thy Sepulcher's reech.

111. Meditation. 1. Cor. 10.16. The Cup of
           blessing which wee bless, is it
           not the Comunion of the body of
           Christ? etc.

7. 10m [Dec.] *1712*. Pub. SMT.

Oh! Gracious Grace! whither soarst thou? How high
      Even from thy root to thy top branch dost tower?
Thou springst from th'essence of blesst Deity
      And grow'st to th'top of Heavens all blissfull flower.
      Thou art not blackt but brightend by the Sin   5
      Of Gods Elect, whom thou from filth dost bring.

Thou Graces Egg layst in their very hearts
      Hatchest and brudl'st in this nest Divine
Its Chickin, that it fledge. And still impartsts
      It influences, through their lives that shine.   10
      Them takest by the hand, and handst them o're
      The Worlds wild waves to the Celestiall Shoare.

And as thou leadst them 'long the way to glory
      Thou hast the Wells of Aqua Vitae cleare.
For them to take good drachms of (Oh! blesst Story)   15
      And Inns to entertain them with good Cheere.
      That so they may not faint, but upward grow
      Unto their ripeness, and to glory Soe.

6 *thou from filth*] orig: from out filth   8 *brudl'st in this nest*] orig: brudlest
up in nest   9 *it*] PW its   12 *to*] orig: unto   15 *good*] orig: their good
17 *faint,*] PW faint.

They take a drachm of Heavenly Spirits in,
    From every Duty. Here is blessed Ware.   20
Thou hast them draughts of Spiritual Liquour gi'n
    And ev'ry Sabbath tenders us good fare,
      But Oh! the Supper of our Lord! What joy?
      This Feast doth fat the Soul most graceously.

Theandrick Blood, and Body With Compleate   25
    Full Satisfaction and rich Purchase made
Disht on this golden Table, spirituall meate
    Stands. And Gods Saints are Welcom'd with this trade
      The Satisfaction, and the Purchase which
      Thy Blood and Body made, how Good,? how rich?   30

Oh! blesst effects flow from this table then.
    The feeding on this fare and Spiritually
Must needs produce a Spirituall Crop for them
    That rightly do this table fare enjoy
      Whatever other Ordinances doe!   35
      This addeth Seale, and Sealing wax thereto.

This is a Common that consists of all
    That Christ ere had to give. And oh! how much!
Of Grace and Glory here? These ripe fruits fall
    Into Saints baskets: they up gather Such.   40
      All fruits that other ordinances which
      Are Edifying, Do this Feast enrich.

But still besides these there are properly
    Its own effects which it doth beare and hath.
Its Spirituall Food that nourisheth spiritualy.   45
    The new born babe to thrive in using Faith
      The Soule it quiets: Conscience doth not sting.
      It seales fresh pardon to the Soul of Sin.

It maketh Charity's sweet rosy breath
    Streach o're the Whole Society of Saints.   50
It huggeth them. That nothing of the Earth

30 *Thy*] orig: The   *made,*] PW made.
42 *Do*] orig: too   49 *breath*] orig: Wings

Or its infection its affections taints.
Grace now grow strong, Faith sturdy. Joy, and Peace
And other Vertues in the Soule encrease.

Gods Love shines brighter now upon the heart: 55
    In that he seals Christ Dying with a Feast
Wherein he smiles doth on the Soul impart:
    With all Christs Righteousness: Joy now's increast.
    The Soul grows valient and resists the foe.
    The Spirituall Vigour vigorous doth grow.   60

Lord, on thy Commons let my Spirits feed
    So nourish thou thy new Born babe in mee.
At thy Communion Table up mee breed
    Communicate thy Blood and Body free.
    Thy Table yielding Spirituall Bread, and Wine   65
    Will make my Soul grow brisk, thy praise to Chime.

112. Meditation. 2 Cor. 5.14. If one died for all then are all Dead.

15. 12m [Feb.] *1712.* Pub. ETP, *W.*

Oh! Good, Good, Good, my Lord. What more Love yet.
    Thou dy for mee! What, am I dead in thee?
What did Deaths arrow shot at me thee hit?
    Didst slip between that flying shaft and mee?
    Didst make thyselfe Deaths marke shot at for mee?   5
    So that her Shaft shall fly no far than thee?

Di'dst dy for mee indeed, and in thy Death
    Take in thy Dying thus my death the Cause?
And lay I dying in thy Dying breath,
    According to Graces Redemption Laws?   10
    If one did dy for all, it needs must bee
    That all did dy in one, and from death free.

58 *Righteousness*] orig: Satisfaction   59 *resists*] PW resist   10 *to*] orig: unto

Infinities fierce firy arrow red
    Shot from the splendid Bow of Justice bright
Did smite thee down, for thine. Thou art their head.   15
    They di'de in thee. Their death did on thee light.
    They di'de their Death in thee, thy Death is theirs.
    Hence thine is mine, thy death my trespass clears.

How sweet is this: my Death lies buried
    Within thy Grave, my Lord, deep under ground,   20
It is unskin'd, as Carrion rotten Dead.
    For Grace's hand gave Death its deadly wound.
    Deaths no such terrour on th'Saints blesst Coast.
    Its but a harmless Shade: No walking Ghost.

The Painter lies: the Bellfrey Pillars weare   25
    A false Effigies now of Death, alas!
With empty Eyeholes, Butter teeth, bones bare
    And spraggling arms, having an Hour Glass
    In one grim paw. Th'other a Spade doth hold
    To shew deaths frightfull region under mould.   30

Whereas its Sting is gone: its life is lost.
    Though unto Christless ones it is most Grim
Its but a Shade to Saints whose path it Crosst,
    Or Shell or Washen face, in which she sings
    Their Bodies in her lap a Lollaboy   35
    And sends their Souls to sing their Masters joy.

Lord let me finde Sin, Curse and Death that doe
    Belong to me ly slain too in thy Grave.
And let thy law my clearing hence bestow
    And from these things let me acquittance have.   40
    The Law suffic'de: and I discharg'd, Hence sing
    Thy praise I will over Deaths Death, and Sin.

21 *unskin'd,*] PW unskin'd.   23 *on*] orig: in   24 *harmless*] orig: Shade
29 *Th'*] PW th'   34 *sings*] PW sing   38 *to me*] orig: in you   *ly slain too*]
PW ly slain to

113. Meditation. Rev. 22.16. I am the
            Root and Offspring of David.

12. 2m [Apr.] 1713. Unpublished.

Help, oh! my Lord, anoint mine Eyes to see
    How thou art Wonderfull thyselfe all ore,
A Common Wealth of Wonders: Rich Vine tree
    Whose Boughs are reevd with miracles good Store.
    Let thy Sweet Clew lead me thy Servant right   5
    Throughout this Labyrinth of Wonders bright.

Here I attempt thy rich delightfull Vine
    Whose bowing boughs buncht with sweet clusters, ripe
Amongst the which I take as Cordiall wine
    This Bunch doth bleed into my Cup delight.   10
    It Cramps my thoughts. What Root, and Offspring too
    Of David: Oh! how can this thing be true?

What top and bottom, Root and Branch unto
    The selfe same tree how can this be? oh-fiddle!
It cannot be. This thing may surely goe   15
    As harder far to read than Sampsons Riddle.
    A Father and a Son to th'selfe same man!
    This wond'rous is indeed: read it who can.

The Root the tree, the Tree the branch doth beare.
    The tree doth run between the branch, and Root.   20
The root and branch are too distinct a pair
    To be the same: Cause and Effect they sute.
    How then is Christ the Root, and Offspring bright
    Of David, Shew, come, read this riddle right.

Lend me thy key, holy Eliakim,   25
    T'unlock the doore untill thy glory shine.

7 *attempt*] PW attemp   9 *as Cordiall wine*] orig: this one most fine
15 *This*] PW this   18 *who*] orig: read

   25: *Eliakim,* steward of King Hezekiah's palace, who Isaiah prophesied
would displace Shebna in the house of the king. The reference here is to

And by thy Clew me thorow lead and bring
    Cleare through this Labyrinth by this rich twine.
Posamnitick's Labyrinth now doth appeare
    An Easy thing unto the passage here.   30

But this doth seem the key unto the Lock.
    Thy Deity, my Lord, is Davids root:
It sprang from it: its rooted on this rock.
    Thy Humane nature is its Offspring-Sute.
    Thy Deity gave David Being, though   35
    Thy Humane Being did from David flow.

Hence thou both Lord, and Son of David art,
    Him Being gav'st, and Being tookst of him.
This doth unbolt the Doore, and light impart
    To shew the nature of this wondrous thing.   40
    Hence two best natures do appeare to stand
    United in thy Person hand in hand.

My blessed Lord, thou art like none indeed.
    Godhead, and Manhood harmonize in thee.
Hence thou alone wee mediator read,   45
    'Tween God, and Man, and setst Gods Children free
    From all Gods wrath, and wholy them restore
    Into that Favour, which they lost before.

Hence give thou me true Faith in thee to have:
    Make me thy branch, be thou my root thyselfe,   50
And let thy Grace root in my heart, I Crave
    And let thy purchase be my proper Wealth:
    And when this Sweet hath in my heart full Sway
    My sweetest musick shall thy praise display.

38 *gav'st*] orig: giv'st   48 *that*] orig: this

Isa. 22:22: "And the key of the house of David will I lay upon his shoulder;
so he shall open, and none shall shut; and he shall shut, and none shall open."
    27–28: And by thy Clew . . . twine. Cf. Herbert's "The Pearl," lines 37–40:

        Yet through these labyrinths, not my groveling wit,
        But thy silk twist let down from heav'n to me,
        Did both conduct and teach me, how by it
            To climbe to thee.

114. Meditation. Rev: 22.16. The bright
          and morning Star.

9. 6m [Aug.] *1713*. Pub. ETG.

A Star, Bright Morning Star, the shining Sun
   Of Righteousness, in Heaven Lord thou art.
Thou pilotst us by night, which being run
    Away, thou bidst all darkness to depart.
    The Morning Star peeps up an usher gay   5
    'Fore th'Sun of Righteousness to grace the day.

All men benighted are by fall, and Sin:
    Thou Graces pole star art to pilote's from it:
The night of Sorrow and Desertion spring,
    Thou morning Starr dost rise, and not a Comet.   10
    This night expired now, is dead and gone:
    The Day Spring of sweet Comfort cometh on.

The Morning Star doth rise, Dews gracious fall:
    And spirituall Herbs, and sweet Celestiall flowers
Sprinkled therewith most fragrantly do call   15
    The Day Star up, with golden Curls, and Towers
    Put back the Curtains of the azure skies
    And gilde the aire while that the Sun doth rise.

The night of Persecution up arose.
    Not Even, but the morning star there to   20
Soon riseth: vant ill looks: the last Cock Crows
    The Morning Star up: out the Sun doth go.
    Farewell darke night, Welcome bright gracious day.
    As Joy Divine comes on, Griefe goes away.

This world's a night-shade, or a pitchy night,   25
    All Canopi'de with storms and Cloudes all darke.
Sending out thunders, Lightnings and with might,

16 *Towers*] orig: Showers

But thou our Pole star art, which we must marke.
While th'morning Star hands dawning light along:
Let Grace sing now, Birds singing time is come.   30

Whilst thou, my Pole-star shinst my Lord, on mee
    Let my poore pinnace saile thereby aright,
Through this darke night untill its harbor bee
    The Daystars bay, the spring of dayly light,
    The Usher bidding of the night, good night   35
    And Day, Good morrow lightend with delight.

If I by thee, my Pole star, steere aright
    Through this dark night of foule hard weather here
My Vessell safely to the harbour bright
    Of thee, my Morning Star, ere shining clear.   40
    I then shall soon Eternal Day possess
    Wherever shines the Sun of Righteousness.

Grant me, my Lord, by thee, my Star to steere.
    Through this darke vale of tears untill I meet,
Thee here my morning Star outshining cleare,   45
    Shewing my night is past, and day doth peep.
    When thou my Sun of Righteousness makst day.
    My Harp shall thy Eternall praise then play.

Thou Jacobs Star, in's Horizon didst rise.
    And fix't in Heaven, Heavens Steeridge Star.   50
To steer poor sinners out from Enemies
    Coasts unto Graces Realm, (Best State by far).
    Thou sentst a star in th'East to lead Wise men
    Thence to thyselfe, when born in Bethlehem.

The golden locks of this bright star, I pray,   55
    Make leade us from sins quarters to the Coast
Of Graces tillage: darkness from, to th'Bay
    Of Consolation and the Holy Ghost.
    And from this Vale of tears to Glory bright
    Where our tunde breath shall ne're be Choakt by th'night.

29 th'morning] PW th morning   31 shinst] orig: shineth   57 darkness
from] orig: from affection

115. Meditation. Cant. 5:10. My Beloved.

Christ is Bride
Christ Bridegroom

4.7m [Sept.] *1713*. Unpublished.

What art thou mine? Am I espousd to thee?
　　What honour's this? It is more bright Renown.
I ought to glory more in this sweet glee
　　Than if I'd wore greate Alexanders Crown.
　　Oh! make my Heart loaded with Love ascend
　　Up to thyselfe, its bridegroom, bright, and Friend.　　5

Her whole delight, and her Belov'de thou art.
　　Oh! Lovely thou: Oh! grudg my Soule, I say,
Thou straitend standst, lockt up to Earths fine parts
　　Course matter truly, yellow earth, Hard Clay.　　10
　　Why should these Clayey faces be the keyes
　　T'lock, and unlock thy love up as they please?

Lord, make thy Holy Word, the golden Key
　　My Soule to lock and make its bolt to trig
Before the same, and Oyle the same to play　　15
　　As thou dost move them off and On to jig.
　　The ripest Fruits that my affections beare
　　I offer, thee. Oh! my Beloved faire.

Thou standst the brightest object in bright glory
　　More shining than the shining sun to 'lure.　　20
Unto thyselfe the purest Love. The Stories
　　Within my Soul can hold refinde most pure
　　In flaming bundles polishd all with Grace
　　Most sparklingly about thyselfe t'imbrace.

The most refined Love in Graces mint　　25
　　In rapid flames is best bestowd on thee
The brightest: metall with Divinest print

1 *Am*] PW am　　*thee?*] PW thee　　2 *It*] PW it　　12 *thy*] orig: up thy
please?] PW please　　15 *to*] orig: with

Thy tribute is, and ever more shall bee.
The Loving Spouse and thou her Loved Sweet
Make Lovely Joy when she and thee do meet: 30

Thou art so lovely, pitty 'tis indeed
That any drop of love the Heart can hold
Should be held back from thee, or should proceed
To drop on other Objects, young, or old.
Best things go best together: best agree: 35
But best are badly usd, by bad that bee.

Thou all o're Lovely art, Most lovely Thou:
Thy Spouse, the best of Loving Ones: Her Love,
The Best of Love: and this she doth avow
Thyselfe. And thus she doth thyself approve.   40
That object robs thee of thy due that wares
Thy Spouses Love. With thee none in it shares.

Lord fill my heart with Grace refining Love.
Be thou my onely Well-Belov'd I pray.
And make my Heart with all its Love right move   45
Unto thyselfe, and all her Love display.
My Love is then right well bestow'd, alone
When it obtains thyselfe her Lovely One.

My Best love then shall on Shoshannim play,
Like David her Sweet Musick, and thy praise   50
Inspire her Songs, that Glory ever may
In Sweetest tunes thy Excellency Glaze.
And thou shalt be that burden of her Song
Loaded with Praise that to thyselfe belong.

33 *should*] PW shoud   34 *other*] orig: any   37 *Lovely*] orig: lovely Lovely
49 *play*] partly canceled and *raise* substituted
52 *tunes thy*] uncanceled insertion between these words: *and may*
54 *belong*] partly canceled and *out blaze* substituted   PW has two extra lines
at the end of this poem: "When thou my breath inspirth, my heart shall
run / Thy praise in sweetest tunes most sweetly sung." Taylor partly revised
the last two stanzas of this poem, but left his revision incomplete. His intentions
were probably to cancel lines 47–8 and to rewrite the last two stanzas as follows:

Lord fill my heart with Grace refining Love.
Be thou my onely Well-Belov'd I pray.

[cont. on p. 294]

Meditation 116. Can. 5.10. My Beloved is White, and Ruddy, the Chiefest among ten thousand.

21.9m [Nov.] *1713*. Unpublished.

When thou, my Lord, mee mad'st, thou madst my heart
    A Seate for love, and love enthronedst there.
Thou also madst an object by thy Art
    For Love to be laid out upon most Cleare.
    The ruling Stamp of this Choice object shows   5
    God's Beauty, beautifuller than the rose.

I sent mine Eye, love's Pursevant, to seek
    This Object out, the which to naturall
I found it mixt with White and Red most sweet.
    On which love naturall doth sweetly fall.   10
    But if its spirituall, then Orient Grace
    Imbellisheth th'object in this Case.

Such Beautie rose in Sharon's Rose and keeps
    Its pleasing blushes of pure White, and Red
Where spirituall blossoms give their Spirituall Reech,   15
    And on thy Spirituall Countenance do bed.
    Thou art this Rose Whose rosy Cheeks are found
    In purest White and Red of Grace abound.

        And make my Heart with all its Love right move
          Unto thyselfe, and all her Love display.
          My Best love then shall on Shoshannim raise
          Like David her Sweet Musick, and thy praise.

        Inspire her Songs, that Glory may ore come
          In Sweet tunes and thy Excellency Glaze.
        And thou shalt be the burden of her song
          Loaded with Praise that to thyselfe out blaze.
          When thou my breath inspirth, my heart shall run
          Thy praise in sweetest tunes most sweetly sung.

5 *shows*] orig: rose

Thou art arrayed in Gods Whitest Lawn
    And with the purest ruddy looks Sweet Rose,   20
White Righteousness, And Sufferings too out drawn.
    Thy purest blood thy blessed veans did lose
    Was Lasht, Gasht slain paying our debts in which
    Thy beauty rose unto the highest pitch.

Hence purest White and red in Spirituall Sense   25
    Make up thy Beauty to the Spirituall Eye.
Thus thou art object to love Spirituall. Hence
    The Purest Spirituall Love doth to thee high.
  * * * * * * * * * * * * * * * * *
  * * * * * * * * * * * * * * * * *   30

Thou art the loveli'st object over spread
    With brightest beauty Object ever wore
Of purest flushes of pure white and red
    That ever did or could the Love allure.
    Lord make my Love and thee its Object meet   35
    And me in folds of Such Love raptures keep.

Oh! thou most beautiful of Objects gay
    Dart out thy Heavenly beams into my breast.
And make thy Beauty Lord, thy Golden key
    For to unlock and open right my Chest   40
    Loves Cabinet and take the best thyselfe
    Of all my Love therein. Its all thy Wealth.

When I bring forth the best of Love to thee
    And poure its purest Streams all reeching Warm
The best of Love, and Beautiest object bee   45
    Then met together, Love by Beauties Charm
    Embrace thyselfe in her pure milke white Hands
    Thy Holy Beauty lays my love in bands.

Thy beauty then shall weare the best of mee.
    My Love shall then the best of Beauties have.   50

22 *thy*] orig: did thy
25 *in*] orig: and   29–30 Two lines omitted from PW at bottom of page.
37 *Objects*] PW Objejects   42 *Its*] PW its

My Love's my best, thy Beauty's best in thee.
    For thy Best Beauty, my best love I save.
    While my best love doth thy best beauty greet
    My purest Love shall sing thy Beauty sweet.

117. Meditation. Cant. 5.10. The Chiefest among ten thousand. דגול

    מרבבות vir illustrus e myriade: Jerom Electus e millebus. Electus ex insignis supra decem. Mar. Standard bearer above ten thousand or the Choice one of ten thousand.

17.11m [Jan.] *1713.* Unpublished.

A King thou art, my Lord, yea King of Kings.
    All Kings shall truckle and fall fore thee down.
Thou hast a Kingdom too Whose great bell rings
    A Passing peale to Worldly Kings and Crowns.
    Thou art the King of Saints and Angells bright.   5
    Thou art the King of Glory, and all Light.

Thy Kingdom is with walls encircled
    Stronger than Walls of Brass or Solid Gold.
Its walld about with fire: Stones Cemented
    With all the Promises Gods booke doth hold.   10
    And all its buildings laid upon the Rock
    Eternall: that Hell gates can't make them shock.

Thou hast a Throne, Crown, Scepter, Mace all Rich
    Richer than golden Crowns, pearld all about.
Thou hast a Body of just Laws, all Which   15
    Transcend all Lawes that ever Kings put out.

3 great bell rings] orig: bells do ring   *12 that*] orig: and

מרבבות דגול *dāggŭl mi-rĕbābōt* 'distinguished out of tens of thousands.' The biblical text has the singular *me-rĕbābāh* 'out of ten thousand.'

Thou also hast both Foes and Enemies
That up against thee and thy Realm arise.

Thou hast a Standard and a Banner greate.
    Thy Gospell and all Gospell Grace, its flag: 20
Thy Standards Colours blancht with Grace compleat
    Enrich thy Banner doth (that is no rag).
    Thou hast a Drum thou beatest up apace
    For Volunteers, that thou enlists with Grace.

Thy Souldiers that unto thy Standard high   25
    Deckt in thy Colours up thou trainst aright
To hande their weapons well and dextrously
    And rightly use shield Arrow, Sworde and Pike.
    And lead'st them out against thy foes, the King
    Abaddon, Divells, Wicked Ones and Sin.   30

Their glittering Swords and Spears Edgd sharp with Grace
    Wherewith they are well arm'd do surely bring
Thy Adversaries under and apace
    Their hearts do pierce that foes do rise to Ring;
    And from the fight to th'Throne triumphantly   35
    Them leadest while Drums beat and Colours fly.

All these thy men under thy flag that fight
    In ranke and file, and Graces Exercise
In all the way go 'till they Come aright
    Unto thy Palace back triumphing wise   40
    Their Colours on their golden Streamers flying
    Do with thy glorious selfe there enter, joying.

Under thy Banner Lord, enlist thou mee.
    Make me to ware thy Colours, SAVING GRACE.
Them flourish in my Life, and make thou mee   45
    To beare thy Standerd and thy Banner trace
    And so me to thy Palace Glory bring
    Where I thy Standards Glory ere may sing.

36 *leadest*] orig: lead   *beat*] orig: do beat   *and*] PW and and

Emblem
Sun

1982

118. Meditation. Can. 5.11. His Head is
most fine Gold.

14. 1m [Mar.] *1713.* Unpublished.

Oh! Hide bound Heart. Harder than mountain Rocks
    Can not one beam of this bright golden Head
Have enterance, thats trim'd with black Curld Locks
    In all its vigrous green up flowerished
    My Child affections thus to touch and thaw.   5
    And to thy golden head their Spirits draw?

The stateliest Head that ever body Bore
    Not gilt but finest gold, of Heavens Gold.
The golden Head that Neb'chadnezzer wore
    Was but a durt ball to't of tainted mould.   *Emblem*   10
    It's true indeed, I call't not Deity,
    But a Bright Emblem of bright Majesty.

This Golden head holds Sovereignity
    And Sovereignity being relative
Constrains a golden body Worthily   15
    Both politick and properly native.
    The Best of Humane Bodies Golden should
    And politicke, ere weare this head of gold.

These Bodies fitted to this Golden Head
    Must needs be golden. Oh the best of all!   20
Because it is their Sovereign: and doth bed
    And board the best things in its golden Hall.
    Faith, Hope and Charity and all graces still
    Out from this Head, and every member fill.

2 *this bright*] PW thus brigh   4 *up flowerished*] orig: and t****
5 *thus to touch and thaw*] orig: till they thee *** touch   8 *gold,*] PW gold.
10 *to't of*] orig: to this Gold of   16 *properly*] orig: also properly
18 *politicke*] orig: bodies politicke   *ere*] orig: do

  9: *The golden Head that Neb'chadnezzer wore.* See Dan. 2:31–38.

The Brains that in this golden brain Pan dwell   25
    Must needs be golden, Golden Wisdom breed.
Its Eyes weare Golden Apples. Th'Senses Cell
    Is all fine Gold, all Golden trade indeed.
    If Wisdom's Palace is the finest Gold,
    Then Golden laws and statutes hence behold.   30

Hence Golden influences out are sent
    To Every member of this Golden Head
The Body Naturall, Whose acts intent
    Upon their Golden Rule are Golden bread
    And hence a golden life my Lord did lead,   35
    From top to toe, most gloriously displayd.

Also the Body Politick, the Realm
    Having its members every one possess
These golden influences from their Helm
    Do make all golden motions ever fresh.   40
    Hence th'golden Laws with Golden influences
    A golden race produce and in all senses.

Thy Golden Head a golden Kingdom hath
    To which it Golden Statutes out doth give
And golden influences it display'th,   45
    That make the Subjects golden lives to live,
    And by these golden Laws thy walke to hold
    Thy glorious City to, whose Streets pure gold.

Oh! glorious Lord, make mee make thy Gold Head
    To bee my Sovereign, and make thou mee   50
A member of thy Golden body led
    By its blesst Golden Lines that lead to thee
    That as my Life thy lines do parallell,
    My Harp shall play: thy Golden head Excell.

30 *statutes*] PW statute
36 *toe,*] PW toe.   42 *senses*] Conj.   44 *Statutes*] PW Statues
47 *thy walke*] PW th'walke[?]   49 *mee make thy Gold Head*] orig: **mee thy**
Golden Head

119. Meditation. Can. 5.12. His Eyes are as
         the Eyes of Doves by Rivers of
         Waters washed with milk, and
         fitly set.

9. 3m [May] *1714*. Unpublished.

My Lord, (my Love,) what loveliness doth ly,
    In this pert percing fiery Eye of thine?
Thy Dove like Eyes ore varnish gloriously
    Thy Face till it the Heavens over shine.
    No Eye did ever any face bedight   5
    As thine with Charming Beauty and Delight.

No Eye holes did at any time enjoy,
    An apple of an Eye like this of thine
Nor ever held an Apple of an Eye
    Like that thine held. Apple and Eye hole fine   10
    Oh! How these Apples and these Eye holes fit,
    Its Eye Omniscient on its fulness sits!

Never were Eyeballs so full trust with might
    With such rich, sharp, quick visive Spirits tite
Nor gave such glances of such beauty bright   15
    As thine, my Lord, nor wore so smart a Sight.
    All bright, All Right, all Holy, Wise, and Cleare
    Or ere discover did such beauty here.

Look here, my Soule, thy Saviours Eye most brisk
    Doth glaze and make't most Charming beauty **weare**   20
That Ever Heaven held or ever kisst.
    All Saints, and Angells at it Gastard stare.
    This Eye with all the beauties in his face
    Doth hold thy heart and Love in a blesst Chase.

Lord let these Charming Glancing Eyes of thine
    Glance on my Souls bright Eye its amorous beams   25
12 *on*] orig: in   19 *most brisk*] orig: in's head

To fetch as upon golden Ladders fine
    My Heart and Love to thee in Hottest Steams.
    Which bosom'd in thy brightest beauty cleare
    Shall tune the glances of thy Eyes Sweet Deare.   30

120. Meditation. Can. 5.13. His Cheeks are as a Bed of Spices, as sweet Flowers etc.

4.4m [June] *1714*. Unpublished.

My Deare-Deare Lord! What shall my speech be dry?
    And shall I court thee onely with dull tunes?
When I behold thy Cheekes like brave beds ly
    Of Spices and sweet flowers, reechs of Perfumes?
    Sweet beauty reeching in thy Countenance   5
    Oh! amorous Charms: that bring't up in a Trance!

Oh! brightest Beauty, Lord, that paints thy Cheeks
    Yea sweetest Beauty that Face ere did ware,
Mans Clayey Face ne're breathd such ayery Reechs
    Nor e're such Charming Sweetness gave so fair.   10
    If otherwise true Wisdoms voice would bee,
    That greater Love belong'd to these than thee;

If so, Love to thyselfe might slacke its pin
    And Love to Worldly Gayes might screw up higher
Its rusty pin, till, that her Carnall String   15
    Did raise Earths Tunes above the Heavenly Quire.
    Shall Vertue thus descend, and have Disgrace?
    Shall brightest beauty have the lowest place?

Shall dirty Earth out shine the Heavens bright?
    Our Garden bed out shine thy Paradise?   20
Shall Earthy Dunghills yield more sweet Delight?
    Be sweeter than thy Cheeks like beds of Spice?

Are all things natur'de thus and named wrong?
Hath God that made them all made all thus run?

Where is the thought that's in such dy pot di'de?   25
Where is the mouth that mutters such a thing?
Where is the Tongue that dare such Speech let slide?
As Cramps the Aire that doth such ditties ding
Upon the Ear that wound and poison doe?
Thy Auditory Temple where they goe?   30

Such things as these indeed are Hells black Smoke
That pother from its Chimny tunnells vile
To smut thy perfect beauty, Damps thence broke
Out of the Serpents Smokehole, to defile
And Choake our Spirituall Smell and so to Crush   35
Thy sweet perfum out of these briezes thus.

But Oh! my Lord, I do abhorr such notes
That do besmoot thy Beautious Cheeks like Spice.
Like Pillars of perfume; thy Cheeks rich Coats,
Of purest Sweetness, decke't in's beauty Choice.   40
My bliss I finde lapt in my Love that keeps
Its Station on thy sweet and Beautious Cheeks.

Lord lodge my Eyes upon thy Cheekes that are
Cloathd ore with orient beauty like as't were
A Spice bed shining with sweet flowers all fair,   45
Enravishing the very Skies so Cleare
With their pure Spirits breathing thence perfumes
Orecoming notes that fill my Harpe with tunes.

23 *natur'de thus*] orig: thus natur'de   30 *Thy*] PW They   33 *broke*] orig:
out broke   40 *decke't*] PW decke[?] decketh[?]   42 *thy sweet and Beautious
Cheeks*] orig: thy Beautious Cheeks and the reecks

121. Meditation. Cant. 5.13. His Lips are
         like Lillies, dropping sweet
         smelling Myrrh.

28.9m [Nov.] *1714.* Unpublished.

Peart Pidgeon Eyes, Sweet Rosie Cheeke of thine
    My Lord, and Lilly Lips, What Charms bed here?
To spiritualize my dull affections mine
    Until they up their heads in Love flames reare.
    The flaming beames sent from thy beautious face   5
    Transcend all other beauties, and their grace.

Thy Pidgen Eyes dart piercing, beames on Love.
    Thy Cherry Cheeks sende Charms out to Loves Coast.
Thy Lilly Lips drop myrrh down from above
    To medicine our spirituall ailes, greate host.   10
    These spirituall maladies that do invest
    The spiritual man are by thy myrrh redresst.

Art thou the Myrrh tree Lord? Thy mouth the Sorce,
    Thy Lilly Lips the bancks, the rivers too
Wherein thy Myrrhie Juyce as water-Course   15
    Doth glide along? And like Choice waters flow?
    Lord make thy lilly Lips to ope the Sluce
    And drop thy Doctrine in my Soule, its juyce.

These golden Streams of Gospell Doctrine glide
    Out from thy Lilly Lips aright, my Lord,   20
Oh! Spirituall myrrh! and raise a Holy Tide
    Of flowing Grace, and graces Sea afford.
    This is the Heavenly Shoure of Myrrh that flows
    Out of this Cloude of Grace thy Lips disclose.

That Grace that in thy lips is powered out   25
    So that these lillie Lips of thine ere bee

7 *on Love*] orig: t'charm   12 *are by*] orig: that by   13 *Thy*] PW thy
14 *bancks*] orig: banks   *too*] PW to   23 *Shoure*] orig: Myrrh

The graceous Flood gate whence thy graces spout.
    My Lord, distill these drops of Myrrh on mee,
    If that thy lilly Lips drop on my heart
    Thy passing myrrh, twill med'cine ev'ry part.   30

If that these Lilly Lips of thine drop out
    These Myrrhie drops into mine hearts dim Eye
And are to mee rich Graces golden Spout
    That poure out Sanctifying Grace Oh! joy.
    This myrrh will medicine my heart that falls   35
    Out of thy Lilly Lips, on graces Hall.

When these thy Lips poure out this myrrh on mee,
    I shall be medicinde with myrrhed Wine
And purifide with oyle of Myrrh shall bee
    And well perfumde with Odours rich divine.   40
    And then my life shall be a Sacrifice
    Perfum'de with this sweet incense up arise.

**122. Meditation. Cant. 5.14. Thy hands are as
gold rings גלילי Orbs set ממלאים
filld with
Berill.**

30. 11m [Jan.] 1714. Unpublished.

My Deare! Deare Lord! While mine Affections act,
    Upon thyselfe, no better words I have
To set them out than this Word Deare, that lack
    Doth length and breadth to show them. Hence I crave
    Thy Pardon Cause such feeble terms I use   5
    Whose Selvedge, Hem, and Web weare Sorry Shews.

32 *These*] orig: this
36 *on*] orig: for   1 *While*] PW while   5 *Cause*] orig: too Cause

גלילי [זהב] ממלאים *gĕlīlē* [*zāhāb*] *mĕmullā'īm:* 'cylinders of gold set with topaz.'

I also crave thy pardon still because
 My Muses Hermetage is grown so old
Her Spirits shiver doe, her Phancy's Laws
 Are much transgresst. She sits so Crampt with cold. 10
 Old age indeed hath finde her, that she's grown
 Num'd, and her Musicks Daughters sing Ahone.

But is the Shine thus of thy Precious hands
 Whose fingers each are girdled rich all round
With Rims of Gold, all Decorated stand, 15
 Puncht with green Berill which therein abound,
 Do by their vivid glances make alive
 My frozen Phancy, that it doth revive.

Thy Hands wherein's thy mighty power displaide,
 Hold out afore us, thy brave Operation 20
Of Mediatory Acts, most golden trade
 Of Spirituall Luster, in thy Holy Station
 May my Chil'd Spirits into raptures put
 Of right delight of an Extatick Cut.

But yet methinks the glory of thy hands 25
 As handling thy mediatoriall Acts
Metaphorized here too faintly stands
 Englishd (gold rings) for th'Hebrew terms exact.
 For in our text the Hebrew predicates
 Thy hands as Golden Orbes of Berill mates. 30

But now, my Lord, are thy brave hands, so bright
 The golden Orbs Celestiall filld up cleare
With this brave Oyle-green Berill all delight
 With all rich Grace of graces Charter Deare?
 Are all th'Celestial Orbs of Graces right 35
 The Spirits predicate of thy hands tite?

In that thy hands this golden Orb is made
 This Orbe is emblem of the Sphere of Grace:

10 *sits*] Conj. orig: is 12 orig: BeNum'd, her Daughters Musick all do sing
ahone 18 *that*] orig: till 23 *Chil'd*] PW Child 26 *handling*] orig: they
handling 28 (*gold rings*)] PW brackets 30 *of Berill*] orig: full of Green Berill
37 *is*] orig: of Grace is

And doth Contain thy mediatory Trade,
    Redemption of thy blesst Elected race.   40
    And Application too, to them, do stand
    With grace laid on, thee on the same to hand.

What are thy hands the golden Orbs of Grace?
    Then they must be the Spirits nest also
Wherein the Spirit doth an holy race   45
    Hatch, and doth rain Sweet Shoures for grace apace
    And hands that hand thy Spouse up, tenderly
    To thy Bride Chamber of Eternall joy.

Lord! let these golden Orbs thy hands that have
    All Graces Operations in them cleare   50
Bestow thy Holy Berill green and brave
    Upon my Soule, and rain Sweet Dews down there.
    Upon my Heart and make the Application
    Of thy rich Grace, and mee its Habitation.

And let this golden Sphere of Grace shoure down   55
    Celestiall Showers of Grace on mee I pray,
And let thy golden hands me lead and Crown
    With glory's Diadem in Graces way.
    Then as I Crownd in Glories Orb do stand
    I'le sing the golden glory of thy Hand.   60

123[A]. Meditation. Cant. 5.14. His Belly:
            (i.e. Bowells) is as bright
            Ivory overlaid with Saphires.

3. 2m [Apr.] 1715. Unpublished.

The Costli'st Gem kept in Christs Ivory Box
    O're laid with Saphires such none else ere had,
Christs Key of grace this Cabinet unlocks
    And offers thee. Why then art thou so sad?

3 *this Cabinet*] orig: most graceiously   4 *sad*] PW sab

Such bright Affection in's bright bowells boiles   5
Up to thyself, may, glaze thy Cheeks with Smiles.

That Precious Gem yea preciousest of all
Embedded in Christs bowells as they shine
Ore Covered with asure Saphirs, Call
To welcome it with brightsome looks of thine.   10
Oh Happy thou! waring the brightest thing
That Christs bright bowells alwayes weare within.

Then why shouldst thou, my Soule, be dumpish sad,
Frown hence away thy melancholy Face.
Oh! Chide thyselfe out of this Frame so bad   15
Seing Christs precious bowells thee Embrace.
One flash of this bright Gem these bowells bring
Unto thyselfe, may make thy heart to singe.

Thy Ivory Chest with Saph'rine Varnish fine
Ope Lord, give me thy Bowells Gem all deare.   20
My lumpish Lookes shall then yield smiles and shine.
Thy brightsomness shall make my looks shine cleare.
If that love in thy Ivory Chest is mine
My Countenance thy bowells Love shall Chime.

Meditation 123[B]. Cant. 5.15. His Legs are as Pillars of Marble set (founded) on Sockets [ארני Bases] of fine Gold.

4m [June] 1715. Unpublished.

My Search, my Lord, now having passed o're
The province of my Soule, to finde some geere

5 in's] orig: in his   boiles] PW boile
10 it] orig: thee   17 these] orig: greet[?]   20 all deare] orig: and then
21 smiles] PW smils   24 thy] orig: shall thy
PW incorrectly dates this poem 1714

ארני adnē 'pillars.'

That for thyselfe is fit to set before
    And Wellcome thee withall, But no good Cheare
    I in my Cogitations Orb can finde: 5
    Whose limits are too little for my minde.

My barren Heart is such an hungry Soile
    No Fruits it yields meet for thyselfe, my King,
Either for food or Raiment, but defile
    What they come nigh. Parden then, what I bring.   10
    Fain I would brighten bright thy glory, but
    Do feare my Muse will thy bright glory smoot.

Thy Spirits Pensill hath thy Glory told
    And I do stut, commenting on the Same,
While some bright flashes of thy glory, Would   15
    If touch my Windows, guild my glasses flame.
    This Pensill Rapts thee up in Glorys fold
    From thy gold head quite to thy Feet of gold.

Thy legs like Marble Pillars streight strong, bright,
    Do beare and Carry all thy Bodie too,   20
That founded are upon thy Feet upright
    As golden Socks or Sockets, Tressles true
    Do fitly hold out that strong might of thine
    That bears up, and mentains thy Realm and'ts Shine.

They shew thy mighty Strength, that doth mentain   25
    Thy Kingdom's Upright, Stately, Welthy, and
Majesticke Righteous, Glorious right and Gain,
    All Conquering and Evermore shall stand,
    And though thy Marble legs with feet of gold
    Treade on the dirty ground, most pure they hold.   30

Thy Marble Pillar-Legs on golden Feet
    Beare up and Carry on thy Realm in State.
Among thy golden Candlesticks most sweet
    Thou Walkst thereon and breakst all that thee hate.
    These are the Pounderall wherewith thy foe   35
    Whether Sins, or Divells dasht to pieces goe.

16 *glasses*] orig: glassey   24 *and 'ts*] PW and 't   35 *thy foe*] orig: Foes

O! let these marble legs and golden feet
 That do uphold, and Carry on aright
Thy blessed kingdom as it is most meet
 And make its shining glory shine most bright   40
 And make my heart unlock its box of Wealth
 And thence its Love, thy treasure, send thyselfe.

Oh! that this Stately, Wealthy Glorious Might
 Of thine, my Lord, inchant my heart might so
That all my heart and hearty Love most right   45
 Leap thence and lodge might in thy heart and go
 And on thy golden head sit singing sweet
 The Glory of thy Legs and golden feet.

125. Meditation. Cant. 5.15. His Countenance is like Lebanon, Excellent as the Cedars.

6. 6m [Aug.] *1715.* Unpublished.

Lead me, my Lord upon mount Lebanon,
 And shew me there an Aspect bright of thee.
Open the Valving Doors, when there upon
 I mean the Casements of thy Faith in mee.
 And give my Souls Cleare Eye of thee a Sight   5
 As thou shinst its bright looking Glasses bright.

If I may read thee in its name thou art
 The Hill, it metaphors, of Frankincense,
Hence all atonement for our Sins thy heart
 Hath made with God: thou pardon dost dispense.   10
 So thou dost whiten us, who were all O're
 All fould with filth and Sin, all rowld in goare.

40 *shining*] orig: shines 44 *heart*] PW heard 47 *singing*] orig: singingst
There is no Meditation 124 in PW

What Costly Stones, red Marble, Porphory
    And Cedars Choice in Lebanon abound
What Almugs and what Vines deliciously
    That smell, are in this Lebanon then found?
    All Grace and gracious Saints are hereupon
    Compared to the Smell of Lebanon.

When thou hast cleard my Faiths round appled Eye
    My Souls peirt Eye and Lebanon display
Her Glory and her Excellency high
    In sweet perfumes and gaudie bright array
    And all grow tall, strong, fragrant up from thee
    And of these Cedars tall I sprung one bee.

Then I shall see these precious square wrought Stones
    Are to thy Zion brought, foundations laid,
And all these Cedars Choice, of Lebanon
    Are built thereon and Spirituall Temples made.
    And still thy Spirits Breathings makes them grow
    And forth they flowrish, and their Smell doth flow.

Lord let me stand founded on thee by grace
    And grow a Cedar tall and Upright here.
And sweeten me with this sweet aire apace
    Make me a grape of Leb'nons Vine up peare.
    Let me then see Thy Glory Lebanon
    And yield the Smell of those sweet vines thereon.

My Circumcised Eare, and Souls piert Eye,
    Having their Spirituall Casements opening
And thou displaying thy bright majesty
    Thy Shine and Smell of Lebanon Crowd in
    At these gold-Casements of mine Ears and Eyes.
    They'l fill my Soul with Joyous Extasies.

Lord, make thine Aspect then as Lebanon.
    Allow me such brave Sights and Sents so sweet
Oh! Ravishing Sweet pour'd out my Soule upon.

15

20

25

30

35

40

45

18 *Compared*] orig: Compar'd are   24 *I sprung one*] orig: tall too
spring in   25 *Stones*] PW Stons   42 *Joyous Extasies*] orig: Extasies of Joy

Fill all its empty Corners and there keep
That so my breath may sing thy praise divine
All smelling of thy Lebanons rich wine.

126. Meditation. Cant. 5.16.

His Mouth   חכו Palate
is most sweet.   or Wind pipe,
latine Guther

9. *8m* [Oct.] *1715.* Unpublished.

My Lord, my Love, my Sov'reign, and Supreme,
    Thy Word's my Rule, thy Law's my Lifes sweet line.
All Law subordinate not to this Beame
    No right contains: but is of Sodoms Shrine.
    Thy mouth's most sweet, the Winde pipe of thy Lungs   5
    Conveighs all Sweetness from thy Heart that throngs.

The Spring of Life, and all life's Sweetness Choice
    Hatcht in thy Heart. (Oh! how sweet is this Chest?)
Comes bubbling up this path of Breath and Voice?
    This Highway is the through fare of thy Breast: 10
    Wherein its Vitall Breath runs in, and out
    Well loaded with sweet languague all about.

The golden Current of Sweet Grace sprung in
    Thy Heart, Deare Lord comes Wafting on thy Tast
Sweetning thy Palate passing by its ring,   15
    And rowling in our borders thus begrac'te.
    Come tast and see How sweet this Current is.
    Oh! sweet breath passage. Sweetend sweet as bliss.

The golden mine of Sanctifying Grace
    That in thy heart is glorious indeed   20

14 *Wafting*] PW Wasting

חכו *ḥikkō* 'his palate.'

In Golden Streames come flowering out apace
    Through thy rich golden pipe, and so in Speed,
    As golden liquour, running thence all ore
    Into thy Spouse's heart from Graces Store.

That golden Crucible of Grace all sweet,   25
    Is thy sweet Heart, The golden pipe of Fame
Is thy sweet Windpipe, where thy Spirits reech
    Comes breizing sweet perfumes out from the Same.
    This is the golden gutter of thy Lungs
    And through thy mouth, by th'Palate sweetly runs.   30

Thy Palate hence not sweet but Sweetness is
    It being made the thorough faire or way
Of all that Sweetness of thy heart, and bliss
    That from thy heart to us thou dost Conveigh.
    How sweet then must thy Holy mouth neede bee   35
    Through which thy sweetning heart breath comes from thee?

Lord, make my Palates Constitution right
    Like to thy Palates Constitution fine.
That what comes from thy heart in heart delight
    Sweet to thy Palate may thus sweeten mine.   40
    Then what disrellish to thy Palate shall
    Shall to my Palate be disrellisht all.

Then what shall to thy tast be sweet indeed
    Shall be most sweet unto my tast likewise.
What bitter to thy Palate doth proceed   45
    Shall to my Palate bitter up arise.
    Thy Hearts sweet steame that doth thy Palate greet
    Will make my Tast with thy heart Sweetness sweet.

Those Hony falls that in thy heart rise high
    Of Grace, and through the pipes of thy pure Lungs   50
Are brought into thy mouths bright Canopy
    And on my Garden herbs are shower'd in throngs
    Will sweeten all my flowers and herbs therein
    And make my Winde Pipe thy sweet praises sing.

46 *up*] orig: bee   **49** *rise*] orig: arise

127. Meditation. Cant. 5.16. He is alto-
         gather Lovely כלו מחמדים
         all of him, or of his eius
         vel ipsius totum is desirable.

4. *10m* [Dec.] *1715*. Unpublished.

My Lord, when thou didst form mankinde the hand
    Of thine Omnipotency then did hold
The Vessell rightly well Engravd, and cleansd
    From dust right stild Omnisciencies Mould,
    Wherein mankinde was run and shapt most bright   5
    With Properties, that fix on Objects right.

Hence I have power to Love and to desire.
    These brave Affections Choose such Objects which
Desirable and Lovely are t'infire
    These bright affections that upon them pitch.   10
    Such objects found by these affections sweet,
    Desire draws in, and Love goes out to meet.

Of all things in the Orbs of Entity
    Such as are best deckt up with such attire
Do these affections onely satisfy,   15
    Whichever to the best of things aspire:
    Though these may in some few things here up thrive
    They're in thee, Lord, Super-superlative.

Some things there bee within this Orb full fine,
    And be desirable. Yet nothing here   20
Do all desirable, and Lovely shine
    But all of thee, and thine most Lovely clear

7 *power*] Conj. orig: proper   9 *are t'infire*] orig: mostly are to infire
21 *Do*] orig: Is   *shine*] orig: mine   22 *clear*] orig: Cleare shine

כלו מחמדים *kullō mahămadīm* 'all of him is desirable.'

For Excellency in thee's the Foundation
That to Desire and Love yieldes firmest Station.

Thou altogether Lovely art, all Bright.   25
    Thy Loveliness attracts all Love to thee.
Yea all of Thee and Thine is Fair and White
    Together or apart in highst degree.
    Thy Person, Natures Properties all thine
    Thy Offices, and Acts most lovely shine.   30

Rich Personated Deity most bright,
    Milk white Humanity by God begot
Deckt with transplendent Graces shining Light
    And Sparkling Operations without Spot,
    All Gods Elect, Angells and Saints All thine,   35
    Thy Word and Ordinances most Divine.

A Spirituall ministry of Gracious Ware:
    A path of Holiness: Blesst Conduct in't.
A way of Right pav'de ore beyond Compare
    To thy Celestiall blissfull Palace mint   40
    Wherein thou intertainst thy Saints in joy
    Oh. Loveliness. Desirable and high.

All thee, and all of thee and thine arise
    Thus Lovely and Desireable appeare
The Object of All Love, and purest joyes   45
    Exactly minted in Love's mold most cleare.
    Be thou the Object then that I attire
    With my best Love, and loveliest desire.

Then thou desirable and Lovely Rose
    Each part alone, or altogether art.   50
Oh! make thy Takingness that thus oreflows
    Take to thyselfe my love and all my heart.
    Then my Desire and Love shall sing this Story
    That all of thee is Lovely, in thy Glory.

25 *art*,] PW art.   *Bright*] orig: White   49 *Rose*] orig: fairest Rose

128. Meditation. Cant. 6.1. Whither is thy
          Beloved gone, Oh! thou Fairest
          among Women? etc.

12. 12m [Feb.] *1715.* Unpublished.

My Deare-Deare Lord, my Heart is Lodgd in thee:
    Thy Person lodgd in bright Divinity
And waring Cloaths made of the best web bee
    Wove in the golde Loom of Humanity.
      All lin'de and overlaide with Wealthi'st lace   5
      The finest Silke of Sanctifying Grace.

Hence ev'ry minim of thy Humane Frame.
    Deckt up with Nature's brave perfections right,
And Decorated with rich Grace, Whose Flame
    In Sparkling Shines do ravish with delight   10
      So that thy Nature, and its Acts all shine
      And never miss the Right an Haire breadth fine.

Thy Soule Divine arrayde in Splendent Grace,
    The Spirituall Temple pinckt with precious Stones:
Like Sparks of Glory glaze thy Spirits Face   15
    And glorious make thy Will with graces tones.
      Not one black tittle ere is in it found
      To dim the Shine that in it doth abound.

Thy Soules a Spirituall Treasury, in Which
    Are Precious Stones and Spirituall Jewells laid   20
The Spirits Spicery the gold mine rich
    Of Precious Grace. And Graces Sugar Trade,
      The Warehouse of all Humane thoughts well Wrought
      In which there never came an Evill thought.

1 *Lord,*] PW Lord.   3 *web*] PW webe   17 orig: And not one tittle black is in
it ere found   20 *Are*] orig: All   *laid*] orig: Cleare   22 *Trade*] orig: geere
23 *thoughts*] PW thougts   24 *thought*] PW thoughtt

Thy Eares and Nose ware Graces Jewells bright.   25
     Thy Sight walks out in Graces Paradise:
Thy Smell is Courted with perfum'de delight.
     Thy Garden Flowers breath sweeter breath than Spice:
     But if the Serpent on these objects spit
     Sighs from thy Soul blow hence the venom quick.   30

Thy Feet o're burnished with glorious Grace
     Make all right Steps and not one strey awry
Leave Every foot step guilt with grace, a trace
     And golden track unto Celestial Joy.
     Thy Tongue's tipt with sweet Heavenly Rhetorick   35
     Ne're spake amiss. Grace from thy lips doth skip.

Thy Hands, milk white, were never yet beguil'd
     In Graces Almond milke washt ware no Spot.
Thy fingers never toucht what Sin defilde.
     Grace at thy fingers ends doth ever drop.
     Thy Head's a golden Pot of Manna fine   40
     A Silver Tower of Gospell Weapons Prime.

Oh! what a glorious Lord have I? See here
     When in the Gospell Glass his Beams dart on
The Bride's twelve bridemaids looking on him cleare   45
     And make them ask, Where, Whither is he gone?
     Oh! Whither's thy Beloved bright declinde
     Declare, thou fairest of All Woman kinde.

Our heart is ravisht with his glory bright.
     Oh! Whither Whither is he turned aside?   50
Wee now indeed do greatly wish we might
     Him seeke with thee, His Spouse and blessed Bride!
     That happiness lodg'd in his Glorious face
     Will thence when seen slide int'our Hearts with Grace.

Lord, let thy Glorious Excellencies flame   55
     Fall through thy Gospells Looking Glass with might,

---

32 *Make all right Steps*] orig: Do gild each foot   33 *Leave*] orig: And leave
grace,] PW grace.   36 *amiss*] PW amise   45 *twelve*] Conj.
52 *Bride*] PW Brde   54 *int'our*] PW in'tour

Upon my frozen heart, and thaw the Same
    And it inflame with flaming Love most Light
    That in this flame my heart may ride to thee,
    And sing thy Glories Praise in Glories glee.   60

129. Meditation. Can: 6.2. My Beloved is gon into his Garden.

25. 1m [Mar.] *1715/6*. Unpublished.

My Glorious Lord. What shall thy Spouse, descry
    That flaming, Glorious Beauty, Rich, Divine,
Before mine Eyes? And shall my heart out cry
    Where's thy Beloved gone hence with his Shine?
    That I may seeke him or shall she me sham,   5
    When saying; to his garden which I am?

This Garden which he's gone to can it bee
    Thyselfe thou fairest of all Women kinde
Can he go from, and yet abide with thee?
    It must be so, if th'Garden's his designd.   10
    It rather shews where his he entertains
    Than th'Sense that saith, and that unsaith the same.

Garden delights when he therein descends
    He makes his entertainments sweet for all,
These dainty Dishes disht up for Choice friends   15
    Who enter there attendents to his Call.
    Eyesight Delights and blushy Rosey Flowers
    Clouds aromatick lodge in our Warm Towers.

Heart Ravishments: Delightful joyes unto
    The highest inchantings of Nose Eares and Eyes   20
With spirituall tunes, Perfumes and Beauties show

60 *thy Glories*] orig: the praise   1 *What*] PW what   10 *Garden's*] PW Garden
designd] orig: Church   13 *he therein*] orig: therein he
18 *aromatick*] PW aromantick

Enriched all with all Celestiall joyes,
The sweet sweet Gales of the sweet spirits sweet Air
With which Clouds aromatick can't compare.

Lord! let thy Holy Spirit take my hand   25
    And opening thy Graces garden doore
Lead mee into the Same that I well fan'd
    May by thy Holy Spirit bee all ore
    And make my Lungs thy golden Bagpipes right
    Filld with this precious Aire, thy praises pipe.   30

130. Meditation. Cant. 6.2. My Beloved is
            gone down into his Garden, to the
            Beds of Spices.

20. 3m [May] *1716.* Unpublished.

My sweet-sweet Lord who is it, that e're can
    Define thyselfe, or Mine affections strong
Unto thyselfe with inke? Who is the man
    That ever did, or can these riches Sum?
    Thy Sweetness no description can define   5
    Nor Pen and Inke can my hearts Love out line.

The Breathings of thy Spice beds Gardens Spot,
    And of thy sweet sweet flowers stowd in th'Aire
This sweet breath breatht out from thy Garden knot
    Perfume the Skies and all their riches fair.   10
    Thy Garden Bed thy Civet Box gives vent,
    To th'Gales of Spiced Vapors, sweetest Sent.

Thy Bed of Spices in thy Garden Spots,
    Perfumes most sweetly as they are inspir'd.
With thy rich Spirits breath, thy flower Pots   15

25–6 *my hand / And opening*] orig: me by / My Hand
1 *sweet-sweet*] PW sweet-speet   8 *sweet flowers*] PW spot [?] flowers

Breathe out such Sweetness, that's by Saints desir'd
Ascending up in gracious exercise
Making these beds of Spices thy sweet Joyes.

Thou dost delight to visit these, and make
  These spicy beds thy blissfull Couches bright   20
And Visits them even from thy Palace Gate
  And walkst their alies with most sweet delight.
    This Sweetness that perfumes bright Glory clear
    Perfumes thy joyes, perfumed joyes are here.

And all the Sweetness of these Beds of Spice   25
  Doth Spiritually perfume these beds of Saints
That they breath in and out perfume, whose price
  Excells all precious jewells, never faints.
    Set me a Lilly in, thy Bed of Spice,
    With sweetend breath, my Lord e're to rejoyce.   30

If thou allowst me setting in this Bed
  Of Spices set in spirituall ranks therein
With Gusts of Spirituall Odors ever fared,
    (Oh! sweet perfum! oh blessed blissfull thing)
    I shall suck in and out as sweetend fare,   35
    As ever did perfume the Clear cleare Aire.

Lord, make my sweetned Lungs out sweet Breath send.
  'Twill make thy Spice Beds still more sweet to bee.
This Aire all sweetned will its sweetness lend,
    And make my heart thereby more sweet for thee.   40
    I shall breath Sweetness in and out to thee
    And in my Spicy Lodgen will lodge thee.

The gales of Graces breath shall rise most sweet
  To thee, my Lord; me sweet with Graces Spice.
A mutuall sweetness then shall be the reek   45
    Thy Garden aire that Carrys there, my voice.
    Then shall my tongue thy Sweetend praises sing
    In tunes perfumed, thus in ery String.

16 *Breathe*] PW Breaths   20 *Couches*] PW Coaches[?]   28 *jewells*,] PW
jewells   29 *a Lilly*] orig: my Lord, a Lilly   30 *my Lord e're*] orig: ever
33 *ever*] PW over.   38 *'Twill*] PW Twill   41 *Sweetness*] PW Sweeness

131. Meditation. Cant: 6.2. To the Beds
          of Spice to feed in the Garden,
          and to gather Lillies.

15.4m [June] *1716.* Unpublished.

Dull, Dull, my Lord, my fancy dull I finde.
    Hast thou allowd no Grindlestone at all,
Unto thy Zion Fancies dull to grinde
    And make sharp edged when that thou dost call
    Thy Servants up to carry on thy worke   5
    That from the Same they may not ever shurk?

Will not the Vine of Lebanon yield Wine,
    To quicken up my Spirits? Or have I
Not tasted of thy Wine, for to refine
    My Fancy at thy feast and't vivify?   10
    How should my heart vent bitter groans, to finde
    Such spirituall deadness deadening my minde?

Dost thou come down into thy garden brave
    To feed and gather Lillies, fragrant, bright?
Shall I no Bed of Spice, or Spices have   15
    Rise up to entertain thee with Delight?
    Nor shall thy Spicy Garden green, and Vine
    Hence entertain thee with her Lilly-Shine?

If thou feedst on my Spice, my Spice must flow;
    Then thou wilt feed my Soull on Spice Divine: 20
Com'st thou to get thy Lillies? Get me so.
    Then I shall be well fed, and made all fine.
    Thine Ordinances then brieze Spicy gailes
    Filling of thy, and my Delights the Sails.

The Clouds of Grace in thy New Covenant Skie   25
    By thy Descent tapt 'still down on this plot,

2 *no*] orig: Zions   3 *dull*] orig: Sharp   8 *Or*] PW or   21 *Get*] PW get
26 *'still*] PW *still* changed to *drill*[?]

Their sweet Spice Showers of Precious grace, whereby
 Sweet Showers of Grace upon thy Garden drop:
 And graces golden Pestill too doth pound
 Her Herbs, and Spices, that sweet Smells abound. 30

Here thus is Entertainment sweet on this.
 Thou feedst thyselfe and also feedest us,
Upon the spiced dainties in this Dish.
 Oh pleasant food! Both feed together thus;
 Well spicde Delights do entertain thee here. 35
 And thou thine entertain'st with thy good Cheare.

And yet moreover thou in thy Spice beds dost
 Thy Elect Lillies gather and up pick
Out of the throng of Stinking Weeds: and stowst
 Their natures with thy holy graces thick. 40
 That they of Lillies are made lillies fresh
 Which thou dost gather glories Hall to dress.

If thou, my Lord, thy Spice bed make my Heart
 My Heart shall welcome thee with spic'de joy.
If I'm thy lilly made by Grace's Art 45
 I shall adorn thy Palace fragrantly.
 And when thou mee thy spic'de bed interst in
 I'le thee on my Shoshannim Spic'de Songs sing.

132. Meditation. Can. 6.3.—He feeds among the Lillies.

9th. 7m [Sept.] *1716*. Unpublished.

Pardon my Lord, I humbly beg the Same
 Of thy most blessed Gracious selfe thy hand.
For if I nothing touch thy glorious name
 Showing its praise I shall unworthy stand.

34 *Both*] PW both 38 *gather*] orig: gatherst *pick*] orig: pickst
41 *made*] orig: pure 48 *I'le thee on my Shoshannim Spic'de Songs*] **orig:**
Spic'de tunes to thee Shall my Shoshannim

And if I 'tempt to celebrate thy fame   5
It is too bright: my jagging pen will't stain.

The words my pen doth teem are far too Faint
And not significant enough to shew
Thy Famous fame or mine affection paint
Unto thy famous Selfe in vivid hew.   10
My jarring Pen makes but a ragged line
Unfit to be enricht with glories thine.

But thus I force myselfe to speake of thee.
If I had better thou shouldst better have.
It grieves me I no better have for thee   15
Finding thou art the Lilly growing brave
Even of the Vally rich where lillies grow
Of Graces Bright making a gracious Show.

These Lillies White all glorious shining bright
Mongst which thou feeding art sweet breathing flower   20
That Entertain thy Sight and Smell most right
With Sweetest Splender of rich Grace in power.
I hope I am one of these Lillies pure
Whose breath and Beauty do thy joy procure.

Lord make my Heart the Vally, and plant there   25
Thyselfe the Lillie there to grow. No Scorns
Shall me amuse, if I'me thy Lilly clear,
All though I be thy Lilly midst of thorns.
If I thy Lilly Fair and Sweet be thine
My heart shall be thy Harbor. Thou art mine.   30

If I thy Vally, thou its Lilly bee.
My Heart shall be thy Chrystall looking Glass
Shewing thy Lillies Face most cleare in mee
In shape and beauty that doth brightly flash.
My Looking Glass shall weare thy Lillies Face   35
As tis thy Looking Glass of Every Grace.

27 *I'me*] orig: thou makest me   34 orig: *In Shape and beauty that gives*
Sparkling Flash uncanceled interlinear line. Line 34 as above in text is written
in margin of PW.   36 *of Every*] orig: held against

My Heart shall then yield thee the Object right
 Of both thy Spirituall Sight and Smell most clear
Standing inrounded in in sweet delight.
  Thou growing Lilly in't dost feed too there   40
  Thus in the Vally and growst very cleare
  And fill my Vally with perfumed fare.

Make mee thy Lilly, Lord and be thou mine.
 Be thou the Lilly, me its vally right.
Thou th'Lillie then shalt make my Vallys shine 45
  Thou feeding mongst the lillies, with delight.
  I then shall weare thy Lillies Whitness fair.
  My Lungues like bellows shall puff out sweet air.

My Vally then shall filld be with Sweet air.
 My Songs shall blow out Sweetend breath therein 50
That shall perfume the very aire that wears
  The aromatick breaths breathd out most thin.
  If thou my Lilly, I its Vally bee.
  My Breath shall Lilly tunes sweet sing to thee.

133. Meditation. Cant. 6.2. I am my
    beloved and my beloved is
    mine.

11.9m [Nov.] *1716.* Unpublished.

Ye Daughters of Jerusalem I pray
 Delude you not yourselves, think not
To steale from me my Souls beloved away.
 I my Beloveds am, and he my lot.

40 *too there*] orig: *indeed*
41 *very cleare*] orig: *oh blest seed* canceled to supply rhyme for the misplaced
final line of stanza seven. 42 This line is written in PW by mistake between
stanzas eight and nine. 44 *Lilly,*] PW Lilly From here until the end of the
Meditations, PW is frequently illegible, and full of errors.
4 *he my*] orig: he is mine

He and his All yea all of him, is mine   5
    His Person, offices, his Grace and Shine.

The Bridsgrooms all the Brids, his all is hers.
    He's not partable nor by parts give out;
Who hath him hath him all, all bright no blurs.
    He's what's hers. Or She's all him without.   10
    He faithfull to his Spouse will ever bee.
    He'l not bag such that to him spoused flee.

Ye Daughters of Jerusalem ne'er please
    Your fancies with such thoughts as tell you do
That you may rob me of my Lord, and seize   15
    Him for your own, oh never deale not so.
    The Bridsgroom, and his bride are Relates sure
    That never Separation can endure.

Christ will not play the knave to shab me thus,
    Though knavishness of such sort youths oft Use: 20
And youthish Damsells to do so don't blush
    Yet shamefull't is and grossly to abuse.
    Your Virgin beauty will not taking bee
    Him by his Eyes t'inchant his love from mee.

Whom Christ espousseth is his Spouse indeed.   25
    His Spouse or bride no Single Person nay.
She is an agrigate so doth proceed
    And in it sure and cant be stole away.
    And if you thus be members made of mee
    He'l be your Bridegroom, you his Spouse shall be.   30

Thus you in me enjoynd shall be made bright
    And thus united, his Choice Spouse be made.
You'll be his Bride, the Bridegrooms Great delight
    And thus we both shall be most True displaid.

Oh! Daughter then ye of Jerusalem   35
    Rest not in your Degenerate case at all.

5 *is mine*] orig: that shines   7 *his all is*] orig: and he's all
8 *He's*] PW He s   9 *all,*] PW all.   12 *bag*] PW bay[?]
16 *deale*] Conj.   31 a four-line stanza in PW   34 *True*] orig: Happy

With all your Soul endevour allwayes then
    To be espousd in heart to Christ, so shall
    Then my beloved in his glory bright
    Discoverd be shall be your hearts delight.   40

Then my Beloved your beloved shall bee
    And both make him one Spouse enrichd with **Grace**
And when dresst up in glory and bright glee
    Shall sing together fore his blessed face
    Our Weddin Songs with Angells mild * * * * *   45
    In ravishing notes throughout Eternity.

134. Meditation. Cant. 6.4. Thou art beautiful as Tirzah
        Oh my Love Comely as
        Jerusalem.

26. 1716. Unpublished.

Thou fairest of the Fairest kinde alive
    Thy Beauty doth ascend above Compare
Thy Shining face Super Superlative
    Like to Jerusalem most comely fair.
    Thy brightness and thy Comeliness shinst like   5
    Most Happy Brides the bravest Beauty bright.

That eye that never did want sight to see,
    Nor to see into the Nature of what's seen
Inravisht with thy Beauty's glorious glee.
    Hath seen't and sets upon it highst Esteem.   10
    Though by Comparison its not to lower
    Its excellence but raise our 'steem on't more.

Oh bright bright Beauty all of glorious Grace
    How doth its beams dance on thy Cheeks all cleare

38 *espousd*] PW esousd   40 *Discoverd be*] be Conj.   42 *Spouse*] PW Spouse
Spouse   12 *'steem on't*] PW steem ont

Setting both beauty and terrour on thy face   15
    Pleasant in Christs Eye and terrour to's foes all here
    A pleasing Shine to Christ and yet sendst darts
    Of Terrour terrifying Wicked hearts.

Hence thou enjoyst a rich Sunshining Grace
    Which most bright beams of beauty ere can play   20
Most gloriously th'alurements of thy face,
    Making the same Christ flower knot thereof gay
    That in this beautious rich thou reeching stand
    That Christ doth Come and take thee by the hand.

And to himselfe presents thee pleasantly   25
    A glorious bride without all Spot or blame
His Eyes and hearts delight eternally
    Oh Bride most beautifull of blissfull fame.
    The Hearts delight Christ wears thee in his heart
    His Eyes delight that ne're doth from thee part.   30

Thy Beauty is made of Heavenly Paint all Grace
    Of Sanctity Holy Within and Out
A Bride most bright for the King of Glorys face
    Whose beauty laid in Heavenly Colours about
    That ravish doth the Eyes of Angells which   35
    Can't but gaze on't and all amaizd at it pitch.

And lest perchance any wrinckle on it light
  Or any freckle on thy beautious face
The Silk and Satin Robes, than milk more white
    Oh Christ's own Righteousness o're all hath place.   40
    Hence all thy Beauty fits thee for Christ's Bed
    And he will Cover thee with's White and Red.

20 *ere can*] Conj.   36 *on't*] PW ont   37 *perchance*] PW perchanch
40 *Christ's*] PW Christ   41 *Christ's*] PW Christ

135. Meditation. Can. 6.4. Terrible as an
                Army with banners.

14. 11m [Jan.] *1716.* Unpublished.

Thou far the fairest of all female dress
    Whose spirituall beauty doth arise with Shine
Of th'Beams of the blesst Son of Righteousness,
    Glazing thy face with glory all Divine.
      All Sparkling Glory like as Moses Face   5
      Shining was dreadfull so is thine with grace.

Thy Intellects a Saphrin Socket bears
    Christ's flaming Torch of Grace that sanctifies.
Thy Will Christs Cabinet of Rich Grace Wares
    Top full of Grace of Every Sort and Sise.   10
      Thy Body's like a golden Lanthorn trim
      Through which the lamps of Grace shine from within.

Thine Eye balls rowle like fiery balled Sparks
    That graces beams like fiery arrows fling
Whose fiery bullets, graces flaming Darts   15
    Most terrible to such as rowle in Sin.
      Thy Mouths Christs Morter piece lets granades fly
      Of th'holy Ghost all wicked ones to 'stroy.

Nay still the more Artiliry is there.
    A Brazeel Bow's thy mouth, thy Tong's the String   20
That shoots his Arrows pild, both in and through
    The Sinners Soules that make deep wounds therein.
      Yet more, thy mouth doth use his furbusht Sword
      By thy bright tongue in truth, his dreadfull word.

Christs golden Canon Balls that dash asunder,   25
    Whereby thou Satans garrisons dost bomb.

8 *Christ's*] PW Christ
13 *Sparks*] PW Sparke   18 *'stroy*] PW stroy   20 *Tong's*] PW Tongs[?]
Tonge[?]

Thy hands cast out like lightening sharp and Thunder
  And herewith thou dost Satan's Souldiers Thump.
  Thy Mouth thy Tongue, thy Eyes and Face are steeld
  With terrour when thou meets the foe in th'field.   30

And thou art armed in thy Coate of Male
  Made all of Graces golden Wyer bright
By th'best of artist ere in Heavens pale
  Thy holy Ghost that made it strong and tite.
  No Arrow that the foe let flies can dint   35
  Or pierce it through or break thereof a link.

Thou'rt rightly trained by thy Captain who
  Hath rightly learnt thee words of his command
Them well doth like and Fiter than the foe
  And makst good use of th'Weapons in thy hand.   40
  Thy Helmet Hope, thy Belt Christ's Truth, thy Shield
  Of Faith all right, thy Fortitude have steeld.

Thy Excellency gracious hath thee made
  Full Terrible, in fight while thou art Eying
Thy bright bright Captain whose rich Skill displaid   45
  Leading thee home with Songs and Colours flying.
  And thus thou terrible in gracious manners
  Appearest like an Armed troop in Banners.

36 *a link*] Conj. These lines following line 36 have been canceled in PW and
rewritten as lines 41–2 above: "Thy Helmet Hope, thy Belt of Truth, Thy
shield / Of Faith all Spirituall will never yield"   37 *who*] orig: and
39 entire line Conj.   41 *Christ's*] Christ   *Shield*] Conj.
42 *steeld*] Conj.   46 *home*] orig: out of th' field

136. Meditation. Cant. 6.5. Turn away thine
          Eyes from mee. For they have
          Over come mee.

6.3m [May] *1717*. Unpublished.

Oh! what a word is this thy Lips Let fall.
    Here in these drops of Honey dews whereby
Thou dost bedew mine Olive Copses all
      Within the garden of my Soul, oh joy?
      Its such a word so wondrous and so high   5
      Hadst not thou said it, sure 'twas blasphemy.

How shouldst it be that thou should charge thy Spouse
    To turn away her glancing face from thee?
Whose Charming glances are quick Flames to rouse
      The dull affections rich flaming Glee   10
      And these glances which most delightful be
      That thou should say they overcome have mee.

What do these Eyes then raise thy Joys so much
    And do they so dilate thy Spirits pure
To such a breadth though thou dost joy in such,   15
      Thy Spirits run so from thy heart, its sure
      * * * * * * * * * * * then robs thy heart of all
      Its Vitall Spirits that it fainting falls?

O wondrous Beauty that doth sorely Cramp
    Our Wondring Faculty and make it strain   20
Untill it feeble grows and groweth faint
      If such Eyes Sparkling start us with their flame!
      Art thou my Lord who are too strong for all
      Orecome hereby when they upon thee fall?

4 *oh*] Conj.
6 *it,*] PW it   9 *Flames to rouse*] Conj.   11 *which most delightful be*] orig:
should like s*** be   19 *Beauty*] Conj.   22 *start*] Conj.

But yet this thy Serprize seems Rationall   25
   In some respect seing thy glorious selfe
Stands graciously portrayed Ever shall
   Within thy Spouses Eyes with richest Wealth
   That Grace's Gold mine hath, so that it seems
   Thou must these Eyes esteem, ere thy heart 'steems.   30

Seeing thy Spouse that doth consist of all
   Gods blesst Elect regenerate within
The tract of time from first to last send shall
   From her bright Eyes her gracious beams and fling
   I wonder't would be topping very high   35
   If that such Eyes should not advance thy joy.

Then let the Beams of my Souls eye ev'n meet
   The brightsome Beams of thy blesst Eye my Lord,
And in their meeting let them sweetly greet
   And back return laded as each affords.   40
   Mine then return'd well loaded with thine flame
   Shall tune my harp to sing thy glories fame.

My Soul then quickend by thy beames brought in
   By my Souls Eye beams and glaz'd be thereby
With glorious Grace that will mee make more sing   45
   Thy praise my Lord, then shall thou have more joy.
   My Soul strung with thy grace as golden Wier,
   Will by its musick Raise thy joy the Higher.

25 *thy*] orig: thing   27 *Ever*] Conj.   30 *heart*] Conj.   31 *consist of all*] Conj.
33 *The tract*] Conj.   35 *be*] Conj.   41 *thine*] PW thines   42 *harp*] Conj.
44 *and glaz'd be*] orig: glazed shall be   45 *will*] orig: make will
46 *shall*] PW sho'nt

137. Meditation. Cant. 6.5. Thy hair is like
a flock of Goats that graze on
mount Gilliad.

14.7m [Sept.] *1717*. Unpublished.

How precious are thy thoughts my Lord, to mee!
    Oh that my thoughts on mee were Crystallizd,
Within the same, like Gems that sparkling bee,
    Like Gilliads Flock of Goats by his so prizde,
      A precious remedy for th'Souls Distempers.   5
      A spirituall Cure on which my Soule adventures.

How doth this praise thy Spouse whose Hair doth shine
    How like a flock of Goats that Gilliad graze
And by their keepers set and Order'd fine
    And stately go in their slick Glory rayes,   10
      These hairs assembled like a flock in fold
      On Gilliads top, there feeding on to hold.

Thy Gilliads top Thy Testimonies place,
    In Zions mount thy testimonies there
Thy spirituall pasture whose frim grass is Grace.   15
    The Spouses Hairs, thy flock, feed on this Cheere.
      With Grace thou feedst and fatst thy flock and down
      Dost make them ly. And in these folds them Crown.

In the High places of the City where
    Wisdome lifts up her Voice and food in't gives   20
Unto the Flock upon her head and there
    Administers them grace that they may live.

Date originally 14 [24?] 5m
2 *mee*] orig: thee   3 *like Gems*] orig: Gems like   *that*] Conj.
4 *of Goats by his so prizde*] orig: he would think on bee prizd
8 *Gilliad graze*] orig: on gilliad doth graze   9 *by*] orig: tended by
10 *go*] orig: going   *Glory*] orig: these[?] Glory   20 *Voice*] orig: head

These Spirituall Hairs do ware a spirituall grace
Feeding in Graces pastures thrive apace.

Are these thy Spouses Curled hairs trimd fine 25
    Adorning her all in rich Graces Shine
Like Gilliads Flocks that Graze her Sweet herbs prime?
    Make me then one of them an hair of thine,
    Fed in thy fold. Assemblies pure and fair
    With Spirituall Crisping pins adorning hair. 30

If thou dost make mee thus one of the Hairs
    Even of thy Spouse and in thy 'Semblies sit
Me with thy Spirits Crisping pins prepare
    Me as a Curled lock thy glory t'hit.
    I'st honour then thy Spouse and thee also 35
    As I like one of Gilliads flock do grow.

138. Meditation. Can. 6.6. Thy Teeth are
        like a flock of Sheep that come
        Up from Washing whereof every
        one bears twins.

25. 9m [Nov.] 1717. Unpublished.

My blessed blessing Lord I fain would try
    To heave thy Glory 'bove the Heavens above,
But finde my lisping tongue can never prie
    It up an inch above this dirt nor move.
    Thy brightsom glory o're this dirty slough 5
    We puddle in below and Wallow now.

But though I can but stut and blur what I
    Do go about and so indeed much marre

27 *prime?*] PW prime   *138. Meditation*] orig: 128. The original day and
month have been obscured by a blot. The date has been written over in PW
as "25:9," but the original date of the day appears to begin with "1."
3 *prie*] PW prise[?]

Do thy bright Shine: I fain would slick up high
    Although I foul it by my pen's harsh jar.   10
    Pardon my faults: they're all against my Will.
    I would do Well but have too little Skill.

What Golden words drop from thy gracious lips,
    Adorning of thy Speech with Holy paint,
Making thy Spouses teeth like lambs that skip,   15
    Oh flock of Sheep that come from Washing quaint.
    Each bearing twins a pleasant sight to spy
    Whose little lambs have leaping play and joy.

* *
    * * * a flock of pure Washt Sheep more white: 20
* * * * * * borne babe and Church that hath relief
    Whose name is in the book of Life wrote right
    The New born Soule and that Society
    I such espoused to my Lord most High.

What are these Teeth? Pray show, Some do suppose   25
    They are the Spouses Military armes:
The Arguments that do destroy her Foes:
    And do defend the Gospell truths from harms,
    But Teeth in Sheep are not their Wepon though
    The Lions teeth and Cur dogs teeth are so.   30

And others do say they note Christ's ministers:
    That dress the Spouses food. Yet such seem Cooks.
When these are 'ployd like teeth 'bout meat as its dresser.
    Yet still this seems a lesson not in books.
    Methinks Christs Ministers may rather beare   35
    The name of Cooks, than Teeth that eat the fare,

Hence methinks they the righter judge, that hold
    These Teeth import true Faith in Christ alone
And Meditation on the Gospell, should
    Be signifide thereby to every one.   40

10 *pen's*] PW pen   12 *too*] PW to   19 line missing; page of
PW torn   25 *What are*] Conj.   *Pray*] PW pray   31 *And*] Conj.
do say] Conj.   *Christ's*] PW Christ   33 *When*] Conj.   *its*] PW it

Teeth are for the eating of the Food made good
And Meditation Chawing is the Cud.

The proper use of Teeth gives the first stroke
    Unto the Meat and food we feed upon
And fits it for the Stomach there to sooke   45
    In its Concoction for nutrition.

And Meditation when 'tis Concocted there
    Take's its rich liquour having nurishment,
And distributes the same Choice Spirituall Cheer
    Through all the new man by its instrument,   50
    And hence that means of Grace doth as I thinke
    Give nurishment hereby as meate and drinke.

This Faith and Meditation a pair appears
    As two like to the two brave rows of Teeth
The Upper and the neather, well set cleare   55
    Exactly meet to chew the food, beliefe.
    Both eate by biting; meditation
    By Chewing Spiritually the Cud thereon.

* * * * two those two exactly answer right
    * * * Grindeing them and operation   60
Those in a naturall Sense in spirituall * * *
    These two, and so they pare, each on their station.
    The fore and hinder teeth, that bite and Grinde,
    So Spiritually these bite and Chew in minde.

They paire each other too, in whiteness cleare   65
    As those like Olivant, these sparkling show
With glorious Shine in a most brightsome geare
    Of spirituall whitness that exceeds pure Snow.
    Christ's milk white Righteousness and splendent Grace
    Faith doth and Meditation ever trace.   70

43 four line stanza in PW   50 *its*] PW it   52 *Give*] PW Gives
66 *show*] orig: white   69 *Christ's*] PW Christ   70 *trace*] orig: shine

Meditation 139. Cant. 6.[7.] Like a piece of
        a Pomegranate are thy Temples within
        thy Locks.

Undated. Unpublished.

My Deare, Deare Lord, oh that my Heart was made
        Thy Golden Vessel filld with Graces Wine
Received from thy Fulness and displaide
        Even by thy Spouse in her sweet Wine cup fine
        Unto thy blessed selfe to drinke at Will,   5
        Of her Sweet Wine unto thy very fill.

Thy Love that's in thy Spouses Countenance
        Is so delighted with her Temples State,
The Seate of Modesty that in't doth glance,
        Her Temples like a piece of Pomegranate   10
        That with Arteriall blood blossom with blushes,
        That in her Temples yield do spirituall flushes.

The Temples where's the purest blood indeed
        Impregnate with the working Spirits ripe.
That Warm and work the Brains as they proceed,   15
        Even from the Heart through the Arteriall pipe.
        Hence modest Looks and head that contemplate
        The Temples proper exercise and State.

The Temples like a piece of Pomegranate
        Import thy Spirituall Beauty and Spirits high   20
In purest heart blood through th'Arteriall Gate
        Into the Head. Hence these thy Visage dy
        Pomegranat like with Ruby blushes Stains
        And sharpen do thine Eyes with Spirituall Strains.

And through thy Temples Silver Wickets go   25
        Int' Contemplations Temple brave and there

Meditation 139] orig: 129   2 Graces] orig: thy Graces   7 that's] Conj.
20 and Spirits high] orig: that up fly   26 brave] orig: where's brave

In Spirituall Contemplations labour do
   On Christs rich Grace, and Glory every where,
   And how to manage well in Grace's wayes
   Sin to destroy. God's Ordinances raise.   30

140. [Meditation.] Cant. 6.7. As a piece of a
        Pomegranate are thy Temples with-
        in thy Locks.

24.9m [Nov.] *1717.* Unpublished.

My all Deare Lord, I fain would thee adore
   But finde my Pen and Inke too faint to do't.
And all my Praise with which my heart runs ore
    Unto thyself is but a poor dull note,
     That thou in thy great love thy blesst Delight   5
     Should set upon thy Spouse and to such hight.

Them thou here thus dost Court saying even thus,
   Like to a piece of a Choice Pomegranate
Thy Temples shine and glaze thy Cheeks that blush,
    With their Arteriall heart blood, modest state,   10
     Whose Vitall heate and Spirits in these pipes
     Make peart thy Countenance in gracious plites.

Th'Arteriall pipes that from thy heart do run
   Conveigh unto thy Temples the best Cheare
Of Hearty Spirits that to thy Temples come,   15
    And dy them like a pomegranate looks cleare,
     And make thy Cheeks to ware a Scarlet Maske
     Of Modest blushes, on thy Cheeks well dasht.

The sixth and final stanza of this poem is illegible. After the final stanza are
these words, partly illegible: "[For] other Meditations see back before the b***"
PW Written at top of page: "Se the following meditations *** which should
have been in the End of the book."   *140. [Meditation]* PW 129 [Meditation.]
9 *that*] orig: with   18 *blushes,*] PW blushes.

Thy Countenance hence is the Looking Glass
    Into thy heart wherein in cleare cleare shapes   20
Appear doth Choice Humility that doth pass
    Most Currant coin in Graces Markets, Mates.
    These pomegranated Temples exercise
    A contemplation of a Spirituall Guise.

A Spirituall Beauty on the Spouse hence flames   *Emblems* 25
    Thats Emblemized by the Pomegranate   *1982*
Unto us on the temples by its grains
    Wearing a scarlet dy upon their Shape
    All holding out a Spirituall Beauty fresh
    And Chiefly to Christ's Eye in loveliness.   30

My Lord my Temples pomegranate make thus
    That I may ware this Holy Modesty
Upon my Face maskt with thy Graces blush,
    That never goes without Humility.
    Thy lovely object then all grace shall bee   35
    Shall Humbly sing forth graces notes to thee.

Meditation 141. Cant. 6.8.9. There are
    threescore Queens, and fourscore
    Concubines, and Virgins without
    number.

2.1m [Mar.] *1717/8.* Unpublished

My Only Dear, Dear Lord, I search to finde
    My golden Arck of Thought, thoughts fit and store:
And search each Till and Drawer of my minde
    For thoughts full fit to Deck thy kindness o're,
    But find my foreheade Empty of such thoughts   5
    And so my words are simply ragged, nought.

22 *Markets*] orig: courts
30 *Christ's*] PW Christ   *Meditation 141*] PW Meditation 130

Thoughts though the fairest Blossoms of my minde
    Are things too loose and light t'strew at the gate
Of thy bright Palace. My words hence are winde
    Moulded in print up thee to decorate.   ·   10
    Hence th'glory of thy Love Whose Sunshine here
    I shall but darken with my dusty geere.

Hence I do humbly stand, and humbly pray,
    Thee to accept my homely Style although
Its too too hurden a bearing blancket, nay   15
    For to lap up thy Love in, it to show.
    When spruiced up therein, it seems like thatch
    Upon a golden Palace (Dirty slatch).

Thy Love dropt on thy Spouses Loveliness
    Out measures all Dimention ne'er so wide.   20
Nay Angills pen can't pencill out its dress
    Nor can its length or breadth ere out describe:
    They never can thy gloryous Love out lay
    Whose brightness doth out shine the brightest day.

All Virgins in their Virginall Attire: 25
    Ladies of Honour eighty in array,
And threescore Queens robde shining out like fire
    Can never match thy Spouses Beauty gay.
    Though these for Number and for Glory rise
    In sparkling glory get not to her Sise.   30

Thy boundless Love thy Spouses boundless prove
    Doth take up all and in't did ever latch.
Oh Boundless Loveliness, and boundless Love
    You neither either ever over match.
    Yet know this thing, thy Boundless Love hath made   35
    This Loveliness thus boundless where its laid.

Oh! let thy boundless Love my Lord, a Kiss
    Bestow on me and joyn me to thy Dove
That is but one, Whose members have such Bliss.

9 *winde*] orig: but winde   19 *Loveliness*] PW Lowliness[?]
22 *out*] Conj.   31 *prove*] orig: Beauty   32 *latch*] orig: laye
33 *Love*] orig: Love so true   34 *match*] orig: *Charged* changed to *dodge*

And in its blissfull beams I'st ever move.   40
My portion then shall far excell the Share
Those Queens and Concubines and Virgins weare.

If one bright beam of this thy boundless Love
    Do light on me, enlightend I shall bee
To Cooe thy praise as joyned to thy Dove   45
    And double back thy Love with songs to thee.
    Thy Love I'le thus requite with Songs Ile sing
    Unto thy lovely selfe, under loves Wing.

142. Meditation. Can. 6.9. My Dove is One
            the onely One of her mother the
        Choice One of her that bare her etc.

4.3m [May] *1718.* Unpublished.

What shall I say, my Deare Deare Lord? most Deare
    Of thee! My choisest words when spoke are then
Articulated Breath, soon disappeare.
    If wrote are but the Drivle of my pen
    Beblackt with my inke, soon torn worn out unless   5
    Thy Holy Spirit be their inward Dress.

What, what a Say is this. Thy Spouse doth rise.
    Thy Dove all Undefiled doth excell
All though but one the onely in thine Eyes
    All Queen and Concubines that bear the bell.   10
    Her excellence all excellency far
    Transcends as doth the Sun a pinking Star.

She is the Onely one her mother bore
    Jerusalem ever above esteems
Her for her Darling her choice one therefore   15

42 *Queens*] PW Queen   *142. Meditation*] PW 131. Medtation
2 *My*] PW my   *spoke are*] orig: spoken then are   3 *Articulated*] orig: Are but
articulated   5 *worn*] orig: and worn   7 *Thy*] PW thy   11 *Her*] orig: Whose
all] orig: doth all   12 *Transcends*] PW Transcend

Thou holdst her for the best that ere was seen.
The Sweetest Flower in all thy Paradise
And she that bore her Made her hers most Choice.

That power of thine that made the Heavens bow,
    And blush with shining glory ever cleare   20
Hath taken her within his glorious brow
    And made her Madam of his Love most Deare
    Hath Circled her within his glorious arms
    Of Love most rich, her shielding from all harms.

She is thy Dove, thy Undefiled, she shines   25
    In thy rich Righteousness all Lovely, White
The onely Choice one of her Mother, thine
    Most beautifull beloved, thy Delight.
    The Daughters saw and blessed her, the Queens
    And Concubines her praisd and her esteem.   30

Thy Love that fills the Heavens brimfull throughout
    Coms tumbling on her with transcendent bliss
Even as it were in golden pipes that spout
    In Streams from heaven, Oh! what love like this?
    This comes upon her, hugs her in its Arms   35
    And warms her Spirits. Oh! Celestiall Charms.

Make me a member of this Spouse of thine
    I humbly beg deck thus, as Tenis Ball
I shall struck hard on th'ground back bounce with Shine
    Of Praise up to the Chamber floor thy Hall,   40
    Possesses. And at that bright Doore I'l sing
    Thy sweetest praise untill thou'st take me in.

20 *ever cleare*] orig: cleare   23 *his*] orig: thy   30 *Concubines*] PW Concubine

143. Meditation. Can. 6.10. Who is she that
        looks forth as the morning. Fare
        as the Moon Clear as the Sun.
        Terrible as an Army With Banners.

13.5m [July] *1718.* Unpublished.

Wonders amazed! Am I espousd to thee?
    My Glorious Lord? What! shall my bit of Clay
Be made more bright than brightest Angells bee,
    Looke forth like as the Morning every way?
      And shall my lump of Dirts ware such attire?   5
      Rise up in heavenly Ornaments thus, higher?

But still the Wonders stand, shall I looke like
    The glorious morning that doth gild the Skie
With golden beams that make all day grow light
    And View the World ore with its golden Eye?   10
      And shall I rise like fair as the fair Moon,
      And bright as is the Sun, that lights Each room?

When we behold a piece of China Clay
    Formd up into a China Dish compleat
All spiced ore as with gold Sparks display   15
    Their beauty all under a glass robe neate,
      We gaze thereat and wonder rise up will
      Wondring to see the Chinees art and Skill.

How then should we and Angells but admire
    Thy Skill and Vessell thou hast made bright thus   20
Out for to look like to the Morning tire
    That shineth out in all bright Heavenly plush?

143. Meditation] PW 134 Meditation
1 *Am*] PW am   2 *What*] PW what   3 *bee,*] PW bee.   6 Between stanzas one
and two are two lines partly canceled: Oh see now too forth like th' morning
very fair / As shines the Moon and bright bright Sun [so cleare?]"

Whose golden beams all Varnish ore the Skies
And gild our Canopy in golden wise?

Wonders are nonplust to behold thy Spouse   25
    Look forth like to the morning whose sweet rayes
Gild ore our Skies as with transparent boughs
    Like Orient gold of a Celestiall blaze.
    Fair as the Moon bright as the Sun most cleare
    Gilding with spirituall gold graces bright Sphere.   30

O Blessed! Virgin Spouse shall thy sharp lookes
    Gild o're the Objects of thy Shining Eyes
Like fairest Moon, and Brightest Sun do th'Fruits
    Even as that make the morning shining rise?
    The fairest moon in'ts Socket's Candle light   35
    Unto the Night and th'Sun's days Candle bright.

Thy Spouses Robes all made of Spirituall Silk
    Of th'Web wove in the Heavens bright Loom indeed,
By the Holy Spirits hand more white than milk
    And fitted to attire thy Soule that needs.   40
    As th'morning bright's made of the Suns bright rayes
    So th'Spirits Web thy Souls rich Loom o're layes.

Oh! Spouse adorned like the morning Cleare
    Chasing the night out from its Hemesphere.
And like the fair face of the Moon: whose Cheere   45
    Is very brave and like the bright Sun peare,
    Thus gloriously fitted in brightest Story
    Of Grace espousd to be the king of glory.

And thus deckt up methinks my Eare attends
    Kings, Queens and Ladies Query. Who is this?   50
Enravisht at her Sight, how she out sends
    Her looks like to the morning filld with Bliss,
    Fair as the Moon Clear as the Sun in'ts Costs
    And terrible as is a bannerd host?

23 *beams*] PW beam   27 *Skies*] orig: Batt[l]ments   *boughs*] orig: Bowers[?]
34 *rise*] orig: as they rise   39 *By*] PW by   orig: All by   *white*] PW whit
40 *that needs*] orig: and feed   46 *peare*] orig: Clear   48 *the king*] PW th king
orig: unto the king

And all in Graces Colours thus bedight   55
    That do transend with glorys Shine, the Sun
And Moon for fairness and for glorious light
    As doth the Sun a gloworms Shine out run.
    No wonder then and if the Bridesgroom say
    Thou art all fair my Love, Yea Everyway.   60

May I a member be, my Lord, once made
    Here of thy Spouse in truest Sence, though it bee
The meanest of all, a Toe, or Finger 'rayde
    Ist have enough of bliss, espousd to thee.
    Then I in brightest glory ere't belong   65
    Will Honour thee singing that Wedden Song.

144. Meditation. Cant. 6.11. I went down
      into the Garden of nuts to se the
      fruits of the Vally, to se whether
      the Vine flowerished and the
      Pomegranate Budded.

14.7m [Sept.] *1718.* Unpublished.

Eternal Majesty, my blessed Lord,
    Art thou into thy Nutty Garden come?
To se the Vallys fruits on thy accord:
    Whether thy Vines do flowrish and thick hange
    To se whether thy Pomegranates do bud,
    And that thy nuttree gardens fruit is good?   5

Am I a grafted Branch in th' true true Vine?
    Or planted Pomegranat thy Garden in
And do I flowerish as a note of Wine?

56 *do*] orig:to   59 *Bridesgroom*] PW Bridesgroon
63 *of all*] orig: member   *144. Meditation*] PW 135 **Meditation**
2 *into*] orig: come into   4 *hange*] PW hunge
9 *note*] PW not[?]

And do my pomegranates now bud and spring?   10
Oh let my blossoms and my Buds turn fruite
Lest fruitless I suffer thy prooning Hook.

And with thy Spirituall Physick purge thou mee:
My very Essence that much fruite't may beare,
Most joyous and delightfull unto thee.   15
The Spirituall Grapes and Pomegranates most fare.
If in thy Nut Tree Garden I am found
Barren thy prooning knife will Cut and Wound.

If in thy nuttery, I should be found
To beare no Nutmegs, Almonds, but a nut   20
All Wormeate, or in barrenness abound
I well may feare thy prooning hook will Cut
And Cut me off as is the fruitless Vine:
That evermore doth fruitfulness decline.

But when thou in thy garden dost descend   25
And findst my branch clusterd with spirituall Grapes;
And my trees limbs with fruits downward to bend,
Each bows full reev'd with Spirituall Pomegranates.
My Vines and blossom and the Grapes thereon
Will smell indeed like Smell of Lebanon.   30

Shall this poore barren mould of mine e're bee
Planted with Spirituall Vines and pomegranates?
Whose Bud and Blossome flowrish shall to thee?
And with perfumed joys thee graciate?
Then Spirituall joyes flying on Spicy Wings   35
Shall entertain thee in thy Visitings.

And if thou makest mee to be thy mold
Though Clayey mould I bee, and run in mee
Thy Spirits Gold, thy Trumpet all of gold,
Though I be Clay Ist thy Gold-Trumpet bee.   40

10 *pomegranates*] PW pomegranate   20 *Almonds, but*]
orig: Almonds filberts, but   25 *in*] orig: dost in
30 *Smell*] orig: Lebanon   38 *run*] orig: therein run   39 *Gold,*] PW Gold
orig: will be Gold

Then in Angelick melody I will
Trumpet thy Glory and with gracious Skill.

145. Meditation. Can. 6.12. Or ere I was aware my soule had made mee like the Chariots of Aminadab.

19.9m [Nov.] *1718.* Unpublished.

Alas! my Lord, how should my Lumpish Heart,
    Ascend the golden Ladder of thy praise
With packs of Sweetest Tunes prest like a Carte
    Loaded with cold hard iron, Sorrows layes?
    Seing thy people tread down under feet,
    Thy will reveald, as dirt within the Street.

I do constrain my Dumpishness away
    And to give place unto a Spirituall Verse
Tund on thy glorious joys and to Conveigh

145. Meditation] PW 136. Meditation
4 *cold hard iron, Sorrows*] orig: iron, prest down Sorrows

    title, line 16, line 24: Chariots of Aminadab (Aminadib). Amminadab is a
Hebrew phrase, *ammi* 'my uncle' or 'my kinsman' plus *nadab* 'has given
freely'; it is a masculine proper name and was often used by the old drama-
tists as a name for a Quaker (*WNI*). Amminadib, according to *A Dictionary
of the Bible* (James Hastings, ed. 4 vols. New York, Scribner's, 1898–1902),
"occurs in A[uthorized] V[ersion] and R[evised] V[ersion] m[argin] of a very
obscure passage, Ca[nticles] 6 [12] 'my soule made me *like* the chariots of
Amminadib.' AV and AVm do not regard the term as a pr[oper] name, but
render 'my soul set me on (RV *among*) the chariots of my willing (RV
princely) people.'" There has been a great deal of interpretation and exegesis
of the phrase *chariots of Amminadib:* see Reuss' *Altes Testament,* vv. 391 ff.
(referred to by Hastings). It seems clear that the Hebrew text here is corrupt.
The Holy Bible (sponsored by the Episcopal Committee of the Confraternity
of Christian Doctrine, St. Anthony Guild Press, Patterson, N.J., 1955) emends
"chariots" out of the text, and notes (p. 474): "The text is obscure in Hebrew
and in the ancient versions. The Vulgate reads: 'I did not know; my soul
disturbed me because of the chariots of Aminadab.'"

My notes upon the Same, and my heart seirce   10
From all such dross till sweet tund prais pierce through
Those Clouds of Dumps to come thy throne unto.

What shall mine Ears, thy Rhetorick displaid
   Be lind with Melancholy Dark and sad?
Whilest thus thou singst, My Soule I wist not, made   15
      Me like the Chariots of Aminadab?
      Whirld up in heart transporting Raptures bright
      And spiced incoms Wonderfull Delights.

Oh! what a Speech is this, thy lips do vent.
My Soul as I walk in my Nut tree Vaile   20
I wist not how its flourishing Vines out sent
      Such reechs about me now within its pales,
      That me enravished and me they did
      Make like the Chariots of Aminadib.

Thy Gardens Graces briezing on thee bring   25
      Thee Welcome when thou Visitst it all bright
Transport thy Soul as it on Angells Wings
      Flyes to thy Paradise of all delight
      Or ears I wist thou saith. And I it see
      To be a word too wonderfull for mee.   30

My Gracious Lord, take thou my heart and plant
      Each Sanctifying Garden Grace therein.
Make it thy nut tree Vaile to have no want
      And tune its graces to thy Songs, My King,
      When thou unto thy praise my heart shalt tune   35
      My heart shall tune thy praise in sweetest fume.

11 *till*] Conj.   orig: and   *through*] PW tho'   14 *Be lind*] PW Belind
16 *Aminadab*] orig: Aminadib   18 *Wonderfull*] orig: of
Wonderfull   22 *me*] PW we   33 *Vaile to have*] orig: Vally to be
36 *sweetest*] PW sweest

146. Meditation. Cant. 6.13. Return, oh
Shulamite, return return.

11.11m [Jan.] *1718*. Unpublished.

My Deare Deare Lord, I know not what to say:
    Speech is too Course a web for me to cloath
My Love to thee in or it to array,
    Or make a mantle. Wouldst thou not such loath?
    Thy Love to mee's too great, for mee to shape   5
    A Vesture for the Same at any rate.

When as thy Love doth Touch my Heart down tost
    It tremblingly runs, seeking thee its all,
And as a Child when it his nurse hath lost
    Runs seeking her, and after her doth Call.   10
    So when thou hidst from me, I seek and sigh.
    Thou saist return return Oh Shulamite.

Rent out on Use thy Love thy Love I pray.
    My Love to thee shall be thy Rent and I
Thee Use on Use, Intrest on intrest pay.   15
    There's none Extortion in such Usury.

I'le pay thee Use on Use for't and therefore
    Thou shalt become the greatest Usurer.
But yet the principall I'le neer restore.
    The Same is thine and mine. We shall not Jar.   20
    And so this blessed Usury shall be
    Most profitable both to thee and mee.

And shouldst thou hide thy shining face most fair
    Away from me. And in a sinking wise

146. Meditation] PW 137. Meditation   2 *too*] PW to   3 *or it to array*]
orig: Such stuff I loath, or thee   4 *Wouldst*] PW wouldst
loath?] PW loath   9 *lost*] Conj.   13–16 a four line stanza
13 *thy Love I*] orig: my Lord I   14 *and*] orig: I pay and

My trembling beating heart brought nigh t'dispare   25
   Should cry to thee and in a trembling guise
   Lord quicken it. Drop in its Eares delight
   Saying Return, Return my Shulamite.

147. Meditation. Cant. 6.13. That wee may
look upon thee.

1. of 1m [Mar.] *1719.* Unpublished.

Had I Angelick skill and on their wheele
   Could spin the purest puld white silk into
The finest twine and then the same should Reele
   And weave't a satten Web there in also
   Or finest Taffity with shines like gold   5
   And Deckt with pretious stones, brightst to behold.

And all inwrought with needle work most rich,
   Even of the Holy Ghost to lap up in,
My Heart full freight with love refinde, the Which
   Up on thy Glorious selfe I ever bring   10
   And for thy sake thy all fair spouse should wear't
   Some glances of the same I to her beare

That Cloath her may who in her mourning Weeds
   As sorrowing she searches thee about
That saith: Oh Shulamite Our eye much bleeds.   15
   Turn turn that it may look on thee right out.
   That we may looke upon thee, and behold
   Thy ravishing beauty that thy sweet face unfolds.

That sparkling Airiness thy Cheeks do lodge
   Laid on them by the Holy Ghost in Grace,   20

27 *Drop*] PW drop   *147. Meditation*] PW 138 Meditation
5 *shines like gold*] PW shins lik'of gold   11 *should*] orig: doth
12 *glances*] PW glance   *beare*] orig: givest[?]   13 *who in her mourning*]
orig: to Cloath in her S***   14 *thee*] orig: to [l]ook for thee

Do send such sparkling flashes without Dodge
  Those Charms that took our Eye in ery place
  A sight thereof which evermore would bed
  Upon those Cheeks of all their sight the head.

The brightest beauty Pensill ever drew   25
  Laid in the Richest Colours gold could gain
The shiningst glory the suns face ere knew
  The sparklingst shine nature did ere attain
  Are but black spot and smoot on brightest faces
  Unto thy beauty all enlaid with graces.   30

The bodies Eyes are blind, no sight therein
  Is Cleare enough to take a sight of this.
Its the internall Eye Sight takes this thing
  This glorious light the Sin blind Eye doth miss.
  Th'Internall Eye with Christ's Eye Salve annointed 35
  Is on this beauteous face alone well pointed.

Hence'noint mine Eyes my Lord with thine Eye salve
  That they may view thy Spouses Beauty pure,
Whose sight passt on thyselfe do thence Resolve
  To lodge and with the Shulamite Endure   40
  That grace shed from this fulness make her shine
  Brightst in mine Eyes to sing her praise and thine.

21 *such*] PW shuch
22 *in ery place*] Conj. 26 *Colours*] PW tinctures[?] *gain*] PW grain[?]
31 *blind,*] PW blind *sight*] PW sights 35 *Christ's*] PW Christ
41 *shed*] Conj.

148. Meditation. Can. 7.1. How beautiful are thy
          feet with Shooes, oh Prince's daughter: the
          Joynts of thy Thighs are as jewells etc.

3. 3m [May] *1719*. Unpublished.

My Blessed Lord, should I arrive unto
     That rich propriety that makes mee thine,
If otherwise though thou thereto say'th noe.
     I am in a bad use indeed and pine.
     If I be thine thou then wilt set thine Eye   5
     Upon my feet their beauty thou wilt spy.

In my returning unto thee, wilt say
     How beautious are thy feet with Shooes, behold
Then thou indeed with praises give my way
     My feet do take, my thigh joynts like rich gold   10
     Adorned with Jewels gloriously do shine
     The work of an Artificers hand most fine.

As I return to thee my errours fro
     Thou wilt mee see and say of Mee behold
Thy feet all beautious with Shooes up grow   15
     Thy walkst more Shines than paths all pavde with gold.
     Thy beauteous Shooes all laid all ore so trim
     And jew'ld thigh joynts grace the way Walkt in.

My walk to thee then in the Way of Faith
     And of Repentance where each step is filld   20
With prints of Grace, of which our Lord Christ saith
     How beautious are thy feet with Shooes that guild
     Hath every step with wealthy grace inlaid
     Thy Huckle joynts with jewells glorious trade.

148. Meditation] PW 139. Meditation   17 *Shooes*] orig: feets
18 *grace*] orig: all grace   23 *step*] PW stept

Shall traitor Beckets tripping Slippers bee   25
    Dawbt all ore with Gold Lace, and studded too
With precious stones? that every step that he
    Didst take that sun like Sparks from thence out flew?
    And shall Christs bride with brightest grace be graced
    With blacksome shew have her bright path defacd?   30

Her Spirituall Shooes ore laid with Spirituall Lace
    Studed with spirituall pearls and precious Stones,
Fitted to stick in glory's Crown where Grace
    Shines in't as brightest Carbuncles ever shown
    Which makes her path she walks in ware a shine   35
    As she walks to Christ, glazd with rayes divine.

Her bright affections and Choice thought, her feet
    Shod all with grace, Choice Shooes indeed the best
In Graces market had, good Cheape most meet
    For th'princes Daughters ware and all her Vests   40
    Are answerable thereunto. That bee
    All beautious for delight in heavenly Glee.

These Shooes do make her walke to Christ appear
    More glorious by far than is Romes Street
Stild Via Auri or triple Crowns costly Geare   45
    Or Bejemd toes of Emperours Passing great.
    How glorious with Shooes blest Madam sweet
    Thy thigh joynts buncht with Pearls so beautious keep.

My Lord, may my Souls feet but wear such Shooes
    And my thigh joynts be lashed, such jewells weare,   50
I then shall statly go and bravely Close

27 *that he*] orig: it*** brightend
28 *Sparks from thence*] PW Sparks thence   30 *With blacksome
shew*] orig: Who with this black shine   35 *ware*] Conj.
36 *walks*] orig: doth walk   *rayes*] orig: these rayes   37 *thought,*] PW thought
40 *ware*] Conj.   41 *bee*] orig: Choose[?]   46 *Bejemd*] PW Besems
50 *such jewells weare*] Conj.

  25: Beckets. Thomas Becket (ca. 1118–70), Archbishop of Canterbury under
Henry II; considered by Taylor a traitor to the king.

Even with thyselfe and keep the way most fair.
But every step will lined be with grace
And fill the Aire with Songs while thee I chase.

149. Meditation. Can. 7.2. Thy Navill is
            a round Goblet אגן bason Exo:
            26. thy belly is a heap
            of Wheate set about with Lillies.

5. 5m [July] *1719*. Unpublished.

My blessed-Glorious Lord, thy Spouse I spie
    Most Glorious in thine Eye that ther is none
That may compare with her under the Skie,
    Nay Heaven itselfe can't shew such other One.
    Her wandring t'seek thee when that thou withdrew   5
    Didst from her, cause her heart ach Sobs renew.

Then thy sweet calls thus said, Return Return
    Oh! Shulamite, return and do not feare:
And as this gladsom Sound forbad to mourn.
    Did touch her heart as it did touch her Eare.   10
    That vitall faith turnd from her wandring State
    Shee findes her Soule enricht with Graces plate.

Her steps returning, her Lord beholds her Shooes
    Ore laid with beauty far out shining Gold.
Her huckle joynts like precious pearls he viewes   15
    Like precious Stones that golden rings enfold,
    Which he beholding doth to her thus crie,
    Oh Beautious daughter and for very joye.

149. *Meditation*] PW 140. Meditation
3 *may*] orig: there is may   6 *renew*] orig: up grew
13 *Lord*] orig: deare Lord   17 *doth to her thus crie, / Oh*] orig: he unto her
cries / Out doth. Oh   18 *joye*] orig: joyes

    אגן *aggan* 'basin.'

Emblem 1982

Thy Spirituall Navill like the Altars Bowle
    Filld full of Spirituall Liquor to refresh   20
The Spirits babes conceived in thy Soule
      The Altars Bason that its blood to dress
      The Altar sprinkled with it and t'atone
      Herself and hers and ease her of her Grone.

Her Belly where her Spirituall Offspring's bred   25
    Is like an heap of Wheate most Choice and fine
With fragrant Lillies richly selvidged
      Making the whole most beautifully shine.
      Her spirituall strength these arteries and nerves keep
      Holding up, and upholding of all most sweet.   30

Here's Spirits of the Spirits Chymistrie
    And Bisket of the Spirits Backhouse best
Emblems of Sanctifying Grace most high
      Water and Bread of spirituall life up dresst.
      Here's Meat and Drinke to nourish grace in Sum   35
      And feed the Spouses infants in her womb.

Hereby is shown her spirituall growth in Grace,
    Whereby she able rises to bring forth
Her spirituall offspring of a spirituall race
      Her Saints, and Sanctifying Grace their growth.   40
      Her Spirituall Navill buttoning all her Store
      Of Liquour rich the Spirits Wine fat pure,

Of spirituall rich distilled Sanctity
    Its sweetest dews to moisten all her fruite.
Here's food to feed her infant Saints whereby   45
      They up are Cherisht well in branch and root;
      Races of Saints do from her belly flow
      That to supply her Spousehood up do grow.

Hence Spirituall Babes hang sucking of her breasts
    And draw thence th'Spirituall milk of these milk bowles
And of this Wheat eat plumb bread too the best.

24 *Herself*] orig: Thyself   *hers*] orig: theirs
34 *Bread*] PW Bead   42 *Wine*] orig: liquour

That nurish do and fatten holy Souls.
My Bisket sop her Basons liquour in
And feed me with, I'le then thy praises sing.

150. Meditation. Cant. 7.3. Thy two
          breasts are like two young
          Roes that are twins.

6. 7m [Sept.] 1719. Unpublished.

My Blessed Lord, how doth thy Beautious Spouse
   In Stately Stature rise in Comliness?
With her two breasts like two little Roes that browse
   Among the lillies in their Shining dress
   Like stately milke pailes ever full and flow   5
   With spirituall milke to make her babes to grow.

Celestiall Nectar Wealthier far than Wine
   Wrought in the Spirits brew house and up tund
Within these Vessells which are trust up fine
   Likend to two pritty neate twin Roes that run'd   10
   Most pleasently by their dams sides like Cades
   And suckle with their milk Christs Spirituall Babes.

Lord put these nibbles then my mouth into
   And suckle me therewith I humbly pray,
Then with this milk thy Spirituall Babe I'st grow,   15
   And these two milke pails shall themselves display
   Like to these pritty twins in pairs round neate
   And shall sing forth thy praise over this meate.

150. Meditation] PW 141. Meditation   3 breasts] PW breast
7 Wealthier] orig: more Wealthy   11 by] orig: and by   like Cades] orig: side
have

151. Meditation. Cant. 7.4. Thy Neck is like
         a Tower of Ivory: thine Eyes are like
         the Fishpools of Heshbon, at the
         Gate of Bath Rabbim: thy Nose is
         like the tower of Lebanon that
         Looketh towards Damascus.

31. 8m [Oct.] *1719*. Unpublished.

My Glorious Lord, how doth the Worlds bright Glory
     Grow great? Yet loe, thy Spouse doth ware a Shine
That far ore shines the Worlds bright Shining Story
     More than the Sun a glow worms glitter prime.
     Thy Neck is like a Tower of Ivory   5
     White, pure and bright, streight upright, neatly High.

Noting thy Pretious Faith which Pillar like
     Bears up the golden Head: and joyns it to
Herselfe thy Body mystick, thy delight:
     And is the very pipe through which do flow   10
     All Vitall Spirits from the head t'revive
     And make the Bodies members all to thrive.

This Neck Compleats thy Spouse, her stately steps,
     As a Celestiall Majesty Upright
Not ry nor Rugged Whight smooth; hath no frets.   15
     Thyselfe her Head fix on her neck all White.
     It never breaks but makes the Spouse a neate
     And statly person, Body and head compleate.

All Spirituall Vitall Influences soaking through
     They through it drench all its passports, or wayes   20
Though never so secret to each member so

151. Meditation] PW 142. Meditation   2 *Yet*] PW yet
3 *bright*] PW brigh   4 *prime*] PW prine   15 *ry*] Conj.   *hath*] orig: and hath
18 *Body*] orig: A Body

And make them grow most gay.
    This office performs and uniting hold
The Head and Body, feet more bright than gold.

Her Eyes the fayer glory, the Looking Glass   25
    Wherein her minde sees all things shining peep.
They are like Heshbon's fish pooles sparkling as
    The Lymphick Rayments Scally Robes there keep
    Her cleare clear knowledge in her Spirituall Eye
    As Viewing things Divine is held thereby.   30

These Fish pools then of Heshbon of rare Art
    And at Bath Rabbim's gate erected cleare
Bright shining do unto us thus impart
    As they stand at the Rabbins Hall door neer
    That bright bright Light that doth thy Spouse attend,   35
    That doth all Hellish darkness quite dispend.

It is the Holy Ghosts bright Lanthorn in Her hand
    That lights her feet to take the path of Grace
And makes the night time daylight. No stop nor stand
    Hence she hath as she doth to glory trace.   40
    The Sun of Righteousness'es beams make day
    Within, through these and out hence she sees th'right way.

Her Nose, the Faces Ornamental Dress
    Like Lebanon's brave tower, that hath its Eye
Upon Damascus which Enemies possess.   45
    And smells the actions of Christs Enemy:
    The Senses and the Neck Eyes, Nose speake beauty bright
    Being Compleat and Watchfull Weights.

And hence these Metaphors we spirituallized
    Speake out the Spouses spirituall Beauty cleare: 50
And morallizd do speake out Enemies
    And hence declare the Spouses Lovely deare

22 A short line in PW
24 *Body*,] PW Body.   28 *Rayments*] orig: garments   36 *darkness*] PW
darknest   37 *Lanthorn*] PW Lathorn   48 Incomplete line in PW
52 *Lovely*] orig: they possess

To be the best and Enemies hath though they
    Assaulting her shall perish in th'assay.

Make me a member of thy Beautious Bride,   55
    I then shall wear thy lovely Spouses Shine
And shall envest her with my Love beside
    Which with thy graces shall a dorn her fine.
    Ist then be deckt up in thy Glorious vests
    And sing the Bridall Melodies out best.   60

152. Meditation. Can. 7.5. Thy Head Upon thee is like
            Carmel and the hair of thy head like Purple.
            The King is held in the galleries.

27. 10m [Dec.] 1719. Unpublished.

My Deare Deare Lord! my Soul is damp Untun'd.
    My strings are fallen and their screw pins slipt.
When I should play thy praise each grace perfumd
    My strings made fit with graces wax most slick.
    My notes that tune thy praise should, pleasantly,   5
    Will onely make an harish symphony.

Thou gildest ore with sparkling Metaphors
    The Object thy Eternall Love fell on
Which makes her glory shine 'bove brightest stars
    Carbuncling of the Skies Pavillion   10
    That pave that Crystal Roofe the Earth's Canopy
    With golden streaks, border'd with Pomell high.

The inward Tacles and the outward Traces
    Shine with the Varnish of the Holy Ghost
Are th'Habit and the Exercise of Graces   15

53 *hath*] orig: possess   55 *thy*] orig: this   56 *I*] orig: I'st   58 *her*] PW here
60 *Bridall*] PW Bidall   *152. Meditation*] PW 143. Meditation
1 *Soul*] PW Soul's   *damp*] PW danp   orig: danpish[?] dunpish[?]
6 *onely make*] orig: make onely   9 *shine*] orig: out shine

Sent out with glorifying a part an host.
Yea every part from leg to toe do shine
Or Rather from the toe to th'top Divine.

Thus waring of the sparkling shine most bright,
    Of Sanctifying Grace in every part   20
She is an Object of thy blesst delight
        That with her beauty doth attack thy heart.
        Hence in her galleries thou'rt held, thy Eye
        Detains thyselfe surprised with such joy.

Then make me Lord a member of thy Spouse   25
    Thus Varnisht with thy spirit, a part of Gold,
A Toe, a Foot, a Navill, Nose or brows,
        An Arm, an Hand, a lock of hair, or fold
        All sparkling with thy Grace in brightest Rayes
        And golden Tunes I'l ever singing praise.   30

153. Meditation. Cant. 7.6. How Fair and
            how pleasant art thou, O love,
            for delight?

12m [Feb.] 1719. Unpublished.

My Glorious Lord thy work upon my hand
    A work so greate and doth so Ample grow
Too larg to be by my Souls limits spand.
        Lord let me to thy Angell Palace goe
        To borrow thence Angelick Organs bright
        To play thy praises with these pipes aright.   5

You Holy Angells lend yee mee your Skill.
    Your Organs set and fill them up well stuft

18 to th'top] PW to'th top   23 her] orig: thy   thou'rt held] Conj.
29 Rayes] PW changed to layse[?]   153. Meditation] PW 144. Meditation
3 Too larg to be by my Souls limits] orig: Too large within my narrow limits

With Christs rich praises whose lips do distill
    Upon his Spouse such ravishing dews to gust   10
    With Silver Metaphors and Tropes bedight.
    How fair, how pleasant art, Love, for delight?

Which Rhetorick of thine my Lord descry
    Such influences from thy Spouses face
That do upon me run and raise thy Joy   15
    Above my narrow Fancy to uncase.
    But yet demands my praise so high, so much
    The which my narrow pipe can neer tune such.

Hence I come to your doors bright Starrs on high
    And beg you to imply your pipes herein.   20
Winde musick makes the Sweetest Melody.
    I'le with my little pipe thy praises sing.
    Accept I pray and what for this I borrow,
    I'le pay thee more when rise on heavens morrow.

154. Meditation. Heb. 11.6. Without Faith
its impossible to please God.

10. 5m [July] *1720.* Unpublished.

Faith! Faith! my Lord! there is none other Grace.
    Like suitable thyself to grace most High.
Of all thy glorious Graces, oh! the place,
    That Faith obtains 'mongst them to magnify
    Thyselfe, it is the Golden twist thou hast   5
    To tie my Soule to thee my Lord most Fast.

That Golden Lace thy Ephod fast to ty
    Unto thy Glorious Breast plate deckt with Stones

9 *whose lips do distill*] orig: tun'de ** *est   11 *bedight*] orig: are bedight
13 *descry*] Conj. orig: display   15 *me*] Conj.   *154. Meditation*] PW [no
number]   2 *thyself*] orig: to this   5 *twist*] Conj.   *thou hast*] orig: that
made[?]   6 *tie*] orig: thy   8 *Unto*] orig: Thy   *deckt*] PW deck   *Stones*]
orig: rich Stones

Rather the golden Button Curiously
    Together on thy shouldier bone alone   10
    Or golden Girdle that the Breast plate ties
    Upon thy breast, my Lord, my High Priest wise.

       ·   ·   ·   ·   ·   ·

    Within whose fold these Oracles Divine
    The Urim and the Thummim doe outshine.

Which utter Oracles of shining Light,   15
    That shine among the Glittering precious Stones
Oucht in their rows upon the Breastplate right
    Dancing among their sparkling glances known
    Upon the High Priest, in his rich Robes drest.
    Stars in his glorious breast plate on his breast.   20

Faith doth ore shine all other Grace set in
    The Soule that Cabbinet of Grace up fild
As far as doth the Shining Sun in'ts run
    Walking within its golden path ore gild
    The little pinking Stars playing boe peep.   25
    As walking in their Azure room they keep.

And though their glorys brave, its borrow Shine
    And when each doth its glorious glory lay
Upon the heap of eachs glory fine
    That lump thus made's but nighty, makes no day.   30
    But when the Sun with its Curld locks out Crowds
    They blush as shamd and hide out in the Clouds.

Even such is Faith amongst these Graces all,
    It is a grace that doth them grace indeed.
It layes a Shine upon their Glory all   35
    That further glory hence on them proceed.

9 *Curiously*] orig: buttoning   10 *Together*] PW together   orig:
Ob**sly together   11 *Breast plate*] orig: Breast ties   13 This line begins the
next page in PW. An undetermined number of lines is missing.
14 *doe*] orig: oracles   17 *Oucht*] Conj.   *rows*] Conj.   19 *Priest*] PW Priests
21 *shine*] PW shines   *in*] orig: Within   22 *Grace*] The word has been crossed
out in PW, but no other word has been substituted.   30 *thus*] PW this
32 *out in*] Conj.

They in its Glory do more glorious grow.
It strengthens and doth nourish them also.

Faith is the Curious Girdle that ties to
    The King of Glory, glorifide with Grace   40
The bundled beams of th'Sun, Gods Son that flow
    In graces Sunshine on the Soul apace
      Making their graces all invest them bright
      In brightest Robes by Faith more light than Light.

It is Golden Bosses of Gods Booke that do   45
    Clasp it, the soule, to God and seals up fast.
The Golden Belt that doth unite also
    Christ and the Soule together: buckled clasp
      Christ and the Soule the seal of Grace and brings
      All grace with't to the Soul Gods praise to sing.   50

155. Meditation. 2 Cor. 13.5. Examine
                 yourselves whether you be in
                 the Faith; know you not your-
                 selves that Christ is in you
                 except you be reprobats?

The 18. of 7m [Sept.] *1720*. Unpublished.

My blessed Lord, I fain would thee advance
    But finde my Pen is workd to the very Stumps.
My tongue my Speeches tabber Stick can't dance
    Unto thy prais as I would have it jump.
      My Drumb Stick thin of Dogtree Wood is made   5
      And is unfit to beat thy praises trade.

44 *more*] orig: bright   45 *It is Golden*] orig: It is the Golden
46 PW Clasp it and soule and yea God and seals up fast   orig: Clasp
it and ***ght soul and God up fast   49 *seal*] Conj.   *155. Meditation*] PW 146.
Meditation   2 *workd*] PW work   6 *trade*] PW Crade

Thou bidst me try if I be in the Faith,
    For Christ's in me if I bee'nt Reprobate.
Thou me dost Check if ignorance displaith
    Itself in me. And I know not my State.
    A Reprobate my Lord, let not this come
    On mee to be the burden of the Song.

Grant me thy Spectacles that I may see
    To glorify aright thy glorious Selfe.
And see this Saving Faith grafted in mee.
    Then thou wilt me inrich with Gospell Wealth.
    This Faith most Usefull is I ever finde
    To glorify thyself, of all Grace-kinde.

It Usefull is for every Duty here
    Thou calst us to, and to the Same fit make
Its Subject doth, for every prayer most deare
    And for the Lord's rich Supper to partake.
    It Oyles indeed the very Wheels of Grace
    And makes them bravely run aright apace.

It is the Grace of Grace begracing all.
    Usefull for Grace, for Sacraments and Prayer.
Religion is without it an empty Call
    And Zeale without it is a fruitless Care.
    Preaching without it's as a Magpies Chatter
    And as a little tittle tattles Clatter.

Prayer without Faith is but as prittle pratle.
    Fasts and Thanksgiving are but barren things
And Sacraments without it but as rattles
    But where this faith is all things gracious spring.
    What ere it fills it Midas like is 'ts told
    It Certainly turns into gospell Gold.

The Heart that it doth make its Feather Bed
    It purifies, makes graces Lodgen Roome.

18 *thyself*] PW thysell   20 *fit make*] orig: prayer **   21 *every prayer*] Conj.
22 *Lord's*] PW Lord   28 *And Zeale*] orig: Prayer   33 *it*] PW its
34 *things*] orig: doth   *spring*] orig: sing[?]   36 *It*] orig: Doth
turns into gospell Gold] orig: *** doth into go . . .
38 *purifies,*] PW purifies   *makes*] orig: and

It makes th'Tongue tipt with it silver, the Couch orespreds
     With Gospell Pillows, Sheets, and sweet perfumes   40
     And sweetest tunes sings in the Spirit Halls
     Sweet musick on the Spirits Virginalls.

Lord give me Saving Faith and then my Heart
     Thou'lt make thy gospell golden mine of Grace.
Studded with precious Stones in every part   45
     Of thy Sweet Spirit gilding ery place.
     If thou wilt give me this my heart shall sing
     On'ts Virginall, thy holy praise, within.

Meditation 156. Cant. 5.1. Eate oh Friendes
and drink yea drink abundantly
oh Beloved.

The 12. 9m [Nov.] *1720.* Unpublished.

Callst thou me Friend? What Rhetorick is this?
     It is a Piece of heavenly Blandishments.
Can I befriend thee, Lord? Grace dost thou miss
     Miss name me by such lushous Complements.
     The Poles may kiss and Paralells meet I trow   5
     And Sun the Full moon buss, e're I do so.

'Twould be too much for Speeches Minted Stamp.
     Sure it would set sweet Grace nigh on the Wrack
To assert I could befriend thee and her Cramp.
     Methinke this tune nigh makes thy Harp Strings crack.   10

39 *Tongue*] PW Thongue
silver,] PW silver   *the Couch orespreds*] orig: *** is ** spredd
40 *With*] PW with   orig: and deckt with   44 *Grace*] orig: richest Grace
45 *Stones*] PW Stone   *Meditation 156.*] PW Meditation 147
4 *name me by such*] orig: nameing by thy   *me*] Conj.   6 *buss,*] PW buss.
e're] orig: than e're   7 *'Twould*] PW T'would   *Minted*] PW Minttd
8 *Sure*] orig: It Sure   *sweet Grace*] orig: sweet sweet Grace
10 *makes*] PW make

Yet Graces note claims kindred nigh this knell
Saying Eate Oh Friend, Yea drinke Beloved Well.

Friend, and Beloved calld to and welcom'd thus
    At thy Rich Garden feast with spiced joy.
If any else had let such Dainties rush   15
    It would be counted sauced blasphemy.
    But seing Graces Clouds such rain impart,
    Her Hony fall for joy makes leape my heart.

A Friend, yea the best friend that heaven hath
    Thou art to me; how do thy sweet lips drop   20
Thy Gospell Hony Dews her sky display'th
    Oh Sweetness such never to be forgot.
    All Trees of Spices planted in this plot
    Rich hung with Hony dews that on them dropt.

Thou drinkst thy Gardens Syllabub in trine   25
    Honide with the drops thy Hony Comb distills.
Thou drinkst a Cup to me of't spiced wine
    And bidst mee pledge thee and I pledge will.
    My heart top full of these sweet dainties comes
    Runs over with thy prais in sweetest songs.   30

157A. Meditation. Cant. 2.4. He brought me into
            the Banqueting house and his banner over
            me was Love.

5. 12m [Feb.] 1720. Unpublished.

How Blesst am I having such blesst a Lord
    If I improve my Happiness a right

13 *to*] orig: unto   15 *let*] orig: saith[?]   *rush*] orig: fall
20 *me;*] PW me   25 *thy*] orig: trine thy   28 a fault· line in PW
29 *comes*] Conj.   30 *Runs over*] Conj.
Meditation 157 is in two versions, of which this is the first.
157A. Meditation] PW 148 Meditation

He loves me so that he doth me afford
    A Banquet such that none can make the like.
    It's not a single meate, but certainly   5
    It life sustains unto Eternity.

The sweetest dainties that were ever disht,
    On any table in best Cookery
In Heavens made. It's Mannah, Angells feast
    The Holy Angells   * * *   10
    That in the Golden poet kept * * * to
    Was a black shadow unto this * * *

Ground in God's mill in Heaven, finest floure
    And made into a pasty paste * * *
And filld with Paschall Mutton that nere soures   15
    Backt in the Backhouse of Free Grace displaid
    Serv'd up in Gospell Chargers pure and bright
    By shining Angells all arrayd milk white.

When this Grist in Free Graces mill ground and
    Bolted most fine into Gospell Tiffiny   20
And made in shew Bread Wafers * * * shew stand
    * * * golden Altar shew bread gloriously
    Yet that of Manna's wheat's but grudgens bakt
    But oh this Banquet is all Shugar Cake.

This Meat and drink is best ten thousand fold   25
    The Paschall mutton th'fattest of the flock
And cookt by Grace in Chargers fine of Gold
    This is the Banquets fare * * * on the rock.

Its Wisdoms rost meat on free graces spit
    All Saints * * * dripping shall   30
And of this table's fare Saints eate each bit
    And never let the least crumb from them fall.
    The Liquour that his table holds is fine,
    Is richer Spirits far than Cana's Wine.

9 *feast*] PW crossed out and illegible word substituted
19 *and*] Conj.   20 *into*] Conj.   24 *Banquet is*] PW Banquet's

157B. Meditation. Can. 2.4. He brought me into the
Banqueting house and his banner
over me was Love.

5. 12m [Feb.] 1720. Unpublished.

How Blest am I having so blesst a Lord
    If I improve in blessedness a right
He loves me so that he doth mee afford
    A Banquet such that none can make the like.
    Its not a single meate but certainly   5
    It life mentains and that eternally.

The sweetest dainties that were ever disht
    On any Table by Best Cookery
In Heavens made. Its Mannah true, a feast
    The holy Angells with your praises joy   10
    That in the golden Pot kept in the Arke
    Was but black smoke to this of Graces Art.

Ground in Gods mill in heaven, finest floure
    Made into Pasty Paste, the Holy * * *
Filld with the Paschall Mutton, spice on it showers   15
    Bakt in the Backhouse of Free Graces Craft,
    Serv'd up in Gospell Chargers pure and bright
    By shining Angells, waiting all in White.

This Grist of Mannah ground in Gods sweet mill
    When bolted in Christ's pure fine Tiffiny   20
And drest in various Dishes by's Cook's skill
    In glorious shine at the Epiphany,
    That of the Mannahs wheat's mere grudgens bakt
    But this Christs Banquet's all of Sugar Cake.

Meditation 157 is in two versions, of which this is the second.
157B. Meditation] PW 148 Meditation
2 in] orig: aright in   5 certainly] Conj.   10 praises] Conj.
13 finest floure] Conj.   16 Craft] Conj.   18 Angells] PW Angell
20 Christ's] PW Christ   22 at] orig: will stand at

This Meate and Drink is best ten thousand fold 25
    Of th'Paschall Mutton the fattest of the Flock
Cookt up by Grace in Chargers all of Gold.
        This Banquits Fare, it's Christ himself, the Rock
        Is Wisdoms rost meat rost in graces sops
        Whose Dripping, Saints their bisket in't do sop. 30

The sweetest dainties cookt most graciously
        Is truly * * * spiced Mess
And tis the Holy Ghost sweet * * *
        This is the Banquets * * * Christ * * *
        The liquour at this table's juyce of the Vine 35
        Far richer spirit than the Cana wine.

This Drinke here drunk is Zions water red
        It is the Blood of the Grape that * * *
In Gods sweet Vineyard on that noblest * * *
        The true true Vine; from this press grape * * * 40
        What wine is this? it's bled out of Christ's side
        Tapt by the speare, Doth always best abide.

Oh! what a banquets here? Saints are its Guests,
        Angells the servitors * * * all on th' Best
The Holy Ghosts spice seasons every * * * 45
        And by the King of Glory it is blesst
        All things hereof super superlative
        All graces in the Guests hereby much make.

Hence banquet me my Lord here mongst thy Feast
        And load my Trencher with his choicest Fare 50
And let my golden Beker too at least
        Be blesst with thy blest Wine beyond Compare
        And then my Violl shall this * * * wing
        All Heaven ore sweet praise on ery string.

29 *sops*] Conj.
30 *Dripping,*] PW Dripping   31 *graciously*] Conj.   47 *things*] PW thing
49 *Feast*] Conj.

Meditation 158. on Joh. 1.14. We beheld
     his Glory as the Glory of the Onely
     begot Son, full of Grace and Truth.

14. 3m [May] *1721.* Unpublished.

My Deare Deare Lord what shall I render thee?
     Words spoken are but breesing boxed Winde.
If written onely inked paper bee.
     Unless truth mantle, they bely the minde.
     Is this sylabicated jumble whist   5
     Out of my pen, for thee fit meed by my fist?

My deare dear Lord, thou king of Gloriousness,
     Who can sufficiently thyself admire?
The Heavens themselves cannot the same express.
     It then their Covering ascends still Higher.   10
     Nor can the Heavens e're thy glory hold.
     Its brightness doth exceed all pearls, and Gold.

I fain would give thee all my Love and all
     Its Cabbinet wherein it keeps its Case.
My heart with it, yea, and myselfe too shall   15
     Go with it to thee, that in holy chase
     Is all too foule and small a thing for thee.
     Yet I no better finde to furnish mee.

If thus my Love dresst with the Quintessence
     Of its choice Faith and dear affection,   20
Extract by thy Spirits Chymistry, Expence
     Being for this thing this rich Ejection
     'Twould be onely Sweate of thy drops of Grace
     Upon my heart, thus trickling down my face.

Meditation 158.] PW Meditation 149   2 *breesing*] Conj.
boxed] orig: agitated   6 *meed by my fist*] Conj.   8 *admire?*] PW admire.
10 *It then*] Conj.   15 *too*] PW to   16 *that*] Conj.   *that in holy chase*] orig:
yet will gifts to thee   21 *Extract*] orig: Extracted   *Expence*] Conj.
23 *'Twould*] PW T'would   *drops*] orig: one drop

These Spirits of Love with th'Quintesses pure   25
    Of all th'affection never could the Eye
Ever behold thy Glory, nor endure
      To look upon it without dazling joy.
      Thy beaming Glory falling on its Sight
      Would make its Vision darke as dark as night.   30

Thy Glory Lord all other glory blinds.
    The glory of thy Nature pure Divine.
The glory that thy Human Nature joyns,
      Out shines all mortall glory that doth shine.
      Thy Persons glory makes all others Smutt   35
      And seem to it but like to Chimny Sut.

The Glory of thy Human birth, by right
    Did make an Host of glorious Angells sing.
And all their spirituall instruments and pipes
      Melodiously tune praises to our King.   40
      Thus when God brought his First born Son to light
      He said ye Angells Worship him aright.

Thy glory shone through ery step thou tookst
    And did attend each word dropt from thy tongue.
Thy Doctrine did shine out thy life like shoots   45
      And glorious miracles were   *   *   *   along
      With * * * * * * * * * this life full cleare
      And made the actions of thy life bright here.

The glory of thy powerfull words did make
    The fiends of hell to tremble and to fly.   50
And made their stoughtest blades their hearts to quake.
      And turn away their feet, and out to cry.
      The wind and Sea amaizd stand still. Divills shrinke.
      The Sun within the Skies hereby's made blinke.

The Grave is gilded where thy body lay   55
    Even with thy glory. That Sting of death puld out.

26 *th'affection*] PW 't affection
45 *like*] orig: alonge[?] (canceled) his booke (uncanceled)
46 *miracles*] PW rayes that *** written interlinearly above and
canceled   53 *Divills*] PW Divill

The Earth a dancing fell when thy bright day
　　Of its uprising shining all about
　　Angells put on their glorious robes to tend
　　Thy tryumph over death and as thy freinds.　　60

And still to make our Happiness compleate
　　Thou art top full of Grace and truth Wherby
The Object art of Intellects the Seate
　　In us and of our Wills, therein to 'ploy.
　　Themselves in truth and Goodness at thy Will　　65
　　These Faculties with happiness, to th'fill.

Then thou upon the Wings of Glories Beams
　　Ridst through the realm of th'Enemies; the Skies:
Unto thy throne of Glorys brightest Streams
　　And hosts of Sparkling Angells glorious wise.　　70
　　And whilst thy Captives thou dost Captive bring
　　The Heavens thy Triumphant glory sing.

Such glory ne'er seen under the Canopy
　　The Copes of Heaven these golden letters savour
This truth, we saw his Glory gloriously　　75
　　As th'glory of th'onely Son of th'Father.
　　Lord ope mine eyes to se thy glory bright
　　And tune thy praise in beams of glorious light.

Meditation 159. Rev. 3.10. He that over comes will I
　　give to eat of the Hidden Mannah.

8m [Oct.] 1722. Unpublished.

Pardon my Lord, this is my great request.
　　For that thy Table of such Spirituall Cheere

65 *at thy*] Conj. at their[?] orig: that will
66 *happiness,*] PW happiness.　　70 *Angells*] PW Angell
73 *seen*] orig: were seen　　74 *savour*] PW favour[?]　　75 *truth*] PW th truth
gloriously] orig: ly gloriously　　*Meditation 159.*] PW Meditation 150
Rev. 3.10.] The correct reference is Rev. 2. 17.　　1 *Lord,*] PW Lord.

Hath been by me so long a time undresst
    My tenderness to the Offender were
    A cause of this long intermission   5
    Yet it at length producde Confession.

And now dear Lord, I do return thee praise
    For such forbearance and such Victory
Over the powers of darkness, that did raise
    The storm to blow the Candle out thereby   10
    But Faith that gains the Conquest over hell
    Hath here tryumphd. And born away the bell.

Thou saist thou'lt feed with hidden Mannah them
    That in the spiritual Combate overcom.
Give mee I pray this Conquouring Faith and then   15
    I'le sing a Tryumph: it shall be my song.
    I honour will my Captain, sing his praise
    Who leads me on and in my song him grace.

He in the War knows well us to Command.
    The word is very ready in his lip.   20
He leads us on, when weary bids us stand.
    Lets not us fall, although we've many a slipp.
    He gives us Heart a grace, come on brave boys
    I'le give you Angells, Dainties, heavenly joyes.

He'l feast us now with such a feast as made   25
    George Nevills Feast although prodigeous 't were
With dainties, things all fat and * * * * trade
    Was but like th'indian broths of Garbag'd deer
    With which the Netop entertain his guests
    When almost starv'd, yea Welcome Sir, its our Mess. 30

Ahashuerus his banquet long and linde
    And larded too with fatness and the Choicest Wine,
Was but a little milk wash * * * * it lin'd

4 *the*] PW that[?]   18 *my song him grace*] Conj.   21 *on,*] PW on
when weary bids] Conj.   22 *not*] PW not.   *many a*] Conj.
25 *such a feast as*] Conj.   28 *like*] orig: to this like   30 *starv'd*] Conj.
31 *linde*] PW lind'e   33 *milk*] Conj.

26: *George Nevills Feast*. See p. 279, note to line 4.

To be compar'd to this that's all divine.
It is a feast so sweet, so taking flavour,   35
That make the very Angells mouths to water.

The Table, Benches Chairs and Cushens and
    Their Table cloaths and Napkins all of Grace
The drinking Cups and Trenchers all at hand,
    Gold hath no market for this feasting place.   40
    The Guests are Saints, the Waiters Angells are
    The Entertainment Mannah. Angells fare.

The Drinking Glass is of Sapharin full of Grace.
    The Pasty past is of the Wheat of Heaven.
The Holy Ghost managed the Cooke choice place   45
    The Venison its filld with free from Leaven
    Was taken in Gods parke and dresst, but where
    By Whom it matter not, its Choicest cheare.

Minced pies most choise spic'd with the richest spice
    Enriched with the Wealthi'st wine indeed   50
And plumbt with raisins, those of Paradise
    Our Mannah thus prepar'd lets now proceed.
    Lord make me then to overcome I 'treat.
    Then thou will give mee hid'n mannah t'eate.

Meditation 160. Cant. 2.1. I am the
Lilly of the Vallie.

Westfield 22. 10m [Dec.] *1722*. Unpublished.

My Lord my Love I want words fit for thee.
    And if't were otherwise, affections want
To animate the words that they might bee

40 *for this feasting place*] orig: but it ** no place
47 *but where*] Conj.   orig: I tell not here   *Meditation 160*.] PW
Meditation 151   2 *affections*] orig: I want[?]   3 *words*] PW word

A mantle to send praise to praises camp
    But want I word and Spirits for the Same;   5
If I omit thy praise I sure have blame.

Lord make my heart in mee an humble thing
    The humble hearts thy Habitation bright.
Its fatted then by thee and thou therein
    Enrich it will with thy Celestiall Light.   10
    Thyselfe, dear Lord, shall be its gloryous Shine
    Wherewith it shall adorned be and fine.

I being thus, become thy Vallie low.
    O plant thyselfe my lilly flower there.
Sure then my lilly in it up will grow   15
    In beauty. And its fragrancy will fleer.
    My heart thy spirituall valie all divine
    Thyselfe the lilly of the Vally thine.

I am thy Vally where thy lilly grows
    Thou my White and Red blesst lilly fresh;   20
Thy Active and thy Passive 'bedience do
    Hold out Active and Passive Right'ousness.
    Pure White and Red making a lovely grace,
    Present thee to our Love to hug and 'brace.

The Medicinall Virtue of the lilly speake   25
    That thou my Lilly are Physician who
Healst all Diseased Souls both small and greate.
    None dy of any Spirituall Sores that to thee goe.
    The Vally lilly then doth Emblemize
    Thy fitness for thy Mediatoriall guise.   30

Shall Heaven itselfe with all its glorious flowers
    Stick them as feathers in thy Cap my king
And in this glory bow to plant in, power
    Them as a lilly flower my Vally in,

---

4 *mantle*] Conj.   6 *I sure*] orig: and hence   12 *fine*] orig: shin
16 *fleer*] orig: spring   20 *blesst*] PW bless   *fresh*] orig: shew
21 *'bedience*] PW bedien   24 *'brace*] PW brace   30 *for*] orig: to appear for
34 *Vally in*] PW Vallin

Which is not onely deepe but durty too,   35
What wonders this? What praise and thanks hence due?

But oh! alas my pin box is too small
    To hold praise meet for such praiseworthiness.
The Angells and Archangells in Gods hall
    Mee your Shoshannim tend then to adress   40
    My Lord with praises bright in highest tunes
    And though they are Stuttings they are sweet perfumes.

If thou the Lilly of my Vally bee
    My Vally shall then glorious be and shine
Allthough it be a barren Soile for thee: 45
    The Lilly of my Vally is divine.
    I'le borrow heavenly praise for thee my king
    To sacrifice to thee on my Harps sweet string.

161A. Meditation. Cant. 2.3. As the apple tree
              among the trees of the wood, so is my
              beloved among the sons.

Westfield 12m 3 day [Feb.] *1722.* Unpublished.

My double Dear Lord, and doubl't ore and ore
    Ten thousand times it would indeed still rise
A bubbe too small to knock at thy blesst doore
    Of Loveliness, ten thousand times to thy sise.
    It would be a gift ten thousand times too low   5
    Though 't is the best I have on thee to bestow.

My Love alas is but a shrimpy thing
    A sorry Crickling a blasted bud

37 *too*] PW to   39 *Angells*] PW Angell
40 *Mee your*] Conj.
Meditation 161 is in two versions, of which this is the first.
161A. Meditation] PW 152 Meditation   3 *bubbe*] Conj. bulke?
small] PW smale   5 *times*] PW time

A little drachm, too light a gift to bring.
    Its but a grain weight and scarce ever good,   10
    And shall I then presume thee to obtain
    If I should rob thee of so small a grain.

Thou art as Apple tree 'mong sons of man
    As was the Apple tree amonge the trees
That many are, (the Worlds geese are white swans   15
    In its account.) but thou excellest all these
    Ten thousand times bearing on every limb
    All golden apples; ripest grace that springs.

Not like the tree that once in Eden grew
    Amongst whose fruits the serpent old soon lops   20
And in his very teeth the poison threw
    Into our Mother Eves her sorry Chops.
    Nor like the Serpents Egge the Squerill held
    Secur'd itselfe from th'venom that on it fell.

Lord shake their bower and let these apples fall   25
    Into my Wicker basket and it fill.
Then I shall have rich spirituall food for all
    Occasions as they essences do still
    And I shall feed on their rich grace my fare
    As they drop from thy Apple tree most rare.   30

9 *too light a gift to bring*] orig: nay not a ***
11 orig: And shall I then presume this, Ist then be blaim
thee] Conj.   12 *if I*] Conj.   13 *'mong*] orig: amongst   *of*] PW each[?]
15 *swans*] PW swans)   21 *poison*] orig: Apple   24 *venom that on it*] Conj.
28 *essences do*] Conj.   29 *on their rich*] Conj.

   23: the Serpents Egge. See also Med. 161B, lines 25 ff. Taylor tells this anecdote (CD): "My Reverend Friend Mr. Samuel Mather Pastor of the Church of Christ at Windsor told me that he had this of Credible hands, that one saw a Squirrell find a Rattle Snakes nest and the Squirrell was surprized by the Rattle Snake; the Snake set upon the Squirrell, the Squirrell held the Egge in her mouth and turned it to the Snake, the snake set on the squirrel another way, the squirrell holds the Egge in her mouth to the Snake that way and which way so ever the Rattle Snake assaulted the Squirrell, the Squirrell would put the Egg in its mouth out to the Snake till at length the Snake turns up and dies and so ended the strife."

And as thou serv'st up in thy Charger bright
    A messe of these rich apples, sweet imbrace
I tasting them do in their reech delight
    And over them will surely sing thee grace.

Thou tree of Life that ever more dost stand   35
    Within the Paradise of God and hast
The Promise to him gi'n whose happy hand
    Doth overcome, shall of it eate and tast.
    Lord feed mee with this promisd food of Life
    And I will sing thy praise in songs most rife.   40

Meditation 161B. Cant. 2.3. As the apple tree among the trees of the wood, so is my beloved among the sons.

Westfield 22. 3m [May] *1723.* Unpublished.

My double Deare Lord, yea doubld ore and ore
    Ten thousand times, it would indeed still rise
Too little for to knock at thy blesst doore
    Of Loveliness ten thousand times its sise.
    'Twould be a gift ten thousand times too small   5
    For my poor love to honour thee withall.

My Love alas is a small shrivled thing
    A little Crickling a blasted bud,
Scarce a grain in weight that can't unto thee bring
    Scarce lump * * * nor give * * *   10
    And shall I then presume therewith to greet
    The precious jewells that adorn thy feet?

31–4 four line stanza
31 *Charger*] orig: choice Charger   33 *do*] Conj.   35 *more dost stand*] orig:
standing host   38 *eate*] orig: *** its surely
Meditation 161 is in two versions, of which this is the second.
Meditation 161 B.] PW Meditation 152
2 *times,*] PW times.   4 *times its*] Conj.   5 *'Twould*] PW T'would
6 *honour thee withall*] Conj.   9 *can't*] Conj.

Thou as the Apple tree, in wood dost rise
    Even such among the Sons and them Excellst
The world   * * * in envy's eyes   15
    But thou these White   * * *   thou tellst,
    Twould this gold Martyre   * * *   relats in's streams
    * * *   indeed its but   * * *   golden dreams.

Not like the tree that once in Eden grew
    Out of whose bows th'old serpent drops   20
Into our Mother Eve's lap the apple threw
    The which she quickly mumbled in her Chops.
    That tree of Life god's Paradise within
    That healing fruite brings froth to heale 'gainst sin.

Its better far then was the snakes eges found   25
    By the poore squerrell, and did arm itselfe
Therewith held in its teeth when th'Snake did round
    Assault it who held them unto this Elfe.
    She tendered the Eggs held in its mouth strange fate
    And so repelld away the Rattle Snake.   30

Oh! Shake the tree and make these apples fall
    Into my Wicker Basket oh how free
Art thou my Apple tree, surpassing all
    Then spirituall Food and Physick, curing mee.
    Then I shall have rich spirituall Balms, once had   35
    The Balm of Gilliad to make me glad.

Lord serve up in thy Saphire Charger bright
    A service of these golden Apples brave
Whose sight and sent will fill me with delight
    As they come tumbling   * * *   Wave,   40
    My food will Food and Med'cine to mee bee
    Which Grace itselfe cooks up aright for mee.

Thou tree of Life yea life erelasting stand
    Within the Paradise of God thou hast
That promisd them that hath that happy hand   45
    As to overcome shall Eating of it tast.

15 *envy's*] Conj.

Lord send me with this promisd branch of Life
And I will sing thy Grace with gracious strife.

Meditation 162. Cant. 2.3. I sat under his shadow with greate delight and his fruit was sweet to my taste.

Westfield 31.12m [Feb.] *1723*. Unpublished.

A shadow, Lord, not such as types show here
    Nor such as Titerus his broad Beech made
In which he with his Oat straw pipe't there
    A Forrest march, such his dark blackish trade.
    But tis a milke white Shadow sparkling bright   5
    That doth excell all excellent delight.

It doth delight the Saints in glorious wise
    As shadow of a rock in weary land.
It doth revive them when the Clouds arise
    And maske the brows of heaven's bright shining hand.   10
    Grace gilds this shade with brightsom shines Godward
    And manward doth bring * * * a blest reward.

A Shadow not a scowling cloud that rose
    Big belli'd with hard Cracks of frightful thunder
And rapid frightful firy flashes throws   15
    A * * * * with horrid rending thunder
    Making the hinds to calve and Lebanon
    To skip like to a frighted Unicorn.

A shade indeed * * * did hap
    * * * cluster of bright Angells * * * up   20
Made a Brave feather to adorn the Cap

Meditation 162.] PW Meditation 153   1 *types show*] Conj.
3 *In which*] Conj.   *there*] orig: there play'd   4 *march*,] PW march
his] PW is   10 *heaven's*] PW heaven   14 *belli'd*] PW belld

Upon the Tabernakles   *   *   *   *   *
By Day and Night the Camp as on they stand
Through the Wilderness to the promisd land.

Lord let this shadow as a Canopy   25
Catch all perfumes that from the Earth arise
* * * * * * * * * in to fill *   *   *
My drinking cup when squezd I shall it prize.
Then when my Crystall Cup grows full to the brim
Thy praise sweet to my tast my harp shall sing.   30

Meditation 163. Cant. 2.3. His fruit
was Sweet to my Tast.

Undated. Unpublished.

Sweet Lord, all sweet from top to bottom all
From Heart to hide, sweet, mostly sweet.
Sweet Manhood and sweet Godhead and ere shall.
Thou art the best of Sweeting. And so keep.
Thou art made up of best of sweetness brast.   5
Thy Fruit is ever sweet unto my tast.

Thou art my sweetest one, my Onely sweet.
From kirnel to the rinde, all sweet to mee.
Thy bitterness is sweet: no choaking reech
Nor damping Steams arise to damp from thee   10
The Sacred Spices. Muske * * * * * * them
Are unto thee, sweet, like to faded gum.

Thou unto mee art onely sweet all sweet
Sweet in the Virgin wombe and horses Manger.
Sweet in thy swath band and thy Childhood meete   15
Yea, sweet to all, to neighbour and to Stranger.

22 *Tabernakles*] PW tabernakes   *Meditation 163*.] PW Meditation 154
12 Two interlinear lines—illegible and canceled except for first two
words *And Onica*—are in PW between ll. 11–12.   *faded*] Conj.

Sweet in thy Life and Conversation, friends.
Thy Sweetness dropest from thy fingers Ends.

My Lord, my Love, my Lilly, my Rose and Crown
    My brightest Glory, and my Hony sweet   20
My Happiness, my Riches, my Renown.
    My Shade for Comfort, in thee good things meet.
    Not one thing in thee that admits of Spot
    All Heavens Scutchen, and a bright Love knot.

Heavens Carnation with most sweet perfume,   25
    Pinkes, Roses, Violets that perfume the Aire
Inchant the Eyes and fancy in their bloome
    Entoxicate the Fancy with their Ware
    That fuddled, turne and reele and tumble down
    From holly sweet to Earthly damps like Clowns.   30

It gathers not the Lillys nor doth Picke
    This double sweet rose in Zions Rose tree breede
Nor climbs this Apple tree, nor doth it sit
    At all in'ts Shade, nor on its Apple feed.
    Its lost within the fog and goes astray   35
    Like to a fuddled person out of's way.

But Oh! my Lord, how sweet art thou to mee
    In all thy Mediatoriall actions sweet
Most sweet in thy Redemtion all way free
    Thy Righteousness, thy holiness most meeke.   40
    In Reconciliation made for mee
    With God offended in the highst degree.

A Cabbinet of Holiness, Civit box
    Of Heavenly Aromatick, still much more,
A treasury of Spicery, rich knots,   45
    Of Choicest Merigolds, a house of Store

18 *thy*] orig: their   22 *meet*] orig: ever meet   24 *and a bright*] orig: carnation
27 *in their*] orig: when they   28 *with their Ware*] orig: make it fuddled ware
30 *like Clowns*] orig: *** brown[?]   31 *nor*] orig: riches[?]
doth] orig: doth't   32 *breede*] orig: breeds   46 *house*] orig: Store house

Of never failing dainties to my tast
Delighting holy Palates, such thou hast.

A sugar Mill, an Hony Hive most rich
    Of all Celestial viands, golden box   50
Top full of Saving Grace, a Mint house which
    Is full of Angells, and a cloud that drops
    Down better fare than ever Artist could,
    More pleasant than the finest liquid Gold.

Then glut me Lord, ev'n on this dainty fare,   55
    Here is not Surfeit; look upon this dish:
All is too little to suffice, this fare
    Can surfeit none that eatest; none eate amiss,
    Unless they eat too little. So disgrace
    The preparation of the banquit place.   60

While I sat longing in this Shadow here
    To tast the fruite this Apple tree all ripe
How sweet these Sweetings bee. Oh! sweet good Cheere
    How am I filld with sweet most sweet delight.
    The fruite, while I was in its shady place   65
    Was and to mee is now sweet to my tast.

47 *dainties*] orig: sweetness   49 *Hive*] Conj. Hall[?]   *most rich*] orig:
omptuary rich   51 *which*] orig: rich   52 orig: Of * top full ***
drops   *Is*] PW is   *Angells*] PW Angell   56 *look*] PW took[?]
58 *eatest;*] PW eatest   62 *To tast the fruite*] PW to tast the fruite to tast the
fruite   63 *Sweetings*] PW Sweeting   *sweet good*] PW sweet sweet good
64 *with sweet*] PW with seet

Meditation 164. Cant. 2.4. He brought mee into his Banqueting house (house of Wine) and his banner over me was love.

Month 6th [Aug.] *Anno 1723.* Unpublished.

Words are Dear Lord, notes insignificant
  But Curled aire when spoke Sedan'd from the Lip
Into the Eare, soon vanish, though don't Cant,
    Yea run on tiptoe, and hence often trip
    Sometimes do poother out like th'Chimny Smoake   5
    Hence often smut the matter, and nigh Choake.

Hence, my Dear Lord, the mantle I would make
  Thee, I do feare will run all Counter buffe,
To my design, and streakt be like a Snake,
    That's new crept out of 'ts garment, a slunk Slough,   10
    Or have a smoaky Smell, and Choaky lodge
    Within its Clasp. And so it proove a blodge.

But, oh Dear Lord, though my pen pikes no gold
  To lace these robes with, I would dress thee in
And its a Shame that Tinsyl ribbon should   15
    Be all the trimming that I own to bring
    Yet seeing, Lord, my shop board hath no better,
    I do presume thou'lt take it of thy debtor.

Thou hast me brought into thy house of Wine,
  The Saphire Caske of thy rich precepts * * *
And thy Carbunkled Firkins tappt divine   20
    And Choicest Nectar in Sweet Promises.
    When thou hath * * * * * * * * * * * * *
    Thy sweetest praise my Muse shall melodiously out sing.

Meditation 164.] PW Meditation 155th
9 *a*] orig: to a   12 *Clasp*] Hasp[?]   13 *gold*] Conj.
16 *own to*] orig: should borrow

165. Meditation. Cant. 2.5. I am sick of Love.

Month 8 [Oct.] *1725*. Unpublished.

Heart sick my Lord heart sick of Love to thee!
    * * * * * * * * * * * * pain'd in Love oh see
Its parchments ready to crack, it was so free.
    It so affects true love * * * * * * * * * *
    As taken * * * * sends my Lords pledge   5
    But seeing its so small and hence not fledge,

It hates confinement, can't confine its Love
    It sends to thee, disdains an Hidebound gift.
But ever doth esteem great Love to move
    Unto thyself my Lord, from all else rifts   10
    All hatcht in heaven of an heavenly Egge
    The Holy Ghost layd there in'ts feather bed.

If it be hatcht in Heaven, and thence brought
    Back in the bill of th'brightest Angel there
My heart would feare it was but stolen, and caught   15
    Thence and me given, unfit for thee most deare.
    The Holy Spirits Egg hatcht in this nest
    Would onely bee a gift, of Gifts the best.

I do bewaile my heart hath little of this
    Thee to assail therewith, but oh the Smell   20
Of such a gift, that thou art pleast with, yes.
    Hence hope there's Something in't will please thee well.
    Hence Lord accept of this, reject the rest.
    I grudg my heart if it send not thee th'best.

165. Meditation] PW 156 Meditation
2 *oh see*] orig: to thee   This stanza has many illegible cancellations.
7–8 orig: My heart is Sick it hold[s] such promisde Love in't bound / It hates
confinement and all hide bound bounds   8 *thee,*] PW thee.
10 *from all else rifts*] orig: thy Lovely breast   11 *hatcht*] PW hatch
14 *Back*] Conj.   15 *and*] PW ore and[?]   18 *onely bee a*] PW be
[canceled] an onely bee a   19 *hath little of this*] orig: so little hath of

Had I but better thou shouldst better have.   25
    I nought withold from thee through nigerdliness,
But better than my best I cannot save
    From any one, but bring my best to thee.
    If thou acceptst my sick Loves gift I bring
    Thy it accepting makes my sick Love sing.   30

Gods Determinations touch-
ing his Elect: and

The Elects Combat in their
Conversion, and

Coming up to God in Christ
together with the
Comfortable Effects thereof.

Part I The creation, the Fall,
      the Decree
      pp 387 - 401

Part II The Elects Combat
      & Conversion &
        Temptation
      pp 401 — 451

Part III Victory of Christ
      Hymns of Praise
      pp 451 - 459

Best Poems
Preface - 387
Christ's ? - 405

The Preface.

Undated. Pub. of *Gods Determinations:* see pp. 499–500. On the title page: "This a MS of the Revd. Edward Taylor of Westfield, who died there A.D. 1728, or 1729. Aetat. circa 88, velsupra. Attest Ezra Stiles D.D. His Grandson 1786." Below these lines, in another hand: "Henry W. Taylor his Great Grandson 1868."

Infinity, when all things it beheld
In Nothing, and of Nothing all did build,
Upon what Base was fixt the Lath, wherein
He turn'd this Globe, and riggalld it so trim?
Who blew the Bellows of his Furnace Vast?   5
Or held the Mould wherein the world was Cast?
Who laid its Corner Stone? Or whose Command?
Where stand the Pillars upon which it stands?
Who Lac'de and Fillitted the earth so fine,
With Rivers like green Ribbons Smaragdine?   10
Who made the Sea's its Selvedge, and it locks
Like a Quilt Ball within a Silver Box?
Who Spread its Canopy? Or Curtains Spun?
Who in this Bowling Alley bowld the Sun?
Who made it always when it rises set   15
To go at once both down, and up to get?
Who th'Curtain rods made for this Tapistry?
Who hung the twinckling Lanthorns in the Sky?
Who? who did this? or who is he? Why, know
Its Onely Might Almighty this did doe.   20
His hand hath made this noble worke which Stands
His Glorious Handywork not made by hands.
Who spake all things from nothing; and with ease
Can speake all things to nothing, if he please.
Whose Little finger at his pleasure Can   25
Out mete ten thousand worlds with halfe a Span:
Whose Might Almighty can by half a looks
Root up the rocks and rock the hills by th'roots.
Can take this mighty World up in his hande,
And shake it like a Squitchen or a Wand.   30

15 *always*] PW alway   16 *down, and up*] orig: a going and up

7 *ff.*: See Job 38:4–8.

Whose single Frown will make the Heavens shake
Like as an aspen leafe the Winde makes quake.
Oh! what a might is this Whose single frown
Doth shake the world as it would shake it down?
Which All from Nothing fet, from Nothing, All: 35
Hath All on Nothing set, lets Nothing fall.
Gave All to nothing Man indeed, whereby
Through nothing man all might him Glorify.
In Nothing then imbosst the brightest Gem
More pretious than all pretiousness in them.   40
But Nothing man did throw down all by Sin:
And darkened that lightsom Gem in him.
    That now his Brightest Diamond is grown
    Darker by far than any Coalpit Stone.

The Effects of Mans Apostacy.

    While man unmarr'd abode his Spirits all
In Vivid hue were active in their hall,
This Spotless Body, here and there mentain
Their traffick for the Universall gain.
Till Sin Beat up for Volunteers. Whence came   5
A thousand Griefs attending on the same.
Which march in ranck, and file, proceed to make
A Battery, and the fort of Life to take.
Which when the Centinalls did spy, the Heart
Did beate alarum up in every part.   10
The Vitall Spirits apprehend thereby
Exposde to danger great the suburbs ly,
The which they do desert, and speedily
The Fort of Life the Heart, they Fortify.
The Heart beats up still by her Pulse to Call   15

   11: *Vitall Spirits.* The vital spirits in 17th-century psychology were com-
posed of airy and fiery matter, which resided in the heart and were dis-
persed by the arteries; they helped carry out the decisions of the sensible soul.

Out of the outworks her train Souldiers all
Which quickly come hence: now the Looks grow pale
Limbs feeble too: the Enemies prevaile.
Do scale the Outworks where there's Scarce a Scoute
That can be Spi'de sent from the Castle out.   20

Man at a muze, and in a maze doth stand,
While Feare the Generall of all the Band
Makes inroads on him: then he Searches why,
And quickly Findes God stand as Enemy.
Whom he would fain subdue, yet Fears affright   25
In Varnishing their Weapons in his Sight.
Troops after troops, Bands after Bands do high,
Armies of armed terrours drawing nigh:
He lookes within, and sad amazement's there,
Without, and all things fly about his Eares.   30
Above, and sees Heaven falling on his pate,
Below and spies th'Infernall burning lake,
Before and sees God storming in his Face,
Behinde, and spies Vengeance persues his trace.
To stay he dares not, go he knows not where   35
From God he can't, to God he dreads for Feare.
To Dy he Dreads; For Vengeance's due to him;
To Live he must not, Death persues his Sin:
He Knows not what to have, nor what to loose
Nor what to do, nor what to take or Choose: 40
Thus over Stretcht upon the Wrack of Woe,
Bereav'd of Reason, he proceeds now so,
Betakes himself unto his Heels in hast,
Runs like a Madman till his Spirits wast,
Then like a Child that fears the Poker Clapp   45
Him on his face doth on his Mothers lap
Doth hold his breath, lies still for fear least hee
Should by his breathing lowd discover'd bee.
Thus on his face doth see no outward thing
But still his heart for Feare doth pant within.   50
Doth make its Drummer beate so loud it makes

17 *hence:*] PW hence   27 *troops,*] PW troops.

The Very Bulworks of the City Quake:
Yet gets no aide: Wherefore the Spirits they
Are ready all to leave, and run away.
For Nature in this Pannick feare scarce gives   55
Him life enough, to let him feel he lives.
Yet this he easily feels, he liveth in
A Dying Life, and Living Death by Sin,
Yet in this Lifeless life wherein he lies,
Some Figments of Excuses doth devise   60
That he may Something say, when rain'd, although
His Say seems nothing, and for nought will go.
But while he Sculking on his face close lies
Espying nought, the Eye Divine him spies.
Justice and Mercy then fall to debate   65
Concerning this poore fallen mans estate,
Before the Bench of the Almighties Breast
Th' ensuing Dialogues hint their Contest.

66 *fallen mans*] orig: mans fallen

A Dialogue between Justice and Mercy.

Offended Justice comes in fiery Rage,
    Like to a Rampant Lyon new assaild,
Array'd in Flaming fire now to engage,
    With red hot burning Wrath poore man unbaild.
    In whose Dread Vissage sinfull man may spy   5
    Confounding, Rending, Flaming Majesty.

Out Rebell, out (saith Justice) to the Wrack,
    Which every joynt unjoynts, doth streatch, and strain,
Where Sinews tortur'de are untill they Crack
    And Flesh is torn asunder grain by grain.   10
    What Spit thy Venom in my Face! Come out
    To handy gripes seing thou art so stoute.

Mercy takes up the Challenge, Comes as meeke
    As any Lamb, on mans behalfe, she speakes
Like new blown pincks, breaths out perfumed reech   15
    And doth revive the heart before it breaks.
    Justice (saith Mercy) if thou Storm so fast,
    Man is but dust that flies before thy blast.

JUSTICE
My Essence is ingag'de, I cannot bate,
    Justice not done no Justice is; and hence   20
I cannot hold off of the Rebells pate
    The Vengeance he halls down with Violence.
    If Justice wronged be she must revenge:
    Unless a way be found to make all friends.

MERCY
My Essence is engag'de pitty to show.   25
    Mercy not done no Mercy is. And hence
I'le put my shoulders to the burden so
    Halld on his head with hands of Violence.
    As Justice justice evermore must doe:
    So Mercy Mercy evermore must show.   30

JUSTICE
I'le take thy Bond: But know thou this must doe.
    Thou from thy Fathers bosom must depart:

8 *unjoynts*] orig: doth unjoynts   11 *Face!*] PW Face

391

Christ is mercy incarnate

And be incarnate like a slave below ,
    Must pay mans Debts unto the utmost marke.
    Thou must sustain that burden, that will make   35
    The Angells sink into th' Infernall lake.

Nay on thy shoulders bare must beare the smart
    Which makes the Stoutest Angell buckling cry
Nay makes thy Soule to Cry through griefe of heart,
    ELI, ELI, LAMA SABACHTANI.   40
    If this thou wilt, come then, and do not spare.
    Beare up the Burden on thy Shoulders bare.

MERCY

All this I'le do, and do it o're and o're,
    Before my Clients Case shall ever faile.
I'le pay his Debt, and wipe out all his Score   45
    And till the pay day Come I'le be his baile.
    I Heaven, and Earth do on my shoulders beare,
    Yet down I'le throw them all rather than Spare.

JUSTICE

Yet notwithstanding still this is too Small,
    Although there was a thousand times more done.   50
If sinless man did, sinfull man will fall:
    If out of debt, will on a new score run.
    Then stand away, and let me strike at first:
    For better now, than when he's at the Worst.

MERCY

If more a thousand times too little bee   55
    Ten thousand times yet more than this I'le do:
I'le free him from his Sin, and Set him free
    From all those faults the which he's subject to.
    Then Stand away, and strike not at the first.
    He'l better grow when he is at the worst.   60

JUSTICE

Nay, this ten thousand times as much can still
    Confer no hony to the Sinners hive.

34 *unto the utmost*] PW unto utmost

  40: ELI, ELI, LAMA SABACHTANI. Cf. Matt. 27:46.

For man though shrived throughly from all ill
    His Righteousness is merely negative.
    Though none be damnd but such as sin imbrace: 65
    Yet none are sav'd without Inherent Grace.

MERCY

What, though ten thousand times, too little bee?
    I will ten thousand thousand times more do.
I will not onely from his sin him free,
    But fill him with Inherent grace also.   70
    Though none are Sav'd that wickedness imbrace.
    Yet none are Damn'd that have Inherent Grace.

JUSTICE

Yet this ten thousand thousand times more shall,
    Though Doubled o're, and o're for little stands.   *hyperbole*
The Righteousness of God should be his all   75
    The which he cannot have for want of hands.
    Then though he's spar'de at first, at last he'l fall
    For want of hands to hold himselfe withall.

MERCY

Though this ten thousand thousand times much more
    Though doubled o're and o're for little go,   80
I'le double still its double o're and ore
    And trible that untill I make it do.

66, 72: *Inherent Grace*, grace which sanctifies the inner man. "There is a double state of grace, one adherent, (which some not unfitly call federall grace) sanctifying to the purifying of the flesh, Hebr. 9:13, another inherent, sanctifying the inner man. And of this latter there be two sorts, one wherein persons in Covenant are sanctified by common graces which make them serviceable and useful in their callings, as Saul, Jehu, Judas, and Demas, and such like hypocrites. Another whereby Persons in Covenant are sanctified unto union and communion with Christ and his members in a way of regeneration and salvation." From John Cotton's "The Grounds and Ends of the Baptisme of the Children of the Faithful," p. 43, as quoted in Peter Y. De Jong, *The Covenant Idea in New England Theology, 1620–1847* (Grand Rapids, Mich., Erdmans, 1945), pp. 88–89. It is clear from the context that Taylor is using *inherent grace* to mean 'saving grace' and not 'common grace.'

How will they save to Elect?

Christ's incarnation

I'le make him hands of Faith to hold full fast.
Spare him at first, then he'l not fall at last.

For by these hands he'l lay his Sins Upon   85
  The Scape Goats head, o're whom he shall Confess
And with these hands he rightly shall put on
  My milkwhite Robe of Lovely Righteousness.
Now Justice on, thy Will fulfilled bee.
Thou dost no wrong: the Sinner's just like thee.   90

Justice agrees

JUSTICE

If so, its so: then I'l his Quittance seale:
  Or shall accuse myselfe as well as him:
If so, I Justice shall of Justice faile
  Which if I do, Justice herselfe should sin.
Justice unspotted is, and therefore must,   95

  *   *   *   *   *   *   *   *   *   *   *

MERCY   *Pride & of cessive humility*

I do foresee Proud man will me abuse,
  He'th broke his Legs, yets Legs his stilts must bee:
And I may stand untill the Chilly Dews
  Do pearle my Locks before he'l stand on mee.   100
  For set a Beggar upon horseback, see
  He'll ride as if no man so good as hee.

Diction locked and Pride

JUSTICE

And I foresee Proude man will me abuse.
  Judging his Shekel is the Sanctuaries:
He on his durty stilts to walk will Choose: 105
  Yea is as Clean as I, and nothing Varies
  Although his Shekel is not Silver good
  And's tilting stilts do stick within the mudd.

MERCY

But most he'l me abuse, I feare, for still
  Some will have Farms to farm, some wives to wed: 110

97 In PW this stanza begins a new page at the top of which is written: *A
Dialogue between* $\left\{ \begin{array}{l} \textit{Mercy &} \\ \textit{Justice} \end{array} \right.$

  83: *hands of Faith.* The phrase occurs in Herbert's "The Sacrifice," lines
45–46.   101 *see*] orig: hee

Some beasts to buy; and I must waite their Will.
    Though while they scrape their naile, or scratch their head
  Nay though with Cap in hand I Wooe them long
    They'l whistle out their Whistle e're they'l come.

JUSTICE

I see I'st be abus'de by greate, and small: 115
    And most will count me blinde, or will not see:
Me leaden heel'd, with iron hands they'l Call:
    Or am unjust, or they more just than mee.
    And while they while away their Mercy so,
    They set their bristles up at Justice do.   120

MERCY

I feare the Humble Soul will be too shie;
    Judging my Mercy lesser than his Sin.
Inlarging this, but lessening that thereby.
    'S if Mercy would not Mercy be to him.
    Alas! poore Heart! how art thou damnifide,   125
    By Proud Humility, and Humble Pride?

Humility
to accept Lord

JUSTICE

The Humble Soul deales worse with me, doth Cry
    If I be just, I'le on him Vengeance take
As if I su'de Debtor, and Surety
    And double Debt and intrest too would rake.   130
    If Justice sue the Bonds that Cancelld are
    Sue Justice then before a juster bar.

MERCY

But in this Case alas, what must be done
    That haughty souls may humble be, and low?
That Humble souls may suck the Hony Comb?   135
    And thou for Justice, I for Mercy go?
    This Query weighty is, Lets therefore shew
    What must be done herein by me, and you.

How to cope
with of cosmic
humility

JUSTICE

Lest that the Soule in Sin securely ly,
    And do neglect Free Grace, I'le steping in   140

130 *rake*] orig: scrape

Convince him by the Morall Law, whereby
    Ile'st se in what a pickle he is in.
    For all he hath, for nothing stand it shall
    If of the Law one hair breadth short it fall.

MERCY

And lest the Soule should quite discourag'de stand   145
    I will step in, and smile him in the face,
Nay I to him will hold out in my hand
    The golden scepter of my Rich-Rich Grace.
    Intreating him with smiling lips most cleare
    At Court of Justice in my robes t'appeare.   150

JUSTICE

If any after Satans Pipes do Caper
    Red burning Coales from hell in Wrath I gripe,
And make them in his face with Vengeance Vaper,
    Untill he dance after the Gospell Pipe.
    Whose Sun is Sin, when Sin in Sorrows shrow'd,   155
    Their Sun of Joy sets in a grievous Cloud.

MERCY

When any such are startled from ill,
    And cry help, help, with tears, I will advance
The Musick of the Gospell Minsterill,
    Whose strokes they strike, and tunes exactly dance.   160
    Who mourn when Justice frowns, when Mercie playes
    Will to her sounding Viall Chant out Praise.

JUSTICE

The Works of Merit-Mongers I will weigh
    Within the Ballance of the sanctuary:
Their Matter, and their Manner I will lay   165
    Unto the Standard-Rule t'see how they Vary.
    Whosever trust doth to his golden deed
    Doth rob a barren Garden for a Weed.

MERCY

Yet if they'l onely on my Merits trust
    They'st in Gods Paradise themselves solace,   170

156 sets] PW set orig: laid[?]

Their beauteous garden knot I'le also thrust
    With Royall Slips, Sweet Flowers, and Herbs of Grace.
    Their Knots I'le weed, to give a spangling show
    In Order: and perfumes shall from them flow.

JUSTICE

Those that are ignorant, and do not know   175
    What meaneth Sin, nor what means Sanctity,
I will Convince that all save Saints must go
    Into hot fire, and brimston there to fry.
    Whose Pains hot scalding boyling Lead transcends,
    But evermore adds more and never Ends.   180

MERCY

Though simple, learn of mee. I will you teach,
    True Wisdom for your Souls Felicity,
Wisdom Extending to the Endless reach
    And blissfull end of all Eternity.
    Wisdom that doth all else transcend as far   185
    As Sol's bright Glory doth a painted Star.

JUSTICE

You that Extenuate your sins, come see
    Them in Gods multiplying Glass: for here
Your little sins will just like mountains bee,
    And as they are just so they Will appeare.   190
    Who doth a little sin Extenuate
    Extends the same, and two thereof doth make.

MERCY

A little sin is sin: and is Sin Small?
    Excuse it not, but aggrivate it more.
Lest that your little Sin asunder fall
    And two become, each bigger than before.   195
    Who scants his sin will scarce get grace to save.
    For little Sins, but little pardons have.

JUSTICE

Unto the Humble Humble Soule I say,
    Cheer up, poor Heart, for satisfi'de am I.   200

178 *brimston*] PW brinston

For Justice nothing to thy Charge can lay,
　　Thou hast Acquittance in thy surety.
　　The Court of Justice thee acquits: therefore
　　Thou to the Court of Mercy are bound o're.

MERCY

My Dove, come hither linger not, nor stay.　　　　　　　　205
　　Though thou among the pots hast lain, behold
Thy Wings with Silver Colours I'le o're lay:
　　And lay thy feathers o're with yellow gold.
　　Justice in Justice must adjudge thee just:
　　If thou in Mercies Mercy put thy trust.　　　　　　　　210

Mans Perplexity when calld to an account.

　　Justice, and Mercy ending their Contest,
In such a sort, now thrust away the Desk.
And other titles come in Majesty,
All to attend Almighty royally.
Which sparkle out, call man to come and tell　　　　　　　5
How he his Cloath defild and how he fell?

　　He on his skirts with Guilt, and Filth out peeps
With Pallid Pannick Fear upon his Cheeks,
With Trembling joynts, and Quiverring Lips, doth quake
As if each Word he was about to make,　　　　　　　　10
Should hackt a sunder be, and Chopt as small
As Pot herbs for the pot before they Call
Upon the Understanding to draw neer,
By tabbering on the Drum within the eare.
His Spirits are so low they'l scarce afford　　　　　　　15
Him Winde enough to wast a single word
Over the Tongue unto one's eare: yet loe,
This tale at last with sobs, and sighs lets goe,
Saying, my Mate procurde me all this hurt,
Who threw me in my best Cloaths in the Dirt.　　　　　　20

note legal terms

Thus man hath lost his Freehold by his ill;
Now to his Land Lord tenent is at Will.
And must the Tenement keep in repare
Whate're the ruins, and the Charges are.
Nay, and must mannage war against his Foes.   25
Although ten thousand strong, he must oppose.
Some seeming Friends prove secret foes, which will
Thrust Fire i'th'thatch, nay stob, Cut throate and kill.
Some undermine the Walls: Some knock them down,
And make them tumble on the Tenents Crown.   30
     He's then turnd out of Doors, and so must stay,
     Till's house be rais'd against the Reckoning day.

Gods Selecting Love in the Decree.   *of Predestination*

     Man in this Lapst Estate at very best,
A Cripple is and footsore, sore opprest,
Can't track Gods Trace but Pains, and pritches prick
Like poyson'd splinters sticking in the Quick.
Yet jims in th'Downy path with pleasures spread   5
As 'twas below him on the Earth to tread.
Can prance, and trip within the way of Sin,
Yet in Gods path moves not a little wing.
     Almighty this foreseing, and withall
That all this stately worke of his would fall   10
Tumble, and Dash to pieces Did in lay
Before it was too late for it a Stay.
Doth with his hands hold, and uphold the same.
Hence his Eternall Purpose doth proclaim.
Whereby transcendently he makes to shine   15
Transplendent Glory in his Grace Divine.
Almighty makes a mighty sumptuous feast:
Doth make the Sinfull Sons of men his guests.
But yet in speciall Grace he hath to some,

general call
speciall call

(Because they Cripples are, and Cannot come)   20
He sends a Royall Coach forth for the same,
To fetch them in, and names them name by name.
A Royall Coach whose scarlet Canopy
O're silver Pillars, doth expanded ly:
All bottomed with purest gold refin'de,   25
And inside o're with lovely Love all linde.
Which Coach indeed you may exactly spy
All mankinde splits in a Dicotomy.
> For all ride to the feast that favour finde.
> The rest do slite the Call and stay behinde.   30

O! Honour! Honour! Honours! Oh! the Gain!
And all such Honours all the saints obtain.
It is the Chariot of the King of Kings:
That all who Glory gain, to glory brings.
Whose Glory makes the rest, (when spi'de) beg in.   35
Some gaze and stare. Some stranging at the thing.
Some peep therein; some rage thereat, but all,
Like market people seing on a stall,
Some rare Commodity Clap hands thereon
And Cheapen't hastily, but soon are gone.   40
For hearing of the price, and wanting pay
Do pish thereat, and Coily pass away.
So hearing of the terms, whist, they'le abide
At home before they'l pay so much to ride.
But they to whom its sent had rather all,   45
Dy in this Coach, than let their journey fall.
They up therefore do get, and in it ride
Unto Eternal bliss, while down the tide
The other scull unto eternall woe;
By letting slip their former journey so.   50
For when they finde the Silver Pillars fair
The Golden bottom pav'de with Love as rare,
To be the Spirits sumptuous building cleare,
When in the Soul his Temple he doth reare
And Purple Canopy to bee (they spy)   55
All Graces Needlework and Huswifry;

Their stomachs rise: these graces will not down.
They think them Slobber Sawces: therefore frown.
They loath the same, wamble keck, heave they do:
Their Spleen thereat out at their mouths they throw,
Which while they do, the Coach away doth high   60
Wheeling the Saints in't to eternall joy.

    These therefore and their journey now do come
For to be treated on, and Coacht along.

The Frowardness of the Elect in the Work
of Conversion.

    Those upon whom Almighty doth intend
His all Eternall Glory to expend,
Lulld in the lap of sinfull Nature snugg,
Like Pearls in Puddles cover'd ore with mudd:
Whom, if you search, perhaps some few you'l finde,   5
That to notorious Sins were ne're inclinde.
Some shunning some, some most, some greate, some small.
Some this, that or the other, some none at all.
But all, or almost all you'st easly finde,
To all, or almost all Defects inclinde   10
To Revell with the Rabble rout who say
Let's hiss this Piety out of our Day.
And those whose frame is made of finer twine
Stand further off from Grace than Wash from Wine.
Those who suck Grace from th'breast, are nigh as rare   15
As Black Swans that in milkwhite Rivers are.
Grace therefore calls them all, and sweetly wooes.
Some won come in, the rest as yet refuse,
And run away: Mercy persues apace,
Then some Cast down their arms, Cry Quarter, Grace.   20
Some Chased out of breath drop down with feare

Perceiving the persuer drawing neer.
The rest persude, divide into two rancks
And this way one, and that the other prancks.

    Then in comes Justice with her forces by her,   25
And doth persue as hot as sparkling fire.
The right wing then begins to fly away.
But in the streights strong Baracadoes lay.
They're therefore forc'd to face about, and have
Their spirits Queld, and therefore Quarter Crave.   30
These Captivde thus: justice persues the Game
With all her troops to take the other train.
Which being Chast in a Peninsula
And followd close, they finde no other way
To make escape, but t'rally round about: 35
Which if it faile them that they get not out,
They're forct into the Infernall Gulfe alive
Or hackt in pieces are or took Captive.
But spying Mercy stand with Justice, they
Cast down their Weapons, and for Quarter pray.   40
Their lives are therefore spar'de, yet they are ta'ne
As th'other band: and prisoners must remain.
And so they must now Justice's Captives bee
On Mercies Quarrell: Mercy sets not free.
    Their former Captain is their Deadly foe.   45
    And now, poor souls, they know not what to do.

Satans Rage at them in their Conversion.

    Grace by the Aide of Justice wins the day.
And Satans Captives Captives leads away,
Who finding of their former Captains Cheates,

24 *other*] PW othe   37 *They're forct into*] orig:
They forct are into   41 *Their*] PW There

To be Rebellion, him a Rebell Greate,
Against his Rightfull Sovereign, by whom   5
He shortly shall to Execution Come,
They sue for Pardon do at Mercies Doore
Bewailing of that war they wag'd before.

    Then Satan in a red-hot firy rage
Comes belling, roaring ready to ingage   10
To rend, and tare in pieces small all those,
Whom in the former Quarrell he did lose.
But's boyling Poyson'd madness, being by
A shield Divine repelld, he thus lets fly.
You Rebells all, I Will you gripe, and fist.   15
I'le make my Jaws a Mill to grin'de such Grists.
Look not for Mercy, Mercy well doth see
You'l be more false to her than Unto mee.
You're the first Van that fell; you're Traitors, Foes,
And Unto such Grace will no trust repose.   20
You Second Ranck are Cowards, if Christ Come
With you to fight his field, you'l from him run.
You third are feeble-hearted; if Christs Crown
Must stand or fall by you, you'l fling it down.
You last did last the longest: but being ta'ne   25
Are Prisoners made, and Jayle Birds must remain.
It had been better on the Turff to dy
Then in such Deadly slavery to ly.
Nay, at the best you all are Captive Foes.
Will Wisdom have no better aid than those?   30
Trust to a forced Faith? To hearts well known
To be (like yours) to all black Treason Prone?
For when I shall let fly at you, you'l fall:
And so fall foule Upon your Generall.
Hee'l Hang you up alive then; by and by.   35
And I'le you wrack too for your treachery.
He will become your foe, you then shall bee

Flanckt of by him before, behinde by mee.
You'st stand between us two our spears to dunce.
Can you Offend and Fence both wayes at once?   40
You'l then have sharper service than the Whale,
Between the Sword fish, and the Threshers taile.
You'l then be mawld worse than the hand thats right
Between the heads of Wheelhorn'd Rams that fight.
        What will you do when you shall squezed bee   45
        Between such Monstrous Gyants Jaws as Wee?

The Souls Address to Christ against these Assaults.

Thou Gracious Lord, Our Honour'd Generall
        May't suite thy Pleasure never to impute,
It our Presumption, when presume we shall
        To line thy Noble Ears with our Greate suite?
        With ropes about our necks we come and lie,   5
        Before thy pleasure's Will, and Clemency.

When we unto the height of Sin were grown,
        We sought thy Throne to overthrow; but were
In this our seeking Quickly overthrown:
        A Mass of Mercy in thy face shone cleare.
        We quarter had: though if we'de had our share   10
        We had been quarter'd up as Rebells are.

Didst thou thy Grace on Treators arch expend?
        And force thy Favour on thy stubborn Foe?
And hast no Favour for a failing Friend,
        That in thy Quarrell trippeth with his toe?   15
        If thus it be, thy Foes Speed better far,
        Than do thy Friends, that go to fight thy War.

39 *You'st*] PW You st   **46** *Wee?*] PW Wee.

42 Cf. Donne, *Progresse of the Soule*, line 351: "The flaile-finn'd Thresher,
and steel-beak'd Sword-fish"

But is it as the Adversary said?
    Dost thou not hear his murdering Canons roare?   20
What Vollies fly? What Ambushments are laid?
    And still his stratagems grow more, and more.
    Lord, fright this frightfull Enemy away.
    A Trip makes not a Traitor: Spare we pray.

And if thou still suspect us come, and search: 25
    Pluck out our hearts and search them narrowly.
If Sin allow'd in any Corner learch,
    We beg a Pardon, and a Remedy.
    Lord Gybbit up such Rebells Arch Who do
    Set ope the back doore to thy Cursed foe.   30

Christs Reply.

    I am a Captain to your Will.
    You found me Gracious, so shall still,
Whilst that my Will is your Design.
    If that you stick unto my Cause
    Opposing whom oppose my Laws   5
I am your own, and you are mine.

    The weary Soule I will refresh
    And Ease him of his heaviness.
Who'le slay a Friend? And save a Foe?
    Who in my War do take delight,   10
    Fight not for prey, but Pray, and Fight
Although they slip, I'le mercy show.

    Then Credit not your Enemy
    Whose Chiefest daintie is a lie.
I will you comfort sweet extend.   15
    Behold I am a sun and shield

4 *If that you stick*] PW If you that stick orig: If you that stick stick Close

And a sharp sword to win the field.
I'l surely Crown you in the End.

His murdering Canons which do roare
    And Engins though as many more
Shoot onely aire: no Bullets fly.   20
    Unless you dare him with your Crest,
    And ope to him the naked breast,
Small Execution's done thereby.

    To him that smiteth hip, and thigh,   25
    My foes as his: Walks warily,
I'le give him Grace: he'st give me praise.
    Let him whose foot doth hit a Stone
    Through weakenes, not rebellion
Not faint, but think on former dayes.   30

The Effect of this Reply with a fresh Assault
from Satan.

    Like as the Shining Sun, we do behold,
Is hot, and Light, when th'Weather waxeth Cold:
Like as brave Valour in a Captain steels
His Armies Courage, when their spirit reels.
As Aqua Vitae when the Vitalls faile:
So doth this speech the Drooping Soul availe.
How doth this Answer Mercies Captives Cheer?
Yet those whom Justice took still Drooping were,
And in this nick of time the Foe through spite
Doth like a glorious Angell seem of Light.   10
Yet though he painteth o're his Velvet smut.
He Cannot yet Conceal his Cloven foot.
Hence in their joy he straweth poyson on,
Those Objects that their senses feed upon.

20 *Engins*] PW Engims

By some odde straggling thought up poyson flies   15
Into the heart: and through the Eares, and Eyes.
Which sick, lies gasping: Other thoughts then high
To hold its head; and Venom'd are thereby.
Hence they are influenc't to selfe Ends: these darts
Strike secret swelling Pride up in their hearts.   20
    The which he fosters till the bladder flies
    In pieces; then joy lies agast and dies.

  Now Satan counts the Cast his own thus thrown:
Off goes the Angels Coate, on goes his own.
With Griping Paws, and Goggling Eyes draws nigher,   25
Like some fierce Shagg'd Red Lion, belching fire:
Doth stoutly Charge them home that they did fall
And breake the Laws of their Choice Admirall.
And his attend: and so were his. For they
Must needs be his whom ever they obey.   30
Thus he in frightfull wise assaults them all,
Then one by one doth singly on them fall,
    Doth winnow them with all his wiles, he can,
    As Wheate is winnow'd with the Sieve, and Fan.

First Satans Assault against those that first Came
    up to Mercys terms.

SATAN

Soon ripe, soon rot. Young Saint, Old Divell. Loe
Why to an Empty Whistle did you goe?
What Come Uncalld? And Run unsent for? Stay
Its Childrens Bread: Hands off: out, Dogs, away.

SOUL

It's not an Empty Whistle: yet withall,   5
And if it be a Whistle, then a Call:
A Call to Childrens Bread, which take we may.
Thou onely art the Dog whipt hence away.

*argument — They were converted
too easily — hence their conversion is
a delusion*

408   GODS DETERMINATIONS

SATAN

If I then you: for by Apostasy
You are the Imps of Death as much as I.   10
And Death doth reign o're you through Sin: you see,
As well as Sin doth reign to Death in mee.

SOUL

It is deni'd: Gods Mercy taking place,
Prepared Grace for us, and us for Grace.
And Graces Coach in Grace hath fetcht us in,   15
Unto her Feast. We shall not dy in Sin.

SATAN

If it be so, your sins are Crucifide:
Which if they be, they struggl'd when they di'de.
It is not so with you: you judge before
You felt them gird, you'de got them out of Doore.   20

SOUL

Mercy the Quartermaster speedily,
Did stifle Sin, and still its hidious Cry,
Whose Knife at first stuck in its heart to th'head:
That sin, before it hard did sprunt, fell dead.

SATAN

A mere Delusion! Nature shows that Life   25
Will strugle most upon the bloody Knife
And so will Sin. Nay Christ doth onely Call,
And offer ease to such as are in thrall.

SOUL

He offer'd unto mee, and I receiv'd
Of what hee wrought, I am not yet bereav'd.   30
Though Justice set Amercement on mee
Mercy hath took it off, and set me free.

SATAN

Is Mercy impudent? or Justice blinde?
I am to make distraint on thee Designd.

10 *much as I*] PW much I

34: *distraint* (see Glossary). Taylor, like Calvin, is fond of using legal terms
in defining God's relation to man.

The North must wake before the South proves Kind. 35
The Law must breake before the Gospell binde.

SOUL

But Giliads Balm, like Balsom heald my wound
Makes not the Patient sore, yet leaves him sound.
The Gospell did the Law prevent: my heart
Is therefore dresst from Sin: and did not smart. 40

SATAN

A likely thing! Oh shame! presume on Grace!
Here's Sin in Grain: it hath a Double Face.
Come, Come with mee I'le shew your Outs, and Inns,
Your Inside, and your out: your Holy things.
    For these I will anatomize then see, 45
    Believe your very Eyes, believe not mee.

The Accusation of the Inward Man.

    You want Cleare Spectacles: your eyes are dim:
Turn inside out: and turn your Eyes within.
Your sins like motes in th'sun do swim: nay see
Your Mites are Molehills, Molehills Mountains bee.
Your Mountain Sins do magnitude transcend: 5
Whose number's numberless, and do want end.
The Understandings dark, and therefore Will
Account of Ill for Good, and Good for ill.
As to a Purblinde man men oft appeare
Like Walking Trees within the Hemisphere. 10
So in the judgment Carnall things Excell:
Pleasures and Profits beare away the Bell.
The Will is hereupon perverted so,
It laquyes after ill, doth good foregoe.
The Reasonable Soule doth much delight 15
A Pickpack t'ride o'th'Sensuall Appitite.

5 do] orig: doth   6 do] orig: doth

And hence the heart is hardened and toyes,
With Love, Delight, and Joy, yea Vanities.

Make but a thorow search, and you may spy
Your soul a trudging hard, though secretly   20
Upon the feet of your Affections mute.
And hankering after all forbidden fruite.
Ask but yourselfe in secret laying neer
Thy head thereto: 'twill Whisper in thine eare
That it is tickled much, though secretly.   25
And greatly itches after Vilany.
'Twill fleere thee in thy face, and though it say,
It must not tell, it scorns to tell thee nay.
But Slack the rains, and Come a Loophole lower:
You'l finde it was but Pen-coop't up before.   30
Nay, muster up your thoughts, and take the Pole
Of what walk in the Entry of your Soule
Which if you do, you certainly will finde
With Robbers, Cut-throats, Theives its mostly linde.
And hundred Roagues you'l finde, ly gaming there.   35
For one true man, that in that path appears.
Your True man too's oft footsore, sildom is,
Sound Winde, and Limb: and still to add to this,
He's but a Traviller within that Way:
Whereas the rest there pitch their Tents, and stay.   40
Nay, nay, what thoughts Unclean? Lacivious?
Blasphemous? Murderous? and Malicious?
Tyranick? Wrathfull? Atheistick rise
Of Evills New, and Old, of e'ry Sise?
These bed, and board here, make the heart a sty   45
Of all Abominable Brothlery.

Then is it pure? is this the fruite of Grace?
If so, how do yee: You and I Embrace.

The Outward Man accused.

[handwritten annotation: You look after the things of this world]

Turn o're thy Outward man, and judge aright.
Doth not a Pagans Life out Shine thy Light?
Thy fleering Looks, thy Wanton Eyes, each part
Are Painted Sign-Post of a Wanton heart.
If thou art weigh'd in Golden Scales; Dost do   5
To others as thou wouldst be done unto?
Weigh weigh thy Words: thy Untruths, all which came
Out of thy mouth, and thou Confest the same.
Why did thy Tongue detract from any one,
Whisper such tales thou wouldst not have be known?   10
When thou was got in such a merry veane
How far didst thou exceed the golden mean?
When that thou wast at such a Boon, or Feast
Why didst thou rather ly, than lose thy jeast?
How wast thou tickled when thy droughty Eares   15
Allay'de their Thirst with filthy squibs, and jears?
Why didst thou glaver men of place? And why,
Scowle, Glout, and Frown, on honest Poverty?
Why did'st thou spend thy State in foolish prancks?
And Peacock up thyselfe above thy rancks?   20
Why thoughtst thyselfe out of the World as shut,
When not with others in the Cony Cut?
Hold up thy head, is't thus or no? if yea,
How then is all thy folly purgd away?

If no, thy tongue belies itselfe, for loe   25
Thou saidst thy heart was dresst from sin also.

The Soul accused in its Serving God.

When thou dost go to serve thy God, behold
What greate Distractions do thy Soule infold?
How thy Religious Worship's much abusde?
And with Confusion greate thy Soul's amus'de?
What thoughts to God on Errand dost thou send   5
That have not Sin therein, or in the End?
In Holy-Waters I delight to fish
For then I mudd them, or attain a Dish,
Of Holy things. I oft have Chiefest part,
And Cutting: nay do Carve the fat, and heart.   10
For in Gods worship still thy heart doth cling
Unto and follows toyish Earthly things.
And what thou offer'st God his Holy Eye
Sees, is an Offering of Hypocrisy.
And if thou saw'st no hell, nor heaven; I see,   15
My Soule for thine, thy Soule and mine agree.
What then's thy Love to God, and Piety?
Is it not selfish? And Comes in by th'by?
For selfe is all thine aim; not God thine end:
And what Delight hath he in such a friend?   20
Lip Love is little else, but such a ly,
As makes the matter but Hypocrisy.

What's thy Repentance? Can'st thou come and show
By those salt Rivers which do Ebb, and Flow
By th'motion of that Ocean Vast within,   25
Of pickled sorrow rising for thy Sin?
For Sin prooves very Costly unto all.
It Cost Saint Peter bitter tears, and Paul.
Thy joy is groundless, Faith is false, thy Hope
Presumption, and Desire is almost broke.   30
Zeale Wildfire is, thy Pray'res are sapless most,
Or like the Whistling of some Dead mans Ghost:

You are weak in worshipping Christ

?

Thy Holy Conference is onely like
An Empty Voice that tooteth through a pipe.
Thy Soule doth peep out at thine Eares, and Eyes   35
To bless those bawbles that are earthly toyes.
But when Gods Words in at those Windows peepe
To kiss thy Soul, thy Soul lies dead asleep.
Examine but thy Conscience, her reply,
Will suite hereto: For Conscience dare not ly.   40
When did thine Eyes run down for sin as sin,
That thus thy heart runs up with joy to sing?
    Thy sins do sculk under a flowrisht paint.
    Hence thou a Sinner art, or I a Saint.

SOUL

Well, Satan, well: with thee I'le parle no more.   45
But do adjure thee hence: begone therefore.
If I as yet was thine, I thus do say
I from thy flag would quickly flag away.
    Begone therefore; to him I'le send a groane
    Against thee drawn, who makes my heart his Throne.   50

The Souls Groan to Christ for Succour.

Good Lord, behold this Dreadfull Enemy
    Who makes me tremble with his fierce assaults,
I dare not trust, yet feare to give the ly,
    For in my soul, my soul finds many faults.
    And though I justify myselfe to's face: 5
    I do Condemn myselfe before thy Grace.

He strives to mount my sins, and them advance
    Above thy Merits, Pardons, or Good Will
Thy Grace to lessen, and thy Wrath t'inhance
    As if thou couldst not pay the sinners bill.   10
    He Chiefly injures thy rich Grace, I finde
    Though I confess my heart to sin inclin'de.

Those Graces which thy Grace enwrought in mee,
    He makes as nothing but a pack of Sins.
He maketh Grace no grace, but Crueltie,   15
    Is Graces Honey Comb, a Comb of Stings?
    This makes me ready leave thy Grace and run.
    Which if I do, I finde I am undone.

I know he is thy Cur, therefore I bee
    Perplexed lest I from thy Pasture stray.
He bayghs, and barks so veh'mently at mee.   20
    Come rate this Cur, Lord, breake his teeth I pray.
    Remember me I humbly pray thee first.
    Then halter up this Cur that is so Curst.

Christs Reply.

Peace, Peace, my Hony, do not Cry,
My Little Darling, wipe thine eye,
    Oh Cheer, Cheer up, come see.
Is anything too deare, my Dove,
Is anything too good, my Love   5
    To get or give for thee?

If in the severall thou art
This Yelper fierce will at thee bark:
    That thou art mine this shows.
As Spot barks back the sheep again
Before they to the Pound are ta'ne,   10
    So he and hence 'way goes.

But yet this Cur that bayghs so sore
Is broken tootht, and muzzled sure,
    Fear not, my Pritty Heart.   15
His barking is to make thee Cling

6 *Is anything*] orig: I thinke   *too*] PW to

*God keeps Satan under control
at all times or uses him for his
own ends —
as the shepherd dos
his dog*

Close underneath thy Saviours Wing.
　　Why did my sweeten start?

And if he run an inch too far,
I'le Check his Chain, and rate the Cur.　　　20
　　My Chick, keep clost to mee.
The Poles shall sooner kiss, and greet
And Paralells shall sooner meet
　　Than thou shalt harmed bee.

He seeks to aggrivate thy sin　　　　　　　　25
And screw them to the highest pin,
　　To make thy faith to quaile.
Yet mountain Sins like mites should show
And then these mites for naught should goe
　　Could he but once prevaile.　　　　　　30

I smote thy sins upon the Head.
They Dead'ned are, though not quite dead:
　　And shall not rise again.
I'l put away the Guilt thereof,
And purge its Filthiness cleare off:　　　　　35
　　My Blood doth out the stain.

And though thy judgment was remiss
Thy Headstrong Will too Wilfull is.
　　I will Renew the same.
And though thou do too frequently　　　　　40
Offend as heretofore hereby
　　I'l not severly blaim.

And though thy senses do inveagle
Thy Noble Soul to tend the Beagle,
　　That t'hunt her games forth go.　　　　45

45 *t'hunt*] PW t'hunts

　　22–24: The Poles . . . harmed bee. Cf. Herbert's "The Search," lines 41–44:

　　　Thy will such a strange distance is,
　　　　　As that to it
　　East and West touch, and poles do kisse,
　　　　　And parallels meet.

I'le Lure her back to me, and Change
Those fond Affections that do range
    As yelping beagles doe.

Although thy sins increase their race,
And though when thou hast sought for **Grace,**   50
    Thou fallst more than before
If thou by true Repentence Rise,
And Faith makes me thy Sacrifice,
    I'l pardon all, though more.

Though Satan strive to block thy way   55
By all his Stratagems he may:
    Come, come though through the fire.
For Hell that Gulph of fire for sins,
Is not so hot as t'burn thy Shins.
    Then Credit not the Lyar.   60

Those Cursed Vermin Sins that Crawle
All ore thy Soul, both Greate, and small
    Are onely Satans own:
Which he in his Malignity
Unto thy Souls true Sanctity   65
    In at the doors hath thrown.

And though they be Rebellion high,
Ath'ism or Apostacy:
    Though blasphemy it bee:
Unto what Quality, or Sise   70
Excepting one, so e're it rise.
    Repent, I'le pardon thee.

Although thy Soule was once a Stall
Rich hung with Satans nicknacks all;
    If thou Repent thy Sin,
A Tabernacle in't I'le place   75
Fild with Gods Spirit, and his **Grace.**
    Oh Comfortable thing!

77 *Gods*] PW God

I dare the World therefore to show
A God like me, to anger slow: 80
    Whose wrath is full of Grace.
Doth hate all Sins both Greate, and small:
Yet when Repented, pardons all.
    Frowns with a Smiling Face.

As for thy outward Postures each,   85
Thy Gestures, Actions, and thy Speech,
    I Eye and Eying spare,
If thou repent. My Grace is more
Ten thousand times still tribled ore
    Than thou canst want, or ware.   90

As for the Wicked Charge he makes,
That he of Every Dish first takes
    Of all thy holy things.
Its false, deny the same, and say,
That which he had he stool away   95
    Out of thy Offerings.

Though to thy Griefe, poor Heart, thou finde
In Pray're too oft a wandring minde,
    In Sermons Spirits dull.
Though faith in firy furnace flags,   100
And Zeale in Chilly Seasons lags.
    Temptations powerfull.

These faults are his, and none of thine
So far as thou dost them decline.
    Come then receive my Grace.   105
And when he buffits thee therefore
If thou my aid, and Grace implore
    I'le shew a pleasant face.

But still look for Temptations Deep,
Whilst that thy Noble Sparke doth keep   110
    Within a Mudwald Cote.
These White Frosts and the Showers that fall

Are but to whiten thee withall.
    Not rot the Web they smote.

If in the fire where Gold is tride   115
Thy Soule is put, and purifide
    Wilt thou lament thy loss?
If silver-like this fire refine
Thy Soul and make it brighter shine:
    Wilt thou bewaile the Dross?   120

Oh! fight my Field: no Colours fear:
I'l be thy Front, I'l be thy reare.
    Fail not: my Battells fight.
Defy the Tempter, and his Mock.
Anchor thy heart on mee thy Rock.   125
    I do in thee Delight.

An Extasy of Joy let in by this Reply
returnd in Admiration.

My Sweet Deare Lord, for thee I'le Live, Dy, Fight.
    Gracious indeed! My Front! my Rear!
    Almighty magnify a Mite:
      O! What a Wonder's here?

Had I ten thousand times ten thousand hearts: 5
    And Every Heart ten thousand Tongues;
    To praise, I should but stut odd parts
      Of what to thee belongs.

If all the world did in Alimbeck ly,
    Bleeding its Spirits out in Sweat;   10
    It could not halfe enlife a Fly
      To Hum thy Praises greate.

If all can't halfe enlife a Fly to hum,
    (Which scarce an Animall we call)

118 *silver-like*] PW silver like   *refine*] orig: refine refine

    Thy Praises then which from me come,   15
        Come next to none at all.

For I have made myselfe ten thousand times
    More naught than nought itselfe, by Sin.
    Yet thou extendst thy Gracious Shines
        For me to bath therein.   20

Oh! Stand amaizd yee Angells Bright, come run
    Yee Glorious Heavens and Saints, to sing:
    Place yee your praises in the sun,
        Ore all the world to ring.

Nay stand agast, ye sparkling Spirits bright!   25
    Shall little Clods of Dust you peere?
    Shall they toote Praises on your pipe?
        Oh! that we had it here.

What can a Crumb of Dust sally such praise
    Which do from Earth all heaven o're ring   30
    Who swaddle up the suns bright rayes
        Can in a Flesh Flie's Wing?

Can any Ant stand on the Earth and spit
    Another out to peer with this?
    Or Drink the Ocean up, and yet   35
        Its belly empty is?

Thou may'st this World as easily up hide
    Under the Blackness of thy naile:
    As scape Sins Gulph without a Guide:
        Or Hell without a bale.   40

If all the Earthy Mass were rambd in Sacks
    And saddled on an Emmet small,
    Its Load were light unto those packs
        Which Sins do bring on all.

But sure this burden'd Emmet moves no wing.   45
    Nay, nay, Compar'd with thee, it flies.

27 *pipe?*] PW pipe.   42 *Emmet*] PW Emmets

Yet man is easd his weight of Sin.
    From hell to Heav'n doth rise.

When that the World was new, its Chiefe Delight,
    One Paradise alone Contain'de: 50
    The Bridle of Mans Appetite
        The Appletree refrain'de.

The which he robbing, eat the fruit as good,
    Whose Coare hath Chokd him and his race.
    And juyce hath poyson'd all their blood,   55
        He's in a Dismall Case.

None can this Coare remove, Poyson expell:
    He, if his Blood ben't Clarifi'de
    Within Christs veans, must fry in Hell,
        Till God be satisfi'de.   60

Christ to his Father saith, Incarnate make
    Mee, Mee thy Son; and I will doe't:
    I'le purify his Blood, and take
        The Coare out of his Throate.

All this he did, and did for us, vile Clay: 65
    Oh! let our Praise his Grace assaile.
    To free us from Sins Gulph each way,
        He's both our Bridge, and Raile.

Although we fall and Fall, and Fall and Fall
    And Satan fall on us as fast.   70
    He purgeth us and doth us call
        Our trust on him to Cast.

My Lumpish Soule why art thou hamper'd thus
    Within a Crumb of Dust? Arise,
    Trumpet out Praises. Christ for us   75
        Hath slain our Enemies.

Screw up, Deare Lord, upon the highest pin:
    My soul thy ample Praise to sound.

66 *assaile*] PW assai'le

O tune it right, that every string
    May make thy praise rebound.   80

But oh! how slack, slow, dull? with what delay,
    Do I this Musick to, repare,
    While tabernacled in Clay
        My Organs Cottag'de are?

Yet Lord accept this Pittance of thy praise   85
    Which as a Traveller I bring,
    While travelling along thy wayes
        In broken notes I sing.

And at my journies end in endless joyes
    I'l make amends where Angells meet   90
    And sing their flaming Melodies
        In Ravishing tunes most sweet.

The Second Ranke Accused.

    You that are branded for Rebellion
What whimsy Crotchets do you feed upon?
Under my Flag you fighting did Defie
And Vend much Venom spit at God most high:
You dar'de him as a Coward, out, and Went   5
Flinging your Poyson'd darts against his tent.
When Grace did sound her parle, you stopt the Eare:
You backward drew as she to you drew neere.
But whats this Grace, which you, forsooth, so prize,
For which you stand your own Sworn Enemies?   10
Whoever saw smelt, tasted felt the same?
Its but an airy notion, or a name.
Fine food for fools, or shallow brains, who know
No better fair and therefore let all go.
Did mercy better Cain, or make him thrive   15

90 *Angells*] PW Angell   11 *smelt*] PW smest

Satan's argument is the opposite of that against Rank I. Here he says your sins are too great for pardon.

When he pronounc'd himselfe a Fugitive?
What Benefit had Esau who did weep
And in Repenting teares did scald his Cheek?
Or what King Ahab, that he softly went?
Or what poore Judas that he did repent?   20
Grace doom'd them down to hellish flames, although
To Court the same they steep't their Souls in woe.
To whom she yields a smile, she doth expect
That with a smile, her smile they soon accept
But you have hitherto like sturdy Clowns   25
Affronted Grace and paid her Smiles with Frowns.
Nay Mercy lookes before she Gives, to see
That those to whom she gives true Christians bee.
That all the Graces of the Spirit do
Like Clouds of sweet perfume from such forth flow.   30
And that their Souls be to the spirits feet
An Aromatick Spicery most sweet.
Is't so with you? You from her scepter fly,
As judging it a grace graceless to dy.
Your Faith's a Phancy: Fear a Slavery.   35
Your Hope is Vain, Patience Stupidity.
Your Love is Carnall, selfish, set on toyes:
Your Pray'res are Prattle, or Tautologies.
Your Hearts are full of sins both small, and Greate.
They are as full as is an Egge of meate.   40
Your Holy Conference and talkings do
But for a Broken Piece of Non-Sense go.
If so, you are accurst; God doth impart
His Blessings onely on the broken heart.
But search your peace turnd o're, and view each side   45
Graces Magnetick touch will it abide?
Doth Mercys Sun through Peaces lattice clear
Shine in thy Soule? Then what's that Uproare there?
Look well about you, try before you trust.
Though Grace is Gracious; Justice still is just.   50

16 *Fugitive?*] PW *Figitive.*

19: Ahab. See I Kings 21, 22.

If so it be with you, say what you can
You are not Saints, or I no Sinner am.

The Third Rank accused.

Not these temptation

What thou art too for Christ, it seems? Yet fain
Thou wouldst the World with all her Pomps mentain.
But such as share of Christ, fall short of these.
And have but faint affections to such fees.
Go Coach thy Eyes about the world, and eye   5
Those Rich inchanting Braveries there Cry
Give us your heart? Wherefore thy heart doth ake
That it such Amorous Objects must forsake.
The Love whereto so stuffs thy heart; no place
Is left therein for any Saving Grace.   10
Its folly then to think that Grace was shown,
When in persute thy heart was overthrown.
It was not Grace in Grace that made thee fall:
For unto Grace thou hast no heart at all.
Thou thoughtst these Objects of thy Love would faile.   15
The thoughts of which do make thy Spirits faile.
And this is easely prov'd: for thou didst goe
Into the field with God, as with a foe.
And bravely didst outbrave the Notion Grace.
And Chose to flee rather than it imbrace.   20
And well thou mightst, A Bird in hand doth far
Transcend the Quires that in the Hedges are.
And so its still: turn o're thy heart, thou'lt finde
As formerly so still thou art inclinde.
In sin thou hadst delight, didst grace defy: 25
And dost so still: For still thou dost reply.
Whoever went to Hell, and Came again
To shew to anyone, what is that pain?

Your heart is still desirous of worldly things

repetition.

a new temptation atheism →

1 _Yet_] PW yet   5 _Eyes_] orig: World

Did ever any slip to Heaven to see
Whether there's there a God? and who is hee?   30
What is that fancide God rowld o're the tongue?
Oh! Brainsick Notion, or an Oldwifes Song!
That He should wholy be in e'ry place
At once all here, and there, yet in no space.
That all should be in any part though small: 35
That any part of him should be him all.
And that he hath no parts though Head, and Heart.
Hands, Ears, and Eyes he hath, he hath no part.
That he is all in all, yea all in thee,
That he is also all that time in mee.   40
That he should be all in each Atom small:
And yet the whole cannot contain him all.
That he doth all things in a moment see,
At once, of things to Come, Past, and now bee.
That He no Elder, he no Younger is,   45
Than when the World began: (What wonders this?)
That time that flies from all with him remains,
These are Chamaera's Coin'd in Wanton brains.
Among which Fopperies mans Soul may go,
Concerning which thou mak'st so much ado.   50
Nay; what? or where is Hell Can any show?
This Bugbare in the Darke, 's a mere Scar-Crow.
But say its true, there is an Hell: a God.
A Soul Immortall in a mortall Clod:
Did God such principles infuse as egge   55
The Soul from him into Eternall plague?
Thou dost Confess that God doth not Command
Such things of us as had are of no hand.
Which sure he doth, if he deny to save
Whom live by Natures Law: which Law he Gave.   60
Yet grant this tenet which thy heart denies,
Christ saveth none but whom he sanctifies.
Thou art not sanctifide in any part:
For sins keepe Centinall within thy heart
And there they train, therein they Rentdevouz.   65

34 *there*,] PW there.   53 *true*,] PW true.   57 *Command*] orig: Demand

But if God does [?] and your [?] is valid — then you are a lost soul because a hardened sinner

Her troops therein do quarter: and do house.
And hence as from a fountain Head there streams
Through ev'ry part Pollution in the Veans.
Hence sprouts Presumption making much too bold
To catch such Shaddows which no hand can hold.   70
Hence Harebrain'd Rashness rushes in the Brain:
Hence Madbrain'd Anger which no man can tame.
Hence Crackbrain'd folly, or a shatter'd Wit
That none Can Plaster: none can med'cine it.
Hence a stiff, stubborn, and Rebellious Will   75
That sooner breakes than buckles to fulfill
Gods Laws: and so for other sins thou'lt find
A Forward Will joyn'd with a froward minde.
Thy Heart doth lip such Languague, though thy Lip
Is loath to let such Languague open slip.   80
I see thy secret thoughts: and such they bee,
That Wish there was no God, or I was Hee.
Or that there was no Holiness, unless
Those sins thou'rt given to, were Holiness.
Or that there was no Hell, except for those   85
Who stand for Holiness, and sin oppose.
Or that there was no heaven t'enter in,
Except for those Who pass their Lives in Sin.
Though thou the Languague of thy heart outface
Dost, yet thou huggest sin, dost hiss out Grace.   90
Set Heaven, and Hell aside its clearly shown,
Thou lov'st mee more than God thou seem'st to own.
Hence was it not for these, it plainly 'pears
Thy God for servants might go shake his ears.
For thou to keep within my booke dost still   95
Ungod thy God not walking by his Will.
        This Languague of thy heart doth this impart
        I am a Saint, if thou no Sinner art.

81 *secret*] orig: secret secret
87 *t'enter*] orig: to enter   90 *dost*] orig: and   97 *impart*] orig: declare

A Threnodiall Dialogue between The
Second and Third Ranks.

Each rank... this to... coming... offer... it is... to... grants... sins (handwritten marginalia)

SECOND

Oh you! How do you? Alas! how do things go
With you, and with your Souls? For once we know
You did as we, Welt, Wallow, Soake in Sin;
For which Gods ire infires our hearts within.

THIRD

Ne're worse, though when secure in sin much worse.   5
Though curst by sin, we did not feele the Curse.
Now seing we no help can see, we, rue.
Would God it was with us as't is with you.

SECOND

With us! alas! a Flint would melt to see
A Deadly foe, in such a Case as wee.   10
God seems our Foe, repent we Can't: but finde
To ill Goodwill, to Good, a wayward minde.

THIRD

This is in you your Grace, we easely spie
The Love of God within your looks to ly.
But oh! our Souls set in sins Cramp stand bent   15
To Badness, and no Grace we have t'Repent.

SECOND

This is your Charity. But if you saw
Those ugly Crawling Sins that do us knaw
You'd Change your minde. You mourn, and pray we see:
We would not for a World, you were as wee.   20

THIRD

Repent! and Pray! Aye, so the Traytor Cast,
Cries, *Good my Lord!* yea, when his Doom is past.

9 *Flint*] PW Flent   10 *such a Case*] PW such Case   16 *no*] orig: we've not
22 *Good my Lord!*] PW These words written in large lower-case letters with
G and L capitalized

You erre through your Abundant Charity.
We dare not wish, as we, our Enemy.

SECOND

Your Low esteemings of yourselves enlarge   25
Ours of you much. But oh, that Dismall Charge!
We don't Repent, Believe, we nothing do:
No Grace we have though something Gracelike show.

THIRD

Is't so with you who do so much out do
Poor nothings us? Oh! whither shall we go?   30
Our Grace a Mockgrace is: of Ulcerous Boiles.
We are as full, as Satan is of Wiles.

SECOND

There's not a Sin that is not in our Heart.
And if Occasion were, it would out start.
There's not a Precept that we have not broke.   35
Hence not a Promise unto us is spoke.

THIRD

Its worse with us: The Preacher speaks no word.
The Word of God no sentence doth afford;
But fall like burning Coals of Hell new blown
Upon our Souls: and on our Heads are thrown.   40

SECOND

Its worse with us. Behold Gods threatonings all;
Nay Law, and Gospell, on our Heads do fall.
Both Hell, and Heaven, God and Divell Do
With Wracking Terrours Consummate our Woe.

THIRD

We'le ne're believe that you are worse than wee,   45
For Worse than us wee judge no Soul can bee.
We know not where to run, nor what to doe.
Would God it was no worse with us than you.

38 *sentence*] orig: Comfort   40 *on*] orig: it on
43 *God*] orig: both God

SECOND

Than us, alas! What, would you fain aspire
Out of the Frying Pan into the Fire?   50
Change States with you with all our hearts we would
Nay, and give boot therewith, if that we could.

THIRD

Say what you can, we can't but thinke this true
That Grace's Ambush hath surprized you.
But Judgment layes an Ambush strong to take   55
* * * * * * * * * * * * * * * * * * * *

SECOND

What Charity have you for us? When thus
You judge amiss both of yourselves and us?
What pitty is't? Yet God will you repay.
Although we perish, and be cast away.   60

THIRD

The Lord forbid the last, and grant we may
Deceived be wherein we be, you say.
We Cannot wish a Toade as wee, but Crave,
Your prayers for us, that we may pardon have.

SECOND

Our Pray'res, are pray'reless: Oh! to what we bee   65
An ugly Toad's an Angell bright we see.
Oh pray, pray you, oh pray, for us that so
The Lord of Mercy Mercy on's may show.

THIRD

O would we could! but oh Hells Gripes do grinde
Yea writh our Souls with Cramps of e'ry kinde.   70
If Grace begrace us not, we go to Hell.
The Good Lord help us both, thus fare you Well.

53 *but*] orig: believe but   54 *Ambush*] orig: tender
Ambush   56 This line is worn away at the bottom of the page in PW.
63 *wee,*] PW wee.

Their Call in this Sad State for Mercy.

We humbly beg, oh Lord, to know our Crime.
That we thus tortur'de are before our time.
Before our Time? Lord give's this Word again.
For we have long ago deserv'de Hells flame.
If Mercy wrought not Miracles none could   5
Us monuments of mercy now behold.
But oh! while Mercy waits we slaves to sin,
Heap up sins Epha far above the brim.
What shall we do when to account we're Calld?
How will abused Mercy burn, and scald?   10
We know not How, nor Where to stay or goe.
We know not whom, nor What to trust or doe.
Should we run hence from Mercy, Justice will
Run hotly after us our blood to spill.
But should we run to Mercy, Justice may   15
Hold Mercies hands while Vengeance doth us slay.
And if we trust to Grace, necessity
Binds us by force at Grace's Grace to ly.
But if we run from Grace, we headlong cast
Ourselves upon the Spiles of Ruine Vast.   20
And if we claim her ours, she'l surely smite
Us, for presuming on an others right.

Who'le with a Leaking, old Crack't Hulk assay,
To brave the raging Waves of Adria?
Or who can Cross the Main Pacifick o're?   25
Without a Vessell Wade from Shore to Shore?
What wade the mighty main from brim to brim,
As if it would not reach above the Chin?
But, oh! poor wee, must wade from brinck to brinck
With such a Weight as would bright Angells sink.   30
Or venture angry Adria, or drown

21 *ours*,] PW ours.   31 *angry*] PW argry

When Vengeance's sea doth break her floodgates down.
If stay, or Go to sea we drown. Then see
In what a wofull Pickle, Lord, we bee.
Rather than tarry, or the rough sea trust,   35
On the Pacificke Ocean forth we thrust.
Necessity lies on's: we dare not stay:
If drown we must, we'l drown in Mercy's Sea.
Impute it not presumption if we high
To Cast ourselves on Mercies Clemency.   40
Is't not as great Presumption, Lord, to stand
And gaze on ruine, but refuse the hand
Which offers help? Or on such Courses fall
Which fall to ruin, ruinating all?
Lord, pitty, pitty us, Lord pitty send: 45
A thousand pitties tis we should offend.
But oh! we did, and are thereto propence:
And what we count off, oft thou Countst offence.
We've none to trust: but on thy Grace we ly,
If dy we must, in mercy's arms wee'l dy.   50
    Then pardon, Lord, and put away our guilt.
    So we be thine, deale with us as thou wilt.

The Soule Bemoning Sorrow rowling upon a resolution to seek Advice of Gods people.

    Alas! my Soule, product of Breath Divine,
For to illuminate a Lump of Slime.
Sad Providence! Must thou below thus tent,
In such a Cote as strangles with ill sent?
Or in such sensuall Organs make thy stay   5
Which from thy noble end do make thee stray?
My nobler part, why dost thou laquy to
The Carnall Whynings of my senses so?
What? thou become a Page, a Peasant, nay,

A Slave unto a Durty Clod of Clay!   10
Why should the Kirnell bring such Cankers forth
To please the shell, as will devour them both?
Why didst thou thus thy Milkwhite Robes defile
With Crimson spots of scarlet sins most vile?

    My Muddy Tent, Why hast thou done so ill   15
To Court, and kiss my Soule, yet kissing kill?
Why didst thou Whyning, egg her thus away ·
Thy sensuall Appetite to satisfy?
Art thou so safe, and firm a Cabinet
As though thou soaking lie in nasty wet,   20
And in all filthy Puddles: yet though thin
Can ne're drench through to stain the Pearle within?
Its no such thing: Thou'rt but a Cawle-wrought Case.
And when thou fallst, thou foulst its shining face.
Or but her mudwalld Lid which, wet by sin   25
Diffuseth all in her that it shuts in.
One stain stains both, when both in one Combine.
A Musty Cask doth marre rich Malmsy Wine.

    Woe's mee! my mouldring Heart! What must I do?
When is my moulting time to shed my woe?   30
Oh! Woefull fall! what fall from Heavenly bliss
To th'bottom of the bottomless Abyss?
Above an angry God! Below, black-blew
Brimstony flames of hell where Sinners rue!
Behinde, a Traile of Sins! Before appeare   35
An Host of Mercies that abused were!
Without a Raging Divell! and Within
A Wracking Conscience Galling home for Sin!
What Canst not finde one Remedy, my Soule,
On Mercies File for mee? Oh! Search the Rowle.   40
What freeze to death under such melting means,
Of Grace's Golden, Life Enliv'ning Beams?
What? not one Hope? Alas! I hope there's some.
Although I know not in what way it come.
Although there is no hope within my minde   45

21 *though*] PW the

The Soul goes to the Wise —
the Saint — (advise —

I'le force Hope's Faculty, till Hope I finde.
Some glimmerings of Hope, I hope to spy
In Mercies Golden Stacks, or Remedy.
I therefore am Resolv'd a search to make,
And of the Pious Wise some Counsill take.   50
Ile then in Pensiveness myselfe apply
To them in hope, but yet halfe hopelessly.
Perhaps these thoughts are blessed motions, though
From whence they are, as yet I do not know.
        And if from Christ, Oh! then thrice Happy mee.   55
        If not, I'st not be worser than I bee.

48 *Stacks*,] PW Stacks.   55 *Christ*,] PW Christ.

Comment on protestant notions
    of Saints

The protestant does not pray to the saints
            in heaven

He seeks advice from the saints on earth

visible or invisible saints

When the protestant soul goes to heaven
    he is also a saint there — or
        above the angels.

The Preface.

SOUL

Long lookt for Sir! Happy, right Happy Saint.
I long to lay before you my Complaint:
And gain your Counsill: but you're strange: and I
Through backwardness lost opportunity.

SAINT

How is't good Sir: methinks I finde there dart   5
Some pleasant Hopes of you within my heart.
What is your Rantery declinde, foregone?
Your looks are like the Earth you Tread upon.

SOUL

Its true: I do, and well may look so, too
For worse than mee the world did never show.   10
My sins are dide in grain: all Grace I lack.
This doth my Soul on tenterhooks enwrack.
Wherefore I Counsill Crave touching my sin
My Want of Grace. Temptations too within.

SOUL] PW omits this first stanza heading   9 *so,*] PW so.

*This is a poem of consolation — for
every sin, M every has a Pardon*

The Souls Doubts touching its Sins Answerd.

Saint comforts the soul

SAINT

Is this thy Case, Poor Soul, Come then begin:
Make known thy griefe: anatomize thy sin.
Although thy sins as Mountains vast do show,
Yet Grace's fountain doth these mountains flow.

SOUL

True, true indeed, where Mountains sinke but where   5
They swim, their Heads above these mountains peare.
Mine swim in Mercies boundless Ocean do:
Therefore their Heads above these waters goe.

SAINT

I thought as you, but loe the Lyon hee
Is not so fierce as he is feign'd to bee.   10
But grant they swim, they'l then swim quite away
On Mercies main, if you Repenting stay.

SOUL

I swim in Mercy: but my sins are sayles
That waft my barke to Hell by Graces Gales.
Is't possible for such as Grace outbrave   15
(Which is my Case) true Saving Grace to have?

SAINT

That's not thy Sin: thou didst not thus transgress,
Thy Grace-outbraveing sin is bashfulness.
Thou art too backward. Satan strives to hold
Thee fast hereby, and saith, thou art too bold.   20

SOUL

Wrong about me

Alas! How are you out in mee, behold
My best is poison in a Box of Gold.
If with mine Eyes you saw my hearts black stain,
You'de judge my Sins were double dide in grain.

SAINT

Deluded Soul, Satan beguiles thee so   25
Thou judgst the bend the back side of the bow

6 *They*] PW The   24 *judge*] orig: my judge

434

Dost press thyselfe too hard: Straite Wands appeare
Crook't in, and out, in running rivlets Clear.

SOUL

You raise the fabrick of your pious hope
Upon such water Bells, as rots denote.
For my Profession doth but cloake my sin.   30
A guilded Maukin's stufft with Chaff within.

SAINT

I love not thus to row in such a Stream:
And if I did, I should so touch my Theme.
But muster up your Sins, though more or few: 35
Grace hath an Edge to Cut their bonds atwo.

SOUL

This is my Sin, My Sin I love, but hate
God and his Grace. And who's in such a state?
My Love, and Hatred do according rise
Unto Sins height, and unto Grace's sise.   40

SAINT

I thought as you when first to make me see
God powred out his Spirit sweet on mee.
But oh strange Fetch! What Love, yet hate to have?
And hate in heart what heartily you Crave?

SOUL

Sometimes meethinks I wish. Oh! that there were   45
No Heaven nor Hell. For then I need not feare.
I'm pestred with black thoughts of Blasphemy,
And after thoughts do with these thoughts Comply.

SAINT

See Satans Wiles: while thou in sin didst dwell
Thou Calledst not in Question Heaven, or Hell.   50
But now thou'rt out with sin he makes thee Call
In Question both, that thou in Hell mightst fall.

SOUL

But, oh! methinks, I finde I sometimes wish
There was no God, or that there was not this.

Or that his wayes were other than they bee.   55
Oh! Horrid, horrid, Hellish thoughts in mee!

SAINT

'Twas thus, or worse with me. I often thought,
Oh! that there was no God: or God was Naught.
Or that his Wayes were other Wayes. Yet hee
In mighty mercy hath bemerci'de mee.   60

SOUL

My Heart is full of thoughts, and ev'ry thought
Full of Sad, Hellish, Drugstery enwrought.
Methinks it strange to Faith that God should bee
Thus All in All, yet all in Each part. See.

SAINT

'Twas so with me. Then let your Faith abound   65
For Faith will stand where Reason hath no ground.
This proves that God is Onely God: for hee
Surpasseth the superlative degree.

SOUL

Methinks I am a Frigot fully fraught,
And stoughed full with each Ath'istick thought.   atheism   70
Methinks I hate to think on God: anone
Methinks there is no God to thinke upon.

SAINT

I thought as much at first: my thoughts, so vain,
Were thus that God was but stampt i'th'brain.
But God disperst these Wicked thoughts. Behold   75
The Various methods of the serpent old!

SOUL

All arguments against mee argue still:
I see not one bespeaks me ought, but ill.
Whatse're I use I do abuse: Oh! shew,
Whether the Case was ever thus with you.   80

74 *i'th'brain*] PW ith'brain

*I A in Satan who is Exaggerating
your sins to
damn you*

SAINT

It was: But see how Satan acts, for his
He troubles not with such a thought as this.
But Wicked thoughts he in the Saints doth fling,
And saith they're theirs, accusing them of Sin.

SOUL

Methinks my heart is harder than a flint,   85
My Will is Wilfull, frowardness is in't,
And mine Affections do my Soule betray,
Sedaning of it from the blessed way.

SAINT

Loe, Satan hath thy thoughts inchanted quite,
And Carries them a pickpack from the right.   90
Thou art too Credulous: For Satan lies.
It is not as you deem: deem otherwise.

SOUL

But I allow of sin: I like it Well,
And Chiefly grieve, because it goes to hell.
And Were it ever so with you, I see   95
Grace hath prevented you which doth not mee.

SAINT

I thought as you: but now I clearly spy,
These Satans brats will like their Curst Sire ly.
He squibd these thoughts in you, you know not how.
And tempts you then to deem you them allow.   100

SOUL

And so I do: would I could Sins disown:
But if I do, thy'l own me for their own.
I have no Grace to do't: this prooves me in
A Lamentable State, a State of Sin.

SAINT

What ambling work within a Ring is here?   105
What Circular Disputes of Satans Geer?

86 *is in't*] Conj.   95 *Were*] orig: if Were   105 *within a Ring is here*] orig:
is here within a Ring

To proove thee Graceless he thy sins persues:
To proove thee sinfull, doth thy Grace accuse.
  Why dost thou then believe the Tempter so?
  He seeks by helping thee thy Overthrow.   110

Doubts from the Want of Grace Answerd.

SOUL

Such as are Gracious grow in Grace therefore
Such as have Grace, are Gracious evermore.
Who sin Commit are sinfull: and thereby
They grow Ungodly. So I feare do I.

SAINT

Such as are Gracious, Graces have therefore   5
They evermore desire to have more.
But such as never knew this dainty fare
Do never wish them 'cause they dainties are.

SOUL

Alas! alas! this still doth me benight.
I've no desire, or no Desire aright.   10
And this is Clear: my Hopes do witherd ly,
Before their buds break out, their blossoms dy.

SAINT

When fruits do thrive, the blossom falls off quite.
No need of blossoms when the seed is ripe.
The Apple plainly prooves the blossoms were.   15
Thy withred Hopes hold out Desires as Cleare.

SOUL

Alas! my Hopes seem but like blasted fruit.
Dead on the Stoole before it leaves its root.

15 *blossoms*] PW blossom

For if it lively were a growth it hath,
And would be grown e're this to Saving Faith.   20

SAINT

* * * * * * * * * * * * I'le make most plain
* * * * * * * * * * * * * * * * * * *
Which lively is, layes hold on Christ too, though
Thou deemst it doth like blasted blossoms show.

SOUL

If it was so, then Certainly I should,   25
With Faith Repentance have. But, oh! behold,
This Grace leaves not in mee a single print.
Mine Eyes are Adamant, my Heart is Flint.

SAINT

Repentance is not argued so from Tears.
As from the Change that in the Soul appears.   30
And Faith Ruld by the Word. Hence ever spare
To mete Repentance out by Satans square.

SOUL

I fear Repentance is not Genuine.
Its Feare that makes me from my sins decline.
And if it was, I should delight much more,   35
To bathe in all Gods Ordinances pure.

SAINT

And dost thou not? Poore Soule, thou dost I know.
Why else dost thou Relent, and sorrow so?
But Satan doth molest thee much to fling
Thee from thy Dutie into e'ry Sin.   40

SOUL

If these were my Delight, I should Embrace
The royall Retinue of Saving Grace,
Peace, Patience Pray're, Meekness, Humility,
Love, Temp'rance, Feare, Syncerety, and Joy.

An interesting fine argument — all you need
to feel is just a little grace. God does
his work gradually.

440   G O D S   D E T E R M I N A T I O N S

SAINT

You do: though not alike at all times sure,   45
And you do much desire to have more.
I wonder that you judge them worth the having,
Or Crave them, if they are not got by Craving.

SOUL

My measure is so small, I doubt, alas!
Its next to none, and will for nothing pass.   50
But if I had but this or that Degree,
Of all these Graces, then thrice Happy mee!

SAINT

You have not what you Would, and therefore will
Not own you have at all. What Sullen still?
If God should fill you, and not work your bane,   55
You would not be Content, but would Complain.

SOUL

What must my vessell voide of Grace be thrust
By you in Glory thus among the Just
As Gracious though the Dose of Grace I finde
Is scarce a Grain? Can this Content your minde?   60

SAINT

God, and His All, 's the Object of the Will:
All God alone can onely it up fill.
He'd kill the Willer, if his Will he should
Fill to the brim, while Cabbined in mould.
What Mortall can contain immortall bliss;   65
If it be poured on him as it is?
A single Beam thus touching him Would make
The stoutest mortall man to ashes shake.
Will nothing give Content unless you have
While here a mortall, all your Will can Crave?   70
If so, the Promise which is made to those
That hunger after Righteousness you'l lose.
For being full, you could not hunger still
Nor Wish for more you having once your Will.

You cant contain Halfe, what in truth you would   75
Or do not Wish for Halfe of what you should.
Can't all the sea o'refill an Acorn bole?
Can't God orefill a little Whimpring Soul?
What Can a Nutshell all the World Enfold?
Or can thy Heart all Heavens Glory Hold?   80
And never break? What! Canst thou here below
Weld Heavens bliss while mortall thus? Oh! No.
God Loves you better than to grant your Cry,
When you do Cry for that which will destroy.
Give but a Child a Knife to still his Din: 85
He'l cut his Fingers with it ere he blin. — *cease*

SOUL

Had I but any Sparke of Grace, I might
Have much more than I have with much delight.
How can I trust to you? You do not know
Whether I have a Grain of Grace, or no.   90

SAINT

You think you might have more: you shall have so,
But if you'd all at once, you could not grow.
And if you could not grow, you'd grieving fall.
All would not then Content you, had you all.
Should Graces Floodgate thus at once breake down   95
You most would lose, or else it would you drown.
He'l fill you but by drops that so he may
Not drown you in't, nor Cast a Drop away.

Doubts from Satans Temptations Answered.

SOUL

But oh the Tempter harries me so fast
And on me falls to make me fall at last.

86 *He'l*] PW Hel

I continue to be
tempted by the
devil —

Had I but Grace surely I might repell
His firy Darts that dart on fire from hell.

SAINT

If you had none, he never would bestow
Such darts upon you Grace to overthrow.
The Bullets shot are blinde, the fowlers eye
Aims at the marke before he lets them fly.

SOUL

But he bewilders me: I scarce can finde
But lose myselfe again within my minde.
My thoughts are Laberryntht, I can't enjoyn
Any thereof the rest to discipline.

SAINT

I once was thus. The Crooked Serpent old
Doth strive to hinder what he can't withhold.
And where he cannot keep from Grace, he's loath,
To keep from keeping Saving Grace from Growth.

SOUL

But if a Pious thought appeare, I finde
It's brambled in the briers of my minde.
Or in those brambles lost, or slinks away:
But Viprous thoughts do in these thickets stay.
With these I pest'red am in Duty so,
I doubt I undo all thereby I do.

SAINT

First Satan envies each Choice thought: then hee
To murder it, or make't short winded bee
Doth raise a Fog, or fude of thoughts most vile
Within the soul; and darkens all that ile.
And when he cannot hinder pray're he'le strive
To spoil the same, but still hold on, and thrive.

5

10

15

20

25

19 *those*] PW thoses   20 *thoughts*] PW thought

SOUL

But yet I feare there oft lurks secretly
Under each Duty done Hypocrisy.   30
I finde no heart unto the Wayes of Grace.
It's but their End my heart would fain imbrace.

SAINT

Why give you Credit to your deadly foe?
He turns ore ery stone Grace t'overthrow.
He'l fight on both sides Grace, Grace to destroy.   35
To ruinate your Souls Eternally.
He makes some thus red mad on mischiefe grow
And not to matter what they say, or do.
He makes Civility to pass for Grace,
With such as hunt riches hot senting trace.   40
To such as God doth Call, he doth reply
That all their Grace is but Hypocrisy.

    Contrarily, a Refuge strong to make
For e'ry sin, he doth this method take.
He tells the Doubting soul, this is no Sin,   45
Until he Diveth over head therein.
But then to breake his Heart he doth reply:
That done is Sin, He sinned willingly.
He to the Sinner saith, Great Sins are small,
Small Sins he telleth him, are none at all.   50
And so to such there is no sin: for why
Great sins are small, Small None. But oh but eye
If God awakes a Soul, he doth begin
To make him count indifferent things as Sin,
Nay Lawfull things wanting a Circumstance   55
Or having one too much although by Chance.
And thus he doth involve the doubting soule
In dismall doubts and makes it fear to rowle,
Himselfe on Christ for fear it should presume.
But if he doth he quickly turns his tune   60

33 *foe?*] PW foe   50 *Sins*] orig: thing

And doth accuse, because he did not take
As soon as mercy did an offer make.
Oh! see the Craft the Serpent old doth use
To hopple souls in Sin, and Sin to Choose.
One while he terms true Grace a morall thing.   65
One while morality a splendid Sin.

SOUL
You shew the matter as the matter is
But shew me how in such a Case as this,
T'repell the Tempter, and the field t'obtain,
To Chaff away the Chaff and Choose the grain.   70

SAINT
Perform the Duty, leave th'event unto
His Grace that doth both in, and outside know.
Beg pardon for your Sins: bad thoughts defy,
That are Cast in you by the Enemy.
Approove yourselfe to God, and unto his   75
And beg a pardon where you do amiss.
If wronged go to God for right, and pray
Hard thoughted Saints black thoughted thoughts away.
Renew your acts of Faith: believe in him,
Who died on the Cross to Cross out Sin.   80
Allow not any Sin: and if you sin
Through frailty, Faith will a new pardon bring.
Do all Good Works, work all good things you know
As if you should be sav'd for doing so.
Then undo all you've done, and it deny   85
And on a naked Christ alone rely.
Believe not Satan, Unbelieve his tales
Lest you should misbelieve the Gospell bales.
        Do what is right, and for the right Contend.
        Make Grace your way, and Glory'l be your End.   90

Yet as a further Caution still I'le shew
You other Wiles of Satan to eschue.
And that a Saint may of a Saint account
Not as a Saint though once with God in th'mount.

[handwritten annotations: "Portrait of Satan", "This Poem is by a saint explains Satans wiles to the penitent Sinner"]

Some of Satans Sophestry.

The Tempter greatly seeks, though secretly,
    With an Ath'istick Hoodwinke man to blinde,
That so the Footsteps of the Deity
    Might stand no longer stampt upon his minde.
    Which when he can't blot out, by blinding quite,   5
    He strives to turn him from the Purer Light.

With Wiles enough, he on his thoughts intrudes,
    That God's a Heape of Contradictions high,
But when these thoughts man from his thoughts excludes
    Thou knowst not then (saith he) this Mystery.   10
    And when the first String breaks, he strives to bring
    Into sins brambles by the other string.

When God Calls out a Soule, he subtilly
    Saith God is kinde: you need not yet forsake
Your Sins: but if he doth, he doth reply,   15
    Thou'st outstood Grace. Justice will vengeance take.
    He'l tell you you Presume on Grace, to fright
    You to despare, beholding Justice bright.

Though just before mans mountain sins were mites,
    His mites were nothing. Now the scales are turn'd.   20
His mites are mountains now, of mighty height
    And must with Vengeance-Lightening be burn'd.
    Greate Sins are Small, till men repent of Sin:
    Then Small are far too big to be forgi'n.

While man thinks slightly, that he will repent,   25
    There's time enough (saith he), it's easly done.
But when repent he doth, the time is spent,
    Saith he, it is too late to be begun.
    To keep man from't, it's easly done, saith he,
    To dant him in't, he saith, it Cannot bee.   30

So Faith is easy till the Soule resolves
    To Live to Christ, and upon Christ rely.
Then Saving Faith he bold presumption Calls.
    Hast thou (saith he) in Christ propriety?
    The Faithfulls Faith, he stiles Presumption great,   35
    But the Presumptuous, theirs is Faith Compleat.

Nay though the Faith be true he acts so sly,
    As to raise doubts: and then it must not do:
Unless Assurance do it Certify:
    Which if it do, it douts of it also.   40
    Faith is without Assurance shuffled out,
    And if Assurance be, that's still a Doubt.

But should the Soule assured once, once Doubt,
    Then his Assurance no Assurance is:
Assurance doth assure the Soul right out   45
    Leave not a single Doubt to do amiss.
    But Satan still will seeke to Pick an hole
    In thy Assurance to unsure thy Soul.

Should any Soule once an Assurance get,
    Into his hands, soon Satans Pick-Lock key   50
With Sinfull Wards Unlocks his Cabinet
    To Steal the Jewell in it thence away.
    The Soul thus pillag'de, droops unto the grave.
    It's greater grief to lose than not to have.

He doth molest the Soule, it cannot see   55
    Without Assurance Extraordinary
Which should it have, it would soon take to bee
    A Mere Delusion of the Adversary.
    Assurance would not serve, should God Convay
    It in an Usuall or Unusuall way.   60

Thus I might search, Poor Soul, the Magazeen
    Of Gospell Graces over: I might paint
Out Satan sculking each side each unseen
    To Hoodwinck Sinners, and to hopple Saints.
    For he to dim their Grace, and slick up sin   65
    Calls Brass bright Gold, bright Golde but brass or tin.

57 *would*] orig: quickly up would

He tempts to bring the soul too low or high,
　　To have it e're in this or that extream:
To see no want or want alone to eye:
　　To keep on either side the golden mean.　　70
　　If it was in't to get it out he'l 'ledge,
　　Thou on the wrong side art the Pale or Hedge.

When God awakes a Soule he'l seeke to thrust
　　It on Despare for want of Grace or get
And puff't with Pride, or in Securety hush't　　75
　　Or Couzen it with Graces Counterfet.
　　Which if he can't he'l Carp at Grace, and raile
　　And say, this is not Grace, it thus doth faile.

And thus he strives with Spite, Spleen, bitter Gall
　　That Sinners might Dishonour God Most high:　　80
That Saints might never honour God at all.
　　That those in Sin, Those not in Grace might dy.
　　And that the Righteous, Gracious, Pious, Grave,
　　Might have no Comfort of the Grace they have.

Lest you be foild herewith, watch well unto　　85
　　Your Soul, that thrice Ennobled noble Gem:
For Sins are flaws therein, and double woe
　　Belongs thereto if it be found in them.
　　Are Flaws in Venice Glasses bad? What in
　　Bright Diamonds? What then in man is Sin?　　90

Difficulties arising from Uncharitable
Cariages of Christians.

When these assaults proove vain, the Enemy
　　One Saint upon another oft doth set,
To make each fret like to Gum'd Taffity,
　　And fire out Grace thus by a Chafe or Fret.

89 *Glasses*] PW Grasses　　4 *fire*] orig: enfire

Uncharitable Christians inj'rous are: 5
Two Freestons rubd together each do ware.

When Satan jogs the Elbow of the one
    To Spleenish Passions which too oft doth rise,
For want of Charity, or hereupon
    From some Uncharitable harsh Surmise,   10
    Then the Poore Doubting Soul is oft oppresst,
    By hard Reflections from an harder breast.

Th' Uncharitable Soul oft thus reflects,
    After each Birth a second birth doth Come.
Your Second Birth no Second Birth ejects.   15
    The Babe of Grace then's strangld in the Womb.
    There's no new Birth born in thy Soul thou'lt find
    If that the after Birth abide behinde.

The Babe of Grace, thinks he, 's not born its sure.
    Sins Secundine is not as yet out Cast.   20
The Soul no Bracelet of Graces pure
    Doth ware, while wrapt in nature's slough so fast.
    And thus he doth for want of Charity,
    The wounded wound Uncharitably.

And thus some Child of God, when led awry   25
    By Satan, doth with Satan take a part,
Against some Child of God, whom frowardly
    He by Reflections harsh wounds thus in heart.
    Pough! Here's Religion! Strange indeed! Quoth hee.
    Grace makes a Conscience of things here that bee.   30

Grace Conscious makes one how to spend ones time
    How to perform the Duties of one's place
Not onely in the things which are Divine;
    But in the things which ware a Sublime Face.
    Do you do so? And order good persue?   35
    Don't Earth and Heaven interfer in you?

Will God accept the service if the time
    Is stolen from our Calling him to pay?

13 *oft*] orig: doth oft   24 *wound*] orig: uncharitably **wound**

What will he yield that Sacrifice his shine,
    That from anothers Altar's stole away?   40
    God and our Callings Call: and th' Sacrifice
    Stole from our Callings Altar he defies.

Yet if it falls on worldly things intense
    Its soon scourgd then with whips of Worldliness:
It gives to many, nay to all, offence   45
    And gathers to itselfe great penciveness.
    Intense on God, or on the world, all's one.
    The Harmless Soule is hardly thought upon.

Such Traps, and Wilds as these are, Satan sets,
    For to intrap the Innocent therein: 50
These are his Wyers, Snares, and tangling Nets,
    To hanck, and hopple harmless souls in Sin.
    If in such briars thou enbrambled light
    Call on the Mighty God with all thy might.

On God in Christ Call hard: For in him hee   55
    Hath Bowells melting, and Expanded arms:
Hath sweet imbraces, Tender mercy free
    Hath Might Almighty too to save from harms.
    Into his Dove streakt Downy bosom fly,
    In Spite of Spite, or Spiters Enmity.   60

These are Gods Way-Marks thus inscrib'd; this hand
    Points you the way unto the Land Divine,
The Land of Promise, Good Immanuels Land.
    To New Jerusalem above the line.
    Ten thousand times thrice tribled blesst he is,   65
    That walketh in the suburbs here of bliss.

His Wildred state will wane away, and hence
    These Crooked Passages will soon appeare
The Curious needlework of Providence,
    Embrodered with golden Spangles Cleare.   70
    Judge not this Web while in the Loom, but stay
    From judging it untill the judgment day.

60 *In Spite*] PW In Spit

For while its foiled up the best Can see
    But little of it, and that little too
Shews weather beaten but when it shall bee   75
    Hung open all at once, Oh beautious shew!
    Though thrids run in, and out, Cross snarld and twinde
    The Web will even be enwrought you'l finde.

If in the golden Meshes of this Net
    (The Checkerwork of Providence) you're Caught   80
And Carride hence to Heaven, never fret:
    Your Barke shall to an Happy Bay be brought.
    You'l se both Good and Bad drawn up hereby,
    These to Hells Horrour, those to Heavens Joy.

Fear not Presumption then, when God invites: 85
    Invite not Fear, when that he doth thee Call:
Call not in Question whether he delights
    In thee, but make him thy Delight, and all.
    Presumption lies in Backward Bashfulness,
    When one is backward though a bidden Guest.   90

The Effect of this Discourse upon the second,
    and third Rancks.

RANK TWO

Whence Come these Spicy Gales? Shall we abuse
    Such sweet Perfumes with putrid noses?
Who did in this Diffusive Aire Diffuse
    Such Aromatick fumes or Posies?
These Spirits are with Graces sweetly splic'te;   5
What Good Comes in them? Oh! they Come from Christ!

79 *Meshes*] PW Mashes[?]
88 *thee,*] PW thee.   *TWO*] PW 2 Numbers designating the ranks in this
poem are indicated by numerals in PW

RANK THREE

Whence Come these Cloudy Pillars of Perfume?
  Sure Christ doth on his Garden blow
Or open Graces Spice Box, I presume
  From whence these Reechs do flow: 10
For oh! heart Ravishing steams do scale my Soule,
And do in Heavenly Raptures it enrowle.

RANK TWO

Sure Grace a progress in her Coach doth ride,
  Lapt up in all Perfumes, whose sent,
Hath suffocated sin, and nullifi'de   15
  Sad Griefe, as in our Souls it went.
Sin sincks the Soul to Hell: but here is Love
Sincks Sin to Hell; and soars the Soul above.

RANK THREE

I strove to soar on high. But oh! methought
  Like to a Lump of Lead my sin   20
Prest down my Soul; But now it's off, she's Caught
  In holy Raptures up to him.
Oh! let us then sing Praise: methinks I soar
Above the stars, and stand at Heavens Doore.

Our Insufficiency to Praise God
  suitably, for his Mercy.

Should all the World so wide to atoms fall
  Should th'Aire be shred to motes, should we
  Se all the Earth hackt here so small
    That none Could smaller bee?
Should Heaven, and Earth be Atomizd, we guess   5
The Number of these Motes were numberless.

18 *Sincks*] PW Sinck

Series of hyperboles — no matter how much, not praise God — it's not enough

But should we then a World each Atom deem,
    Where dwell as many pious men
    As all these Motes the world Could teem
       Were it shred into them?   10
Each Atom would the World surmount wee guess
Whose men in number would be numberless.

But had each pious man, as many Tongues
    At singing all together then
    The Praise that to the Lord belongs   15
       As all these Atoms men?
Each man would sing a World of Praise, we guess,
Whose Tongues in number would be numberless.

And had each Tongue, as many Songs of Praise
    To sing to the Almighty ALL   20
    As all these men have Tongues to raise
       To him their Holy Call?
Each Tongue would tune a World of Praise, we guess
Whose songs in number would be numberless.

Nay, had each song as many Tunes most sweet   25
    Or one intwisting in't as many,
    As all these Tongues have songs most meet
       Unparallelld by any?
Each song a world of Musick makes we guess
Whose Tunes in number would be numberless.   30

Now should all these Conspire in us that we
    Could breath such Praise to thee, Most High?
    Should we thy Sounding Organs be
       To ring such Melody?
Our Musick would the World of Worlds out ring   35
Yet be unfit within thine Eares to ting.

Thou didst us mould, and us new mould when wee
    Were worse than mould we tread upon.
    Nay Nettles made by Sin wee bee.
       Yet hadst Compassion.
Thou hast pluckt out our Stings; and by degrees   40
Hast of us, lately Wasps, made Lady-Bees.

Though e're our Tongues thy Praises due can fan
    A Weevle with the World may fly,
      Yea fly away: and with a span 45
        We may out mete the Sky.
Though what we can is but a Lisp, We pray
Accept thereof. We have no better pay.

The Soule Seeking Church-Fellowship.

The Soul refresht with gracious Steams, behold,
    Christs royall Spirit richly tended
With all the guard of Graces manifold
    Throngs in to solace it amended
    And by the Trinity befriended. 5

Befriended thus! It lives a Life indeed
    A Life! as if it Liv'd for Life.
For Life Eternall: wherefore with all heed
    It trims the same with Graces rife
    To be the Lambs espoused Wife. 10

Yea, like a Bride all Gloriously arraide,
    It is arrai'de Whose dayly ware
Is an Imbrodery with Grace inlaide,
    Of Sanctuary White most Faire,
    Its drest in Heavens fashion rare. 15

Each Ordinance and Instrument of Grace
    Grace doth instruct are Usefull here.
They're Golden Pipes where Holy Waters trace
    Into the spirits spicebed Deare,
    To vivify what withering were. 20

Hence do their Hearts like Civit-Boxes sweet
    Evaporate their Love full pure,
Which through the Chincks of their Affections reechs

To God, Christ, Christians all, though more,
  To such whose Counsills made their Cure.   25

Hence now Christ's Curious Garden fenced in
  With Solid Walls of Discipline
Well wed, and watered, and made full trim:
  The Allies all Laid out by line:
  Walks for the Spirit all Divine.   30

Whereby Corruptions are kept out, whereby
  Corrupters also get not in,
Unless the Lyons Carkass secretly
  Lies lapt up in a Lamblike skin
  Which Holy seems yet's full of sin.   35

For on the Towers of these Walls there stand
  Just Watchmen Watching day, and night,
And Porters at each Gate, who have Command
  To open onely to the right.
  And all within may have a sight.   40

Whose Zeale, should it along a Channell slide
  Not banckt with Knowledg right and Good,
Nor Bottomed with Love: nor wiers ti'de
  To hinder prejudiciall Blood
  The Currant will be full of mud.   45

But yet this Curious Garden richly set,
  The Soul accounts Christs Paradise
Set with Choice slips, and flowers: and longs to get
  Itselfe set here: and by advice
  To grow herein and so rejoyce.   50

26 *Christ's*] PW Christ
38 *Porters*] PW Porter   49 *by advice*] orig: Heavenly wise
50 *and so rejoyce*] orig: it seeks and joyes

The Soul admiring the Grace of the Church
Enters into Church Fellowship.

How is this City, Lord, of thine bespangled
    With Graces shine?
With Ordinances alli'de, and inam'led,
    Which are Divine?
Walld in with Discipline her Gates obtaine   5
Just Centinalls with Love Imbellisht plain.

Hence glorious, and terrible she stands;
    That Converts new
Seing her Centinalls of all demand
    The Word to shew;   10
Stand gazing much between two Passions Crusht
Desire, and Feare at once which both wayes thrust.

Thus are they wrackt. Desire doth forward screw
    To get them in,
But Feare doth backward thrust, that lies purdue,   15
    And slicks that Pin.
You cannot give the word, Quoth she, which though
You stumble on't its more than yet you know.

But yet Desires Screw Pin doth not slack:
    It still holds fast.   20
But Fears Screw Pin turns back or Screw doth Crack
    And breaks at last.
Hence on they go, and in they enter: where
Desire Converts to joy: joy Conquours Fear.

They now enCovenant With God: and His:
    They thus indent.   25
The Charters Seals belonging unto this
    The Sacrament

11 *Passions*] PW Passion   21 *turns*] orig: slips   27 *Seals*] PW Seal's

So God is theirs avoucht, they his in Christ.
In whom all things they have, with Grace are splic'te. 30

Thus in the usuall Coach of Gods Decree
    They bowle and swim
To Glory bright, if no Hypocrisie
    Handed them in.
For such must shake their handmaid off lest they 35
Be shakt out of this Coach, or dy in th'way.

The Glory of and Grace in the Church set out.

    Come now behold
  Within this Knot What Flowers do grow:
    Spanglde like gold:
  Whence Wreaths of all Perfumes do flow.
Most Curious Colours of all sorts you shall 5
With all Sweet Spirits sent. Yet thats not all.

    Oh! Look, and finde
  These Choicest Flowers most richly sweet
    Are Disciplinde
  With Artificiall Angells meet. 10
An heap of Pearls is precious: but they shall
When set by Art Excell: Yet that's not all.

    Christ's Spirit showers
  Down in his Word, and Sacraments
    Upon these Flowers
  The Clouds of Grace Divine Contents. 15
Such things of Wealthy Blessings on them fall
As make them sweetly thrive: Yet that's not all.

    Yet still behold!
  All flourish not at once. We see 20

While some Unfold
Their blushing Leaves, some buds there bee.
Here's Faith, Hope, Charity in flower, which call
On yonders in the Bud. Yet that's not all.

But as they stand   25
Like Beauties reeching in perfume
A Divine Hand
Doth hand them up to Glories room:
Where Each in sweet'ned Songs all Praises shall
Sing all ore heaven for aye. And that's but all.   30

The Souls Admiration hereupon.

What I such Praises sing! How can it bee?
Shall I in Heaven sing?
What I, that scarce durst hope to see
Lord, such a thing?
Though nothing is too hard for thee: 5
One Hope hereof seems hard to mee.

What, Can I ever tune those Melodies
Who have no tune at all?
Not knowing where to stop nor Rise,
Nor when to Fall.   10
To sing thy Praise I am unfit.
I have not learn'd my Gam-Ut yet.

But should these Praises on string'd Instruments
Be sweetly tun'de? I finde
I nonplust am: for no Consents   15
I ever minde.
My Tongue is neither Quill, nor Bow:
Nor Can my Fingers Quavers show.

But was it otherwise I have no Kit:
Which though I had, I could   20

Not tune the strings, which soon would slip
        Though others should.
    But should they not, I cannot play:
    But for an F should strike an A.

And should thy Praise upon Winde Instruments   25
        Sound all o're Heaven Shrill?
My Breath will hardly through such Vents
        A Whistle fill,
    Which though it should, its past my spell
    By Stops, and Falls to sound it Well.   30

How should I then, joyn in such Exercise?
        One sight of thee'l intice
Mine Eyes to heft: Whose Extasies
        Will stob my Voice.
    Hereby mine Eyes will bind my Tongue.   35
    Unless thou, Lord, do Cut the thong.

What Use of Uselesse mee, then there, poore snake?
        There Saints, and Angels sing,
Thy Praise in full Cariere, which make
        The Heavens to ring.   40
    Yet if thou wilt thou Can'st me raise
    With Angels bright to sing thy Praise.

The Joy of Church Fellowship rightly attended.

In Heaven soaring up, I dropt an Eare
        On Earth: and oh! sweet Melody:
And listening, found it was the Saints who were
        Encoacht for Heaven that sang for Joy.
    For in Christs Coach they sweetly sing;   5
    As they to Glory ride therein.

31 *joyn*] orig: Lord, joyn   33 *heft*] orig: thee fly

Oh! joyous hearts! Enfir'de with holy Flame!
    Is speech thus tassled with praise?
Will not your inward fire of Joy contain;
    That it in open flames doth blaze?   10
    For in Christ's Coach Saints sweetly sing,
    As they to Glory ride therein.

And if a string do slip, by Chance, they soon
    Do screw it up again: whereby
They set it in a more melodious Tune   15
    And a Diviner Harmony.
    For in Christs Coach they sweetly sing
    As they to Glory ride therein.

In all their Acts, publick, and private, nay
    And secret too, they praise impart.   20
But in their Acts Divine and Worship, they
    With Hymns do offer up their Heart.
    Thus in Christs Coach they sweetly sing
    As they to Glory ride therein.
Some few not in; and some whose Time, and Place   25
    Block up this Coaches way do goe
As Travellers afoot, and so do trace
    The Road that gives them right thereto
    While in this Coach these sweetly sing
    As they to Glory ride therein.   30

11 *Christ's*] PW Christ

Miscellaneous Poems

[1. When] Let by rain.

Undated. Pub. *W*.

Ye Flippering Soule,
   Why dost between the Nippers dwell?
Not stay, nor goe. Not yea, nor yet Controle.
   Doth this doe well?
      Rise journy'ng when the skies fall weeping Showers.   5
      Not o're nor under th'Clouds and Cloudy Powers.

Not yea, nor noe:
   On tiptoes thus? Why sit on thorns?
Resolve the matter: Stay thyselfe or goe.
   Be n't both wayes born.   10
      Wager thyselfe against thy surplice, see,
      And win thy Coate: or let thy Coate Win thee.

Is this th'Effect,
   To leaven thus my Spirits all?
To make my heart a Crabtree Cask direct?   15
   A Verjuicte Hall?
      As Bottle Ale, whose Spirits prisond nurst
      When jog'd, the bung with Violence doth burst?

Shall I be made
   A sparkling Wildfire Shop   20
Where my dull Spirits at the Fireball trade
   Do frisk and hop?
      And while the Hammer doth the Anvill pay,
      The fireball matter sparkles ery way.

One sorry fret,   25
   An anvill Sparke, rose higher
And in thy Temple falling almost set
   The house on fire.
      Such fireballs droping in the Temple Flame
      Burns up the building: Lord forbid the same.   30

In PW at top of page is written: "*** occurrants occasioning what follow"
Title means: when hindered (from going on a journey) by rain.

2. Upon a Spider Catching a Fly.

Undated. Pub. *W*.

Thou sorrow, venom Elfe.
    Is this thy play,
To spin a web out of thyselfe
    To Catch a Fly?
      For Why?   5

I saw a pettish wasp
    Fall foule therein.
Whom yet thy Whorle pins did not clasp
    Lest he should fling
      His sting.   10

But as affraid, remote
    Didst stand hereat
And with thy little fingers stroke
    And gently tap
      His back.   15

Thus gently him didst treate
    Lest he should pet,
And in a froppish, waspish heate
    Should greatly fret
      Thy net.   20

Whereas the silly Fly,
    Caught by its leg
Thou by the throate tookst hastily
    And 'hinde the head
      Bite Dead.   25

This goes to pot, that not
    Nature doth call.

8 *clasp*] Conj. word torn away in PW. *W* conjectures hasp
17 *pet*] orig: thee ***set   21 *Fly*,] PW Fly.

Strive not above what strength hath **got**
    Lest in the brawle
        Thou fall.   30

This Frey seems thus to us.
    Hells Spider gets
His intrails spun to whip **Cords thus**
    And wove to nets
        And sets.   35

To tangle Adams race
    In's stratigems
To their Destructions, spoil'd, made **base**
    By venom things
        Damn'd Sins.   40

But mighty, Gracious Lord
    Communicate
Thy Grace to breake the Cord, afford
    Us Glorys Gate
        And State.   45

We'l Nightingaile sing like
    When pearcht on high
In Glories Cage, thy glory, **bright**,
    And thankfully,
        For joy.   50

3. Upon a Wasp Child with Cold.

Undated. Pub. ETG.

The Bare that breaths the Northern blast
Did numb, Torpedo like, a Wasp
Whose stiffend limbs encrampt, lay bathing
In Sol's warm breath and shine as saving,

28 *what*] orig: thy
43 *Cord,*] PW Cord   49 *And*] Conj. W conjectures Yea   1 *blast*] PW blast.

Which with her hands she chafes and stands   5
Rubbing her Legs, Shanks, Thighs, and hands.
Her petty toes, and fingers ends
Nipt with this breath, she out extends
Unto the Sun, in greate desire
To warm her digits at that fire.   10
Doth hold her Temples in this state
Where pulse doth beate, and head doth **ake**.
Doth turn, and stretch her body small,
Doth Comb her velvet Capitall.
As if her little brain pan were   15
A Volume of Choice precepts cleare.
As if her sattin jacket hot
Contained Apothecaries Shop
Of Natures recepts, that prevails
To remedy all her sad ailes,   20
As if her velvet helmet high
Did turret rationality.
She fans her wing up to the Winde
As if her Pettycoate were lin'de,
With reasons fleece, and hoises sails   25
And hu'ming flies in thankfull gails
Unto her dun Curld palace Hall
Her warm thanks offering for all.

    Lord cleare my misted sight that I
May hence view thy Divinity.   30
Some sparkes whereof thou up dost hasp
Within this little downy Wasp
In whose small Corporation wee
A school and a schoolmaster see
Where we may learn, and easily finde   35
A nimble Spirit bravely minde
Her worke in e'ry limb: and lace
It up neate with a vitall grace,
Acting each part though ne'er so small

11 *in*] orig: and   16 *Volume*] PW Volumn   18 *Apothecaries*] orig: in't
Apothecaries   20 *ailes,*] PW ailes   28 *warm*] Conj.   32 *downy*] Conj.
39 *each*] orig: in ery

Here of this Fustian animall.   40
Till I enravisht Climb into
The Godhead on this Lather doe.
Where all my pipes inspir'de upraise
An Heavenly musick furrd with praise.

4. Huswifery.

Undated. Pub. ETP, *W*.

Make me, O Lord, thy Spining Wheele compleate.
    Thy Holy Worde my Distaff make for mee.
Make mine Affections thy Swift Flyers neate
    And make my Soule thy holy Spoole to bee.
    My Conversation make to be thy Reele   5
    And reele the yarn thereon spun of thy Wheele.

Make me thy Loome then, knit therein this Twine:
    And make thy Holy Spirit, Lord, winde quills:
Then weave the Web thyselfe. The yarn is fine.
    Thine Ordinances make my Fulling Mills.   10
    Then dy the same in Heavenly Colours Choice,
    All pinkt with Varnisht Flowers of Paradise.

Then cloath therewith mine Understanding, Will,
    Affections, Judgment, Conscience, Memory
My Words, and Actions, that their shine may fill   15
    My wayes with glory and thee glorify.
    Then mine apparell shall display before yee
    That I am Cloathd in Holy robes for glory.

40 *Here*] orig: Exactly   41 *Climb*] orig: up Climb
42 *on*] orig: upon

5. Another upon the Same.

Undated. Pub. ETG.

Make me thy Spinning Wheele of use for thee,
    Thy Grace my Distaffe, and my heart thy Spoole.
Turn thou the wheele: let mine Affections bee
    The flyers filling with thy yarne my soule.
      Then weave the web of Grace in mee, thy Loome   5
      And Cloath my soule therewith, its Glories bloome.

Make mee thy Loome: thy Grace the warfe therein,
    My duties Woofe, and let thy word winde Quills.
The shuttle shoot. Cut off the ends my sins.
      Thy Ordinances make my fulling mills,   10
      My Life thy Web: and cloath me all my dayes
      With this Gold-web of Glory to thy praise.

6. Upon Wedlock, and Death of Children.

Undated. Pub. ETP, *W;* stanzas 5 and 7 only, *RTS,* SCP.

A Curious Knot God made in Paradise,
    And drew it out inamled neatly Fresh.
It was the True-Love Knot, more sweet than spice
    And set with all the flowres of Graces dress.
      Its Weddens Knot, that ne're can be unti'de.   5
      No Alexanders Sword can it divide.

The slips here planted, gay and glorious grow:
    Unless an Hellish breath do sindge their Plumes.
Here Primrose, Cowslips, Roses, Lilies blow
    With Violets and Pinkes that voide perfumes.   10

10 *mills*] PW mulls

Whose beautious leaves ore laid with Hony Dew.
And Chanting birds Cherp out sweet Musick true.

When in this Knot I planted was, my Stock
    Soon knotted, and a manly flower out brake.
And after it my branch again did knot   15
    Brought out another Flowre its sweet breathd mate.
    One knot gave one tother the tothers place.
    Whence Checkling smiles fought in each others face.

But oh! a glorious hand from glory came
    Guarded with Angells, soon did Crop this flowre   20
Which almost tore the root up of the same
    At that unlookt for, Dolesome, darksome houre.
    In Pray're to Christ perfum'de it did ascend,
    And Angells bright did it to heaven tend.

But pausing on't, this sweet perfum'd my thought,   25
    Christ would in Glory have a Flowre, Choice, Prime,
And having Choice, chose this my branch forth brought.
    Lord take't. I thanke thee, thou takst ought of mine,
    It is my pledg in glory, part of mee
    Is now in it, Lord, glorifi'de with thee.   30

But praying ore my branch, my branch did sprout
    And bore another manly flower, and gay
And after that another, sweet brake out,
    The which the former hand soon got away.
    But oh! the tortures, Vomit, screechings, groans,   35
    And six weeks Fever would pierce hearts like stones.

Griefe o're doth flow: and nature fault would finde
    Were not thy Will, my Spell Charm, Joy, and Gem:

17 orig: One *** knot gave tother tothers place   38 *my Spell*] orig: my Spell,
my joy

    Four children are mentioned in this poem: line 14, "a manly flower"
(Samuel, born Aug. 27, 1675, survived until maturity); line 16, "another
Flowre" (Elizabeth, born Dec. 27, 1676, died December 25, 1677); line 32,
"another manly flower" (James, born Oct. 12, 1678, survived until maturity);
and line 33, "another, sweet" (Abigail, born Aug. 6, 1681, died Aug. 22, 1682).
Taylor's fifth child (Bathshuah, born Jan. 17, 1683/4) is not mentioned; the
date of this poem, then, is probably 1682 or 1683,

That as I said, I say, take, Lord, they're thine.
   I piecemeale pass to Glory bright in them.   40
   I joy, may I sweet Flowers for Glory breed,
   Whether thou getst them green, or lets them seed.

7. The Ebb and Flow.

Undated. Pub. ETP, *W*.

When first thou on me Lord wrought'st thy Sweet Print,
   My heart was made thy tinder box.
   My 'ffections were thy tinder in't.
     Where fell thy Sparkes by drops.
Those holy Sparks of Heavenly Fire that came   5
Did ever catch and often out would flame.

But now my Heart is made thy Censar trim,
   Full of thy golden Altars fire,
   To offer up Sweet Incense in
     Unto thyselfe intire: 10
I finde my tinder scarce thy sparks can feel
That drop out from thy Holy flint and Steel.

Hence doubts out bud for feare thy fire in mee
   'S a mocking Ignis Fatuus
   Or lest thine Altars fire out bee,   15
     Its hid in ashes thus.
Yet when the bellows of thy Spirit blow
Away mine ashes, then thy fire doth glow.

5 *came*] orig: fell

8. Upon the Sweeping Flood Aug: 13.14. 1683.

Dated as above. Pub. ETG.

Oh! that Id had a tear to've quencht that flame
    Which did dissolve the Heavens above
    Into those liquid drops that Came
        To drown our Carnall love.
Our cheeks were dry and eyes refusde to weep.   5
Tears bursting out ran down the skies darke Cheek.

Were th'Heavens sick? must wee their Doctors bee
    And physick them with pills, our sin?
    To make them purg and Vomit, see,
        And Excrements out fling?   10
We've griev'd them by such Physick that they shed
Their Excrements upon our lofty heads.

A Funerall Poem Upon the Death of my ever Endeared, and Tender Wife Mrs. Elizabeth Taylor, Who fell asleep in Christ the 7th day of July at night about two hours after Sun setting 1689 and in the 39 yeare of her Life.

Undated except as above. Pub. TVT.

PART. 1.

My Gracious Lord, I Licence of thee Crave,
Not to repine but drop upon the Grave
Of my Deare Wife a Teare, or two: or wash

9 *Vomit, see,*] PW Vomit see   *see*] orig: as wee

A Funerall Poem] This is the only poem in which Taylor comments directly on the death of his wife.

Thy Milk White hand in tears that downward pass.
Thou summond hast her Noble part away: 5
And in Salt Tears I would Embalm her Clay.
Some deem Death doth the True Love Knot unty:
But I do finde it harder tide thereby.
My heart is in't and will be squeez'd therefore
To pieces if thou draw the Ends much more.   10
Oh strange Untying! it ti'th harder: What?
Can anything unty a True Love Knot?
Five Babes thou tookst from me before this Stroake.
Thine arrows then into my bowells broake,
But now they pierce into my bosom smart,   15
Do strike and stob me in the very heart.
I'de then my bosom Friend a Comfort, and
To Comfort: Yet my Lord, I kiss thy hand.
I Her resign'd, thou tookst her into thine,
Out of my bosom, yet she dwells in mine: 20
And though her Precious Soule now swims in bliss,
Yet while grim Death, that Dismall Sergeant is,
Between the Parts Essentiall now remote,
And hath this stately Tabernacle broke
My Harp is turnd to mourning: Organ sweet   25
Is turn'de into the Voice of them that weep.
Griefe swelling girds the Heart Strings where its purst,
Unless it Vent the Vessell sure will burst.
        My Gracious Lord, grant that my bitter Griefe
        Breath through this little Vent hole for reliefe.   30

PART. 2.

        My Dear, Deare Love, reflect thou no such thing,
Will Griefe permit you at my Grave to sing?
Oh! Black Black Theme! The Girths of Griefe alone
Do gird my heart till Gust of Sorrows groan
And dash a mournfull Song to pieces on   35

4 *Thy*] orig: That   29 *bitter Griefe*] orig: Griefe

13. *Five Babes thou tookst from me.* Elizabeth, died 1677, aged one year;
Abigail, died 1682, aged one year; Elizabeth, died 1685, aged five months;
Mary, died 1687, aged ten months; Hezekiah, died 1688, aged two weeks.

The Dolefull Face of thy Sepulcher Stone.
My Onely DOVE, though Harp and Harrow, loe,
Better agree than Songs and Sorrows doe,
Yet spare me thus to drop a blubber'd Verse
Out of my Weeping Eyes Upon thy Herse.   40
What shall my Preface to our True Love Knot
Frisk in Acrostick Rhimes? And may I not
Now at our parting, with Poetick knocks
Break a salt teare to pieces as it drops?
Did Davids bitter Sorrow at the Dusts   45
Of Jonathan raise such Poetick gusts?
Do Emperours interr'd in Verses lie?
And mayn't such Feet run from my Weeping Eye?
Nay, Dutie lies upon mee much; and shall
I in thy Coffin naile thy Vertues all?   50
How shall thy Babes, and theirs, thy Vertuous shine
Know, or Persue unless I them define?
Thy Grace will Grace unto a Poem bee
Although a Poem be no grace to thee.
Impute it not a Crime then if I weep   55
A Weeping Poem on thy Winding Sheet.
Maybe some Angell may my Poem sing
To thee in Glory, or relate the thing,
        Which if he do, my mournfull Poem may
        Advance thy Joy, and my Deep Sorrow lay.   60

PART. 3.
        Your Ears, Bright Saints, and Angells: them I Choose
To stough her Praises in: I'le not abuse.
Her Modesty would blush should you profess,
I in Hyperboles her praises dress.
Wherefore as Cramping Griefe permitts to stut   65
Them forth accept of such as here I put.
        Her Husbands Joy, Her Childrens Chiefe Content.
Her Servants Eyes, Her Houses Ornament.
Her Shine as Child, as Neighbour, flies abroad
As Mistress, Mother, Wife, her Walke With God.   70

52 *define?*] PW define.   70 *Wife,*] PW Wife.

As Child she was a Tender, Pious Bud
Of Pious Parents, sprang of Pious Blood
Two Grandsires, Gran'ams: one or two, she had
A Father too and Mother, that englad
The Gracious heart to thinke upon, they were   75
Bright Pillars in Gods Temple shining cleare.
Her Father, and her Mothers Father fix
As shining Stars in Golden Candlesticks.
She did Obedient, Tender, Meek Child prove
The Object of her Fathers Eye, and Love.   80
Her Mother being Dead, her heart would melt
When she her Fathers looks not pleasant felt.
His smile Would her enliven, Frown, down pull
Hence she became his Child most Dutifull.

    As Neighbour, she was full of Neighbourhood   85
Not Proud, or Strang; Grave, Courteous, ever good.
Compassionate: but unto none was Soure.
Her Fingers dropt with Myrrh, oft, to her power.

    As Mistress she order'd her Family
With all Discretion, and most prudently   90
In all things prompt: Dutie in this respect
Would to the meanest in it not neglect.
Ripe at her Fingers Ends, Would nothing flinch.
She was a neate good Huswife every inch.
Although her weakenesse made her let alone   95
Things so to go, as made her fetch a groan.
Remiss was not, nor yet severe unto
Her Servants: but i'th' golden mean did goe.

    As Mother, Oh! What tender Mother She?
Her bowells Boiled ore to them that bee   100
Bits of her tender Bowells. She a share
Of her affections ever made them ware.
Yet never chose to trick them, nor herselfe
In antick garbs; or Lavishness of Wealth.
But was a Lover much of Comeliness: 105
And with her Needle work would make their Dress.

81: *Her Mother being Dead.* Mrs. Taylor's mother died Sept. 9, 1659,
when Elizabeth was about seven years old.

The Law of Life within her Lips she would
Be dropping forth upon them as shee should.
Foolishly fond she was not but would give
Correction wisely, that their Soules might Live.   110
    As Wife, a Tender, Tender, Loving, Meet,
Meeke, Patient, Humble, Modest, Faithfull, Sweet
Endearing Help she was: Whose Chiefest Treasure
Of Earthly things she held her Husbands pleasure.
But if she spi'de displeasure in his face,   115
Sorrow would spoile her own, and marr its grace.
Dear Heart! She would his Joy, Peace, Honour, Name,
Even as her very Life, seeke to mentain.
And if an hasty word by chance dropt in:
She would in secret sigh it or'e with him.   120
She was not wedded unto him alone
But had his joy, and sorrow as her own.
She, where he chanc'd to miss, a Cover would lay
Yet would in Secret fore him all Display
In meekness of sweet wisdom, and by Art,   125
As Certainly would winde into the heart.
She laid her neck unto the Yoake he draws:
And was his Faithfull Yoake Mate, in Christ's Cause.

    As to her walk with God, she did inherit
The very Spirits of her Parents Spirit.   130
She was no gaudy Christian, or gilt Weed:
But was a Reall, Israelite indeed.
When in her Fathers house God toucht her Heart,
That Trembling Frame of Spirit, and that Smart,
She then was under very, few did know: 135
Whereof she somewhat to the Church did show.
Repentance now's her Work: Sin poyson is:
Faith, carries her to Christ as one of his.
Fear Temples in her heart; Love flowers apace
To God, Christ, Grace Saints, and the Means of Grace.   140
She's much in Reading, Pray're, Selfe-Application
Holds humbly up, a pious Conversation

119 in] orig: from   124 fore him all Display] orig: it
before him lay   128 Christ's]PW Christ   131 gaudy] PW gaudy,

In which she makes profession * * * * * * *
Which unto Westfield Church she did disclose.
Holy in Health; Patient in Sickness long.   145
And very great. Yet gracious Speech doth throng:
She oft had up, An Alwise God Doth this.
And in a filiall way the Rod would kiss.
When Pains were Sore, Justice can do no wrong,
Nor Mercy Cruell be; became her Song.   150
The Doomsday Verses much perfum'de her Breath,
Much in her thoughts, and yet she fear'd not Death.

An Elegy upon the Death of that Holy and Reverend Man of God, Mr. Samuel Hooker,

Pastor of the Church of Christ at Farmington, (and Son to the Famous Mr. Thomas Hooker, who was a Pastor of, and began with the Church of Christ at Hartford on Connecticut in New England) who slept in Christ, the 6th day of November, about one a Clock in the morning in the 64 year of his age entered upon. Annoque Domini 1697.

Undated except as above. Pub. TVT.

Griefe sometimes is a duty yet when **Great**
And geteth vent, it Non-Sense sobs, doth spea**ke**

144 *she*] Conj.

151: Doomsday Verses. Michael Wigglesworth's *The Day of Doom* (1662), a best seller in New England in the 17th century.

Samuel Hooker was a son of the famous Thomas Hooker of Hartford. He was born ca. 1635, perhaps in Cambridge, Mass., and graduated from Harvard in 1653—a classmate of Taylor's father-in-law, Samuel Wyllys. He preached in the colony of Plymouth, where he was married, in 1658, to Mary Willet, by whom he had eleven children. A daughter, Mary, was the mother of Sarah Pierpont, wife of Jonathan Edwards. In 1661, Hooker was ordained at Farmington, Conn., and remained there until his death Nov. 6, 1697. He was considered a good preacher. John Sibley, *Biographical Sketches of Harvard University*, Cambridge, 1881.

Cutting off Sentences by Enterjections
Made by the force of hard beset Affections.
Should I in mine pass through this Hemisphere   5
And beg of ev'ry Eye a Trickling teare
To wash thy Tombe, Deare Hooker, bright therein,
All would not Drown the Griefe that thence doth spring.
Shall thy Choice Name here not embalmed ly
In those Sweet Spices whose perfumes do fly   10
From thy greate Excellence? It surely would
Be Sacraledge thy Worth back to withhold.
Lord spare the Flock. Shall brave brave Jon'than dy?
And David's place be empty? Sling ly by?
Before their heads those Almond Trees are white   15
And ere they're mellow'd by old age's weight?
When Birds new Hatcht ware, as in nest they ly,
Presbytick Down, Pinfeatherd Prelacy
(Young Cockerills, whose Combs soare up like Spires
That force their Dams: and Crow against their Sires?)   20
Dost thou withdraw? and now? Where are thy Spurs
Then to be had? Whose sight would work demurrs.
Where hast thou left thy Strenth, and Potency?
And Congregationall Artillery?
We need the Same, and need it more and more.   25
For Babels Canons 'gainst our Bulworks roare.

2 TO NEW ENGLAND.

Alas! alas! New England go weep.
Thy loss is greate in him: For he did keep
Within thine Orb as a bright shining Sun
To give thee Light, but now his race is run.   30
And though his Epicycle was but small
His shining Beams did fly to lighten all.
He was in Person neat, of lesser Sise,
With Ruddy Looks, and with quick rowling eyes.
His Head a Magazeen of Wisdom rich,   35
With Spirits fand from foggy Vapors which
Do Reason cloud: a Fine spun Fancy, Quick,

13 *Shall*] PW shall   26 *'gainst*] orig: do against   *Bulworks*] orig: Walls do

Producing Notions brave, and Rhetorick.
A Son of such a Father, whose name Flew
Like sweet Perfume o're Englands Old, and New.   40
A Son, though youngest, yet that did inherit,
A noble portion of his Fathers Spirit,
Wise, Pious, Prudent, had a Strong, Cleare Head,
That entertaind the Strength of what he red.
Grave, not Morose, Courteous; yet did Command   45
A Distance due: and by a gentle hand.
Not Verbous, yet, his lips would oft distill
Brave Apophthegms: Facete Wit, and Skill.
In Councill Choice, deliberate, and full.
In Disputation, Acute. Home, not Dull   50
Meek as a Lamb, yet as a Lion, hee
Could put on Majesty, if't needs must bee.
Keen in Rebukes yet Candid, Corrosive
Where Cases calld, would to the bottom rive.
A True Peace-Maker, Farmington may say,   55
Offt in the fire and Flame of others fray
Calazy-Gem like quencht it. And as fring'd
With Salamanders Woole, he was not sindg'd.
He steady was: Not on, and Off. His Minde
John Baptist like's no Reed shook with the Winde.   60
Concocted not, though neatly minced Slops,
A mess of Windmills, or of Weather-Cocks.
Not Esau like selling his choice Free Sockage
Then left his Birthright for a bowl of Pottage.
He, and the best of Queens, we thus describe'm   65
Agreeing in one Motto Semper idem.
A Box of Jewells, string of Pearls bright, High.
Of Heavenly Graces a sweet Spicery.
Humble, and full of selfe abasement, though
Such Excellency did in him e're flow.   70

63 *selling his choice Free Sockage*] orig: that in his hungry dottage
64 *Then left*] orig: Parts with   *bowl*] orig: mess

65: *best of Queens.* Probably the Protestant queen Mary, who died in 1694.
Taylor, of course, was well disposed toward the revolution of 1688 and to-
ward William and Mary.

A Rich Divine: a Pastour very choice
Dispensing Grace, with a sweet piercing voice
(Like to the still small Voice Elijah heard)
That rended Rocks, and Satans Intrest marr'd.
In Prayre sweet, the musick of which String   75
Celestiall Wealth unto the Earth would bring
Like little Paul in Person, Voice, and Grace
Advancing Christ and sinfull things out race.
The Sacred Writ with joy he did attend.
And Scriptures dropt even at his fingers end.   80
A Weighty Preacher: never notion Sick:
An Angel in a Golden Candlestick.
He had the knack of Preaching: and did dart
Christs fiery Shafts into the flinty heart;
Till it was broken: Then the smarting wound   85
Would dress with Gilliads Balm to make it sound.
The Gospell Bow and balsom well he knew—
Barjona was; and Boanerges true.
Great Gregry, its said, did Peters Coffin Wrest
Wide ope, and found his Keyes in't. (Ah! well Blesst)   90
But Hooker bravely handed Aaron Rod
Christ's own Choice Keyes, and gently, and for God.
  A Loving Husband; tender Father, who
In sweet affections oft would overflow
With Pious, Rich Discourse, that was well spic'd   95
With Gospell Grace, to bring them up to Christ.
And holy Counsill on them he would shoure
With Death Bed Charges till his dying hour.
But seeing Death Creep on his Fingers ends,
And on his Hands, and Arms, bespake his Friends   100
Thus, saying, They are Dead, you see, and I

74 *rended*] orig: did rend
76 *Wealth*] PW Weath orig: blessing   87 orig: The Gospell Brand he usd,
and salve well knew   90 *Ah*] orig: Oh   101 *you*] orig: and I you
and I] orig: them thus

88: *Boanerges*. Name given by Christ to the two sons of Zebedee (Mark
3:17)—literally, 'sons of thunder,' hence 'a loud, vociferous preacher.' How-
ever, Taylor seems to be using the word in a favorable sense.

Have done with them: warm cloaths thereto apply,
But Death admits no check mate. Out he poures
His Soul on Christ. On him they weep in showers.
       But art thou gone, Brave Hooker, hence? and Why?   105
What, wast thou weary of thy Ministry?
Or weari'd out by thy fed flock? Alas!
Or did the Countrey's Sins it bring to pass?
He was a Samuel in his place, and breath.
Let Israel do him honour at his Death.   110
       Mourn, mourn, New England, alas! alas!
To see thy Freckled Face in Gospell Glass:
To feele thy Pulse, and finde thy Spleen's not well:
Whose Vapors cause thy Pericordium t'swell:
Do suffocat, and Cramp thee, and grow worse   115
By Hypochondrik Passions of the purse,
Affect thy Brains toucht with the Turn, till thou
Halfe sick of Preachers false, and Gospell Plow.
Such Symptoms say, if nothing else will ease,
Thy Sickness soon will cure thy sad Disease.   120
For when such Studs, as stop, and scotch the Way
Of thy Declensions are remoov'd thy bay,
Apostasy wherewith thou art thus driven
Unto the tents of Presbyterianism
(Which is refined Prelacy at best)   125
Will not stay long here in her tents, and rest,
But o're this Bridge will carry thee apace
Into the Realm of Prelates arch, the place
Where open Sinners vile unmaskt indeed
Are Welcom Guests (if they can say the Creed)   130
Unto Christs Table, While they can their Sins
Atone in Courts by offering Silverlings.
Watch, Watch thou then: Reform thy life: Refine
Thyselfe from thy Declentions. Tend thy line.

104 *weep in showers*] orig: tears do shower
in] orig: *new* changed to *may*   115 orig: Stiffen the Patchwax of thy neck
and taint   Two lines canceled between 115–16: "Thy Brow with Crocus
Metallarians' paint / Enfeebles too thy Spirits which distill grow worse"
116 *Passions*] orig: Sickness   117 *toucht*] orig: do   118 *Gospell*] orig: the
Gospell   126 *stay*] orig: here stay   129 *Sinners*] PW Sinner

Steeples ware Weathercocks: but Turrits gain   135
An Happiness under a Faithfull Vane.
And weep thy Sins away, lest woe be nigh.
    For Angells with thy Lots away do high.

PART. 3. TO CONNECTICUT.

Mourn, mourn, Connecticut; thou'st lost a Gem;
A Carbuncle, (and thou hast few of them)   140
Is fallen from thy Crown, a Sun full bright
Is set, bidding thine Horizon good night.
Mourn Hartford, mourn; a bud of thine is gone:
A Gem that grew on thy Foundation Stone
(Not Stone's, but Hooker's who did in thee Shine   145
In Light, Life, Line, and Gospell Discipline)
Who griev'd to see thee warpe from thy foundation
And leave thy first Love thus, and Education.
Of all thy Sons thou hast not such another
To stay thy Head, and heart from ill recover.   150

PART. 4.

    Alas poor Farmington, of all the rest
Most Happy, and Unhappy, Blesst unblesst:
Most Happy having such an Happiness:
And most unhappy losing of no less.
Oh! mourn, and weep, remember thou the Call   155
Thy Prophet gave thee to't before his fall.
Oh Daughter of my people, (that last text)
Gird thee with Sackcloth, Wallow thee perplext
In ashes. Mourn thou lamentably
As for an onely Son: weep bitterly,   160
For lo, the Spoiler suddenly shall come
Upon us. And his Sermon being done
The motive to the Call, the Prophesy

159 *Mourn*] PW mourn

136: Faithfull Vane. Evidently a pun on the name of Sir Henry Vane, the
English Puritan, executed by Charles II in 1662.
   145: Stone's. A pun on the name of Thomas Hooker's close friend and
colleague at Hartford, Samuel Stone (1602–63) (TVT).

Had an accomplishment before your eye.
For he much spent desired you to sing   165
A Psalm while he refresht and rested him,
Which done he prayed over you intent,
Dismist you with a blessing briefe, and bent
Under the Spoiler down that suddenly
Assaulted him. And gave discharg thereby   170
Unto his pulpit from all right of Claim
For ever after in this man of Fame.
He bowing goes unto a neighbours, whence
After a while he rideth home from thence
Betook him to his dying Bed perfum'd   175
With prayers to God, and Charges he assum'd
And laid his friends and Wife and Children under
While five dayes run, and Illiak pains did thunder.
That Hooker now by this sharp tyranny
Forcing things back that should go on, should dy   180
Lord grant it be n't an Omen of our Fate
Foreshewing our apostate following State.
Then mourn poore Church, thy Prophets race is run
As for a Father, or an onely Son.
After three tens, and seven years were past   185
Under thy rocky hill by him, at last
He thus doth leave thee. Search into thy Sin,
Repent, and grieve that ere thou grievedst him,
Or rather God in him, lest suddenly
The Spoiler still should on thee come and stroy.   190
Lord, art thou angry with the Flock, that thou
Dost slay their Shephard? Or dost disallow
The Fold, and lay it Common that thou smite
Down dost the shory that upheld it right?
Shall angling cease? And no more fish be took   195
That thou callst home thy Hooker with his Hook?
Lord, spare the flock: uphold the fold from falling.
Send out another Hooker of this Calling.

169 *Under*] PW under   orig: Down under   171 *from*] orig: of
181 *of our Fate*] orig: to recite

PART. 5. TO THE FAMILY RELICT.

Thou mourning Family, what shall I say?
Shall Passion, or compassion o're me sway?   200
It is a day of Griefe: Tears are a Dress
Becoming us, come they not to excess.
Then keep due measure. Should you too much bring,
Your too much is too little far for him.
         Thou mourning Widdow! oh! how sad? how sharp?   205
Poor bleeding Soule! how turned is thy Harp
Into the Voice of mourning? Organ sweet
Into the bitter Voice of them that weep.
But yet cheere up: New England layes her head
To thine, to weep with thee over thy Dead.   210
Thou may'st therefore spend fewer tears of Sorrow
Out of thine own, thou dost so many borrow.
Christs Napkin take, Graces green Taffity
And wipe therewith, thy Weeping, watry eye
And thou shalt see thy Hooker all ore gay   215
With Christ in bliss, adorn'd with Glories Ray,
And putting out his shining hand to thee
Saying, My Honey, mourn no more for mee.
That Love wrongs both, that wills mee with thee hence.
But joy to see my Joy, and Glory mence.   220
In Faith, Obedience, Patience, walk awhile
And thou shalt soon leape ore the parting Stile,
And come to God, Christ, Angells, Saints, and Mee.
So wee in Bliss together e're shall bee.
When we did wed, we each a mortall took.   225
And ever from that day for this did look
Wherein we parted are; and one should have
Griefe, I o're thy, or thou over my grave.
The Lot is cast on thee. I first must go
And leave thee weeping o're my Grave in woe.   230
But stay thy Sorrow: bless my Babes. Obey.
And soon thou shall with mee enjoy good day.

224 *So*] orig: And So
230 In PW at the bottom of the page following line 230 is this line which
Taylor probably intended to cancel: "In Prayre Sweet, the musick of which may"

And as for you his Buds, and Blossoms blown,
Stems of his Root, his very Flesh and Bone,
You needs must have great droopings, now the Tree   235
Is fallen down the boughs whereof you bee.
You have a Father lost, and Choice one too.
Weeping for him is honour due from you.
Yet let your Sorrows run in godly wise
As if his Spirits tears fell from your eyes.   240
Strive for his Spirit: rather Christ's, than His
To dwell, and act his Flesh, yourselves, to bliss.
Its pitty these in him conjoyn'd, up grew
Together, should be parted here in you.
Plants of a Noble Vine, a Right, Right Seed.   245
Oh! turn not to a Strange Wild vine or Weed.
Your Grand sire were a Chiefe Foundation Stone
In this Blesst Building: Father was well known
To be a Chiefe Good Builder in the Same
And with his might did ever it mentain.   250
Your Grandsire's Spirit through your Father breathd
In Life, on you, and as his Life he leav'd,
Striving to breath into your hearts his Spirit
As out of him it passed, to inherit.
Be n't like such babes as parents brains out pull   255
To make a Wassill Bowle then of the Skull.
That Pick their Parents eyes out, and the holes
Stuff up with folly, as if no braind Souls.
You are of better form than this sad guise
Yet beare this Caution: Some apostatise.   260
And strive your Sires, and Grandsires Life and Line
Through you their Flesh and blood may brightly shine.
Imminde your Father's Death bed Charge and aime.
You are his Very Flesh, and Blood, and Name.
The NAME of HOOKER precious in our story   265

236 *whereof*] PW wereof   251 *Spirit*] orig: Spirit Spirit
252 *on you, and as*] orig: and on you, as   *leav'd,*] PW leav'd.
256 *then*] orig: of the then   263 A couplet written in the margin was to be
inserted following this line. The first line of the couplet is worn away with the
edge of the page. The second line reads: "God doth delight in filial Piety."

Make you more precious, adding to its Glory,
At the Bright flaming Sun of Righteousness,
With a Celestiall Light, e're burning fresh.
A Cabbinet of Vertue, ever brave.
A Magazeen of Counsill, Weighty, Grave.   270
A Treasury of Grace, th'Imbroideries
Of th'Holy Ghost in Heart, and Life here lies.
A Temple bright of Piety in print,
To glorify that God that dwelled in't.
A Stage of War, Whereon the Spirits Sword   275
Hew'd down the Hellish foes that did disturb.
A Cage whose bird of Paradise therein
Did sing sweete Musick forth to glories King.
A Silver Trumpet of the Temple bright
Blown by an Angell of Celestiall light   280
A Temple deckt, and with all graces spic'de
For God the Father, Spirit, and for Christ.
A Golden Pulpit Where an Angell Choice
Preacht Zions Grace with Sinai's thundering voice.
An Oratore of Prayre, which, rapt up, hopt   285
Up Souls to Heaven, Heaven down to Souls oft knockt.
Were there a Metempsychosis, we say
Greate Hookers Soule, sure, once possest this Clay.
Elijah's Mantle: and the dust that fell
Of th'Charriot, and the Horse of Israel,   290
Scarce ever dust more glorious made for bliss
With glorious Grace, or better usd than this,
That here now stript of all that Wealth, and Station
Doth lie, yet firmly holds its high Relation.
And here we leave it, till the last Dayes Shoute   295
Breaking its Coffin brings it glorious out.
And wipe those drops wrung from thy Winding Sheet
Brave Sir, off from our Eyes, that weeping keep,
With thy White Lawn thou wearst in Glory Gay,
    Charming our Griefe therewith, Amen we say.   300

267–300 These lines, out of place in PW, are on a separate page,
opposite the page which concludes the elegy on Mrs. Taylor.
298 *keep*] Conj.

HIS EPITAPH.

A turffe of Glory, Rich Celestiall Dust,
A Bit of Christ here in Death's Cradle husht.
An Orb of Heavenly Sunshine: a bright Star
That never glimmerd: ever shining faire,
A Paradise bespangled all with Grace: 305
A Curious Web o'relaid with holy lace
A Magazeen of Prudence: Golden Pot
Of Gracious Flowers never to be forgot
Farmingtons Glory, and its Pulpits Grace
Lies here a Chrystallizing till the trace   310
Of Time is at an end and all out run.
Then shall arise and quite outshine the Sun.

A Fig for thee Oh! Death.

Undated. Unpublished.

Thou King of Terrours with thy Gastly Eyes
With Butter teeth, bare bones Grim looks likewise.
And Grizzly Hide, and clawing Tallons, fell,
Opning to Sinners Vile, Trap Door of Hell,
That on in Sin impenitently trip   5
The Downfall art of the infernall Pit,
Thou struckst thy teeth deep in my Lord's blest Side:
Who dasht it out, and all its venom 'stroyde
That now thy Poundrill shall onely dash
My Flesh and bones to bits, and Cask shall clash.   10
Thou'rt not so frightfull now to me, thy knocks
Do crack my shell. Its Heavenly kernells box
Abides most safe. Thy blows do break its shell,
Thy Teeth its Nut. Cracks are that on it fell.

301 *Rich*] orig: and   302 *here in Death's Cradle husht*]
orig: is in this Cellar husht   308–9 Interlinear line canceled "Here lies a
Chrystallizing, till"   Rewritten as line 310   7 *Lord's*] PW Lord
8 *'stroyde*] PW stroyde   12 *Its*] PW it

Thence out its kirnell fair and nut, by worms   15
Once Viciated out, new formd forth turns
And on the wings of some bright Angell flies
Out to bright glory of Gods blissfull joyes.
Hence thou to mee with all thy Gastly face
Art not so dreadfull unto mee through Grace.   20
I am resolvde to fight thee, and ne'er yield,
Blood up to th'Ears; and in the battle field
Chasing thee hence: But not for this my flesh,·
My Body, my vile harlot, its thy Mess,
Labouring to drown me into Sin, disguise   25
By Eating and by drinking such evill joyes
Though Grace preserv'd mee that I nere have
Surprised been nor tumbled in such grave.
Hence for my strumpet I'le ne'er draw my Sword
Nor thee restrain at all by Iron Curb   30
Nor for her safty will I 'gainst thee strive
But let thy frozen gripes take her Captive
And her imprison in thy dungeon Cave
And grinde to powder in thy Mill the grave,
Which powder in thy Van thou'st safely keep   35
Till she hath slept out quite her fatall Sleep.
When the last Cock shall Crow the last day in
And the Arch Angells Trumpets sound shall ring
Then th'Eye Omniscient seek shall all there round
Each dust death's mill had very finely ground,   40
Which in death's smoky furnace well refinde
And Each to'ts fellow hath exactly joyn't,
Is raised up anew and made all bright
And Christalized; all top full of delight.
And entertains its Soule again in bliss   45
And Holy Angells waiting all on this,
The Soule and Body now, as two true Lovers
Ery night how do they hug and kiss each other.
And going hand in hand thus through the skies

16 *new formd forth*] orig: such forms
out   17 *flies*] orig: highs   40 death's] PW death   *finely*] PW findly
41 *death's*] PW death   46 *Angells*] PW Angell

Up to Eternall glory glorious rise.   50
Is this the Worst thy terrours then canst, why
Then should this grimace at me terrify?
Why camst thou then so slowly? Mend thy pace.
Thy Slowness me detains from Christ's bright face.
Although thy terrours rise to th'highst degree,   55
I still am where I was, a Fig for thee.

From the *Metrical History of Christianity*.

Graces Bright Shine.

Undated. Unpublished.

Oh! Glorious Day of Glorious Light!
Guilded with Grace that shines more bright
Than any Pen, and Ink can write
                              Thy Beams out shine.

Bringing thy Holy Servant John   5
From Patmos Ile, Where that Vile one
Had banisht him: Yet here upon
                              He's made Divine.

How should I choose but make my Feet,
Ware Sapphick Slippers when this sweet,
And Glorious Grace breaks forth to greet   10
                              Us with such gales?

Whose Golden Pen so cleare doth write
Those Glorious Visions that did light

50 *rise*] PW wise
51 *canst,*] PW canst   53 *Mend*] PW mend   54 *detains*] PW detain
Christ's] PW Christ   55 *highst*] PW higst   *Metrical History of Christianity*]
MH has no title   *Graces Bright Shine*] MH pp. 9–11

Before his Eyes in open Sight   15
               That't us assails.

How came he thence, thus in his hands
Holding those Letters Christ Commands
Be gi'n to th'Candlesticks that stand
               Made all of gold: 20

And clearly 'fore our eyes doth fix
How middst these golden Candlesticks
Christs walking doth his glory mix,
               And Shines unfold?

How his Right hand doth hold these Stars?   25
These shining Lights? These Trumpiters?
Angells of Peace, and Gospell wars:
               'Gainst Hellish Hosts?

Doth Chide for Sin, Doth Call to Grace,
Doth Threaton, yet Shines fill his Face,   30
With Promises doth us imbrace
               Draws to his Coasts.

Whose golden Pen doth still describe
How he Christs Court in Heaven spide
When heavens Gate op'to him Wide: 35
               Whose Throne was lac'te,

With a Smaregdine Rainbow rounde,
Where in a glorious One he found
Like to a Sardine Jasper sound
               His lookes were grac'te,   40

And round about this Throne of State
The Courtiers, Saints and Angells waite.
Saints Glorifide Crown'd with rich Plate
               Yea Crowns of Gold,

And clothed in White Robes pure, trim,   45
On foure and twenty seats sitting.

27 *and*] orig: and Wars   45 *trim*] orig: fine and trim

Christs Officers within the Rim
     This Throne doth hold.

Before it stand Christs Angels bright
Sparkling like Lamps of firy light
And all the Works Worke of Delight   50
     With blissfull noyse.

The matters that transacted were
In this Bright Court of Glory Cleare
Were bravely done, yet to the eare   55
     In Dreadfull wise.

And in the Throned Persons hand
A seald Book was none understand,
Untill the Seals were opend and
     Pluckt off the same.   60

At which the Courtiers sang forth praise
On Viols, Harps, and other wayes
Which with their Incense they araise
     To spread Christs fame.

And in the opening each Seale   65
He doth Gods Providence reveale
Unto his Church, both Woe, and Weale
     Of Pagan Rome.

Yea till she Antichrist doth rise
And play the Rex in Cruilties
Untill the Glorious one Destroyes   70
     Her by his Doom.

And now he also shews ag'en
The Heavens send Jerusalem
New like a bride adornd down then   75
     Heart-Ravishingly.

And that the Wicked then shall goe
Into the firy Lake of Woe
Where mercies stream doth never flow
     Nor grain of joy.   80

How Glorious Saints, With Angells harp
These blissfull songs of Praise which starte
Forth Warblingly as glorious sparks
                Of Honour Coild

All up in a bright thankfull Theame   85
And isshue like a living streame
From Souls bathd all in glories gleame,
                And nothing soild.

As in this City stately known
Walld all with sparkling Pretious Stone   90
Whose Gates are Pretious Pearles, each one,
                And streets pure gold

They get, and eate the Fruites that grow
Upon the Tree of Life also
Within Gods Paradise whence flow   95
                Joyes manifold.

Thus John came from his Patmos Ile
With this bright Glory thus to foile
The Evills of the times that spoile
                The Gospell shine.   100

And with these Glorious brightsome beames
To Counter buff all Darkining streames
While this Discoverie outgleams
                Things such, Divine.

Still a Prophetick Spirit doth   105
Attend the Gospell as it go'th,
And wondrous things it often shew'th
                To win poore hearts.

Hence Gospell Grace doth much assaile
The Pagan World, and doth prevaile.   110
Conversion worke hence doth not faile
                But fills all parts.

89 *City*] orig: City thy

Saints rising up in Churchood fix,
Encrease the Golden Candlesticks.
The Gospell Sun hath no Ecclipse   115
               As yet, Oh Praise.

Their Officers like Angells shine
Or like the Stars in glories line
And flame forth Rayes of Light Divine
               In holy Wayes.   120

Christs sparkling Image bright forth shines
Through these Choice Persons Lives, and Lines
Which they receiv'd from such Divines
               As went before.

Both ministers of Gods rich Grace   125
And other Saints that had a place
In Gospell Causes truth to trace,
               Whereof are store.

The Sparkling Shine of Gods Justice.

Undated. Unpublished.

Patience thus Exercisd, Gods Providence
    Doth in her Checker'd Mashes hang the Shine
Of Justice in such Spangles as from thence
    Dropt here and there are by the hand Divine.
    Some instances where of I blazon would   5
    Upon this Flag, all blancht therewith like gold.

Justice persues the Jews still for their Sin,
    Poor Nation now, how hast thou banisht Grace,
Quite from thy Tents? Vengeance red hot steps in.
    Oh, thou art plunged in a dismall Case.   10

127 *In*] orig: In is   *The Sparkling Shine of Gods Justice*] MH pp. 24–26.

Thy land is by thy wickedness well nigh
    Laid Desolate, thou must not in it ly.

The Jews Rebell; full fifty thousand slain:
    By Adrians Sword, have fifty Castles stroi'de.
Nine hundred fourscore towns untownd again,   15
    By Sickness, Sword, Fire, Famine almost void.
    Jerusalem new built, new namde, and new
    Enpeoplde, by the Gentile, not the Jew.

At Rome in Trajans reign the Pantheon
    And Nero's Golden House the lightning burnd.   20
In Asia Dreadful Earth Quakes whereupon
    Four Cities were in Asia overturnd.
    The very Earth doth tremble at the Flood
    That overflows it thus of Martyres blood.

And Antioch while Trajan there perchance   25
    So shaken was, that neighbouring mountains tall
Were tore, and Casus that did high advance
    Ore all in Syria tumbling down did fall,
    And Rivers dry did grow: the Earth moreore
    An horrid lowing made, the Sea did roare.   30

The ruind building dreadfully did Clash,
    The Schreeching of sad men was high and greate,
Such darkness made by dust that mixed was
    One Could not heare another, se or speak.
    The Emperour took through a window there   35
    Out of the ruind building sav'd thus were.

And in the Agarean War did rise
    Thunders and Lightnings, strange Rainbow, storms
Vast Hails, Stones too and mighty Swarms of Flies,
    That did anoy them, who were full of scorns.   40
    They did infest the Romans meat and drinck
    They swarmed on with a most nautious Stinck.

God still comes nigher; he now takes in hand
    The Wicked man his members do unjoynt,

27 *tore*] orig: tore to pieces   43 *nigher;*] MH nigher

His body's numbd, his senses, lose command;   45
    He thinks he poyson'd is (Gods hand doth point)
    Then swells with Water twixt the flesh, and fell.
    His Gost doth bid his Carkass thus farewell.

In Adrians time great Earth Quakes too God brings:
    That Nicomedia, and Nice nigh stroy.   50
Soon after these Nicopolis down flings
    Yea, and Cesaria as utterly,
    Then Inquest makes for Blood. Blood new so skips
    From Adrian's nose as frighted out of'ts wits.

And now therewith such torments him surprize,   55
    He Calls for Death, seeks to dispatch his life:
He wasts away, then doth a Dropsy rise
    Which did refuse his Charms, and Spells so rife.
    His blood breaks down all dams still, and will flow.
    His Tortures too will not be Charmd but grow.   60

He asketh Poyson of his Doctor then
    But such a Potion never can obtain.
Then Craves a Sword, bids mony for't to's men
    But none do reach him this to end his pain.
    At length by torments more than can be told   65
    He is dispatcht, and tumbled down to mould.

And in the Reign of Pius, sad things light,
    As Famine, Earthquakes that did towns destroy
In Rhodes, and Asia, the Circk stroyd quite.
    Three hundred forty houses burnt down ly   70
    At Rome, and Narbon City, Antioch,
    And Carthage Market place, burnt turnd to Smoake,

Tyber oreflows its bancks: a boy is born
    With two heads, then five babes born at a time.
A mighty Cristed Snake was seen off shorn   75
    And eat itself up halfe in Arabs Clime.

57 *away*,] MH away.   60 *Charmd*] orig: Charmd down
74 *heads*,] MH heads.

A mighty Plague rag'd in Arabia.
Barly from tree twigs grew in Morsia.

In Commodus his reign then Lightning turn'd
    The Capitoline Temple into dust.   80
The neighboring Famous Library burnd.
    The Temple too of Peace soon after Crusht,
    And Vesta Temple and the Palace by her
    Much of the City too, and all by fire.

Then Commodus the Senate did define   85
    More Cruell than Domitian, and impure
Than Nero, comes unto his tragick time
    Doth drinke a draught of Poyson for a Cure,
    Which failing, he with Nariss scuffling
    In jest, in earnest throtled was by him.   90

Touching Narcissus of Jerusalem
    Gainst whom three wicked guilty persons rose
He taxed is before the Church by them.
    They do the Crime under dread Oaths depose.
    Which done, the Good Old man for griefe retires;   95
    Although the Church did not believe those liers.

The first doth wish he might be burnt if he
    Spake not the truth; the second if he li'de
By Cruell Sickness might surprised bee.
    The third that's Sight might out be pluckt or glide   100
    If he spake false. And this they did, its said
    Lest by Narcissus they ashame be made.

But see the Case. The first mans house by night
    And he and all therein are burnt by fire.
The second is surprizd in all mens sight   105
    By Cruell sickness and thereby expires.
    The third much terrifide, the Fact descries
    And With repenting tears weeps out his Eyes.

Now Justice hath Narcissus made more shine.
    He from his solitary Place doth pass   110

79 *turn'd*] orig: laid   89 *he*] orig: he was   109 *Justice*] MH Justices

Unto his sacred Charge, a grave Divine,
When aged eight score years and three he was.
Thus Justice, see, doth see, and show her Shine
While Patience doth Gods providence enline.

The Martyrdom of Deacon Laurence.

Undated. Unpublished.

Laurence another Deacon of Choice fame
Of Romes blesst Church the third day after came
Unto his Martyrdom Whose Case runs thus.
The greedy Tyrant being very flush
With hopes to get the Churches Treasure all   5
Doth Deacon Laurence now charge, whom they call,
To shew him where the Churches Treasure were
Who therefore causd great number to appeare
Of Christian Poore ore whom with arms displayd
These are the Churches treasures then he said.   10
These Treasures are indeed, in them the Faith
Of Christ doth reign: in them Christ mansion hath.
Oh now what tongue is able to express
The Tyrants fury, and enragedness.
He stampt, star'd, Rampt, and far'd as lost his Wit.   15
His Eyes did glow, Mouth foam, Teeth gnasht and bit.
And like a Lyon out doth breake thus roar
What! hath this Villain mockt the Emperour.
Away with him! Away with him! Him Whip
With Scourges, Scurge with rods, and buffit flip   20
With fist, him brain with bats. What, doth he slur?
What joke, and jybe upon the Emperour?
Pinch him with firy tongs and gird him up

The Martyrdom of Deacon Laurence] MH, pp. 37–38   Title not in MH
Excerpted from that section of MH entitled "The Eight[h] Persecution"
17 *roar*] MH arr[?] orig: saith   19 *him! Away*] MH him, away
Him Whip].MH him Whip   21 *What*] orig: What slur

With burning plates. Strong Chains upon him put.
The firy Forkes, and Gridiron bed out bring,   25
Make it red hot, this Rebell on there fling.
Him Rost, him broyle, him toss, him turn again
Oh ye Tormentors on your sorest pain.
They whirle him on't, but oh God made this Bed
Like to a Down bed, where he's nourished   30
And broyling long on this red firy Grate
Presst with red forks was patient, and thus spake,
This side is rost, turn't up, thou Tyrant great.
Try whether rost or raw is better meat.
And in this wise he did to Christ ascend   35
And by a glorious martyredom did end.

The Persian Persecution.

Undated. Unpublished.

For Isdegerdes dead, Gorones reigns,
His kingdom, and his Cruelties mentains
Against the godly and he also dies
And hands them both unto his son likewise.
The Cruelties they mannaged were sore.   5
To hear the same may make one shake all ore.
They fley'd the skin off of the hands of some
Off of the backs of others as they come,
Off of the Heads of others: and begin
Upon the brow and to the neck unskin,   10
Then leave them in this wise. Some naked quite
They Cover ore with reeds split down aright
Fitting the Cutting reeds upon the flesh
And bind with Cords from head to foot this dress.
This done they drew with violence away   15

27 *toss*,] MH toss
The Persian Persecution] MH p. 77   Excerpted from that section of MH
entitled "Persian Persecution"   2 *His*] orig: And His

From ery part, that their sharp Edges may
Thus drawn upon the flesh, cut, gash and Wound
Thereby to make their tortures more abound.
They many close in filthy Valts up shut
And many Dormice caught and to them put,   20
And having tide the martyres hands and feet
That so they might not fright them when they Creep
Upon them. And the bats by hunger greate
Being compelled do peck them up as meat.
And so by little bits greate torments rise   25
While being peckt and eate to Death: each dies.
And thus these Saints did for Christ's holy Cause
Sustain and overcome all hellish jawes.

27 *Christ's*] MH Christ

Appendix 1. Editions

Poems

Taylor published none of his poems. However, stanzas five and seven of "Upon Wedlock and Death of Children," together with an extract of Taylor's letter of condolence to Samuel Sewall, were printed after the last page of Cotton Mather's sermon *Right Thoughts in Sad Hours,* London, 1689. There are a few variations between the printed version of the poem and the version in PW. Both versions appear in Thomas H. Johnson's "A Seventeenth-Century Printing of Some Verses of Edward Taylor," *New England Quarterly, 14* (1941), 139–141. See also T. J. Holmes, *Cotton Mather: A Bibliography of His Works* (Cambridge, Mass., 1940), p. 927.

Johnson is Taylor's first editor. In "Edward Taylor: A Puritan 'Sacred Poet,'" *New England Quarterly, 10* (1937), 290–322, he published "Huswifery"; "Upon Wedlock and Death of Children"; "The Ebb and Flow"; the following poems from *Gods Determinations*—"Christs Reply," "The Soul Admiring the Grace of the Church Enters into Church Fellowship," "The Glory of, and Grace in the Church Set Out," "The Souls Admiration Hereupon," "The Joy of Church Fellowship Rightly Attended," "Prologue"; *Meditations,* first series, 1, 7, 8, 25, 38; "The Experience," "The Reflexion"; *Meditations,* second series, 3, 112; eight lines from "My Last Declamation in the Colledge Hall," and excerpts of thirty-four lines from *Gods Determinations.*

In "The Topical Verses of Edward Taylor," *Publications of the Colonial Society of Massachusetts, 34* (1943), 513–54, Johnson edited the following poems: "Elegy on Mr. Sims," "Elegy on Francis Willoughby," "Declamation in the Colledge Hall," "Elegy on Mr. John Allen," "Elegy on Mr. Charles Chauncey," "Acrostic Love Poem to Elizabeth Fitch," "Elegy on Mrs. Elizabeth Taylor," "Elegy on Mr. Sam Hooker," "Elegy on Mrs. Mehetabel Woodbridge," "Elegy on Dr. Increase Mather," "Verses made upon Pope Joan."

Johnson also edited *The Poetical Works of Edward Taylor,* Rockland Editions, 1939; Princeton University Press, 1943. This selection contains the following: *Gods Determinations* (complete); "An Address to the Soul Occasioned by a Rain"; "Upon a Spider Catching a Fly"; "Huswifery"; "Upon Wedlock and Death of Children"; "The Ebb and Flow"; "The Experience"; "The Reflexion"; *Meditations,* first series, 1, 6, 7, 8, 12, 19, 20, 25, 28, 29, 30, 33, 38, 42, 49; second series, 3, 7, 11, 18, 30, 33, 56, 60, 62, 76, 77, 82, 110, 112.

In Thomas H. Johnson, "Some Edward Taylor Gleanings," *New England Quarterly, 16* (1943), 280–96, were the following poems: "Upon a Wasp Chilled with Cold," "Huswifery II," "Upon the Sweeping Flood," *Meditations,* first series, 3, 10, 37, 40, 47; second series, 40, 80, 114.

More recent publications: Morris A. Neufeld, "A Meditation upon the Glory of God," *Yale University Library Gazette,* 25 (Jan. 1951), 110–11 (transcript of *Meditations,* first series, 21). Barbara Damon Simison, "Poems by Edward Taylor," *Yale University Library Gazette, 28,* Jan. and April 1954; *29,* July and Oct. 1954 (*Meditations,* first series, 2, 13, 22, 24, 26, 32, 34, 35, 39, 43, 46; second series, 4, 14, 19, 25, 29, 37, 41, 42, 43, 46, 49, 64, 65, 69). Donald E. Stanford, "Sacramental Meditations by Edward Taylor," *Yale University Library Gazette, 31* (Oct. 1956), 61–75 (*Meditations,* second series, 104, 105, 106, 107, 108, 109, 111). Donald E. Stanford, "Nineteen Unpublished Poems by Edward Taylor," *American Literature, 29* (March 1957), 18–46 (*Meditations,* first series, 16, 18, 23, 31, 36, 41, 45, 48; second series, 8, 16, 17, 26, 27, 28, 75, 78, 79, 84, 95). Donald E. Stanford, "The Giant Bones of Claverack, New York, 1705," *New York History,* 40 (Jan. 1959), 47–61.

Diary and Letters

An extract of a letter to Samuel Sewall, dated "14th 6m. [August] 1686" in Cotton Mather's *Right Thoughts in Sad Hours,* London, 1689; reprinted by Thomas H. Johnson, in the *New England Quarterly, 14* (1941), 139–40.

"Edward Taylor to Increase Mather," *Collections of the Massachusetts Historical Society,* 4th ser. *8* (1868), 629–31. This is a letter dated Westfield, "22d 1m [March] 1682/3." It describes the hail storm of July 26, 1682, which brought down hail stones "like musket bullets," "wallnuts," and "hen's eggs," a strange light in the sky on August 16, 1681, shaped like a scythe and encompassing a third of the horizon; a strange vapor; and other remarkable phenomena.

A love letter to Elizabeth Fitch, dated Westfield, 8th day of the 7th month [September], 1674. Printed in *The Westfield Jubilee*, Westfield, Mass. (1870), pp. 157–58; John T. Terry, "Religious Influences in American Civilization—Its Founders," *Journal of American History*, 5 (1911), 132–33; John H. Lockwood, *Westfield and Its Historic Influences* (Springfield, Mass., 1922), *1*, 156–58; John T. Terry, *Rev. Edward Taylor* (New York, 1892), pp. 16–19; W. B. Goodman, "Edward Taylor Writes His Love," *New England Quarterly*, 27 (1954), 510–15.

"Diary of Edward Taylor," *Proceedings of the Massachusetts Historical Society, 18* (1880), 5–18. Dated from April 26, 1668, to January 12, 1671/2. It describes Taylor's journey from England to the Bay Colony, his life at Harvard, and his trip to Westfield. The original is in the Redwood Athenaeum, Newport, Rhode Island.

A letter to the Council at Boston, dated 3 April, 1676. Reprinted from the State Archives in Lockwood, *Westfield and Its Historic Influences, 1*, 234–36. This letter presents the decision of the citizens of Westfield not to move to Springfield during King Philip's War. It is not signed by Taylor but it is attributed to him by Lockwood.

A letter to the Council at Hartford written in 1676. Excerpts from this letter, attributed to Taylor, are in Lockwood, *Westfield, 1*, 237–38.

A letter to the Council at Hartford, dated March 15, 1676, printed in Lockwood, *Westfield, 1*, 226–28, from the Judd MS, Forbes Library, Northampton, Mass. Attributed to Taylor but not signed by him. Requests reimbursement for quartering Hartford soldiers.

A letter to the Reverend James Fitch of Norwich (Taylor's father-in-law), dated July 1679, printed in Lockwood, *Westfield, 1*, 109–10. Taylor invites the Reverend Fitch to the organization of the Westfield church.

Appendix 2. Manuscripts

Poetical Works.

This manuscript was once in the possession of Ezra Stiles who probably inherited it from Taylor's son-in-law Isaac Stiles. On the title page of *Gods Determinations* is written "This a MS of the Revd. Edward Taylor of Westfield, who died there A.D. 1728 or 1729. Aetat. circa 88, vel supra. Attest. Ezra Stiles His Grandson, 1786." The manuscript eventually came into possession of Taylor's great grandson, Henry W. Taylor. Beneath the signature of Ezra Stiles is written "Henry W. Taylor his Great Grandson 1868." According to a note on the margin of the first page of the manuscript, Henry W. Taylor presented it to the Yale University Library in 1883.

The four hundred quarto pages of the "Poetical Works," measuring 5½″ by 7⅜″, were originally bound in leather, probably by Taylor himself. Seventy-eight pages of poetry were discovered in the binding when it was removed for the purpose of laminating the manuscript. For a description of these poems see below. The pages of the manuscript are unnumbered except for those of *Gods Determinations*. The "Poetical Works" contain the following items:

1. A Latin elegy on Charles Chauncy (1592–1671/2), president of Harvard College. 20 lines. Right edge of page worn away. Partly undecipherable.

2. "Aliter." A Latin elegy, also on Charles Chauncy. 32 lines. Right edge of page worn away. Partly undecipherable.

3. "An Elegie upon the Death of that holy man of God Mr. Sims late Pastor of the Church of Christ at Charlestown in N. England who departed this life the 4th of 12m Ano. Dni. 1670/1." 66 lines.

4. "An Elegie upon the Death of the Worshipfull Francis Willoughby Esq. Deputy Governour of the Mas[s]ach[usetts] Colony in New England who departed at Charlestown 3d.2m. 1671." 65

lines. 17 lines form a triple acrostic spelling Francis Willoughby.

5. "My last Declamation in the Colledge Hall May 5, 1671, Where four Declaim'd in the Praise of four Languages and five upon the five senses. Those upon the Languages Declaim'd in the Language they treated of: and hence mine ran in English." 212 lines.

6. "An Elegy upon the Death of that Holy man of God Mr. John Allen, late Pastor of the Church of Christ at Dedham, who departed this Life 25th. 6m. 1671." 64 lines.

7. "An Elogy upon the Death of the Reverend and Learned Man of God Mr. Charles Chauncey President of Harvard Colledg in New Englend Who Depart[ed] this Life 20th. 12m. 1671/2. And of his age 80." 72 lines. An elaborate poem with double and quadruple acrostics on Chauncy's name.

8. An elaborate acrostic love poem to Elizabeth Fitch with a dove inscribed on the body of which is "This Dove & Olive Branch to you/Is both a Post & Emblem too."

9. A love letter in prose to Elizabeth Fitch dated Westfield 8th. 7m. 1674. One and one-third pages.

10. "A Funerall Poem upon the Death of the Hon'd Captain John Mason, son to Major John Mason, Captain of Connecticut Souldiers against the Pequods. . . ." 108 lines, tetrameter alternating with trimeter, rhyming *abab* (*The Day of Doom* stanza). At the conclusion of the poem is this note: "These made and sent by Mr. Bradstreet minister of the Gospell at New London to the Captain." The verses are evidently by Simon Bradstreet.

11. "These for my truely deare and Endeared Mrs. Elizabeth Fitch mine Onely Love, in Norwich . . ." Dated Westfield "27. 8m. 1674." 64 lines.

12. "A Funerall Poem Upon the Death of my ever Endeared and Tender Wife Mrs. Elizabeth Taylor Who fell asleep in Christ the 7th day of July at night about two hours after Sun setting 1689 and in the 39 yeare of her Life." 152 lines.

13. "An Elegy upon the Death of that Holy and Reverend Man of God, Mr. Samuel Hooker Pastor of the Church of Christ at Farmington (and Son to the Famous Mr. Thomas Hooker, who was a Pastor of, and began with the Church of Christ at Hartford on Connecticut in New England) who slept in Christ,

the 6th day of November, about one a Clock in the morning in the 64 year of his age entered upon. Annoque Domini, 1697." 312 lines.

14. "An Elogy upon the Death of My Honoured Sister in Law Mrs. Mehetabel Woodbridge, wife of the Reverend Mr. Timothy Woodbridge, Pastor of the first Church in Hartford, who departed this life 20th day of 10m 1698." 86 lines.

15. "Upon my recovery out of a threatening sickness December . . . 1720." Written in a shaky hand, partly illegible. 52 lines.

16. "A funerall Tear dropt upon the Coffin of [that holy man of] God, Dr. Increase Mather, Teacher of the North Church in Boston and pro tempore President of the Colledg at Cambridge." 86 lines.

17. "A nipping Epigram upon that so much advanced bishop Laud . . ." These verses, which have been crossed out, appear to have been written during Laud's lifetime, hence are not by Taylor. 8 lines.

18. "Verses made upon Pope Joan." A bitter and coarse attack on the legendary female Pope of the ninth century. Partly illegible. 110 lines.

19. "A nipping Epigram . . ." Another copy of item 17.

20. ". . . Let by rain." These are the three final words of a title incomplete because part of the page is torn away. A lyric on the decision of the soul to come to Christ. 30 lines.

21. "Upon a Spider Catching a Fly." 50 lines.

22. "Upon a Wasp Chil[l]d with Cold." 44 lines.

23. "Huswifery." 18 lines.

24. "Another upon the Same." 12 lines.

25. "Upon Wedlock and Death of Children." 42 lines.

26. "The Ebb and Flow." 17 lines.

27. "Upon the Sweeping Flood Aug: 13. 14. 1683." 12 lines.

28. "The Description of the great Bones dug up at Clavarack on the Banks of Hudsons River A.D. 1705. An Account of which is to be seen in the Lond. Phil. Transactions." This inscription on the title page appears to be in the hand of Ezra Stiles. On the first page is written "By Edward Taylor of Westfield Ezra Stiles." This poem of 190 lines consists of a brief introduction in prose, followed by "The Prologue," "The Gyant described," "The De-

scription thus Proved," "His Deeds." The last section bears only
the title. Accounts of the discovery of these bones appeared in the
Boston News Letter of July 23–30, 1705; a letter by Governor
Dudley to Cotton Mather dated July 10, 1706, published in the
Collections of the Massachusetts Historical Society, 2d ser. 2
(1814), 263–64; *Philosophical Transactions of the Royal Society
of London,* 29 (1714), 62–63; and C. R. Weld, *History of the
Royal Society* (London, 1848), *1,* 421–22.

29. "A Valediction to all the World prepatatory for Death 3d
of the 11m. 1720."

"Cant. 1. To the Stars and Sun and Moon and Aire." 42
lines.

"Cant. 2." [no title] 42 lines.

"Cant. 3. Valediction to the Teraqueous Globe." 106 lines.

"Cant. 4. A sute to Christ hereupon." 50 lines.

"Cant. 5." [no title] 31 lines.

"Cant. 6." [no title] 38 lines.

"Cant. 7." [no title] 48 lines.

"Cant. 8." [no title] 16 lines.

30. "A Fig for thee Oh! Death." 56 lines.

31. *Gods Determinations touching his Elect and The Elects
Combat in their Conversion, and Coming up to God in Christ to-
gether with the Comfortable Effects thereof.*

32. *"My Valediction to all the World preparatory to Death."*
A revision of no. 29.

"1." [no title] 18 lines.

"2 Cant." [no title] 20 lines.

"3. Cant. Adjue to the Aire" 39 lines, of which six have been
crossed out.

"4. Cant. To the Terraqueous Globe Adjue." All except the
last word of this title is crossed out. 18 lines.

33. "Prologue." Evidently intended as introduction to Pre-
paratory Meditations. 30 lines.

34. "Sacramental Meditations for 35 y. from 1682 to 1725.
Preparatory Meditations before my Approach to the Lords Sup-
per Chiefly upon the Doctrin preached upon the Day of admin-
istration." The original figure 1717 has been crossed out and
changed to 1725. The figure 35 has not been corrected. The words

"Sacramental Meditations for 35 y. from 1682 to 1717" are written across top of page in the hand of Ezra Stiles. The correction "1725" is in another hand. 28 Meditations—the last Taylor wrote —are out of place between "The Prologue" and Meditation 1 (first series) which bears the title "Preparatory Meditations."

Poems found in the Binding of "Poetical Works."

Forty-one sheets written on both sides, or eighty-two pages.

1. Notes and scribblings. 4 pages.
2. Fair copies of *Preparatory Meditations* one to eight and the first two stanzas of Meditation nine (all of the first series), and "The Experience," "The Return," and "The Reflexion." 12 pages. Variant readings in these copies are collated with the poems in the "Poetical Works" under the symbol Z.
3. A metrical paraphrase of the book of Job from 3:1 to 17:16. 32 pages. Complete except for two verses—13:28 and 14:10.
4. Another version of the metrical paraphrase above from Job 3:1 to 15:16. 23⅔ pages.
5. A metrical paraphrase of 2 Samuel 1:19–27, entitled "Davids Lamentation for Saul and Jonathan." 1⅓ pages.
6. A metrical paraphrase of 1 Samuel 2:1–10 entitled "The Song of Hannah." 1¼ pages.
7. A metrical paraphrase of Judges 5:1–31 entitled "The Song of Deborah and Barak." 4 pages.
8. A metrical paraphrase of Deut. 32:15–43. 3¾ pages.

All of these paraphrases appear to be written in four-line stanzas, tetrameter lines alternating with trimeter lines, rhyming *abab*. The style and form is similar to that of Wigglesworth's *The Day of Doom*. All of the paraphrases are partly illegible.

Manuscript Book.

Presented to the Yale University Library on March 15, 1921, by Henry T. Terry of New York in the name of his branch of the Terry family. 54 unnumbered pages 3⅝ × 6 1/16," of which 18 pages are blank except for occasional scribbling or numbers. Taylor's name appears on one of the otherwise blank pages. The first sheet of the book is a fragment. All lines unless otherwise noted are decasyllabic.

1. Rough drafts of "Verses on Pope Joan." About 99 lines, of which 7 are crossed out. Another draft of this poem is in the "Poetical Works."

2. "A Valediction to the Whole World."

"Cant. 1. To the Celestiall Bodies." 49 lines.

"Cant. 2. Farewell to the Aire." 50 lines.

"Cant. 3. Farewell to the Terraqueous Globe." 70 lines.

"Cant. 4." [no title] 34 lines.

"Cant. 5." [no title] 70 lines.

"Cant. 6." [no title] 10 lines.

"Cant. 7." [no title] 6 lines.

"Cant. 8." [no title] 48 lines.

Another draft of the above poem is in the "Poetical Works."

3. "A Fig for thee Oh Death." 58 lines. Another version of this poem is in the "Poetical Works."

4. Rough drafts of "Verses on Pope Joan." 163 lines.

5. A page of writing in shorthand or code.

6. "A . . . nipping Epigram made upon the so much admired by our Cutler and his apostate party Laud Archbishop of Canterbury . . ." 8 lines, octosyllabic. With commentary in prose on Laud and King Charles etc. Poem and commentary one page. Two other copies of this epigram appear in the "Poetical Works."

7. "I wrote these made by a girl[?] call[ed] Maria[?] . . . at Northfield, not for the Wit sake nor for the Verse sake but for the History sake, she being at the place when the mischief was done in February 1723/4." 68 lines, *Day of Doom* stanza. Describes incidents in Father Rale's War.

8. A page has been cut out. On the next page are seven lines of verse (irregular metre) beginning "Though I am a child . . ." which may refer to item 7.

9. "An Elegie on the Death of that holy Man I.M." [Increase Mather]. 73 lines. Another version of this poem is in the "Poetical Works."

10. "An Elegie or funerall Verses made upon the Death of that Holy man of God the Reverend Mr. I.M." 76 lines. Another version of item 9.

11. [no title] Verses on a silk worm. 30 lines, of which 8 have been crossed out, 4 of these being almost completely faded.

12. Rough draft of "Verses on Pope Joan." 88 lines.

13. Another draft of the beginning of "Verses on Pope Joan." 8 lines.

14. Another draft of the elegy on Increase Mather. 50 lines. See item 9 above.

China's Description and Commonplace Book.

Approximately 335 pages, of which 28 are blank, measuring 5¾" by 7½", bound probably by Taylor himself.

1. "China's Description. This account of China is Chiefly taken out of the Letters of Lovis Le Compte Jesuit." 142 pages. [Louis Daniel LeComte, *Memoirs and Observations . . . Made in a Late Journey through the Empire of China,* London, 1697.]

2. Taylor's commentary on the above book. 13 pages.

3. A commonplace book in which are entered records of miracles, remarkable providences, monstrosities, etc., copied from various books or recorded from Taylor's personal experiences or those of his friends. 152 pages. The chief sources of the entries are Peter Heylyn, *Cosmographie,* London, 1657; Patrick Gordon, *Geography Anatomized,* London, 1702; and John Seller, *The History of England,* London, 1696.

Metallographia.

Bound, probably by Taylor, with pages measuring 3½" × 5½". On the first page is written "Such things as are Herein contained are the Principalls of Physick as to the Practicall part thereof in the Knowledge of Diseases and their Cures, being Extracted of of [sic] that famous Physian [sic] Riverius." This is followed by a few notes on page two and three. Then follow 125 blank pages indicating that Taylor had intended to copy Riverius' book on them. There follow a page of notes on the use of castor oil, a blank page, a three-page memoir of Taylor by Ezra Stiles and three pages of index drawn up by Stiles of the work that follows. This is entitled "Metallographia or the History of Metalls Written by [no name] A Brief Collection or an an [sic] Epitomy of the Metallography. Something changing the method, and some few things added where the matter respects not the Arcana's of the Chymists." 115 numbered pages followed by a few notes evidently in Ezra Stiles' hand. There are 86 blank pages at the end of the book. Ezra Stiles has written this note on these extracts: "I do not know the Author from whom my Grand-father TAYLOR extracted this Piece; but the Book, as should seem, was originally written in 29 Chapters at least, all of which except 3 are preserved in this extract, but very much transposed and reduced. . . . It is observable that Gold, Philosophic Mercury and Transmutation make the principal Subjects." The extracts, sometimes in a condensed form, were taken from John Webster, *Metallographia,* London, 1671.

Dispensatory.

Over 500 pages $3\frac{7}{8}'' \times 5\frac{3}{4}''$, bound probably by Taylor, consisting mainly of a description of the medicinal properties of herbs, drugs, oils, gums, etc.

1. "Some of the rare Fruits and Trees of China tooke out of the Memoirs of Lovis Le Compte, Jesuit Missionary sent from Paris Ano Dni 1685. Printed London 1698." 10 pages.

2. The medicinal properties of earths, waters, minerals, stones, etc. 40 pages.

3. The medicinal properties of herbs, roots, gums, etc. 426 pages.

4. Index. 64 pages.

The herbal portion of Taylor's Dispensatory appears to have been extracted from Nicholas Culpeper, *The English Physitian Enlarged,* London, 1666. Other parts of the Dispensatory may have been taken from William Salmon, *Pharmacopoeia Londinensis or The New London Dispensatory* (London, 1685) or from one or more of Culpeper's medical books.

Christographia.

"CHRISTOGRAPHIA, or A Discourse toching Christs Person, Natures, the Personall Union of the Natures. Qualifications, and Operations Opened, Confirmed, and Practically improoved in severall sermons delivered upon Certain Sacrament Dayes unto the Church and people of God in Westfield." In another hand "15 Sermons." A quarto of 340 pages, $5\frac{5}{8}'' \times 7\frac{3}{16}''$ bound prob-

ably by Taylor himself. Sermon 14 is missing; therefore, there
are a total of fourteen sermons. Meditations 42–56 of the second
series bear the same dates and texts (with one exception) as the
sermons. Meditation 47 has the same date as the corresponding
sermon, but a different text. Meditation 55 which would cor-
respond with Sermon 14 is missing from the manuscript of the
"Poetical Works." Several sermons have been transposed, an
error probably made when the manuscript was bound. In the de-
scription below, the sermons are numbered according to their
present position in the manuscript. The first 100 pages only are
numbered.

1. Sermon 1 (not numbered in the MS). "Westfield 26: 8m
1701. Rom. 9.5.—God blessed for ever." Meditation 43 has the
same text and date.

2. Sermon 2. "Westfield 31 6m 1701. Heb. 10.5. A Body hast
thou prepared me." Meditation 42 has the same text and date.

3. Sermon 3. "Westfield 28. 10m 1701. John 1.14. The word
was made flesh etc." Meditation 44 has the same text and date.

4. Sermon 4. "Westfield 15. 12m 1701. Col. 2.3. In whom are
hid all the treasures of wisdom and knowledge." Meditation 45
has the same text and date.

5. Sermon 5. "Westfield [10. 3m 1702] Col. 2.9. For in him
Dwelleth the fulness of the Godhead bodily." Meditation 46 has
the same text and, probably, the same date. The date of the
sermon has been obscured by a blot.

6. Sermon 6. "Westfield 12: 5m 1702. Col. 1.19. For it pleased
the Father, that in him should all fulness dwell." Meditation 47
has the same date but a different text: John 5:26—"The Son
hath life in himselfe."

7. Sermon 7. "13. 7m 1702. Rev. 1.8. I am α and ω, the Be-
ginning, and the Ending, saith the Lord, which Is and was and
is to Come, the ALMIGHTY." Meditation 48 has the same text and
date.

8. Sermon 8. "Westfield 8. 9m 1702. Joh. 1.14. Full of Grace."
Meditation 49 has the same text and date.

9. Sermon 9 (not numbered in the MS). "Westfield 27 10m
1702. Joh. 1.14. Full of Truth." Meditation 50 has the same
text and date.

10. Sermon 10 (not numbered in the MS). "Westfield 14. 12m 1702. Eph. 1.23. Which is his body, the fulness of him that filleth all in all." Meditation 51 has the same text and date.

11. Sermon 11 (not numbered in the MS). "Westfield 13th 4m 1703. Math. 28.18. All power is given unto me in heaven and Earth." [Note in Taylor's hand] "This sermon should follow that that follows it." Meditation 53 has the same text and date.

12. Sermon 12 (not numbered in the MS). "Westfield 11. 2m 1703. Math. 28.18. All power is given me in Heaven and Earth." [Note in Taylor's hand] "This sermon is misplaced and should stand before that before it." Meditation 52 has the same text and date.

13. Sermon 13 (not numbered in the MS). "Westfield 22th 6. 1703. Math. 28.18. All Power in Heaven and Earth is given unto mee." Meditation 54 has the same text and date.

14. Sermon 15. "Westfield 10th 8m Ano. Dom. 1703. Joh. 15.24. If I had not done among them the Work that none other man did, they had not had Sin." Meditation 56 has the same text and date. The Yale College Library Seal on the inside back cover states: "Presented by Hon. Henry W. Taylor Ll.D. 1883."

Westfield Church Record.

"The Publick Records of the Church at Westfield Together with a briefe account of our proceeding in order to our entrance into that State." A folio volume, pages measuring 9½″ × 11⅝″ first bound in the eighteenth century and rebound in 1929. During the first binding many pages were transposed. Those in Taylor's hand, dating from 1679 to 1726, are 1–109 [75–80; 103–6 missing], 123–51, 243–54, and 307–8.

1. Brief account of Taylor's arrival in Westfield, his marriage, King Philip's War, pp. 1–2.

2. Letters of invitation to the organization of the church and Taylor's ordination (August 27, 1679), pp. 2–5.

3. Taylor's profession of faith, pp. 5–74.

4. Taylor's spiritual "Relation," pp. 81–83.

5. The "Relations" of the six foundation men of the church, pp. 83–87.

6. Sermon by Taylor preached on the day of his ordination, Eph. 2:22, "In whom you also are builded up . . ." pp. 87–100.

7. Final details of the ordination service and the words of the Church covenant, pp. 100–2.

8. Record of admissions, baptisms, etc., pp. 107–9.

9. Ordination of deacons, p. 123.

10. Confessions of sin by various members of the church; letters concerning the character and activities of members of the church, pp. 125–51.

11. Record of baptisms and church admission, 1679–1726, pp. 243–54.

12. Church dismissions, pp. 307–8.

This volume, which carries the church record down to 1836, is in the Westfield Athenaeum.

Copy Book of the Council of Trent.

"An Extract of the Councill of Trent which was set forth at large by P[i]etro Soave Polano . . . and Faithfully Translated into English by Nathaniel Brent . . . London . . . 1629." Presented to the Westfield Athenaeum by Taylor's lineal descendant Dr. Oliver Brewster Taylor, 1897. Quarto, bound in paper, 5¾″ × 7⅛″.

1. "A Chronicle from Adam to Christ dated according to the Yeare of the World, of the Flood, and of Christ." 1⅔ pages.

2. Extract from the Council of Trent. 293 numbered pages. An index of 15 unnumbered pages.

3. "The creed of P. Pius 4," 1½ pages.

Origen's Contra Celsus and De Principiis.

A manuscript copy book in English of about 500 pages bound in hogskin parchment. The first seventy pages of Contra Celsus are missing. The title page of De Principiis states that the work was translated by Rufinus. The copy book was presented to the Westfield Athenaeum by Oliver Brewster Taylor in 1897. Information communicated by Francis E. X. Murphy who discovered the manuscript.

Commonplace Book.

This manuscript, bound in vellum with pages measuring 3½″ × 5½″, was presented to the Massachusetts Historical Society in 1900 by William P. Upham.

1. Extracts of Origen against Celsus. 7 pages.

2. Letter from George Phelps, Joseph Whiting, and Samuel Loomis to Edward Taylor requesting him, in the name of the town, to continue his work among them. Westfield, "3 of 5m, 1673." 1 page.

3. Letter from Phelps, Whiting, and Loomis to the church at Northampton advising of their intention to organize the church at Westfield and requesting that David Wilton of Northampton be allowed to settle at Westfield "for further encouraging of Mr. Taylor" and to help in their proceedings. Dated Westfield "11. 5. 1673." 2¼ pages.

4. Letter from Solomon Stoddard and John Strong to Whiting, Phelps, and Loomis, encouraging them to organize their church but denying the request that Wilton settle at Westfield. Dated Westfield, July 29, 1673. 2 pages.

5. "An Answer [to the above] by way of Reply sent Aug. 21, 1673" from Whiting, Phelps, and Loomis, renewing their request for Brother Wilton, stating that Taylor refused to organize the church without further encouragement from Northampton. 2¾ pages.

6. A letter from Peter Bulkly to his father. Dated London "17th 11m 1676/7." 2 pages. Published in *Proceedings of the Massachusetts Historical Society*, 2nd ser. *14* (1900), 213–15.

7. "The Determination of the Differences at Windsor," sent by John Talcot and thirteen others. Date obscure, probably May 2, 1677. 1¾ pages.

8. "To the Church of Christ in Lebanon." Advice as to admonished brethren in the Lebanon Church by a council of ministers and elders including Taylor and Stoddard. April 10, 1706. 1½ pages.

9. "A Letter sent to Edward Culver and Thomas Hunt." These men had been admonished at Lebanon. In shorthand. Dated N.H., May 20, 1706.

10. "The King's Letter," Sept. 30, 1680. Another copy of this letter is bound up in Taylor's "Harmony of the Gospels." 2 pages. Published in Thomas Hutchinson, *A Collection of Original Papers* (Boston, 1769), 522–25. This is a copy of a letter from King Charles to the Bay Colony.

11. Letter from Colonel Pynchon [?] to his brother, London, Oct. 15, 1691, concerning negotiations for the new charter. 3 pages. Published in *Proceedings of the Massachusetts Historical Society*, 2d ser. *14* (1900), 215–17.

12. "To the Worshipfull Peter Tilton Esq." from Edward Taylor. The letter is concerned with "the bleeding and almost dying interest of Christ at Hadly" caused by the scandalous accusations of Abigail Warner. Dated "26. 11m. 1684." 9 pages.

13. "A Briefe account of some speciall Observances of brother Dewy upon the Death of his Daughter Hepzibah who died of a Putrid Fever in child bed." ". . . if she did belong to eternall life she should be saved: but if not all that I could do could not help her . . ." 4 pages.

14. "A Letter sent to the Reverend Mr. Solomon Stoddard Pastor of the Church of Christ at Northampton When he was about to bring all Civilized and Catechised above 14 years old to the Lord's Supper, and throwing away all relations of the account of their hope to the Church." Violently attacks Stoddard's innovations on twelve counts. Westfield, "13: 12m 1687/8." 3 pages.

15. A letter from Solomon Stoddard to Edward Taylor. In answer to the above. Dated N.H., June 4, 1688. 1 page.

16. Six arguments arranged in syllogisms against Stoddardeanism, prefaced by a brief account of Stoddard's devious success in persuading his congregation to accept his notions about the Lord's Supper. 3 pages.

17. A further account of experiences by Deacon Dewy. 3⅓ pages.

18. A letter from Edward Taylor to Richard Edwards on the question of Edwards' desire for a divorce. Taylor's position is that when the essence of marriage is subverted, as in adultery, then the marriage tie may be dissolved. Dated "26 7m 1691" or 1692? 6 pages.

19. A letter to the General Court at Boston from William

Bates and others. Congratulates the Court on the restoration of the charter. Dated Oct. 17, 1691. Followed by Increase Mather's "Brief Account." 3 pages. Published in *The Andros Tracts,* The Prince Society (Boston, 1868–74), *2, 273–98.*

20. "A Brief Account concerning severall of the Agents of New England, their Negotiations at the Court of England," by Increase Mather. London, November 16, 1691. 18¼ pages.

21. A letter from Taylor to Samuel Mather of Windsor arguing that rape is a capital crime. Westfield, "17 12m 1693/4." 3½ pages.

22. A letter from Taylor to Samuel Sewall on the interpretation of the seven vials. Westfield, "29. 7m 1696." ". . . the Foggy damps assaulting my Lodgen in these remotest swamps from the Heliconian quarters, where little save Clonian Rusticity is . . ." 6½ pages.

23. A letter from Samuel Sewall in response to the above. Boston, Oct. 28, 1696. A copy of this letter is in Sewall's Letter Book. 6½ pages. Published in *Collections of the Massachusetts Historical Society,* 6th ser. *1* (1886), 171–78.

24. A letter from Taylor to Solomon Stoddard on the refusal of two of the Westfield Church brethren to join in the monthly fasting and prayer. Westfield, "6. 2m 1710." 2 pages.

25. A letter from Taylor to Mr. Nathaniel Rise of Wallingford concerning a case of conscience. June 1715. 4 pages.

26. "The Farewell Sermon of that Worthy Man of God Mr. Thomas Leadbeater, Minister of Gods Work at Hinckly . . . preached . . . up on the solemn Day (hence calld black Bartholomew 1662) . . ." December 20, 1662. 34½ pages.

27. "An Answer against kneeling at the Lord's Supper, pend by that Famous Man of God Mr. Arthur Hildersham . . ." Dated 1618. 30½ pages.

28. "A Letter of Mr. Increase Noel sent to his Mother Mrs. S. Perkins out of New England. Charls Town the 17th of the 7th month . . . 1638." 1½ pages. Published in *Proceedings of the Massachusetts Historical Society,* 2d ser. *13* (1899), 126.

29. "Mr. Christopher Loves Scaffold Speech." Note in a hand not Taylor's: "The Reverend Mr. Love was executed on Tower Hill London Aug. 22, 1657." 10½ pages.

30. "The Last Will and Testament with Profession of Faith

of Humphry Fon, some times Minister of one of the Churches in
Coventrie . . ." 7½ pages.

31. "Mr. Cottons work [words?] shewing The grounds on
which Conformity is built together with a discovery of the sandi-
ness thereof." Against kneeling at the Lord's Supper. 25 pages.

32. "Reasons why the Service Booke urged upon Scotland
ought to be refused." 6 pages.

33. "Grounds of Exceptions Against the Oath required in the
sixth Canon established by the Synod." 2½ pages.

34. "A Briefe Relation of one Mr. Barkers Speech 14 of July
An. Do. 1637." 9 pages.

35. "The effects of the young Gentlewomans speech." This
and the above were delivered just before the speakers were ex-
ecuted.

36. Lines on the above warning against murder and adultery.
Sixteen lines in decasyllabic couplets, perhaps by Taylor.

37. Visions of John Holland just before death. "Clarks Exam:
142 p. taken out of Leigh."

38. George Nevil's feast. "Ao Dmi 1470 in the 10 year of King
Edward 4 George Nevil, brother to the greate Earle of Warwick
made this prodigious feast at his instalment into his Arch-
bishoprick of York wherein he spent of . . . Ale 0300 Tuns . . .
Oxen 0080 Fat, Bulls 0006 wild etc." There follows a long
itemized list of the amount of food and drink consumed. See
Meditation 109 (second series). ½ page.

39. "Remarkable Providences in the life of Mr. Dod." ½ page.

40. Magical performances by a juggler and other wonderful
narratives. 8½ pages.

41. Extracts from a medical book or books, chiefly on diseases
of the head. 12 pages.

42. Scattered throughout the manuscript are extracts from
various authors in Greek, Latin, and English classified under
such headings as Angels, Anatomy, Blasphemy, Body, Castle, etc.

The Redwood Athenaeum Manuscripts

The Redwood Library and Athenaeum at Newport, Rhode Island, in 1951 received three volumes of Edward Taylor manuscripts from the estate of Roderick Terry, Jr., a descendant of Taylor. A description of these manuscripts follows.

Diary, Theological Notes, and Poems.

146 unnumbered pages approximately 4″ × 5¾″, of which 30 are blank. Bound in full red levant with a printed title page: Diary of Atlantic Voyage / Life at Harvard College / Settlement at Westfield, Mass., / April 26, 1668–December 3, 1671 / Theological Essays / 1655 / Recantation of a Penitent / A Play, 1663 / By Rev. Edward Taylor, D.D. / His Original Manuscript.

1. Diary from April 26, 1668, to January 12, 1671/2. 22 unnumbered pages, of which one is blank. This is the diary referred to by John L. Sibley in his *Biographical Sketches of Graduates of Harvard University* (Cambridge, Mass., 1881), *2*, 397, and published in *Proceedings of the Massachusetts Historical Society, 18* (1880), 5–18.

2. Shorthand notes or code, two-thirds of a page. See item 12.

3. Theological notes dated June 20, 1655, comprising arguments under sixteen headings proving the divine authority of scripture, the existence of God, etc. About 38 pages. The first heading on the divinity of scripture is attributed to a Mr. Ford, Minister at Neather Seale. The sections on Election, Reprobation, and God's Decrees appear to be in accord with the orthodox Calvinism of the period.

4. Bound in with the above notes is a fragment of a page describing remarkable occurrences including a blazing star, a rain of blood, and a troop of men in the air—the latter seen near "Hinkly market." These events are dated from September 1664 to April 1665.

5. "The Recantation of a Penitent / Proteus or Changling / As it was Acted with good applause / in St. Maries in Cambridge and / St. Pauls in London, 1663. / To the tune of Dct. Faustus." 136 lines in decasyllabic couplets. A copy of Robert Wild's "The Recantation of a penitent Proteus," London, 1663. *Short Title Catalogue,* No. W2148.

6. "Rome for good newes / or / good news from Rome." 434 lines (of which the last 64 lines bear a separate title "An Exhortation to Bishops") in quatrains 4343. A copy of Ralph Wallis' "Rome for good news," 1662? *Short Title Catalogue,* No. W618.

7. "The Lay-mans Lamentation upon the / Civill Death of the late Labour[ers] / in the Lords vinyard by way / of Dialogue between a / proud Prelate and / a Poor Professour / Silenced on Bartholomew day 1662." 208 lines in decasyllabic couplets, lamenting the ousting of the dissenting clergy by the Act of Uniformity of 1662. Perhaps by Taylor.

8. "A Letter sent to his Brother Joseph Taylor and his wife after a visit." An acrostic poem of 40 lines in decasyllabic couplets, the initial and final letters forming the acrostic EDWARD TAYLOR TO HIS BROTHER AND HIS SISTER JOSEPH AND AL[I]CE TAYLOR RR. Written in another hand at the top of the letter: "He had also a Br. Richard. Jorimal[?] A. May."

9. An epigram on the Archbishop of Canterbury. 8 lines. Copies of this epigram are also in the "Poetical Works" and in the "Manuscript Book."

10. "A Reasonable Motion In behalfe of such / of the Clergie as are now questioned in / parliament for their places." 106 lines in decasyllabic couplets. Copy of "A Rreasonable [*sic*] Motion / in / The behalfe of such of the Clergie, / As are now questioned in PARLIA- / MENT for their places." 1641. *Short Title Catalogue,* No. R462. Three lines of Latin and two of English inserted between the title and the poem in the MS do not appear in the printed poem.

11. A Dialogue in verse between the writer and a Maypole dresser. The writer attacks the custom of Maypole dancing. A Latin couplet is followed by 92 lines of English in decasyllabic couplets. Perhaps by Taylor.

12. ". . . this in a Letter I sent to my schoolfellow. W.M." 24 lines in decasyllabic couplets followed by a page of shorthand notes or code similar to item 2 above. In the couplets the poet explains he is weaving a web out of an alphabet of love. He is taking the web out of the loom to send to his friend, but he is keeping the thrum. Probably by Taylor.

13. "Dea Wild to Mr. / Calamy imprison'd for Preaching a /

Sermon to his people out of 1 Sam. 4: 13 / after hee were si-
lenced." 114 lines in decasyllabic couplets. Copy of Robert Wild's
"A poem upon the imprisonment of Mr. Calamy in Newgate"
[London, 1662]. *Short Title Catalogue,* No. W2146.

14. "A Valediction made by one of those gentlemen that was
put to death upon the Death of King Charles 1st by Charles
the 2d." 54 lines of decasyllabic couplets arranged in 9 stanzas
of 6 lines each. Author unidentified.

15. "An answer to a Popish Pamphlet cast in London Streets
not long after the city was burnd, composed by Dr. W." 34 lines
of octosyllabic couplets. Author unidentified.

16. "Another answer wherein is recited everie verse of the
Pamphlet and answered particularly, by E.T." 191 lines in
octosyllabic couplets, of which 20 lines are quotations from the
pamphlet, one line of the pamphlet being left unrhymed. The
pamphlet states that the London fire is a foretaste of eternal fire
for heretics. By Taylor.

17. "Vox & Lacrimae Anglorum / Or / The true English-men
Complaints / to their Representatives in / PARLIAMENT." 408
lines in decasyllabic couplets. Copy of George Wither's "Vox &
lacrimae Anglorum," London? 1668. *Short Title Catalogue,* No.
W3208. A general attack on the king's ministers and his pro-
French policies.

A Metrical History of Christianity.

438 pages, of which 4 are blank, measuring 5¾" × 7⅜", bound,
apparently by Taylor himself. A copy of the *Boston News Let-
ter* dated 1710 is in the binding. There is no title page. On the
binding inside is pasted this note: "This Book is the property of
Miss Meacham of Beach Street Bloomfield New Jersey. It was
found by her family hidden away under the eaves of the garret
roof in their old homestead in Mass. It appears to be at least 300
years old." In another hand in pencil: "Enfield, Conn." A note
inserted in the MS reads "A metrical history of the world from
the beginning to 1558. This curious old manuscript covers
several hundred octavo pages, and is bound in hogskin. It was
written in various styles of verse and seems to be mainly in re-

ligious topics. It was probably written by one of the pilgrims
as it was found under the eaves of a garret in Enfield, Conn. Its
date is probably 1620 to 1630. Bound in the cover as filling are
copies of the Boston Newsletter of 1710, showing it was bound
about that date. This might be called the work of the first
American poet." Another note inserted in the MS, signed by
Roderick Terry, states: "This book bought by me in April 1905
was written by my great great great grandfather—Rev. Edward
Taylor, because 1. Two experts on handwriting have so un-
hesitatingly declared. 2. It was found in an attic in Enfield,
Conn., where his grandson Rev. John Taylor who inherited a
large part of E.T.'s library lived. 3. He wrote many books of this
style and bound them himself. Hon. Henry W. Taylor says (in
E.T.'s life) that many which belonged to Rev. John Taylor were
lost—this is undoubtedly one of them."

Both the handwriting and poetic style appear to this editor
to be that of Taylor. The poem begins with graphic and some-
times rather crude descriptions of the sufferings of the martyrs
of the primitive Church. About the first 50 pages covering the
ten persecutions of the Church appear to be metrical paraphrases
of similar material in John Foxe's *Actes and monuments,* a
copy of which was in Taylor's library. The poem proceeds cen-
tury by century until the year 1100 and, leaving a gap of four
and a half centuries, begins again with the reign of Queen Mary
and terminates with the year 1558. The emphasis throughout is
on persecutions and martyrdoms. The narrative portions are in
decasyllabic couplets. Interspersed among the narrative sections
are verses of varied stanzaic pattern in praise of God's mercy,
truth, patience, and justice which usually function as a com-
mentary on or summing up of the preceding narrations.

In binding the manuscript a number of pages were transposed.
those describing the century 900 appearing after those dealing
with the century 1,000.

Harmony of the Gospels.

Folio of 485 unnumbered pages measuring 8¼″ × 12¹⁵⁄₁₆″.
Bound with the MS is a letter by Taylor's second father-in-law,

Samuel Willis, dated 1693/4, and a copy of a letter sent by com-
mand of King Charles II to the governor and magistrates of the
Massachusetts Colony dated the 30th day of September 1680,
calling for a meeting of the General Court. The following notes
in the MS are by Ezra Stiles: "This is the Work and original
Hand Writing of my Grandfather the Reverend Edward Taylor
pastor of the Church in Westfield . . . Grandfather Taylors
Commentary and Harmony of the Gospels written about AD.
1690 to 1710 as I judge." On the first page of the MS in its pres-
ent state Taylor indicates his purpose as follows: "My design
is if God assist to gather up a compleat account of our Lord and
Saviour and of the things done by him in order as they may be
gathered up out of all the Evangelists according to a rationall
Conjecture of their Order; and so to open the same; and gather
some practical and doctrinal improvement thereof." The work
is incomplete, beginning with John 1:1 and ending with Mat.
12:34. The commentary is organized according to Ramistic
practice with many dichotomies, points of doctrine, and "rea-
sons." Frequently the style is one of exhortation, urging sinners
to repent, promising salvation to the elect and damnation to the
wicked. This suggests that Taylor incorporated passages from his
sermons into his Gospel Harmony.

Glossary

Words and phrases of obsolete, dialectal, or otherwise unusual meaning are listed and identified in this section. Dubious or speculative identifications are queried by a parenthetical question mark: (?)—e.g. *Chase*. Included for the sake of convenience are some proper names, as well as theological terms defined or discussed by Taylor elsewhere in his writings. Words in this latter category appear in small capital letters. The primary sources for glosses are first the *OED,* second, the *EDD,* but these works are cited only when direct or paraphrased quotations are used. Books of the Bible are abbreviated as in the *OED.* For other abbreviations see above, p. xi. References to the text of the poetry are by page and line of the present edition: "12.25," e.g., means page 12, line 25.

Taylor's spellings and punctuation are retained, but his capitalization is disregarded: all words are capitalized initially, but no others unless they are normally spelled with capital letters. Variant spellings as used by Taylor appear in alphabetical order under the word (e.g. *Alembick, Alimbeck*) unless, under this scheme, a little-used spelling would appear first (e.g. *Pother, Poother*).

Nouns and verbs are given in their uninflected form except where it seems preferable for one reason or another to cite them just as they appear in the poetry (e.g. *Almugs*). Taylor is fond of interchanging parts of speech—sometimes by syntactic means alone (e.g. *Cabbinet* used as a verb, 6.17), sometimes by affixation (e.g. *Myrrhy,* 236.5, adjective from noun; *Heavenizing,* 238.13, *bebride,* 100.14, *Dayify,* 186.13, verbs from nouns; *adepts,* 241.25, verb from adjective; and so on). Such altered forms are not listed unless there is a special reason for doing so.

Abaddon, destroyer, angel of the bottomless pit (Hebrew name—the Greek equivalent is Apollyon: Rev. 9:11)

ADAM. Taylor, like many of his New England contemporaries, considered Adam to be the head of all mankind, and Christ—a second Adam—the head of the elect. "Se[e] hence how God hath Confounded Satan in the greate Design managed by him to the ruine of mankinde. His Design discovers itself—it was to ruine mankinde in the Head of all mankinde [Adam] that was the Originall of all men; and the Head Covenanter for all with God so that overthrowing of him and destroying of Grace in him, all mankinde ever after might never have any such thing as sanctifying grace amongst them. But God hath utterly befoold this subtill piece of hellish policy. For he hath made another Adam to be advanced to be head of his Church, in whom there is a greater Fulness of grace than ever there was in the first, and he is the Head and Originall of all that obtain grace, Their spirituall Head from whence their gracious Nature flows, and their Head Covenanter with God in the New Covenant" (C, Sermon 8)

Adepts (241.25), makes adept, makes proficient

ADOPTION. "Adoption is a gracious Act of God, passt upon a true believer in Christ, whereby, translating him out of Satans famaly, as a Childe into his own houshould, he constitutes him a rightfull heire of all the privilidges of his own child" (CR)

Ahone, alas; = *ohone,* Scottish and Irish exclamation of lamentation

Alembick, Alimbeck, apparatus used for distilling

Alkahest, the "universal solvent" of the alchemists (probably coined by Paracelsus, after the Arabic, in medieval Latin)

Almugs, variant of *algums,* i.e. algum trees—variously surmised to be a species of acacia, cedar, or cypress, but probably a kind of sandalwood (said to have been brought from Ophir: cf. e.g. 1 Kings 10:11–12)

Altaschat, Altaschath, Al-tashcheth, i.e. Al-Taschith, Al Tashcheth, literally 'destroy not'; found in the introductory verse to Psalms 57, 58, 59, 75 and probably designates the tune to which the Psalm is to be sung (*DB*). In Taylor, followed in each occurrence by *Mic(h)tam,* q.v.

Amercement, imposition of a penalty or fine at the "mercy" of the inflicter; hence, an arbitrary penalty or fine

Amoring, aphaeretic form of *enamoring*

Amuse, divert the attention of, beguile, mislead

Anakims, anglicized plural of the Hebrew plural *anakim* (singular, *anak*); "an Old Testament race of giants of southern Canaan, who were virtually annihilated by the Israelites. *Josh.* xi.21" (*WNI*)

Angelica, an aromatic plant used for culinary or medicinal purposes and believed to be a preservative against poison

Angell, English coin (1470–1634) showing archangel Michael slaying the dragon

ANGELS. "Angels are compleat spirits created, probablie in the morning of the first day, with Intellectual faculties to attend the glorious Throne of God, and to be sent out for the good of Gods elect" (CR). ". . . the Holy Angels appearing to do their Messages do attend upon those forms and modes of good manners which are esteemed acts of Honour by those places where they are sent. The Angel doth not come in as a mere Clown, no, but as soon as he is entred, he doth as it were moove his hat and bow his body and say how do you" (HG, 30). "The visibility of Angels is not proper to their own nature for the Angelicall nature is spiritual and Invisible but they appeared visible in an Elementary body which they either assume or make to array themselves withall when they are dispensing their Message, for as an Ambassador coming into another contry arrayeth himself in apparrell suitable to the mode and Condition of those to whom he is sent, but layeth aside the same apparrell when he returns if it is not according to the Custom at home, so do the Angels sometimes array themselves in visible shape when they approach with Ambassies to Men which they lay by when they return into their own Countrie againe" (HG, 16). "Hence se[e] what love God manifests unto his own people. He hath special tokens to send them; a token is from a loving friend. So here is a token, a love token sent out of heaven unto thee, here is love indeed, nay and it is sent by an angel; this much more manifests Gods love, the Angels of God, those Courtiers of glory, that stand attending Gods royall Throne of Glory are not too glorious to be imployed in this work. God sends them with good things in their hands to his people; he spares his own royall Guard for this work! oh! then what love is here! . . . Hence se[e] what excellent wayes the wayes of God are to walk in; here the Angels of God are Conversant; here the soul may meet with the Holy Angels flocking from heaven unto him and may see them herein upon Jacobs Ladder flocking backward and forward in a way of divine favour to the people of God. Hence se[e] what fools all those are that will not walk in Gods way. Oh poore souls! they walk Just in the Divels way; they shall not meet the Holy Angels coming down from God out of heaven with love tokens unto them, but with the wicked angel rising out of the bottomless pit with damnable delusions to tole them on in the wayes to hell and eternall Damnation" (HG, 16)

ANTITYPE, that which is shadowed forth or represented by a type (q.v.) or symbol

Aqua vitae, any brandy or spiritous liquor; originally applied by alchemists to ardent spirits. Taylor often uses it in its literal meaning 'water of life'

Archont, i.e. archon, ruler, chief magistrate

Arrians. believers in the doctrine of Arius (4th-century presbyter of Alexandria), who denied that Christ was consubstantial, i.e. of the same substance with God

Aurum vitae red, possibly aurum potabile 'drinkable gold'—a blood-red gummy or honey-like substance taken as a medicine and cordial

Awn, "beard" of grain sheath of barley, oats, etc.; often spelled yawn as a result of the frequent combination barley awn

Baalzephon. See Hiroth

Bag (324.12), catch, seize (?); or, jilt (dialectal) (?)

Baracadoes, barricadoes, barriers

Barath'rick, adjective coined from Barathrum (Greek βαρα θρον) 'pit, gulf; the abyss, hell.' More particularly, the name was applied to a deep pit at Athens into which condemned criminals were thrown

Barjona, patronymic of Simon Peter

Barlybreaks, a game played by six persons, three of each sex, formed into couples. One couple stands in "hell" (a plot of ground between two other plots) and tries to catch other couples as they pass through

Bay (480.122), evidently the architectural meaning 'division of a wall or space lying under a gable'

Bdellium, a fragrant gum (also the name of the tree yielding it) used in medicine and perfume; from Hebrew בדלח b'dolakh, rendered by Josephus as βδελλα, in Genesis as ἄνθραξ 'carbuncle,' and in Numbers as κρύσταλλος 'crystal' but explained by the Rabbins and Bochart as 'pearl, pearls' (OED): hence Taylor's pearly Bdellium

Bear the bell, have foremost position, win the prize, take first place (the phrase, according to the OED, represents a merging of two denotations: bear the bell, i.e. take first place, as the bell-wether or leading sheep of the flock, which wears a bell on its neck; and *bear*, or *carry away, the bell*, i.e. carry off the prize —perhaps a golden or silver bell presented to a victor)

Bearing blancket, cloth or blanket used to wrap a newborn baby

Bedotcht, soiled, bedaubed (?); origin not known

Beetle, heavy mallet used for driving stakes, etc.

Bell: Bells (noun, 435.30) 'bubbles'— cf. 1576, J. Woolton, *The Christian manuell*, "Mans life flieth away . . . as the bells which bubble up in the water" (quoted in *OED*); *belling* (verb, 403.10) 'bellowing.' See also *Bear the bell*

Bemegerim, inflict with a severe headache (*be-* + *megrim* 'severe headache')

Bepinckt, Bepinkt, cut in small scallops; worked or pierced with eyelet holes. Cf. *pinkt*

Besprindge, variant of *besprenge* 'sprinkle (something) over' (*be-* + *sprindge*, q.v.)

Bib, drink

Bibble, dabble with the bill like a duck

Bindg'd, past participle of *binge* 'make (a wooden vessel) watertight by filling it with hot water, in order to swell the wood'

Black-Cap, chickadee

Blancht, whitened, made white; (57.2) made pale with fear or awe

Blin, cease

Blodge, possibly *blotch* 'discolored patch; pustule, boil'

Bloomery, the first forge in an ironworks, where the metal is made into blooms (ingots)

Boanerges, a loud, vociferous preacher (see also p. 479, note to line 88)

Bob, strike, buffet

Boon, favor, gift

Booths. See *Feast of Booths*

Boss: [as noun] a round prominence in hammered or carved work, as in the cover of a book; [as verb] furnish or ornament with bosses

Bowl, Bowle, roll, like a ball in a bowling alley

Bozrah, capital of Edom (Hebrew word for 'sheepfold'). Cf. p. 23, note to line 3

Brancht, adorned with a figured pattern

Brazeel Bow, a bow made of brazilwood, a wood noted for its hardness and red color

Bruddled, Brudled [past participles], *Brudl'st* [2d singular], from *broodle* 'brood over, fondle'

Bubs, pustules

Bucking tub, a tub used for bucking, i.e. for steeping or boiling yarn, cloth, or clothes in a lye of wood ashes, etc.

Buffe. See *Counter buffe*

Burr'ing, burrowing, sheltering

Buskt, dressed, attired, adorned

Buss, buzz, hum

Butter teeth, buckteeth, large projecting front teeth

Cades, pets (cf. cade-lamb 'pet lamb')

Calamus, sweet calamus, an aromatic plant (cf. Song of Sol. 4:14)

CALLING, EFFECTUAL. "Effectual-Calling is the Regenerating Work of the Spirit of God in the means of Grace upon the Soule, whereby the Soule turning from sin, is inseperably joyn'd unto Christ in a new Covenant. . . . The Principall of the Souls returning to God is the passive principle of Grace wrought upon the Will by the free grace of God" (CR)

Cant, pitch, turn over

Cassia, aromatic wood, ingredient of anointing oil (cf. Ps. 45:8)

Casts (62.34), defeats (in an action at law)

Catholicon, universal remedy, panacea

Catochee, catochus, catalepsy or similar affection

Cawle, caul, net, spiderweb; *anat.,* any investing membrane. Taylor probably used the word in the anatomical sense in the phrase *Cawle-wrought Case*

Chalybdine, of steel, steely. From Greek χαλυβδικος or χαλυβικος (derived from the name of an Asia Minor nation famous for iron working) with the adjectival suffix -ινος

Chase, box or setting for gems; grooves (?), stone troughs used in cider-making (?)

Chat, small branch used for kindling

Cheape. See *Good cheape*

Checkling, chuckling

Chokewort, chokeweed (a weed which chokes other plants)—a species of Broomrape

Chuffe, swollen, puffed out as with disease

Cittern, a guitar-like instrument, the Tyrolean zither

Clagd, Clag'd, bedaubed with some sticky substance

Clew, ball, round bunch, cluster

Clout, cloth

Collops, thick folds of flesh on the body evidencing a well fed condition

Concoct, digest

Conjue, congee, bow

Consents (457.15), concents, harmonies

Consonant, harmonious

Cony cut, probably 'rabbit run' (*cony* 'rabbit,' *cut* 'way, passage'—cf. *short cut*)

Cordilera, Spanish for 'mountain chain'; the Spaniards applied the plural form *Cordilleras* originally to the parallel chains of the Andes in South America and later to the same system through Central America and Mexico as well

Corinthian brass, "an alloy, said to be of gold, silver, and copper, produced at Corinth, and much prized in ancient times as the material of costly ornaments" (*OED*); figuratively, 'effrontery, shamelessness'

Counter buffe, in a contrary direction

Coursey park, course-a-park, a country game in which a girl calls out a boy to chase her

COVENANT OF GRACE. Taylor believed that the Covenant of Grace became operative after the fall, when God promised that the seed of Eve would bruise the serpent's head. This new covenant, which supplanted the Covenant of Works, was made out of the free grace of God with sinning and undeserving man. "God doth forthwith plight a New-Covenant with all mankinde in Adam, Gen. 3.15. The seed of the Woman shall breake the serpents Head. Herein God did Confound the Master piece of Hellish Policy, And translate his Dispensations towards man, from the First Covenant Administrations to the New . . . and so . . . shewing signalls of his Favours to his own people, As the Blessing of Abraham, His presence with Moses, and his Advancing of David" (C, 85–86). The Covenant of Grace left man unable to be saved by his own efforts. "Whether or no a man be able of himself to come up to the terms of the Covenant. He is not able . . . from the Condition in which hee lieth till a Change be wrought . . . he is without strength" (DTP). The Covenant of Grace in New Testament times is not confined to the elect; a man under the Covenant of Grace may fall away from Grace and so be damned. "Whether or no the Covenant of Grace in new Testament times be restrained onely to the Elect. Answer: It is not . . . Because Gods call in New Testament times is of far greater latitude than the Grace of Election" (DTP). In commenting on Matt. 3:10 Taylor writes: "there are many in Covenant Relation unto God that bring not forth good fruit . . . Such as bring not forth Good fruite Gods judgments shall advance against . . . Gods judgments which he advanceth against a people in Covenant Relation to himselfe are Compared unto a Sharp Ax . . . those that are Cut off by Gods Ax from the Root of their Relation to God shall be Cast as fuell in Gods fire or hell" (HG). For further explication of the covenant see below, OLD AND NEW COVENANT

COVENANT OF WORKS. "The Covenant of works with Angels and Men is Gods tr[a]nsacting with them upon their Creation, in put[t]ing them into his service, whereby he gave them his Law as the condition of injoying life, binding of them to perfect Obedience upon pain of death and for the confirmation of mans faith therein he instituted the tree of Knowledge and Life to be the Sacramentall Seales thereof" (CR)

Cribb, house, lodgings

Crickling, small, wrinkled, dried apple (dialectal variant of *crinchling, crinklin'*)

Crincht, cringed

Crosswort, name for various plants having leaves in the form of a cross

Crouce, pert, brisk, lively, jolly

Cue, one-half pint of beer or cider (DAE); Taylor uses it to mean *cue-cup,* a cup which holds this amount

Cupping glasses, glass vessels applied to the skin during the operation of cupping, i.e. scarifying the skin and applying to the opening a vessel having the air within it rarefied

Dead head, the residuum remaining after distillation or sublimation; figuratively, worthless residue

Declensions, falls

DECREES OF GOD. "The Decree is an Internall Act of God, whereby hee hath for his own Glory appointed whatsoever should come to pass from all eternity" (CR). "Hence he saith Counsill is mine and Prudence is mine, and the Lord possessed me in the begining of his Way, before his Works of old, before there was any time, before the world was I was anointed, before the beginning. . . . It hath drawed out as a map, an Exemplar of all things whatsoever from the Highest Heavens to the lowest dust of the Earth, yea and from the brightest Angell in Celestiall Glory to the smallest nit in animall Nature" (C, 80–81)

Delph, quarry, mine

Dide in grain, dyed in fast colors

Distraint, (law) action of distraining, i.e. forcing a person to perform an obligation by seizure of a chattel or thing

Divells bit, devil's-bit, a meadow plant

Dozde, Doz'de, Dozed, Dozie, dozed, dozy 'in a state of incipient decay [of timber]'; refers in 203.19 to the cold light given off by rotting wood

Dragons (192.14), dragonwort, plant of the genus *Araceae*

Drugstery, drugs (?); cf. the *-ery* of *Rantery,* q.v.

Dub, array, adorn; (84.35) strike

Dunce, puzzle

Edom, mountainous country southeast of Palestine, about 100 miles long and 20 miles broad

Effectual-Calling. See CALLING, EFFECTUAL

ELECTION AND THE ELECT. According to Calvin's and Taylor's thinking, the elect are chosen by God to be saved and glorified, the choice being made before the foundations of the world were laid and without foresight of the good works or faith of the elect. "Whether God of his good pleasure doth elect some to life eternall, or of foreseen Faith and good Works, or of foreseeing some good in the Creature. Answer. It is of Grace . . . Rom. 9.11. . . . Because God could foresee no good in us but what he himselfe had determined to worke in us. . . . Because the end is alway[s] in intention before the means. But Gods will to elect men to glory is his end and therefore is intended, and goes before his calling them to faith and good works . . ." (DTP). The elect may be assured of salvation. "Whether or no a man may be assured in this life he is Elected. [Answer] He may be assured of it and it is proved by Scripture 2 Pet. 1.10 . . . its assured by the testimonies of our own spirit as our spirit witnesseth with Gods spirit and this is two ways: 1. By inward tokens, as sorrow for sin, faith in Christ . . . love of Righteousness and praying for pardon. 2. By outward fruits, as a holy life and Conversation" (DTP). Taylor, of course, was not a universalist. "Whether or no Christ in the intention of his Father did die for, and redeem all men. Answer: Christ did not die for all . . . Because of the absurdity which will follow if we grant he died for all, as That Christ did actually shead his blood in the last age of the world for them that were damned in hell in the first age of the world as Kain, etc. Christ calls all with a Common call in regard of the means. But the Elect onely with a speciall call in regard of the effectuall working" (DTP). "Art thou an Elect vessell? oh! Gods providences are signall touching thee. Looke on Moses, and you shall finde he and all other Males of the Israelites are under a Decree of Death to be executed upon them as soon as they peep out into the World at their birth. Well, Provi-

dence hides him in a boate of Bulrushes: Pharoah's Daughter findes him and will fauster him as her own son, puts him to Nurse to his own Mother, takes him and trains him up with all the Wisdom of Egypt, then Providence banishes him into the land of Midian and there Calls him and makes him Greate" (C, 86). The number of the elect compared with the number of the non-elect are few. ". . . there are but some of Israels unconverted Children brought up to the Lord their God by the means of Converting Grace allowed them . . . hence saith Christ few enter into the streight gate Mat. 7.13.14. and Paul calls them a remnant Rom. 9.27" (HG, 21). The Calvinist preacher, although in theory he believed that man was incapable of achieving saving faith through his own efforts, nevertheless in practice, that is in his sermons, preached as if man could make an effectuall effort to achieve saving grace, and he held man morally responsible if he did not make the effort: "O most lovely Jesus! O most wonderfull One. O most necessarie unto the sons of men. There is no Life but what is in thy hand, and comes from thee. But o the folly and Hellish folly then in men, before whom thou art propounded as Life, as life for them, as the Way of Life to them: and without whom they are dead, and shall possess Eternall Death, Death the Death of Death to all Eternity, and yet they will not come to Christ. Ye will not come to mee that you may have a Life. O their folly shall be written in letters as black as Eternall Death and imbellished in the fire of Hellish flames for ever" (C, Sermon six)

Eliakim. See p. 288, note to line 25
Elim, second encampment of the Is-

raelites after passage of the Red Sea (Exod. 15:27)

Emmet, ant

Empon'd, past participle formed from *pond* 'store up, dam' (*em-* + *pond* + *-ed*); *up Empon'd* (231.8) 'stored up, as by damming' (*up* placed before *Empon'd* for metrical reasons)

Empt, empty, exhaust

Engedi's Vineyard, an oasis celebrated for its palms, vineyards, balsam, and rich tropical vegetation, created by hot water from the fountain Engedi (in the town of the same name) on the west shore of the Dead Sea (*WDB;* cf. Song of Sol. 1:14)

Enkentrism, a Greek-derived coinage describing a theological conception of the Trinity with Christ as the center (?); or *Encratism,* doctrine of an early Christian sect whose members abstained from flesh, wine, and marriage (?)

Enrin'de, past participle formed from *rind* "To prepare . . . for preservation by melting and clarifying; to render; to melt" (OED) (*en-* + *rind* + *-ed*)

Enucleate, extract the kernel from; hence, lay open, make clear, explain

Epha, a Hebrew dry measure, 4½ to 9 gallons (*DB*) (cf. Exod. 16:36)

Ephods shoulder piece. An *ephod* was a sacred garment worn by the high priest, with the shoulder piece held by an ornamental stone. Attached to the ephod was a breastplate set with 12 precious stones, in four rows, symbolizing the 12 tribes of Israel; each was engraved with the name of one of the children of Israel. These stones constituted the *Urim and Thummim* (q.v.) and symbolized the glory of the New Jerusalem

Epinicioum, song of triumph, ode in honor of a victor

Eshcol's Grapes, the celebrated grapes from Eshcol valley, near Hebron (*WDB*) (cf. Num. 13:23)

Etham, first encampment of the Israelites after leaving Succoth (q.v.) (cf. Exod. 13:20)

Euxine, Black Sea

Facete, elegant, graceful, polished

FAITH. "Faith is the first saving act of Reversion, wrought in the heart by the spirit of God in its effusing the principle of Grace therein whereby the soule doth inseperably cleave unto Christ Jesus his Saviour for life and salvation" (CR)

FALL OF MAN. "The Fall itselfe is a Consequence of the Covenant of Workes consisting in a Volentary disobedience unto the Command through the instigation of Satan, by eating the forbidden fruit, whereby all mankinde fell from God into a State of Sin" (CR)

Fardells, bundles, especially burdens or loads of sin (cf. *Hamlet* 3.1.76, "Who would these fardels bear . . . ?")

Fat (258.21), vat

Fawnbain, a plant (species unknown) which is harmful to fawns

Feast of Booths. See p. 125, note to line 26

Ferula, giant fennel (see p. 226, note to lines 1-2)

Fet (388.35), fetched

Filberd, filbert, fruit or nut of the hazel

File, polish

Fillitted, bound or girded as with an ornamental band

Fincht. See *Gold-fincht*

Finde (305.11), fined, brought to an end

Fistula'es, long, narrow suppurating canals of morbid origin

Fleer, Fleere, make a wry face, laugh in a coarse manner; mock, sneer; (373.16), flare

Flippering, crying (?); swinging, fluttering in the air (?)

Florendine, pie, tart

Flory, showy, flowery

Flout. See *May game flout*

Flur, Flurr, scatter; flutter

Flyer (467.3), the part of a spinning wheel that twists the thread as it leads it to the bobbin

Foil, apply a thin sheet of metal to; see also p. 17, note to line 16

Foist, stink, musty smell

Fox and geese, a boys' game played with marbles or pegs

Frame (401.13), constitution, nature

Freestone, any fine-grained sandstone or limestone

Frim, vigorous, flourishing, luxuriant

Frize, frieze, a kind of thick, warm woollen cloth used for rough outer garments

Frob, variant of *throb*

Frog, disease of the throat or mouth

Froppish, froward, fretful, peevish

Fude, feud

Full, beat (cloth) with wooden mallets and cleanse it with fuller's earth or soap. *Fulling mill,* mill in which cloth is fulled

Furrd, trimmed, covered

Fustian, thick twilled cloth

Gam-Ut, musical scale; technically, the "Great Scale," consisting of all the recognized notes used in medieval music

Garland tuns, probably tuns with garland insignia

Garnisht, adorned

Gastard, Gasterd, astonished; terrified; struck with amazement

Gayes, toys, childish amusement

Geer, Geere, gear, apparatus; matter, stuff

Gilgal, first encampment of Israelites west of the Jordan, where those born during the march through the wilderness were circumcized; cf. *Gilgal's Razer* (210.6). See also p. 97, note to Med. 10

Giliad, Gilliad, mountainous country east of the Jordan, where the famous balm grew. *Giliads Balm,* Balm of Gilead, or Mecca balsam, which exudes an agreeable balsamic resin

Gird, strike, smite; (472.34) bind tightly

Girths, tight bands

Glaver, flatter

Glore, Scottish form of *glory*

GLORIFICATION. "Glorification is a Reall Change of State whereby a Person is translated out of a state of misery into a state of felicity that shall be compleated in the full fruition of heavenly Glory to all eternity" (CR)

Glout: [as noun] frown, sullen look; [as verb] frown, look sullen

Gold-fincht, having a golden streak on its back *(gold + finched* 'streaked along the back')

Good cheape, a cheap market

Goshen, the part of Egypt where the Israelites dwelt throughout their sojourn in that country

GRACE. The effect of the working of God's free grace upon the soul was a very real experience to Taylor and resulted in some of the most moving passages in the Meditations as well as eloquent passages in prose. "What can all the Powers of Hell and Darkness do or Effect, think you, against God? If God be for us who can be against us? The sweetest Consolation attainable for man comes in with this Relation. Oh! with joy shall you draw water out of the Wells of Salvation. What Comfort is here for all in Christ. All God is in Christ, therefore all Comforts of God are in Christ. If the Influence of God in the outlets of his providence, makes a Pinke, A Rose, a Violet so sweet to us, if a touch of such influences make the liquour of the Grape, the fertility of the Field, the Cookery of our food, the Labour of the Bee. the sati[s]faction of the Cane juyce, yea and the Influences of a sorry mortall acting gratefully, leave such a Delightsomeness upon our spirit and senses and are so Edulcorated for us, What then are the sweet heart enravishments of the Consolations that are Contained in the Godhead itselfe from a little vent of whose influences these things are made so sweet unto the hearts of saints in Christ?" (C, Sermon 1). "O let this stir up all to be bathing their souls in this sunshine; all heavenly Excellencies are here to be had; here is Warmth to revive thy soule; Life to Enliven thy dead soule; Light to Enlighten thy Blinde soul, and to direct it in the right Way and Glory to make all glorious thy black deformed soule! Oh what would thou have more; nay here is a glorious golden scaling Ladder made of this shine to carry thy soul up into the Body of the son of Righteousness and so into the Throne of Eternall Glory" (HG, 6). The saving grace of Christ is imparted to the elect and the elect only. "But oh how doth he . . . worke Graciously to and for his own people? This lies as a foundation for all that he hath done and suffered for them. His Grace and Favour to them lies as the Corner Stone that bears up the Whole of this building. His undertaking the work lies upon this rock. His sufferings ly upon this bottom. Because he hath a Favour for them, he died for them, and he pours out his prayers to God for them, yea and Conferrs all Grace in them and on every one of them and advanceth every one of them into Eternal Glory" (C, Sermon 8). "Grace, furnishing the soule for glorie and Glory the Felicity and Reward of Grace. O! what Comfort and Con-

solation is here. Hands off: its Childrens bread; a Crumb of it may not fall to dogs. But all of it belongs to every Child in the Family" (C, Sermon 8)

Grain. See *Dide in grain*

Grindlestone, dialectal form of *grindstone*

Grudgens, gurgeons, coarse meal

Gudgeon, bait

Gum'd Taffity. See *Taffity*

Gust: (24.20) blow; (359.10) taste

Halls (391.22), hauls

Hanck, hank, fasten by a loop or noose; entangle

Harish, mad

Harle, filament or fiber of flax or hemp; tangle, knot, confusion

Haump, smock-frock (Yorkshire: "a hardin' hamp" *EDD*)

HEAVEN. Taylor had a literal conception of heaven, typical of the Puritan idea of his time. ". . . what transporting contentment will it yield? to se[e] God face to face, to se[e] Jesus Christ, to se[e] the wayes of God in the World! to se[e] the Golden Checker work of the Draw net of Providence hung open before the view of the soule, to behold how in the Mashes of the same the Saints are Cought and carried to Glory and the Sinners cought and Cast into hell. . . . to see the glorious outgoing of Gods Essential Properties . . . oh how will this amount the Soule . . . it sets the Soule a singing forth the Praises of the Lord God having made the soule such a glorious Musicall Instrument of his praise, and the holy Ghost having so gloriously strung it with the golden Wyer of Grace and heavenly Glory, having screw'd up the strings to sound forth the songs of Zions King; the pouring forth of the Influence of Glory play upon the Soule Eternall praises unto God, and Now the soule be-

gins to sing forth its endless Halle-
lujahs unto God; if it were possible
it would fly in pieces under its
glory, if this glory got no vent; and
therefore it being filled with glory
for Gods glory it falls to singing
most ravishingly out the Glory of
God in the highest strains" (CR)

HELL. Taylor had a very literal and
vivid conception of this place where
the wicked are tormented: "The
sentence is thus given Depart from
me, thou accursed into eternall
flames . . . the place where the
Damned and Divels are tortured
forever . . . oh this must needs be
a dreadfull, dolefull, darksom,
gloomy, dismall, and Deadly place
indeed; it is called in scripture
utter darkness; Hell fire; Wrath to
come; a Lake of fire and brimstone;
Everlasting Distruction; Everlasting
torment and everlasting flames.
Whether by this fire or flame is in-
tended the Pure wrath of God as
some, or also material fire as most
probable I shall not determine, yet
this is plain, it doth import the
most extream tormentor which is,
for nothing acts more furiously
than fire upon any thing. Hence
this place is the most terrible, tor-
turing, tormenting, burning, scald-
ing, Enfiring, stincking, strangling,
stifling, Choaking, damping Dun-
geon immaginable" (CR)

Henbain, henbane, common name of
a certain weed having an unpleas-
ant smell and narcotic and poison-
ous properties

Herba Trinitatis, an herb; old name
for pansy or anemone hepatica

Herb-a-grace, herb of grace, an old
name for the herb rue; in a gen-
eral sense, an herb of virtue or
valuable properties

Hesbon, Heshbon, city of Sihon (cf.
Song of Sol. 7:4)

Hift [noun, verb], heft, lift, help,
heave

Hilt, foil

Hin, Hebrew liquid measure, a little
over a gallon

Hint, occasion, opportunity (cf.
Othello 1.3.142, "It was my hint to
speak")

Hiroth, Pi-hahiroth, site of the last
encampment of the Israelites before
they left Egypt, between Migdol
and the sea, near Baal-zephon
(Exod. 14:2)

Hopple, fasten together the legs of
an animal to prevent it from stray-
ing; fetter, hobble

Hopt, happed, covered, wrapped

Horeb, the mount of God in the pen-
insula of Sinae where the Law was
given to Israel (*WDB*)

Hurden, harden, a coarse fabric made
from the hards of flax or hemp;
often used attributively, 'coarse'

Hyssop, small herb used by Hebrews
to sprinkle blood on door posts
during Passover

Ignis lambens, a lightly licking fire

Iliak, Illiak, ileus, a painful afflic-
tion caused by intestinal obstruc-
tion; also called *iliac passion*

Imply (359.20), employ

Issick Bay, a bay in the northeast
corner of the Mediterranean

I'st, I shall (*I* + *'st,* reduced enclitic
form of *shall*)

Jet, swagger

Jews trump, Jew's harp

Jing, Jinks, Jink Game—a card game
derived from Spoil-five

JUDGMENT DAY. "The day of Judg-
ment is the Generall Assise of Jesus
Christ who summoning all sinners
to appeare before his Tribunall
shall in a glorious manner render
to every one exactly according unto
their Deeds" (CR). In CR there are
seven and a half folio pages of very
close, minute writing by Taylor de-
scribing this great event, much of it
reminiscent of Wigglesworth's "The
Day of Doom." For example: "The

Arreignment of the Miserable Miscreant and Damnable wretch who shall stand in his sin and guilt and ugliness and filth trembling and that every one of them, not one whether wicked men or Divells, none over-lookt, none omitted; none can get away from the wrath of the judge, or make an Escape." See also above, HEAVEN; HELL

JUSTICE. With respect to the non-elect, that is the majority of mankind, God's justice takes precedence over his mercy. Like Jonathan Edwards and other Calvinists, Taylor preached that Christ would take a just and terrible vengeance on his enemies: "What a terrour will it be to thee to have Christ thine Enemy that is Almighty? O think of this. No terrour on this side hell like this. Can thy heart endure or thine hands be strong in the day that he shall deale with thee? Alass, if he come against thee in the form of a Lamb, though thou was the greatest Monarch or Mightiest mountain on earth, thou wouldst be ready to run into [a] mouse hole to hide thyselfe from his Wrath . . . He will put on Might as a garment and Majesty and strength as a Robe. He will array himselfe With glory and come in flames of fire to take Vengeance of his Enemies and revenge upon his Adversaries, to render his anger with fury and his rebukes with flames of fire. Now then what a terrour wilt thou be in when he shall thus come to deale with thee? Thinke of it. His Maje[s]ty shall bee so great that the Angells of Glory Will shout at it, the Heavens Will ring again, the Aire and skies filld with his host will Quaver and the earth Will tremble, and now the most amazing sight that poor sinners set their Eyes on will appear before their eyes to their utter Con-

fusion. Thou mayst as easily toss away the earth as a tennis ball or turn the World out of doores as a puppy dog or Pull down the Heavens over the heads of all things as a tilt Cloath, as easily recover the time that is passt away, Weigh the Whole Empyreall battlements in a pair of Gold Scales, Contain the Winde in the Hollow of thy hande and lade the Sea dry with an acorn bowle as stand before the Lord Jesus Christ who is Almighty and thine Enemy" (C, Sermon 7)

JUSTIFICATION. "Justification is a gracious sentence of God passt upon a true believer in Christ whereby on the accou[n]t of Christs Righteousness, he being freed from guilt of sin, is pronounced truely Righteous in the sight of God eternally" (CR). Taylor, like all Calvinists, believed that man was justified by faith alone, and not by works. "Whether or no we be justified by Faith alone. Answer: We are justified by Faith alone" (DTP)

Keck, retch, reject with loathing
Ken, catch sight of, discover by sight
Kerfe, incision
Kid, faggot or bundle of twigs, brushwood, etc., either for burning or for embedding in sand to give it firmness
Kit, small fiddle
Kit-cat, a boys' game rather like baseball on a small scale
Knops, knobs, ornamental studs, bosses
Knot, flower bed

Lade, take up or remove water from a river, vessel, etc.
Lake of Meris, Lake Moeris, an artificial lake in Middle Egypt (*Cent. Dict.*)

Lather, ladder

Layes, layers or courses (of masonry)

Learch, lurk

Let, hindrance

Lign aloes, the aromatic wood of the Agalloch, noted for its fragrance (cf. Song of Sol. 4:14)

Lignum vitae, wood of life; wood from the *Guaiacum* tree

Linsy-Wolsy, an inferior material of wool and cotton

Lug, pull, as by the ear

Lythargy, lethargy

Macie, mace-like; adjective formed from *mace*, the spice consisting of the dried outer covering of the nutmeg

Mammocks, scraps, shreds, broken pieces

Mammulary, nipple, breast. See also p. 7, note to lines 18 ff.

Mara, fountain of bitter water (Exod. 15:23). See also p. 184, note to lines 81–82

Mates, pairs

Maukin, scarecrow

May game flout, a flout (i.e. butt or object of flouting, mocking) in a May game

MEDIATION. "The Mediation itselfe is Christs appearing before his Father on the account of his people who by making full satisfaction to Justice itselfe, hath purchased them unto Eternall Salvation" (CR)

Mence, adorn, grace

MERCY. With respect to the elect God's mercy takes precedence over his justice. "Now by Mercy we are to understand that speciall Favour which God doth bestow upon his own people for here in our Text [Luke 1:50] all other are exempt from it . . . onely those that are the true fearers of God in any generation have a right propriety in the Mercy of God" (HG, 44). God's mercy will sustain the elect, and

even satan is powerless against it: "Satan by all his Wiles and Temptations can't . . . touch them. He is a Conquer'd Enemy. He is cast down out of his throne, out of his first habitation. Those Starrs that are struck down by his Taile out of Heaven were but Wandering stars for Whom is reserved the blackness of darkness for ever. None in Christ be harmed by this Enemy of Christ . . . Christ is Almighty and Will blow the old Serpent and his Serpentine subtilty away as a feather in the Winde. Now is not this sweet Comfort?" (C, Sermon 7)

Meris. See *Lake of Meris*

Michtam, Mictam, term applied to certain psalms to indicate their musical character; in the phrase *Michtam-David*, apparently 'psalm.' Usually preceded by *Altaschat* (etc.), q.v.

Migdol. See Hiroth

Minced, chopped

Miserere mei, name for iliac passion (see *Iliak*)

Morrice, Nine Men's Morris, a game rather like checkers or chess, but played in a field (or on a table or board); cf. *Midsummer Night's Dream* 2.1.96–98, "The fold stands empty in the drowned field, / And crows are fatted with the murrion flock; / The nine men's morris is fill'd up with mud"

Mullipuff, fuzz-ball (used as a term of contempt)

Mummy, a medicinal preparation of the substance of mummies

Muscadalls, the grapes from which muscatel wine is made; or the muscadell pears

Neatly, finely

Neckt, dialectal pronunciation of *naked*

New Covenant. See OLD AND NEW COVENANT

Nine holes, a boys' game played with a ball and nine round holes in the ground (or in a board)

Nine pins, skittles, a bowling game played with nine pins

Ninus, Nineveh

Noddy, a card game like cribbage (ETG)

Non-suites, subjects to a *nonsuit,* "the stoppage of a suit by the judge, when, in his opinion, the plaintiff fails to make out a legal cause of action or to bring sufficient evidence" (OED)

Note (343.9), sign, token, indication

Nymps, imps

Obsignation, ratification, action of sealing

Oculated, observant

Officine, workshop, laboratory; office in a monastery (cf. medieval Latin *officina,* "applied to a store-room of a monastery, in which medicines, etc. were kept"—OED)

OLD AND NEW COVENANT. Taylor defines the differences between these in his theological notes (old refers to Old Testament times, new to New Testament times)

SIMILARITIES:

"1. In the Authour of them, which is God.

2. In regard of the Mediator of them, Christ. Moses indeed was called a Mediator of the old Covenant, but he was but Typical.

3. In regard of the parties accepting of them, i.e., man.

4. In regard of the moving Cause, to wit Free-Grace.

5. In regard of the Conditions of them for they are the same.

1. On Gods part, as remission of sins and happinesse.

2. On Mans part, As Faith and Repentance."

DIFFERENCES:

"1. In their extent and latitude. For the old Covenant received onely the Jews, but the new, all Nations.

2. In the parties impl[o]yed in the administration of them. The old Covenant was administred by Priests and Prophets, but the New by Christ.

3. In their Duration. The old had its date and time, but the New continues to the end of the world.

4. In the Seales annext to them. The old had Circumcision and the Passeover, but the New Baptism and the Lords Supper.

5. In the Way of Consecrating of them. The old by the blood of Bulls and Goats, etc., the New by the blood of Christ.

6. In their Clearenesse of the Doctrine of Salvation; it is more cleare and distinct by Christ than before.

7. In the time of the Exhibition of Christ; in the old there were onely Christ in a promise, but in the New he is set forth as already come.

8. In the liberties injoyed under the New Covenant above what was under the old. For those under the New lie not under the yoake of Ceremoniall bondage.

9. In the large effusion of the spirit under the New above what was under the old. For the application of the spirit is more effectuall and his gifts more perfect under the New than under the old" (DTP)

Olivant, horn of ivory

One-and-thirty, a card game resembling vingt-un

Ophir, a place of uncertain locality mentioned in the Old Testament (e.g. 1 Kings 10:11), where fine gold was obtained

Ophthalmicks, medicines for the eye

ORIGINAL SIN. "Originall Sin . . . is the want of Originall Righteousness together with a strong inclination unto all actuall evill flowing from the guilt of Adams first Sin over all his posterity descending from him by ordinary generation, and is the spawn and spring of all Actuall transgressions" (CR). The guilt of original sin extended to children. "Whether or no Infants, and so all men bee borne guilty of Originall Sin? Answer: All men by nature are sinners. . . . Children are part of the world, and if so then guilty of sin before God" (DTP). Man in a state of sin is completely helpless without the free grace of God: ". . . we may see what an accursed, poisonous, ruinating Evill thing Sin is, and what a dismall, Woefull, Miserable, and forlorn Condition man is cast into by Sin. The Case is such that the Elect of God, the Object of Gods Everlasting Love are sure on the account of sin to sustain the Vengeance of Gods Everlasting Wrath, and the torments of Eternall flames in hell unless they be relieved and their condition is so Execrable that it is beyond the relief of all Created help whatsoever. None But the Eternall son of God could succor them. There is no remedy the whole world can procure them: All man Kinde is lost, and beyond its own Reliefe. His state is remediless; as to the Holy Angells of God—No help in their hand. Its onely Godhead Power that could do it" (C, Sermon 1)

Paintice, penthouse, a sloping roof, awning, canopy, shed, etc.

Palate fallen, relaxed uvula (1664, Pepys Diary, 23 Sept., "the palate of my mouth falling, I was in great pain"—quoted in *OED*)

Pald, enclosed with pales, surrounded, fenced in

Palma Christi, the castor oil plant

Panchins, pancheons, circular pans made generally of earthenware

Parg'd, covered with parget or plaster

Pargings, pargeting, ornamental work

Passover, Passo're. See p. 119, note to line 10

Patmos Ile, the island in the Aegean Sea to which St. John was banished and where he saw his vision

Peare, aphaeretic form of *appear*

Peart, Piert, quick to see, sharp (of the eye); lively, brisk (of a person)

Peckled, speckled

Peere, (be the) equal (of)

Pegs, pins or points of the rowel of a spur

Pensile orchards, hanging gardens

Peps, pepse, pelt, throw at

Pericarde, Pericordium, pericardium, the sac which encloses the heart

Petro oyle, probably Peter's oil

Phlebotomized, bled by having a vein opened

Pia-mater'd, covered with a pia mater, i.e. with "a delicate fibrous and very vascular membrane which forms the innermost of the three *meninges* enveloping the brain and spinal cord" (*OED*)

Pick, pitch (cf. *Coriolanus* 1.1.204, "As high as I could picke my Lance")

Pickpack, pick-a-back, on the shoulder or back, like a bundle

Piert. See *Peart*

Pild, tipped with a pile, i.e. "the pointed metal head of a dart, lance, or arrow" (*OED*)

Pillard, one who is peeled or stripped (from the obsolete verb *pill* 'peel'; Taylor also uses *pilled* 'peeled' in his diary)

Pimping, small, petty, mean, insignificant

Pinck, Pink, peep, blink, wink; *pin(c)ked, pin(c)kt* 'adorned,' see also *Bepin(c)kt*

Pincky eyes, small, narrow eyes; cf. *pinkeny* 'blinking, peering eye' (17th-century usage)

Pingle, small piece of enclosed ground

Pink. See *Pinck*

Pipkin, small earthen pot or glazed earthenware saucepan

Plastrum Gratiae Dei, plaster of the grace of God

Pledgets, small compresses for applying to wounds

Plites, plights, conditions, states, moods

Pomills, ornamental knobs on a chair

Poole of Shiloam, pool built by Hezekiah on the west side of Jerusalem, to which sick persons were brought to bathe in Jesus' time (cf. John 9:7–11)

Poother. See *Pother*

Posamnitick's Labyrinth. See *Psammitich's Labyrinth*

Post-and-pare, a card game played with three cards each in which the players bet on their own hands

Pother, Poother: [as noun] commotion, tumult; [as verb] move, pour, or roll in a cloud, as smoke or dust

Pottinger, porringer, small soup bowl

Pounderall, pounder, pestle, instrument for crushing

POWER. Taylor emphasizes God's use of his power in punishing sinners and rewarding saints. ". . . hence this power which is matter of joy to Gods people, is matter of amazing Astonishment to the wicked; as sure as God is a God of power he will put forth his Power in scattering the Wicked before him, and in succoring his own people. Oh then all the Enemies of his people comming out as a mighty host against him shall not be able to stand before him; but he will breake all their Ranks and scatter

their power into the four winds togather. But oh! the joy then of his own people! Oh happy day!" (HG, 45)

Pranck, caper with an arrogant air

Print: [as noun] an image or character stamped on the mind or soul, especially the divine likeness; [as adjective] perfect, neat, precise, hence *in print* 'in a precise and perfect manner, to a nicety'

Pritch, grudge, spite

Propence, inclined

PROVIDENCE. "Providence in Generall is an externall worke of God whereby he disposeth of all things with all their Actions" (CR)

Psammitich's (Posamnitick's) Labyrinth, labyrinth built by Psammetichus, an Egyptian ruler of the 13th dynasty (*Cent. Dict.*)

Purdue, perdue, concealed

Purse, scrotum

Pursevant, pursuivant, messenger

Put, a card game

Quaver, a shake or trill in singing

Quicken'd metall, probably quicksilver

Quill, piece of reed or other hollow stem on which yarn is wound

Quilting, blanketing, (all-)covering (?)

Quinsie throate, inflammation of the throat; tonsillitis

Quintesses, quintessences

Quorn, quern, a simple mechanism usually consisting of two stones, the upper one turned by hand, for grinding corn

Radien, radial, pertaining to light in the form of rays

Ragnell, coinage meaning vagrant (?)

Ragwort, an herb of a bitter, cleansing quality

Rameses, Ramesis, town in Goshen (q.v.), starting point of the Exodus; first stage of the journey was from here to Succoth

Rantery, ranting (cf. the *-ery* of *Drugstery*)

Recepts, receipts

REDEMPTION. "Redemption is the first part of the Recovery of the Elect out of the Fall by the Redeemer, Who laying down for them the full price satisfactory to justice itselfe, hath purchased them unto eternall salvation . . . Christs Humiliation is the first part of Redemption whereby yielding obedience unto the whole Law of God perfectly satisfactory to justice itselfe, he hath purchased eternall salvation for his people" (CR)

Reech, reek, odor (either sweet or bad)

Reev'd, intertwined, wreathed (?)

Refelld, repelled

REPROBATION. "Unbeliefe and bad works are the Cause of Damnation, but not of Reprobation. Because sin doth not go before but follows after Reprobation. For we must distinguish between the Decree and the Execution of it. The Decree is eternall and before sin. The Decree respects man in generall as a Creature; the Execution looks on man as he is in sin" (DTP). Like Calvin, Taylor found it difficult to resolve the conflict between man's moral responsibility and the decree of Reprobation, and like Calvin he insisted that in spite of the Decree, God was not the author of sin. The following verbal quibbling by Taylor is typical: "Objection: Reprobation brings men into a necessity of sin[n]ing; therefore God is the Author of Sin. Answer: Gods Decree infers no necessity of constraint but onely of immutability" (DTP)

Riggalld, verb formed from the noun *riggal* 'ring-like mark' (or 'groove in wood or stone'?)

Rinde, strip the rind or bark from

Rive, pierce

Rowell, spur with a rowel

Rowle upon, meditate on; *Rowle oneself upon,* entrust oneself to. The word occurs in the poetry of Taylor's contemporary Anne Bradstreet:

> Hide not thy face from me, I cry'd,
> From Burnings keep my soul;
> Thou know'st my heart, and hast me try'd;
> I on thy Mercyes Rowl.
>> (From "For Deliverance from a feaver")
> O stay my heart on thee, my God,
> Uphold my fainting Soul!
> And, when I know not what to doe,
> I'll on thy mercyes roll.
>> (From "In my Solitary houres in my dear husband his Absence")

Mrs. Bradstreet's 19th-century editor J. H. Ellis offers an interesting interpretation of the expression:

> This singular expression . . . is probably taken from Ps. xxii.8, —"He trusted on the lord *that* he would deliver him: let him deliver him, seeing he delighted in him"; or from Ps. xxxvii.5, —"Commit thy way unto the Lord; trust also in him; and he shall bring *it* to pass." The marginal reading for "trusted on" is *"rolled* himself," and for "Commit thy way unto," *"roll thy way upon."*

The "Bay Psalm Book" translates the former verse as follows:

> Vpon the Lord he rold himself,
> let him now rid him quite:
> let him deliver him, because
> in him he doth delight.

Winthrop uses the same expression in a letter to his son ("Life and Letters," p. 250).

> But such as will roll their ways upon the Lord, do find him always as good as his word.

J. H. Ellis, *The Works of Anne Bradstreet* (Charlestown, 1867), pp. 35–36 n.

Rubston, rubstone, a kind of whetstone

Ruff-and-trumpt. Ruff, "a former card-game. . . . The act of trumping at cards, esp. in whist" *(OED)*

Sabellians, followers of Sabellius (3d century), who believed that the Father, Son, and Holy Spirit are merely different modes of one divine being

SACRAMENTS. The New England Puritans had two sacraments, the Lord's Supper and Baptism. "The Seales of the Covenant of Grace (called the Sacraments) are means instituted of God whereby the benefits of Redemption by outward signs represented are sealingly applied unto believers, as in Baptism and the Lords Supper" (CR)

Saints Johns Wort, plants of the genus *Hypericum*

Salamanders Woole, asbestos

Sampler, an example to be imitated; model, pattern, archetype

SANCTIFICATION. "Sanctification is a Reall Change of State whereby the Person being cleansed from the filth of sin, is renewed in the likeness of God by the graces of the Spirit" (CR)

Saphrin, sapphirine, sapphire-like

Sapphick, seraphic (?)

Sawceboxes, persons addicted to making saucy or impertinent remarks

Scar-fire, scare-fire, a sudden conflagration

Searce, Seirce: [as noun] sieve, strainer; [as verb] sift, strain (past participles *searcde, searst*)

Secundine, placenta

Sedan, carry, as in a sedan

Seirce. See *Searce*

Selvedge, border, edge; literally, edge of woven material finished to prevent ravelling out of the weft

Set, at a, at a standstill, in difficulties, nonplused

Shab, get rid of, get (a person) out of the way

Shackeroon, -oon variant of *shackerell* 'vagabond'

Shalm, Shawm, a musical instrument

Sheed, variant of *shed* 'cause (blood) to flow, by cutting or wounding'

Shew-bread, "the twelve loaves that were placed every Sabbath 'before the Lord' on a table beside the altar of incense, and at the end of the week were eaten by the priests alone" *(OED)*

Shiloam. See *Poole of Shiloam*

Shittim wood, a species of acacia—supposed to be hard, resistant to insects, and not subject to rot—of which the ark of the covenant was made. Cotton Mather judged it to be the black acacia: see *Philosophical Transactions of the Royal Society of London,* 29 (1714), 63

Shivers, splinters, fragments

Shooclout, shoe cloth, cloth for wiping the shoes

Shory, shorry, short pole

Shoshannim, probably a stringed instrument *(DB).* Word occurs in Psalms 45 and 69

Shulamite, woman of Shulem (cf. Song of Sol. 6:13)

Shutts, shutters

Sibma, Sibmah, 'balsam-place'—a town east of the Jordan famous under the Moabites for its grapes *(WDB)* (cf. Isa. 16:8–9)

Sillibub, Sillibubb, Syllabub, "a drink or dish made of milk or cream, curdled by the admixture of wine, cider, or other acid, and often sweetened and flavoured" *(OED)*

Silverlings, shekels

Simnill, simnel, "rich currant cake, usu. eaten on Mid-Lent Sunday in certain districts [of England]" *(OED)*

Sin-falling mallady, probably epilepsy (the "falling sickness"—*OED*)

Sippits, small pieces of toasted bread, often served in soup

Skeg: (74.1) variant of *keg* (?); (179.12) wild plum

Slatch, lazy idle vagabond

Slickt up, made elegant or fine

Slops, food

Slunk, cast

Snick-snarls, tangles

Socinians, members of a sect founded by Laelius and Faustus Socinus (16th-century Italian theologians), who denied the divinity of Christ

Sockage, socage, tenure of land; most usual in the phrases *free socage* and *common socage*

Sogd, soaked, steeped, saturated

Sory, a kind of mineral ore yielding vitriol; a kind of vitriol

Soul Blindness, defective power of recognizing objects seen, caused by cerebral lesion, without actual blindness and independent of other psychic defect (*Cent. Dict.*)

Spagyrist, alchemist

Spermodote, giver of seeds

Spic'd, seasoned

Spicknard, spikenard, the aromatic plant *Nardostachys Jatamansi* of North India

Spiles, spoils

Spiricles, diminutive form of *spires*

Sprindg, Sprindge, variant of *sprenge* 'sprinkle; scatter, disperse, spread about'

Spruice, brisk, smart, lively

Sprunt, struggle, lash out, kick

Squibd, attacked as with a squib, i.e. with a sarcastic hit or lampoon

Squitchen, variant of *scutcheon* 'piece of bark used in grafting' (?)

'St, reduced enclitic form of *shall;* see also *I'st*

Stale, butcher's stall; lure

Standish, inkstand, inkpot

Stem (56.24) shoot, as advanced by a growing plant

Stob, stab

Stoole (438.18) head of a tree stump, from which new roots are produced

Stowhouse, variant of *stovehouse* 'hothouse (for plants)'

Stranging, wondering

Strout, strut

Stut, stutter

Sub Forma Pauperis, in the form of a poor person exempted from liability to pay the costs of a legal action

Succoth, sukkoth, Hebrew holiday also known as the Feast of Booths (see p. 125, note to line 26). See also *Rameses*

Surdity, deafness

Swash: [as noun] swaggering; [as adjective] showy (cf. printing: swash letters, capital letters made with flourishes)

Sweetspike, the sweet flag, a rush-like plant with sword-shaped leaves, from whose roots *Calamus aromaticus* (a stomachic) is extracted

Syllabub. See *Sillibub*

Syncopee, heart failure

Tabber, tabor, drum; *tabber stick,* drumstick

Taffity, taffeta; *brancht taffity,* taffeta adorned with a figured pattern; *gum'd taffity,* taffeta stiffened with gum

Tag'd, fitted with ornamental ends or points of metal

Tantarrow'd, verb formed from *tantara* 'trumpet flourish.' Cf. PW, Canticle 3, item 32, appendix 2: "I trumpet out tantarroes"

Tazzled, tangled, fuzzy, twisted, knotty (from *tazzle,* dialectal form of *teazle* 'entangle')

Tenent, tenon, join together with tenon and mortise

Tent: [as noun] probe; [as verb] (74.6) reside, (84.4) past participle of *tend* 'kindle, light, set fire to'

THEANTHROPY, THEANTHROPIE, the fact of being both God and man; the union of the divine and human natures in Christ

Thresher, or thrasher, a shark which attacks with its tail

Thrum, fringe of warp-thread ends remaining on the loom when the web is cut off

Thrump, variant of *frump* 'mock, flout'

Thummim. See *Urim*

Tilt-clothe, awning, canvas; tent, tabernacle

Ting, ring

Tipple, topple

Tole-Dish, toll-dish, vessel of the proper dimensions for measuring the grain which is the miller's fee for grinding

'Tony Cross, St. Anthony's Cross, the *crux commissa,* in the shape of the letter T; so called because it was supposed to have been worn on the cope of Sir Anthony, who suffered from frequent temptations of the devil (John McClintock and James Strong, *Cyclopaedia of Biblical, Theological, and Ecclesiastical Literature,* 12 vols. New York, Harper's, 1894–96).

Topping, ascending

Trancifide, put in a trance

Tread, cicatricula, the round white spot on the yolk bag of a bird's egg, consisting of the germinal vesicle

Trig, trip

Trine, group of three, threefold

Tuck up, enclose, fold in

Tumberill, tumbrel, tumbril, "A cart so constructed that the body tilts backward so as to empty out the load; *esp.* a dung-cart" (*OED*)

Turn, Turns, a brain disease characterized by giddiness

TYPE, analogy, foreshadowing; "a person, object, or event of Old Testament history, prefiguring some person or thing revealed in the new dispensation; correl. to *antitype*" (*OED*). In 83.13, 19 possibly used in the more general meaning 'symbol, emblem—especially of something or someone yet to appear'

Ubiquitarians, believers in ubiquitism, the doctrine of the omnipresence of Christ's body

Ubiquity, the omnipresence of Christ or his body

Unguent Apostolorum, unguent of the Apostles

Unlute, remove lute—tenacious clay or cement used to stop an orifice —from a vessel

Urim and Thummim. Taylor believed that the Urim ('light'?) and Thummim ('perfection'?) were used to determine the will of God—that God spoke through them: ". . . for in the Temple God did discover his minde by Urim and Thummim but probably the Urim and Thummim there were burnt when Solomons Temple was burn[t] or left in the Captivity" (HG, 15); "that God sometimes doth reveale his will unto his people worshiping him, not according to the manner of his own Institution . . . the way wherein he gave forth Oracles in his Temple was by Urim and Thummim" (HG, 17). See also *Ephods shoulder piece*

Varnishing, polishing

Verjuicte, sour; past participle from *verjuice* 'acid juice of unripe fruit; make sour'

Wamble, feel nausea; *womble-crop* 'nauseate, make sick,' formed from the phrase *wamble-cropped* 'affected with nausea, sick'

Wards, ridges of a lock

Wash (401.14), swill

Waybred, Waybred Leafe, plantain, an herb used medicinally

Wedden, wedding

Welt, roll

Welted, adorned or trimmed as with welts, i.e. borders or fringes

Whelm'd-down, turned with the concavity downward; buried under a load

Whiffle: [as noun] trifle, insignificant thing; [as verb] blow or puff about as by slight gusts

Whimsy, dizziness

Whorle, small flywheel on a spinning wheel

Wisp, small bunch of straw, etc., used to wipe something dry or clean

Womble-crops. See *Wamble*

Wooling, woolgathering

Writh, writhed, wrenched; wreathed

Yawn. See *Awn*